PIMLICO

342

OSBERT SITWELL

Philip Ziegler was born in 1929 and educated at
Eton and New College, Oxford, where he
gained first-class honours in Jurisprudence. He
then joined the Diplomatic Service and served
in Vientiane, Paris, Pretoria and Bogotá before
resigning to join the publishers William Collins,
where he was editorial director for more than
fifteen years. His books have included biographies of William IV, Melbourne, Lady Diana
Cooper, Mountbatten, Edward VIII and Harold
Wilson, as well as a study of the Black Death.
His most recent book is *London at War*.

OSBERT SITWELL

———

PHILIP ZIEGLER

PIMLICO

Published by Pimlico 1999

2 4 6 8 10 9 7 5 3 1

Copyright © P.S. & M.C. Ziegler & Co 1998

Philip Ziegler has asserted his right
under the Copyright, Designs and Patents Act 1988
to be identified as the author of this work

First published in Great Britain by
Chatto & Windus Ltd 1998
Pimlico edition 1999

Pimlico
Random House, 20 Vauxhall Bridge Road,
London SW1V 2SA

Random House Australia (Pty) Limited
20 Alfred Street, Milsons Point, Sydney,
New South Wales 2061, Australia

Random House New Zealand Limited
18 Poland Road, Glenfield,
Auckland 10, New Zealand

Random House South Africa (Pty) Limited
Endulini, 5A Jubilee Road, Parktown 2193, South Africa

Random House UK Limited Reg. No. 954009

A CIP catalogue record for this book
is available from the British Library

ISBN 0-7126-6531-5

Papers used by Random House UK Limited are natural,
recyclable products made from wood grown in sustainable forests.
The manufacturing processes conform to the environmental
regulations of the country of origin

Printed and bound in Great Britain by
Mackays of Chatham PLC

To Diana Baring, who is alas no longer my agent,
and to Christopher Sinclair-Stevenson, who,
for different reasons, is alas no longer my publisher.
They kept the flag of civilised values flying in a world
increasingly falling prey to the barbarian.

Contents

List of Illustrations

List of Illustrations

Acknowledgements

Sir Reresby Sitwell and his wife Penelope have advised and encouraged me along my way with endless patience and kindness. Without unlimited access to the archive at their home, Renishaw Hall, this book could never have been written. I also owe an immense debt of gratitude to Mr Francis Sitwell and his wife Susanna for much help and wise counsel and for allowing me to see the smaller but extremely important collection of papers at Weston Hall.

Mr Frank Magro, Sir Osbert Sitwell's devoted companion, secretary and literary executor, has done everything to facilitate my work and has provided invaluable recollections of the years which he shared with the subject of this biography.

I am most grateful to Her Majesty Queen Elizabeth for talking to me about Sir Osbert and for allowing me to quote from her unpublished letters. Her Royal Highness Princess Margaret was also most kind in sharing with me her recollections of Sir Osbert.

I have been singularly fortunate in my recent predecessors. In 1978 there was a study of the Sitwells as a group and since then there have been individual biographies of both Dame Edith and Sir Sacheverell. Mr John Pearson's *Façades* was both a formidable work of research and a sensitive and penetrating study of this extraordinary family. He was able to interview many critically important witnesses who have since died and his admirably complete and vivid records of these meetings are deposited at the University of Tulsa. They have proved invaluable to me in my work. Mrs Victoria Glendinning's biography of Edith Sitwell is perceptive, eloquent and wholly convincing; Mrs Sarah Bradford's accomplished biography of Sacheverell provided a skilful evocation of an era and a society as well as of a man. To these three, as well as to the late Mr John Lehmann, Mr Derek Parker, Dr Richard Greene and other workers in the field, I owe an inestimable debt of gratitude.

Acknowledgements

It was Sir Stephen Tumim who first pointed out to me how odd it was that, while Edith and Sacheverell Sitwell had both been the subjects of their own biographies, Osbert figured only in a group study. From the moment he had spoken I realised that this was the book I wanted to write.

Mr Howard Usher has performed a Herculean task in sorting the papers at Renishaw into some sort of order. His labours both made my work possible and ensured that anyone wishing to do so would be able to track down any document that I cite without spending too many hours in the quest.

Mr Anthony Thwaite has kindly read those parts of the book which relate to Osbert Sitwell's poetry and has reassured me that, while he does not necessarily agree with what I say, he does not think I have made too many foolish errors.

Mr Neil Ritchie has been most generous in introducing me to his treasure house of Sitwelliana. His knowledge of the subject is so comprehensive that he should have undertaken this biography himself.

Mr Roger Cazalet of Chatto & Windus has shown himself a skilled and conscientious editor. Miss Jenny Overton picked up a distressingly large number of inconsistencies, repetitions and other such infelicities. I hope not too many remain. Mr Douglas Matthews, that prince among indexers, worked with his customary diligence.

I would like to thank all those who have allowed me to see and quote from papers in their possession or of which they control the copyright, who have shared with me their memories of Sir Osbert Sitwell, and have helped me in many other ways over the last few years. Not all their names appear below, but I acknowledge with gratitude Lord Aberconway, Mr Nicolas Barker, the Duke of Beaufort, Sir Martyn Beckett, Mr Philip Bobbitt, the Hon. Raymond Bonham Carter, Mr Edward Chaney, Mrs Anne Chisholm, Mr John Colvin, Mr Michael De-la-Noy, the Duke of Devonshire, Mrs Jessica Douglas-Home, Mrs Valerie Eliot, Mr T. M. Farmiloe, Sir Ewen Fergusson, Sir Brinsley Ford, Sir Edward Ford, Mr Richard Garnett, Lord Gladwyn, Dr Richard Greene, Mr John Gross, Sir Rupert Hart-Davis, Mr Simon Heneage, Mr Anthony Hobson, the late Lord Horder, Mr Bruce Hunter, Mr David Fraser Jenkins, Mr Francis King, Mr James Knox, Professor Hermione Lee, the late Mr James Lees-Milne, Mr Mark Le Fanu, Mrs Clarissa Lewis, Professor and Mrs Roger Louis, Mr Michael Meredith, the late Lady Alexandra Metcalfe, Mr Roger Morgan, the Hon. Lady Mosley, Mr Nigel Nicolson, Mr Eric Norris, Mr Derek Parker, the late Mrs

Acknowledgements

Myfanwy Piper, Dr Mark Pottle, Mr Anthony and Lady Violet Powell, Mr Piers Paul Read, Mr Kenneth Rose, Mr Anthony Rota, Mr John Saumarez-Smith, the late Sir Stephen Spender, Mr Thomas Staley, the Earl of Stockton, Sir Peter Ustinov, Mr Hugo Vickers, Sir Marcus Worsley, Mr Adrian Wright, Mr Martin Young.

Librarians and archivists never cease to astonish me by their patience and generosity. In particular I must thank Mrs Margaret Richards of Badminton, Ms Jacqueline Kavanagh of the BBC Written Archives, Dr Vincent Giroud of the Beinecke Library, Ms Lisa Brower of the Berg Collection, Mr Timothy Rogers and Mr Colin Harris of the Bodleian Library, Dr Elizabeth James of the British Library, Ms Kathleen Cann of the Cambridge University Library, Mr Peter Day of Chatsworth, Mr Matthew Phillips of Christ Church, Oxford, Mr Alan Kucia of the Churchill Archives Centre, Ms Tracey Earl of Coutts & Co., Ms Elizabeth Rainey of the University of Durham Library, Ms Sue Usher of the English Faculty Library at Oxford, Major P. A. Lewis (ret'd) of the Grenadier Guards, Ms Barbara La Borde and all of the staff of the Harry Ransom Humanities Research Center, Mr Nick Wood of the Hertfordshire County Record Office, Ms Melanie Wisner of the Houghton Library, Mr Robert McCown of the University of Iowa Library, Mr Peter McNiven of the John Rylands Library, Ms Jacqueline Cox of King's College Library, Mr Christopher Sheppard of Leeds University Library, Mr Alan Bell and all the staff of the London Library, Ms Carol Ibrahim and Ms Ruth Vyze of London University Library, Mr Sidney Huttner of the McFarlin Library, Mrs Fiona Wilkes of Merton College Library, Mr Howard Gotlieb of the Mulgar Memorial Library, Mr Michael Bott of the University of Reading Library, Mr Richard Olney of the Royal Commission on Historical Manuscripts, Ms Julia Abel-Smith of the Royal Society of Literature, Mrs O. M. Geddes of the National Library of Scotland, Ms Elizabeth Inglis of the University of Sussex Library, and Mr Robert Evans of the National Library of Wales.

My final and greatest debt is to my wife Clare for her endless patience and generous help and for understanding people so much better than I do.

The Eye of Childhood

The eye of childhood faithfully records
The destined figures creaking on the boards . . .
(Introduction to England Reclaimed)

FRANCIS Osbert Sacheverell Sitwell was a man whose pride in his aristocratic ancestry coexisted uneasily with his conviction that the artist was the sole truly superior being. Only in his auto-biography, where his background and upbringing were triumphantly transmuted into art, did these two ill-suited elements achieve complete reconciliation.

His ancestry was, indeed, imposing; if not quite so splendiferous as he, and still more his sister Edith, were accustomed to assert. The Sitwells – or Cytewelles, as they were spelt in the fourteenth century – had been landowners in Derbyshire for over six hundred years. In the seventeeth century they ventured into industry, set up a large iron-works at Eckington, became one of the world's pre-eminent manufacturers of nails, and built themselves a fine new house at Renishaw, a few miles from their previous home. The direct line ended with the death of William Sitwell in 1776. William's nephew, Francis Hurt, inherited Renishaw. Francis evidently had great reverence for the family name: not only did he give it to his son as a Christian name but on succeeding to Renishaw he adopted it as his own surname. Young Sitwell Hurt, when he eventually inherited the estate, thus did so as Sitwell Sitwell: 'Perhaps his hypersensitive descendant should resume the patronymic and call himself Sir Hurt Hurt,' remarked Evelyn Waugh in 1961.[1]

In his autobiography Osbert* ignored his manufacturing forebears by

---

*I dislike implying a non-existent intimacy by the use of a Christian name, but so many Sitwells will be referred to so often in this book that any other course would seem inexpedient.

leaping boldly from the early Cytewelles to the first baronet, Sir Sitwell Sitwell. 'There are precious few Englishmen who could not assume a mediaeval name if they chose to pick about in their pedigree,' Waugh wrote to Nancy Mitford.[2] This was less well justified than his earlier jibe; though it may have strayed through the female line, Osbert's direct descent from fourteenth-century Derbyshire landowners could not be questioned. But Osbert certainly preferred not to dwell on the family's brush with trade four hundred years later; he left the source of Sitwell Sitwell's wealth discreetly obscure.

He showed no similar reticence when it came to the zest with which Sitwell Sitwell and his heir dissipated the fruits of their ancestors' industry; this, indeed, Osbert felt more a matter for congratulation than for shame. Sir Sitwell, as he was to become after the Prince Regent visited Renishaw and repaid the hospitality with a baronetcy, displayed the incontinent extravagance that was to mark his descendants. He built stables, gates, triumphal arches; imported marble chimney-pieces which had been discarded by the Duke of York, pictures and tapestries, fine furniture; flung out a ballroom: all so that the Regent could be entertained in the style to which he was accustomed. Fortunately for posterity, he had excellent taste and left a much embellished property behind him; unfortunately for his heir, he also left a much diminished fortune to match the lavish train of life which he had established.

Undeterred, the second baronet, Sir George, behaved with equal prodigality. Horses and politics were his particular indulgence but he also made unwise investments, was the victim of a crooked solicitor and lost a fortune in the crash of the Sheffield Land Bank. In 1846 he was forced to shut up Renishaw and eke out a – relatively – penurious existence in the small towns of Germany. He died not long afterwards and the family fortunes showed no signs of reviving under the third baronet, Sir Reresby. It was left to Sir Reresby's widow to pull things together during the minority of her son, George. Her astuteness, coupled with the discovery of rich seams of coal beneath the land at Renishaw, ensured that when the fourth baronet came of age in 1883 he found himself master of an estate which was not merely unencumbered but conspicuously profitable.

Sometime in the early 1860s a small boy, escorted by a nurse, was travelling by train across England. A kindly old gentleman sitting opposite asked him who he was. 'I am Sir George Sitwell, baronet,' the child is said to have replied. 'I am four years old and the youngest baronet in

England.'[3] By this response he demonstrated both an alarming awareness of his own consequence and an inability to conceive what impression he might make on other people. Both characteristics were to mark him throughout his life.

In the four volumes of his autobiography Osbert Sitwell portrayed his father as an eccentric on the grandest possible scale, grotesque yet awe-inspiring, a cross between Don Quixote and Lewis Carroll's White Knight. Given Osbert's freely admitted dislike of Sir George, it is tempting to assume that this was a caricature, largely the fruit of his imagination; an attempt to avenge himself on, or perhaps come to terms with, a man who he believed had done much to ruin his life. Elements of exaggeration there certainly were and many of Osbert's best anecdotes were embellished so as to make a point more forcibly or just to raise a laugh at his father's expense. But few seem to have been wholly invented. Sir George was a very curious figure; in some ways remarkably appealing, in some ridiculous, in some curmudgeonly and mean.

Anthony Powell, who often met him at Renishaw, insists that he was every bit as bizarre as his son described him; indeed, that the portrait was, if anything, too generous: 'In depicting the figure of Sir George Sitwell ... the less pleasant sides are toned down, rather than exaggerated.'[4] This is not the impression of most observers, however. The weight of evidence suggests that, though little may have been made up in Osbert's portrayal, a great deal was suppressed or distorted; the impression given of Sir George's personality was unfair. 'He wasn't nearly as comic a figure as [Osbert] made him appear,' Osbert's younger brother, Sacheverell, told the historian of the family, John Pearson. 'He was a much nicer person. I think he was much nicer than Osbert.'[5] Kenneth Clark felt the same: Sir George was 'nicer and sadder than Osbert allowed in his ungenerous portrait'.[6] Again and again in reading of his dealings with other people one feels that, though he must often have been infuriating, his intentions were nearly always excellent and his courtesy immaculate. Osbert, with some reason, makes fun of his ridiculous inventions – a musical toothbrush, a small revolver for killing wasps; his self-proclaimed omniscience – continuously putting right lawyers, architects, doctors, gardeners, on the more arcane details of their professions; his megalomaniac building plans – remove that hill, divert that stream, here we must have a triumphal arch! But his son takes too little account of the fact that much of Sir George's ingenuity was usefully and practically employed; that his knowledge was unusually wide and his advice by no means always silly; that his plans quite often came to fulfilment and both his Derbyshire home at Renishaw and his Tuscan palace at Montegufoni were rendered immeasurably more beautiful by his activities. Osbert mocks his father's genius for financial obfuscation and his tendency to keep careful count of the pennies while allowing the pounds to flood away, but gives no hint that Sir George had a shrewd financial brain, was one of the first people to see the potential in South African mining shares, and made quite as much money on the Stock Exchange as he squandered on visionary projects.

If Sir George had been idle or stupid he might have been less resented by his son, but he was clever and alarmingly energetic – the cleverest in the family, Alan Pryce-Jones believed: 'On the rare occasions when I observed him in action, he struck me as a move or two ahead of his children.'[7] He wrote better than they did too, Kenneth Clark maintained: 'I believe that *au fond* they were all jealous of him.'[8] This opinion is harder to accept. His finest book, *On the Making of Gardens*, is clearly based on much travel, study and reflection, but the style is lush and over-romantic; the judgments dogmatic – 'Flower beds in stars or moons or rounded figures cannot be right; they are simply unquiet.' His advice to his readers was no doubt soundly based but not always entirely practical: 'The great secret of success in garden-making [is] that we should abandon the struggle to make nature beautiful round the house and should rather move the house to where nature is beautiful.'[9] But he did know a great deal about Italian gardens in particular, his knowledge of the Middle Ages was extensive and peculiar and his views were taken seriously by genealogists and social historians of established reputation.

His problem was that, almost since childhood, there had been no one to curb his whims, challenge his views, even to make fun of him. An only son, he had grown arrogant and aloof. His appearance fitted his character: 'a suitable model for Van Dyck', Harold Acton described him; while Peter Quennell wrote of 'his height, his patrician good looks, the air of dignified remoteness and self-sufficient impassivity with which he travelled through existence'.[10] Quennell saw something in him of Meredith's Sir Willoughby Patterne, and certainly few people can have been so complete an egoist. His view of contemporary life was almost entirely solipsistic and rendered the more eccentric by his firm assumption that, whatever subject might be in question, it had almost certainly been done better in the Middle Ages. Inevitably this led to a certain remoteness from contemporary life and an indifference to the views, the activities, the very existence of other people. Indeed, he rarely even noticed other people, never knew his constituents in the days when he was in the House of Commons, and was capable of walking past his children in the street without a hint of recognition.[11] At Renishaw, when confronted by his guests, he would be polite, even convivial, but he would usually lunch alone an hour before the others got to table.[12] When Beverley Nichols was introduced to him, Sir George 'merely sniffed and went away to sit by himself in a corner'. Such rudeness was unusual and suggests an exceptional degree of preoccupation; it was entirely in character, however, that he should look up in the course of the meal that followed this aborted introduction and observe plaintively, 'I never know anybody in this house.'[13]

'Sir George is the strangest old bugger you ever met,' his butler, Henry Moat, once remarked to the composer Constant Lambert.[14] He was prodigal when it came to acquiring works of art or constructing grandiose architectural follies, but would parsimoniously examine the smallest item on a bill or an estimate and was convinced that everyone except himself was guilty of the most wanton extravagance and must be curbed in their excesses. Osbert attributed this obsession to the depredations made on the family fortune in the nineteenth century by the army of poor relations who took up residence at Renishaw and exploited their host with parasitic vigour: 'To be financially safe, he felt, one should be friendless. "Such a mistake," he remarked to me once without explanation, "to have friends." '[15] Sir George devoted much of his energies to worrying about money and was preoccupied by thoughts of his incipient pauperdom. His fears were fanned by the monumental extravagance of his wife.

Sir George's father-in-law, Henry Denison, first Earl of Londes-borough, spent on a scale which made the Sitwells seem like cheese-paring niggards. The family had amassed an immense fortune in the City of London in the mid-eighteenth century and their wealth was augmented by Elizabeth Denison, Marchioness of Conyngham, mistress of George IV. Osbert gallantly defended the reputation of his forebear in his autobiography but she remains one of the most rapacious harpies ever to have plundered the royal coffers. The Conynghams' son, Lord Albert, inherited the Denison millions, took their name, and became first Baron Londesborough. *His* son, Henry, became an earl and pushed still further into the upper reaches of the aristocracy by marrying a daughter of the Duke of Beaufort. He thus ensured that their younger daughter Ida, the future Lady Ida Sitwell, could claim direct descent from the Plantagenets. History was not Lady Ida's strong point and she seems to have taken little pleasure in her royal ancestry; to her children, however, it was a subject for infinite satisfaction. With alarming zest, Lord Londesborough squandered the huge fortune that he had inherited on race-horses, grand houses, theatrical productions and other such diversions of the very rich. By the time Ida needed to look for a husband her family's wealth had been dramatically reduced; she, on the other hand, had been imbued with the conviction that there was nothing which she could not afford, no whim which it was not merely permissible but desirable to indulge.

Sir George Sitwell was an ardent genealogist and regarded his wife's lineage with all due deference. Lady Ida was also beautiful, and charming in a vapid, prattling way. By the standards of the time she was a most suitable match for a wealthy but not particularly grandiose baronet. In fact the combination proved disastrous. She was a stupid woman, 'slightly mentally retarded' thought Harold Acton,[16] and she was neither able nor willing to accompany her husband on his intellectual adventures. 'I have been much alone all my life,' Sir George told Osbert sadly, 'as your mother could not be and did not try to be a companion.'[17] Confronted by his indifference she retreated into a twilight life of bridge, bad novels and social fatuity. Until disaster struck she was never actively miserable – most strong emotions were beyond her – but she suffered from a nagging discontent. 'Have you ever been happy?' she one night asked her daughter Edith. 'Yes, Mother. Haven't you?' 'Never *bird-happy*.'[18] Perhaps with encouragement she could have learned to tread new territories but she lacked both animation and application: 'One always felt boredom was just round the corner,' her cousin by marriage, Constance Sitwell, remembered.[19]

She loved flowers – preferably when out of season and expensive – rich scents and fabrics, beautiful jewels, but was inordinately generous and scattered her valuable possessions among her friends and relations with the same unthinking prodigality as she had acquired them. She recognised her extravagance but could do nothing to control it: 'I can't go to Paris,' she once explained to Anthony Powell. 'I'll spend money like a drunken sailor.'[20] It was as if only by spending could she keep ennui at bay; an attitude which filled her hyperactive husband with perplexed alarm. Her profligacy drove a fresh wedge between them; by the time their youngest child was born their relationship oscillated between cool neutrality and out-and-out dislike.

When talking to the nine-year-old Osbert about his ancestors, Sir George once murmured pensively: 'We've been working up towards something for a long time, for well over a century.'[21] Though he was in fact to take considerable pride in his children's achievements it is unlikely that he was contemplating a career in literature when he predicted this resplendent future – something more political or pro-consular must have been what he had in mind. It was therefore something of a disappointment to him when his first child was a daughter, a disappointment that grew ever more severe as it became obvious that Edith was not going to mature into the sort of amiable, attractive and intellectually unassuming girl who could be expected to marry well and thus redress the initial solecism of her sex.

> To you, sad child, upon the darkened stair,
> Poor flaxen foundling of the upper air,

Osbert dedicated one of his earlier books of verse,[22] and the image of Edith as a sad child – lonely, unfulfilled, at odds with the world in which she lived – emerges strikingly from all recollections of her family at the time. 'I had a very terrible childhood and youth, so terrible that I *never* think of it and *never* mention it,' she told Stephen Spender many years later.[23] In fact, she rarely ceased to brood on it and mentioned it repeatedly, but to the outside eye it does not seem that it was so very terrible. She was not treated cruelly, nor even seriously neglected. She might have been happier if she had been. Her trouble was that her parents tried to turn her into something that she could never be and failed to understand, or even to try to understand, her true potentiality. 'What are you going to be when you are grown up?' a friend of her mother asked her. 'A genius,' Edith replied.[24] Sir George, though with some doubts, might have accommodated a genius as a son but in a daughter such pretensions had to be resolutely curbed: the weapons used were gymnastics, the cello, and horrific contraptions of rubber and steel intended to adjust physical deficiencies which the doctors had detected or imagined in her legs, back and nose. 'I doubt whether any child was ever more mismanaged by her parents,' wrote Osbert.[25] Whether or not, objectively, she had good grounds for being so miserable is neither here nor there: as Victoria Glendinning has remarked in her brilliantly sympathetic biography, 'I have ended up with a great respect for her, and a very protective feeling, because of the loneliness and fear that were her almost constant companions.'[26]

Any illusions Edith might have cherished about her importance in her parents' eyes were dispelled at the birth of Osbert on 6 December 1892 when she was five years old. The rejoicing in the household, the ringing of bells in the churches of his birthplace, Scarborough, must quickly have convinced her that something of great consequence had occurred. An heir had been born, and a mere daughter found herself relegated even further into the background. It was not just a matter of status or comparative importance: Lady Ida, whom Edith would have loved with passion if she had been given even the least encouragement, made a fuss of her son in a way her daughter had never experienced. Osbert was allowed to crawl over her bed, disorganise her papers, inspect her scents and jewellery; Edith had barely been tolerated in her bedroom. This was not just a tribute to the generally accepted myth of male superiority. Edith was gauche and superficially unattractive: a silly mother who relished pretty things was unlikely to find many charms in such a child, or to extend to it any great part of her limited capacity for affection.

Another five years on, and the family was completed by the birth of Sacheverell. Sachie, as he was invariably called, found life less stressful than his elder siblings. He was an attractive and relatively uncomplicated child for whom it was as natural to love and be loved as it was difficult for his sister. Five years between brothers is a formidable gap but Edith's disappearance into a world of governesses and music lessons left Osbert hungry for companionship. 'I suppose that when he was a very small child I understood him better than did anyone else,' wrote Osbert. 'I instinctively comprehended what he wanted to say, before others could: and on this foundation our friendship was soundly based.'[27] Friendship was an inadequate word for a relationship that was emotionally and intellectually intense; until Osbert went to boarding school the brothers shared a room, talked endlessly, and were as near inseparable as the demands of grown-ups would allow. They did not wilfully exclude their sister but inevitably at this stage of their lives she was a distant figure. Their father was still more remote but Lady Ida showed Sachie the same warm affection as Osbert already enjoyed. Edith later accused her younger brother of inventing a relationship which had never existed; Sachie 'created for himself a wonderful dream-mother who understood everything and shielded him in some extraordinary way'. The facts 'were sadly and terribly different'. She conceded, though, that Sachie had been sheltered from the worst afflictions of an unhappy childhood; 'the horror was all mine'.[28] 'The facts' seem to have been that Lady Ida was put off and slightly frightened by her intransigent daughter while regarding her sons as delightful playthings to be indulged and exhibited to her friends. Such an attitude did not provide a promising basis for a lifetime's relationship between a mother and her children but it served well enough while the boys were uncritical and undemanding.

The Sitwell children, whether viewed as a pair or as a trio, endured a strangely isolated existence. They made close relationships with game-keepers, gardeners, retainers of every kind, but did not play with the children of the – anyway scanty – neighbours or even estate employees. While at Renishaw they remained usually within the confines of the great house and its immediate surroundings. When they ventured out it was as if into a jungle populated by an alien and probably hostile fauna. Sacheverell described meeting a group of miners' children when black-berrying in the woods near his home. 'They were of a very flaxen, long-headed, Danish type, and their hands and faces were of an indescribable blackness which accentuated the pallor of their skin . . . Their speech was slurred and clipped to a degree that made it hard to understand, and their noise, like the sparrow twittering in a low spray of leaves, seemed out of all proportion to the mark they made on the landscape.'[29]

But even among children of their own kind they felt isolated and ill at ease. At Madame Augustine's dancing classes in Scarborough the offspring of the local *noblesse* chattered away happily and made plans for bicycle rides or picnics; the Sitwells clung together, left to themselves by contemporaries who found them strange and unappealing. It was not for another fifteen years, wrote Osbert, that he realised he and his siblings were indeed different: they were artists in embryo 'with nerves and brains created for the one purpose of a certain kind of sensitive perception',[30] the others were not. As an explanation of their social isolation this is hardly adequate; many 'artists in embryo' have contrived to mingle happily with their contemporaries and draw pleasure from their pastimes. A crippling compound of arrogance and shyness was more to blame. But for all these reasons the Sitwells shrank from any intercourse with other children. Children's parties Osbert described as 'those fearful ordeals imposed on the young by their elders';[31] it evidently never occurred to him that some of the young might positively have relished such encounters. It was not until he became a Guards officer many years later that he belatedly discovered the 'comfort to be derived from friendship with those of one's own age'.[32] Much misery was to have been experienced before that revelation. In the meantime the Sitwell children existed in a remote half-world of their own – self-sufficient, suspicious, like snails tentatively venturing from their shells, poised to retreat at the first signs of hostility. A visitor to Renishaw in 1900 saw them about to leave for some expedition or other: 'I was struck by their strange quietness and restraint – so unusual for their age – as they descended the stairs in slow, dignified steps.'[33]

Osbert's natural diffidence was reinforced by ill-health. When only eighteen months old he was seriously ill, subjected to a course of mustard baths and ipecacuanha, and left a delicate child much plagued by croup. A year later he had serious convulsions when suffering from chicken-pox. Then Sir George, on what must have been an infrequent visit of inspection, saw Osbert in his bath and noticed several spots. He told Lady Ida and the nurse that they should call a doctor in case the child had measles. The women ridiculed this idea, assuring him that it was only heat-rash. Sir George left for London 'and had a telegram a day later saying that two doctors were with Osbert. The clever nurses had given him a nice cold bath that morning, with the result that his life was in danger.'[34] By the standards of the day Osbert was not a disastrously sickly child, but nor was he strong. The inevitable childish ailments seemed to afflict him more severely than they did most of his contemporaries and inculcated a lifetime tendency to believe that he was ill unless positive evidence to the contrary was forthcoming.

Perhaps in part as a result of this he was slow to develop, learning to read late and having trouble over the enunciation of certain consonants. This was an offence in the eyes of his father, compounded by Osbert's precocious appreciation of flowers and sunsets and his reluctance to engage in the more robust pursuits appropriate to boyhood. Sir George was himself an aesthete with a genuine appreciation of beauty in every form. He was in time to foster his son's artistic interests. But he also believed – provided he did not have to indulge in them himself – in cold baths, bracing walks and character-building sports. 'Unless you learn to play ping-pong properly, you can never hope to be a Leader of Men,' he assured Osbert gravely.[35] Osbert was never to play ping-pong properly and viewed the sport with detestation. He was frightened of horses and fell off them painfully and promptly. Guns bruised his shoulder. Worst of all, he was bored by cricket. His grandfather, Lord Londesborough, arranged for Osbert to be put down for the MCC at birth; if Osbert ever entered the Pavilion at Lord's it must have been with deep reluctance. Londesborough was given cause to suspect this unhealthy tendency when he invited his four-year-old grandson to the Scarborough Cricket Week, of which he was president. Osbert fell asleep at a critical moment and tumbled off his seat at the feet of his scandalised relations. Almost the only exercise which he took with any pleasure was walking. 'I adore it,' he told his friend the writer and philanthropist Bryher, 'and always normally go, *very fast*, for long walks.'[36] The pursuit was solitary, offered opportunities for looking at flowers or landscapes, was free from competition and left time for thought. Sir George would not have felt it at all a proper activity for a growing boy.

Osbert never felt that his distaste for the traditional pursuits of the English country gentleman was in any way a weakness, or regretted the days he might have spent with rod or gun. He was saddened, however, by the disappointment his aversion to blood sports and similar activities caused to people he liked and respected: Mark Kirkby, the gamekeeper, or Maynard Hollingworth, who was already employed at Renishaw when Osbert was a child and remained as agent until after the Second World War, where he handed on the charge to his son. Hollingworth, in particular, fostered his interest in birds and flowers, showed him where a Camberwell Beauty was to be seen and where the white kingfishers were nesting. Another source of country lore, indeed of knowledge on almost any subject, was the inimitable Henry Moat. Sancho Panza to Sir George's Don Quixote, Moat had entered Sitwell service in 1893. 'You were a fine young lady then,' he wrote to Lady Ida many years later, 'full of high spirits and fun. I would not have missed the career for the earth . . . I never feel lonely when I think of my past life, the cinema is not in it.'[37] The remark suggests both the enjoyment which Moat derived from his work, and the robustness with which he expressed his views. His relationship with Sir George combined veneration with affectionate contempt. He was always ready to apply a touch of stern common sense to Sir George's more exotic conceptions – when his employer recommended the use of condensed milk in the manufacture of knife handles Moat gloomily pointed out that there would be trouble if the cat got at them – but was quick to defend his master against attacks from outside. 'Ain't it amusin',' Lady Ida would say, after recounting some anecdote about her husband in the strangulated cockney that was then commonly affected among the upper classes. Moat kept a stony silence; not by a flicker of his eye would he concede that Sir George could ever be ridiculous.[38] Only with the Sitwell children would he in time allow himself the luxury of sharing their amusement.

Moat came from a family of fishermen who had lived in the same house in Whitby for more than two centuries. Though himself not particularly drawn to the sea, he somehow managed to exude a nautical self-confidence and, temporarily at least, convinced Osbert that a life on the ocean wave must be the noblest of vocations. His brother Bill had a pet seal which he would bring over by train to Renishaw: the children were devoted to it – 'We used to ride on his back, which caused us to stink, permanently, of fish,' Edith remembered.[39] To Osbert, Henry Moat was the source of all wisdom, in many ways the most important adult figure of his childhood. Moat in 1938 heard of Osbert's *Who's Who* entry, in which he claimed that he had been 'educated in the holidays from Eton'. 'Well, sir,' he wrote, 'I make bold to claim some of that: because whether you were at Scarboro', Renishaw or abroad and you or Master Sachie wanted to know anything about things on the earth, the sea under the earth or in the air above, you generally came to me, even when you had a tutor, and often the tutors came too.'[40]

More formal education was provided by a series of governesses and the tutors whose knowledge Moat had thus dismissed. One of the former kept a detailed diary for 1901. Osbert weighed four stone nine pounds in March and three pounds more seven months later. There seems to have been an orthodox routine of lessons and walks, with fishing at Renishaw and riding at Scarborough to relieve the monotony. The doctor came once a week; 'Edith's boots and spinal stays arrived,' was an entry that struck a chilling note.[41] It does not seem that any of the teachers did much to inculcate a love of learning in their charges, but they encouraged Osbert to read, or at least did nothing to curb the habit. History was his favourite subject; he devoured every book on which he could lay his hands, his conclusions coloured by one governess who was a strong Imperialist and 'considered History as a nice, motherly, white-haired woman, robed in a becoming Union Jack'. Osbert was inclined to believe that, since things could hardly be expected to improve, history might safely be assumed to have come to an end; his governess told him that he was very probably correct.[42] This robustly anglocentric view of world affairs did not survive maturity; the habit of reading history lasted an even shorter time – 'a practice of which school quickly broke me', he remarked drily. Early in 1902 an expedition undertaken in the cause of history yielded a richer dividend. A governess took him and Sachie to Kensington Palace. It was the first time he had entered a public building except for the purpose of religion; the visit enthralled him and set the pattern for a lifetime of passionate sight-seeing. For the time being, he had to confine himself to what was immediately at hand, but his eyes were opened to wider horizons by an undergraduate tutor who had just paid a first visit to Rome. His tutor's incoherent and ardent enthusiasm provided the nearest approach to real inspiration that Osbert encountered in all his schooling; he vowed that one day he would visit not only Rome but the whole world besides.

Renishaw was home, he wrote in his memoirs; arrival a delight, departure painful.[43] The family went there only for August and the first part of September, otherwise it lay uninhabited, almost, indeed, uninhabitable, for it was grimly cold in winter, damp at any time, with only one bathroom before the First World War and precious little else by way of comfort. 'That ancient hall of yours looks like a place that needs 1400 slates a year to keep the rain out and is a museum of inconveniences,' wrote Bernard Shaw. 'Still, if you knock it down and replace it by a dozen bungalows you will die a rich man.'[44]

In origin it was a Carolean hall, extravagantly enlarged during the Regency. It was long, low and gloomy, crouching in its park above the seams of coal which had provided the money for its expansion. From the cellars could be heard the clanking of the trolleys in the pits below, at night the park was lit by the furnaces of the nearby iron foundries, from the pit-heads the black dust drifted, lying thick upon the lawns, besmirching the dresses of any female guest rash enough to venture out. 'Renishaw was a quite horrible house, I always thought,' wrote Harold Acton,[45] and most of those who went there described it as grim, hostile, sinister. It was infested with ghosts as another house might be by rats: Sir Sitwell Sitwell calling from his deathbed; young Henry Sacheverell, who had drowned in the river at the edge of the park and returned to give unsuspecting women guests a damp and chilly kiss. Beverley Nichols found it 'a frightening house. I remember lunching there ... It was midsummer but I could not rid myself of the impression that I was in the depths of winter; not because the day was cold but because the whole vast pile seemed to be over-shadowed by ... something.'[46] Today, with the pits closed, the ghosts exorcised, a family cheerfully ensconced, it is hard to imagine what all the fuss was about. To a child it must have seemed forbidding. Yet Osbert loved every bit of it and barely noticed the pervading gloom that struck the rest of the world so forcibly.

The annual agricultural and flower show at Renishaw was for Osbert the signal that time was nearly up; the return to their home in Scarborough would take place a few days later. Scarborough, with its combination of curative waters and bracing sea air, had been for a long time a resort much patronised by the nobility and gentry of north-east England. For Osbert it was

> A town of musty churches, built
> By regiments of cackling, dry ghosts in feather boas
> Who sought their souls to ransom for their gold –
> A town devoted to the rich, the old.[47]

He never felt that he belonged there, as he did at Renishaw or, later, in Italy, but it left the most vivid impression on his childish mind and figured largely in his poetry, short stories and only successful novel. The Sitwells had been going there since the eighteenth century and in 1880 had bought Wood End, a dull, massive, oblong house in the fashionable Crescent, built some sixty years earlier in orange-yellow stone. Sir George's mother had handed it over to her son in 1886 and herself retreated to Hay Brow, a smaller house with a much larger garden three miles or so from the centre of town. Sir George at once set to work reshaping the gardens and constructing a huge conservatory to contain one of the tallest palm-trees to be found in Britain.[48] 'There was an odd mixture of extreme comfort and the opposite in that house,' wrote Constance Sitwell; 'there was the all-pervading smell of gardenias and white lilacs and carnations; and always that big vase of tuberoses, and soft sofas and wood fires, and good coffee and cigarettes, and the feeling that no one *need* do anything, and the more money they spent, the better.'[49]

Scarborough was the home of Miss Lloyd, an exquisitely pretty old lady of artistic talent who served as an honorary poor relation to the Sitwells and achieved the rare distinction of being liked and respected by both Sir George and Lady Ida. By profession, in so far as she had a profession, she was a painter of china; Sir George installed her in a workshop in a tower in the garden of Wood End, where she gave lessons to members of the family. 'The house itself was full of hideous pieces in sky-blue china, twisted with white designs,' Osbert told Lady Desborough, 'made by all my relations, even my poor darling mother, who was taught the accomplishment as a bride of seventeen, and seems to have been far worse at it than anyone else!'[50] Miss Lloyd was a valued ally of Osbert, spoiling him, giving him presents, and doing her best to persuade Sir George that his son was neither idle nor degenerate and would thrive on liberal treatment. Osbert used to give her presents too, and 'soon discovered that I preferred the pleasure of giving to that of receiving'.[51] It is possible to see the baser side of this – Osbert longed to be loved and valued; he relished the power which the donor can exercise over the recipient; he disliked being beholden to others. But whatever the qualifications, generosity is still an amiable trait. It was one which Osbert manifested all his life.

Another old lady who bulked large in Scarborough life was Osbert's grandmother, Louisa, Lady Sitwell. Lady Sitwell was a power-house of good works, one of those gentle and unassuming creatures whose apparent diffidence conceals an unshakeable will and considerable organising powers. Today she might be making a fortune in the City or, more probably, running one of the larger health authorities; in Scarborough in 1900 she wrestled with drunkenness, rescued fallen women, ministered to the clergy and worried about her grandchildren. For Osbert she provided thoughtful attention, measured affection and a set of unwavering standards, none of which was a feature of his life at home. For this, her role in his life was of prime importance. But though he loved her, it was more because he felt it was expected of him than with real ardour. She did little to enhance the joys of his life and deplored the pleasure he derived from dancing, barrel-organs, and other such trifling diversions. After a prolonged dose of uncompromising rectitude it was, he wrote, 'a greater pleasure to me to visit my more hedonistic relatives on the maternal side'.[52]

He did not have far to go. Londesborough Lodge – a house a little larger and far more elegant than Wood End – was also in the Crescent, only a door or two away. The Sitwell children treated it as a second home, and one even more luxurious than their own. Lord Londesborough liked to have a lot of children around and enjoyed organising treats for them; not all of these were to his grandson's taste – the Cricket Week being a pre-eminent example – but visits to the circus, parties to view the fireworks, expeditions to the woods around Scarborough, gave Osbert enormous and enduring pleasure. Christmas at the Londesborough country home of Blankney was less agreeable; to live in propinquity with an army of young cousins proved daunting and the plays in French which they were forced to perform before the grown-ups on Twelfth Night provided an especially painful deterrent. Sir George, reclusive, scholarly, weak on small talk, found the annual ritual distasteful but endured it for the sake of the family. He assumed, without ever asking, that his children relished the festivities. 'Ida would take them there,' he told his daughter-in-law many years later, but 'I found out after two Christmases that they simply hated it'.[53] The annual visits did not stop, however: tradition and the pull of the Londesborough connection proved too great.

There cannot have been many such occasions when Sir George sacrificed his own comfort or convenience for his family. He was a supremely selfish man and took it for granted that whatever suited him best must also be best for other people. He imposed his whims with arbitrary, even despotic authority. In 1900 he decided that a family conversation-piece should be painted, to match the fine late eighteenth-century group by John Singleton Copley which already hung at Renishaw. Since the chosen painter, John Singer Sargent, refused to leave his studio, the family came south, accompanied by a commode designed by Robert Adam and built by Chippendale, a Brussels tapestry, and other possessions designed to lend territorial verisimilitude to the finished painting. Sir George instructed Sargent in the minutiae of his trade, Sargent kept his temper and all went swimmingly. The only fracas arose when Sir George urged the painter to emphasise the slight crookedness of Edith's nose. Sargent not only refused to do so but introduced a slight crookedness into the nose of Sir George himself. The final portrait was a miracle of stylish artificiality: Sir George in riding-boots, though in fact he rarely rode; Lady Ida in evening dress and a hat suitable for Ascot, arranging flowers, a task she preferred to leave to others; Edith affectionately close to a father she would never willingly have approached; the boys unconvincingly contented as they played together on the floor. The episode was notable for Osbert in another way. While the work was going on the family settled in a house belonging to Winston Churchill's aunt. The room where the children did their daily lessons was festooned with photographs of Churchill, ranging from the baby to the young MP. 'Wherever we looked,' wrote Osbert, 'that face, already so well known, followed us with intent gaze, determined and dramatic.'[54] The children took an intense dislike to their enforced companion and would cover his photographs with newspapers before beginning work.

By now their relationship with their father was becoming difficult. Sir George noticed with concern that his children did not conform to the pattern which he deemed desirable, for their own good their excesses must be curbed and more proper instincts inculcated. Osbert in particular showed a disconcerting tendency to laugh at things which his father did not think funny and to fail to see jokes which Sir George found hilarious. This, Sir George felt, showed a weakness of understanding which potentially might prove most damaging. When their senses of humour *did* coincide, however, the results were not always happy. Sir George – it was the age of practical jokes – provided a collapsible chair for a luncheon guest, a portly alderman. Osbert sought to enhance the joke by changing the chairs around so that it was Sir George who ended on the floor. His father was outraged: 'I might have most seriously injured my back,' he remarked as he clambered to his feet. Osbert was in disgrace for weeks.[55]

But it was his children's extravagance that most alarmed the baronet.

In the early 1900s a lawsuit over the mines around Renishaw threatened to reduce his income. At once a reign of economic terror was introduced: not, of course, curbing serious or worthwhile expenditure such as the building of a new folly or the importation of statues for the garden, but involving a reduction in the children's pocket-money and the substitution of useful presents – cakes of soap, hairbrushes – for the more usual sweets or toys. The children, their father felt, could not learn soon enough how to make both ends meet in a hostile world. It was a lesson Osbert resolutely ignored; his main conflicts with his father lay far ahead but by the age of eight or nine he had learnt to consider him an adversary, to be circumvented if possible, but in the last resort to be fought to the death.

2

Educated in the Holidays
from Eton

IF one was required to devise the ideal English schoolboy one could do worse than start with Osbert Sitwell and search for the opposite to every characteristic. He had a few points in his favour. He was, for instance, never late for lessons: 'A martyr to a morbid punctuality,' he described himself,[1] and in the course of his life he wasted innumerable hours by arriving five minutes early for appointments with people who arrived five minutes late. To be on time for a class was not a guarantee of success, but at least it eliminated one potential point of friction. So also did his unfailing courtesy. 'I was brought up to be polite,' said his sister. 'It is the greatest possible disadvantage.'[2] Like his sister, Osbert was capable of appalling rudeness, but unless provoked was at pains to behave with an exquisite civility. He would have subscribed to the ancient adage: 'a gentleman is one who is never rude unintentionally'. This cut little ice with his fellow schoolboys; probably, indeed, did more to alienate them; but with the masters it went down well.

That was about all that could be said for Osbert as a schoolboy, however. He wrote of his 'race-horse-like eagerness to win',[3] but he rarely broke out of an apathetic trot during the years devoted to his education. Partly this was incapacity; mathematics, for example, seemed to be entirely beyond him – 'to add up twice-two would keep me awake at night'. Much more, however, it was disinclination, a revulsion against the drear learning by rote which was the order of the day. He was not actually lazy – 'I cannot bear to be idle for a moment and am, congenitally, a fusser, a plodder, one who takes trouble,' he wrote much later,[4] and this was almost as true when he was a boy as in maturity – but he rarely applied his industry where it could best have served his interests, in the eyes of his teachers, at least. He took, for instance, no trouble over the presentation of his work – his handwriting was atrocious – and few schoolmasters take the trouble to look beyond a messy and ill-spelt page to the imagination and sensibility that might underlie it.

No amount of application and academic success, however, would have made him popular among his fellows. Probably it would have made matters worse – Sitwell might have little to recommend him, seems to have been the accepted view, but at least he was not a swot. As it was, he liked in later life to portray himself as a victim of persecution. 'So bad . . . was the atmosphere of those days,' he wrote, 'so hopeless and lonely, that it becomes almost impossible for me to write of them without seeking to protect myself by ridiculing them.'[5] He simultaneously feared and despised most of his fellows. Always he felt himself an odd man out. When the houses of pro-Boers were stoned during the Boer War and Osbert found that his sympathies lay with the victims, he realised that: 'My heart did not beat with the heart of the herd.'[6] Schoolboys in any numbers are the herd *par excellence* and if one hopes to survive unscathed it is unwise to let one's heart beat too conspicuously to another rhythm. Osbert was not of the material from which contented schoolboys can be made. One of his few consoling reflections at the time was provided by a friend of his mother's who told him not to believe that school was the happiest time of his life – 'It isn't. You'll hate every moment of it!'[7] At least there were better things to hope for in a life thereafter.

But with the luxury of hindsight he remembered things as blacker than they were. His heart may have beaten to another rhythm but he was usually prudent enough to conceal his feelings. His sins were of omission rather than commission: he was a lamentable athlete, which meant that he could enjoy no trace of the heroic; he lacked charm, which meant that he found it difficult to make friends; he shrank from human contact – 'for all his urbanity he was fundamentally shy,' wrote Harold Acton of the mature Sitwell.[8] Photographs of the time show him as a heavy, slightly sullen child, withdrawn and self-contained. This was his protective armour and on the whole it worked. He was unpopular rather than hated; a nonentity to be ignored, not a martyr to seek out and destroy.

Sometimes the carapace cracked. 'I was born with a violent temper as my birthright,' Osbert wrote. When he indulged it, 'it would poison my blood for three whole days, making me feel wretchedly ill'.[9] At school he usually managed to keep it in check, but not invariably. His father was perceptive enough to recognise the risk. 'The first lesson in life is always to keep one's temper,' he told Osbert. 'Boys are always inclined to go on teasing anyone who gets huffy, though if he looked good-tempered and amused at their chaff they would stop.'[10] It was good advice but more easily accepted than followed. Osbert found the amusement and good temper hard to simulate but usually he managed at least to keep the huffiness under control.

Sir George specialised in injunctions that were sound in principle but not always easy to obey. 'The way to be popular is to look pleased when you meet people and always to look *at* them when you are talking to them,' was another piece of his advice. 'You will get on capitally with the other boys if you are friendly; and if you take every opportunity of doing a good turn to another boy . . . That is part of what I should call the art of being popular. Another part of it is always to take the most favourable view you can of other people's characters and actions and motives, and as far as you can without hypocrisy, to say things which will please them.'[11] Osbert's schooldays, indeed his whole life, would certainly have been happier if he had followed these precepts. So, for that matter, would Sir George's. But the behaviour suggested was hardly compatible with being a Sitwell. Even in the years of his ripest urbanity Osbert was never to be generally popular; at school the most he could hope for was not to be actively disliked.

Before launching into his boarding-school career Osbert was granted a brief warming-up period at a Scarborough day school. The experience was supposed to prepare him for the sterner tests ahead; in fact it thoroughly demoralised him at a time when encouragement was badly needed. The school was intended for the sons of 'superior tradesmen and rich farmers' and, if Osbert's somewhat hysterical account is to be trusted, these provincial worthies resented the fact that he was the son of a baronet and as such deemed certain to think himself superior to his fellows. Osbert, who had been taught by Lady Ida to consider baronets pitifully small fry, was baffled by this attitude. Not seeing how he could have offended, he was unable to defend himself. His reticence, however, did not protect him; he returned from his first day at school with 'two black eyes, an aching body and a sore heart'.[12] His father felt this to be rather a good sign; his son was obviously mixing with the other boys and learning to hold his own; luckily for Osbert, Miss Lloyd perceived his plight and did something to restore his self-confidence and his morale. Sir George, in fact, had other and more pressing problems to contend with.

At the best of times he was in a state of repressed agitation; as Osbert began his schooldays the defences cracked and he suffered a nervous breakdown which drove him into long periods of residence abroad and greatly reduced his activity within the family. Lady Ida in her turn was preoccupied by her husband's illness and often joined him in exile. The children were not neglected – the two grandmothers, in particular, took a keen interest in their well-being – but there was nobody at home to give Osbert the concentrated attention that he required. Miss Lloyd was the nearest thing to a mother-substitute; better than nothing but far short of what was needed.

By the time that Osbert moved on to his boarding school he had concluded that little if any pleasure was to be derived from learning and that the years ahead were likely to be at the best tedious, at the worst grimly painful. But the most immediate victim of his departure was his brother. In spite of the difference in their ages Osbert and Sachie had become almost inseparable, Sachie was an adoring younger brother who believed his senior to be a figure of infinite wisdom and understanding. Their relationship was not invariably harmonious – Osbert wrote of 'violent quarrels, such as only brothers can engage in'[13] – but the reconciliations were as satisfying as the quarrels had been brief. Sachie was always capable of passionate affection and as a child the greater part of it was lavished on his sibling. Sarah Bradford, in her perceptive biography,[14] has described the agony Sachie experienced when he saw his brother disappear to another, alien existence, abandoning him to a desolate solitude.

> And in one of the agonies of childhood,
> It would be in the second or third week of September,
> Going our hateful different ways to school . . .[15]

He solaced himself in an orgy of letter-writing: 'It will be so dull today after tea without you, darling.' 'I will write again tomorrow morning. I love you so much, darling. I miss you so much, darling.'[16] (The fact that Osbert never called Sachie 'darling' in return probably did no more than reflect the difference in their ages.) Time did little to make such partings less painful. Through all the years in which Sachie was preparing to follow in his brother's painful footsteps, he remained inconsolable every time that Osbert disappeared to school and mourned his absence until the end of term. Five years after his first venture into boarding-school life Osbert returned to Eton and told his father, with mingled satisfaction and dismay: 'On arriving here I found 7 postcards from Sachie!'[17]

Osbert was little less bereft and his letters to his parents were punctuated by appeals that they should visit him: 'Do come and see me *soon*.' 'When are you coming to see me?' 'I do wish you or Mother would come down and see me.'[18] Sir George rarely responded; Lady Ida did a little better but her ailing husband was her first priority and her inability to cope with the minutiae of everyday existence meant that, when she did come, she was usually late and sometimes arrived on the wrong day altogether. If she got there, she could be embarrassing. She took him to school on his first day and wept copiously on leaving him. The other parents looked disapproving at this un-British display of temperament. Osbert refused to shed a tear.

Osbert's first boarding school, Ludgrove, was a preparatory school in the south of England which prided itself on its athletic achievements and its close links with Eton. It was only a couple of miles from the celebrated lunatic asylum Colney Hatch; a coincidence which gave much innocent pleasure to the boys, who assumed that most of their masters had recently escaped from the neighbouring establishment. The asylum caught fire a few weeks after Osbert arrived; the boys stood on the lawn to admire the distant flames and speculate gleefully about the numbers of the dead.

'It is rather fun here,' Osbert gallantly told his mother in his first letter. 'Four new boys came here as well as myself. It is very pretty round about.'[19] In later life he was to describe his time at Ludgrove as if it had been passed in a hell painted by Hieronymus Bosch. As usual, he made too much of his miseries, but whatever he might tell his mother, Ludgrove was never fun. The worst affliction was not the brutality of the masters nor the hostility of the boys but the omnipresent threat of boredom, boredom in his lessons and boredom in his games, boredom in the chapel, boredom in the conversations with the other boys. The teaching was uninspired, the curriculum unimaginative, the only master from whom Osbert derived any pleasure was the champion of the English folk-song, Cecil Sharp, who taught music but – as befitted the importance of his subject in the eyes of the authorities – made few appearances in the school.

'I am sorry to say I am at the bottom of the school,' Osbert admitted ruefully in an early letter.[20] Inevitably, he rose in the school, but he stayed always near the bottom of his class. Almost the only subject at which he shone was history. Here not even the efforts of his masters could wholly curb his enthusiasm; the final order for his first term showed him top with 176 marks to the next boy's 139 and a bottom mark of 34. Far from gaining him credit, this success merely confirmed his head-master in the conviction – by no means unjustified – that Osbert was not trying at subjects that absorbed him less. Except in history he was judged to be 'slow, careless and inattentive'. 'Though I know he has had many difficulties to contend with, yet I confess to being a little disappointed with his progress in work as a whole. It is *so* essential for him to do his very best and I do not think that he always does. His conduct has been fair, but I wish he would employ his time more usefully out of school.'[21]

The 'difficulties' must have related to his health. Osbert seems to have spent an inordinate amount of time in the throes of one disease or another. Part of this was no doubt self-induced – the sanatorium provided a welcome refuge from the rigours of Ludgrove – but the sickly child had become a sickly schoolboy. Osbert was not robust and the illnesses that another boy might quickly have thrown off, with him lingered and became more complicated. He himself would probably have ascribed his poor health to malnutrition; his letters home refer to the need for supplementing the school diet almost as often as they do to parental visits. 'These are the things I need and if possible *do* remember them,' he enjoined his mother: 'Chocolate cake with icing, plain cake, fruit, honey, ginger biscuits and butterscotch. *Don't forget* the butterscotch. I also want country life' (presumably the magazine *Country Life*, rather than the woods and farms of Renishaw). His Sitwell grandmother offered to provide a hamper of emergency supplies: 'I hope she won't send me any more figs, as the others were not as good as they *might* have been.' If more figs were sent they were presumably of better quality, but all was still not well: 'The apples were *nearly* as good as the figs,' he reported gloomily.[22]* No boy has ever admitted that the food at his school was even moderately palatable, but it does sound as if Ludgrove rivalled Dotheboys Hall in its cuisine. 'In a pretty hectic and varied life,' a contemporary told him long afterwards, 'I have only once had the experience of eating food which was so nasty that I retched between mouthfuls but ate it from sheer desperate hunger. That was at Ludgrove!'[23]

The school had the advantage of being reasonably close to Gosden, the

---

*Some of these extracts appear in Osbert Sitwell's autobiography. Though he is faithful to the meaning he has frequently collated passages from different letters, introduced or corrected spelling mistakes, and edited the texts in the interests of artistic effect. Wherever possible, I have reverted to the original.

southern home of Osbert's Sitwell grandmother. Gosden, like Hay Brow, was a centre of austere rectitude with much prayer and an almost unceasing routine of good works. Osbert found few charms in such an existence but valued greatly the stability and sure affection which he found there. With his father so much abroad, his mother *distraite* and elusive, it was only at Gosden that he received the concentrated attention which he craved. Lady Ida viewed her mother-in-law's *ménage* with unconcealed distaste; even the knowledge that her son was to be found there rarely induced her to make the short journey from London. When she did promise to come she as often as not cancelled at the last minute, leaving Osbert bereft and asking himself why he was so unlovable that even his mother could not endure his company.

In his autobiography Osbert indulged in a searing indictment of his preparatory school:

> I had gone there, a tall, well-made boy, with a strong temper, high spirits, and, although of nervous temperament, possessed of a naturally social disposition ... I read Greek, Roman and French history, in addition to English, and certainly knew more of all four of them than I do today ... The school restored to my parents a different boy, unrecognisable, with no pride in his appearance, no ability to concentrate, with health impaired for many years, if not for life, secretive, with no love of books and an impartial hatred for both work and games, with few qualities left and none acquired, save a love of solitude and a cynical disbelief, firmly established, in any sense of fair play or prevailing standard of humane conduct.[24]

It must be Ludgrove which is particularly the subject of this diatribe, but in fact, though he barely mentions it in his autobiography, in the spring of 1905 he was removed and, after a period recuperating from an illness, sent to St David's, Reigate. Presumably his parents had concluded that he was getting nothing out of Ludgrove and would do better to make a fresh start elsewhere. What evidence there is suggests that St David's proved in every way more satisfactory and that he was, if not happy there, then at least much less actively miserable. He was so backward that he was placed among boys who were a year his junior, a decision which caused him some initial humiliation but was probably of benefit to his self-confidence. 'I like the boy very much and only regret that we did not have him earlier,' wrote his head-master, evidently grateful to have a chance of scoring off a rival school; 'He is at least 2 forms too low!!'[25] The same complaints were made, about his slowness, his carelessness, his handwriting, but he was consistently among the top two or three in his class except in arithmetic and even in that subject he was soon 'doing very much better'. One of the last of his preparatory school reports concluded that he had done well and showed a marked improvement, both in his work and in his outward bearing: 'He must work very hard now or his place at Eton will bring no credit to himself or to his school.'[26] A kindly master took Osbert aside and assured him that he would find Eton both jolly and healthy – 'a topping place'. He went on to give him a complicated explanation of the facts of life, drawing his analogies from the world of plants. The only result, Osbert wrote in an autobiographical passage thinly disguised as a short story, was that it was 'quite two years before I could look a primrose in the face again'.[27]

'I liked Eton,' Osbert wrote balefully, 'except in the following respects: for work and games, for boys and masters.'[28] 'Public schools are to private schools as lunatic asylums to mental homes; larger and less comfortable,'[29] was another of his epigrams on the same theme. Osbert Sitwell was not prone to understate his case. He was a polemicist, who felt that any attempt to see, let alone state, both sides of a question would make his work less readable and much less fun to write. When considering his diatribes against Ludgrove, Eton or a host of later targets, one should remember that he did not take them entirely seriously himself and did not expect other people to do so either. The same was true of his anecdotes; an art form to which he attached much importance and which he practised with great skill and brio. It would be a shame, he felt, to spoil a good story by undue preoccupation with its accuracy. A case in point is a tale which he enjoyed telling about his early days at Eton. He was alarmed and depressed, he maintains, when he heard the boys bellowing the words of the Eton Boating Song: 'We'll all swing together, and swear by the best of schools.' He misunderstood, and 'imagined the hangman at his grim task, and the band of juvenile criminals, myself among them, crying out, in a final contemptuous gasp, as the noose tightened round each neck, "*Floreat Etona!*"'[30] At the risk of belabouring a trivial point, it is worth remarking that he could not possibly have imagined anything of the sort. The title of the song; its first words, 'Jolly boating weather'; the reference to those who swing as being 'steady from stroke to bow'; the swaying from side to side by which the song is traditionally accompanied: these make its real meaning unmistakably obvious. No doubt the image of hanging schoolboys flashed through his mind and he thought it a joke worth elaborating. So it was; but he no more expected it to be taken literally than he did his blanket condemnation of Eton life.

His dislike of the school was genuine, though. In one of his short stories, 'Charles and Charlemagne', he describes the anglicised Jew Simon de Montfort as having

> very quickly seized on the principles of English public-school education, for he openly refused to learn anything, became maniac about cricket, exulted in the correct shibboleths of dress, speech and deportment and adopted ostentatiously the public-school-boy-code-of-honour; which, summed up, encourages bullying, but forbids 'sneaking' – thereby assuring the bully of an absolute impunity. And a jolly good code it is, too, if you mean to be a bully.[31]

Though Osbert in later life was to show that he had more of the instincts of a bully than he would have cared to admit, at Eton he saw himself as being decidedly among the bullied. Boys would kick footballs at him in a hostile manner or throw his books out of a window. But he does not pretend that the bullying amounted to much. Harold Wernher, a contemporary at the same house, remembered that Osbert loathed games: 'He spent most of his leisure at Westbrook's, the Eton florists, arranging flowers. In anyone else this conduct would have been resented, but Sitwell was such an amusing sort of person that anything was forgiven him.'[32] It was at Eton that Osbert discovered he could make people laugh. Equipped with so effective a defence, it was certain that he would never again be among the seriously persecuted.

His house-master – the individual who, above all, dictates whether a young Etonian will thrive or founder – was H. F. W. Tatham. He should have been at Luxmoore's, Macnaghten's or Benson's, reflected that great schoolmaster George Lyttelton, then he 'would have had a pleasanter spring-time'. In the other houses philistinism was too often rife.[33] Certainly Tatham was no aesthete. He was an enthusiastic athlete, each year assembling a team to wallow and grunt in the mud in Eton's notorious wall-game. But he did not attach extravagant significance to games. 'He might, perhaps, be keener on outside things,' he remarked mildly of Osbert, 'though I am far from thinking them all-important, or even chiefly so. It is mainly with him a matter of health.' Tatham appreciated the fact that Osbert was 'intelligent and friendly' and that he had 'plenty of interests in things outside the ordinary run of boys' needs'.[34] Osbert found him consistently kind, encouraging his pupils to read widely and always ready to discuss the books they chose, himself writing 'homely tales in Churchwarden English' and reading them aloud with enthusiasm.[35] The other boys in the house do not seem to have been a particularly memorable lot; the list shows a fair sprinkling of grand dynastic names, but none, except perhaps the millionaire industrialist Wernher, who achieved great distinction in later life. Such a judgment has little significance, however; the mass slaughter of Osbert's generation between 1914 and 1918 means that it is impossible to judge how far his contemporaries would have got or in what fields they might have excelled.

Certainly few would have picked out Osbert himself as destined for success. His reports over a period of three years, without being damning, are far from enthusiastic. 'Poor written work. Very slow to learn but willing,' was a comment on his French. His classics master found that he had 'a very sluggish manner and an inaudible voice, while his hand-writing is cramped and indistinct'. 'Very slow and ponderous in his work,' was the verdict on his mathematics: 'I think he had done his best, in his own heavy way; but his geometry is feeble, and he does not take in new ideas readily. I should like to make him run round the room occasionally to wake him up.'[36] The impression emerges of an inert and lumpen youth, bored by his studies, unenthusiastic, not a disruptive force but uninspiring material for a schoolmaster to work with.

Meanwhile, as Tatham if nobody else detected, Osbert was quietly educating himself; both 'in the holidays from Eton' and, though he would have denied it, at Eton itself. It was at Eton that he learnt to read for pleasure, and part of that at least was his tutor's doing. A notebook which he kept at the time shows that his reading was omnivorous and energetic.[37] Between 22 and 24 June 1909 he managed to read *The Merchant of Venice*, *The Winter's Tale* and *A Midsummer Night's Dream*. On 25 June he took a brief break from Shakespeare with *Green Ginger* by Arthur Morrison. 'Humorous short stories after style of W. W. Jacobs. Best story: "Dolby's Parrot".' After that it was back to Shakespeare, *Othello* and *Romeo and Juliet*; another brief break with *The Green Curve* by Ole Luk-Oie – 'Short stories. All deal with military affairs, 1st story, "The Green Curve" is very clever'; then back to a course of Shakespeare alternating with Jane Austen: 26–27 June, *King Lear*; 27–28 June, *Pride and Prejudice*; 27–29 June, *Julius Caesar*; 29–30 June, *Mansfield Park*. 'I read an enormous amount . . .' Osbert later boasted, 'and was much laughed at by my family for reading the whole works of Shakespeare right through in a week! This was considered rather quick going!'[38] The going was not quite as quick as that, but it was still impressive for a boy of sixteen, especially for one who was considered sluggish and intellectually unambitious by his masters. His tastes quickly widened: the following month's entry shows that he read Fanny Burney's *Evelina*, Meredith's *The Ordeal of Richard Feverel*, Sheridan's *The Rivals* and *The School for Scandal* and Oliver Wendell Holmes's *The Autocrat of the Breakfast Table*. It was an eclectic list, to which Shelley, Pope, Ruskin, Pater and Gissing were soon added. 'I read, in fact, without purpose, as cattle browse,' Osbert later wrote; 'Osbert reads for style; I read for information,' commented his father disapprovingly.[39]

Cattle browse for sustenance, so as to keep alive. By the time he left Eton books were food and drink to Osbert, life without them inconceivable. He later claimed that he also by then considered himself a writer: 'My first writing was done at the age of fourteen when I wrote a dreadful and horrific play in blank verse on the subject (I regret to say) of Jezebel! My sister kindly advised me to wait – and tore it up; for which I'm now intensely grateful.'[40] There is nothing in his school reports to suggest that he was seen as a future author, though this perhaps reflects more on the lack of importance which Eton gave to the writing of English than to Osbert's abilities. More curiously, he did not join the Literary Society, where he would have been expected to write an essay as well as listen to E. K. Armstrong read a piece about Charles Dickens or the Hon. J. N. Manners on R. L. Stevenson.

Whether or not Eton encouraged his literary bent, it certainly did nothing to sharpen his aesthetic instincts. On the other hand, it did nothing to repress them. At Ludgrove, indeed at most English public schools of the time, to spend one's spare time arranging flowers in the local florist's would have given rise to fierce derision, probably to persecution. Eton, however, was big, relaxed and adult enough to tolerate, indeed mildly to enjoy, any display of eccentricity which was not too flamboyantly provocative. Only if Osbert had been in an aggressively bone-headed house would he have suffered for his predilections; the boys at Tatham's seem to have been as amiably accepting as their tutor. Osbert was left to develop in his own way. By the time he was fifteen or sixteen he was already showing a genuine appreciation of beauty and a keen eye for detail. When Edward VII and Queen Alexandra visited Eton to open the new School Hall, Osbert told his mother: 'The Queen, who looked about 30, much younger than her daughter, wore *yellow* hair and mauve dress. Lord Rosebery appeared in a scarlet robe with pink sleeves. What he looked like!'[41] The judgment may not be strikingly sophisticated, but it shows discrimination and an unusual range of interests for a schoolboy. Constance Sitwell describes him following her around at Renishaw. She found him spoilt but very friendly: 'Osbert, who really does love colour, used to pick me flowers constantly to wear with different dresses.'[42]

She noted too 'the terrible nervousness, apparently innate' shown by both Osbert and Sachie.[43] Under the heaviness and indolent air which so struck his masters Osbert was highly-strung and dangerously vulnerable. He was unusually responsive to the atmosphere around him, and the patent inability of his father and mother to make any sort of a harmonious life together preyed heavily upon him. As their marriage became more fraught and crisis-ridden, so his own nerves became more fragile. His sensitivity, he believed, gave him unusual intuitive powers: he claimed always to know if his mother or sister was going to visit him at school even though he had been given no warning in advance. The gift, if gift it was, never wholly deserted him. Sometimes it was the cause of worry and confusion, sometimes it could be turned to advantage. In 1939 he told the publisher Rache Lovat Dickson that three times he had 'dreamt true', most recently at Monte Carlo when he had been told in his dreams to back the number 15 at the moment the Casino clock struck six. 'Most successful. At precisely six pm I produced the maximum and won.' He told Dickson he had caught sight of a ghost from time to time, but that he 'would not like anyone to think I believed in that arrant nonsense "spiritualism" '.[44] He was, in fact, selective in his irrationality: ghosts were acceptable – he had, after all, been brought up at Renishaw – but they must manifest themselves of their own accord, and not be called from the vasty deep by charlatans or self-deluded zealots. He made no claims to consistency. Writing to another friend, he dated a letter 14 March, then corrected himself and substituted 13: 'You'll see a trace of character in this letter,' he apologised, 'for I am so superstitious that instinctively, though I knew quite well it was the 13th, I jumped a day ahead.'[45]

Eton, however, notably failed to inculcate any religious convictions into the growing boy. Probably nobody tried very hard: evangelical fervour was contrary to the ethos of the school and the rituals of the Church of England were taken for granted as part of the social order. His masters would anyway have had an uphill struggle. Sir George was a convinced agnostic, if not a card-carrying atheist, and he never hesitated to express his scepticism to his children. Constance Sitwell found him 'singularly prejudiced on the subject'. Of course I talk to the children about it, he told her. She wondered what he could find to say.[46] One thing he said gave Osbert much comfort when he was going through a brief religious phase at the age of ten. Osbert was worried that he might end up in hell. Don't let it frighten you, his father reassured him. You'll find all the people you most admire there – Wellington, Nelson, the Black Prince.[47] It is a mark of Eton's easy-going approach to religious matters that, when Osbert showed reluctance to be confirmed, no pressure was brought on him to change his mind. Many years later the clergyman at Renishaw called to ask Osbert why he never went to Holy Communion. 'Didn't tell him, because I refused to be confirmed!' Osbert told Lady Aberconway, his close friend and confidante.* 'But if he is tiresome, I will.'[48]

'The boys' had been one of the elements of Eton which Osbert claimed to have disliked. In his autobiography he maintained that it was only some years later that he discovered 'what brave, generous, loyal and often lovable companions these young boors, dullards and bullies' could turn out to be.[49] As usual, he overstated his case. His house-master told Sir George that he 'soon seemed to settle down and make friends with the other boys'.[50] Tatham, too, may have been pitching it a bit high; Osbert does not seem to have found anyone in his own house particularly sympathetic. But he did find several kindred spirits in his generation at Eton; notably William King, who was later to become an important figure at the British Museum, and a precocious young aesthete, Peter Lycett Green. Several letters from Lycett Green survive. He credits Osbert with having taken charge of his reading programme, rebuking him for wasting his time on trash and launching him on Thackeray. Lycett Green proved an apt pupil and his letters were bookish, mannered and affectionate. The two boys stayed with each other in the holidays; when life at Eton seemed more than usually drear they would console themselves that their schooldays could last only a year or two more and that an infinity of liberty lay ahead.

It was in the holidays that Osbert was first able to indulge the passion for travel which his undergraduate tutor had inspired in him a few years before. His first expedition of any consequence was to San Remo in the winter of 1904, when he was recovering from the illness that heralded his retreat from Ludgrove. San Remo, he later observed, was intrinsically

---

*Christabel Aberconway was in fact the Hon. Mrs McLaren until her husband succeeded his father as second Baron in 1934. To save confusion, however, I have called her Lady Aberconway throughout.

no more romantic than Margate, but from the moment that he arrived there he sensed that he had discovered something infinitely precious, which was to sustain him for the rest of his life: 'I realised that Italy was my second country, the complement and perfect contrast to my own.'[51] From then onwards he went with his parents to Italy every spring, sometimes staying briefly in France on the way but usually hurrying through as if to the promised land. After the first year or two Sachie joined the party: 'Do you remember sitting at a window in Danieli's with me and watching a ship called the *San Marco* sail out into the sunset, going to Dalmatia?' Sachie asked him many years later. 'It must have been in 1908.'[52]

In the same year Sir George sent Osbert with his tutor to Rome. He had intended to leave them to their own devices, but when it came to the point he could not resist the temptation to join the party himself and take over the role of *cicerone*. In three gruelling days they visited the Forum (twice), the Capitol, the Palatine (twice), the Pantheon (twice), St Peter's (three times), the Borgia apartments, the Pope's garden, the church of St Cecilia, the best Greek statues in the Capitoline and National Museums, the Appian Way, the Colosseum (twice), the remains of Nero's Golden House, the model of ancient Rome restored, Tivoli to see the cascades and the Villa d'Este, 'and a good many other things'. 'It is charming to find how strong Osbert seems to be,' his father reported approvingly. 'No amount of travelling or sight-seeing tires him and he always sleeps and eats well. He is such a dear boy altogether.'[53] Sir George always assumed that everyone must share his own enthusiasms. In this case he was right: Osbert was as indefatigable as even his father in the pursuit of culture. Intellectually as well as physically it was assumed that nothing was beyond him. Sir George made no concessions to the age and immaturity of his son. When he wrote to the eight-year-old Osbert from Nuremberg he explained that the charm of the city was due chiefly 'to the high-pitched red roofs and the air of inimitable antiquity which pervades the whole town', and expounded its architectural merits over fifteen hundred words.[54] But though he was remorselessly didactic, his enormous enthusiasm, range of curious interests and genuine learning made him an excellent mentor. Osbert enjoyed himself immensely during their Roman holiday; he became an insatiable sight-seer and until his final illness crippled him could exhaust companions far younger than himself in his quest for new sensations.

Though he got on well with his father on such occasions, Osbert could not ignore the fact that the life of his family was far from harmonious.

His first loyalty was always to his mother, and he watched with increasing anxiety for signs that she was distressed or in any way estranged from her husband. 'Of course I love you and am quite devoted to you and am not in the least bit huffy with you,' she reassured him when he found that he had given offence; and then again: 'I do miss you dreadfully and I do love you dreadfully . . . You are everything to me. I do wish we had longer time together.'[55] As her relationship with her husband soured, Lady Ida became more and more determined to enlist Osbert as an ally. When Sir George rallied to Asquith in the battles which he waged in 1911 and 1912 against the House of Lords she was convinced, probably quite correctly, that he did it in part at least to spite her and as a gesture against her family. 'I am very unhappy your Father has joined the Radical Party,' she wrote to Osbert. 'He has behaved very unkindly to me in never saying a word till he has done it. I am perfectly miserable. I hope you will persuade him he is not to be too bad about it. I do want him to leave the House of Lords alone. I think a word from you will make him leave it alone.'[56]

The idea that he might try to change his father's political opinions must have struck Osbert as both comical and alarming. But it was over money that ill-feeling between his parents was festering most painfully. 'Write to your Father about money,' Lady Ida besought Osbert. 'He is perfectly dreadful over money matters now, worse than ever.'[57] But Osbert himself was quite as much a victim of Sir George's economy campaign. 'You must come down 3rd Class,' his mother told him in June 1909 when he was about to go from Eton to Scarborough. 'Father says it is cheaper. And take a return.'[58] Osbert watched in dismay as his parents grew ever more fiercely alienated. 'I never hear from Father,' Lady Ida told him. 'I suppose he is cross with me. He generally is.'[59] It hardly made for a happy atmosphere in which to spend the holidays.

School holidays, however, were almost at an end. Osbert's third-class journey from Eton to Scarborough was the last of its kind. In the same year his house-master was killed climbing in the Alps. Osbert made this a reason for arguing that he had no more to gain from Eton and should now leave. His father was quick to agree: with money so short and Sachie still to educate he felt that it was high time Osbert made a start on his real life and settled down to a career. It was obvious that trouble lay ahead over the choice of what that career should be. For the moment, however, there was precarious harmony. In July 1909 Osbert left Eton. A new life began.

3

The Great Free World

I was a proud citizen of the great free world of 1914.

(Laughter in the Next Room)

'I loathe English Universities and most "Varsity men",' Osbert wrote in 1940; '... they're tinged with all the things I dislike, Church of England priggishness, unwarranted intellectual airs, sniggering, snobbishness, cliqueyness, clergymen, "a regular life", lectures, games, and even, at any rate at Cambridge, science!'[1] His views might have been less bilious if Sir George had listened to his pleas and sent him on from Eton to Oxford. He did not plead with particular vigour, however. The truth was that he had no real idea what he wanted to do. Subsequently he claimed that already he had determined to become a writer, but he does not seem to have mentioned it to anyone at the time. He thought vaguely that he might be suited to life in the Diplomatic Service; but Sir George considered diplomats to be degenerate and their way of life effete, and Osbert lacked the conviction which might have induced him to argue the point more strongly. The Church was inconceivable to both father and son, the City hardly less so, the Bar did not appeal. There remained the armed services.

Osbert maintained that his father forced him to become a soldier for no reason except that he knew his son loathed the idea. It followed logically that, since Osbert hated horses, the cavalry would be Sir George's chosen arm.[2] It is probably fair to say that, if his children particularly wanted to do something, Sir George usually thought it wise to check them, but his intentions were not so malign as Osbert imagined. His elder son at Eton had showed himself idle and unambitious, prone to extravagance and reluctant to settle with any diligence to tasks that were even slightly uncongenial. Many fathers faced by such a problem

33

would have felt that an injection of self-discipline and determination was what was needed, and that in the world of 1909 the Army offered one of the few possibilities for such a treatment. The Royal Navy might have done as well, but seventeen was unusually late to start and there had anyway never been a sailor in the Sitwell family. Osbert protested feebly but offered no serious resistance. Almost without noticing it, he found himself at the Army College, Heath End, Farnham, preparing for the examinations that would, with luck, secure his entry into Sandhurst and then the regular Army.

In a short story called 'Happy Endings',[3] Osbert described the Army College in a disguise so thin that he found himself threatened with a libel action by the outraged wife of its proprietor. The crammer of his story and in real life occupied a dingy and undistinguished house perched on a ridge about two miles from Farnham. The country around was attractive, which was lucky since it was almost impossible to remain inside, 'for in the rooms which we were given to sit in there were only two armchairs, with black, frizzy clouds of horse hair peeping out of dark, split purple leather'. It was too cold in winter, too hot in summer, there were no lights fit to read by, the food was execrable – 'but please do not write about it,' Osbert enjoined his father anxiously.[4] According to the prospectus – or Osbert's version of it in any case – the tone was one of dour and resolute asceticism: 'The hours of study are rigidly observed. Supervision and Discipline are unremittingly exercised and the moral tone is high.' In fact the teaching seems to have been lack-lustre, discipline slack and the expectations of academic success so slight as to be almost spectral. The head-master, Mr Welch, had had a varied career, Osbert told his father: 'On leaving Harrow he went on the stage and married an actress ... He then left the stage and wrote, at one time, leading articles for *The Times*. As well as managing this crammer's, I think he has much to do with the examinations for the "Territorial Forces".'[5]

His fellow students did not impress Osbert any more favourably than had his contemporaries at Eton. They were mostly drawn, he wrote in 'Happy Endings', from that layer of the wealthy middle classes upon which, before the war, a commission in the Army, particularly in one of the 'crack' regiments, was felt to bestow a certain social prestige. 'A few of them', he generously conceded, were 'not without some interest', but the majority were just 'ordinary, if kindly, middle-class snobs'.[6] In later life he was to be slightly ashamed of this supercilious disdain for lesser mortals, referring to the 'more than ordinary share of pride and vanity that in those days I possessed'.[7] His repentance, however, was only superficial. All his life he laboured under the illusion, common in the aristocracy, that he enjoyed an instinctive rapport with the working classes, which, in his case, meant domestic servants, gamekeepers and miners. The lumpen middle class that lay between he viewed with incomprehension and distaste: 'He always said he couldn't stand middle-class people,' his secretary, Lorna Andrade, recorded.[8] Osbert once claimed to draw no distinction between classes but only between 'those who create and those who do not'.[9] Such admirable broadmindedness did not run deep, however. He chose to ignore that many, probably most, of the artists whom he so much admired were drawn from the *petite bourgeoisie*. If the point was forced upon him he would dismiss it as a freak of chance. There *might* be a few exceptions, but little of real intrinsic worth could be expected to emerge from the 'greedy, ravening hordes of the middle-classes' who had destroyed traditional England and imposed their pettifogging standards on society.[10]

Surprisingly, his fellow students did not seem to resent their new companion's air of innate superiority. 'So glad you are getting on well with the others,' his father wrote to him. 'I hope there are games and that you are playing whether you like it or not.'[11] Sir George would have been disappointed by the games, which were at the most perfunctory and easily avoided, but he was right about Osbert's popularity. In 'Happy Endings' Osbert wrote that 'in some odd way I had succeeded in establishing a kind of leadership over them'.[12] Nevill Meakin, a friend of Lady Sitwell who knew the Army College well and visited it often, confirmed that this authority was no illusion. Osbert, he wrote, was 'so like Sir George in manner and everything it would seem. Being so extremely calm he puzzles the average budding army youth not a little. They like him very much, I find, and despite his youth, his opinions are often quoted.'[13] Possibly they were awed by his Etonian polish and grand connections; possibly they admired his wit and obvious intelligence: whatever the cause, he seems by the age of seventeen or eighteen to have become an imposing personality, a massive presence which might sometimes be disliked or resented but was rarely scoffed at or ignored.

Intelligent or not, he was far from being an apt examinee. He failed the Sandhurst exam first time round – 'in those days no easy matter', as he ruefully admitted[14] – and though Sir George congratulated him on his prowess as an essayist there was not much else in his academic life to deserve commendation. Mr Welch was 'very keen that I should do science instead of Latin, and I think it would be more use', he told his father,[15] but his head-master's proposal had more to do with his inaptitude for the classics than his probable prowess among the test-tubes. He made touching efforts to impress Sir George with his diligence. 'I am being very *systematic* with my accounts,' he wrote proudly. 'I keep rough accounts in pencil in one book, and tidy ones in another.'[16] His attitude towards his father showed respect verging on obsequiousness; however he may have chosen to present the relationship in later life, Sir George in 1909 and 1910 was still a fearsome figure, to be derided only covertly if at all. Towards the end of 1909 Osbert told his father that two of the teachers at the Army College had suggested he would be well suited to the Diplomatic Service. The French master, in particular, thought he would be up to the necessary standard; 'However, I am quite content to do what you think best, and if you think the Army would be best, I am sure it will be.'[17]

Sir George did think the Army would be best and made it clear that Osbert was not to escape so easily. Possibly his son would have done better in his studies if he had devoted rather more time to his set work and less to promiscuous reading. At the Army College he used to retreat to his bedroom and read his books, 'to keep in touch with a life that was real'.[18] His record of books read shows a constant competition between the demands of the curriculum and the delights of literature. Usually the curriculum lost. 'Working for Qualifying Exam. Not much time for reading,' he wrote gloomily, but he still managed to fit in a dozen novels by Wells and as many plays by Shaw. Surprisingly, he did not read Samuel Butler's *The Way of All Flesh* – that classic study of the generation gap and the conflict between a smug and overbearing father and his oppressed and sensitive son – until December 1911, eight years after it was first published. He delighted in it, read it for a second time within six months, and gave a copy to his father. The experiment was not a success; according to Osbert, Sir George was so put out by Butler's irreverence that he took to his bed in protest. Towards the end of his time at the crammer Osbert discovered the Irish romantics – Yeats, Synge, James Stephens – as well as Strindberg, Ibsen and Chekhov. He began to read the works of Dostoevsky and Turgenev though there is no mention of Tolstoy, another curious omission. It was the reading list of an energetic, intelligent and discriminating youth but almost entirely irrelevant to the demands of the army examiners.[19]

'I do hope your exam will be all right this time,' Osbert's old friend, Miss Lloyd, wrote from Scarborough in March 1911. 'I know you will be very anxious but cheer up, it will all come right in the end.'[20] It did not come all right in the end. Osbert failed the exam and, to his dismay, found himself back at the Army College in the autumn for yet another try. 'Why are you back at that old crammer's?' asked his Aunt Blanche. 'What for? I thought Sandhurst was given up and that you had joined the Sherwood Foresters . . .'[21] Sir George did not abandon the quest so easily but even he was convinced after Osbert failed his exams for a second time that a course at Sandhurst – not essential for a regular soldier but the traditional route to distinction in the Army – was no longer a possibility. He was, however, unshaken in his view that his son was destined to be a soldier; was reinforced in that conviction, indeed, since Osbert's failure at the Army College merely proved the need for a further stiffening of the delinquent's will. He pulled strings busily, while saying nothing to his son. The first intimation that Osbert had as to what was in store was an announcement in *The Times* that a certain F. O. S. Sitwell had been commissioned a Second Lieutenant in the Yeomanry and posted to a regiment of the Hussars. Like it or not – and it was most decidedly not – Osbert was now an officer in the cavalry.

Osbert's six months with the XIth Hussars were among the most miserable of his life. Aldershot was a deeply dispiriting town; a drear, colourless litter of buildings set in a drear, colourless countryside. It was dedicated to the service of the Army, which he hated – and of all arms of the service the one he hated most was undoubtedly the cavalry. He was ill-qualified to be a peacetime officer of any kind. Any sort of machinery left him helpless; his claim that he could not even put on a gramophone record for himself was no doubt affectation but changing a needle would certainly have been beyond him.[22] He could not read a map or understand the simplest detail in the Drill book: intellectually such things were no doubt well within his grasp but he was paralysed by boredom, distaste and a conviction of his own inadequacy. He was ill at ease with either a rifle or a shot-gun – a frailty which, as it turned out, was relatively unimportant in his professional life but considered an unforgivable solecism by his fellow officers. Miss Lloyd wrote to thank him for a present of two pheasants: 'I am so pleased to have them from your first shooting-party.'[23] It must have been almost his last shooting party. 'I was a profoundly, almost an inspired, bad shot,' he boasted in his autobiography. 'I never, I am thankful to say now, approached so near my mark as to wound a bird, or a beater, even.'[24] He exaggerated his incompetence but he never displayed even a flicker of talent for anything that called for co-ordination of eye, mind and muscle.

But if he was ill-adapted to be a soldier of any kind, he was doubly disqualified for the cavalry. Horses both intimidated and bored him – a combination otherwise induced in him only by the aeroplane. His mounts instantly detected that he feared and loathed them, reciprocated the latter sentiment at least, and delighted in humiliating him in public by ignoring his increasingly hysterical commands or by pitching him ignominiously to the ground in front of the Commanding Officer.

Even worse than the horses were his fellow officers. In *Great Morning*, the third volume of his autobiography, Osbert has left a memorable picture of his first dinner in the mess, his frantic efforts to conduct a conversation only to be ignored or met with surly grunts, his failure to make even the slightest dent in the listless stupor which hung about the table. Only later did he realise that every effort he made to entertain increased his unpopularity: any sort of cultivated conversation was anathema in the mess, conversation of any kind from so junior an officer was a gross breach of taste.[25] Only once did he hear any reference to a figure of cultural significance, and that was when a newspaper reported that the Polish pianist Paderewski had been insulted while travelling on a liner to South Africa. A purple-faced Major flung down the paper carrying this news. 'I wish to God the fellow'd killed him,' he bellowed. 'I don't believe he could play a choon if he wanted to! He ought to be shot, that – Paderoofsky!'[26]

Much of this, of course, was fantasy. Not all regular officers, even cavalry officers, were philistines; when Edmund Blunden shamefacedly admitted to his Commanding Officer that he was something of a poet the Colonel merely remarked that he had noticed a good review of Blunden's latest collection in the previous week's *Times Literary Supplement*.[27] But Osbert's fellow officers for the most part seem to have confined their interests to shooting, women (not to be mentioned in the mess except in the most general terms) and every aspect of the horse. The most notable exception was the adjutant of the regiment, a saturnine intellectual called Louis Spears, who was bilingual in French, had spent much of his life on the Continent and was to write several excellent books.

In 1948 Spears read Osbert's account of his unhappy experiences in *Great Morning* and wrote him a perceptive letter of congratulation:

Your picture of your attachment to the XIth is a satirical masterpiece. I might have seen it through your eyes had it not been for the love of horses and the deep feeling of solidarity engendered by the Regiment itself . . . I realised at the time how uncongenial it all was to you, and my Continental upbringing made me sympathise with you and understand. We both felt the void. Personally, and quite deliberately, I lived two separate lives. The one of books, study and friendship with people who thought in other terms than those of horses or dogs . . .

Osbert's reply betrays some softening, even a little nostalgia for the past. Though he had passionately hated Aldershot, he said, he looked back on it with interest. 'I quite understand the good points the system possessed – alas, it has all gone, with things better or worse . . . with the vilest of mankind everywhere in the ascendant. And what a set of timid clerks and nincompoops govern us! Give me the old-school horse gang any day!'[28] Written at a time when a Labour government – deeply loathed by Osbert – was still in power, this can hardly be called a ringing endorsement of the values of a cavalry regiment, but it is at least less black than his mood in August 1912 when he fled the mess to join his father in Italy. Osbert has left obscure how he obtained leave for this escapade or, if he went without permission, how he avoided court-martial. He seems to have suffered something of a nervous breakdown, serious enough to persuade the authorities that his disappearance should be tacitly condoned. Probably the regiment was as glad to see him go as he was to escape it. His state of mind was sufficiently grim to convince his father that the experiment had failed; Osbert would never make a cavalry officer. He must remain in the Army, Sir George concluded, but he should try his luck where he might find the atmosphere more congenial, the Brigade of Guards. Given his record, it was remarkably generous of the Grenadier Guards to accept this unpromising recruit. In 1912, however, it was still possible to fix such things in a way unthinkable today. After three months of almost unbroken delight in Italy, Osbert in November returned to London as a Second Lieutenant in the Grenadier Guards – stationed in Wellington Barracks, a few hundred yards from Buckingham Palace.

The life of a junior Guards officer before 1914 was – or at least could be – one of sybaritic indolence. Officers were required to behave like gentlemen, and not much else. Even a Second Lieutenant enjoyed more than three months' leave a year, and when an officer was on duty in London the routine was so leisurely as to make the line between work and play almost indistinguishable. Company Orders, which officers could attend in civilian clothes, took place at ten, followed by Commanding Officer's Orders and a glass of port in the mess. The rest of the day was free. Few officers slept in barracks, fewer still dined there;

they were not supposed to carry parcels or a suitcase in public, reverse when waltzing or smoke Virginia cigarettes but otherwise it was up to them how they passed their time. Most of them played polo, went racing or conducted elaborate flirtations but if their tastes tended more to the aesthetic then that was their own affair.[29] The pace became slightly more animated in the summer when there were divisional exercises but even on such occasions the Guards contrived to ensure their comfort. In September 1913 Osbert wrote to his mother from Tring, where Alfred Rothschild was providing tents and food for 2,500 men and 100 officers: 'Yesterday afternoon I went over his house, the most monstrous affair, perfectly hideous, but with the most priceless things in it. All over gilded, etc. We also had a performance of his private band and private circus. In the evening 60 of us went to dine with him. The most wonderful food, and the band again, which is extraordinarily good.'[30]

Into this background Osbert fitted as if he had been born for the role. Long after his time in the Army Osbert admitted to Anthony Powell that, almost unconsciously, he had absorbed the ethos of the Guards; 'you never get used to not being saluted,' he added wistfully.[31] With the help of his soldier servant, John Robins, who had come with him from the Yeomanry and was to remain in his service until a long-delayed retirement, he managed to look spruce on the relatively few occasions that he was required to appear in uniform. Out of uniform, he blossomed as a dandy, rejoicing in expensive suits from Savile Row, silk shirts from Pall Mall, constant visits to Trumper's – that most Attic of London barbers. Once he had become concerned about his appearance he devoted endless time and money to its embellishment. The habit remained with him until ill-health made all such efforts futile. Cyril Connolly remembered him as being above all preoccupied by his hair, parting it 'in the style he had supposedly copied from Beau Brummell or someone. It took an enormous amount of time and resulted in two partings in front and the hair brushed somehow up the back of his head.'[32] His ties, usually procured from Charvet in Paris, bordered on the extravagant. Geoffrey Gorer, a friend of the family best known as an anthropologist, once remarked to Edith Sitwell that one simply *could not* wear ties like those which Osbert sported. '*You* can't,' Edith replied severely. 'But Osbert can. He can wear anything.'[33] Always, he had with him an elegant cane with amber or agate top. 'I'm so glad he carries it,' wrote the novelist and painter Denton Welch. 'It is nice to like nice, showy things all through one's life.'[34] The butterfly had not emerged in its full glory in 1912 but already Osbert's refulgence would have caused dark suspicions in the mess of the XIth Hussars.

With maturity Osbert had become a handsome man, rather too ponderous for everyone's taste but not a figure easily ignored. His sister Edith described him in her poem 'Colonel Fantock', from *Troy Park*:

> And Dagobert my brother, whose large strength,
> Great body and grave beauty still reflect
> The Angevin dead kings from whom we spring.

German dead kings were more often invoked in his description: 'pale, morose and early Hanoverian', Beverley Nichols called him, while Virginia Woolf referred to his 'very sensual Royal Guelf face'.[35] His features were large, his nose long and bridged – a point to which he attached considerable importance: 'with becoming modesty,' he wrote, when considering a statue of Sir Charles Napier, 'one must again emphasise the importance, and even beauty, of a large nose, and the degeneracy and deterioration of type that a "snub" proclaims in a man.'[36] His body was substantial in proportion. Ada Leverson, who adored him, observed him through a bathroom window and reported excitedly that he looked like a wingless swan.[37] An ostrich would perhaps be an apter simile; he had the same slightly ponderous dignity and air of one who might suddenly overbalance and tip forwards.

Lady Diana Manners, the future Diana Cooper, one day innocently asked Lady Cunard what a 'Guardee' might be. She would find out that evening, she was told, for she was sitting next to one at dinner. 'My Guardee opened the conversation by asking me if I thought much of Stravinsky. It was Osbert.'[38] However naive, she can hardly have supposed that this was a gambit normally to be expected from a Second Lieutenant in the Guards. Few of Osbert's brother officers would have known who Stravinsky was, nor have had the smallest interest in Lady Diana's views on his importance. But they thought none the worse of Osbert for his curious preoccupations. They were a tolerant lot. When the Captain of the King's Guard asked him whether he liked horses and Osbert replied that he preferred the giraffe, it had such a beautiful line, they found the retort amusing. In the Hussars it would have been a matter almost for court-martial.

Thus liberated, he plunged contentedly into the cultural life of London. All his life he derived great joy from music; he was not, strictly speaking, musical, William Walton judged, but he '*liked* music and appreciated it'.[39] Mozart, Scarlatti, Bach and Handel were his favourite composers, with Debussy, Rimsky-Korsakoff, Delius and Stravinsky pre-eminent among the moderns. 'But then where is one to stop?' he wrote, in answer to a questionnaire. 'For I like music of all kinds, including the Elizabethans. I have interests ranging from harpsichord to barrel-organ. I dislike intensely Wagner though I suppose he was a genius.'[40] Debussy was a particular hero. When introduced to him in the summer of 1914 Osbert was so overcome that afterwards he could not even remember what the composer looked like: 'The intensity of the emotion killed memory.' He first saw ballet at the Alhambra music hall and thought it of little interest, then was overwhelmed by the apparition of the Russian ballet with Diaghilev, Nijinsky, Bakst and Karsavina at the top of their miraculous powers. Tchaikovsky's ballet music he judged to be 'the greatest music of the theatre ... ever composed',[41] but it was Stravinsky's *Firebird* which above all enthralled him and sent him intoxicated into the London night. Henceforth, he wrote, he knew where he stood: 'I would be, for so long as I lived, on the side of the arts.'[42] His taste was eclectic but he detested Elgar and drew the line well short of Gilbert and Sullivan – 'I reserve, in the matter of *opéra-bouffe*, my reverence for Offenbach alone.'[43]

The great Russian bass Chaliapin for opera, Shaw and Granville-Barker for drama, even the wraith-like figure of Sarah Bernhardt gallantly battling on against illness and old age: it was an epoch of miracles on the London stage. But Osbert was almost equally interested in painting. He had been introduced to the art by his father, who showed him when he was still a child a picture by George Morland of the Westminster Election and explained, detail by detail, what was going on.[44] Osbert was enthralled but quickly moved beyond such homespun stuff: 'I love Italian painting beyond all. Piero Della Francesca is one of my favourites, and El Greco. On the other hand I also love the late Venetian decoratives (such as Tiepolo) and the paintings of the Golden Age such as Titian or Tintoretto.'[45] In 1912 he still knew most of such work only through reproduction and his knowledge of contemporary art was limited. He had been impressed, however, by the turbulent views of the Italian Futurist Filippo Marinetti, as expounded in the manifesto 'Art and Literature'; he did not particularly like Marinetti's painting but it intrigued and excited him and he wanted to see more like it. The artist in the Futurist school whom he most admired was another Italian, Gino Severini, who was one day to be commissioned by the Sitwells to paint what is probably his best-remembered work.

Osbert's interests were by no means confined to the aesthetic. He joined the Marlborough Club: 'I *am* so glad,' wrote Sachie. 'It will be so nice for you to be able to go there.'[46] It was; the other members were for the most part no more artistic in their tastes than his fellow officers in the Guards – many of them, indeed, *were* his fellow officers – but they were friendly and congenial and the club was a pleasant place to while away the hours. Still more, he went to balls, routs, dinner parties, the endless diversions of London society. For a young Guards officer, personable, of good family, almost every door was open; and immediately before the First World War the doors were numerous and the houses into which they led were sumptuously grand. Osbert preferred the drawing-rooms of those hostesses – like Lady Cunard or Mrs George Swinton – who did not recruit exclusively from the ranks of the upper classes but lion-hunted among writers, artists and musicians, but he had conceived a passion for ballroom dancing and would go anywhere if the floor and music were likely to be good. Given his striking lack of agility in other physical pursuits, it is surprising that he was a good dancer, but he had a great belief in his own ability and seems to have persuaded everyone that his confidence was well founded.

He even had something approaching a flirtation. Violet Keppel was the daughter of Alice Keppel, mistress of the recently deceased King Edward VII and among the grandest of *grandes dames* on the London scene. Violet was turbulent, flamboyantly emotional, at first exhilarating, soon exhausting; 'We called her the White Devil,' remembered David Horner, Osbert's long-time lover. Either through mischief or because she was genuinely attracted to him, she made a frontal assault on Osbert and suggested it would be a good idea if they married. According to Horner, Osbert made some sort of non-committal reply, whereupon Violet rushed off to her mother, shouting that they were engaged.[47] Osbert's own account, recorded in old age, is slightly different; he claims that he avoided making any reply by pleading an urgent engagement and fleeing from the house. Whatever the truth, it seems, at any rate, that Violet actually proposed: 'By Jove, I wish he'd accepted her,' her husband, Denis Trefusis, remarked feelingly when told of the incident many years later.[48] Possibly Violet's enthusiasm owed something to the fact that her true love, Vita Sackville-West, had recently married Harold Nicolson. She may have suspected that Osbert as a husband would provide the same sort of partnership as that described so vividly by Nigel Nicolson in his remarkable *Portrait of a Marriage*.

In the months which followed his flight from Aldershot and during his years in the Grenadiers, Osbert fortified his love for Italy and all things Italian – except for the language, in which he never advanced far beyond a gingerly use of the infinitive. Sir George had by now bought himself a house. 'Is it actually the fact, as I have heard, that Montegufoni is the largest private house in the world?' a friend asked Osbert.[49] It was not; but it was still built on an alarming scale. There were more than a hundred rooms of decent size and the total could be pushed up to over two hundred given a little ingenuity in definition. Nearly three hundred peasants were living in the castle at the moment Sir George stumbled on it in 1909 – or, perhaps more accurately, was led to it, since it seems likely that his 'discovery' was a put-up job contrived by a crafty land-agent. Its appearance was spectacular: a great tower rearing above a massive castle which had been built mainly in the twelfth century. Montegufoni – the hill of the white owls – had been the home of the Acciauoli, who had been Dukes of Athens and then, after being expelled from Greece, had returned to their Tuscan roots. Sir George was enraptured by its seedy magnificence and at once conceived the project of buying it and restoring it to its previous glory. He paid £4,000; a bargain, he felt, since, as he told Osbert, 'the roof is in splendid order, and the drains can't be wrong, as there aren't any'. For some reason, probably connected with tax, he bought it in Osbert's name and wrote proudly to describe the excellent investment he had made on his son's behalf: 'I do hope, my dear Osbert, that you will prove worthy of what I am trying to do for you, and will not pursue that miserable career of extravagance which has already once ruined the family. I am sure you will try to be straight in money matters.'[50] Osbert quoted from this letter in his autobiography, though he chose to omit the final sentence. 'I was not conscious of having been extravagant,' he commented. 'I had not bought a castle big enough for three hundred people.'[51]

Not everyone liked Montegufoni. Constance Sitwell found the vaults terrifying and deplored 'the horrible well, at the bottom of which, I was told, were some woman's bones', while Harold Acton described it as pure Charles Addams – 'a very ugly house full of second-rate furniture'.[52] There were indeed drawbacks enough: it could look forbidding in bad weather, was grimly cold in winter, damp when it rained, difficult to run without a regiment of servants. But it had many advantages as well: some splendid rooms, a fine setting, a majestic courtyard, ranks of generously laid-out terraces cascading below the castle walls, a grotto of beauty and originality. Osbert loved the house from the moment he first visited it in 1912. At one point his father supposed him to be itching to dispose of this grotesque white elephant. 'Nothing would induce me to sell it unless I were absolutely forced into doing so,' he protested. 'I am devoted to the house, and would like you to understand this.'[53] He knew that its purchase had been foolhardy and that its restoration would cost many times the original investment, but he never doubted that the enterprise had been worthwhile.

With his father he also went south to stay with his godfather, Lord Grimthorpe, at Ravello. Grimthorpe, Osbert wrote, was 'a wicked and sometimes disagreeable old man', but he had built a house on a site of surpassing beauty with a terrace perched a thousand feet above Amalfi and the Mediterranean. 'The position, the view from the terrace, is perhaps the most lovely in the world,' Osbert told Lady Aberconway. 'Very much like Brueghel's *Fall of Icarus*.' All his life he believed that Ravello and Amalfi in the bay below it were unrivalled in all the world, 'infinitely more strange and subtle than anything in Sicily. The sea has more colour in it here.'[54] Amalfi for twenty years was to be almost a second home; he spent many winters there writing and enjoying the milder climate and never tired of its elegant tranquillity.

Things meanwhile were going badly wrong in the Sitwell family. The parents wrangled bitterly between themselves and constantly criticised their children for their idleness, ill-discipline and prodigality. Edith admitted that all the fault might not lie on their side. 'I do wish Osbert wouldn't write Mother cross letters,' she told Sachie; '. . . after all, he *is* extravagant and we are all being punished for it more than he is.'[55] But she rarely blamed her brother; far more often she was preoccupied by Sir George's meanness and repressive nature. She wrote angrily to Osbert: 'Do you think Father will be able to pay for my funeral expenses? I think he will soon be called on to do it. I hope it won't interfere with his being able to buy Italian furniture, that being the most important thing in life.' Edith was incapable of moderation and whipped herself into paroxysms of fury or despair, but her life at Renishaw or Scarborough, with her two brothers away at school or in the Army, was singularly cheerless. There seemed no possibility of escape. 'I feel I shall go *mad* if I have much more of it,' she told Osbert. 'I don't want to worry you, but I have no one to talk to, and we are good friends, you and I.'[56] Sachie too importuned Osbert with cries of woe about his loneliness and estrangement from his parents. He wrote from Eton: 'Neither of them are really fond of me and neither is Edith. I am hated here, and consequently you are the only person who could be fond of me . . . I wish you could realise that I love you much more than I have ever imagined.'[57]

Osbert rejoiced in his siblings' affection, but it must at times have seemed something of a burden. He had enough problems of his own without taking on the woes of Edith and Sacheverell. Many of the problems were of his own making. As Edith had admitted, Osbert was grossly extravagant. He constantly complained that he was kept in penury but in fact his allowance was generous by the standards of anyone except the most pampered sons of the very rich. When with the Hussars he received £530 a year: in theory his Army pay was deducted from this but there is no reason to think that Sir George ever received any reimbursement. Multiplying by forty – which for the period before the First World War is a rough-and-ready way of establishing current values – this meant that he was receiving more than £20,000 a year: not bad for a young man of twenty whose basic living expenses need only have been a few pounds a week. When he transferred to the Guards his allowance was increased to £700 a year. By the end of the first year in his new regiment all this had been spent and Osbert was £500 in debt: 'What made the matter worse', wrote his father reproachfully, 'was that so much of it went on restaurants and for cigarettes, theatres, hot-house fruit etc. Obviously, you were then unfit and unable to exercise control.'[58]

Sir George was perplexed as well as indignant. He himself derived satisfaction from keeping intricate accounts and he could not understand why Osbert did not do the same. His belief that, with a little help and encouragement, his son would become 'careful and systematic'[59] was a delusion quickly dispelled. Osbert at first made a few inadequate efforts to keep track of the money which vanished with such disconcerting speed but soon concluded that the exercise was beyond him: if the money was there he would spend it, if it was not he would buy on credit; the idea that he should forgo any of life's little luxuries so as to balance his budget was inconceivable. His father grumblingly paid his debts: 'Though I am not satisfied with your letter. What I want is some indication that you are sorry about them, that you realise that it is a mean thing to spend much on oneself, especially on things . . . such as food, clothes, cigarettes.'[60] Sir George spent on a far more grandiose scale himself, but his extravagances were landscape-gardening, building, pictures, furniture: all of them – as he saw it – sound investments for the benefit of his family. Osbert did not agree, and felt no inclination to restrain himself when his father was guilty of such profligacy. Sir George fell back on threats. '£340 seems no great sum,' he wrote, 'but what about the thousands it *must* cost you in unnecessary death duties because I have lost confidence and dare not hand over property, at least until time has re-established confidence.'[61] With his father an exceptionally vigorous fifty-three, who had till then shown no propensity to hand over anything to his elder son, Osbert was unmoved by such a menace and continued on his self-indulgent way.

Sir George was in many ways ridiculous but it was his own money that he was spending and he never ran into debt. He was genuinely, and not unreasonably, concerned about the perils to the Sitwell estates if Osbert did not mend his ways. The dreadful example of his brother-in-law was always in his mind: 'Who would have believed that Lord Londesborough would have got through the two million and have been on the point of bankruptcy ... all because of a tendency in youth to be generous to [himself]?'[62] But he could not find the right tone in which to couch his warnings so that they were taken seriously by Osbert rather than dismissed as the objurgations of a tiresome niggard. He was endlessly censorious, critical not just of his son's prodigality but of his taste in books and architecture, his choice of ties, his flippancy. In March 1913 he directed yet another grand remonstrance at his errant son:

> This difference between us has long been growing like an evil tree until it has now led to a breach of the old relations. I dislike all that set of ideas intensely. I think people who spend profusely on their bodies are really swine. One ought to be self-denying with one's expenses, except when the mind is concerned. Loyalty to your regiment will oblige you to dress well and in some ways to live expensively, but there should be some feeling of shame not only at spending on clothes, cigarettes etc much more than I do, but at having to be self-indulgent at all.
>
> I hope that presently, when you have reflected, you will accept my doctrine on this subject. You should determine to be reasonably careful and endeavour to arrange your expenditure for this year so as to keep within your income. You should try to be self-denying in small things, should realise that you must make some return to this world, must work and take trouble without grumbling, must not complain about boredom when you have a single dull day. Then I shall be able to feel respect for your character and other people will feel it too.[63]

Coming as they did from so palatial a glass house, Sir George's stones were ill received. An elderly family lawyer once warned Osbert: 'You will not have an easy time with Sir George. In talking to him it will be better if you always bear in mind, as I do, that he has never made a mistake in the whole of his life.'[64] Osbert could not endure his father's assumption

47

of inviolable rectitude; he argued, contradicted and reduced himself to such a lather of resentment that he rejected without consideration a great deal of advice that was in fact perfectly sensible and that he would have done well to heed.

Lady Ida from time to time made ineffective efforts to improve relations between her husband and her son. 'I spoke to your Father this morning and told him you were hurt with his letter,' she wrote to Osbert. 'He says he never meant to be unkind, but that he never spends much on hankeys himself.'[65] But it was her own example, more even than Lord Londesborough's, which led Sir George to look so severely on his son's overspending. Lady Ida had never been out of debt but now had reached a point where she no longer dared tell her husband how much she owed. Her children watched sympathetically but could not help: 'Mother is rather troubled, as she has to pay the *concierge* £3.11.0. for some tickets and he wants the money at once,' Sachie wrote to Osbert from the Hotel Curzon. 'She is going to try to win a prize tonight at the bridge tournament. If she does not, she will have to sell that diamond and sapphire brooch, or try and borrow the money.'[66] Prizes at bridge tournaments were few and far between, the stock of diamond and sapphire brooches began to dwindle, more and more Lady Ida had recourse to borrowing. Osbert was anxious to help: 'You know I do not think it your fault,' he told her. 'I do love you so and you must not worry yourself.'[67] On the advice of a friend of Osbert's from Aldershot, a Lieutenant Martin, Lady Ida was put in touch with a certain Julian Osgood Field, who was said to be a dab hand at helping those in high places solve their financial problems with discretion and despatch.

The results were catastrophic: Field was a plausible rogue, concerned with nothing except the feathering of his own nest. Lady Ida was persuaded to borrow and to borrow again, usually on no security except a promise that she would bestow unspecified social benefits on her benefactors. She received only a tiny part of what she borrowed; Field or other intermediaries retained the lion's share for themselves. When she panicked and tried to check her rake's progress, Field threatened to reveal all to her husband. By the end of 1912 she was more than £11,000 in debt, creditors were pressing, her letters to Field – disastrously indiscreet and damning to her own reputation – became ever more desperate. Osbert had already been responsible for persuading Lieutenant Martin to back a bill for a relatively small amount, and was pressed to find other rich friends who would come to the rescue; 'he quite hopes,' Lady Ida told Field, 'if he joins the XIth Hussars, there must be

48

some boy he can get hold of'.[68] Even if Osbert did agree to exploit his more gullible fellow officers in this way, he does not seem to have done much about it. Probably his involvement with Martin caused him more than enough embarrassment and worry. Francis Bamford, who was very close to Sir George towards the end of his life, believed that Osbert profited personally from some of Field's transactions and used his mother's name to back bills to settle his own debts.[69] If any evidence exists to show that Osbert gained serious benefit, then it is well concealed. It does not seem likely. Nor could he be shown to have played any significant role in the murky transactions which had brought his mother to court. He could not do much to help her in her plight. He offered her moral support but little if anything else; Lord Grimthorpe told Sir George how relieved he was 'that Osbert had the firmness and good sense to refuse to put his name to anything'.[70]

Sir George, perhaps through a wilful determination to ignore what he did not wish to see, knew little about his wife's folly before the situation got out of control towards the end of 1912. Then his first preoccupation was to protect his son: 'If any attempt is made to draw you in to this business of your mother's, or to work on your feelings, please go and see Mr Wasborough [the family lawyer] . . . who will advise you. And leave at once the hotel or house in which your mother is staying as she deliberately "puts herself into a state" with the idea of working upon people's feelings.'[71]

With the possibility of legal action becoming every day more likely, it seemed that Osbert's career might be in jeopardy. 'Pray do not let this reflect on your children,' wrote Lady Londesborough to Sir George. 'Cannot Osbert pledge his future money (as yr eldest son) to help *himself* in this? . . . I am absolutely sure from what I am told (from high places) Osbert will be sent out of the Regiment.'[72] Lady Ida used the same weapon to try to persuade Osbert to work on his father and ensure a settlement of her debts. 'It is absolute ruination for me and I fear for you in the Guards . . . They could settle it for £2,500–£3,000. It seems very hard all this, and yet your Father is going about spending a lot of money in buying furniture.'[73]

For Osbert one of the most disturbing features of the scandal must have been his mother's misery. Sachie was disposed to condemn her for her selfishness and idiocy. She 'does not seem at all to realise what she has done, and thinks that poor Father has behaved shockingly,' he told Osbert. Yet Sir George had already paid out £1,750, not to mention formidable bills from lawyers. 'So it really is rather hard on him. She really is hopeless.'[74] Osbert knew she was hopeless but as a small child he had loved her intensely and he hated now to see her in such pain. When she was compelled to give evidence in court at a preliminary hearing she broke down and was seriously ill; another appearance in the witness box, the doctor ruled, 'would very seriously affect her health and might kill her'.[75] She was exiled to Scarborough and her cries of anguish became increasingly distraught. 'I am all by myself and the days are dreadfully long . . .' she told her husband. 'I care for nothing and have no wish to live . . . darling, I shall have a collapse. Do be kind and reasonable to me, darling, and see the torture I am going through.'[76] Sir George was unmoved. Lady Ida was doing much better than might have been expected, he told Osbert, and should be quite well in a couple of months. 'I very much doubt if she suffered as much as you and I did.'[77] To look at his impassively robust exterior one might well have thought that Osbert's sufferings too were inconsiderable. In fact his mother's plight and the imminence of scandal weighed heavily upon him. The breakdown which had led to his retreat from the Hussars was certainly in part induced by this miserable imbroglio and Sir George would probably not have acquiesced so readily in Osbert's transfer to the Guards if he had not realised the strain under which his son was suffering.

The more pressing of the debts were paid off and a precarious tranquillity returned. One important account, however, Sir George refused to settle, on the grounds that Field had obtained the loan by criminal misrepresentation and that he should not be allowed to profit from it. It was a principled stand – it seems unlikely that he would have been so stout if he had foreseen the eventual consequences for his wife. As it was, he told himself that the matter was now closed. The scandal had confirmed him in his belief that it was all-important to reclaim Osbert from the wicked ways which might lead him to his mother's fate. In the summer of 1914 he abruptly withdrew his son from the Guards and hauled him back to Renishaw to improve his handwriting and master the intricacies of double-entry accounts before he began work in the Town Clerk's office at Scarborough. Osbert saw this as an act of gratuitous spite; Sir George, he heard, had been disconcerted to find that his son appeared actually to enjoy Army life and so decided to find him some less congenial occupation. It is much more likely that Sir George was genuinely concerned for Osbert's salvation and acted in a way which, though misguided, was not intended to be vengeful. Misguided it was, however; Osbert was as little cut out to be a town clerk as a cavalry officer and the few weeks that he spent at Renishaw practising pot-hooks and making a mess of accounts showed vividly what miseries lay ahead both for Osbert himself and for whatever luckless official might be responsible for his activities in Scarborough. Those miseries, however, were subsumed in a greater tragedy. On 3 August 1914, Germany declared war on France. On the same day Osbert left Derbyshire to join the Grenadier Guards. He hoped that, even though he might not become the first to leave for France, he would still be in time for the closing stages of what would inevitably be a brief campaign. Like many other officers he packed his evening clothes for use in occupied Berlin.

4

Splendid Soldier Strife

> ... for each life
> Laid down for us, with duty well imbued
> With song-on-lip, in splendid soldier strife –
> For sailors too, who willingly were sunk –
> We'll shout 'Hooray!'
>
> (From 'Peace Celebration', *Argonaut and Juggernaut*)

OSBERT Sitwell was with a friend in Pratt's, that dining club cum nursery play-pen in St James's, when war was declared. He moved on to the Marlborough Club before writing to his father: 'The excitement, as you may imagine, is intense, especially on the part of the rowdy individuals who intend to cheer but not to fight . . . I should so like to know whether the Germans always intended us to fight. Have they a plan?'[1]

Though he resented the jingoists who bellowed bloodthirsty encouragement from the sidelines, there is no suggestion that Osbert at this time had doubts about the wisdom or the propriety of the war. It had been forced on the British and was a disagreeable necessity. But nor did he rejoice. Much of the youth of Britain went to war in a spirit of exaltation. 'Now, God be thanked Who has matched us with His hour,' wrote Rupert Brooke, 'and caught our youth, and wakened us from sleeping.'[2] This was not at all Osbert's thinking. He would not have felt inclined to thank God, even if he had had any serious belief in Him. The last thing he wanted was for his youth to be caught, and so far from being wakened by the war, he felt it more likely that it would draw him into a morass-like stupor in which all the joys of life if not life itself would be extinguished. It had to be endured, however. The best, indeed the only, course for him would be to accept its demands with resignation and seek to survive it by the exercise of all appropriate professional skills.

He assumed that he would be leaving almost at once for the continent, probably bound for Belgium. 'The Prophets of Evil say the war will last a good year,' he told his father; his main preoccupation was to pass that year in whatever comfort and security were compatible with doing conscientious work as an officer. Money was the prime requirement: £25 to £50 in gold and notes would be 'absolutely necessary'; he would have to buy field-glasses, which could easily cost £15; he had had to pay cash for a revolver since the gunsmith's, Wilkinson's, would no longer accept credit. 'I hate worrying you about these things, as I know how dreadfully the war will affect you,' he added apologetically, 'but one's chance of survival in this war seems so small that it is not worth taking small risks on account of expense ... I hope we shall some of us get through this blackest year.'[3]

In the event he was posted to the Reserve Battalion and after a few days found himself in the London Docks, on guard against some unspecified enemy threat. One of his duties was to keep watch on a warehouse full of enemy aliens – men of prominence and a danger to the state, he was assured. Osbert felt that a few of the faces were familiar but could not identify them until one prisoner asked him cheerfully: 'Which table would you like tonight, sir?' The internees were waiters from West End restaurants. After a few days of this distasteful work Osbert was ordered to take his platoon back to the barracks in Chelsea. The day was hot, the march long and dusty, Osbert drew his sword, stopped a bus and commandeered it for the journey. The displaced passengers were indignant, unappeased by Osbert's explanation that they were being given a chance to do what civilians claimed always to want to do – to make a sacrifice for the boys in khaki. Their protests filtered back to the authorities, who huffed and puffed but feared to make too much of it in case word of Osbert's exploit spread abroad and his example was copied by other junior officers.[4]

His social life went on much as before. If anything the atmosphere in the regiment was still more relaxed and tolerant than in peacetime. Osbert was spotted having a drink in the Café Royal with a private soldier and was denounced to the Lieutenant-Colonel for what was, in military eyes, a gross breach of good order. He was summoned to explain this misdemeanour and protested that the soldier was Jacob Epstein, who was both one of Britain's leading sculptors and a personal friend. The Lieutenant-Colonel found this defence entirely reasonable and dismissed the charge.[5] But though the drinking and the dancing went on unchecked, the carnage in Flanders was always in the background. By the time Osbert himself left for the Front many of his friends and contemporaries were already dead; Osbert's casual words to his father about his small chance of survival – probably written with little in mind except his need to extract some fresh financial subvention – had become terrifying reality. Nor was the danger only across the Channel. A day or two before Osbert embarked for France three German cruisers had emerged from the morning mist and shelled Scarborough, leaving Wood End scarred though not severely damaged. Sir George took refuge in the cellar. 'Directly you hear the first shell,' he advised his son, 'retire; as I did, to the Undercroft, and remain there quietly until all firing has ceased.' Lady Ida stalwartly remained in bed, emerging once the raid was over to gather up a large fragment of a German shell and bear it up to London, where she was going to say goodbye to Osbert. 'Here you are, darling!' she cried. 'I've brought it with me specially for you to take to France. I'm sure it'll bring you luck.'[6]

'I leave by the 9.25 train from Waterloo tomorrow,' Osbert told Sir George on 16 December. 'I think the base is at Rouen. I shall probably be there a day or two, before going to the Front.'[7] A photograph of the officers of the 4th Battalion taken at this time shows a somewhat sheepish Osbert standing next to the future Prime Minister, Harold Macmillan. His less than military appearance struck his Colonel unfavourably and he was ordered to smarten himself up by growing a moustache. 'What colour, sir?' asked Osbert in a spirit of amiable co-operation.[8] To his brother and mother his departure meant agonising sorrow. 'I am sure if anything happened to you I should go mad, and slowly decay,' wrote Sachie; while Lady Ida was hardly less distraught: 'I miss you too dreadfully it is all too awful, Darling, I could not stand seeing you leave . . . My darling, if I have ever been hard or cruel, please forgive me and realise I adore you.'[9]

It is more difficult to be sure what his father felt about it, so thick was the carapace which Sir George had built around his emotions. Osbert chose to portray him as a heartless curmudgeon, who profited by his son's departure for the Front, where there would be nothing on which to spend money, by cutting off his allowance. He claims that on one occasion Sir George burst into his wife's bedroom and announced that he had been looking ahead. 'We may hear at any moment that Osbert's been killed, and the other dear boy will probably go too; in which case you will certainly pass away, and what I want to know is, would the money in your settlement be available for the sons of my second marriage?'[10] All this is good fun, but it is not borne out by the surviving letters. A few days after the outbreak of war Sir George wrote of his 'unspeakable relief' that Osbert had not been in the first expeditionary force; when departure seemed imminent he reassured his son that the insurance companies estimated it was eleven to one against an officer being killed in a year's fighting, 'so I hope we may get you back safe and sound, though I realise the danger'. He took considerable pains to ensure that Osbert was supplied with the necessities of life, and more besides. In January 1915 he reported that he had just despatched twelve tins of Keating's powder (a sovereign remedy against fleas and lice), a bottle of eucalyptus oil, a cake of disinfectant soap and four pounds of plain chocolate. The boots would be ready the next day: 'The leather of the uppers is very light and the boots themselves are of a kind of leather which has had India rubber forced into the pores under pressure. The maker tells me he has used it frequently.' He seems to have realised something at least of what his son must be going through. 'Don't trouble to write nice or amusing letters, if you are tired or don't feel equal to it,' he urged Osbert, 'but tell me what you want, just as a schoolboy does, and I will see to it.'[11] Sir George was certainly eccentric and egocentric, but in 1914 and 1915 at least he does not seem to have been indifferent to the welfare of his son.

Second Lieutenant Sitwell joined the 1st Battalion of the Grenadier Guards in the trenches near Fleurbaix in December 1914, three days after a brigade attack in which the battalion had suffered severely. The battalion stayed at or near the Front till the end of February, boxing and coxing with the Scots Guards, four days in the line, four days in billets two or three miles back. On 3 March the battalion was relieved and Osbert shortly afterwards sent on leave to London. He thus missed the battle of Neuve Chapelle, in which four out of the eleven Second Lieutenants were killed. He rejoined the 2nd Battalion, Grenadier Guards, of the newly formed Guards' Division in the summer of 1915 and took part in the battle of Loos. There were 45,000 British casualties and at the end of the day nearly all the German territory taken in the first push had been recaptured, but Kitchener deemed it 'a substantial success' on the grounds that 'German casualties must have been as heavy as, if not heavier than, our own'. Osbert's battalion had been in reserve during the battle, but they occupied the former German front line a few days later and were attacked fiercely while in these positions. The battalion remained at or just behind the line until the spring of 1916; early in May Osbert went on leave to England.[12]

From this cursory record it is clear that Osbert's fighting war was not particularly dramatic nor, when compared with that of some of his fellow subalterns, hazardous or onerous. He spent the best part of ten months in or near the trenches, however, enduring discomfort and danger. He was never injured, except for the accidental cut which was to end his fighting life, but men were killed or maimed at his side and on a dozen occasions at least it might just as easily have been he who was the victim. While he showed no signs of being a military genius, or even a better than average soldier, he proved himself a conscientious and hard-working officer who cared for the welfare of his men and who, without being notably heroic, made no effort to avoid any necessary risk. Leonard Scriven was a Private in his platoon. Osbert took over as acting Captain on the death of a Captain Penn:

> The first time Captain Sitwell took us from the trenches when we were being relieved, he made a manoeuvre that almost led us into the German trenches. We found out later that someone had moved markers that he had placed on the trench sides. Only the Captain's knowledge of German saved us. As time went by we learned that Osbert Sitwell was very clever and possessed courage. Another thing that made him a favourite was his in-sistence that we get our full allowance of rations. He checked and hounded the supply services and mess sergeants so that we were better fed than at any other time I was with the Company in France. He also at Christmas time dipped into his own private funds to ensure us a fine turkey dinner.[13]

Whether it was his error that led to the platoon almost blundering into the German lines, and how his exiguous command of German saved the company, is neither here nor there. In the eyes of Private Scriven he was courageous and resourceful, an officer whom the men liked, trusted and respected.

'I am writing in a very dark dug-out,' Osbert told his father a week or so after he arrived in the trenches. 'It is difficult to write. Snow on the ground today.' If anyone wanted to send him a Christmas present it should be food, thick clothing or cigarettes. 'Nothing else is any use here. The cold is very trying. Up to our knees in some places in slush. We all seem to live on hot rum, which sounds very drunken, does it not?'[14] As with so many of his colleagues, the war for most of the time seemed to be as much against boredom and squalid discomfort as German shells or bullets. The trenches were more than a foot deep in water, he reported a fortnight later: 'As for the weather, "The rain it raineth every day".'[15]

To escape, he retreated into his own private world. Behind the lines there was access to a gramophone of a sort but it was usually churning out American dance music. In the trenches he sought to recreate in his mind the music he had most loved in the preceding years, particularly the ballet music of Stravinsky. But it was above all in books that he sought refuge. 'I should have gone mad from boredom and misery in the trenches,' he told a French friend, Madame Guéritte, many years later, 'had I not read Dostoevsky and been able to say to myself, "This would have been worse than what I am going through. So perhaps things are not really so bad." '[16] To solace one's misery by dwelling on the woes of others seemed to suit Osbert. He found *Lear* and *Othello* particularly efficacious. He read Dickens too, reflecting how well that novelist would have described life at the Western Front, 'rats and mud, and the particular horror they hold for human beings, he already understood'.[17] He was only just beginning to write himself but the instincts of a writer were quickening within him; more and more he was seeing things in verbal terms. Osbert wrote little poetry while in France, but nevertheless when he left France he was a poet.

He also left France with whatever illusions he had once held about the war dispelled for ever. He was away from the battalion on the occasion that General Horne inspected it, deplored the recent death of their Commanding Officer, and told them 'no losses must deter them; it was their duty to prosecute the war with their utmost energy, until the German Empire lay at the feet of England and her Allies', but if he had been there he would have been confirmed in his hatred of all such bombast and rodomontade:

> Eternal Moloch, strong to slay
> Do not seek to heal or save.
> Lord, it is the better way
> Swift to send them to the grave.[18]

By the middle of 1916 Osbert had already been consumed by the bitter resentment at the waste and futility of war which suffused most of his early poetry. When a young man was shot dead a foot or so away from where he was standing he felt, not fear, but 'sick with sorrow, with a sense of pathos'.[19] It was a sickness that never left him and was revived, with corrosive force, when the Second World War renewed the horrors of the First.

The extended leave which saved Osbert from a high chance of death in the battle of Neuve Chapelle was far from being a time of pleasant relaxation. He had hoped that the sordid scandal of his mother's debts had finally been ended in November 1914 when judgment had been given in favour of Lady Ida and Field branded as a cheat and liar. But certain of the debts remained unpaid, the creditors clamoured for settlement. Sir George insisted that *he* would not repay a penny; Field had been deemed responsible and must be made to suffer. Field had no resources, however, and was determined that, if he were brought down, Lady Ida would accompany him. He made available to the prosecution all the foolish letters that his dupe had written to him. In an effort to induce Sir George to take a more conciliatory line, the creditors threatened to join Lady Ida with Field in charges of fraud. Sir George dismissed this as bluff; so it may have been at first, but as so often happens with bluffs, it was caught up in its own momentum and, almost accidentally, transformed into reality. In March 1915 Lady Ida found herself in the dock.

Osbert personally, if not in the clear, was not particularly vulnerable. Field had induced Lady Ida to say that one of the main objects in her frantic quest for funds had been the settlement of her son's debts, but the debts, in fact, for the most part remained unsettled and Osbert had received only £20 from Field and relatively trivial sums through his mother. But he could not escape involvement. 'It is always trying to have to appear in court, but if you are still in England we shall put you first in the box, and I think your evidence will materially damage Field,' Sir George told him. 'A young officer about to leave for the Front carries great weight at this moment. Your answer that you refused to speak or write on the subject to any of your friends protects you completely.'[20] Osbert would anyway have wished to be present during the trial; he knew his mother had been guilty of startling folly and less than scrupulous behaviour, but he knew too how much she had been the pawn of others and how little benefit she had gained from her idiocy. A lot of dirty linen was about to be washed in public, but that it would end in Lady Ida's acquittal with no more than a token stain on her character seemed to him certain. Only as the trial progressed did he realise how black things could be made to look; even at the end he was astonished and horrified when the judge, in suitably shocked tones at this deplorable falling of the mighty, sentenced Lady Ida to three months in jail.

It seems unlikely that Sir George, if he had realised what the end of the trial would bring, would not have settled with the creditors; not so much out of consideration for his wife as to save the family name from further disrepute. But by the time he saw that there was a serious risk his wife would be found guilty, it was too late; the wheels were turning and nothing could stop them. In later years he adopted a vengeful tone and spoke as though he had master-minded the entire operation; 'I could have saved her,' he told Francis Bamford, 'but thought it better she should learn a lesson.'[21] This sounds like the braggartry of an old man who hated to admit that he was wrong; it is much more likely that he misjudged the situation and was as surprised by the verdict as anyone else. But whether by mischance or volition, the fact remains that he *could* have saved his wife yet failed to do so.

Osbert never forgave him. The spectre of his mother's humiliation haunted him all his life; Frank Magro, his closest companion in old age, said that, even when near death, he was still reduced to tears by any mention of the trial.[22] He knew his mother was a fool, was irritated by her whenever they met, yet loved her all the same. Julian Field figured thenceforth in his calendar of demons; as late as 1945 he was having enquiries made into the circumstances of his death – of a heart-attack, in Kilburn, his gross estate being valued at £13 2s 6d.[23] His resentment against Sir George was less all-consuming, yet little the less potent; from 1915 there is a new stridency in Osbert's railing against his father. Previously he had bickered, argued, criticised, but there had been an element of affection and respect underlying the relationship. Now the affection and respect had died. Fear remained, fear of a man who still wielded power and held the purse-strings, but it was accompanied by something close to hatred. Osbert's guerrilla warfare with Sir George soured his life and ate up a wholly disproportionate part of his time and energies; only after his father was dead could it be transmuted into the unfair but marvellously entertaining portrait that emerges in the autobiography.

David Horner, who was to see more of him over the next fifty years than any other friend or relation, ascribed to the scandal much of the shyness and nervousness which he could see so clearly yet which was concealed by the façade that Osbert presented to the outside world. Certainly it scarred him deeply. For the moment, however, there was nothing to be done but carry on: 'We'll go to all the parties, be seen everywhere, make a name for ourselves to show that we don't care what anybody thinks.'[24] The genesis of the Sitwells as the literary *enfants terribles* of the post-war world can at least in part be traced to the events at the Old Bailey in 1915. It was fortunate for Osbert that, while the scandal was still at the forefront of people's minds, he found himself posted back to France. By the time he returned to England for a second period of leave it had largely been forgotten. Lady Ida was back in Scarborough, Sir George grumbling angrily in London; life went on.

Osbert's life went on, too; as it might well not have done if he had returned a third time to France. A few days before his return to London in the spring of 1916 he had somehow cut his finger* while in the trenches. He went to hospital for several weeks, convalesced for a further month at Renishaw, did not report to the barracks until the late summer of 1916. Probably the authorities had already concluded that he was not likely to be an important asset in the front line. For a while he was kept at home; imperceptibly the while lengthened until it became a permanency. Osbert never returned to the Western Front; for him the fighting war was over.

*Some accounts refer to a foot but Osbert himself told the literary critic Frank Megroz that it was a finger.

5

We Are Poets and Shall
Tell the Truth

You hope that we shall tell you that they found their happiness
        fighting,
Or that they died with a song on their lips,
Or that we shall use the old familiar phrases
With which your paid servants please you in the Press:
But we are poets,
And shall tell the truth.

(From 'Rhapsode', Argonaut and Juggernaut)

AUDEN once wrote that, if biographies of writers could be justified at all, it must be because, in their case, 'the ways in which they accept and revolt against their immediate situation are peculiarly easy to watch, and the acceptance of and revolt against the immediate is the central human problem of free will'.[1] By the middle of 1916 Osbert Sitwell was most markedly in revolt against his immediate situation. Whatever belief he had once had in the necessity, still less the desirability, of war had faded. He was not by nature a crusader, and did not think it necessary or suitable to thrust his unpalatable views down the throats of his fellow officers. But nor did he keep them secret; it must have been well known in the Grenadier Guards that Sitwell was unsound about the war and that he was from time to time guilty of a measure of indiscretion. It says much for the tolerance and good sense of the authorities that they chose to pay no attention; if he was ever warned to behave more prudently it was done with tact and in such a way as to ensure that scandal could be avoided.

'The war came and went,' wrote Osbert in one of his short stories, 'rolling me over, submerging me as it did most of the younger generation, filling our souls with anger, rancour and hatred, with pity and love.'[2] In the summer of 1916 he began to pick himself up from the spume and foam of the war in France and to consider where he stood. His illness and long convalescence gave him a chance for reflection which had so far been denied him. He realised that he was out of sympathy with the great majority of his fellow citizens. Thomas Hardy, a greater poet than he would ever be, put into the mouth of the radical politician Francis Burdett words that summed up the conclusion of Osbert's thinking:

> I have beheld the agonies of war
> Through many a weary season; seen enough
> To make me hold that scarcely any goal
> Is worth the reaching by so red a road.[3]

There could be no such thing as a righteous war, Osbert was later to argue: 'A righteous war is only one degree less wicked than a wicked war.'[4] The war against Germany should never have been begun; it must be brought to an end as soon as possible. When Lord Lansdowne, himself a former Foreign Secretary, wrote his celebrated letter to the *Daily Telegraph* in 1917, urging the merits of a negotiated peace, Osbert praised the utterance as 'moderate and direct', and wrote to Lansdowne to support it.[5] He never wavered from this point of view. Some years later the parish council of Eckington, a village near Renishaw which was largely owned by Osbert, asked if they could have a piece of land on which to erect a cannon as a war memorial. Osbert agreed, but made it a condition that the cannon should bear an inscription reading: 'This gun has been erected here to remind the people of Eckington of the wicked folly and waste of war . . . and in the hope that its ugliness will frighten the children so that they grow up with a natural hatred of war.'[6]

Increasingly his heroes became those who not merely shared his views but were able and ready to trumpet them abroad: Bernard Shaw; H. W. Nevinson, the journalist and philanthropist whose mastery of irony appealed particularly to Osbert; above all, H. W. Massingham. Massingham was editor of the Liberal weekly, the *Nation*, which he shaped into a powerful engine for reform as well as a vehicle for some of the most interesting young writers of the day. Sassoon, in his auto-biographical novel *Sherston's Progress*, describes his eponymous hero as stoking his bitterness 'by gobbling up liberal reading matter like Markington's *The Unconservative Weekly*'.[7] Osbert not merely gobbled it up but contributed largely to it. He had first met Massingham through Robbie Ross, that loyal friend of Oscar Wilde and champion of innumerable young writers and painters. Massingham read some of Osbert's earliest poems, liked them, and encouraged him to write more and publish them in the *Nation*. Osbert's pseudonym was '*Miles*' – the Latin word for a soldier; probably his superior officers knew who the author really was but they did not see it as being their business to make any formal enquiries.

Shortly before he left for France, Osbert had visited a fortune teller; you will survive, he was told, and continue your career as a writer.[8] The fortune teller was both prescient and premature; in 1914 Osbert had no career as a writer to continue. By 1916, however, he was poised to embark on one. He had no doubt that it was in poetry that he most wished to express himself; had been in no doubt, indeed, since that June evening at Scarborough many years before when he had evaded his governess, run to the clifftop and looked out at the sunset across the sea: 'The clouds began to take on a deeper and more rosy hue, and it was time for me to return home; but this strange peace, of which poetry is born, had for the first time descended on me and henceforth a new light quivered above the world.'[9] Now the words to express that vision were beginning to form within him. His sister Edith had already led the way; by 1916 she was establishing a small but not insignificant reputation as a poet. In seeking to follow her, Osbert felt that he was taking on a quest of the utmost seriousness: 'Already, even at the start, I realised the sacredness of my task.'[10] His contemporaries were apt to dismiss him as a dilettante, rich, idle, dabbling in all the arts. By his conduct and his activities, he did much to foster this prejudice. But to him his poetry was something apart, a vocation demanding reverence and dedication. It suffused all his writing: 'I can claim never to have written a book, or a short story, or an essay that I did not conceive as if it were a poem, and in that resides the value, such as it is, of my work.'[11]

It did not come easily. As a journalist, Osbert had the reputation of being able to dash off a thousand words at the drop of a hat on any subject that occurred to his editor: London squares, the state of the contemporary theatre, English food, Venice in December. The pieces read like that: casual, relaxed, with all the air of spontaneity. Yet even these light-weight pieces were the source of much agonising. 'Osbert really had to *construct* his talent,' remarked the Marxist poet and critic

Jack Lindsay. 'He wasn't a natural writer. It was an effort of will-power.'[12] His poems grew painfully, phrase by phrase, word by word, from rough beginnings to highly finished products. Partly this was a fortuitous by-product of his handwriting. This was so hard to read that he was forced to write everything out two or three times before it was fit to be sent to a typist; he took advantage of the exercise to refine his original conception. But far more it was a quest for perfection, that restless discontent which torments writers in the endless search for words which will express with total precision and vividness whatever it is that they are trying to say. 'He worked extremely hard at whatever he was writing, taking extraordinary pains over it,' remembered his long-time and long-suffering secretary, Lorna Andrade. 'He used to get me to ring every word that he used twice on the same page.'[13]

Beverley Nichols describes[14] how one evening at the Café Royal Osbert scribbled on the back of a menu the lines from 'The Modern Abraham'[15] in which an armaments manufacturer – one of the poet's favourite targets – complains that it is unreasonable to ask him to subscribe to the 'Disabled Soldiers' Fund':

> I've fought for Britain with my might and main;
> I made explosives – and I gave a son.

It is a bitter and accomplished poem on a theme that Osbert had often pondered. Nichols claims that the hurried draft was in all important respects the same as the finished article. Such a way of working would be wholly contrary to Osbert's accustomed practice. It seems much more likely that the spontaneity was an illusion; that Osbert had already worked out what he wanted to say and had revised it in his head or even on paper. If he could hoodwink Nichols into believing that his work was an efflux of sudden inspiration, then so much the better; he knew himself that this was not the way he worked.

His first poem – or, at least, the first poem by which he wished to be remembered – was in fact written before his return to London in 1916, when he was in a billet behind the front line not far from Ypres. Nothing, he wrote in his autobiography, astonished him more than to find 'how entirely I lost myself in the process, and yet was able to concentrate'.[16] The result was 'Babel', an unexceptionable if not particularly distinguished denunciation of war describing a scene of devastation to which night and moonlight have lent a spurious serenity.

The shimmering sands where once there played
Children with painted pail and spade
Are drearily desolate – afraid
To meet night's dark humanity,

Whose silver cool remakes the dead,
And lays no blame on any head
For all the havoc, fire, and lead,
That fell upon us suddenly,

When all we came to know as good
Gave way to Evil's fiery flood,
And monstrous myths of iron and blood
Seem to obscure God's clarity.

Deep sunk in sin, this tragic star
Sinks deeper still, and wages war
Against itself; strewn all the seas
With victims of a world disease
– And we are left to drink the lees
Of Babel's direful prophecy.[17]

This poem, which, as John Pearson has pointed out, echoes the rhythm of Thomas Campbell's ever-popular 'Hohenlinden', was in spirit far from the fierce diatribes which Osbert was soon to aim at those who directed or profited by the war. The tone was mournful rather than condemnatory; its images, though presaging much that was to feature prominently in Osbert's poetry, were not such as to cause disapproval in the West End clubs or regimental messes. Certainly the author felt no hesitation in claiming credit for the lines and was delighted when *The Times*, after some judicious string-pulling, agreed to publish it. It was a curious decision on the part of that paper, which only a little while before had given prominence to Julian Grenfell's passionate hymn in glorification of the martial spirit, 'Into Battle', but it elevated Osbert to the status of published poet and convinced him that this was where his future lay. 'Though rather immature,' Osbert wrote many years later, 'I like to think that it has some point even today.'[18] The point was one which he was to make again and again throughout his life but particularly over the next few years.

Satire was his favoured weapon with which to attack the stupidity and evil of war. Dr Johnson defined a satire as 'a poem in which wickedness or folly is censured', and Osbert, though usually under the cloak of anonymity, became ever more pungent in his censure of what he believed to be a war indefensible on grounds of either morality or *realpolitik*. The poem in which he took most pride, 'Rhapsode', like many others of what he called his 'war (or rather peace) poems',[19] appeared first in the *Nation* and was dedicated to its editor, H. W. Massingham. The theme was that of much of Osbert's verse: in a society dominated by vested interests and their jackal propagandists, only the voice of the poet could be relied on to ring true – 'But we are poets and shall tell the truth.' However anxious those in power might be to create a cosy, acceptable image of war, however ready the people at large might be to be beguiled by such siren images, there would be at least one astringent note of honesty:

> We know you now – and what you wish to be told;
> That the larks are singing in the trenches,
> That the fruit trees will again blossom in the spring,
> That Youth is always happy;
>
> But you know the misery that lies
> Under the surface –
> And we will dig it up for you![20]

Viewed from the 1990s such sentiments may seem boringly predictable, but in the autumn of 1917 the heroics of Brooke and Grenfell still held sway. Siegfried Sassoon was only just beginning to be spoken of, Wilfred Owen was unknown; if not blazing a solitary trail, Osbert was at least in the forefront of the new poetic movement. 'Rhapsode' was a brave poem; more remarkable, perhaps, in its message than in its form, but a sincere and moving affirmation of something that was always in need of saying and never more so than when the war had more than a year to run and seemed to be going on for ever.

But it was not only in his pacifism that Osbert wanted to say something new. He was self-consciously in revolt against what he felt to be the prevailing spirit in contemporary poetry. In fact he was no more than a relatively minor player in a revolution that was already under way: Eliot's *Prufrock* first appeared in London in 1917, by which time Ezra Pound had already published eight volumes of poetry. But to Osbert, and indeed to many of those who read him, it seemed that he was an isolated figure, almost alone with his sister and a tiny handful of kindred spirits in challenging the stultifying grip of the 'Georgian' versifiers. It is easy to overstate the decadence of English poetry immediately before and during the First World War.[21] The previous decade had perhaps been undistinguished by the highest standards, though no period which could boast Hardy, Housman and the early Yeats, as well as the considerable skills of Rudyard Kipling, could be lightly dismissed. Since then there had been much movement. The first volume of *Georgian Poetry*[22] – a series which was to become identified in the minds of the Sitwells with everything that was most dismal about English versifying – included poems by D. H. Lawrence and W. H. Davies as well as the more conservative contributions of Masefield and John Drinkwater. The first three volumes, indeed, contained much that was fresh and innovative; before the end of the First World War, Robert Graves, Sassoon, Edmund Blunden, Ralph Hodgson and Isaac Rosenberg had all appeared within its pages. By then, however, the movement was in decadence; its editor, Edward Marsh, had lost touch with the contemporary world and clung to outdated standards and shibboleths. In distancing himself from this increasingly unpleasing environment, Osbert chose also to ignore the good things that *Georgian Poetry* had fostered and dismissed the entire movement as trite and sentimental, encapsulated in the dreadful couplet with which William Kerr began his poem 'Counting Sheep':

> I lingered at a gate and talked
> A little with a lonely lamb.

Alfred Noyes was his favourite butt and was to remain so for many years; as late as 1927, he wrote derisively of a 'loud-pounding goods train', heard in childhood, which:

> Lumbered along, had I but known it then,
> To the precise rhythm of Mr Alfred Noyes's verse.[23]

(Noyes struck back to some effect when, in his poem 'The New Duckling', he described his Sitwellian hero as not wanting

> to waddle like mother
> Or quack like me silly old dad.
> I want to be utterly other,
> And *frightfully* modern and mad.[24])

But it was not so much individuals that Osbert detested as the cosy, middle-class society, ruled by philistine aspirations and conservative views, hidebound, smug, fearful of novelty and resentful of anything that seemed to challenge its unquestioned and unquestionable beliefs. It was the world of the athletic curate from Osbert's novel *Miracle on Sinai*, who was 'very literary, a great admirer of *A Shropshire Lad* and of Miss Clemence Dane'.[25] With the athletic curate he lumped not merely Alfred Noyes, J. C. Squire and other such pillars of neo-Georgianism but a whole movement of English poetry which contained much of merit as well as dross. In this he was not alone; T. S. Eliot for one was equally ready to categorise the Georgian movement as inbred and insipid. It was, Eliot wrote, characterised by 'pleasantness' of the 'insidiously didactic, or Wordsworthian' variety, or 'the decorative, playful or solemn minor-Keatsian'.[26] The neo-Georgians of 1917 or later might be worse than their predecessors, but the basic weaknesses were the same. In this Sitwell and Eliot concurred: the most notable distinction between the two was that Eliot, intellectually and poetically, had established a new world from which to rail at the shortcomings of the old. Osbert sniped effectively at the feebler follies of the Georgians but, as was to become evident when he published his first collections of verse, essentially he stood upon the same ground as those he attacked.

His own tastes were by no means confined to the avant-garde. To his biographer Frank Megroz he said that his favourite poets were Chaucer, Dryden, Marlowe, Marvell, Milton, Pope, Shelley – 'and Shakespeare – but is it necessary to state anything so obvious?'[27] Only one of these poets wrote even as late as the early nineteenth century. His list of favourite poems came closer to the present day, including as it did his sister's 'Heart and Mind' and Owen's 'Strange Meeting', as well as several extracts from Pope and Dryden, Shakespeare's 'When icicles hang by the wall', and, probably also by Shakespeare, 'The Phoenix and the Turtle' – 'always to me the most mysterious and lovely poem'.[28] The incantatory power of that marvellous poem – 'Let the bird of loudest lay, On the sole Arabian tree . . .' – was something for which Osbert often strove; it is ironic that his most effective verse – none of which appeared for another decade or more – eschewed mystery and incantation but described with warmth and simplicity the minutiae of the people and places that he had known.

Most of his early work that did not appear in the *Nation* was to be found in the anthology *Wheels*, which appeared erratically between 1916 and 1922. *Wheels* was the inspiration of Edith Sitwell and the minor poet and social rebel Nancy Cunard; the latter's contribution, considerable at first, dwindled as other preoccupations took their toll. It set out to revolt against the prevailing ethos, to surprise and, with luck, offend the leaden bourgeoisie. The leaden bourgeoisie, as was their wont, paid not the slightest attention but *Wheels* caused a stir among a small group of intellectuals and would-be intellectuals. It contained some good things but the prevailing tone was sour and flippant, its prime objective to destroy rather than to create; it was 'on the whole dour and morose', wrote the *Times Literary Supplement*; 'they see nothing bright in the present, and no bright hopes in the future'. T. S. Eliot complained that its authors had 'a little the air of smattering'. In seeking to escape from the rainbows, cuckoos, daffodils and timid hares beloved by the neo-Georgians, they had given the reader 'Lancret rather than Watteau'.[29]

The reaction to *Wheels* from those whom the Sitwells would have considered their peers was cautiously scornful. Aldous Huxley wrote to Lady Ottoline Morrell in June 1917 to report that he was on his way to meet Edith Sitwell, 'who is passionately anxious for me to contribute to her horrible production. The Wheelites take themselves so seriously: I never believed it possible.'[30] Horrible or not, he contributed, and was secretly flattered to be asked to do so. But he continued to scoff. He was writing for 'the well-known Society Anthology,* *Wheels*', he told his brother Julian:

> The folk who run it are a family called Sitwell, alias Shufflebottom, one sister and two brothers, Edith, Osbert and Sacheverell – isn't that superb? – each of them larger and whiter than the other. I like Edith, but Ozzy and Sachy are still rather too large to swallow. Their great object is to REBEL, which sounds quite charming; only one finds that the steps they are prepared to take, the lengths they will go, are so small as to be hardly perceptible to the naked eye. But they are so earnest and humble . . . these dear solid people who have suddenly discovered intellect and begin to get drunk on it . . . it is a charming type.[31]

Huxley's charge, that they were amiable amateurs playing at being revolutionaries, was to haunt the Sitwells throughout their careers.

One of the more endearing – if sometimes infuriating – features of Osbert, Edith and Sacheverell was that each believed his or her siblings to be transcendent geniuses and saw it as essential to point this out *ad nauseam* to a largely disbelieving world. Edith Sitwell conceived *Wheels*

---

*An offensive phrase borrowed from the *Evening Standard*.

as being mainly a vehicle for the promotion of her family's talents. Its first number contained ten of Osbert's poems, as well as a maiden effort from nineteen-year-old Sacheverell. In later life Osbert did not rate these juvenilia highly, dropping most of them from collections of his poetry. 'Twentieth Century Harlequinade' echoed the bleak mood of most of his earlier verse:

> The pantomime of life is near its close;
> The stage is strewn with ends and bits of things,
> With mortals maim'd or crucified and left
> To gape at endless horror through eternity

but most of his offerings lent force to Eliot's complaint that in *Wheels* there were too many 'garden-gods, guitars and mandolins'. One poem in particular, 'The Lament of the Mole-Catcher', which told of an ancient peasant who was now enfeebled and blind like his former victims, could just as easily have found a place in the despised columns of *Georgian Poetry*.

'On Saturday I dined in the sullen magnificence of St James's Palace with Osbert Sitwell, who is Captain of the Guard,' that literary panjandrum Edmund Gosse told his protégé, another young war poet, Robert Nichols. 'He is writing poems zealously. What a poetical animation there is everywhere!'[32] There is a note of mild mockery about the final comment, yet Gosse was an admirer of the Sitwells and would strongly have urged Osbert to be yet more zealous in his labours. It was not till October 1919, however, that he had accumulated enough work to make a reasonable selection. By then he had already co-operated with his sister on a slim pamphlet called after his own poem, *Twentieth Century Harlequinade*, and gone solo on a spirited if somewhat laboured polemic against Winston Churchill, *The Winstonburg Line*.[33] Churchill already seemed to Osbert to be the supreme warmonger and in 1919 he compounded his sins by championing intervention against the Bolsheviks in Russia. Osbert held no brief for the Bolsheviks but he could not forgive what seemed to him a wanton will to prolong the war. He denounced Churchill in three satirical poems, two of which the left-wing *Daily Herald* was happy to buy and publish in its leader column.[34] There were some good lines and some telling points, but the poetic content was limited: 'He often falls into prose,' wrote Rose Macaulay of his satire, 'but never into vague and facile wordiness':[35]

> I consider
> That getting killed
> Should be
> The normal occupation
> Of other people.
> I enjoyed
> Doing my bit in France
> Immensely
> And am only sorry
> That the war stopped
> Before I could go out again.

And so it went on; neither vague nor wordy perhaps, but not strong enough to cause Churchill a sleepless night. Now it was time for something more substantial. *Argonaut and Juggernaut* registered his claim to be not just an occasional satirist but an established poet.

The poem by which he would most have wished to be remembered, 'How Shall We Rise to Greet the Dawn?', appeared as the preface to the collection. It provided the most accomplished statement yet, both of his view of life and of his poetical aspirations. It also offered some potent weapons to the hostile critic:

> How shall we rise to greet the dawn?
> Not timidly,
> With a hand above our eyes,
> But greet the strong light
> Joyfully;
> Nor will we mistake the dawn
> For the mid-day . . .
>
> Let us prune the tree of language
> Of its dead fruit.
> Let us melt up the clichés
> Into molten metal;
> Fashion weapons that will scold and flay;
> Let us curb this eternal humour
> And become witty.
>
> Let us dig up the dragon's teeth
> From this fertile soil;
> Swiftly,
> Before they fructify;

Let us give them as medicine
To the writhing monster itself.

We must create and fashion a new God –
A God of power, of beauty and of strength;
Created peacefully, cruelly,
Labouring from the revulsion of men's minds.
Cast down the idols of a thousand years,
Crush them to dust
Beneath the dancing rhythm of our feet.
Oh! let us dance upon the weak and cruel:
We must create and fashion a new God.

Osbert was no Lord Byron, who woke to find that he had become famous overnight. Chatto & Windus printed a thousand copies of *Argonaut and Juggernaut* and still had 412 in stock when the title was transferred to Duckworth in 1927.[36] But the book was taken seriously by the critics and talked of, if not always kindly, by his fellow poets. It fell substantially into two parts: the satires, most of them directed at warmongers or profiteers and for the greater part printed already in the *Nation*; and the more exotic and florid poems, which had earned Eliot's censure:

Slowly the torches die. They echo long,
These last notes of a Bacchanalian song,
Of drifting drowsy beauty, born of sleep,
– Vast as the sea, as changing and as deep,
In thanksgiving for shelt'ring summer skies.[37]

These latter poems, with their post-Tennysonian lilt and redolent with owls, moons and mermaids, seemed the weaker part of the book to most of Osbert's critics. 'I think you are more successful in irony and anger than when you try to create beauty,' wrote Richard Aldington, while the *Globe* considered that the 'tinkling title' indicated the nature of much of the poetry, which was 'melodious descriptive reporting of his emotions rather than depth of thought, and when these [the emotions] become forcible, they tend to be hysterical'.[38] The *Athenaeum* was harsher still about the more romantic poems, complaining about the absence of 'precision, point and critical certainty'. Not everyone agreed, however. Rose Macaulay, in the *Daily News*, praised Osbert's 'rich fantastic imagination' and said that he was at his best 'when furthest from the realism of life, when writing of the hot colours of tropical seas and colours, of sailors on the swinging seas of adventure', while Edmund Blunden, in a letter which was no doubt intended to please the recipient but still sounds essentially sincere, told him: 'You have a great host of beautiful words at your elbow, strong words, colour words, words that are like trumpets – and the imagination in these poems is odd and, attracting some, repelling some, of an intense cumulative effect.'[39] But the consensus was strongly that it was in satire that Osbert was both more original and most at home. *The Times*, in a review which Osbert relished and often quoted in the future, observed that 'Captain Sitwell in his combative moods is one of the swiftest pursuers of Mrs Grundy, and this volume shows him tripping her up several times with ease and adroitness.'[40]

Osbert could be well satisfied with the scale of his coverage, which was extensive beyond anything a poet of his slender reputation could have expected to command. The content too, on the whole, did not displease him, though some reviews disturbed him deeply. The one which annoyed him most was a short review in the *London Mercury*, unsigned but patently from the pen of its editor, J. C. Squire, and thus emanating from the heart of the Georgian establishment.[41] It was the more vexatious for following a larger and laudatory notice of Siegfried Sassoon's new collection and a review of the most recent volume of *Georgian Poetry*, which included contributions from Graves, D. H. Lawrence, W. H. Davies, Walter de la Mare and Sassoon himself. It was thus difficult to dismiss the review, as Osbert would have liked, as the product of a sour and disappointed philistine who saw himself left behind by the current of literary life. At first sight, wrote Squire of *Argonaut and Juggernaut*, the book looked like a revolutionary manifesto. 'Its title is vehement and original, and its paper "jacket" is decorated with the photograph of a Negro head surmounted with a towering and tapering wickerwork structure. It has no bearing on the contents, and we can only assume that the author puts it there to arrest attention.' But attention having been arrested, expectation was disappointed. Unkindly quoting the injunction in the Preface Poem to melt up the clichés and become witty, Squire complained that clichés abounded in Osbert's poems while the wit did not emerge. 'He cannot really play the revolutionary with gusto ...' concluded Squire; 'and when he lapses into more ordinary forms and more connected statements he is revealed as an ordinary immature writer of verses. He has some gift of observation which he will waste unless he treats it more conscientiously, but observation will not make a poet.'

The review was uncharitable and more brutally dismissive of the work of a young and inexperienced poet than was necessary or kind. It was provoked by the contempt which Osbert had ostentatiously displayed towards everything that Squire and his associates stood for in literary terms, and it inspired in return a hatred out of all proportion to the offence. Osbert's indignation was the more splenetic because the review contained an essential truth. His hatred of war and all who championed it was unfeigned but he made an unconvincing revolutionary. His power of observation was indeed acute, his gift for word-play considerable, but these alone were not enough to make a poet. 'I'm so glad you dislike Osbert's book,' wrote Virginia Woolf to Ethel Smyth when his *Collected Satires and Poems* was published in 1931. 'So do I. All foliage and no filberts.'[42] The florid fruitlessness to which she took exception was less apparent in much of his later work, but the charge would never totally be dismissed. Harold Monro, whose Poetry Bookshop provided a sanctuary where poets of every style and size could graze peacefully side by side, was something of a champion of Osbert's. 'Winter the Huntsman' appeared in one of the bookshop's rhyme-sheets and several of Osbert's poems featured in the monthly chapbooks which Monro published from July 1919. In his critical study *Some Contemporary Poets*, Monro praised the younger, more controversial poets of the avant-garde, in particular Aldous Huxley. About Osbert he was laudatory but more equivocal: 'Though his mind works in a painted over-heated atmosphere, it has a considerable power of feeling its way back into the past or peering into the psychology of the present.'[43] The kind words were justified, but so also was the criticism. Yeats used to praise people who were creatures of intellectual passion, Geoffrey Grigson told John Pearson: 'The Sitwells weren't that.'[44] Osbert's intellect was sound enough, the passion was lacking. Honed by experience and directed into the channel where it was most at ease, his poetry was to become proficient, often moving, sometimes even memorable. But that indefinable quality that separates the truly great from the highly competent was never to be found. All his life he hankered for the stature of a major poet; long before he died he had realised that it would never be his.

There were other poets on the scene who seemed more, or at least as, likely to achieve greatness. One of them was Robert Nichols. Early in 1918 Cynthia Asquith, diarist and daughter-in-law to the former Prime Minister, recorded a conversation which she had had with Nichols about contemporary poetry: 'We skimmed over the Sitwells, and he said he thought Osbert – unlike most of the poets – *had* got something to say, but he considered him inarticulate.'[45] So utterly did Nichols's own poetic talent splutter out that it is hard now to remember that towards the end of the First World War he was acclaimed as the great hope of English letters. Edmund Gosse rated him, with Graves and Sassoon, as 'a sound Georgian' and admired him extravagantly, though describing him as 'distractingly violent, mercurial and excessive'. He compared him with the Sitwells: 'Impossible to think of a greater contrast,' he told John Drinkwater. 'The Sitwells are alert, rather elegant, with beautiful manners and a formidable reserve of humour. But whether really gifted or not, I do not know. Of Nichols' gifts there are no doubts.'[46] Edith had no doubt either; her life was punctuated by wild enthusiasms, many of them ill-judged, and Nichols was one of her earlier and most eagerly promoted heroes. Osbert was more cautious; he was probably jealous of Nichols's fame and reputation but also had doubts about the reality of his talent. He makes many references to Nichols in his autobiography but is significantly silent about the quality of his writing.

There was another great star in the London firmament about whom he had no such reservations. Osbert never spoke or wrote of T. S. Eliot's work except in tones of admiration. The respect was not entirely mutual. He was reviewing two anthologies of poetry, Eliot told his mother in March 1918, 'one mostly by some young friends of mine; two young Guards officers with literary aspirations'.[47] This somewhat patronising note characterised the relationship; but the friendship was real. Osbert had been a staunch ally when Eliot was trying to wangle his way into the US Navy, pulling strings with Lady Cunard and joining J. C. Squire, St John Hutchinson and other such 'prominent official people' in a recommendation of Eliot's abilities to anyone concerned.[48] In 1918 and 1919 he and Sachie would often take themselves to a dank London tea-shop. There Eliot's ill-fated first wife Vivienne would be awaiting them, to be joined later by the poet himself, emerging from his work at the bank to consume hot tea and muffins. On Thursdays of most weeks they would dine together at a restaurant in Piccadilly, and would often lunch at the weekend in Eliot's flat. They were never intimate but the relationship was much more than casual. *The Love Song of J. Alfred Prufrock*, though published in Chicago in 1915, did not appear in London till 1917. Eliot was still little known; he had no doubts about the merits of his poetry but much about his status in English society; the friendship of a family as well-connected and relatively affluent as the

Sitwells was of more importance to him than he liked subsequently to admit.

Another close friend, whose influence was not so great in literary matters but far more profound in forming Osbert's attitude towards the war, was the young infantry officer and poet, Siegfried Sassoon. Sassoon had gone far further than Osbert in defying public opinion and the authorities, throwing away his Military Cross and inviting court-martial by refusing to serve in future battles. Osbert had first met him through that tireless promoter of literary friendships, Robbie Ross. He admired Sassoon's principled stand, more indeed than he admired his poetry, but felt no urge to emulate him; martyrdom, he knew, was not for him. Nor, as it turned out, was it for Sassoon; the authorities wisely ignored his protest and treated him for a nervous breakdown rather than court-martialling him for mutiny. In time his relationship with Osbert was to become tempestuous, for the moment they felt themselves to be comrades in a tiny minority against a largely hostile world. Osbert prudently hid his light under a denser bushel than Sassoon could bring himself to use, but they were both on the same side and could talk to each other with a freedom and common terms of reference that they could only with difficulty find elsewhere.

In July 1917 Sassoon sent Osbert an advance copy of his new book – presumably *The Old Huntsman*, a collection of his subversive war poetry. 'I hope you'll not be disappointed,' he wrote. 'It is highly suitable for people of a funereal disposition and should have a great success among undertakers. The word death, die, dead, occurs more than 40 times in the 39 poems – Dark 4 and darkness 16 – War 15 – Night 13 – Gloom 9 – Doom 7 – Killed 5 – Corpses only 3. I am afraid I really must try and invent some new words for these light subjects.'[49] Osbert's preoccupations were much the same; in a similar group of fifteen poems the words dead/death/dying/die occur ten times, war five times, blood five times – the difference in emphasis is perhaps accounted for by his preference for the more oblique approach. So far as the spirit of the poems was concerned, as distinct from the style, there was little to choose between them. When Sassoon sought an ally to help nurture a new poetic talent, he was in no doubt where to turn. 'Have you met Wilfred Owen, my little friend, whose verses were in the *Nation* recently?' Sassoon asked Osbert in July 1917. 'He is so nice, and shy, and fervent about poetry, which he is quite good at and will do *very well* one day.'[50] Osbert had not met Owen at that point, but did so a few weeks later, again with the ubiquitous Robbie Ross. Osbert was 'not to frighten him', Ross insisted; an injunction which proved unnecessary since the two men established within a few minutes that they took a common delight in 'the company of our friends, a love of books, and a hatred of modern war'.[51] Owen rapidly found himself assimilated into the little world of kindred spirits in which Ross, Sassoon and Osbert played so prominent a part. He and Sassoon went with Osbert to hear Mrs Gordon Woodhouse play her harpsichord and then went back to Osbert's house for 'a sumptuous tea which culminated in – was it raspberries and cream? and ices of incredibly creamy quality'.[52]

The friendship throve. Owen wrote regularly from camp. He had broken out to order a copy of *Wheels* at the Scarborough bookshop, he told Osbert in July 1918. The shop assistant denied all knowledge of it. Owen protested so vociferously that 'the Young Lady loudly declared she knew all along that I was "Osbert himself". This caused consternation throughout the crowded shop; but I got the last laugh by – "No, Madam; the book is by a friend of mine, Miss Sitwell."' It was the 1917 volume that he was seeking; the 1918 version was still in preparation. Owen played with the idea of contributing a poem to the next collection. Would it continue the crusade against the war? he asked; was it designed to 'go on the caterpillar wheels of Siegfried's Music Hall Tank?' – the tank that Sassoon wished would lurch down the stalls to rag-time tunes and ensure that there would be no more jokes in music halls 'to mock the riddled corpses round Bapaume'. If so, 'I might help with the ammunition'.[53] He did not live to see it happen. A few days later he was back in France. A week before the end of the war he was killed. No poem of his had been published when he died.

'I was so dreadfully sorry to hear about Wilfred,' Osbert wrote to the poet's mother, from the hospital where he was recovering from an almost lethal bout of Spanish influenza. 'I can't tell you how much I feel for you – and how personally we all feel the loss.' Owen's poems would appear in the following year's collection of *Wheels* but the priority must be to bring together all his manuscripts and publish a collected edition of his work. 'It must be a success – and I think it would be a good thing to get Siegfried Sassoon (who is better known as a poet than I am) to write a short preface.'[54] He continued the campaign and when Mrs Owen seemed dilatory he wrote to urge her on: 'Wilfred's poems ought to be seen about at once. I am sure I could get them taken by Blackwell at Oxford . . . but I advise a London publisher – and would act for you in this matter or get Siegfried to do so. So will you command me about this?'[55]

For Edith the eventual publication came as something of a disappointment: she had longed to edit Owen's poems herself and present them to the world as her own discovery. Instead Sassoon took on the task and gained most of the credit for Owen's phenomenal posthumous success. Osbert rejoiced unreservedly in Owen's ever-growing reputation. He sometimes showed a lack of generosity towards those whom he considered his rivals and was often grudging in his praise of his fellow poets. Towards Owen, though, he behaved with selfless magnanimity and never ceased to mourn his loss. A mutual friend once remarked how much easier all their lives would have been if Owen had lived. 'These words', wrote Osbert, 'bear true witness, both to his influence on his friends and to their feeling for him.'[56]

It was Edith who had the greatest influence on her brother's development as a poet. Her interventions were not wholly beneficial. Anthony Powell believed that the unstinted and often extravagant praise which she heaped on Osbert's slightest efforts was damaging in that its recipient began to believe everything that she said.[57] Equally, however, but for Edith's unremitting encouragement and support Osbert might never have become a poet at all, or have stuck to it when he met with setbacks. His surface arrogance, even complacency, masked deep self-doubt. Edith's insistence that hostile critics were blind and bigoted, probably jealous as well, reassured him when his confidence was at its lowest. The history of English poetry might not have been very different if Osbert had abandoned the enterprise in despair, but his own development would have taken another course and the crowning achievements of his maturity might never have come about. Osbert will not be remembered primarily as a poet, but if he had not first been a poet he could never have written the books by which he earned whatever claim he has to immortality.

Without Edith's energy and enthusiasm it is unlikely that there would have been a poetry reading in Lady Colefax's drawing-room in December 1917; an event memorable, among other things, in that it provided the first recorded sighting of the three Sitwells operating publicly as a team. Gosse was in the chair – 'the bloodiest little old man I have ever seen', Huxley described him[58] – and distinguished himself by snapping nervously at all the participants and scolding T. S. Eliot for being a few minutes late in arriving from his bank. Other readers included Robert Nichols, Graves, Sassoon and Aldous Huxley. Gosse had been dubious about the affair from the start; he had hardly met the Sitwells at the time and knew little of them – 'I pray Apollo that they be not pacifists,' he wrote to Drinkwater.[59] They were pacifists, of course, which may have accounted for some of his tetchiness, though it does not seem likely that their political views were much in evidence on such an occasion. Eliot was another contributor who wondered why he had let himself be dragged into so uncomfortable an outing. The bigwigs, he told Ezra Pound, were 'OSWALD and EDITH SHITWELL, Graves, Nichols and OTHERS'.[60] He made various suggestions to Pound about obscene verses which he might read on such an occasion, but, according to Huxley, when it came to the point: 'Eliot and I were the only people who had any dignity.' Nichols 'raved and screamed and hooted', Viola Tree was 'syrupy and fruity and rich', while 'the Shufflebottoms – alias Sitwells – were respectable but terribly narrow'.[61] Cynthia Asquith in the audience was less censorious; she thought the Sitwells looked notably Germanic but found the reading as a whole 'very moving'.[62] For the Sitwells, nervous or not, it had been an unequivocal success. They had been, if not the stars of the show, at least among the most prominent. Their names would in future be remembered in any discussion of the London literary scene. They had arrived.

So preoccupied was Osbert by his writing and literary politicking that it must sometimes have been hard for him to remember that he was still a professional soldier. He could never wholly forget that the war was not just an abstract issue, but there is little evidence in his writings, public or private, to suggest that he gave much thought to the doings of his regiment or to the survival of his contemporaries. He can hardly be blamed for a feeling of detachment. Most of his closest soldier friends were dead even before he left France; Sacheverell was too young to be in much risk of finding himself at the Front. It was not by any doing of his that he was deemed unfit to return to France himself; he made no strenuous efforts to reverse the decision of the authorities, but equally he pulled no strings to ensure that he remained in London. He had hated his time in the trenches but had done his duty; now he wanted to forget all about it except in so far as he could use his experiences as raw material for pacifist polemics.

His duties with the Grenadier Guards were little more arduous than in peacetime. From time to time he found himself forced to play a more active role – in March 1917, for instance, he wrote gloomily from Seaford that he was 'down in this wretchedly cold place for some time – in a hut'[63] – but far more often a more or less token appearance in barracks would be followed by afternoons and evenings at liberty. This suited him admirably; as a civilian he would have had to explain himself from time to time to those who were on the look-out for cowards and shirkers, as a Guards officer, however under-employed, he was beyond reproach. Usually he wore uniform, partly as protective colouring and partly because he thought it suited him, but he never looked wholly convincing as a soldier. The painter Nina Hamnett persuaded him to pose for a portrait – not that much persuasion was needed for one so markedly narcissistic. 'He came and sat in his uniform, but it was not a success,' recorded Miss Hamnett. 'I painted another one of him in a small "John Bull" top-hat, a head and shoulders, and that was much better.'[64] Colonel Repington, the military correspondent of *The Times*, spent a weekend at Mrs Keppel's house, Watlington Park. He travelled back with two young Guards officers who had been in the party, one of whom was Osbert. 'Instead of discussing soldiering we talked of nothing but pictures, Palladio and palaces. They were extraordinarily well-informed, and knew Italy well. The war has brought a strange medley of capacities and incapacities into the Army.'[65]

The three Sitwells were now beginning to assert themselves as the nucleus of a social and artistic group. They distanced themselves from their parents with an unhealthy compound of rage, fear and disdain. Lady Ida, reported Edith with habitual exaggeration, was 'drunk all the time now, and I think has really come to imagine that she had done the right things and covered herself with glory'. Osbert could not bring himself to denounce his mother and reserved his worst bile for Sir George: 'Father, *Gott strafe* him, is being bloody. He has nearly got me turned out of the Guards' Club . . . by giving me no money so that I can't pay my subscription.'[66] Nearly always money was the cause of his worst rancour. The family papers present a depressing picture of embittered bickering. Sir George had made over the house at Renishaw to Osbert on the understanding that he would continue to live there as tenant for a moderate but still substantial annual rent. This was a generous move – though it seems to have been activated more by a wish to avoid taxes than by altruism – but it gave rise to protracted guerrilla warfare and a conviction on each side that the other was behaving with unscrupulousness if not dishonesty. In the middle was the luckless agent, Maynard Hollingworth. On the whole, Hollingworth seems to have felt that, between father and son, Osbert was the less unreasonable but his first loyalty was to his employer, Sir George, and he tried gallantly to steer an honourable course between the two. Meanwhile, fomenting the hostility, with an eye always to her own interest, was Lady Ida. 'I am rather fussed about Mr Osbert's affairs,' she told Hollingworth in April 1917.

> Sir George informed me two nights ago that the next rent for Renishaw he intends to keep back as he has advanced so much to Mr Osbert. I have heard from Mr Osbert that you meant to pay him the rent on April 1. Can this be safely done without Sir George's knowledge? The boy can not come up for another fortnight as he is in camp. Would it be possible for you to come up for the day to London to see me, and then we go on to Mr Osbert? Can all this be done without your getting into serious trouble? I do feel very strongly that ... all his money affairs ought to be put into order. A reckoning day must come and I don't think he realises it and only lives from day to day and thinks that somehow everything will go right. I do not see how things are to go on unless we take a firm hand.[67]

Hollingworth had no intention of being caught in this web of intrigue. Coming to London would serve no purpose. He knew nothing of any private arrangements between Osbert and his father, he told Lady Ida, and had no wish to do so. When she persisted, he replied flatly that he would pay over any surplus if ordered to do so, 'but of course it will appear in the accounts and if Sir George asks me what I have paid I shall be compelled to tell him. I absolutely refuse to adopt any other course.'[68] Probably Osbert knew nothing of his mother's machinations; certainly he bore no grudge against the agent for refusing to co-operate. Only two months after this exchange of letters he asked Hollingworth to act as executor of his will. But he did not conceal the fact that he found his father tiresomely ridiculous. 'I hear Italy is having revolutionary troubles,' he wrote to Hollingworth in the autumn of 1917. 'I think Father ought to go and defend the Castle!'[69] Hollingworth did not respond to such badinage but he went as far as he could to help and to warn Osbert when a fresh storm seemed to be in the offing. 'For some reason I do not understand,' he wrote later in the same year, 'Sir George does not expect you to draw any money from me, so evidently there is trouble in store.'[70]

Meanwhile, as Lady Ida had predicted, Osbert lived merrily from day to day and never allowed the uncertainty of his income to curb his spending. By early 1918 he had installed himself with Sachie in a tall, modern house in Swan Walk, Chelsea, with a view over the river in one direction and the Physic Garden in another. It was a house 'with much better pictures and bric-à-brac than furniture', recorded Arnold Bennett. 'In fact there was scarcely any what I call furniture. But lots of modern pictures, of which I liked a number. Bright walls and bright cloths and bright glass everywhere.'[71] The lack of furniture was often commented on: 'Just the bare luxuries of life and not the necessities,' explained Osbert. Sassoon was more sceptical than Bennett about the pictures, many of which looked 'peculiar to my inexperienced eyes. In some instances I am inclined to suggest that they were more startling and experimental than well drawn.'[72] Probably he was right; most of them were jettisoned by Osbert over the next decade. Osbert was always inclined to flirt with the latest movement; in these first years in London he was particularly disposed to worship all that was new and look with caution on, if not reject, the old. The painter Walter Sickert, another regular visitor, would probably have shared Sassoon's view of the paintings but he thoroughly enjoyed his visits there: for him, he said, the atmosphere of Swan Walk was summed up by Gray's line: 'Youth on the Prow, and Pleasure at the Helm.'[73]

In Swan Walk the Sitwells entertained, far more lavishly than their funds permitted, and from it they sallied forth to savour everything that London had to offer. They favoured High Bohemia. Beverley Nichols met Osbert dining with Epstein and Augustus John at the Café Royal. 'Osbert was the conversational star of the evening,' he remembered. 'A very silly woman sat herself down with us and, *à propos* of nothing, said "No woman ever gained anything from domesticity". Osbert stared at her with a beady eye. "What about Nell Gwyn?" he demanded. A stranger paused beside us and began to rebuke him for his tirades against British imperialism. Osbert cut him short. "If the British were turned out of India tomorrow all that would be found is a broken-down bathroom and an empty whisky bottle." '[74] As conversational stardom goes, this hardly coruscates, but dinner-table wit rarely reads happily when recorded. There are too many reports of the pleasures of Osbert Sitwell's conversation to leave doubt that he was an asset at almost any party. But enthusiasm for his company was not invariable. Cynthia Asquith, for one, was cooler; she found him no more than 'quite agreeable to talk to', though she was impressed when he told her that he read every night till three or four in the morning.[75] Diana Manners also had reservations. Since he was a soldier she assumed he would have information about the fate of her future husband, Duff Cooper, now at the Front, and so spent her days 'telephoning unceasingly to Osbert for news, which he never had, and even lunching with him' (she considerately omitted the word 'even' when she quoted from this letter in her autobiography).[76] Duff Cooper more than shared her hesitation. 'I don't like the very new novelists and the very new poets,' he wrote to Diana in July 1918. 'They make me think of Osbert and Elizabeth [Asquith], of mean restaurants and bad wine.'[77]

In the last years of the war it seemed that Osbert was to be sighted everywhere of fashionable or cultural renown. One night he was playing poker till 3.00 a.m. with the Cabinet minister Edwin Montagu, the next he and Sachie joined the writer and editor David Garnett in Massine's dressing-room after a performance of *La Boutique Fantasque* – 'two tall, extremely elegant young officers with fair hair and rosy complexions', Garnett remembered them. 'Osbert was self-possessed and talkative, Sacheverell seemed even shyer than I.'[78] Aldous Huxley was not surprised to find them at the private view of Gaudier-Brzeska's paintings – 'There I saw almost everybody – the glorious company of Sitwells, the noble army of poets, including Graves and Davies and Eliot.'[79] Huxley wrote mockingly but to some the company of Sitwells was indeed beginning to take on the aura of glory. C. R. W. Nevinson, the painter, dined at Swan Walk. 'It was one of the most memorable nights I have ever spent. Here at last were some wonderful English people, not only of great culture, but of understanding, in love with all the finer achievements of men, yet full of wit and diabolical cynicism.'[80]

Inevitably there were frequent contacts with members of the Bloomsbury Group, inevitably the two camps regarded each other with slight suspicion not untouched by contempt. The Sitwells, in the definition of the leading authority on the subject, Ellen Moers, were true dandies, 'free of all human commitments that conflict with taste: passions, moralities, ambitions, politics or occupations'.[81] The Bloomsberries had some elements of the dandy in their make-up but they were more serious, more high-minded, less cynical. The great figures of Bloomsbury, wrote Osbert, were Roger Fry, Virginia Woolf, Clive and Vanessa Bell, Lytton Strachey and Duncan Grant, followed by 'a sub-rout of high mathematicians and low psychologists, a tangle of lesser painters and writers'[82] (Keynes was presumably lumped under the mathematicians). Unsurprisingly, it was not one of these great figures but Strachey's worshipper, the painter Carrington, who was most impressed by Osbert, though his appeal seems to have been more physical than intellectual. She went to tea with him late in 1918 and found: 'His appearance was too wonderful! Lying on two chairs, surrounded by silk shawls and cushions, writing poetry on a large sheet of paper. His collar turned up straight against his cheeks, like Byron, with a black tie wound round. His hair was brushed . . . from the back forwards and the front backwards, and the most lovely striped silk vest underneath which he showed us, and striped drawers, the circles running round like a football jersey.'[83]

Possibly Virginia Woolf would have been more enthusiastic if she had seen the striped drawers. As it was, she was cool, critical of his writing, doubtful about his sincerity and seriousness of purpose. Osbert was 'at heart an English squire', she wrote, 'a collector, but of Bristol glass, old fashion plates, Victorian cases of humming birds, and not of foxes' brushes and deer's horns'. She liked him, she concluded, but 'why are they thought daring and clever?'[84] There was never any outright hostility between the two groups; on the contrary, each saw the other as an ally against the common enemy, the philistine. They met frequently, conversed amicably, were at least publicly tolerant of each other's work. But it went no further. 'It was a charming party. I think the Sitwells are charming,' wrote Duncan Grant, after he and Virginia Woolf had been to tea at Swan Walk, and then again, after staying till 3.00 a.m. at another Sitwell occasion: 'It was a charming party.'[85] 'Charming' is hardly the strongest word and it reflected the slightly tepid nature of the relationship, but it could have been a lot more frigid, and Osbert would certainly have counted Virginia Woolf, if not Lytton Strachey, among his closer, though not closest, friends.

In spite of his problems with his father and the war looming horribly in the background, life was very pleasant for Osbert towards the end of 1918. The Armistice should only have made it better. In fact it was quickly followed by an almost fatal illness. In January 1919 he fell prey to the killer Spanish influenza which swept Europe at the end of the war and left more dead behind it than the belligerents had managed to notch up in four years. He spent six weeks in King Edward VII's Hospital for Officers and at one point his father was told that his prospects for survival were not good. The illness left its mark, though doctors could never decide whether the greater contribution to his general ill-health had been made by his acute pleurisy in youth, which had left him with an abscess at the base of his left lung, the blood poisoning, which had been the first cause of his not being sent back to France in 1916, or the influenza of 1919, which probably included an undiagnosed element of encephalitis. From this time onwards Osbert was increasingly preoccupied with his health, racked by constant problems with his teeth, a victim of insomnia who could only find relief by imagining himself in a gondola floating through Venice under a full moon. So persistent were his moans about his ailments that it would be tempting to describe him as a hypochondriac; yet in fact he had a great deal wrong with him and every reason to complain. His chronic bronchitis recurred almost every year and furnished an admirable excuse, if not necessarily a valid reason, for wintering abroad. Within a few years he was experiencing the first symptoms of what was supposed to be rheumatism in the feet. In 1935 gout was diagnosed and from then on it was downhill all the way. If he had known what lay ahead of him when he left hospital at the end of February 1919 he might have wondered whether the battle could really be worth waging. As it was, he returned to the brave new post-war world in the conviction that many great and enjoyable things lay just around the corner.

6

The Delightful but Deleterious Trio

'WE do not like to be treated as if we were an aggregate Indian god, with three sets of legs and arms, but otherwise indivisible,' Edith wrote indignantly to the publisher Rache Lovat Dickson. 'We have all three suffered very much from this. It vulgarises and cheapens everything, and deprives all the work of its importance.'[1] By 1949, when she delivered this rebuke, she had some grounds for complaint, but in the years after the First World War it was entirely by their own doing that the Sitwells were perceived as a literary troika by the world at large. This was how they chose to behave. When Edmund Gosse ushered them from his front door with the words 'Goodbye, you delightful but deleterious trio',[2] he was saying no more than they would have wished; it was their intention to be seen as delightful, certainly, but dangerous, unpredictable, marauders in a literary jungle; also, most definitely as a trio.

From 1917 or so, when Sachie joined his brother and sister in London, the Sitwells hunted as a pack. Mutual promotion was their intent; avowed to themselves if not to others. Sachie extolled zealously the merits of his elder siblings; Osbert hawked around publishers the manuscript of Sachie's first work, *Southern Baroque Art*, 'this magnificent and now celebrated book'; Edith urged Robert Nichols to smooth Osbert's path on a planned but subsequently aborted visit to the United States.[3] Publicity was a tool which they used with skill and satisfaction. Evelyn Waugh believed that this was part of their 'aristocratic disdain' for middle-class conventions: 'Popular newspapers with all their absurd vulgarity were just a part of the exciting contemporary world in which the Sitwells romped. They were weapons in the total war against dullness.'[4] Still more, they were weapons in their

86

campaign to make the name of Sitwell known in every house where books were read and, with luck, in many less favoured homes as well. Waugh could as well have substituted the word 'artistic' for 'aristocratic'; the Sitwells did indeed feel disdain for the middle classes but it was more because they did not feel the middle classes to be capable of appreciating the finer things of life, than because of any deficiency of purse or breeding. When Gérard de Nerval took his lobster for a walk on a golden chain or Sebastian Flyte aired his teddy bear in the Oxford streets, they did it because they wanted to attract attention to themselves and enjoyed showing off. The Sitwells had a slightly more serious purpose – than Sebastian Flyte at least – in that they wanted to persuade people to read their books, but they were quite as much exhibitionists as any undergraduate aesthete.

To secure this attention the indivisibility of the trio was of the first importance; 'The Sitwells' were far more worthy of attention than one Sitwell, or indeed six Sitwells taken in isolation, could possibly have been. Unfortunately the campaign also trivialised their work. 'The triune nature of the family cartel,' wrote Anthony Powell, 'fatally effective at the time as a vehicle of publicity, has not otherwise been advantageous to the Sitwells as individual writers.'[5] 'Fatally' is a strong word; 'damagingly' would be nearer the mark. The Sitwells became well known, but as the price of their celebrity they forfeited the approval of many of those they most wished to impress. But about the effectiveness there can be no argument. They contrived to radiate a sophistication, a sublime self-assurance, which seemed almost overpowering to those who were easily impressed and even to some of the less susceptible. Edmund Gosse's daughter Sylvia was amazed to learn that the Sitwells had been in awe of her father and had lingered on the doorstep before daring to ring the bell: 'You three always seemed to me to enter so calmly, so assured, and to be "experienced conversationalists", whereas we felt and were such dumb adolescents.'[6] Even a hardened bully like Wyndham Lewis, the author and Vorticist painter, could be slightly in awe of the Sitwells' public armour. 'You know how inexpert I am in the social art,' he wrote to Osbert in March 1922. 'You, with your traditional and personal experience, should befriend me if you see me going into the wrong door or, "bewildered".'[7]

Arnold Bennett saw Osbert as being the leader of the trio in their unrelenting campaign: 'Osbert is a born impresario – the Charles B. Cochran of the muse ... Osbert "presents" the family and does it with originality.'[8] Certainly Osbert was the one who got the most fun out of the flamboyance and vulgarity, just as he extracted the most pleasure from the endless rows in which the Sitwells became embroiled. Edith cared too much. For her the issues were of passionate importance; she was the most belligerent because the enemy were to be hated, the most exhibitionistic because what was being exhibited was so close to her heart. Sacheverell cared too little. He disliked rows and had to be dragged reluctantly behind his siblings' chariot; he liked dressing up and showing off but found the cruder aspects of self-publicity distasteful, even vulgar. Osbert treated his writing with great seriousness, as he did that of his brother and sister, but the publicity and the rows were part of an elaborate game. If other people chose to take them seriously then that was their own affair and their own funeral. His detachment was not always perfect, sometimes he became so caught up in some extravagant enterprise that he began to confuse fantasy with reality, but a keen awareness of the ridiculous and a sense of proportion which was never totally extinguished saved him from taking too tragically vicissitudes which to Edith or Sacheverell would seem from time to time intolerable. He knew his propensity to dramatise and stage-manage, knew how much of his time and energies it absorbed, mildly deplored it but had no serious wish to mend his ways. 'That is the worst of being both a born impresario and a born writer,' he told an American friend, 'a condition which I understand, as I have a little of both in myself.'[9]

The rows were much the most time-consuming. It seemed at times as if the Sitwells had only to meet another writer for a feud to the death to develop. The war with John Collings Squire and his coterie – the Squirearchy – was the longest and the most embittered. Squire was no nonentity. As a young man he had been a Fabian and a translator of Baudelaire; from 1913 he was also literary editor of the *New Statesman* and thus the wielder of real influence. A poem he published in the third volume of *Georgian Poetry* was one of the few contributions to win praise from T. S. Eliot. By 1919, however, when he began to edit a new magazine, the *London Mercury*, and was also reviewer-in-chief of the *Observer*, he was running out of steam. His power waxed as his ability to absorb new impressions or encompass new ideas inexorably faded. By nature a kindly man, he elected himself champion of traditional values against a modern movement that seemed to him mischievous, obscure and possibly communistic as well. He conducted his campaigns with some brutality. He knows nothing about poetry but is 'the cleverest journalist in London', judged Eliot.[10] His power base was strong, his connections formidable, his criticism trenchant and designed to hurt.[11] If he had been as insignificant as the Sitwells liked to pretend, Osbert would not have been so upset by his hostile review of *Argonaut and Juggernaut*, nor Edith by his contemptuous dismissal of almost everything in *Wheels*.

Osbert retaliated vigorously. He denounced the propensity of Squire and his acolytes to win control of Britain's literary prizes and then to ensure that these were awarded only to their followers. By way of an addendum, he invented his own annual prize for the dullest literary work of the year. Squire was one of the first winners (another was Harold Nicolson, whose prize, a 'curiously mangy cat, playing with some diseased mice and surmounted by a huge dome of glass', was sent round to him at the Foreign Office). But his most considered thrust at the Squirearchy was an angry pamphlet, *Who Killed Cock-Robin?*, which he published in December 1921.[12] This tendentious tract professed to establish what poetry was supposed to be; 'the conversation of the Gods through the medium of Man,' Osbert opined loftily if a little vaguely. In fact it devoted itself far more to what poetry was not. It was not 'a nebulous painting of Highland cattle in a Scotch mist'; it was not 'the monopoly of lark-lovers, nor rustic rhymesters – Peasant poetry is like peasant pottery. The best thing about it is the smashing of it.' This angry outburst suggested that smashing was Osbert's speciality, creation a secondary occupation. 'We modern poets have brought poetry into touch with the other modern arts, and with other modern countries,' he announced grandly but no satisfactory definition was offered of modernity – whether as applied to poetry, or to other arts or, for that matter, to countries. Geoffrey Grigson, then an undergraduate, the future critic, poet and arch-enemy of the Sitwells, read *Who Killed Cock-Robin?* and found it 'smart, but intolerant and stimulating'. He resented the way Osbert spoke for modern poetry, 'seeming to exclude even Eliot and Pound from the new Pantheon. I was *not* Sitwellian: with doubts and timidities I was now for Eliot.'[13]

Osbert submitted the typescript of *Who Killed Cock-Robin?* to Chatto & Windus, who returned it the same day on the excuse that they did not publish polemical pamphlets.[14] It appeared under the imprint of a less celebrated house three months later and enjoyed some success. Reviews were for the most part inconsiderable and tepid, but it sold well and achieved its aim of stirring up controversy. Nor was it only a nine days' wonder. Years later Osbert was despatching a mild protest to a Mr Edward Thompson. 'I see you're about to issue a pamphlet called "*Who Killed Cock-Robin?*". May I, at the risk of being a bore, point out that I wrote a similar pamphlet on the *same* subject and under the *same* name some seven years ago? This still enjoys a good sale, being in its 3rd or 4th edition.'[15] That such a letter was necessary suggests that Osbert's pamphlet was not particularly well known, but it must have had a certain potency to have survived so long.

Not everyone found the Sitwells formidable, or at least was prepared to admit the fact. In 1969, when John Lehmann published his book about the family, *A Nest of Tigers*, Leonard Woolf wrote to congratulate him on his use of the word 'nest' in the title, 'showing what they were, cuckoos in tiger's clothing'.[16] They were as much derided as abused: Paul Selver, translator of Karel Čapek, neatly misappropriated Jesse Collings's slogan for land reform and described them as 'Two wiseacres and a cow'.[17] And they were as much the victims of other writers' satires as they were the aggressors. W. J. Turner, a minor poet and dramatist who had once been a friend of Edith's in spite of being accepted as an established member of the Squirearchy, in 1924 offended by writing a play patently based on the Sitwells, *Smaragda's Lover*.[18] Osbert's initial response was to be loftily dismissive; he had heard, he said, of 'an idiotic play by that poor, simple Turner, which is, I believe, a sort of skit on my family'. Once he had read it, however, he grew indignant: the play was 'offensive and vulgar', it had 'put me in an awful temper'. Why could people not look for their own ideas? he asked his publisher. Perhaps his own latest book could be advertised on the basis that the Sitwells seemed 'to afford about as many ideas to other authors as we do to ourselves'.[19]

Turner, however, was no more than retaliating for a skit in which Osbert, writing under the pseudonym of Augustine Rivers, had parodied him and, to a lesser extent, Robert Graves and Edmund Blunden. This squib, inoffensive in itself, was of importance since it embroiled Osbert with a closer friend and a far better writer than Turner, Siegfried Sassoon. Sassoon had been an intimate friend of Osbert's since he had taken refuge for ten days in Swan Walk when in agony from sciatica. The brothers, he said, had 'behaved like angelic and agitated turtle doves. Almost always in a hurry, one or other seemed continually to be dashing up the steep stairs to look in and ask "How are you?" '[20] The relationship prospered, but Sassoon, exaggeratedly sensitive and far less sure of himself than his new friends, felt overwhelmed by Osbert and resentful of his preoccupations. 'How petty they are with their endless family lampoons on the *London Mercury*,' he wrote in his diary. 'As long as they go on like that they can hardly expect to be taken seriously . . . I have the advantage of being more successful as a writer. I have no cause to be jealous of Graves and Blunden, etc., as Osbert has always been.'[21] When Osbert produced his attack on Turner, Sassoon commented that it was not merely mean, spiteful, amateurish and ineffective but was inspired by jealousy of Turner's friendship with Sassoon. There is not the slightest reason to believe that this was so; Sassoon, however, was obsessed with Osbert and mulled over their relationship with a brooding fascination that would have startled the latter if he had known of it. A few weeks after this diary entry he deliberately pursued Osbert out of a concert in the Wigmore Hall, just so as to have the satisfaction of cutting him on the pavement outside. 'I suddenly realised that my attitude towards O is strongly sadistic,' he wrote that night. 'I saw, quite calmly, that my (supposed) stab at his feelings this afternoon aroused in me acute sexual feelings towards him. (I'd never before been conscious of any sexual feelings towards him except a slight repugnance.)' Osbert, he concluded, stirred strong reactions in him because he was 'such a vivid (though unsympathetic) character. I can't hope to blot him out of my life and thoughts.'[22]

The feud grumbled on, with Osbert making occasional conciliatory gestures, Sassoon rejecting them with the stridency of a virgin who is tempted but dare not fall. 'I intend to keep him at more than arm's length for several more months,' he wrote in June 1922. 'He is a case where one must assert one's independence.' He tried to analyse his feelings.

> Something in his character makes it impossible for me to feel kindly towards him. His neurotic spite and jealousy are ill-concealed by his 'social charm'. He seems incapable of serenity, or of tolerance of his contemporaries. His portrait should be a restless reflection in a valuable gilt Chippendale mirror. Peacock *en casserole* should be his staple diet. How tiresome he can be with his everlasting chatter about his antiquarian father; and his disreputably aristocratic mama; and his untidy financial affairs. Perhaps I am severe on him, but he is always merciless to everyone but himself and his brother and sister.[23]

When they met in Venice later that summer Sassoon once more looked through him: 'It is the arrogance of the artist. Until I have humiliated or dominated him I will not be satisfied.'[24] This satisfaction was denied him – Osbert was neither humiliated nor dominated, remained indeed infuriatingly unconscious that anything of the sort was required of him, but the feud nevertheless died down. First Sassoon, meeting Osbert unexpectedly in Pall Mall, abstained from smiling but 'forgot to scowl'; then came an exchange of jokey but offensive postcards; then a long letter from Sassoon setting out all that he found wrong in Osbert's character. Arnold Bennett stage-managed a reconciliation, at a lunch at the Reform Club. 'Sort of silly feud between [Siegfried] and O,' he wrote in his diary. 'SS drew back but I made him come.' Not merely did he make him come, but he made him escort Osbert from the club. When the two next met in the street they chatted amicably and Osbert gave Sassoon a small glass globe containing a toy fish.[25] The rapprochement did not mean that they became close friends again, but at least the horrors of Osbert ceased to be an obsessive refrain in Sassoon's diary.

'Are the Sitwells worth worrying about?' Sassoon asked himself, when the fires of his indignation still burned high.[26] The Bloomsberries might have doubted it; so might the first precocious swallows of a new and more rigorous intellectual summer, like Geoffrey Grigson; but for many of the post-war generation the Sitwells provided a unique and refreshing inspiration. They were within the establishment and yet against it, they were serious and yet light-hearted, hard-working hedonists. They 'radiated an aura of high spirits, elegance, impudence, unpredictability, above all sheer enjoyment', wrote Evelyn Waugh. 'They declared war on dullness.'[27] For his generation, Cyril Connolly told John Pearson, Bloomsbury seemed dowdy and puritanical; the Sitwells supplied the two things they craved for – 'Edith had genius and Osbert panache'.[28]

Whether Edith's principal contribution to the Sitwell legend was a work of genius is at least open to question. *Façade*, an entertainment in which Edith's poetry was set to music by William Walton and declaimed through a megaphone by members of the family sheltered behind a screen, was *prima facie* absurd. Disembodied voices intoning nonsense verses to a musical accompaniment was unlikely to appear as serious art to a Virginia Woolf or a Grigson. Nor did it appeal to Harold Nicolson, who found it a dreary muddle and wrote to his wife, 'I am quite sure that in 50 years from now no one will ever have heard of those frauds the Sitwells, any more than they will of George Robey.'[29] The fact that the verses were always ingenious and sometimes strangely beautiful, and that William Walton's music included some of the most accomplished pieces that he ever wrote, redeemed the performance from mediocrity but could not invest it with the *gravitas* required by a critic who took himself and expected to be taken with becoming seriousness. As for the philistines: they thought it was a joke in doubtful taste, designed to shock and patently without artistic merit.

Façade had a cosy outing before an audience of friends in Osbert's house in Chelsea, an under-rehearsed and disastrous first public showing in the Aeolian Hall in June 1923 – 'a shambles', William Walton described it, 'that's the simple truth of it' – and a considerable success when the performers finally got it right at the Chenil Gallery three years later. Osbert's role was a minor one: he recited some of the poems and picked Frank Dobson, the sculptor who was working on his bust, to paint the curtain that divided the speakers from the audience. From the point of view of publicity, though, it was very much a Sitwell enterprise: Osbert took the lead in orchestrating the build-up to the earlier performances and in dramatising the fiasco of the first night. According to most witnesses it was an exceptionally hot evening and a lethargic audience greeted the performance without enthusiasm but also without marked hostility. This was not nearly interesting enough for Osbert, who claimed that the first night 'created a scandal and involved all connected with it in a shower of abuse and insult'.[30]

He reacted angrily when Noël Coward parodied the Sitwells and *Façade* in his new revue, *London Calling*. 'To this day,' wrote Coward in 1937, 'I am still puzzled as to why this light-hearted burlesque should have aroused [Osbert], his brother and his sister to such paroxysms of fury.'[31] It would certainly have been far more sensible either to pretend to enjoy the joke or to ignore it altogether. Osbert's first impulse does seem to have been to dismiss it as a triviality. He is supposed to have said that, as he had to be out of town for two or three nights, he would unfortunately miss the run of the revue, to which Coward retorted that, on Osbert's return, he would gladly make a box available to him so that he could invite all his friends (an exchange which, with variations, has been attributed to different protagonists and to different eras). But Edith took extreme exception, apparently because she had been told, quite wrongly, that she was represented as a lesbian. Osbert wrote Coward an outraged letter, and then another, even more indignant. There was a grudging reconciliation in New York in 1926, the accounts of which could hardly be more dissimilar. 'The brute wrote me a letter of apology,' Osbert told Sachie. He felt that he could hardly reject it flatly, in case the persecution of Edith was renewed, so telephoned Coward to insist that he must write to Edith to apologise. 'The point is that he's just intelligent enough to realise his floater.'[32] Coward for his part agreed that he offered the initial olive branch but claimed that Osbert then came round in person and proposed 'quite pleasantly that I should apologise to Edith publicly in all the papers. I gave him an old-fashioned look and explained gently that he was very silly indeed which he seemed to understand perfectly and we parted very amicably. It really was becoming a bore because he wasn't being asked anywhere, poor dear, owing to my popularity being the greater.'[33] Coward did write a private note of apology to Edith but the aftermath was far from 'very amicable'. Relations, though formally reopened, remained frigid. Even as late as 1942 Osbert was writing of Coward's 'silly and spiteful music-hall skit' and it was not till after the Second World War that he actually shook Coward by the hand.

William Walton, who provided the musical element of *Façade*, had been discovered by Sachie when the future composer was the youngest undergraduate at Christ Church, Oxford. Sachie concluded he was a genius whose potential was being stifled by the demands of university life. Osbert, whose prejudice against university education was by now well established, did not need much persuading that this was indeed the case. The brothers removed Walton to London, installed him in Swan Walk and encouraged him to pursue his music outside the traditional academic circles. Walton quickly settled in and became part of the family; so much so, indeed, that he took on some of the Sitwell mannerisms and was thought by many to be a by-blow of Sir George's.[34] But there were limits to the indulgence Osbert showed him. Walton was an inveterate womaniser, and while working with Edith on *Façade*, he flirted mildly with her. Edith rather enjoyed it, but Osbert 'quickly put an end to any romantic attachment by warning William not to court his sister, otherwise he would be shown the door'.[35] It seems unlikely that either Walton or Edith had a serious entanglement in mind, but Osbert was always ready to look with regret, if not disfavour, on anything which seemed to threaten the cohesion of the family triad.

It was Sacheverell rather than Edith who made the breach. Osbert had the additional chagrin of knowing that he had brought it on himself. At a dance given by Arnold Bennett in the spring of 1924 he met an attractive young Canadian, Georgia Doble, and asked her to tea. Georgia was delighted. She longed to know the Sitwells – 'I was very, very highbrow in those days' – and accepted with alacrity. Sachie was there, then as always susceptible to charm and good looks, and asked her out to dinner. From that moment things moved rapidly and inexorably towards an engagement.[36] (John Rothenstein, the future Director of the Tate Gallery, claims that it was he who asked if he might bring the Doble sisters to tea. 'If you must,' said Osbert gloomily. Next day Rothenstein thanked his host for being so nice to the visitors. 'But we *liked* them,' replied Osbert. 'Sachie particularly one.'[37])

Osbert tried hard both to like Georgia and to make his liking obvious to her, Sachie and the outside world. 'Mr Sachie is engaged to be married to Miss Georgia Doble, a charming Canadian lady,' he wrote to his housekeeper.[38] To Georgia he was extravagant in his protestations. 'Enclosed is my cheque for £40,' he wrote to her (a sum which in 1925 was equivalent to £1,000 or so), 'the outward and visible sign of my affection for you. This is also a written testimonial to my belief that you are an *angel*: in any case, you have behaved like one. And if you have your deserts you ought to be very, very happy.'[39] But though he tried gallantly to put a brave face on it, he was himself far from very, very happy. Until the last moment he told himself that something would happen to prevent the marriage. He managed to curb himself from trying directly to dissuade his brother but still could not resist a last-minute signal to that effect: 'Darling, I do hope you will be happy, and I am sure you will be. But if you have *any* doubt, even now, say so. It would be better for everyone in the end.'[40]

Sachie had no doubts and Osbert must have known that the chance was a slender one. His mood as the wedding approached would have been more appropriate for a funeral. Lady Ida begged his friend, Christabel Aberconway, to travel with Osbert to Paris for the ceremony, which was to take place on 12 October 1925, and then return with him to Montegufoni: 'It would be a great kindness as I think Osbert will be very sad about Sachie and it will help to cheer him up.'[41] Osbert had no illusions about the loss he was going to suffer; since 1917 he had been living in the same house as Sachie, they had done everything together, shared their friends and interests, travelled always as a pair. He had convinced himself that their partnership would endure throughout their lives. Much as he liked Georgia, he told his publisher, Grant Richards, 'the marriage will naturally make a great difference to me'.[42] Secretly, he was not at all sure that he did like Georgia: he found her hard, insensitive, not particularly intelligent. But he had to make the best of it and prepare for life without Sachie, or at least life with a Sachie shared with someone who would always have a prior claim on his time and attention. 'I think there is no doubt, really, that we must look for a house together,' he told Georgia, 'but divided into two different establishments. When you come back we must look for it, and find a really amusing house, preferably in Regent's Park, and covered with statues from head to foot.'[43] The prospect was better than nothing, but it was bleak enough.

*

Sir George grumbled that Sachie could not afford to get married, but accepted the inevitable with surprising equanimity. He announced, according to Osbert at least, that he intended to stay close at hand during the honeymoon, 'in case the boy needs me'.[44] Osbert managed to dissuade him. It must have been as nearly amicable an exchange as the two contrived in the decade after Osbert returned from the Western Front. Sir George, infuriating though he could often be, on the whole preserved a decorous politeness towards his son. Osbert showed no such restraint. Sir George had grown a reddish beard, and a taxi-driver, dissatisfied with the size of his tip, had concluded the argument with a baleful: 'After the war, Ginger, I'll get even with you!'[45] 'Ginger' now became the name by which his children usually referred to him. Edith and Osbert in particular missed no chance to ridicule or abuse their father. Usually this was behind his back, but Osbert was quite ready to be offensive to his face. Peter Quennell was a friend of Osbert's and disposed to support the younger generation but he was still dismayed by Osbert's rudeness, the way he would interrupt his father and his maddening habit of imitating the opening of a champagne bottle and punctuating Sir George's monologues with reverberant popping noises.[46] When Diana Guinness, third of the celebrated Mitford sisters and future wife of Oswald Mosley, stayed at Renishaw she found Sir George 'charming', Lady Ida 'vague', and the three children 'egging on the guests to be rude'. Such discourtesy was as vulgar as it was uncharacteristic of Osbert; that he should have resorted to such childish boorishness says much about the state to which the relationship between father and son had been reduced. But Sir George did have a gift for helping those who sought to make him seem absurd. His children always claimed that he made a buzzing noise when a little anxious. Once he had arranged to lunch with his sons at a restaurant and, failing to see them, roamed around the tables buzzing nervously. 'Father sounds just like a bluebottle fly,' Osbert remarked to Sacheverell, whereupon Sir George spotted them and came up, saying, ' I was just wondering which table to settle on.'[47]

In his fascinating study of the inter-war generation, *Children of the Sun*, Martin Green argues that this conflict was a common phenomenon. The young who had suffered on the Somme felt that they had been betrayed 'by their fathers, by England's fathers'. They rejected the values and shibboleths that had been held sacred by the previous generation, 'they looked for decadence and for the flag of rebellion against their fathers'.[48] Such feelings may well have underlaid Osbert's antipathy, but the peculiar virulence which charged his rejection of Sir George was more than just a manifestation of a collective *Zeitgeist*. Money was almost always the trigger for the uglier exchanges. Neither shone in the encounters; it was Sir George who most retained his dignity, but that perhaps is easier to do if one is the putative donor rather than the would-be recipient. Siegfried Sassoon, staying at Renishaw, complained about 'this incessant wrangling about money, Osbert trying to snatch money from Ginger, etc. Why does O let himself be under G's thumb? A complete break would be more dignified, surely? But O is too fond of luxuries and prestige to sacrifice a single square meal.'[49] Sassoon had never had to sacrifice many square meals himself, but it is easy to sympathise with his point of view.

The truth is that Sir George had been very generous. In the years after the end of the First World War Osbert's annual income varied between £1,500 and £2,000 a year, not vast riches but a more than comfortable income for a bachelor. Of this Osbert contributed on average less than £50 a year as a writer; not that he was idle or unsuccessful, but because while his output consisted mainly of poetry he had little prospect of earning an income of any significance. 'I think you ought to make good your position as a poet, and am all for your having leisure to bring out a volume,' Sir George told him. 'But I don't think your whole life should be sacrificed to this. You have mentioned to me that an ordinary balance-sheet is Greek to you, and it is quite obvious that at present you have no capacity for dealing with business matters. You would do well to try and fit yourself for that and for public life.'[50] Osbert thought that his whole life, or the greater part of it at least, *should* be sacrificed to his poetry. This posture was noble enough in principle but was rendered less impressive by his reluctance to sacrifice an iota of his comforts and indulgences.

Osbert raised extravagance to the level of a religion, convincing himself that it was an essential element in the artistic temperament. 'Self-indulgence and extravagance seemed to make people tolerant and generous,' he wrote in his autobiography; 'avarice and even carefulness have always seemed to me to be vices.'[51] However generous his income, he contrived to overspend it; he was perpetually in debt. The archive at Renishaw abounds in unpaid bills and protests from indignant tradesmen. Usually the latter believed that they would be paid in the end, grumbled fretfully, but were content to wait for better times. Sometimes they were tried too far. In April 1921 Osbert's London housekeeper, the long-suffering Mrs Powell, sent an SOS to Hollingworth at Renishaw:

the bailiffs were on the premises, demanding settlement of a bill from the furniture store, Heal's. 'Please see to this at once,' she urged, 'as I have to find food for 2 men and it will be 8/6^d every day they are here.'[52] For Sir George, with the grisly memory of his wife perpetually at the back of his mind, his son seemed guilty of almost criminal irresponsibility. Constantly he demanded that Osbert should mend his ways:

> I think, as with Lloyd George's government, some signs of amendment in the stoppage of extravagant waste should precede a call for larger supplies. Do you intend to stop it or not? If so, when may I have evidence that you have stopped it? Many people are under the domination of some idea which is certain to ruin or kill them sooner or later. Your suggestion that a larger allowance can be used to pay the debts of the year before gives one the horrors! Do you realise that it was wrong ideas which ruined and killed Lord Londesborough and have ruined your mother?[53]

Osbert's replies to such *cris-de-coeur* were flippant or evasive. When his father warned him that, if he did not take care, the bailiffs would take possession of his house in London, he replied that he never went to sleep without first looking under the bed in case one was already ensconced there.[54] He was convinced that he was being unfairly treated, fortified in this belief by the fact that the spending at Montegufoni continued unabated. 'I suppose I shall return,' he told Ronald Firbank from Monte Carlo, 'but I fear in a bad way as "Ginger" is going to snatch my little remaining money from me. So I suppose Sachie and I will have to earn our living, by street-singing or something of that sort.'[55] They might have done worse. Even the faithful Maynard Hollingworth from time to time rebelled at the constant demands made on the estate by Osbert's whims. 'I do not in the least want to pay for your fancy dress,' he protested, when Osbert expected to be kitted out for some gala occasion. 'I shall be in trouble enough for the payments I have already made when Sir George goes through them, but fancy dress would simply put the lid on it.'[56] Not until the autumn of 1925, when Sir George finally quitted Renishaw and settled in Italy, did the guerrilla warfare between father and son dwindle in intensity; it continued even after that, but at a distance, and with some of the acrimony departed.

In Derbyshire, where Sir George was still often to be found even after he had formally resigned the field in favour of his elder son, his presence could prove something of an embarrassment. He neither invited the guests nor felt it was his responsibility to entertain them, yet his presence brooded over the proceedings and he could not safely be ignored. Osbert tried to present him as a decorative feature, to be ranked with the Copley portrait or the tapestries. 'I am very grieved that you cannot come here,' he wrote to Arnold Bennett. 'There are some nice (old) pictures and my father to look at.'[57] His friends did not always share his prejudice. Sir George was a 'very civil gentleman', Wyndham Lewis reported, who took a well-informed and benevolent interest in his guest's headache, while Lady Ida had sustained a thoughtful discussion of the merits of Eno's fruit salts: 'they are altogether a very agreeable family and live in an agreeable house'.[58]

This somewhat bland depiction of life at Renishaw was untypical. More of Osbert's guests referred to the tension in the atmosphere, the brooding sense of storms about to burst. Raymond Mortimer, literary critic and fringe member of the Bloomsbury Group, was disconcerted to discover that his room was one of the most heavily haunted in the house. He contemplated a rapid flight to London but was partly reassured when told that the ghost had never been known to do more than hiss in a meaningful manner. In the end the ghost failed to manifest itself at all. Mortimer settled down and cautiously enjoyed his weekend. It was nice, Osbert commented, 'to hear, for the first time, echoes of Bloomsbury laughter lingering under the oak beams or spidery plaster ceilings'.[59]

One of the livelier, if more bilious, accounts of life at Renishaw came from Siegfried Sassoon, who spent a few days there in August 1921. 'Blighted skies and blasted trees and blackened exhaustion,' he recorded gloomily. 'Atmosphere of nerve-twitching exhaustion . . . What time is the next meal? Look at this! Look at that! Ancestor-worship in oil paintings . . . Rich food: the house a stronghold; decayed and morose dignities fronting encroachments of industry. An oasis of landscape-gardening and terraced formality, girdled by iron and tunnelled by coal mines.' This was but a start; his phantasmagoric reveries became more hectic, envisaging 'harassed and skulking servants; furtive gardeners. Undoubtedly wicked influences. Crazy behaviour late at night.' The lake was large, ornamental 'but too shallow for an effective suicide' – an escape from the house party which Sassoon evidently meditated. The crazy behaviour late at night seems to have consisted of nothing worse than 'some dreary charades – variations on the "Ginger" theme, with Edith dressed up in a suit of his clothes. I made hectic attempts to be "hearty", assisted by champagne (which appeared after Ginger had gone to bed).' And to cap it all were the Sitwells themselves: 'The three are an absolute climax! Regency relics. The trouble is they've all got too much taste.' Sassoon was particularly irritated by Osbert's refusal to 'discuss anything for more than two minutes'. He could never allow anyone to hold the floor to any serious purpose without breaking in on a different theme, 'he cannot sustain his interest until the end'.[60] Most visitors to Renishaw seem to have enjoyed themselves rather more, but references to the rich food and febrile atmosphere abound and the inconsequent snipe-like quality of Osbert's conversation was a frequent source of comment, if not complaint.

In London, at least, the skirmishing between Sir George and his children did not provide a discordant background to the entertaining. Towards the end of 1919 Osbert and Sachie had left Swan Walk and taken a long lease on a house in Carlyle Square, off the King's Road in Chelsea. Though on four storeys the house was narrow and there was actually less space than in their former home. This, at first at least, was a minor problem since, as Osbert wrote in 1946, 'I possessed practically no furniture, but *masses* of glass ornaments. I had to go backwards and forwards in taxicabs for days.'[61] For two years they camped in Carlyle Square, with little except half a dozen beds and a few armchairs; they dined off a kitchen table from the Omega workshop which had been painted for them by Roger Fry. Gradually the house took on a more settled appearance. Alan Pryce-Jones, one of the more regular guests, remembered it in its prime as being 'a fine jumble: from sketches of decor for Diaghilev to the Neapolitan conch-shaped silver chairs round the dining room table. Small pretty things abounded – the house was a temple of a now-forgotten style called the "amusing".'[62] In pictures the tone was predominantly modern; and over the years were added works by Picasso, Severini, Gaudier-Brzeska, Modigliani, as well as by local painters such as Sickert, Gertler and Paul Nash; but there were older paintings, too, though the more valuable of these were not added for twenty years or more. The ornaments were still more eclectic: much Victorian bric-à-brac, sea-shells, wax flowers, ships of spun glass, and the best-known feature, a huge bowl filled with press cuttings, for the most part displayed in a drawing-room with a lilac-blue ceiling and blue woodwork. The dining-room was still more bizarre, a lean-to shed erected in the yard at the back of the house and reached by a draughty passage. This, once Fry's homespun kitchen table had been banished, was transformed into a grotto, with the chairs Pryce-Jones had described, of black ebony encrusted with sheets of mother-of-pearl forming shell-shaped backs, and side tables supported on the tails of gilt dolphins – 'The walls shimmered, covered in a greeny-gold material that gave the visual effect of an undersea cave.'[63]

The house was run by Osbert's housekeeper, Mrs Powell, with a dedication that enabled her to transcend any temporary inconveniences such as the last-minute apparition of half a dozen guests or the still less welcome incursions of the bailiffs. Mrs Powell had been trained at Castle Howard and with the Londesboroughs but accepted the Bohemian ways of Osbert and Sachie with equanimity. She loved them and they her, so much so that Osbert professed nothing but the most delighted enthusiasm when she committed one of her rare errors of taste and presented him with a cushion of black satin embroidered with a rose in ice-cream pink. Osbert resigned himself to putting up with this object manfully for many years, but Mrs Powell thought better of her gesture and the cushion disappeared after a day or two.[64]

Osbert made it his object to invite to Carlyle Square anyone whose company he enjoyed or who could contribute usefully to the Sitwell legend. Usually the two categories coincided. When Arnold Bennett dined there, the painter Sickert and Wyndham Lewis were also at table. 'Very good dinner and the most fantastic and hazardous service,' he remembered. After dinner the group moved on to a party given by Ottoline Morrell: 'It was like Osbert's effrontery to insist on taking us. He marched into Ottoline's at the head of his squad with much quiet and noble pride.'[65] 'Outwardly uproarious' but 'indefinably out of harmony' was Anthony Powell's verdict on a dinner party that had included Harold Acton, Evelyn Waugh, Robert Byron and Constant Lambert,[66] and an uneasy feeling that something was awry was marked on many of these occasions.

Members of the Bloomsbury set were often there; the occasions were convivial enough, but their presence created a vague unease, as if the Macdonalds were wassailing with the Campbells at Glencoe and nobody was quite sure whether the daggers would appear. Stephen Tennant, a talented epicene of unwavering frivolity, was dining with the Sitwells when Osbert announced that the last guest – yet to arrive – would smell of camphor balls and be wearing an old lace curtain from some Notting Hill lodging house. 'Would you like to know the form her madness takes?' he asked. 'Osbert, how can you say such obscene and vile things about Virginia Woolf?' Tennant exclaimed. On the same occasion Mrs Woolf was heard to remark that she knew what horrible things Osbert said about her.[67] Yet she went on coming to Carlyle Square and the two enjoyed each other's company in a pleasantly malicious way. 'Yesterday I was in mischief – in the arms of Osbert, and very fat they are too,' she told Vita Sackville-West; 'on the carpet of Mrs Courtauld, and that is as thick and resilient as Osbert's arms. Lord! What a party.'[68]

Lytton Strachey was as regular a visitor to Carlyle Square and was at least as censorious. After a 'dreadfully dull' dinner with the Sitwells he was taken on to an 'incredibly fearful function' at Arnold Bennett's house. An 'imbecile frog' lectured inadequately on Rimbaud, then Edith appeared, 'her nose longer than an ant-eater's, and read some of her absurd stuff'. Finally came T. S. Eliot, 'very sad and seedy . . . As a study in half-witted horror the whole thing was most interesting . . . Why, oh why does Eliot have any truck with such coagulations?'[69] Strachey was no better pleased when a party, including Siegfried Sassoon and led by Osbert Sitwell, descended on him in the country from Stephen Tennant's house, Wilsford. They seemed to be entirely preoccupied with dressing up: 'The night before they had all dressed up as nuns, that morning they had all dressed up as shepherds and shepherdesses. In the evening they were all going to dress up as – God knows what – but they begged and implored me to return with them to share their rapture.' He resisted the invitation: 'Strange creatures,' he mused, 'with just a few feathers where brains should be. Though no doubt Siegfried is rather different.'[70] Osbert would have been enraged by this uncharitable judgment, especially since he himself had resolutely refused to dress up on this occasion.

Osbert tried to involve Strachey in another of his odder enterprises. 'We are making a presentation to Chaliapin at the Savoy tomorrow from the *Writers* of England,' he wrote. 'Will you join us? No excuses will be taken.'[71] No excuse seems to have been offered but Strachey did not turn up; David Garnett did, though, as well as Raymond Mortimer, William Walton and a cohort of journalists and photographers summoned by Osbert. The occasion was something of a débâcle. The great singer kept his admirers waiting for more than two hours while the journalists gradually slipped away, then accepted the olive wreath from Osbert with a warm but somewhat perfunctory embrace and went about his business.[72] Osbert was genuinely an ardent admirer of Chaliapin and anxious to do him honour, but he had it just as much in mind to win some credit and free publicity for the Sitwells. Usually such undertakings were successful; on this occasion he largely failed.

Until Sachie's marriage in 1925 the two brothers almost always took part jointly in such adventures; Osbert to the fore, Sachie a diligent if sometimes mildly reluctant second. Edith, though very much part of the trio in the public mind, led a life apart. She lived in a dingy flat in Bayswater and entertained principally at tea. Her brothers loyally attended such occasions but came and went with some speed; they 'generally produced the impression of having descended from a different plane', wrote Peter Quennell. They would circle rapidly round the room, shaking any hand they encountered. 'And how are *you*?' they would ask, 'in a tone that, although kindly and courteous, did not suggest that they required an answer.' Soon they completed the circuit and swept gracefully towards the door. 'Their fine heads, as they turned to vanish, recalled twin faces stamped on a single coin.'[73]

Edith was incomparably the most important woman in Osbert's life; he revered her poetry, hungrily sought her plaudits and automatically took her side in any quarrel. As confidante and personal companion, though, he would probably have opted for Christabel Aberconway. Lady Aberconway was the daughter of a former head of Scotland Yard and the wife of a rich industrialist. She was beautiful, intelligent and, on the whole, kind-hearted; she was also a mischief-maker and inordinately possessive towards the many men who admired her. Some of these were her lovers; Osbert's appeal may have been partly that he was entirely safe in such matters and thus presented a relaxing alternative to the more fraught relationships which she enjoyed with his rivals for her affections. In her autobiography she listed him as one of her closest friends;[74] he was expected to demonstrate this closeness by treating her on every occasion as being of paramount importance in his life. She was most put out when she found Anthony Powell's wife, Lady Violet, seated on Osbert's right at dinner. As the daughter of an earl, Lady Violet was quite correctly given precedence over the mere wife of a baron, but Christabel scorned to ask why the other guest had been preferred, addressed her coldly as 'Mrs Powell', and rang up peevishly next day to demand who 'that woman' had been.[75] Osbert was more than happy to put up with her exigency and occasional tantrums. He loved her as much as he ever loved any woman; she was so clever and subtle, he told Lady Desborough, and besides that 'she is an angel of kindness and real *niceness* (such an awful word)'.[76] On Jubilee Day, in May 1935, he wrote to her:

While others praise their sovereign, I propose to praise you . . . The other day, facing you at luncheon, I thought how frightful it was that one always waited until people were dead to say what one felt about them; and especially someone of my nature, diffident in that direction and shy of complaints. And so I decided, as I watched your lovely sweetness and sweet loveliness, and remembered that you had once told me that the most I had ever said was that I liked your hat, that I would put on record what I did feel about you ... Certainly you've been much the most important and lovely happening in my life ... And from any point of view – I only hope from yours – what a wonderful friendship it is and what warm and wonderful companionship you've given me. Whatever my faults, at least I can say that my heart is always lifted when I see you ... and that everything in your company becomes 100% nicer, or, if a painful occasion, 100% less so.[77]

Osbert was allowing himself to be carried unduly far on a wave of sentimentality when he told Christabel that she had been 'much the most important and lovely happening' in his life, but her importance to him was great and he would have found it most painful to contemplate existence without her.

The other women in his life were inconsiderable. The Ladies Cunard and Colefax, those rival high priestesses of London polite – or more-or-less polite – society, were used, abused and made the victims of relentless satires. Sibyl Colefax was a particularly favoured butt, thinly disguised in a starring role in many of his more bilious verses. Emerald Cunard fared a little better – he once described her as 'a highly intelligent and cultivated American with a streak of genuine originality in her character', but at the time of the Abdication he made little attempt to distinguish her from the rest of the 'gay, courageous pirate crew' whom he excoriated in his doggerel polemic Rat Week.[78] Ada Leverson, 'The Sphinx', novelist and friend of Oscar Wilde, meant more to him than either of these more coruscating ladies. She met him at the house of her sister, Violet Schiff. She conceived a passion for all the Sitwells, but Osbert in particular – 'Ada Leverson was in love with Osbert,' said Harold Acton. 'It was as simple and as pathetic as that.'[79] After the death of her husband she turned to Osbert for protection against her domineering daughter and almost equally proprietorial sister and bombarded him with appeals for help and counsel: 'This is only my 2nd letter and I haven't sent more than 2 wires today,' she once wrote proudly. 'Quite moderate when such events go on.'[80] Osbert found her a bore but appreciated her qualities and behaved with exemplary kindness; he 'treated her crepuscular passion with a rare combination of sympathy and delicacy', wrote Peter Quennell.[81] He drew the line only when she prowled beneath his window at Renishaw at 7.00 a.m.; a message was sent out by a footman that Mrs Leverson must go back to bed. In the spring of 1922 he extended his charity so far as to take her with him to his cherished retreat at Amalfi. 'You and Sachie are releasing a Sphinx, Andromeda or somebody like that, in arranging for me to fly to Italy,' she wrote gratefully. 'It is very sweet and generous and good of you to care. But you are exactly like the Gods of the Greeks, Antinous and Apollo.' The experiment was not a total success. Once there, she maddened the brothers by her constant demands for conversation and her absent-minded losing of possessions which they then had to search for – Osbert invented a motto for her: 'Silence and Self Help'.[82]

Mrs Ronald Greville – 'Mrs Ronnie' to everyone – was perhaps of greatest importance to Osbert for the link she provided with the royal family. Shrewd, vulgar, snobbish and extremely rich, Mrs Ronnie was a loyal and generous friend to those who were accepted into her little band; an honour whose award called for a certain amount of charm and social distinction, the latter being the more significant. Osbert was a particular favourite. After he had been so ill with flu in 1919 she swept him up and took him to Monte Carlo and Biarritz to convalesce. The visit to Biarritz was particularly memorable since it was there that he learned that he had been demobilised. At once he stuffed his uniform, grey overcoat and gold-braided hat into a hamper and launched it ceremoniously into the Bay of Biscay.[83] But it was back in England, where Mrs Ronnie entertained lavishly and frequently at her country house, Polesden Lacey, that her friendship with Osbert really flourished. Whenever the Duke and Duchess of York came to stay, Osbert was included in the party. Before he met the duchess, Osbert had been, or claimed to have been, sceptical about assurances that he would find her 'remarkably charming and intelligent', but he was swiftly converted and became a devoted follower, not only at Polesden Lacey but at Philip Sassoon's house, Trent, and the Yorks' own house in Piccadilly.

This weakness for the highest of high life illustrated vividly the dichotomy which was so prominent in Osbert's career. He considered himself a *grand seigneur*, yet also a hard-working professional writer. He himself saw no incompatibility between the two but those with whom he associated in either camp were not always so broad-minded. The Prince of Wales looked askance when Osbert told him that he had retired from the Grenadier Guards to take up a life of literature;[84] his literary friends were suspicious if not contemptuous of his social acrobatics. Osbert tried valiantly to reconcile the two. Sometimes he brought it off successfully, quite as often he encountered hostility or ridicule. In October 1919 he sent a brace of pheasants to T. S. Eliot, the following season it was two brace of partridges to Harold Monro of the Poetry Bookshop, one and a half brace to W. J. Turner and the painter Bernard van Dieren, and a brace to Robert Graves and W. H. Davies. It was a perfectly sensible thing to do and no doubt welcome to most of the recipients but Robert Graves – who, incidentally in his reply, showed that he could not tell a partridge from a grouse – thought the gesture exquisitely pompous. The birds had come with a card reading: 'With Captain Sitwell's compliments to Captain Graves.' Graves replied with equal formality: 'Captain Graves acknowledges with thanks Captain Sitwell's gift of Captain Grouse.'[85]

Some people believed that Osbert's work was the worse for his failure to shuffle off the clouds of glory which he had trailed since his illustrious birth. In a review of *Tales My Father Taught Me* in 1962, Philip Toynbee wrote that the book was 'suffused with that curious but widespread fantasy which leads so many members of so many different classes to believe that their social origins are somehow a credit to themselves'. The author had adopted a 'self-consciously aristocratic' tone of voice. Is it the case, Toynbee asked, that Osbert's 'profound sense of social superiority has done much to vitiate his natural talents as a writer?'[86] Osbert's aristocratic tone of voice was not 'adopted' or in any way self-conscious but was entirely natural. The question, however, is still valid. Would Osbert have become a better writer if he had been, say, a younger son or some still more distant connection, and had eschewed society and his grander connections in favour of the austere life of a penurious author? Certainly, he would have been a very different animal. It does not follow, though, that he would have benefited from this deprivation. Siegfried Sassoon was a richer man than Osbert, even if his Jewish blood and merchant ancestry meant that his social status was more equivocal. Would he have been a better writer if he had renounced *his* past? Both Osbert and Sassoon drank so deeply from their personal sources that it is questionable whether they could have flourished at all if those sources had dried up. It is, indeed, arguable that Osbert's 'aristocratic tone of voice' was one of his greatest assets, the ideal instrument for the kind of writing for which he was to be best remembered. The way Osbert wrote fused intimately with the subjects that he chose to write about; the one can hardly be conceived without the other. Of no one was de Buffon's aphorism '*Le style est l'homme même*' more evidently true. If Osbert had shed his heritage he *might* have been a better writer; it is at least as possible that he would not have been a writer at all.

The problems of being simultaneously artist and patron were particularly apparent in Osbert's relationship with his protégé, the composer William Walton. Though the credit for Walton's success was more Sachie's than Osbert's (and more Walton's than either's) Osbert played an energetic part in his promotion, once inviting Diaghilev and his entourage to Carlyle Square to hear three movements of a ballet which Walton had recently composed.[87] According to Angus Morrison, a pianist and close friend of Walton's, the Sitwells had been ideal patrons, 'Completely undemanding and never eager for their pound of flesh. They simply let him get on with his work.' Walton himself described Osbert to John Pearson as being 'half an elder brother, half a father. I wouldn't go against his wishes.'[88] The Sitwells never complained about the rate of his progress or his inability to make a living. But a posture of dependence is wearing to maintain, however benign the regime. 'I think the Sitwells a little bit swamped his personality,' said Stephen Tennant. They would tease him affectionately, but sometimes painfully, about his 'low' Oldham background and social inexperience. In the end he revolted. 'But we must honour Osbert for discovering and nurturing his genius.'[89] Walton's friendship led to another young composer, Constant Lambert, joining the circle. Lambert more or less invaded Carlyle Square towards the end of 1921 and endeared himself to Osbert by his wit, intelligence and exceptional good looks – a 'fast-talking, cigarette-smoking, "job lot Apollo"', his biographer, Andrew Motion, called him. Soon he too was visiting Renishaw and playing duets with Walton on the antiquated Bechstein.[90]

The brothers took Walton with them when they wintered in Amalfi. If the young composer had envisaged a relaxing holiday he was soon disabused: 'I saw how they slogged away at their books,' he remembered ruefully. 'No drinking and no socialising. Just hard work.'[91] In fact there was drinking and socialising but only in strict moderation; nothing was allowed to interfere with the designated hours of work. The Hotel Cappuccini, a former monastery perched three hundred steps above the road running along Amalfi's sea-front, with its one-time cells austerely furnished and devoid of central heating, was not surprisingly largely empty in winter and well suited for any literary work which did not call for constant reference to a library.[92] Osbert told T. S. Eliot that there were a thousand steps and said that it was 'rather like being in a lighthouse only without the light'. The climate was all that could be expected and for a man as easily distracted as he was the lack of company and entertainment was a necessity, but he hankered after London and looked forward to the arrival of *The Times* and the *Nation* as the 'great events respectively of the day and week'.[93]

Once Walton had adapted himself to the way of life he worked well there, among other things completing his *Sinfonia Concertante*, the first movement of which he dedicated to Osbert. Not all visitors behaved as dutifully. Peter Quennell stayed there in 1925 and described how everyone was expected to lurk within their cell, emerging only just before lunch and dinner 'for one or two of the anodyne cocktails that were then called "White Ladies"'. He drew restive under this regime; provoked rows and, when he went off for a brief visit to friends in another part of Italy, received a letter politely suggesting that he should not return.[94] Edith, another occasional visitor, told Richard Aldington that she was working hard, 'indeed, it is difficult not to work, for there is nothing else to do'. But there were still interruptions; the previous week she had looked from her window to see Sir George advancing up the steps towards the hotel, 'looking, with his long red beard, rather like the cover to *Dracula*. He did not know we were in Italy, and altogether it was a mutual shock.'[95]

Sir George believed – or was supposed by his children to believe – that Osbert and Sachie were far away on a mythical yacht, the SY *Rover*, for which they had had a supply of writing paper printed which they would get friends to post from far-flung corners of the Mediterranean or even remoter destinations. Dodging Sir George became a favourite sport; once Osbert hid behind the counter of Thomas Cook's office in Piccadilly until his father had done his business and departed.[96] Whether Sir George was deceived by these devices is debatable. Sassoon thought that he was not. He sighted Sir George in Florence and noted sceptically: 'He is supposed to be unaware that his sons are in Italy, but no doubt he *is* aware.'[97]

Rapallo was for a time a rival to Amalfi as a resort for wintering. Osbert described how unpopular he had become in the hotel there. The 'pathetic drudge of a niece' of two old ladies named the Misses Oakover was unwise enough to boast to Osbert in the lift how her aunts belonged to this ancient and distinguished family. 'Oh! Oh! How awful!' exclaimed Osbert. Thinking he had not heard, the niece persisted: 'You know, the *Derbyshire* Oakovers.' 'Then you should inform the Director,' said Osbert angrily. 'That sort of thing wants stamping out!' The unfortunate niece could not decide whether Osbert was mad, deaf or gratuitously offensive but evidently plumped for the latter because 'her aunts glare at me venomously' and organised an anti-Sitwell movement in the hotel.[98] Osbert delighted in telling stories of this kind, in which he described himself rending importunate acquaintances who invaded his privacy. In fact he was genuinely anxious not to hurt unless hurt first. He was capable of ferocious rudeness when aroused but would never have savaged an innocent if foolish woman in this way. Still less would he have insulted a 'poor relation', a category for which he had great sympathy, and one kindly portrayed in many of his novels and stories. No doubt, as twenty years before with the Eton Boating Song, he thought to himself how amusing it would have been if he had responded in such a way and decided the story was too good to waste.

Whether or not he was unpopular in the hotel, he had other friends in Rapallo. Max Beerbohm, a writer and artist for whom he had high regard, lived there; Osbert called on him often and Beerbohm did several brilliantly perceptive cartoons of him and Sachie which caught their languid yet febrile dandyhood with delicate precision. Ezra Pound also stayed there. Rapallo, Pound once remarked, was a place for people who were immediately recognisable by their Christian names; until Osbert Lancaster appeared on the scene, Max, Ezra and Osbert could have meant only one thing to habitual readers. Osbert wrote to tell Harold Monro's wife, Alida, that Pound was there 'in that open blue collar and with all the triangular red cornelian buttons and cuff-links'. He was 'in perfect form, and poor Mrs Pound seems quite to have recovered from that distressing accident . . . You remember the incident, I suppose. Ezra was just beginning his career as a sculptor when he asked Mrs Pound to hold a block of wood for him while he shaped it, but by mistake he shaped Mrs Ezra's index finger.' Osbert's main diversion was visiting the English Library run by a retired major-general who was reduced to purple fury by the mere mention of a book. But then why, Osbert wondered, take on a library? 'It's as though a bull were put in charge of a china stall, or had set up for itself a shop solely dedicated to selling red flags.'[99]

'Will you be very kind and send me any postcards of the house and gardens there may be?' Osbert wrote to Hollingworth at Renishaw. 'I have got a sudden attack of homesickness.'[100] It was an unusual admission. Habitually Osbert spent the four or five months of the winter abroad, usually at this period in Italy, and travelled widely during the rest of the year. In the autumn he would pass a few weeks at Montegufoni, his guests coexisting uneasily with Sir George's friends: 'The only disadvantage', reported Edith from Montegufoni, 'is a constant incursion of tarantulas, scorpions, Mrs Hwfa Williams and Mrs George Keppel — these ancient and malevolent women are always here.'[101] Not everyone was deterred by such a threat; even Lytton Strachey pronounced the castle ' a truly outstanding place', while Aldous Huxley liked it so much that he proposed to take up residence there while writing 'a gigantic Peacock in an Italian scene'. 'I would live for very little in the Sitwells' enormous house,' he told his brother hopefully.[102] The 'enormous house' duly featured as the palace of the Cybo Malaspina in Huxley's novel *Those Barren Leaves*.

Osbert and Sachie cherished a wish to hire some contemporary artist to paint frescoes in one of the principal rooms in Montegufoni. Their first choice as artist was Picasso, who was absorbed at that time by the works of Benozzo Gozzoli and relished the challenge of interpreting them in contemporary idiom. Sir George vetoed the idea; more, it seems, on grounds of cost than of the artist's suitability. Gino Severini was then approached. He found Sir George 'cordial but distant'; his two sons 'intelligent and pleasant ... ready to discuss any subject on any plane. They were both poets, so we were necessarily destined to be either enemies or friends straight away; we became friends.' A sixteenth-century salon was selected and Severini commissioned to paint it with the *commedia dell'arte* scenes which had recently become his speciality.[103] Sir George, according to Osbert, had confused Severini with Mancini, another Italian painter, who had been much admired by Sargent and had died a few years before.[104] On this basis he agreed to the work being carried out. Severini believed that he was entirely satisfied with the result, so much so that he appropriated the painted room for his own use. This says much for Sir George's good manners. Osbert told Sachie a year or two later, 'Ginger has become the most fearful snob and still cries out when he looks into the Severini room "*Non è mio gusto!*"'[105]

Osbert was the ideal tourist: well briefed, indefatigable, endlessly enthusiastic yet discriminating. Sachie was the better and more thoughtful scholar but it was usually Osbert who got the enterprise under way. Cyril Connolly, then an Oxford undergraduate, spotted them in Granada where they had gone for Holy Week in 1925 and thought them 'witty and cultured and kind'. The two brothers echoed each other completely, though Sachie was 'rather nice looking and Osbert rather bloated'.[106] They were at the centre of a gang which included Walton, Constant Lambert and the dilettante painter Richard Wyndham. 'Alarming rather than forbidding,' Connolly found them. 'They all wore black capes and Andalusian hats and looked magnificent.' He approached them timidly, was judged acceptable and absorbed into the party.[107] The picture he paints of a noisy, hedonistic and exhibitionist crew, shouting down a group of American tourists whose conversation they deemed insufficiently interesting, is not an attractive one. *En masse*, the Sitwells and their entourage could be overpowering and, in a cultured sort of way, distinctly boorish. But they were not wasting their time.

Osbert and Sachie devoted many hours a day to intensive sight-seeing, absorbing and thinking about what they saw and storing away their impressions for use in future writing. There was nothing amateurish about their tourism.

They were not preoccupied solely by their aesthetic pursuits and the wish to have a good time. In Germany, in the summer of 1922, Osbert was horrified by what he saw. 'Berlin is too terrible for words,' he told Ada Leverson, 'the whole scene laid for some appalling catastrophe which can't be far off . . . All the middle-classes are absolutely starving . . . It is really ghastly! And all the hotels are full of guzzling foreigners, stuffing themselves with food.'[108] Osbert realised that he was a guzzling foreigner himself, but in the years after the First World War, as at no other time of his life, he convinced himself that he could and should do something about the parlous state of the world around him. Though he had stood for parliament as a Liberal, his preferred solutions tended towards the right-wing and the authoritarian. The peace of 1918, he believed, had made the world safe for 'a beer-logged trades-unionism in the victorious countries' and the worst excesses of dictatorship elsewhere.[109] There must be another way. For a time he believed he had found it in the so-called 'Regency' that the Italian poet Gabriele d'Annunzio set up in Fiume. Blithely ignoring the disorder and philosophical incoherence which attended this ill-considered venture, Osbert concluded that d'Annunzio's small domain might develop 'into an ideal land, where the arts would flourish once more on Italian soil', and might offer an escape from 'The Scylla and Charybdis of modern life, Bolshevism and American Capitalism'. After trying to persuade the *Daily Mail* to send him to Fiume as a special correspondent, he settled for the *Nation* and hastened off with Sachie to interview d'Annunzio. The Regency was in its death throes by the time he got to Fiume and, well disposed though he was, Osbert could see the absurdity of much of what was going on and the prominence of the criminal element among d'Annunzio's followers. But he never lost his belief that the adventure had been a noble one and that it might have succeeded. Nor did he deplore the rise of Italian fascism, to which d'Annunzio's enterprise contributed. Even after the evidence to the contrary was becoming overwhelming, Osbert persisted in his belief that Italian fascism was a movement of high ideals and disinterested values. He deplored those Englishmen who admired fascism as a 'money-grabbing, castor-oil administering weapon of law and order'. They had missed the point, he maintained. The hymn of the fascisti was 'a libel on the thousands of eager, energetic, clever men who compose that body'.[110]

Though by the standards of the time Osbert was in no way exceptional, his writings and recorded speeches are filled with examples of anti-Semitism. He insisted always that the Jews were members of a separate race, not merely of a separate faith, and regretted that they had been allowed 'to adopt European dress and ape European manners. Their life is one round of pretence, of pretending to be Europeans, Christians, Englishmen, English Gentlemen, Peers and Viceroys.'[111] More often than not, such views were put into the mouths of characters in his fiction and as such, he could have claimed, did not represent his personal opinions. Yet the Jewish characters in his fiction are consistently unattractive; the paradigm being Sir Levy Lollygo, who resembled 'a very fleshy and aged wild boar' and was 'plainly of so low and wallowing a vanity, of a baser and more repulsive order'.[112] Nor was it only in his books that Jews figured badly: there was only one person of any interest in Brides-les-Bains, he told David Horner, 'all the rest are Jews'; Sachie's new book had a frightful jacket, which was unsurprising since Faber & Faber always employed a Jew and 'he gives them a horrid, heavy, oily quality'.[113] Some of my best friends are Jews, he protested when speaking of John Rothenstein: 'I just can't stand a Japanese Jew.'[114] The disclaimer is hardly convincing. He couldn't bear the Jews being chivvied, he wrote, when the first intimations of Nazi excesses were becoming known, 'though I can't help appreciating Hitler's statement that all that is needed to put the world right is a "one-way road to Jerusalem"'.[115] His views on colour were hardly more enlightened. A friend, Zena Naylor, was said to have black lovers: 'Poor Zena Naylor', wrote Osbert:

> Finds white men fail 'er
> So that the coon
> Comes as a boon;
> But after coons, soon
> She will have a baboon![116]

In 1928, when this was written, it was perhaps as much as could have been expected at the bar of some provincial rugger club; one might have hoped for better, however, from a man who dreamed of an ideal state where poets would rule and the arts flourish undisturbed.

When final demobilisation was impending, Osbert conducted a brief foray into politics himself. In the general election of November 1918 he decided to stand for Scarborough, the seat which Sir George had once occupied and where residual family loyalties might still be of value. His father applauded the move; politics might be more expensive than poetry but as a pastime they were more becoming for a gentleman. Osbert elected to stand as an Asquithian Liberal – the genteel and more obviously doomed wing of that anyway decaying party. 'I am hanged if I have ever seen any traces of Radicalism in you,' expostulated Hollingworth.[117] It was, indeed, difficult to find traces of any very coherent political philosophy in Osbert's electioneering: he wanted a platform from which he could proclaim the wickedness of war, otherwise a sense of *noblesse oblige* and a vague conviction that the social order required remodelling were the most conspicuous features of his programme. He proved to be a competent speaker, unexpectedly good at making an audience laugh and getting it on his side, but this was not enough against the tide which swept the Conservatives to power. He polled a respectable 8,000 votes but still lost by nearly 4,000. 'He did not "get in". I suppose they found out he is a poet,' Edith told Robert Nichols.[118] More probably they found out he was a Liberal.

The election went well enough to convince Osbert that, once the post-war euphoria had faded, he might well capture the seat. His father encouraged him. Only a few months after the general election Sir George was urging him to show himself in Scarborough and confer with his leading supporters: 'If you lose this chance it may be 20 years or more before another chance of *success* offers itself.'[119] Osbert complied, but without great enthusiasm. He found electioneering a bore. 'As for what one does at Whitby,' he told a friend in 1921, 'one speaks on politics, making oneself as amiable as circumstances can allow and, if depressed, reflects on the life of the Blessed Hilda; who resided at the Abbey opposite, and must have been at least 4 times as bored as I ever am.'[120] Sir George put up the money for Osbert's campaigning and offered advice as well. Try to avoid talking about politics, he suggested; nobody is interested. 'If you must talk on politics, *don't go in for rhetoric*. Give them good facts and good reasoning.' And at all costs avoid jokes or irony; 'Be careful of your humour, which is dangerous.' So far as possible, Sir George believed, Osbert should conduct his electioneering with a minimum of stress. He had only recently been seriously ill and his health preoccupied his father as much as his platform manner. An absolutely regular life was essential, including 'two good walks a day, at exactly the same hours. I think you rather regard exercise as a duty, and therefore something a really clever person would shirk.' On the contrary, it gave a glow of health. 'It would certainly help to cure your constipation, but continue the oil treatment if there is any doubt.'[121]

For light relief while in the constituency Osbert relied on the visits of friends. Aldous Huxley joined him several times at the Pavilion Hotel in Scarborough, where conversation in the dining-room was conducted only in decorous whispers. Huxley defied the prevailing gloom and would continue 'in his clear emphatic unclouded voice to give details of the remarkable love-life of the octopus, or the latest news of life at Garsington'.[122] A visit from Mr Asquith was more relevant to Osbert's political career. Since Edith refused to have anything to do with his electioneering, his cousin Constance was drafted in to act as hostess. Asquith addressed two rallies and enjoyed himself thoroughly, particularly the supper at Wood End when Osbert brought in his charwoman 'to sing revivalist hymns and dance, just like a performing bear'.[123]

But Osbert's enthusiasm for politics, never marked, waned rapidly. 'My life has been a hell of public meetings and cross letters from parents,' he wrote early in 1921. He claimed that it was the cross letters, in particular a change of heart on the part of his father who took alarm at the thought that Osbert might actually *win* the next election,[124] which led him to abandon the field. In fact the public meetings were more to blame. Osbert became increasingly desultory in his appearances and finally withdrew as candidate. Henceforth he was a Conservative in name, though never orthodox or even partisan. In 1925, when the Labour Party wanted to hold a rally in the park at Renishaw, Hollingworth advised against it: 'The farm tenant would not be pleased to see the Red Flag tramping his grass down.' 'I think we should let them hold this meeting,' Osbert replied. 'I very much regret that I shall not be there to receive them in person.'[125] The rally duly took place. It was an admirably civilised response, which he would have made even when political passions ran much stronger. It suggests, perhaps, that Osbert would never have prospered as a member of a parliamentary party.

7

Not a Story but a Sketch

OSBERT Sitwell had no doubt that he was a writer first and foremost. In 1924, when he first appeared in *Who's Who*, his only biographical note was 'Contested the Scarborough Election', but by 1925 he categorised himself as 'Writer and Poet'. This he remained until 1929 when he briefly styled himself 'Poet and playwright', to become 'Poet, playwright and novelist' in 1932 and 'Poet, playwright and novelist, writer of essays' the following year. Short stories never featured; presumably in his mind subsumed under 'novelist'. *Who's Who* was used too as a vehicle in which to air his more idiosyncratic prejudices in the form of facetious entries. In 1925 he declared that he was 'deeply interested in any manifestation of sport, founded the Renishaw Park Golf Club 1913 ... played against Yorkshire Cricket Eleven (left-handed when 7 years old), was put down for MCC on day of birth by W. G. Grace', while in 1929 he added to these proud boasts (the last two of which happened, curiously, to be true), 'but has now abandoned all other athletic interests in order to urge the adoption of new sports such as: Pelota, Kif-Kaf and the Pengo'. His most celebrated entry, 'Educated in the holidays from Eton', also appeared for the first time in 1929.

But though a professional writer, he prided himself on taking an informed interest in other arts and being in the vanguard when it came to welcoming new artists and new movements. It was a typical joint enterprise between the brothers: Sachie contributed a greater share of the taste and knowledge, Osbert provided the impetus that got things done. A case in point was the Exhibition of Modern French Art at the Mansard Gallery in 1919, hailed by Roger Fry as 'the most representative show of modern French art seen in London for many years'.[1] The collection was billed as having been brought together by the Sitwell brothers, though the selection of the paintings was mainly done by the Parisian dealer Léopold Zborowski. Certainly it would never have got to London without Osbert's energy and enthusiasm. It was an impressive achievement: the exhibition introduced to London the work of Modigliani and Utrillo, as well as containing important contributions from Vlaminck, Picasso, Matisse, Derain, Dufy, Léger and a dozen or so others. Indeed, Bonnard and Braque were almost the only significant omissions among those who were then doing important work in France. Clive Bell, in the *Nation*, gave the show an ardent welcome: 'The grand and thrilling fact that emerges is that French art is vital still.'[2] The exhibition was a critical but not a commercial success. Most of the work that was for sale returned to France. Osbert and Sacheverell tried to persuade their father to buy what was left unsold; if he had taken their advice he would have secured for a few hundred pounds paintings and drawings that are now worth many millions. For £4 Osbert procured Modigliani's *Peasant Girl*, now a cherished treasure of the Tate Gallery.

In the hope of averting public wrath through the championship of a solid and well-respected figure, Osbert had persuaded Arnold Bennett to write a foreword to the catalogue. The tactic availed him nothing. Conservative opinion was outraged. Clive Bell's review in the *Nation* gave rise to a spirited correspondence in which a self-styled 'Philistine' questioned the sanity of the cubists and of painters who produced 'distorted ladies with flesh the colour of underburnt brick', while in *Everyman* Modigliani was accused of employing sitters who had been 'squeezed long and hard in a lemon squeezer'. Spending the weekend at Polesden Lacey with Mrs Greville, Osbert and Sachie found themselves assailed by a furious chorus of elderly dignitaries who had no time for Bolshevism in art and who thought Cézanne should have been shot.[3]

Osbert enjoyed the furore; he would, indeed, have been disappointed if all had passed off placidly. But his restless craving for new sensation also led him, paradoxically, into some of the lesser known of the older, classical schools of art. Sachie and the Finnish savant-cum-art-dealer Tancred Borenius steered him along the way. He did not abandon the avant-garde, but as the 1920s advanced he became progressively more involved in baroque painting of the seventeenth and eighteenth centuries, the school today identified above all with Caravaggio but including Tiepolo, Guido Reni, the Caracci and the relatively little known Magnasco. Either because he owned two of his paintings or because he preferred to be seen as champion of a minor figure, Osbert adopted Magnasco as the patron saint of the movement. In 1924 he and

Sachie founded the Magnasco Society under the presidency of the future Duke of Wellington, Gerald Wellesley. Wellesley resigned two years later, saying that the society had been a flop,[4] but he was proved wrong. The society not only held convivial dinners for its members at the Savoy but organised a series of exhibitions which did something to convince the average English picture-viewer that there was more to post-Renaissance Italian art than Guardi and Canaletto. The first exhibition included six Tiepolos, a Salvator Rosa lent by the Duke of Beaufort, a Caravaggio from the Duke of Wellington, a Longhi from Lord Harewood; while later exhibitions contained a hitherto unknown Caravaggio from Lord Harcourt and many pictures from the royal collection. The exhibitions gave much pleasure – not least to the organisers, awakened interest in a neglected school of painting and provided a substantial contribution to artistic scholarship. Osbert took justified pride in the achievement. Neither his own temperament nor the material available, however, made it likely that the society would endure for long. After a few years it began to lose steam and to grow diffuse in its aims. The final exhibition included works by Richard Wilson, Rubens, Tintoretto, Cranach and Corot. It was a distinguished and enjoyable collection but it had little to do with Magnasco. Softly and silently the Magnasco Society vanished away.[5] Some years later Osbert was asked whether he could give any information about the Magnasco Society or the 'Remember Bomba' League, which he claimed in *Who's Who* to have founded. The Bomba League – named after the best-forgotten King of Naples who was nicknamed Bomba because of the zeal with which he bombarded the cities of Sicily – was a joke, he replied: the Magnasco Society, however, was 'an accomplished fact, associating for the appreciation of later Italian painters'.[6]

Through his father Osbert found himself already the possessor of a collection of impressive if minor old masters on the walls of Renishaw. To them, and to his modern pictures in Carlyle Square, he never ceased to add. Borenius guided him, and indeed actively intervened to purchase pictures on his behalf. In May 1929 he reported that he had successfully bid for a Francavilla head (£60), a Cézanne lithograph (£42) and three Romney drawings (£90). Osbert was delighted; Hollingworth, who had to find the money, was unsurprisingly less enthusiastic.[7] Borenius was not a crook, Harold Acton judged, but he had 'one foot in the art world and one in Sotheby's'.[8] On the whole he gave good advice: the Magnasco Society furthered his own passionate enthusiasm for the Italian seventeenth century; if it also happened to promote trade in a commodity in which he was well qualified to deal, then that was an agreeable bonus but not the primary objective.

But it was writing that absorbed by far the greater part of Osbert's energies. The decade after the First World War, Cyril Connolly argued, was the age of the Mandarin, to be supplanted by the age of the Realist as the Second World War approached. In the history of literature, he wrote, there can have been few names more mentioned than those of 'Proust, Joyce, Lytton Strachey, Virginia Woolf, the Sitwells and Paul Valéry. Their moment was propitious. After the post-war disillusion they offered a religion of beauty, a cult of words, of meanings understood only by the initiated at a time when people were craving such initiations.'[9] *Wheels* had been an early manifestation of this movement. Now Osbert sought to further it in another periodical. *Art and Letters* was a quarterly review which had been founded in 1917 by a former director of the Leeds City Art Gallery, Frank Rutter, and the critic and socialist Herbert Read, to encourage all kinds of creative art. Any enterprise so high-minded was likely to run into financial problems, and by the autumn of 1918 capital was urgently needed. The Sitwells seemed a possible source and in October Read met Osbert and Sachie at the Café Royal to talk the matter over.

Read was enchanted. He considered the Sitwells aristocratic – which he felt regrettable but excusable; wealthy – which was essential; and, best of all, 'furious socialists'. 'They are crammed full of enthusiasm for the future and it is with them that I can imagine myself being associated in the future.' Anyone who could take Osbert for a furious socialist must have had a considerable capacity for self-deception, and Read soon had afterthoughts: 'The Sitwells are rather too comfortable and perhaps there is a lot of pose in their revolt.'[10] But he did not doubt that they were basically well intentioned and that it would be possible to work harmoniously with them. Osbert hoped to get Arnold Bennett interested and to buy out Rutter altogether but he mishandled the negotiations and left Bennett with the impression that he was an incompetent dilettante. 'The thing must be conducted in an absolutely business-like and prompt fashion if there is to be anything in it at all,' wrote Bennett sternly, 'and in my opinion you have too many engagements to permit you to do this.'[11]

In the event, Sydney Schiff, the rich brother-in-law of Ada Leverson, who himself wrote novels under the pseudonym of Stephen Hudson but achieved greater distinction as patron of other artists, bought a third share of the paper. He installed Osbert as joint literary editor with Read: 'Sitwell and I would run the literary part on very modernist lines,' wrote Read, 'and there would be a good chance of making things go.'[12] Osbert sent Bennett a prospectus for the refurbished magazine. I have already received seven others, the novelist replied. 'I hope it will be a success. It certainly will not be a success if it is not produced with absolute regularity.'[13]

At first things did go and *Art and Letters* was produced with acceptable if not absolute regularity. Wyndham Lewis was among the most frequent contributors; Robert Graves sent a poem with the proviso that it should be inserted 'between Sassoon and one of the few others of whom I am not terrified, as for instance Aldous Huxley (douce man), Lytton S – or you yourself, my dear Osbert, with whom I feel a genuine tie, if not of a common artistic perception, at any rate of a common desire to champion losing causes';[14] Richard Aldington sent two poems, though with private doubts: 'If they can make a "do" and get their subscribers it might be worthwhile going on with them,' he told his wife. 'But I doubt very much if they [will] get anywhere.'[15] Osbert was assiduous in routing out new or under-recognised talent. He was enthusiastic about the artistry of Ronald Firbank and persuaded him to contribute a chapter of his as yet unpublished novel *Valmouth*: 'If people are such fools as not to appreciate the wit and beauty ... they must, somehow or other, be made to.'[16] But the world at large chose to ignore not only Firbank but *Art and Letters*; even among the literati there was hostility. Vita Sackville-West wrote to Hugh Walpole about the possibility of starting a rival periodical: 'I do so want to do something to stem the tide of Osbert Sitwellism and all that slovenly, slipshod beastliness. I hate worms, and Pierrots, and peg-top trousers and all the rest of that paraphernalia.'[17]

As the subscription list failed to grow, the management became nervous and bad-tempered. Osbert fell out with Herbert Read. Read claimed that this was because he had got married without first telling his fellow editor. 'Conceit isn't the word to describe their attitude,' he told Denton Welch angrily. 'It's a sort of arrogance due, I think, to their loveless childhood.'[18] Read's discourtesy – if discourtesy it was – may have been the immediate cause of the rift, but the two men were so very different that it would not have been difficult to predict that trouble would eventually occur. Deteriorating morale was evident when Osbert thought he detected a conspiracy to oust him in favour of T. S. Eliot. He wrote indignantly to Schiff, demanding to know whether the rumour was true. If he was to stay on, he insisted, then it must be on the basis that he was in sole charge of the poetry pages: 'at present ... the only advantage I have in being an editor is the non-payment of my contributions'.[19] He wrote a similar letter to Eliot, who was perplexed and rather cross; he had no wish to join the staff of *Art and Letters* and found the suggestion somewhat insulting.[20] Schiff did not have too much trouble in disabusing Osbert of his suspicions. He had written only because of 'the mischief-making of his enemies', Osbert explained. 'The rumour, such as it was, was evidently intended to cause a breach between Eliot and myself. The truth of the matter is that, because, I suppose, I am a satirist, I have plenty of people who hate me.' To Eliot he explained that the contretemps had arisen from the mischievous gossiping of Schiff's chatterbox nephew, Beddington Behrens. 'If I meet him,' he told Eliot, 'there will be a pogrom ... he ought to be flayed alive.'[21] But he was uneasily conscious that his intemperate reaction had made him look a fool. 'It sometimes seems to my "diseased egoism" that almost everyone outside my own immediate friends, and my brother and sister, are bent on the sole purpose of harassing me.'[22]

Osbert's friendship with Eliot survived these vicissitudes. But new strains were imposed when Eliot in 1923 asked if Osbert could think up some scheme which would enable him to give up working at the bank and devote himself to poetry. Before Osbert had been given a chance to oblige, Eliot's hysterically unbalanced wife, Vivienne, ferociously denounced him for his jealousy of her husband and accused him of working actively to ensure that Eliot should never escape from his imprisonment. For a time Eliot seems to have been convinced by this improbable accusation, but he soon realised the extent of his wife's derangement. He took refuge in a flat in the Charing Cross Road where he was able to work undisturbed. Osbert and Sachie dined with him there several times and were surprised to find that he styled himself 'Captain Eliot' and that to gain admission they had to ask the porter for 'the Captain'. They were even more disconcerted to find that, on one occasion, Eliot appeared to have covered his face with a fine green powder. Virginia Woolf had observed the same phenomenon; discussing it together they decided that Eliot must be trying to emphasise the strain that he was under.

Fresh complications arose when Osbert and Edith in May 1926 received cryptic messages from Vivienne in Rome. She was involved in some unspecified scandal, she wrote; she urgently needed their advice. Having no idea what was going on, and uncertain how much Eliot knew and what he would wish them to do, the Sitwells dallied in replying; whereupon Vivienne reappeared and told her husband that his so-called friends had spurned her appeals for help. Once more Eliot was initially taken in; once more he soon became convinced of Vivienne's unreliability and made it up with Osbert. His tempestuous marriage tottered on. When Vivienne emerged from a spell in a nursing home, her husband invited Osbert and Edith to dinner to celebrate her return. The other guests were James Joyce with his mistress and the publisher Geoffrey Faber with his wife. Vivienne came late. 'It *is* splendid to see you again,' said Osbert heartily. 'I don't know about *splendid*,' replied Vivienne, 'but it is strange, *very* strange.' After this unpropitious opening things got worse; anything Eliot said his wife contradicted, the atmosphere grew more strained every minute, and the Joyces, who were planning to get married the following day after many years of cohabitation, became visibly depressed. Finally, the party broke up. 'It's been lovely, Vivienne,' said Mrs Faber, more in hope than conviction. Vivienne looked at her mournfully and replied: 'Well, it may have been lovely for you, but it's been dreadful for me!' 'Nonsense, Vivienne,' Mrs Faber countered stoutly. 'You know it's been a triumph.' 'A triumph!' was Vivienne's parting shot. 'Look at Tom's face!'[23] After this the two men drifted apart. In 1930 Osbert made an attempt to bridge the gap by inviting Eliot to stay at Renishaw. Eliot politely declined. 'It is indeed a long time since we have met,' he wrote, 'but I am not aware of that being due to any unwillingness on my part. On the contrary! I have thought of you often and wondered whether I should ever have a chance to see you again.'[24]

Their friendship cannot have been made easier by Eliot's disdain for Osbert's poetry. Osbert can hardly have been unaware of Eliot's contemptuous dismissal of 'the poets who consider themselves most opposed to Georgianism and who know a little French'. They were the sort of people, Eliot wrote, who would imagine 'the Last Judgment as a lavish display of Bengal lights and Roman candles, Catherine wheels and inflammable fire balloons'.[25] The Sitwells were not mentioned by name, but must have felt themselves among the victims of the attack. In private Eliot was no less sharp. 'Osbert Sitwell tells me that Knopf is publishing his poems in the spring,' he wrote to his friend and confidant John Quinn. 'Did you know this? I hope they do not appear at the same time as mine. Some of them are rather clever imitations of myself and other people.' The conviction that Osbert had aped his style became stronger as publication approached. 'Heaven preserve me from being reviewed in the company of Osbert,' he wrote two months later. 'I may say that any poems of his which appear to have any affinity with any of mine were published *subsequent* to mine.'[26] Osbert for his part was quite as sensitive to charges of plagiarism:

> Though a younger man than Eliot, I have been published for a much longer period* [he wrote to the American editor Horace Liveright] and if there is any likeness in our poetry – which there may be in form as we both use occasionally the *Hymns Ancient and Modern* metre – I was writing and publishing this kind of verse long before I had ever seen that of Mr Eliot. In content we cannot be too much the same – for I am of English origin and upbringing, whereas Mr Eliot, who is in my opinion the most interesting living American poet – is very distinctly Transatlantic. Furthermore, I have never yet been able to be anything or anyone except myself, and any effort in that direction would be futile and, since I am a well known poet in England, unnecessary.[27]

Art and Letters expired in 1920. Osbert had enjoyed his involvement enough to want to try something of the sort again. Within a couple of years he was suggesting to Sydney Schiff that there was room for a revised and improved version. Wyndham Lewis and Sachie might also be directors. Something was badly needed to show that 'there really was an *English* modern movement in prose, poetry and painting – serious as well as witty – but not *dull* and not edited by vague ladies with literary friends'.[28] Presumably he had canvassed Lewis first, for only a few days later Schiff received a letter from the latter to urge the creation of a 'Sitwell Review' of which he would control the Art side.[29] Schiff seems to have resisted the idea and it was not long before Lewis turned against his putative co-director.

Osbert was busy picking other literary quarrels at the time. The fashionable novelist Michael Arlen caused great offence when he allegedly adopted one of Osbert's short stories, 'covered it with slime; missed any point there may have been', and put it in his latest book, the formidably best-selling novel of 1924, *The Green Hat*. According to Osbert, the 'horrible little Armenian' had then added insult to injury by congratulating him on the excellence of the story, which he claimed only just to have read.[30] Osbert complained to his publisher, who evidently persuaded him that no redress was possible. All seems to have been soon

---

*An extravagant boast, since *Prufrock* appeared in the United States more than a year before Osbert published his first poem.

forgiven; within a few years he was happily accepting a commission to write a portrait in verse of the offending author.[31] The link between *The Green Hat* and Osbert's story was anyway so tenuous as to be almost unnoticeable.

Another short-lived breach was with Aldous Huxley. Huxley notoriously cannibalised his friends and enemies when writing his books. In his first novel, *Crome Yellow*, in 1921, he had caricatured Garsington and the Morrells with a vigour which caused much distress to the hostess of Garsington, Lady Ottoline. But he had also endowed Henry Wimbush – the Philip Morrell figure – with certain characteristics patently lifted from Sir George Sitwell, notably his antiquarian interests and remoteness from humanity.[32] For him or his siblings to mock their parents was one thing, Osbert felt; for others to intrude on the same ground was quite another – bad taste if not actually breach of copyright. The following year, however, still worse offence was given. In a short story, 'The Tillotson Bequest', Huxley all too obviously based on Osbert the character of an enormously rich aristocrat, Lord Badgery, who 'refused to have anything to do with politics or war' but instead patronised the arts. Like Osbert, he 'had an alarming habit of changing the subject of any conversation that had lasted for more than two minutes'; like Osbert he relished situations that others found painful or embarrassing: 'Behind the heavy waxen mask of his face, ambushed behind the Hanoverian nose, the little lustreless pig's eyes, the pale thick lips, there lurked a small devil of happy malice that rocked with laughter.'[33]

The portrait was hardly charitable and it stung. Osbert, however, preferred to base his objections on the fact that Huxley had taken his story from an incident which he himelf had told him about a certain Harry Melvill, once a great figure in London society, whom Osbert had encountered in his dotage in Monte Carlo, pathetically rehearsing to himself the monologues for which he had formerly been celebrated. It was *his* story, and Huxley had stolen it. Though he was in time to resume his friendship with Huxley, Osbert never forgave the offence; twenty years later he told a friend that Huxley was 'a preacher by nature, a charming intelligent, kind preacher who is always discovering the obvious . . . with a shock of surprise. He is . . . never original, always derivative.'[34] For Osbert, however, the incident had an unexpected and, on the whole, beneficial consequence. In the foreword to his *Collected Stories* in 1953 he wrote that he had turned to short stories because they, and novels, had always been his favourite reading, because he wanted a rest from the ferocity of the poetry critics and, 'thirdly, because I designed to save my stories for my own pen, since a friend of mine . . . had taken to writing the tales I could not resist relating to him, and to producing them either as his own short stories, or as episodes in the witty, rather bumpy novels he wrote'.[35] His first short story, 'The Machine Breaks Down', recycles the story of Harry Melvill which Huxley had poached for his own purposes. To this, for good measure, Osbert added a caricature of Aldous Huxley himself, William Erasmus, a writer 'very much on the look-out for copy . . . always watching, listening and peering'. He echoed Huxley's pasquinade by referring to 'my fleshy Hanoverian face and big body', but contrasted this appearance with that of Erasmus, 'tall and thin as a young girl, with the small head of some extinct animal, some kind of vegetarian creature that subsisted on the nibbled tops of young palm-trees in the oases – the Giant Sloth, for example'.[36] He read this story to Ada Leverson, who had previously deplored his decision to abandon politics. 'I feel happy now, you were right to give up the thought of Scarborough,' she exclaimed enthusiastically, and was instrumental in getting it published in the *English Review*.[37]

'The Machine Breaks Down' was one of Osbert's more successful short stories, witty, elegant and compact, but he could not base a career as a short-story writer solely on episodes in his own life. In Amalfi, probably at the end of 1922, he began seriously to address himself to the writing of fiction. He admired the masters of short-story writing – Kipling, Maugham, de la Mare – but he decided that he did not wish to model himself on any one of them. He held that 'each story should be conceived as a poem and fashioned in the style, couched in the language that itself and its theme imposed'.[38] The principle was admirable, but first catch your theme. Osbert found himself floundering. He sent what he had written to Arnold Bennett with an appeal for help: 'I have been writing something which I suppose, but I can't help feeling quite wrongly, to be a novel. I can't quite make out what it is really.' Bennett's reply does not survive but its substance is clear enough. 'I see exactly what you mean,' Osbert responded. 'I had realised that it was not a story but a sketch – in fact I had contemplated a 'Book of Characters' – but what I had not realised . . . is the importance of anecdote. It is a terribly difficult thing to begin writing short stories.'[39]

Osbert never stopped producing sketches. His main qualification for writing short stories, he claimed, was 'a love and understanding of human beings'.[40] He was indeed exceptionally adept in creating characters and in placing them firmly in their social and geographical environment, but he did not know what to do with them once they were there. His stories often petered out; when he arrived at a climax more often than not it seemed contrived. He once admitted to Beverley Nichols that he was not really an imaginative or creative writer. He could not write a story from nothing. 'Everything had to come out of his experience.'[41] The same could be said of many, perhaps most, great writers, but the test of artistry lay in the extent to which the experience was digested and transmuted into something new. Too often, with Osbert, the raw material remained recognisably raw and once he had exhausted it he fell back on sterile and sometimes tedious word-play. 'What a lot of words you know,' the Duchess of York wrote to him after reading *Dumb Animal*, his second collection of short stories, 'pleasant-sounding words strung pleasantly together and entrancing to read or listen to. I wish that I knew more.'[42] The comment was kindly meant but it was also a shrewd and valid criticism. 'Pleasant-sounding words strung pleasantly together' may be entrancing to read but they do not in themselves constitute great art or anything near to it. A few of Osbert's short stories are of outstanding quality, nearly all are agreeable to read, but by the highest standards he is no more than second rate.

He was also inclined to use his stories as a vehicle to attack those who had offended him – and sometimes those who had not. 'Triple Fugue', the longest story in the collection with that title, which was published in 1924, took swipes at Ottoline Morrell, Gosse and John Squire, and also contained a sustained caricature of Edward Marsh, who had done Osbert no harm at all except by his association with the various volumes of *Georgian Poetry*. Marsh became Mattie Dean, 'a great patron of the arts, ancient and modern; a patron of advanced art even – as long as it has not advanced too far to make safe its retreat'. For good measure Osbert added an attack on literary prizes, the award of the Pecksniff Prize for English Literature being described in entertaining if somewhat laboured detail. He wrote to his publisher to point out that Chatto were advertising a new book as 'Hawthornden Prize Winner'. 'I wish you would insert an advertisement in *The Times*: "*Triple Fugue* by Osbert Sitwell, which did *not* win the Hawthornden Prize for 1924." It's so much more distinguished.'[43]

Osbert always maintained that the characters in 'Triple Fugue' were creatures of his imagination, and that therefore no one had the right to take offence. He can hardly have expected Lytton Strachey to believe it when he protested to him that Lady Septuagesima Goodley was in no way based on Ottoline Morrell;[44] the caricature was cruelly accurate and the author had barely troubled to add even a modicum of camouflage. He had slightly more of a defence in the case of Professor Crisscross. The professor recognisably owed some features to Gosse but, as Osbert told the latter's biographer, the character was 'a fantasia on certain themes', and its portrayal in no way affected the fact that 'I very much liked and respected Sir Edmund'.[45] Gosse took no offence; nor did Ottoline Morrell, who had never considered Osbert a close friend and had been far more upset by the insults of Huxley and D. H. Lawrence, but Marsh was hurt by the attack and became a dangerous enemy.[46]

Siegfried Sassoon read the account of the prize-giving and protested angrily that it all seemed pathetically trivial: 'I can't understand Osbert thinking such stuff worth printing.'[47] 'Triple Fugue' is, indeed, unduly preoccupied with in-jokes and parish-pump polemics. Its harsh treatment of all the main protagonists lends force to the accusation in the *Times Literary Supplement* that 'Dislike, contempt or ridicule is Mr Sitwell's cardinal feeling for his characters'.[48] 'Low Tide', another story included in *Triple Fugue*, and one of Osbert's best evocations of life at Scarborough, gave rise to the same charge. Osbert was accused of having no sense of pity. Pity 'is for the reader to feel and for the writer to make him feel', Osbert retorted. The very fact that this reader had complained showed that pity had been aroused; 'As to the writer, it is difficult to write between sobs.'[49] In this case one's sympathies are with Osbert. The grotesque yet gallant Misses Cantrell-Cooksey, who are the main characters in 'Low Tide', are described with a clinical dispassion which is far more poignant for not being sentimental. Few readers will not feel pity for them or doubt that the author felt it too. But when Osbert was grinding one of his literary axes or lashing out at some cherished butt, then dispassion yielded to dislike and pity disappeared.

Triple Fugue was successful enough to make the publisher want a second volume. It was six years before sufficient stories were available. *Dumb Animal*, published in 1930, showed all the strengths but also the weaknesses of the earlier collection: the characters still more exaggerated; the satire unrelenting; the wit sharp, some of the descriptive passages genuinely eloquent.[50] The same old Aunt Sallies were disinterred for a fresh drubbing. Joe Bundle was a minor and obviously 'Georgian' poet: 'Apart from his altogether exceptional knowledge of bird-life (the only other qualification, besides ill-health and its latent promise of an early decease, that is demanded by the public as essential in an English poet) it was understood from the very beginning that in some peculiar, almost mystic way he was not only connected, but positively identified with the soil of Sussex.' One of the funnier stories, 'That Flesh is Heir to . . .', featured Muriel Chitty, a 'walking microbe', who carried disease around with her, gleefully spreading it to all she met. Mrs Chitty was very obviously based on a celebrated London hostess and friend of Osbert's, Violet Hammersley. Mrs Hammersley was not amused. Osbert wrote hopefully to appease her: 'Read this story twice and you will realise it was a great compliment.' 'Dear Osbert,' she replied coolly, 'I am unable to realise the compliment as I am unable to read the story twice.'[51]

Another story got him into worse trouble. The longest piece, almost a novella in its own right, was called 'Happy Endings'. It had made Sir George 'rather cross', Osbert reported with satisfaction.[52] Unfortunately Sir George was not the only one to take offence. The story described Osbert's time at the Army College, with some exaggeration but so much identifiable detail as to make the source of his inspiration indefensibly obvious. With an irresponsibility that verged on the suicidal he endowed the head-master, Mr Welch – called, for the occasion, Mr Slowcombe – with a wife who was both separated from him and demented, without first taking the trouble to find out that the real Mrs Welch had had a nervous breakdown, but was disastrously alive and quite *compos mentis* enough to sue for libel. 'I hardly know her,' Osbert protested unconvincingly, 'but probably the character is, as always with imaginative writing, exactly as she is.'[53] Mrs Welch demanded the destruction of the 600 copies left in stock, the withdrawal of the book from libraries, the omission of the story from future editions, £500 in damages and 50 guineas in costs.[54] Osbert subsequently claimed that he had asked his publisher whether there was a risk of libel, but Thomas Balston, the editor responsible, was a careful and experienced man and it seems likely that, if consulted, he would at least have suggested that the facts be checked before printing. Osbert had nobody to blame but himself, though this did not stop him lashing out angrily at his victim. 'That horrid old woman,' he wrote. 'It must, in any case, be the first book she's ever read, and I suppose if you do read a book, suddenly, after seventy years, it's a bit of a shock.'[55] In the end a compromise was worked out which left Osbert battered but unbankrupted; his publishers very decently advanced him £545 to enable him to pay the costs and damages. The settlement was unexpectedly good, Balston considered, 'but I realise that even so they are cruel enough for you. It must be exasperating to have lost nearly all the profits of many months of labour in this way.'[56]

The supportive publisher was Duckworth. Osbert's publisher until 1925 had been Grant Richards; a man of charm and taste but bad at business and, as it turned out in the end, decidedly unscrupulous. Ada Leverson had put them in touch and at first all went swimmingly. Increasingly, however, Richards had become more unreliable and reluctant or unable to pay the anyway exiguous royalties. Osbert told Christabel Aberconway in November 1925 that he was 'doing very dirty and nefarious, and for me very expensive tricks. But don't tell anyone . . . as I can't help liking the brute and am not certain that it may not be alright in the end.'[57] It wasn't, and throughout that winter Osbert bombarded his peccant publisher with demands for money. Finally he struck, and announced that he was moving to another house: 'It is a great grief to me to lose you as a publisher and I hope that it will not mean that I lose you as a friend as well.'[58] His plan had been to take his existing books with him as a dowry but Richards clung on to them. Then, in 1933, Richards sold the rights in two titles, *Triple Fugue* and *Discursions on Travel, Art and Life*, to two publishers at once and went off to Paris to squander the £800 he had netted from the deal.[59] In the end the rival owners sorted matters out more or less amicably; Osbert's publishers swopped the two Sitwell titles for two books by D. H. Lawrence which Martin Secker wanted. The Lawrence books were *The White Peacock* and *Sons and Lovers*;[60] given the subsequent publishing history of the two authors it is difficult not to feel that Secker had the better of the deal.

Duckworth, who had stood by Osbert so stoutly during the libel action, was an altogether more solid firm than Grant Richards, though not among the most powerful or thrusting in the field. Most of the work in the house was done by Thomas Balston, a conscientious and sensible man who had put some money into the firm and, perhaps for this reason, was viewed askance by the eponymous publisher, Virginia Woolf's half-brother and bugbear, Gerald Duckworth. It was Balston who travelled to Amalfi early in 1926 and signed up all three Sitwells.[61] Osbert had the greatest respect for Balston's judgment and liked him as a man, but his only personal friend in the organisation was a young junior editor, Anthony Powell. Osbert was apt to spend several hours in the Duckworth office, conferring with Balston, gossiping and discussing the merits of other authors on the Duckworth list. These, at various times, included Evelyn Waugh, Ronald Firbank, Elinor Glyn, Galsworthy, Gerhardie and Ford Madox Ford, but Osbert, Powell remembered, 'could feel competitive about the most insignificant of writers'. Always he was asking about his rivals' sales, questioning the extravagant

amounts poured out on their advertisements, deploring the par-
simonious publicity which his own works were granted. When he had
finished what he supposed to be his business, Osbert would often suggest
to Powell that he should accompany him as far as the end of the street.
Since Henrietta Street was long and Osbert walked slowly, often stopping to talk, the outing could sometimes take an hour or more.[62]

Grant Richards had urged Osbert to widen his repertoire as a
professional writer by producing a book of travel pieces. Little
persuasion was needed. Though Osbert disliked trains, was terrified by
aeroplanes and took little pleasure in sea voyages, travel for him was 'a
necessity, almost a mania'. He loved to write about his experiences: 'To
all writers,' he declared, 'whether chiefly concerned with the exterior or
the interior of the world, books of travel are the most stimulating,
lending wings to head and pen, effecting an absolute, if transient rescue
from care, from pain, even from the nearness of death itself.'[63] He had
begun to place his travel articles in journals like the *Nation* or the
Weekly Westminster Gazette as early as 1922 and quickly built up a
considerable body of work. His speciality was the baroque, in particular
Italian baroque, a field where Sachie led the way but which was as yet so
little exploited that there was plenty of scope for both brothers to work
without intruding on each other's preferred areas of exploration. One of
the first articles that he published was on Lecce, a small town far down
in the heel of Italy, fifty miles south-east of Taranto. The piece illustrates
vividly the limitations but, still more, the great strengths of his travel-
writing. Osbert was not a serious scholar; there was already a perfectly
adequate if little-known book by Martin Briggs which dealt thoroughly
with Lecce and Osbert offered no new information or insights of serious
significance. What he could do, sometimes marvellously well, was to take
a subject almost unknown to the average English reader and make it
comprehensible and interesting by the intensity of his observation, the
virtuosity of his writing and the explosive warmth of his enthusiasm. His
style was particularly well suited to its subject. Writing of the palace at
Lecce, he says of the windows that they are

> works of a rich fantasy; each one a separate work of art, yet each essential
> to the design of the whole building. The themes upon which these fantasies
> are built up are culled from the common sights of the Leccese countryside.
> They are drawn from the full, formal curl of the cabbage-leaf, as lovely as
> any acanthus . . . , from the swags of flowers that drop in such architectural
> form under each side of a swelling Spanish balcony, from the wreaths and

strings of tomatoes and pimentoes, the clusters of water melons, grapes, mellowing apples and fissuring pomegranates, that are hung up to dry or ripen beneath the flaming autumn sun.[64]

Cultural cross-references abound. He watched the procession on Good Friday in the Piazza della Prefettura, 'curling like a dragon, with mournful cries, wailing, and the brazen tongue of a trumpet, while high above were held up the illuminated sacred images and relics', and was reminded of 'figures from some ballet by Callot, or from a drawing of the Inquisition by Della Bella or Goya'. Sometimes such parallels seem precious or intended to impress the reader, more often they are genuinely illuminating. Osbert did have, as the cliché has it, 'a well-stocked mind'; images from one art form did intrude upon him when he was contemplating another, his writing was sometimes extravagantly rococo but it was never meretricious or insincere. He was at his best when describing what appealed to him most: the juxtaposition of people and places, the crowd celebrating the feast of St Andrew in Amalfi, the young bucks of Catania, 'whose dress is almost too elegant, though, as they think, thoroughly English, whose cloth-topped patent-leather boots are too shiny, whose suits are too carefully cut'.

By 1925 he had enough pieces accumulated to make a book, the pretentiously named *Discursions on Travel, Art and Life*. As well as the article on Lecce, there were other pieces on southern Italy – notably a memorable account of the great but almost forgotten Carthusian monastery, the Certosa di Padula – a report of his visit to d'Annunzio in Fiume and an excursion to the German baroque of Bayreuth and Würzburg. Inevitably Osbert slipped in the occasional jibe against his father – the only Englishman competent to describe the gardens of Lecce but who had 'the misfortune to be elderly, and to disapprove of anything later than the first Black Death'. Nor did he spare 'the democratic noisy dadaism of Mr Alfred Noyes and – if such there be – his like'. Such solecisms, however, were mercifully few and far between. On the whole, the *Discursions* were impressive and enjoyable; Cyril Connolly said that they had had an important educational influence on him,[65] and though they did not blaze a trail as significant as Sachie's earlier *Southern Baroque Art*, they contributed substantially to opening the eyes of the English to a world of which they were deeply ignorant. Osbert, however, saw them in later life as slightly embarrassing juvenilia. 'What a badly written book it is,' he observed when Macmillan proposed a new edition. 'It astonishes me, and I don't know that I dare risk republishing.'[66]

Two years later Osbert contemplated another literary departure. A publisher planning a series of short biographies suggested that he should contribute one on Augustus John. Osbert was attracted by the idea and wrote to Christabel Aberconway, a friend of John's, to ask her to sound him out.

> He's a splendid fable and a legend, and I should see that he remained one; and the fact that we don't know each other fearfully well, would help it. And between us we could lie and spin stories as much as we would like. All this, of course, on the assumption that I think he's a grand man really, and would see to it that others did: which is the reason that I might write a biography; not a form I care for. But, just when every little person is busy knocking off the corners of the great dead, and removing the statues from their pedestals, it would be interesting to try to substitute a living figure, on the grand scale, for one of them.[67]

Augustus John admired Osbert's writing. The previous year he had read his first novel, *Before the Bombardment*, and had reported to Lady Aberconway that he was 'happy but rather weak with laughter'.[68] Possibly he could not bear the thought of being the subject of a biography; possibly Lady Aberconway, for her own obscure reasons, took against the idea; possibly Osbert himself thought better of it. Whatever the reason, it came to nothing. It would anyway have been no more than an extended essay, but it might still have been perceptive and entertaining. Osbert wrote at some length on Rowlandson and Sickert; a biography of John, however slight, would have completed an intriguing triptych.

The fact that he was put forward for what would have been an important commission shows how Osbert's reputation had grown since the days of *Wheels*. His fame was not reflected in his earnings. His literary income in the tax year 1923/4, he told Hollingworth, was £20: 'Two articles for *Vogue* brought me in £14 and odd poems, I believe, 6.' In the following year he expected a considerable increase, perhaps to as much as £100. 'You can tell the Inspector,' he concluded, 'that as regards earning money, his profession is more lucrative than a poet!'[69] But his fame was out of all proportion greater than these humble rewards suggested. The Sitwells collectively had established a reputation, particularly among the young, which had outstripped their actual achievements. When Cecil Beaton asked what he should do in life he was told not to bother, 'Just become a friend of the Sitwells and wait and see what happens.'[70] Gosse, addressing the Literary Society at Lincoln

College, Oxford, in 1927, concluded that the authors who interested the undergraduates were the Sitwells, Joyce, T. S. Eliot and Sassoon.[71] For every one person who had read, let alone bought, the books of Osbert Sitwell, ten knew something of him and his family; it was not exactly the sort of renown he would have chosen but it was a great deal better than nothing.

A sign of fame, or at least notoriety, is that somebody thinks it worth writing one's biography. Osbert did not have a biography of his own but in 1925 a minor literary figure called R. L. Megroz announced that he wanted to do a book about all three Sitwells. 'On the whole I think Megroz's book will be a good thing,' Osbert told Grant Richards. He judged that the would-be biographer was an admirer and a safe man and he liked the idea of being commemorated in this way. 'I will give him all the help I can when I return.'[72] He kept his word, inviting Megroz to Renishaw, showing him papers and holding forth endlessly on the literary principles of the three Sitwells. The result was not as appalling as it might have been; *The Three Sitwells* was hagiographic and insipid but the author was not stupid and he made some perceptive and even sometimes modestly critical remarks about his heroes' writings. Osbert was gratified. 'I think you've done us an amazing amount of good,' he wrote appreciatively. 'For though many of the papers are not very polite about it, in dealing with us, all proceed to quote what you say as if it was their own idea! . . . I shall always be grateful to you.'[73]

Frank Megroz was already hard at work when Osbert paid his first visit to the United States. Siegfried Sassoon had tried to organise a lecture tour for him in 1919 but had failed to raise sufficient interest in somebody who was still relatively obscure in England and unknown across the Atlantic.[74] Now his fame had spread, if only to a small and anglophile section of society. He was sped on his way by a luncheon given in his honour at the Savoy: Augustine Birrell was in the chair and among the sixty guests were Clive Bell, Arnold Bennett, C. B. Cochran, Gerald du Maurier, Gosse, the cartoonist David Low, Sassoon, Walton, H. G. Wells and Humbert Wolfe. That so many dignitaries took the trouble to turn up – and indeed pay – for such a luncheon was an impressive tribute to Osbert's standing. 'It was exceedingly well done,' recorded Bennett. Birrell, aged seventy-six, made two excellent speeches and was 'lively as a boy'.[75]

The ostensible reason for Osbert's visit was to help with the promotion of his first novel, but not much seemed to be done in this direction. George Doran, his publisher, gave a large dinner in his honour and he was lavishly fêted, but he never left New York and did little lecturing. Muriel Draper was one of the many hostesses who entertained him. She invited the novelist Ford Madox Ford 'to meet Captain Osbert Sitwell'. 'You cannot ask *Colonel* Ford to meet *Captain* Sitwell,' she was told sternly.[76] (Possibly someone had told Ford that Osbert's nickname for him was Freud Madox Fraud.) Osbert was on the whole well behaved, but could not resist from time to time making a little mischief. One of the starchier New York hostesses enquired anxiously about 'the exact social position of Lady Colefax in London'. 'Well,' Osbert replied, 'you see, we have no colour prejudice at all in England. But it does seem to me odd that here, where you mind these things, you should receive her.' A look of consternation came over the face of the enquirer: 'Why, you don't mean to say she's a Black, Mr Sitwell? Do you mean that . . . we were receiving a negress in our house without knowing it? Well, I call that a dreadful thing for her to do.'[77]

Osbert found New York noisy and exhausting but on the whole enjoyed it. He wrote on his return about the kindness and lavishness of American hospitality, but also about the respect for intelligence and expert opinion which he had encountered across the Atlantic. There was none of that 'silly rudeness towards modern art and artists' which was met with so regularly in England.[78] His private opinion was rather more equivocal. He never went to bed before 5.00 a.m. and lived off cocktails, he told Sachie: 'I don't think there's much hope for the future here, tho' it's amusing and interesting. And I've never before realised how intensely European I am.'[79] D. H. Lawrence, more bluntly, said Osbert had told him he loathed America.[80] So categoric a denunciation certainly overstated his feelings, but for another twenty years he cherished the illusion that the sensibilities of American readers were less subtle than those of their European counterparts. When in 1945 he discussed an American edition of one of his books with his friend, the formidably blue-stocking Madame Guéritte, he admitted: 'In general, my attitude to America has been "It's your money I want!" Their good opinion is of less value to me.'[81] Only after the Second World War, when the love affair between Osbert, Edith and the American people began to flourish extravagantly, did he conclude that, after all, the good opinion of his transatlantic readers was something to be greatly prized.

8

No Love and No Buried Treasure

LITERATURE exists perpetually in a state of transition, but in the decade after the First World War the transit appeared unusually tempestuous. When Osbert began work on his first novel in 1925 he could have looked in widely different directions for role-models to guide him along his way. If the average British reader, of sound but conservative taste, had been asked to name the leading novelists of the day, he would probably have opted for John Galsworthy, Arnold Bennett and H. G. Wells. The first was anathema to Osbert; when Galsworthy died he remarked how curious it was that the author of the *Forsyte Saga* should have succumbed to 'precisely the thing which has made the success of all his work, anaemia!'[1] Bennett he admired but had no wish to emulate. Wells he believed to be a genius but, as he told Rebecca West a few years later, he felt that his political utterances had become repellent and had 'almost ruined him as a writer'.[2] For the more adventurous yet still anglocentric readers, Virginia Woolf and D. H. Lawrence ranked highest in the pantheon. Woolf, Osbert esteemed, but equivocally. 'She can make a fender of consuming interest to the lover of fine prose,' he wrote, 'but alas! the day may come when equality ceases to reign, and fenders will once more yield precedence to man as the proper study of mankind.'[3] Lawrence he rated far higher as a novelist, but he knew that he never could nor wanted to write books like *Sons and Lovers* or *Women in Love*.

In the background, still little known except to a tiny coterie, loomed gigantic figures like Joyce, Kafka, Proust. Joyce, Osbert dismissed as an amazing freak, building a new language 'for the use of generations yet unborn – and in the opinion of many, likely to remain so'.[4] Kafka he admired; Proust he revered. 'What an amazing author he was,' he wrote.

'After you have read his book nothing is ever the same as it was before, everything is bathed in a new and revealing light.'[5] He freely admitted that *Remembrance of Things Past* had influenced him more than any other work when he came to write his autobiography. But his grasp of French was weak enough to force him to depend on Scott-Moncrieff's translation – a source of double chagrin since he detested Scott-Moncrieff even more than he deplored his own dependence on a second-hand version of the masterpiece. He could have read *Swann's Way* by the time he started his own first novel but he makes no recorded reference to Proust till some years later. If any contemporary writer influenced Osbert in the mid-1920s, it was probably that rococo fantasist Ronald Firbank, whose extravagant and innovative creations did so much to shape the development of the English novel in the 1930s. If challenged, Osbert himself would probably have claimed Dickens and Flaubert as his twin lode-stars, widely disparate geniuses, the one for his explosive imagination and passionate interest in human nature and human society, the other for his balance, his discipline, the exquisite precision of his writing.

Osbert stated his own ideals in a lecture on the modern novel:

> The first necessity of the novel – which is art – is that it should conform to the rules that govern every other art form: it must be considered as an entity, not a thing to be chopped up and changed: it must be dreamt rather than thought out: it must well up from the sub-conscious mind, not be forced down: it must, in fact, be a poem, an empty poem, as it were, a shape to be filled at the imperious discretion of the artist.[6]

As a blueprint for the embryo writer this may be considered a little imprecise, but Osbert followed the precept conscientiously in his own first novel. *Before the Bombardment* was a work of art, a concept skilfully crafted but emerging intact from the subconscious, an entity. It did not follow that it was a wholly successful novel. It was set in Scarborough – Scarborough, under the name of Newborough, was indeed the leading character of the book. The plot was exiguous. A rich old lady, Miss Collier-Floodgaye, and her companion, Miss Bramley, winter in Newborough. Miss Bramley jealously defends her employer against the advances of a local family, the Floodgays, who are no relation but who take advantage of the similarity in names to claim distant cousinship. Her efforts avail nothing; the Floodgays ingratiate themselves successfully and when the old lady suddenly falls ill and sends for a lawyer, her companion suspects that a new will is about to be drawn up, depriving her of the legacy which she had been promised. She plays for time, Miss Collier-Floodgaye dies before the lawyer arrives, it then transpires that she wanted only to sign her existing will, by which her companion would have benefited. As it is, she dies intestate, a distant cousin inherits everything, Miss Bramley is left to seek another job. The 'Bombardment' of the title – based on the German bombardment of Scarborough in 1914 – occurs in an epilogue and is almost entirely irrelevant to the action.

There are many good things about *Before the Bombardment*, some very good things. Life in pre-1914 Scarborough is vividly evoked and the picture of this snobbish, introverted, limited society could hardly be improved. The central characters are well described and totally convincing; especially the companion, a class for whom Osbert felt a strange sympathy, and Miss Collier-Floodgaye herself, who 'yearned for friendship . . . and since, through lack of charm, by a total deficiency in all social qualities, she was debarred from making friends in the usual way, she was in the end obliged to buy one'. The *Tatler* complained, 'All the time one's sympathies are rather with his victims than with the author,' and concluded, 'Captain Sitwell has no pity.' This is presumably the source of the comment which Osbert had attached to 'Low Tide' in the preface to his collected short stories, and his defence is as valid in either case.* It was the author's job to evoke pity in the reader, not to manifest it himself. Miss Collier-Floodgaye is conspicuously un-appealing. Osbert's treatment of her could fairly be called cool, even clinical. Yet in the end the portrait is compassionate as well as understanding.

The wit, too, is often sharp, even if those acquainted with Osbert's prejudices will be unsurprised by its targets. One of his rasher sallies was against the horse, which, he wrote, though occasionally beautiful, was the stupidest of animals, 'merely an obsolete method of locomotion, an animated, strong-willed and headstrong Stephenson's Rocket'. This got him into fearful trouble. Mr Lawrence A. Booth for one wrote indignantly that the book deserved to be boycotted, 'if only because of his un-English remarks regarding the horse. I wonder if he saw the splendid service which the horse rendered in France during the war.'[7] Did Mr Booth not know, Osbert's friend, the painter C. R. W. Nevinson, retorted, that the horse had done equally splendid service for the Germans? Perhaps it was this that Captain Sitwell had seen, and he was

*See p. 126 above.

merely voicing patriotic disapproval. Mr Booth subsided. Where the minor characters are concerned, however, the satire sometimes grows depressingly broad, and the sketches are perfunctory. The clergyman who has grown rich by inventing a device for retrieving ping-pong balls from under a sofa, or the ladies running the flower-stall at a bazaar – 'Hon. Mrs D. Rickety Rudyer, Miss Persephone Rudyer, Lady Racket, Mrs Rolls, Mrs Rump and Miss Ruby Rump' – seem depressingly trivial when contrasted with the finely realised portraits of the sad old ladies at the heart of the book.

Constant Lambert remembered Sir George remarking shortly before publication that it would be a strange novel, with 'no love and no buried treasure. I fear it may not find great favour with the public.'[8] Osbert told the same story but made his father complain that there was 'no love interest and no hero or heroine'.[9] Whichever formula is preferred, Sir George had a point. *Before the Bombardment* has many merits but it is emotionally etiolated and short on plot. Osbert hopefully sent copies to certain fellow authors: Virginia Woolf's was inscribed 'Tremblingly from the Author', Arnold Bennett's to 'dear good uncle Arnold from a nephew'. Woolf's views are unknown but can be guessed without too much difficulty. Bennett wrote in his journal: 'Well, it is difficult to read. Very brilliant, or perhaps rather brilliant: but it doesn't seem to have much form and much individual interest. The man *describes* characters instead of showing them.'[10] Comments on books can generally be graded in sincerity according to whether they are made directly to the author, for the public eye in a review, to a friend, or for the writer's private satisfaction. Bennett's comment came in the last, and usually most reliable, category; Logan Pearsall Smith's judgment that it was 'a sustained masterpiece of irony' was in the first and least reliable.[11]

It should not be discounted totally for that reason, however. Many people thought highly of *Before the Bombardment*. Years later, James Agate in the *Daily Express* was to call it 'one of the twenty best novels written since the death of Dickens'. On publication, Mary Webb, in the *Bookman*, said that it was 'packed with wit, humour and subtlety';[12] 'A masterpiece,' concluded the *Morning Post*, while the *Irish Times* said it was 'difficult to praise too highly'. The insults, too, were often of a nature to encourage the reader to try his luck. 'Greenjade', in the *Sunday Express*, claimed that Osbert 'spat on the whole Victorian age' and the book should be called 'Great Expectorations'. The *Yorkshire Post*, its local pride affronted, judged that 'The literary coteries of London will, with justice, find this book clever. The people of Scarborough, with equal justice, will find it merely caddish.'[13] It was just as well that Osbert had renounced his political ambitions: the Mayor of Scarborough said that it was 'in thoroughly bad taste', while the Vicar pronounced it 'a vulgar caricature which should be treated with silent contempt.'[14]

It was D. H. Lawrence in his portrait of Sir Clifford Chatterley who made the most penetrating comments on Osbert's fiction-writing. Sir Clifford's production, he wrote, was 'curious, very personal stories about people he had known. Clever, rather spiteful, and yet, in some mysterious way, meaningless. The observation was extraordinary and peculiar. But there was no touch, no actual contact. It was as if the whole thing took place in a vacuum.'[15] This was as true of Osbert's short stories and later novels as of *Before the Bombardment*. The latter was his personal favourite, Osbert wrote twenty years later, 'because, I think, it is the first real vehicle of my particular view of life'.[16] He was right; Lawrence was describing not just Osbert's literary style but his innermost nature. Perhaps 'no touch, no actual contact' is too absolute a dismissal, but whatever Osbert wrote, whoever he was with, there would always be that quality of remoteness. The fact that he was able to appreciate *Sons and Lovers* is remarkable; the fact that he did not want to write such a book himself is unsurprising. Osbert did not just write books very different from those of Lawrence; he was almost a member of another race.

Lawrence was fascinated and slightly horrified by Osbert. He met Sir George first, he and his wife calling at Montegufoni in the summer of 1926. A queer old place, he found it 'a bit disheartening. He collects of all things, beds – room after room, bed after bed, as if he were providing for all the dead.' Do you put your guests in them? Lawrence asked. 'Oh! They're not to sleep in. They're museum pieces.' Lawrence sat in one of the 'gilt and wiggly-curved chairs. Oh! said Sir George in dismay. "Those chairs are not to sit in!" So I wriggled on the seat in the hopes it would come to pieces. Depressing!'[17] Sir George was equally perplexed, particularly by Frieda Lawrence. 'She jumped on all the beds,' he reported, 'to see if the mattresses were soft . . . When they signed their name in the visitors' book, she put, after hers, "*Geborene*", and then something I couldn't read. So extraordinary. *Of course* she was born. Everybody is.'[18]*

*The 'something' that Sir George could not read was Mrs Lawrence's maiden name, von Richthofen. It was perfectly legible – which suggests that Sir George was as ready as his son to adjust the truth for the sake of a good remark or story.

Next year Osbert and Edith repaid the compliment and went to tea with the Lawrences. They were very nice, reported Lawrence, 'and we liked them much better than we had thought'. But he found them extraordinarily absorbed in themselves and their parents, 'as if they were marooned on a desert island and nobody in the world but their lost selves. Queer!'[19] In his study of the Sitwell family, John Pearson has skilfully analysed how Lawrence's observations during this visit were grafted on to his portrait of Sir Clifford Chatterley, so that that unfortunate baronet ended up with some of Osbert's characteristics to add to those which he had enjoyed in an earlier draft.[20] Edith would never accept that the character had not been modelled on Osbert from the start. A baronet who wrote – who else could it be? The impotency with which Lawrence endowed Sir Clifford was a gratuitous insult, perhaps a smear at Osbert for being still unmarried and apparently uninterested in women at the age of thirty-six.[21] She clung to her view with all the rancorous determination that blighted her life; nearly forty years later she was still denouncing *Lady Chatterley's Lover* as 'a very dirty and completely worthless book, of no literary importance'. Sir Clifford, she claimed, was loathed by Lawrence because he had been 'so criminally offensive as to be a Baronet and he, with most men, fought like a tiger in the First World War, instead of remaining at home, fornicating and squealing shrilly about the oppressions from which he had suffered'.[22] In fact Lawrence does seem to have extracted several of Osbert's most marked characteristics – his alienation from so much of contemporary society, his rebellion against fathers, governments and all figures of authority, his morbid sensitivity – and given them to Sir Clifford. Wragby, the Chatterley home, had features of Renishaw; details of Sir George and Lady Ida, too, were apparent from time to time in earlier drafts; but the war injury, which left Sir Clifford impotent and rendered him the most celebrated cuckold of the twentieth century, had been part of Lawrence's concept long before his acquaintance with the Sitwells led him to modify his original idea.

Edith's furious denunciation of *Lady Chatterley's Lover*, as so often with her rages, rebounded on the very people she sought to protect. People who would never have thought of identifying Osbert with Sir Clifford now wondered whether they should do so. Lawrence himself wrote dismissively that the Sitwells, 'of course, want to be important at any price; poor souls'.[23] Osbert himself was for once wise enough to keep quiet. He had no doubt where Lawrence had drawn much of his inspiration. William Walton, he told Sachie from Amalfi, 'had an acute attack of sexual mania after reading Lawrence's book (about us) and his conversation is in consequence somewhat tedious'.[24] But he rarely referred to it at the time. The slur did rankle, though. In 1933 Lawrence's step-daughter, Mrs Barbara Barr, contemplated making a film of *Lady Chatterley's Lover* and cabled Osbert asking for permission to inspect Renishaw, presumably with a view to using it as a setting. It is hard to tell whether she was being ingenuous or gratuitously offensive. Osbert thought the latter and at once telegraphed Hollingworth instructing him to deny access to any representatives of a film company who might present themselves. He told Mrs Barr that he found her request as 'gross as it is libellous'.[25] In 1957 Edward Nehls, engaged in his study of Lawrence, asked Osbert if he could quote from this letter. He was welcome to publish 'my far too amiable telegram', Osbert replied. 'Of course Lawrence was a man of genius and one would put up with a good deal from him, but one cannot be expected to put up with as much from poor Mrs Barr.'[26] He did not endure Lawrence's offence as docilely as all that. In a novel published in 1933, *Miracle on Sinai*, he included a spirited assault on Lawrence as T. L. Enfalon, who liked to pose as a collier's son and whose 'nervous, ladder-like body was crowned, upon its long stooping neck, by a thinly bearded head of weak though intellectual order'. Such then, Osbert trumpeted, 'was the chief apostle of force, or, as he loved to call it, *guts*, in literature: a weak, weedy bearded man, stooping and emaciated: a belated, mid-nineteenth-century intellectual, despite the Italian mould in which his hypnotised admirers affected so clearly to see him'.[27] Osbert was 'perfect on the subject of the D. H. Laurence [*sic*] ménage,' rejoiced Edith, 'but they really deserve everything they have got, for Laurence's scandalous attack on Osbert'.[28]

Osbert did not consider C. K. Scott-Moncrieff, another of his bitterest enemies, to be anything approaching a man of genius; nothing, therefore, should be put up with from him. He had first come into the Sitwells' life as an admirer of Wilfred Owen but had not lasted long in this role; later Osbert even accused him of having 'in effect murdered' the young poet.[29] His first conspicuous offence, however, came in 1926 when he published a silly squib, 'The Strange and Striking Adventures of Four Authors in Search of a Character' – the authors being the Sitwells and William Walton. The four 'dear little children' live in a stately home, venture out in a barge, arrive, by way of the Alimentary Canal, at a dinner table in South Belgravia, hie here and there, and eventually return to their parents where they 'spend the remainder of their days in opulence and inanity'.[30] Osbert was not the most objective of critics when attacks on him or his family were in question but in this case the pointlessness of Scott-Moncrieff's satire justified his comment that 'the very folly and futility of it will tend one day to give it a certain interest as an example of what modern poets have had to endure at the hands of the jackals and boot-snatchers of the literary world'.[31] Shortly after this, Scott-Moncrieff met Osbert in a theatre and tried to shake hands. Osbert refused to reciprocate; Scott-Moncrieff asked why. 'Because I have for a long time disliked you, and because you have been impertinent,' Osbert answered loftily. He never relented; twenty years later he dismissed Scott-Moncrieff as 'a sad, twisted creature with an Anglican mind gone Catholic and an Academic mind struggling after modernity, but only really happy in the pages of *Punch*'.[32]

Robert Graves caused similar though less sharp offence by mildly disparaging comments about Osbert and Sachie in his autobiography. 'I haven't read *Goodbye to All That*,' wrote Osbert somewhat unconvincingly to Lady Aberconway, 'as I know it would infuriate me. He's so tiresome: schoolboy and schoolmaster in exact proportions of 50–50. At present the latter is more in evidence. He now behaves (on the strength of having left his wife and living with . . . Laura Riding, a bad modernist poet who copies G. Stein) as though he were Stein herself, Whitman, Picasso, Matisse and Stravinsky, rolled into one.'[33] Graves remained a friend of Edith's, which, given her passionate loyalty to her brothers, suggests that Osbert did not feel seriously disturbed by Graves's observations. When Osbert and Edith were instrumental in persuading Gertrude Stein to come to England to lecture at Oxford and Cambridge, Graves was among those invited to help fête the high-priestess of modernist literature. Stein was delighted by her reception and by the pains the Sitwells took to smooth her path. Osbert was a great comfort, she wrote – referring to herself in the third person. 'He so thoroughly understood every possible way in which one could be nervous that as he sat beside her in the hotel telling her all the ways that he and she could suffer from stage fright she was quite soothed. She was always very fond of Osbert. She always said he was like the uncle of a king. He had that pleasant kindly irresponsible agitated calm that an uncle of an English king always must have.'[34]

Another friend who fell temporarily out of favour was Cyril Connolly. The almost idolatrous enthusiasm which Connolly had felt for the Sitwells when an undergraduate had evolved into a more critical, sometimes even hostile stance. 'I don't hold with the Sitwells, you know,' he told his friend Noel Blakiston. 'I think they are very tiresome . . . Edith is tedious, humourless and combative, Osbert advertises, Sachie is the most remote, but none is really our style.'[35] He mocked Osbert in his journal:

> O Osbert father Osbert
> to whom the young men pray
> a Sitwell voice and Sitwell face
> bestow on me this day
> and teach me in society
> to cleave to what is best
> and ogle, flatter, boast, till I
> may stink like all the rest.[36]

But publicly, and as far as the Sitwells knew, he was still a devotee, even a disciple. Then, sometime in 1927, Connolly met up in Paris with a drunken set of friends, including William Walton. Walton turned on Connolly and said that he was just Desmond MacCarthy's bumboy. Connolly retorted: 'I'm no more Desmond MacCarthy's bumboy than you are Osbert Sitwell's.' Helpful friends reported to Osbert that Connolly had been going round Paris saying that Walton was his bumboy. The next Connolly heard of it was when he received a stiff letter from Osbert's solicitor demanding a recantation and an apology. 'I'm told that you daren't set foot in England lest you should be sued for libel by Osbert Sitwell,' his friend, the diplomat Gladwyn Jebb, wrote to him admiringly. 'I should have thought that your reputation would be made if only you could persuade him to sue you.'[37] Connolly took the threat more seriously. He abased himself, but a chill continued for several years. Then he did something to put himself back into the Sitwells' good books and found himself best friend again. 'This was typical of them,' he told John Pearson. 'You were either out in the cold or else you were with them. When you were out of favour nothing was too bad. But when you were in favour, they would take all the trouble in the world.' In fact, even when he was at his most censorious, Connolly never ceased to have considerable respect for Osbert's talents and some affection for him as a man. They were never the most intimate of friends, but their relationship was agreeable and useful to both of them.

To the casual acquaintance Osbert, towards the end of the 1920s, would have seemed contented and successful. Siegfried Sassoon, who was far more than a casual acquaintance, might have been expected to be more perceptive, but his account of a dinner party in Carlyle Square in June

1927 does not suggest much was amiss. He arrived a little early to be greeted by an urbane Osbert, wearing a white waistcoat, waving at him, hairbrush in hand, from an upstairs window. Francis Birrell was already there, speculating about the probable dreadfulness of a couple of unknown American guests. Osbert surged in, brandishing a cocktail-shaker full of some powerful ruby concoction. An indignant cry of 'I am disgusted' from outside proved to be Mrs Belloc Lowndes remonstrating with her taxi driver. Arthur Waley, scholar, translator from the Chinese and close friend of Osbert, arrived, and Steven Runciman, 'heavy-faced with rather affected gestures of hands (and voice)'. The Americans turned out to be dull and literary, 'laying waste tract after tract of conversational territory'. The food at least was delicious: excellent soup, lobster '*à la* something jaundice-producing', richly roasted chicken, strawberry ice. Sassoon catches a glimpse of Osbert conjuring with wobbly asparagus. He raises saturnine eyebrows, mutely querying 'ain't it a go?' After dinner Sachie arrives; he has lost his voice and talks in a husky undertone. Edith would be there too but has a sore throat. Waley and Osbert 'discuss the poetry of "Humbug" Wolfe. They think it should be stopped.' And so to bed; 'Don't like parties much,' Sassoon concluded.[38]

Wherever he was spotted Osbert seemed to be the centre of attention and a moving force. At dinner at Boulestin, where Rex Whistler and Cecil Beaton enjoyed 'Osbert's talk, the cheese sauces and red wines. Osbert has very early in life acquired the grand manner without pomposity. He tells a story with interruptions of "Huh Huh" as he himself enjoys the humour and looks quickly from one face to another for approval. He is generous in his appreciation of others' attempts at wit, snorting with painful grunts of suppressed laughter during an imitation of some friend or rival.'[39] At tea with the Charles Morgans, where their two-year-old son is brought down. He falls instantly in love with Osbert and gazes at him 'with such fixity as to prevent all conversation for ten minutes, at the end of which he is sick from sheer adoration'.[40] In the National Gallery, where Boris Anrep features him as the god of music in the mosaic pavement in the entrance hall. Virginia Woolf is Clio, Greta Garbo the muse of tragedy. He even acts as marriage counsellor to his more favoured friends, advising Somerset Maugham's interior-decorating wife Syrie to put off or abandon her divorce. Syrie took his advice. 'She told me that I was the *only* person who had suggested that it might not be a good thing.'[41] It was bad advice, anyway; the doomed marriage foundered shortly afterwards.

The Sitwell family painted by Sargent in 1900. The group portrait is a miracle of stylish artificiality: Sir George in riding-boots, though he rarely rode; Lady Ida arranging flowers, though she invariably left this task to others; Edith nestling up to a father she would never willingly have approached; the boys unconvincingly contented on the floor (p. 16)

The family photographed by Cecil Beaton thirty years later. Sacheverell's wife Georgia and their son Reresby have joined the group. Osbert is seated behind the table.

Renishaw from the south, photographed in 1910

Montegufoni in 1905, the south front and east baroque façade

Osbert painted by Nina Hamnett at the end of the First World War. She painted him in uniform and was dissatisfied, then tried again with him wearing 'a small "John Bull" top-hat … and that was much better'.

Osbert and Sacheverell by Max Beerbohm. Osbert's parrot says, 'Bravo, Sacheverell', Sachie's, 'Well done, Osbert'. Siegfried Sassoon thought the cartoon rather cruel and asked Osbert how he liked it. 'He said it made him look too thin (an attempt at a joke)'. But Osbert enjoyed it enough to put it in his autobiography.

The original plaster model for the sculpture of Osbert by Frank Dobson.
T. E. Lawrence described it as 'appropriate, authentic and magnificent …
as loud as the massed bands of the Guards'.

Wilfred Owen by John Gunston, 1916

Siegfried Sassoon by Pirie MacDonald,
*c.*1920

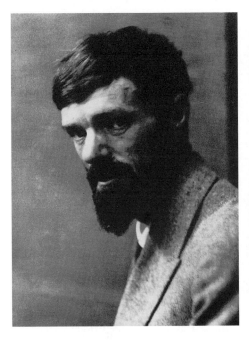

D. H. Lawrence by Nickolas Muray, 1920

William Walton by Cecil Beaton, 1926

Osbert and Edith at the wedding of Sacheverell and flanked by the bride's parents.
The occasion, as is only too apparent, filled Osbert with deep gloom.

All At Sea. 'It is a sort of *Charley's Aunt*,' Osbert told Grant Richards. 'I do trust it will succeed. It seems to me very amusing.'[56] It ran for only five nights, at the Arts Theatre Club in November 1929, with, Osbert wrote ruefully, 'unparalleled lack of success'; nobody appeared to be enjoying it except the two authors. In later life he admitted that he was 'rather ashamed of it' and felt that it was too facetious.[57] Arnold Bennett went to the first night. 'Not a play,' he noted. 'An entertainment. Funny in parts, but in more parts tedious.'[58]

The judgment erred on the side of charity. The play was dire. The action – if action is the proper word – was set on a luxury liner and turned on the fact that a lion-hunting hostess, Lady Flinteye, based on Sibyl Colefax, confused a young passenger of no importance with a celebrity and fêted him accordingly. The flimsy plot was a vehicle for some vaguely sub-Wilde epigrams – psychoanalysis was 'the young person's way of accounting for the older generation', while war was 'the old person's way of accounting for the younger generation'. It contained a few good lines but also others which must have been among the least sayable in twentieth-century drama. Even Coward would have quailed when confronted by: 'The camaraderie of the millionaire class is amazing and to my mind much more touching than that of the poor: for though they hate one another far worse than they hate any Bolshevik, yet there's nothing they won't do for one another.' The surprising thing is that the critics were not entirely hostile: the *Times Literary Supplement* said it was 'far wittier than most revues', while the representative of the *Morning Post* 'smiled gently most of the time'. Abuse was more common, however: the *New Statesman* described it as 'absurdly superfluous and fundamentally ineffective', while the *Sunday Express*, always quick to revile the Sitwells, found it 'Dreary drivel'.[59] When considering it in 1943 for adaptation and broadcasting, the BBC reader found it 'very visual, very thin, very incoherent'.[60]

The play was published at the same time as the Arts Theatre production, with a bad-tempered preface by Osbert rather longer than the play itself. He took the opportunity to restate all his complaints about the plight of the artist in Britain in the 1920s. 'A Few Days in an Author's Life', as Osbert entitled it, lashed out at critics, literary jackals (notably Scott-Moncrieff), fashionable modern comedies, democracy, the cult of the amateur, poverty, actors and actresses, gossip-columnists and 'the stupidity and supreme lack of interest in everything except motor-cars and night clubs of most of the young super-rich'. It was a 'long-drawn-out whine', said the *New Statesman*, 'utterly unnecessary and utterly unworthy either of the writer or of his brother and sister'. Siegfried Sassoon was more sympathetic but took Osbert to task with equal vigour:

> I must confess that I am rather perplexed by parts of your preface – 'good reading' though it is. Is it intended to be taken seriously? (when you refer to 'artist-baiting'). Haven't you and Edith and Sachie received adequate praise and recognition in the last few years? And if you object to gossip-writers, etc., why don't you close your door (and mouth) to them? I was under the impression that publicity has always been your favourite recreation . . . If you and the other two want to be free from annoyance by stupid and spiteful people, why don't you adopt my own method and give the whole caboodle the cold shoulder? . . . I am not preaching to you; I know how dreary most 'quite consistent' persons can be. My main reason for writing so candidly, is that if anyone asks me what I think of this week's *New Statesman*, I shall say very much the same as I am to you now. You can't accuse me of being envious or unfriendly. One more word – I have felt lately that your mind is too much occupied with 'what Lady Cunard said' to someone about you, or what Baba said to Georgia, and so on *ad infinitum*. Result: Nil.[61]

Sassoon slightly regretted the tone of this 'parental letter' when Christabel Aberconway sent him a sheaf of offensive attacks on Osbert and all his works which she had culled from the press. 'This is a time when their friends should stand by them,' he agreed. But they had still brought their trouble on themselves. 'If Osbert goes down into the arena he must expect to be insulted by the cads who are down there.' He considered himself, said Sassoon, one of Osbert's few real friends, 'most of the people he finds amusing in everyday life are not my friends and I have no use for them'.[62] Osbert seems to have taken Sassoon's strictures without bearing any grudge but he always believed that the preface to *All At Sea* was one of the most telling things that he had written. It was 'terrific', he told Sachie at the time. 'It is really rather good. Too good perhaps.' Even after he had lost all faith in the play itself he still felt the preface was well worth re-reading. As for *All At Sea* – 'I hope I shan't ever do anything like that again. It came from high spirits.'[63]

This débâcle, which had included an appearance by Osbert and Sachie playing themselves and reciting poems through megaphones, did not assuage their appetite for public spectacles. In June 1929 the three Sitwells were together again, at a poetry reading in the Mayfair home of Baroness d'Erlanger. The audience were 'mostly more diamonds than brains', noted William Plomer, a young writer recently arrived from

South Africa. Plomer was not much impressed by the performance, though he admired Edith's voice control, but what struck him most was the lack of rapport between the Sitwells and their audience, 'as if performers and hearers did not quite trust one another. There did not seem any reason why they should, nor was it possible to imagine a bridging of the gulf between them.' After all, he reflected, the Sitwells had led a resistance movement against the philistines of their own class why should they expect to be acclaimed in a Mayfair salon?[64] In fact they were received with perfect politeness, even moderate enthusiasm. They might have met with a less cordial reception at the dinner table of some hunting squire in Leicestershire but on the whole the upper classes endured the insults of the Sitwells with remarkable good humour. Some of the audience at Baroness d'Erlanger's may not have understood much of what was going on, but that they turned up at all was a tribute both to the Sitwells' prestige and their own tolerant curiosity.

The high spirits, to which Osbert had attributed *All At Sea*, were not much in evidence at the end of the 1920s; gloom shot through with a certain febrile gaiety was more apparent. Edwin Lutyens, whom Sir George from time to time consulted about new architectural excesses planned for Renishaw, visited there in 1928. He found Osbert 'as ever self-possessed and growing more like his grandfather George IV than ever.* Sachie is quick-tempered and with selfish Papa and unhappy dipsotic Lady Ida it was like being on a volcano.'[65] The gardens looked as if the volcano was already in eruption; Sir George had launched an extensive redevelopment which left his agent aghast. 'The amazing thing is that we are allowed to go on and finish the whole thing unless he writes and stops us,' Hollingworth told Osbert.[66] Inside the house the baiting of Sir George continued relentlessly. When a friend of his children, Ankeret Jackson, came to stay, Sir George asked Osbert what her interests were so that he could draw her out. Osbert improvised wildly and told his father that Miss Jackson was an authority on polar exploration, the embroidery of church vestments during the latter part of the thirteenth century and, above all, Sardinian silverware. For the next few days the unfortunate woman found herself quizzed remorselessly on subjects about which she knew and for which she cared nothing.[67] After dinner William Walton and Lord Berners would play duets until Sir

---

*Even if the decidedly questionable premise about the parentage of Lord Albert Conyngham were accepted, Lutyens missed out a couple of 'greats'.

George was driven to bed, after which Osbert would entertain his guests with 'unkind, amusing stories' about people he disliked, or sometimes whom he liked.[68]

Prominent among the former were his parents. Osbert wrote in despair to Sachie to report that Sir George was about to visit Vienna so as to have monkey glands injected – a then fashionable counter to the ageing process. 'This is really a bit *too much*,' he wrote indignantly. 'It means 170. I don't mind an ordinary 100. I shall therefore frighten him away with news of a mysterious epidemic. So if you hear that a new plague has broken out in Vienna, don't be disturbed.'[69] Although he treated his relationship with his father as a joke, the constant tension and Sir George's real or imagined onslaughts wore him down: 'Sleep eludes me constantly and consistently,' he told Virginia Woolf. His mother had installed at Renishaw two former ladies-in-waiting from the Greek Court, 'who bore me literally to death'. A year before he would have ignored them; now he was reduced to a frenzy of irritation.[70]

Many of Sir George's wilder enterprises existed only in Osbert's imagination or, as in the case of the expedition to Vienna, were little more than a vague idea which was never followed up. There was one initiative, however, which was certainly not dreamt up by Osbert, though it was neither as sustained nor as ferocious as he represented it. His father's campaign opened in the summer of 1928. 'You know, my darling, I am really devoted to you, and anxious to do all I can for you,' wrote Sir George, but he felt certain that, in the long run, Osbert would find it impossible to live at Renishaw. Why not sell up and buy a flat in Venice? 'After I am gone, being abroad will save you £1,500 a year in taxes, while entertaining one's friends there costs half or a third of what it costs in England.'[71] In none of his letters does he directly propose that Osbert should become an Italian citizen, but Osbert convinced himself that this was his intention. 'Yesterday was a bloody day,' he reported at the end of 1929. 'Ginger bullies and storms. He wants me to become an Italian subject and to give up living in London. I've refused.'[72] He refused also to give up Carlyle Square, and when Sir George protested that he was living far beyond his income, threatened to take out a £10,000 mortgage on Renishaw. The arguments were protracted and indecorous; Osbert could, of course, have averted them by cutting down on his expenses, but obstinacy as well as disinclination seemed to render this impossible. In the meantime he was distracted from his writing and a fresh worry was added to the maelstrom of doubts and distresses which throbbed behind that bland exterior.

*

Another distraction had come in 1926 when labour unrest had culminated in the General Strike. Osbert believed that the upper classes had let down Britain and that they were now about to pay the price in the shape of violent revolution. He would never be on the side of the revolutionaries, but nor could he unequivocally support those in authority. In *The Man Who Lost Himself*, a novel published three years later, Osbert set out his view of England and English society:

> In days when the owners of hereditary wealth were bent solely on their own pleasure, when to make use of the privileges which had been handed on to them, or to adopt any definite standard, was apt to be regarded as 'priggish' or 'stuck-up', when, in consequence, all round them the class to which they belonged, and which up till this moment had for many centuries held and wielded the power in England, was now sinking down, uneducated, helpless, inert and each day poorer . . .[73]

there was not merely room but a vital need for the few enlightened patricians who remained to bestir themselves to save the country. Osbert fancied himself in such a role. He deplored the 'thug-militia of St James's Street, the bands of young steel-helmeted clubmen',[74] who saw things only in terms of standing firm and asserting law and order. It was essential to build bridges between the men of goodwill on both sides. Whether he could himself achieve anything effective he did not know, but he was ready to try.

First, in the early hours of the morning, a day or two after the General Strike had been called, he and Siegfried Sassoon went to see Beverley Baxter, editor of the *Daily Express*. They explained that they wanted to end the strike. Baxter pointed out that this was difficult because of the mood of the unions. 'That's right,' shouted Sassoon furiously. 'Shoot them down! Shoot them down! You're like all the rest!' Osbert remained calm and managed to appease his tempestuous colleague. Then he set out his formula for peace. 'It was clear, sane and wise,' Baxter observed. They agreed that the next step should be for Osbert to approach Lord Wimborne, a former Cabinet minister with connections over the whole political spectrum, and ask him to put the plan to J. H. Thomas, the trade union leader and politician, who was better qualified than anyone else to speak for the Labour movement as a whole. As a preliminary, Osbert took Lord Wimborne's wife Alice out to lunch and expounded his ideas. Already an admirer of Osbert and his books, Lady Wimborne was easily convinced. She talked to her husband and persuaded him to hold a lunch at Wimborne House, where Thomas, Snowden and Henderson for the workers could meet the former Viceroy and Foreign Secretary, Lord Reading, and selected representatives of the employers. Lady Wimborne debated the guest list with Osbert at hourly intervals: Lord Hugh Cecil, it was felt, was too intransigent; Lord Londonderry, a great coal owner, was 'more pliable and broad'.[75]

The lunch lasted until 4.00 p.m. – its chief weakness was that, although the people at it were influential and important, none was in a position to deal directly with the Prime Minister, Baldwin, nor the even more pugnacious Chancellor of the Exchequer, Winston Churchill. There was still a lot that could be done, however, and Osbert convinced himself that he was the right man to do a large part of it. 'No one is working harder than you,' Alice Wimborne assured him, 'and your help means a lot.'[76] He made it his particular task to convince Arnold Bennett that he should lend his voice to those working for a settlement. Bennett was unconvinced: he neither saw that he had a role nor would have wished to play it if there had been.[77] In the end the strike crumbled. How much, if anything, the Wimborne House group contributed to the outcome can hardly be assessed; probably not much, though Lady Wimborne claimed great credit for her husband and for Osbert:

> You will let me tell you what a big part your ability and drive played in bringing about the result we are so happy about. Perhaps only you and I know exactly how it was done ... It is a great link of friendship to have thus worked together through every stage of these last feverish days – and they have brought me a sense of mutual understanding with you which I value more, much more than you know.
>
> All this has made me regret slightly that you are not of those who devote their minds to influencing current affairs in an active way. There are too few with such powers as yours dealing with these things.[78]

Osbert fantasised about the career he might have had, 'arriving at some different, perhaps – who knows? – some more glorious destination'.[79] It would be easy to ridicule his role in the General Strike as no more than the meddling of a vain and self-important man. Even if he achieved nothing, however – and this would probably be unfair to him – he did at least try. He was active in the cause of moderation and common sense at a time when a majority of his peers were striking belligerent attitudes or trying to pretend that nothing very much was going on. For this, at least, he deserves credit.

9

Enter a Golden Squirrel

You are my golden squirrel,
My heart, a nut for you to crack.

(Unpublished poem dedicated to David Horner)

BY the end of 1929 Osbert was thirty-seven years old, an age at which one is usually deemed to be mature. The term, reasonably precise when applied to a wine or a pear, means little when used about a human. Osbert had shed, or at least learnt successfully to conceal, some of his youthful doubts and inhibitions; his judgment was perhaps a little sounder; he was less impetuous, less quarrelsome. Yet he was still essentially the same human being: no childish weakness had been wholly banished, no inhibition exorcised. He had failed to reconcile, perhaps did not even wish to try to reconcile, the dichotomy between the artist and the aristocrat which so clearly marked, and in the eyes of some marred, his life.

The aristocrats still felt Osbert to be extravagantly artistic; to the artists he seemed suspiciously aristocratic. At the Marlborough Club or the St James', Osbert was viewed with tolerant astonishment. Like Evelyn Waugh at White's, he was the token aesthete, a source of occasional irritation, some merriment and a quiet pride. It was known that he wrote poetry and was unsound on fox-hunting, but he was far too well mannered to thrust his prejudices on unwilling listeners. They accepted him because they believed that, at heart, he was one of them. Anyway, the English upper classes, at any rate as observed in the West End of London, were not nearly as philistine as Osbert liked to pretend. There were at least some members of the St James' Club, Kenneth Clark and Tancred Borenius among them, who could tell a Perugino from a Pinturicchio and who took an interest in modern ballet or the verse of T. S. Eliot: even those who could not would probably have echoed Lady

Colvin's tolerant judgment that the Sitwells were 'quite nice and amusing young people, if only they would not write poetry'.[1] It took a Russell, cousin of the Duke of Bedford, to ridicule Osbert's aristocratic pretensions. When reading the first volume of Osbert's memoirs, Conrad Russell told Diana Cooper that he had been amused by the way the author sought to establish his descent by including collateral relations as if they had been of the same blood. 'Baronets are the only class-conscious people in England. The inferiority of their rank tortures them . . . How can a man exhibit himself as such a donkey?'[2]

The artists had graver doubts. Virginia Woolf saw and resented the ambivalence of Osbert's status when she wrote of his 'extreme uneasiness; his childish vanity always striking the two notes: rank and genius'. But, she concluded, 'I like him – why, I don't know'.[3] The same note of slightly grudging, occasionally exasperated affection marks the comments of many of those whom he would have considered his literary peers. Wyndham Lewis, who was to become the main protagonist in some of the Sitwells' most spectacular battles, recollected in his memoirs that he had always liked Osbert:

> rather in spite of myself – for those fox-hunting men I can never really respect. The very name *Sitwell* is suggestive of the horse-master, the hereditary 'fox-hunting man'. But Osbert is a 'hearty' who has taken the wrong turning – he has looked at pictures, he has listened to music too much – he has loved the Ballet not wisely but too well. I doubt if he could catch a fox today for all the equestrian aplomb of his patronymic.
>
> Osbert was once a minor Maecenas. He has *le bel air* . . . A Hanoverian hauteur and a beautiful lisp – which helped him out as a *raconteur*, and he was one of Chelsea's best. He threw quite a good dinner party in his salad days, and he was about the last person in London to mix 'mind' with his Mayfair. He would have been a 'baronet with a butterfly' under happier circumstances.[4]

That Osbert looked, behaved as if, and indeed considered himself to some degree, royal was an article of faith among the literary. Opinions differed about the dynasty. Usually it was Hanoverian but Richard Church told Osbert that Wilfred Owen was alarmed by him because 'in your social approach you are the incarnation of Louis XIV'. Somerset Maugham also favoured the French connection. At a dinner party, he wrote with a touch of mockery but also genuine admiration, Osbert had impressed the company by his wit, amiability and presence: 'That is what I have always envied in him – his presence, Louis XV.'[5] Even when trying most energetically to be outrageous, such a figure was hard to accept as a revolutionary. Harold Macmillan, who had served with Osbert in the Grenadiers as well as being his publisher for many years, told John Pearson that he did not believe the author was a rebel at all; he was more of a radical Whig aristocrat in the old tradition who, a hundred years before, 'would have fitted in among the young aristocrats in *Endymion*'.[6] Osbert, he maintained, was more at home at Renishaw or in the West End clubs than among the artists.

In answer to what he would have considered a wounding accusation Osbert might have replied that he was at home neither at Renishaw nor in Bohemia but at his desk. Though in London he did allow the delights of civilised existence to distance him from his labours, in the country or abroad he was a dedicated professional, ruthless in putting his writing before anything else. He hated the word 'dilettante', he said. The hours he spent at work suggest that he had some right to reject the description, but the pained irritation with which he did so shows that he felt himself vulnerable to such a charge. He did indeed work hard at his writing, but he did also dabble in other art forms and revel in the diversions offered by civilised but upper-class society. John Piper, who was both a protégé and a close friend of Osbert, judged that he was a nice man, and a serious one, with 'all the right reactions about the artist in society', but that he was diverted, and often made ridiculous, 'by his pretensions as a man of fashion and a social figure'.[7] Osbert recognised the danger. He had tried, he wrote, to free himself from the shackles of class – 'but voluntarily to unclass oneself is no easy matter!'[8] Certainly his efforts were unavailing; indeed, at times they were far from strenuous. He complained about his shackles but at the same time rejoiced in and boasted about them. As is usually the fate of those who try both to have their cake and to eat it, he ended up with a pair of inadequate slices. He performed this operation, however, with good humour and a certain amount of grace; and made a very passable showing in both the worlds of which he felt himself a member.

The 'sensual Royal Guelf face', to which Virginia Woolf had referred, crowned a substantial Guelf body. Osbert was a big man who ate and drank a great deal and took little exercise except for walks when he was at Renishaw. By 1929 he had become ponderous. His heavy frame, however, was always presented to best advantage – 'pink, fair, spick-and-span, well tailored, well shorn and shaven', his editor Rache Lovat Dickson remembered him[9] – and many women considered him handsome, even alluring. Lorna Andrade, his loyal but by no means uncritical secretary, found him 'extremely good looking – much more so than any photograph I've ever seen of him. He was so pink, so very big, and his hair was marvellous.'[10] Miss Andrade seems to have admired Osbert solely on aesthetic grounds, but William Walton claimed to know of various women who were more or less in love with him.[11] Osbert proudly endorsed the claim. He told of one girl who had applied for the job of secretary. When she was turned down on the grounds that she could not write shorthand she asked to see Osbert on a private matter of urgency. Osbert suspiciously asked for further details in writing. 'I am in love with you, madly, passionately in love,' she replied. 'I know no peace day and night and must be at your side.' She threatened suicide unless she gained this cherished propinquity. 'Such an infernal bore,' commented Osbert with obvious gratification. 'She says she has seen me once and it "produced an over-powering emotion". On the boat I had similar trouble.'[12] His charms did not always have this effect. Ethel Mannin, the popular novelist and journalist, in a volume of memoirs, described him as looking like 'a large elegant fish, a salmon, or a sturgeon, perhaps, or a very superior cod. Colourless. Sexless. Complacent.'[13] (She later repented of this gratuitous offensiveness, excised it from further editions of the book, and wrote to Osbert to apologise for her 'bad taste, ingratitude and discourtesy'.[14])

Evelyn Waugh, like so many others, wrote of Osbert's bland, patrician features and tall, well-dressed figure but added a caution: 'Closer scrutiny reveals a hint of alertness and menace, as though a rattle-snake may be expected round the next corner.'[15] Some would have said that the rattle-snake was to be found within the well-cut suit; indeed, Osbert might have made such a claim himself. He took pride in the belief that he was formidable, dangerous, a bad man to offend. Musing on the propensity of members of the public to be rude to authors, in particular to those authors who were most likely to respond with equal violence, he asked: 'Is it kind . . . to be rude to Pope or Dr Johnson or Sheridan or Shaw – or Sitwell? Is it *kind*; but, above all, is it *wise*?'[16] His choice of such exalted company was perhaps immodest but not wholly unjustified. He was capable of alarming savagery, sometimes out of all proportion to the provocation. Annoyed by what he considered to be a somewhat off-hand invitation from a fashionable hostess, he replied that unfortunately he could not accept, 'but won't you dine with us, last Thursday at eight?'[17] The examples of his wit that admirers quote are almost always malicious. When William Jowitt, political turncoat and Labour Lord Chancellor, was about to take a title, Osbert suggested: 'Lord

Whittington. You know, turn again Whittington'; to a Jewish lady who annoyed him he enquired: 'Would you like a cup of tea or some vinegar on a sponge?'[18] Even his closest friends were cautious. 'I like Osbert Sitwell very much and enjoy his stories,' Leslie Hartley told Marie Belloc Lowndes. 'But they're not very kind, are they? He keeps giving me searching looks, as though committing some defect to memory, for subsequent use.'[19] He seemed to take pleasure in the solecisms of others; his sister-in-law Georgia referred to him as 'enjoying, as he always does, everyone's discomfiture'.[20] But though the characteristic was hardly amiable it stemmed more from his delight in making a good story out of a disaster than from any deep-seated misanthropy. He loved to mock others but, though he did not relish being the butt of other people, was perfectly ready to mock himself. Like Mr Bennet in *Pride and Prejudice* he would have asked: 'For what do we live, but to make sport for our neighbours and laugh at them in our turn?'

His arrogance was unashamed. Denouncing the stupidity of English 'art-lovers' when talking of El Greco, he added in parenthesis: 'I know the mere mention of the word "stupid" is taken as an indication of an attitude of self-adopted superiority, yet I must declare my belief: which is that there are in England still a great many of them.'[21] 'I hate the million readers,' he wrote in a poem called 'Personal Prejudices'. 'I love their money, but shall never see it.'[22] But brazen self-assurance concealed doubts and frailties. He required constant reassurance: that he was loved, that he was honoured, that his writing was properly esteemed. He once told Georgia Sitwell that he could never believe people were fond of him unless they were continually telling him so – 'some form of inferiority complex,' he supposed.[23] Any artist, he wrote in the preface to *All At Sea*, must have 'as part of his necessary equipment, nerves more sensitive and susceptible than those of other people'.[24] One manifestation of this susceptibility was his extreme resentment of hostile criticism. Even though he might despise the critics, he was no less wounded by their insults. He knew it was absurd but could not protect himself. 'I must have a very naif character,' he told a friend, 'for each time I bring out a book, a stupid review puts me in a rage. I am always expecting to be popular and welcomed and am surprised at the reception I get.'[25] He tried to convince himself that if the criticism was well intentioned and came from a well-wisher it would be more acceptable. He never succeeded. Faint praise was almost as intolerable as outright abuse; only the best butter was sufficient for his needs.

An undated palmist's report in the archive at Renishaw reads:

'Disappointed in his fellow men, Sitwell seeks and at the same time shuns their company. He hovers between society and solitude, joy and melancholy.' This emotional cycle neither could nor should be corrected, the palmist concluded; it was 'the particular basis of his work'.[26] Osbert would not have disputed this verdict; indeed, it might have gratified him. He knew that he was subtly ill at ease with almost every other human being and took some pleasure in the belief that he was different from and, in certain respects, superior to those around him. The impression he made when he came into a room, wrote John Lehmann, 'was of princely apartness'.[27] But this apartness did not imply any lack of interest in his surroundings. It was the detachment of the professional observer: 'I am a watcher of human beings,' wrote Osbert, 'as others are, for instance, bird-watchers.'[28]

'You ask if Osbert Sitwell is conceited,' wrote Violet Woodhouse's husband many years later. 'I should say the answer is Yes.'[29] Most others would have given a similar reply. But it is sometimes hard to say where a proper pride in one's own accomplishments ends and vanity begins. It was all right to be an exhibitionist, Osbert might have argued, if you have something that is worth exhibiting. He used to say that anyone who called himself a poet but who did not take pleasure in reading his poems aloud to an audience was unworthy of the title.[30] He himself needed little persuasion to treat any gathering to a recitation; sometimes, indeed, the problem was to check him in full flow. Any audience, he felt, was privileged to be so regaled. He hankered for their applause and for other rewards, the more conspicuous the better. When Val Gielgud, the head of drama at the BBC, won an honour, Osbert wrote to congratulate him. 'I *long* for the Garter, the OM, the Bath, the KCVO and the OBE,' he confessed. 'I have none, and so hope that they will all be awarded to me *together*.'[31] If no Garter was forthcoming, encomia would be the next best thing: 'I need praise like a salamander needs flame,' he wrote, though adding that the praise must be of the right kind.[32]

This craving for attention and applause made it inevitable that he would show off outrageously: whether reading his poems in a village hall in Derbyshire or holding forth at some sophisticated London dinner table. He preferred the monologue to conversation, though he was sensitive and sensible enough to realise that by perpetually holding the floor he would alienate the very people whom he sought to impress. He was at his happiest as raconteur, letting other people have a turn from time to time and heartily appreciative of their efforts, but relishing the starring role. He played it uncommonly well. Cecil Beaton remembered

telling Frank Magro that Horner had neve[r]
forty years.[75] The surviving papers do no[t]
story, but they support Osbert's account o[f]
behave like a man of independent means. In
are frequent references to presents of mon[ey]
August 1930, for instance, Osbert wrote: 'I[f]
it's not enough, let me know'; in May 193[?]
advancing you £100, if you behave nicely, s[...]
your debts for the moment. I expect it will
to tide over the moment till yr ship sails in
did seem to sail in, or perhaps was maroon[ed]
war, for in the 1940s the subsidies became a
presents – 'Do you think £50 would be a h[...]
– were followed in 1943, 'as a slight token
more substantial £4,000 – getting on for
Osbert had told his bankers, he said, that h[e]
Horner in his will but had now decided to
That might have been thought sufficient
months later Horner was saying that money
as a birthday present. 'How do you know
birthday present?' asked Osbert. 'Tell me i[f]
would be gratefully received, always bearin[g]
my poorer moments, but that all the same I'[...]
In November 1944 Horner was acknowle[dged]
gigantic present. It was quite overwhelmin[g]
quite believe my eyes.'[79] His letter probably
which Osbert had sent him some two week[s]
may have intervened. Another £500 on 3 J[...]
a week later by a similar amount: 'It's be[...]
Tuesday. But it's best to present while the m[...]
sake don't spiffle it on greyhounds!'[80]

Whatever he may from time to time ha[ve]
large his personal fortune, it seems certain t[...]
gained substantially from the relationship
happiness. It is not unreasonable to look on
whom one was far the richer and therefore
the joint income. If Osbert thought he was
did not begrudge supporting the partner he
a biographer should be more censorious. T[...]
immeasurably more satisfying for Osbert b[...]

---

credited him with.'[44] But the benevolence cou[...]
felt that he was being imposed on or taken
Scott wrote him a long, rambling begging lett[er]
earned a terse negative. Sir Osbert, replied a
except in the matter of advice. His advice i[s]
someone for help, always write in ink and
what you say. Sir Osbert had to spend tw[...]
letter.'[45]

Though Osbert rarely allowed the state o[f]
his spending – whether philanthropic or self-[...]
that most of this casual charity occurred aft[er]
the prosperity which followed. This was eq[...]
subventions to his siblings. Before 1939 th[...]
could do. In 1931 he offered Sachie the use,
but he was far more concerned with extrac[ting]
than supplying it to his brother and siste[r]
however, was that though he was by instin[...]
was likely to stop short of anything that mig[ht]
the recipient. Whether his brother, his lov[...]
involved, Osbert liked to remain in a po[...]
wilfully hold back payments which morally,
to make, with no aim except to assert that h[...]
not the funds were forthcoming must be his
was unequivocally the patron, he could be
suggestion that money or services were due
procrastination if not outright hostility.

John Piper once told how Osbert had enjo[...]
man called Parker who had come up befor[e]
magistrate, on a charge of assaulting a smal[l]
girl had been offensive to him and was aske[d]
embarrassment he asked if he could write it
fucking Parker, you can fucking well fuck o[ff]
This unmemorable anecdote is of interest
recorded instances of Osbert indulging in
risqué story. 'Sachie liked talking about s[...]
Waugh recorded in his diary after a wee[k]
Acton noted how he would shrink from an[...]
change the subject if the conversation seem[ed]
gossipy to the prurient.[48] Lorna Andrade m[...]

---

his charm and 'crackling warmth, and then there was that wonderful voice of his. A deep sonority, and as he told the story he would stoke the fire with his hum-hums and his own obvious enjoyment of what he was saying ... he told jokes and stories with a fruity richness – fatness, plumpness, magnanimity.'[33] Anthony Powell made the same point: Osbert was 'best adapted to the set-piece ... He dominated a dinner table with geniality.'[34] Tributes to his prowess did not come only from his peers. C. R. W. Nevinson gave a dinner party for what he modestly described as 'some of the most distinguished men in London, all leaders in their own spheres'. His butler and ex-batman was resolutely unimpressed by this galaxy until he took in Osbert, then drew Nevinson to one side and asked who it was who was talking. Nevinson explained. 'I can tell a master of men when I see one,' said his servant reverently.[35]

Brinsley Ford, the connoisseur and art historian, rated Osbert as one of the best conversationalists he had ever met: 'His voice is so rich, his way of relating something supremely funny and frivolous in a solemn manner, the brilliant interjection when least expected ...'[36] Most people would have agreed on the mastery of technique, not so many on Osbert's skills in conversational give-and-take. The butterfly agitation which Huxley had satirised in his description of Lord Badgery had become more than a mere mannerism. Except when at work, at which time his powers of concentration were remarkable, he was consumed by a febrile restlessness. David Higham, Osbert's literary agent, described luncheon at Carlyle Square with Sachie also present. The meal concluded, the brothers loped up and down, their feet soundless on the soft carpet – 'One had the feeling ... of being caged with a couple of the greater cats, of picking up a golden glint, even, in the pale blue eyes* they both had.'[37]

The restlessness, the paranoia, the latent aggression: for most of the time these were well under control. Unprovoked, in congenial surroundings, he could even appear tame. Angela, Lady Brocket, by all accounts a singularly insensitive woman, met him at Christabel Aberconway's house and wrote to tell her hostess how taken she had been by 'your gentle and kindly friend Osbert Sitwell. What a charming and loveable personality ... He belongs to a peaceable world of his own.'[38] His courtesy could, indeed, seem almost daunting; Lovat Dickson remembered him 'sweeping off his tweed cap to a cottager's wife, bending his head to enquire solicitously after the cottager or his children'.[39] His relationship with those whom he regarded as clearly his

---

*Sachie's eyes, in fact, were more green than blue.

social inferiors was almost always admirable;
considerate, loyal, tolerant. From men like He
what higher level, Maynard Hollingworth, h
and accept criticism, dealing with them on th
each party knew its role and would play i
authority. Evelyn Waugh, fascinated by every
observed how Sitwells and servants lived tog
familiarity'. A footman would announce to t
wanted to see Miss Edith upstairs. Edith w
already spent an hour with her mother, it
would try to pass the poisoned chalice to Sa
said the footman impatiently, 'one of you's g
the oldest of old retainers, once burned a ho
expected, or professed to expect, instant di
together for so many years, you can't im
difference?' said Osbert consolingly.[41]

Though he liked the relationship to be de
indeed be singularly generous. The impecuni
only one of the many whom he helped to kee
sent him £50, then another £50 a few mont
letters of introduction, paid for his journey t
from Barker contained a reference to som
Thomas, his sister's protégé, was another rec
you for the lovely present, wrote Thomas. '
birthdays the morning of getting it . . . it was
the voley river cold, and school bills paid
Algerian, and books I've wanted for months,
and more things and more, and such happi
thinking of us and could spare, in this taxed
gift.'[42] Nor was it just gifts of money. Whe
Bates found himself during the war doing w
and uncongenial, Osbert put himself to seri
to some more suitable occupation. Bates
Relations, a contented man. 'I want to tell y
you have been in trying to get me someth
gratitude. 'You don't know me personally,
than many people who do know me. I can
your trouble and unselfishness.'[43] John Pip
most generous person I've ever known, in t
of himself, emotionally . . . He had a self

With that of flames, and so my h
But most of all, my ever dearest
I love you for *yourself*; a grace s
And yet mysterious, that pervad
Transcends the senses, even that
Is in your voice, your hands, an
Depicts for me shy satyrs in a gr
The turning of your head, the –
How to define the scent within a

In Algeciras, in September 1929, when
blood poisoning, Horner described himself
playing the roles of 'nurse, scribe, bully, con
the most significant omission would have b
had felt it described his status, Horner wo
such a letter. Lady Aberconway had no ill
between the two men but had no wish to
out).

Within a few days of Horner's letter, Os

You are all that I love in life or art,
The only easing for an aching heart,
And where you hate me, there not o
Myself, but fade out blossoms, trees

You are my golden squirrel
My heart, a nut for you to crac
But when you've peered at it, and th
Remember I can never have it b

For me to say 'I love you' means 'I li
To live without you is but wast
Remember all the love I hourly give
And that without you even life i

David Horner finally moved into Carlyle
taking over the room of the recently decea
left a substantial fortune by d'Hendecourt
something near half a million pounds de
Horner's family believe that his relationsh
between client and patron but between two
a fair share to the expenses of their life to

David Horner. Horner never gave all that Osbert asked of him; it is possible that the frenzied benevolence of the wartime years was in part accounted for by the fear that, once Horner had escaped into the Royal Air Force, he might decide never to return. Osbert, though the patron, was always the suitor; Horner, though the protégé, dictated the terms of their relationship. But the two complemented each other admirably. Horner 'was absolutely right for Osbert', judged Lorna Andrade, who disliked him heartily. He 'was like a big gay butterfly, fluttering around and drawing honey from all the flowers'.[81]

In one respect Osbert was the leading figure. Horner had literary aspirations, Osbert was already a well-established and influential author. When Osbert locked himself in his cell at Amalfi and wrote, Horner would do the same. Eventually this resulted in a book. 'The great news is that Macmillan (without the raising of a finger on my part) have accepted David's book on France,' Osbert wrote exultantly to Christabel Aberconway. 'I am *so* pleased. It should make a gt difference to him and he has worked so hard without much result up to now.'[82] He may not have raised a finger to speed its publication, but when *Through French Windows*, a lively travelogue with more emphasis on people and meals than on buildings or landscapes, finally appeared, the most important single review, praising its 'unusual qualities', was by Osbert Sitwell; the second, extolling its 'charm, wit and perception', was by Edith. Macmillan published a second book, a childhood memoir, the following year,[83] and there was a subsequent, rightly forgotten, novel, but then Horner's career as an author petered out. He told Lady Aberconway that he had not yet dared show the manuscript of the novel to Osbert 'as I am terrified of either acid criticism or tolerant appreciation'.[84] He received neither, but lavish praise. When Macmillan nevertheless rejected it, Osbert procured a copy of the report and was indignant when he found the novel damned for its muddle and mawkish humour, a 'vaguely meretricious, vaguely kittenish effusion'. The reader obviously had no sense of humour, Osbert told Horner, adding consolingly that 'a reader's report has always to be rather severe and impartial'.[85]

'The more I see of little D, the more I am certain that he makes the most hellish mischief about us all,' wrote Edith to Sachie at the end of 1931.[86] Both Osbert's siblings disliked Horner, resented his influence over their brother, and viewed with dismay the lavish gifts that were heaped upon him. Edith in particular felt herself threatened; she already resented Osbert's friendship with Christabel Aberconway, this was far worse. A combination of the two was almost unbearably perturbing.

Alan Pryce-Jones was at Renishaw one weekend when Horner, Rex Whistler and Lady Aberconway were among the other guests, and watched Edith 'glowering at any evidence of a close triangular friendship, however unalarming, between Osbert, Christabel and David'.[87] It was not as unalarming as all that. Horner did not consciously set out to undermine Osbert's relationships with other people but he resented challenges to his authority and would subtly disparage anyone whom he felt might pose a threat. Edith was frightened of him and tried to avoid any confrontation since she was not certain that in the last resort Osbert would not take his friend's side rather than his sister's. Horner for his part was equally anxious to avoid a quarrel; it was to be twenty years before anything close to open warfare was declared. In the meantime, an appearance of amity was preserved, with occasional sniping from concealed positions and much backbiting to confidantes on either side. It was not a happy relationship, but both parties took care not to let it impinge on Osbert, who missed most of it and turned a blind eye to what remained. With Sir George, relations were at first positively warm; Horner worked hard to be charming and took a pleasing interest in all the baronet's arcane pursuits. Things were never the same, however, after the episode of the bath. Henry Moat had run his employer a hot bath, emptying into it the last sachet of a very special preparation which Sir George had had made up for him. Horner found the bathroom empty, assumed he was supposed to be the beneficiary, and set to work. Sir George, finding the door locked, demanded another bath and was outraged to be told that the last of his special mixture had been hijacked by his guest. A fresh brew was hurriedly prepared by Moat – an unholy compound of oil, soap and soda water – but it was not the same. Sir George knew that he was being fobbed off with an inferior substitute and regarded Horner with resentment for months thereafter.

The main trouble with Horner was not that he tried to weaken Osbert's links with the outside world but that he reinforced Osbert's baser prejudices. He was a snob, who would put up with Osbert's middle-class literary friends but sneer at them once they were departed. He was a racist, who as an Englishman felt himself unequivocally top of the global pack: 'David says that I am far too nice to the natives,' Osbert wrote from Corfu, 'and has developed a quite terrifying "imperative" manner in the Great British Raj style.'[88] He was an anti-Semite, of a virulence which made Osbert's previous tendencies seem almost benevolent. His wit was almost invariably unkind; the tinge of malice which suffused Osbert's anecdotes was altogether more lurid when

Horner was in play. His impatience and fretfulness were notorious: 'David is giving up being bad-tempered for Lent,' reported Osbert to Christabel Aberconway. 'At present it seems to be working well.'[89] Certainly the good resolution did not outlive the fast; it seems unlikely that it survived as long. All these were frailties which Osbert shared and all of them became more marked as time wore on. If Osbert had fallen in love with an amiable, kindly, patient, gentle man his development in the second half of his life might have been very different; but any such speculation is singularly unfruitful. If he had fallen in love with an amiable, kindly, patient, gentle man, he would not have been Osbert.

10

Phantoms

Now watch the phantoms,
How they tremble into being,
Amble, tremble into ample phantoms.

(From the Prologue to *England Reclaimed*)

ABOUT halfway between the two world wars, Osbert Sitwell
found his poetic voice. It was not a very loud voice nor necessarily one well calculated to resound down the centuries, but it
was individual, authentic, and in its own way curiously beguiling.

After the publication of *Argonaut and Juggernaut* in 1919, Osbert
for some years continued with the same mix of satire and heady lyrics.
At the House of Mrs Kinfoot and *Out of the Flame* fell into these
categories. The Mrs Kinfoot poems, transparently if not specifically
aimed at Lady Colefax, appeared first in 1921 in a private edition of
101 copies and recurred in *Out of the Flame* two years later, and many
of the other poems in the later collection had been published previously
in the *Spectator*, the *Saturday Westminster Gazette*, the *Nation* and
other journals. Osbert was indignant when he was accused of passing
off old goods as new. 'Though not perhaps a popular poet in the sense
that Jessie Pope or Mr Noyes can be said to be one,' he retorted
haughtily to his publisher, 'yet I can still manage to get my poems
accepted by a few papers and should be foolish not occasionally to
avail myself of this opportunity. It is therefore inevitable that one or
two of my poems should have appeared in print before, though
probably less of mine are seen before their publication than would be
the case with other poets.'[1] In fact nearly 90 per cent of the poems in
Out of the Flame had been already published in one way or another,
though often they had been revised in the meantime. Osbert abhorred
waste, and in both prose and verse liked to recycle his material for a

second, or sometimes even third, appearance. The targets of his satire did not change greatly with the years. Warmongers, armaments manufacturers, philistines, hypocrites, society hostesses and the middle classes remained his favourite butts, the first two gradually dwindling in significance as the war receded from his mind. 'The Subtlety of the Serpent' – a poem from *Out of the Flame* – was 'so very great, so fine, so marvellous', said Ada Leverson, that it would be a classic long after the *English Review*, which had rejected it, had itself been forgotten.[2] It was not and hardly deserved to be, but it had an attractively rancorous flavour. The serpent mused over the difference between apes and humans, and concluded:

> 'But now, O Lord,
> Give me a good old-fashioned ape
> Every time;
> – An ape who tries to kill me
> Without a chatter of clean-hands, law-and-order,
> *Crime Passionel*, self-defence,
> Or helping-me-to-help-myself.
> I may be a snake in the grass,
> But I am not a hypocrite:
> I may change my skin,
> But I am not ashamed of it.
> I have never pretended to be a super-snake
> Or to walk except on my belly –'
>   *   *   *   *
> 'It is not only the ignorance of good and evil,'
> The serpent continued,
> 'That raises the monkey above the man
> (Though the man knows evil and therefore prefers it),
> But the fact that the monkey
> Cannot yet disguise the good with bad words
> Or the bad with good ones.'[3]

But it is Mrs Kinfoot, that paradigm of the smug, snobbish, self-seeking society lady, with resolutely closed ears, eyes and mind, who most offended him. She was the ultimate British bourgeoise:

> Nothing exists which the British *Bourgeoisie*
> Does not understand;
> Therefore there is no death
> – And, of course, no life.

> The British *Bourgeoisie*
> Is not born,
> And does not die,
> But, if it is ill,
> It has a frightened look in its eyes.*[4]

In 'Malgré Soi' Mrs Kinfoot is sent to heaven but finds to her discomfiture that all the most fashionable spirits whom she would like to invite to dinner are below in hell. She tries to join them, but every time she starts the descent the angels intercept her with glad cries of: 'Dear Mrs Kinfoot – you are good! We know!' Finally, in 'Paradise Regained' she accomplishes her escape and arrives triumphantly in hell. The Devil hesitates but in the end yields, saying:

> . . . for Persistence
> You have no equal, so, though free from Sin
> We here create you Honorary Member,
> Beginning on the Fifth day of November,
> (A Saint's day here).' Now authors and Debrett
> Mingle their laughing tears to music's swell,
> For here are some whom she has never met
> – And Mrs Kinfoot finds her Heaven in Hell![5]

'While the book has abundant claims on us as pure poetry,' claimed the *Glasgow Herald*, 'it is its satire that puts it in a class by itself. Nothing so brilliantly witty has appeared for years, and behind the wit lurks humour.'[6] The praise seems extravagant, and was not echoed by many critics, who tended to nod approvingly towards the satire – 'savagely witty', said the *Observer* – but find the real hope for the future in Osbert's lyrics. Previously he had looked on Osbert as a satirist, wrote Arnold Bennett, but now, 'Lo, he is creating ideal beauty . . . The satirical part of the volume, while it contains the best satire that Osbert Sitwell has yet done, is inferior in essential quality to the first part. And I am inclined to think that Mrs Kinfoot is definitely slain and should be buried.' Richard Aldington declared that Osbert was 'one of the few living English poets with a poet's mind . . . he scatters beauties recklessly through pages which are bright and glittering with fine sensual appreciations'. *Out of the Flame*, he concluded, was one of the most stimulating books of poetry to have appeared in England since the war.

---

*In spirit strikingly close to D. H. Lawrence's 'How beastly the bourgeois is' (*Pansies*, 1929).

Aldington's praise indicates the weakness as well as the strength of Osbert's poetry. He was a poet who loved words and flashing turns of phrase, could capture detail with a perceptive, sometimes even visionary, eye, but did not have much to say. His pages were indeed set with 'bright and glittering' images, but the settings for such jewels were often inadequate, sometimes tawdry. At times his poetry read as if it had been written for inclusion in *Façade*, but had come too late; 'Fox Trot', for example:

> Thus the Queen met the King at Jerusalem
> And he
>   Seemed wiser
>   Than Methuselem
> With a great black beard,
>   And a nose like a scythe,
> He lived in the palace,
>   And subsisted on a tithe![7]

Sometimes the shadow of Eliot seems to have fallen over him, as in the title poem, 'Out of the Flame':

> It is not thus in the Northern cities,
> Where the cold breathes close to the window pane;
> Where the brittle flowers of the frost
> Crackle at the window's edge.
> From my window in the Northern city
> I can hear the rattle and roar of the town,
> As the carts go lumbering over the bridges,
> As the men in dark clothes hurry over the bridges.
> They do not parade their hearts here,
> They bury them at their lives' beginning.[8]

'Derivative, in the lowest sense,' wrote Squire's acolyte, Edward Shanks, in the *Daily Mail*. So harsh a judgment was unjust. Osbert was not innovative as a poet nor did he enjoy intensity of vision, but his eye was clear and perceptive and the language with which he expressed it was precise and sometimes eloquent:

> From my window in a Southern city,
> Floating above the geometrical array
> Of roofs, squares and interlacing streets,

Do you remember Mr Goodbeare,
Who remembered a lot?
    Mr Goodbeare could remember
        When things were properly kept up:
    Mr Goodbeare could remember
        The christening and the coming-of-age:
    Mr Goodbeare could remember
        The entire and roasted ox:
    Mr Goodbeare could remember
        When the horses filled the stable,
And the port-wine coloured gentry rode after the tawny fox:
    Mr Goodbeare could remember
        The old lady in her eagle rage,
            Which knew no bounds:

    Mr Goodbeare could remember
        When the escaped and hungering tiger
Flickered lithe and fierce through Foxton Wood,
When old Sir Nigel took his red-tongued, clamouring hounds
And hunted it then and there,
        As a Gentleman Should* . . .

, do you remember, do you remember,
I remember and deplore,
at day in drear and far-away December
en dear, god-fearing, bearded Mr Goodbeare
uld remember
more?[17]

ction ended with a rhetorical flourish:

        Sound out, proud trumpets,
        And you, bugles blow,
        Over the English Dead . . .

ynote was a skilfully contrived simplicity and a warmth that
o Osbert's work. He knew and loved these people, and both
edge and the love shone through.
w note was greeted enthusiastically by the reviewers.

o an incident which had taken place in 1798. In spite of Osbert's claim person-
ber Mr Goodbeare's death, the original of the portrait, Frank Elliot, had died
us age before Osbert's birth and the details of his life had been recorded by

One can see beyond
Into far valleys,
That seem at first
To be open blue flowers
Scattered here and there on the mountains.

The forests are so far away,
They creep like humble green moss
Over slopes that are mountains,
And there sounds other music
Than the falling streams,
Or the deep penetrating glow
Of sunlight piercing through green leaves.[9]

Osbert the lyricist was at his most satisfying in the scenes of linked but discrete poems called 'Winter the Huntsman', which first appeared in a collection by the three Sitwells, *Poor Young People*, published in October 1925. The title poem, conventional in expression, reveals a romantic attachment to the countryside and to the forces that traditionally govern it, which was to figure increasingly in his future work:

        Through his iron glades
        Rides Winter the Huntsman.
        All colour fades
        As his horn is heard sighing. ·

        Far through the frost
        His wild hooves crash and thunder
        Till many a mighty branch
        Is torn asunder

        And the red reynard creeps
        To his hole near the river,
        The copper leaves fall
        And the bare trees shiver.

        As night creeps from the ground,
        Hides each tree from its brother,
        And each dying sound
        Reveals yet another.

> Is it Winter the Huntsman
> Who gallops through his iron glades,
> Cracking his cruel whip
> To the gathering shades?[10]

In the three poems, wrote Osbert, he was trying to show 'in the simplest terms applied to the most radical and obvious causes, the reasons, as I saw them, of the plight in which we found ourselves; that religion, intuition, even superstition had been banished from the modern world, and a worship of brute knowledge – science – and of material things had replaced them'.[11] Virginia Woolf's derisive dismissal – 'All foliage and no filberts' – was probably directed at these poems.[12] Sometimes the charge was justified: but in this case he curbed his natural extravagance and achieved a purity of line that was as moving as it was economical.

But Osbert's poetry was about to take a new direction. People, he often claimed, were his obsession and his chosen field of study. Children habitually collected many useless things; as a boy he had collected pens and people, 'and later these two passions grew united'.[13] It was in his poetry that his pens and people found their fusion. He resolved to write a series of portraits in verse of the people he had known as a child at Renishaw or elsewhere: the gamekeeper; the estate carpenter; Mary-Anne, the old woman who fed the ducks on the lake at Blankney; Mrs Hague, the gardener's wife at his grandmother's home, Hay Brow. The names were changed, some poetic licence was allowed, but the sketches were unquestionably taken from life; any subjects who were still alive would have recognised themselves, have been surprised, disconcerted even, but, since the poems were affectionate and never malicious, have been gratified by their apparition. He had had to make up his own rules, Osbert maintained, since portraiture in verse had not been seriously practised in Britain for several centuries; there had been caricatures, as those of Alexander Pope, but little intended to catch the essence of a human being without distortion or exaggeration. Chaucer had established the art in, for example, *The Pardoner's Tale* ('No, I am not comparing myself to Chaucer,' he disclaimed to Dr Connie Guion), and, perhaps because he had set so intimidating a model, few later poets had essayed the genre. The modern influence Osbert most gratefully acknowledged was that of the Kansas poet and novelist Edgar Lee Masters, whose collection of poems, *Spoon River Anthology*, portrayed the inhabitants of a small Midwestern town; and incidentally, he told Dr Guion, 'on the last occasion I talked with Dylan Thomas I asked him,

apropos of *Milkwood*, whether he knew the work yes, and greatly admired it'.[14]

Osbert called his collection, which was publi *Reclaimed*, a choice which earned him some criti reviewer who complained of the 'dreadful priggi was, Osbert explained, because the critic had r of spiritual reclamation, 'instead of using it i connection of physical reclamation, such as that clue should have been given by the subtitle, 'eclogue' being a term for a pastoral or idyllic certain works of Virgil. (Louis MacNeice liked tell T. S. Eliot a few years later that he had which, 'for want of a better name, I am callir did not discard the characteristics which had There is the same extravagant word-play –

> Now watch these phantoms,
> How they tremble into being,
> Amble, tremble into ample ph
> Tumble into their small wants

the same use of pictorial analogies – Mrs Hag by Botticelli . . . a Rousseau portrait, inflate signed Van Eyck inserted in a Gauguin par sounding and exotic words – 'proligerous', at its best the poetry displays a new certai who was working within his powers and w trying to do. The 'Elegy for Mr Goodbear

> Do you remember Mr Goodbea
> Godfearing and bearded Mr Go
> Who worked all day
> At his carpenter's tray,
> Do you remember Mr Goodbe
> Mr Goodbeare, that Golconda
> Living, thin-ground between
> Pressed thus close against Alf
> Mr Goodbeare, who had nev
>
> Do you remember Mr Good
> Mr Goodbeare, who never t

The
but the was ne the kno This

*A referen ally to rem at an enor Sir George.

'Sympathy has replaced indignation,' declared Naomi Royde-Smith in *Time and Tide*; Osbert had attained a new maturity. He could be 'a really big writer', wrote the *Daily Express*. 'If he can be satiric, he also has the gift of understanding. If he can hate he can also love.' 'Nothing could be more quietly harmonious in expression, or more humanly simple in theme,' said Arthur Waugh in the *Daily Telegraph*. 'No recent poem, not even the best of John Masefield, has recreated a world more thoroughly or more fascinatingly English.'[18] This cheering reception encouraged Osbert to try again. Two years later, in 1929, he published, though only in a minuscule edition, a portrait in verse of Miss Lloyd, his old ally from Scarborough, under the title of *Miss Mew*:

> This little, feathery old woman
> Was bright and kind and gentle as a flower,
> And clever with no cleverness human . . .

It was a charming piece, but too slight in itself to interest any commercial publisher and, since it was privately printed, it almost entirely escaped critical attention until it reappeared more than twenty years later as part of a second volume of verse portraits, *Wrack at Tidesend*. Not that *England Reclaimed* had done much to relieve Osbert's chronic overdraft at Coutts. His royalties, he wrote, 'though gratifying to any poet and, indeed, wildly in excess of any sum I had, when younger, ever dreamt of making, would yet hardly have been deemed by a business man to compensate him for an equivalent amount of labour'.[19] In an effort to put this right, but more than half in joke, he put an advertisement in *Miss Mew* offering portrait poems at 100 guineas for full length, 50 for head and shoulders and 200 for a family group. Given that only a hundred copies of *Miss Mew* were printed, this device might have been expected to escape attention but the press took it up with an interest that was denied the poem itself. Osbert now decided to extend his campaign to the personal columns of *The Times*. At first no order followed, but at a party at Arnold Bennett's house a few weeks later Michael Arlen asked what the response had been. On being told that there had been none, he at once commissioned his own portrait, a three-quarter-length being judged appropriate.

Three-Quarter-length Portrait of Michael Arlen, a pamphlet of twenty-four thinly covered pages, appeared in 1931, in an edition of 520 copies of which 500 were offered for sale, half in Britain and half in the United States. The technique of a Van Dyck was called for, Osbert wrote, but Van Dyck's cavaliers were always defeated:

> While Arlen is anything, is everything
> Except an unsuccessful cavalier.

It was an ingenious piece of work which contrived to be flattering in what at first glance seemed to be a mildly offensive way. Arlen belonged, Osbert wrote, either in 'the picture-postcard delta of the Nile' or on 'the sun-baked plains of Asia Minor'. Imagining him in Southport on a rainy day:

> I comprehended why,
> Alone of all the popular writers
> He dares to use the arts of Imagery.

Following Arlen's lead, according to that obsequious chronicler of all things Sitwellian, Max Wykes-Jones, 'many persons hastened to be limned by Mr Sitwell'.[20] If they did, they covered their tracks remarkably well. Only one other 'three-quarter-length portrait' survives, and that privately printed. The subject was Alice Wimborne, Osbert's collaborator at the time of the General Strike.[21] If Osbert's portrait of Arlen was flattering, that of Lady Wimborne was fawning. To gild a lily, Osbert declared:

> However unalloyed my gold,
> Is silly.

He extolled her pallor, 'whiteness of stephanotis and magnolia', her 'thrilling, deep-throated laughter', her valour:

> More brave than any candour
> Of those who make their insolence their trade.

The poem was printed for Christmas 1931, and was probably a present, but even if Lady Wimborne paid the full 100 guineas she still got her money's worth.

Three years later the result might have been less fawning. Alice Wimborne, in Osbert's eyes, was in disgrace. The reason was William Walton. Ten years after Walton had taken up residence among the Sitwells, he remained firmly ensconced, making himself a considerable

One can see beyond
Into far valleys,
That seem at first
To be open blue flowers
Scattered here and there on the mountains.

The forests are so far away,
They creep like humble green moss
Over slopes that are mountains,
And there sounds other music
Than the falling streams,
Or the deep penetrating glow
Of sunlight piercing through green leaves.[9]

Osbert the lyricist was at his most satisfying in the scenes of linked but discrete poems called 'Winter the Huntsman', which first appeared in a collection by the three Sitwells, *Poor Young People*, published in October 1925. The title poem, conventional in expression, reveals a romantic attachment to the countryside and to the forces that traditionally govern it, which was to figure increasingly in his future work:

Through his iron glades
Rides Winter the Huntsman.
All colour fades
As his horn is heard sighing. ·

Far through the frost
His wild hooves crash and thunder
Till many a mighty branch
Is torn asunder

And the red reynard creeps
To his hole near the river,
The copper leaves fall
And the bare trees shiver.

As night creeps from the ground,
Hides each tree from its brother,
And each dying sound
Reveals yet another.

Is it Winter the Huntsman
Who gallops through his iron glades,
Cracking his cruel whip
To the gathering shades?[10]

In the three poems, wrote Osbert, he was trying to show 'in the simplest terms applied to the most radical and obvious causes, the reasons, as I saw them, of the plight in which we found ourselves; that religion, intuition, even superstition had been banished from the modern world, and a worship of brute knowledge – science – and of material things had replaced them'.[11] Virginia Woolf's derisive dismissal – 'All foliage and no filberts' – was probably directed at these poems.[12] Sometimes the charge was justified: but in this case he curbed his natural extravagance and achieved a purity of line that was as moving as it was economical.

But Osbert's poetry was about to take a new direction. People, he often claimed, were his obsession and his chosen field of study. Children habitually collected many useless things; as a boy he had collected pens and people, 'and later these two passions grew united'.[13] It was in his poetry that his pens and people found their fusion. He resolved to write a series of portraits in verse of the people he had known as a child at Renishaw or elsewhere: the gamekeeper; the estate carpenter; Mary-Anne, the old woman who fed the ducks on the lake at Blankney; Mrs Hague, the gardener's wife at his grandmother's home, Hay Brow. The names were changed, some poetic licence was allowed, but the sketches were unquestionably taken from life; any subjects who were still alive would have recognised themselves, have been surprised, disconcerted even, but, since the poems were affectionate and never malicious, have been gratified by their apparition. He had had to make up his own rules, Osbert maintained, since portraiture in verse had not been seriously practised in Britain for several centuries; there had been caricatures, as those of Alexander Pope, but little intended to catch the essence of a human being without distortion or exaggeration. Chaucer had established the art in, for example, *The Pardoner's Tale* ('No, I am not comparing myself to Chaucer,' he disclaimed to Dr Connie Guion), and, perhaps because he had set so intimidating a model, few later poets had essayed the genre. The modern influence Osbert most gratefully acknowledged was that of the Kansas poet and novelist Edgar Lee Masters, whose collection of poems, *Spoon River Anthology*, portrayed the inhabitants of a small Midwestern town; and incidentally, he told Dr Guion, 'on the last occasion I talked with Dylan Thomas I asked him, apropos of *Milkwood*, whether he knew the work of Masters and he said yes, and greatly admired it'.[14]

Osbert called his collection, which was published in 1927, *England Reclaimed*, a choice which earned him some criticism from an American reviewer who complained of the 'dreadful priggishness' of the title. This was, Osbert explained, because the critic had read the title in the sense of spiritual reclamation, 'instead of using it in the right sense in this connection of physical reclamation, such as that of the Zuyder Zee'.[15] A clue should have been given by the subtitle, '*A Book of Eclogues*', 'eclogue' being a term for a pastoral or idyllic poem, usually applied to certain works of Virgil. (Louis MacNeice liked the conceit sufficiently to tell T. S. Eliot a few years later that he had been writing some poems which, 'for want of a better name, I am calling "Eclogues" '.[16]) Osbert did not discard the characteristics which had marked his earlier poetry. There is the same extravagant word-play –

> Now watch these phantoms,
> How they tremble into being,
> Amble, tremble into ample phantoms,
> Tumble into their small wants;

the same use of pictorial analogies – Mrs Hague was 'a Mrs Noah limned by Botticelli ... a Rousseau portrait, inflated by Picasso', Mr Hague 'a signed Van Eyck inserted in a Gauguin panel'; the same delight in rich-sounding and exotic words – 'proligerous', 'corrugant', 'phanariot'. But at its best the poetry displays a new certainty, the product of an artist who was working within his powers and who knew exactly what he was trying to do. The 'Elegy for Mr Goodbeare' is an excellent example:

> Do you remember Mr Goodbeare, the carpenter,
> Godfearing and bearded Mr Goodbeare,
> Who worked all day
> At his carpenter's tray,
> Do you remember Mr Goodbeare?
> Mr Goodbeare, that Golconda of gleaming fable,
> Living, thin-ground between orchard and stable,
> Pressed thus close against Alfred – his rival –
> Mr Goodbeare, who had never been away.
>
> Do you remember Mr Goodbeare,
> Mr Goodbeare, who never touched a cup?

Do you remember Mr Goodbeare,
Who remembered a lot?
    Mr Goodbeare could remember
        When things were properly kept up:
    Mr Goodbeare could remember
        The christening and the coming-of-age:
    Mr Goodbeare could remember
        The entire and roasted ox:
    Mr Goodbeare could remember
        When the horses filled the stable,
And the port-wine coloured gentry rode after the tawny fox:
    Mr Goodbeare could remember
        The old lady in her eagle rage,
            Which knew no bounds:

    Mr Goodbeare could remember
        When the escaped and hungering tiger
Flickered lithe and fierce through Foxton Wood,
When old Sir Nigel took his red-tongued, clamouring hounds
And hunted it then and there,
        As a Gentleman Should* . . .

Oh, do you remember, do you remember,
As *I* remember and deplore,
That day in drear and far-away December
When dear, god-fearing, bearded Mr Goodbeare
Could remember
No more?[17]

The collection ended with a rhetorical flourish:

        Sound out, proud trumpets,
        And you, bugles blow,
        Over the English Dead . . .

but the keynote was a skilfully contrived simplicity and a warmth that was new to Osbert's work. He knew and loved these people, and both the knowledge and the love shone through.

This new note was greeted enthusiastically by the reviewers.

*A reference to an incident which had taken place in 1798. In spite of Osbert's claim personally to remember Mr Goodbeare's death, the original of the portrait, Frank Elliot, had died at an enormous age before Osbert's birth and the details of his life had been recorded by Sir George.

reputation as a composer but still largely dependent on Osbert for his bread and butter. On the whole the relationship was harmonious. Osbert liked to treat Walton as a feckless and irresponsible artist who could thrive only with tactful direction and a certain amount of bullying. He acted as manager, agent and spiritual director. There could be no question of Walton giving a talk on the radio, he told Joe Ackerley. 'I dread to think what he would say. His language is always appalling, and he would probably end in getting the whole of the BBC the sack.'[22] For the most part Walton was prepared to put up with this bossiness, and when he struck out on his own line he did so with some caution. Osbert never tried to interfere with his composing, and everything else was negotiable. But there were points of friction. 'The girls were an early issue,' Walton said much later,[23] and the girls were not only early but numerous as well. Walton was attractive to women and himself susceptible. Osbert had little sympathy for such escapades, resented the fact that entanglements with women might reduce the control which he felt that he and Sachie must exercise over the volatile composer, and most of all deplored the waste of time and energy which would better be directed to the writing of music. He realised, however, that there were limits to his power. Towards the end of 1929 Walton wrote to say that he was now fixed up for life with his current girlfriend: 'We have more or less decided to be abroad together in the winter (subject to your august approval) . . . I don't see why it shouldn't all work well.' The remark about 'august approval' was jokingly expressed but concealed a real disquiet; if Osbert disapproved, Walton's financial future might be bleak. 'I think you will get on with her,' Walton continued nervously. 'You won't find her a bore, whatever Little David may say.'[24] Osbert was disquieted by the news. 'All my hatred of change – not conservatism but more a dislike of crystallisation, as much for myself as for others, is aroused by it,' he confessed to Christabel Aberconway. But he saw no grounds on which he could object.[25] Anyway, he felt reasonably confident that the relationship would not endure – a judgment which, as several times before, proved to be sound.

It was a different matter when Walton took up with Lady Wimborne, whose husband, as well as being complaisant, was immensely rich. Alice Wimborne, though still strikingly beautiful and youthful in appearance – 'with the tall litheness of a young tree in the wind,' Osbert had described her in his portrait – was more than twenty years older than Walton, and Osbert's sense of propriety was offended. Still worse, however, was the fact that Walton was *his* protégé, Alice Wimborne *his* special friend. A liaison between them was a double betrayal, which Osbert found it hard to forgive. 'There has been a slight chilliness between me and Carlyle Square,' Walton told Siegfried Sassoon. He had been installed by Lady Wimborne in a flat in South Eaton Place, 'and I must say I appreciate being on my own'.[26] For a time, indeed, the chilliness was glacial. Walton told John Pearson much later that his affair with Lady Wimborne ended his relationship with Osbert: 'he never really spoke to me again'.[27] In 1937 it was even said that Osbert was trying to block the income which Walton was receiving from a trust set up earlier by some of his admirers. Lord Aberconway, who was in charge of the fund, was outraged at the rumour and called it a vile libel on Osbert. 'Never for one moment have I believed you capable of such a proceeding,' he wrote to Osbert; '. . . since the days when the Trust was first made, neither you nor anyone else has ever spoken to me about WW's financial affairs.'[28] Such reports were indeed unfair; Osbert would not have tried so mean as well as risky a manoeuvre. He and Walton never entirely lost touch and, particularly after Walton married Susana Passo in 1948, saw each other quite often and discussed plans for co-operation on various, usually abortive enterprises. But their friendship never really revived. Probably unfairly, Walton blamed David Horner for securing his expulsion from Carlyle Square and ensuring that the breach was never completely healed.[29]

Osbert and Walton could hardly have avoided a certain amount of contact, for they had worked together on a project which was to be revived constantly over the next sixty years. In 1929 the BBC approached Walton with a proposal that he should write the music for an oratorio with an Old Testament theme, and agreed with alacrity when it was suggested that Osbert should contribute the libretto. Osbert put forward the story of Belshazzar's feast, from the Book of Daniel, with its superbly dramatic vision of the writing on the wall. This, he argued, would have the advantage of being familiar to everyone. It was not familiar to Walton, who confused Belshazzar with his father Nebuchadnezzar and vaguely imagined that there would have to be a scene in which the eponymous hero of the oratorio would be observed grazing grass, but once this misunderstanding was cleared up the partnership prospered.[30] Walton was starting a new work for the BBC, Horner reported from Amalfi: 'Words biblical (very biblical) by Osbert and music (very oratorio) by Willie. I had to censor the words as I found them too anti-Semite. I have now almost worked myself into a pro-Jew frenzy.'[31] Osbert makes no mention of such amendments but admits that certain changes were made at Walton's insistence. He had wanted to conclude with the nursery rhyme 'How Many Miles to Babylon?' Walton insisted on something more dramatic and secured the 'pagan shout of triumph' which now ends the work.[32]

The oratorio was immediately and immensely successful, though *The Times* so far agreed with David Horner to describe the text as 'Stark Judaism from first to last. It culminates in ecstatic gloating over the fallen enemy, the utter negation of Christianity.'[33] Osbert's contribution had been more one of arrangement than original writing, though he allowed himself considerable licence with the text. Christabel Aberconway claimed that she, anyway, had done most of the donkey work of research and selection. It is notable that in 1996 by far the largest single royalty earned by Osbert's literary estate came from the libretto which he wrote for *Belshazzar's Feast*. He was less fortunate with his other musical ventures. A short ballet for which he wrote the scenario, *The First Shoot*, in spite of having music by Walton, designs by Beaton, choreography by Ashton and a place in a C. B. Cochran review, made no real mark and was never repeated, while *The Princess Caraboo*, a fantasy featuring an escaped slave girl who hoodwinked Bath society into believing she was a visiting princess, never even reached production. 'I read it and thought it very good. It's for the de Basil ballet,' wrote a friend of Walton's; but though Walton himself believed a production had been guaranteed, the project foundered without trace.[34]

England Reclaimed was dedicated to his sister Edith, 'To you, sad child, upon the darkened stair . . .' The poem showed that, however mellow the tone of the book that followed, Osbert still nursed sharp resentment against 'the sillies and the dullies', the 'crowds of giggling, chic cads' and, by implication if not specifically, his own parents. Graham Greene told the author that he found it 'more moving each time I read it',[35] and it is obvious that it was written with feeling and complete sincerity. The relationship between Sir George and his children – Osbert and Edith in particular – in the late 1920s and early 1930s was as unpleasant as it had ever been. Sir George was an opinionated, selfish, irrational old tyrant. He must have been infuriating to live with, worse still to be dependent on financially. Yet the pity is that the evidence suggests he loved his children, took pride in their achievements, and would have been immensely relieved to be on good terms with them if only he had known how to bring about such a state of affairs.

Francis Bamford, who saw much of Sir George in his old age, bore witness both to the fondness the father felt towards his children and to the difficulty he found in expressing it. 'He would often talk of you with pride and affection,' he told Osbert, 'and those were real feelings, even though . . . he would finish up with one of his raps over the knuckles for one or other of you.'[36] Sachie could never understand why his brother and sister failed to grasp this fact, which seemed to him so obvious. 'It is most painful to realise your hatred for your father,' he wrote. 'It is, I know, useless to try and persuade you that in his heart, he is in his queer way devoted to you.'[37] It *was* useless. Even when Sir George protested his love, Osbert dismissed it as hypocrisy. When the financial squabbling was nearing its peak, Sir George ended a bleak statement of Osbert's debts with the words: 'You wrote me such a dear letter, and there is truly great love and affection between us and I am proud of all your literary successes.'[38] The 'dear letter' does not survive; but Osbert told his sister-in-law Georgia two days before that he had written his father 'a sensible letter' and now awaited developments. 'What it amounts to is simply that he sees some money and is after it.'[39] To Hollingworth he said that he had received a short letter from his father saying that, in spite of Osbert's dreadful behaviour, 'he remained very fond of me. I thought, after due consideration, that it was best not to answer . . . What a time we've had!'[40] The response was hardly gracious. Yet his scepticism was not wholly unreasonable. Bamford himself admitted that, though Sir George genuinely admired his children's achievements, 'he felt it very unfair that you had succeeded while he (who considered himself so much better equipped than was anyone else) had failed'. Harold Acton detected an equivocal, slightly grudging note in Sir George's warmest encomia: 'When he spoke of "the boys" it was with an odd mixture of pride and faint disapproval, as if they were not sufficiently serious.'[41] He liked to score off his children: if he failed to do so he was resentful, if he succeeded he was surprised when they retaliated.

But in his odd way he was benevolent and concerned for their well-being. When Osbert complained of feeling tired he explained that this was probably caused by 'food not being properly assimilated, owing to overwork and worry. You should therefore put yourself on to a light and really nourishing diet, and be very careful what you eat. Small meals at short intervals, a beef tea or chicken broth between meals, a Horlock's [*sic*] malted milk in the night. Best love, darling. Ever your loving father.'[42] Osbert's financial future preoccupied him as much as did his health. On one occasion he suddenly said: 'Excuse my mentioning the subject, Osbert, but why not marry a widow? There's such a number of nice widows nowadays.' Osbert replied that he could not envisage needing more than one; but though his father's advice struck him as bizarre, it was still kindly meant.[43] If his children were in trouble Sir George was usually supportive. In 1929 in North Africa Osbert was bitten on the hand by some malevolent insect and suffered blood-poisoning as a result. At one moment there seemed to be a serious risk that a finger might have to be amputated. Sir George at once telegraphed him £100, 'and sent two pre-paid wires, which is a hitherto unknown event'.[44]

To reconstruct in any detail the financial dealings between Osbert and his father between 1929 and 1934 would be tedious, otiose and probably impossible. Nor is it easier to establish a balance sheet of rights and wrongs. Sir George felt himself ill-used. He had made over Renishaw itself and a substantial part of the income from the estate. 'I have spent a month in the summer with you about once in two years,' he wrote in 1929. 'Beyond that I have never entered the house except with your permission. On these occasions I have not slept in the house, but have put up at the Sitwell Arms.'[45] It is true that this exaggerated propriety was motivated more by the need to convince the tax authorities of his non-resident status than out of deference to the new owner, but the fact still remained that he had given away a good deal which he could easily have retained. He subsequently undid much of the good of this magnanimity by haggling over details and resurrecting questionable debts from the past, but his initial generosity was no less great because of this.

It is difficult not to sympathise with Sir George over an imbroglio which arose in 1929. As an unintended consequence of the elaborately complex web of transactions by which Sir George was seeking to outwit the British taxman, Osbert found he was receiving £600 a year more than had been intended. Sir George wrote to point out that the plan had been to allow this money to accumulate, and asked for a refund. 'Something very, very funny has happened,' Osbert told Christabel Aberconway. Instead of repaying the money, or even admitting that he had received his father's letter, he wrote to tell Sir George that he had heard from a private source that the revenue authorities were taking an unhealthily close interest in the transactions of the Sitwell family. A day or two later, Sir George's original letter having, by then, supposedly been received, he wrote again to say that he thought it would be risky to repay the money. Unless they were careful, all the financial arrangements so far made would be invalidated.[46] Sir George professed to take Osbert's protestations at face value but it does not sound as if he were deceived. 'You are right to be careful,' he replied, 'but I could not view with equanimity any attempt on your part to take personal advantage at my expense of a legal slip made in a settlement which already involves great sacrifices by me in your favour.'[47] There is nothing to show that the money was ever repaid; certainly if it was, Osbert made his father work for it.

From Osbert's point of view his father had saddled him with a large country house which he could not afford to keep up and was now trying to claw back what little income his son enjoyed so as to pay for his own monstrous extravagance at Montegufoni. As Sir George saw it, Osbert insisted on keeping up an expensive house in London even though he only lived in it for a few months each year and made not the slightest attempt to relate his income to his increasingly lavish tastes. In 1930 Sir George, whose favoured plan was still that Osbert should replace him in Italian exile, produced a variant on this proposal. His new game, Osbert told Hollingworth, was 'Musical Chairs'. All the employees at Renishaw, whether they liked the idea or not, were to be sent to live at Weston, the Sitwell house in Northamptonshire which had been Sachie's home since 1927. The servants and gardeners at Weston, for their part, were to move to Renishaw. Sachie was to go to Renishaw, Osbert to Montegufoni, while Sir George himself would take over the Tudor dower-house, Long Itchington, near Rugby, which had been freed by the death of his sister, Florence. 'This may sound exaggerated, but watch and pray, and you'll see I'm right.' Hollingworth replied that he was amused to hear of this project: 'After all, it is not more fantastic than some of the ideas one has heard in the past from the same source.'[48] Such a remark, coming from an eminently sane and loyal employee, shows how impossible Sir George could be; Osbert behaved ungenerously, even ungratefully, but he was not unprovoked.

Through 1931 and 1932 the quarrel grumbled on; Osbert, perpetually in financial straits, raising an ever larger overdraft with a reluctant Coutts Bank, yet living as if his income was twice as large and assured for life. He had had a very bad go of business worries, he told Georgia: 'They have not cleared up yet by any means, and I have been quite knocked out for a little.'[49] Far from clearing up, they became still worse the following year; agricultural depression had led to a fall in rents and Coutts were growing menacing: Hollingworth interviewed their Mr Hadock in January 1933 and found him alarmed at the increase in Osbert's overdraft, which was rising by more than £1,000 a year. Osbert was only slightly perturbed – he had been receiving similar ultimatums since he was eighteen years old and the effect, he told Lady Aberconway, was always the same, 'A moment of frightful nausea, followed by slight nervous hilarity.'[50] In the spring of 1933 he prolonged his stay abroad until mid-June, thus making it possible to let the house in Carlyle Square. Otherwise he would have had to succumb to his father's pressure and sell it, a prospect which he found intolerable.[51] When he finally did return, however, he found that his circumstances were in no way improved; because of the slump his income was likely to be only a third of what he had been expecting and, still worse, 'Ginger, behind my back, has put in a claim for . . . £1,000 for some debt long ago incurred, not by me, but by the estate. So I get nothing.'[52]

The battle over the alleged debt raged through the summer of 1933. Osbert's first impulse was to be conciliatory; 'the point is, as far as possible, to achieve what one wants *without* a break with him,' he told Sachie.[53] Sir George, for his part, resorted to pathos. 'My time is getting so short now that I should much like to spend August at Renishaw with you.' He could manage a rent of £25 a week, and wished it could have been more.[54] But this was no more than a lull. As soon as the debts came under discussion, Sir George proved obdurate. They were 'most undoubtedly *legally* due from you *personally*', he insisted, the fact that the money had gone into an estate account and that Osbert had not had the spending of it was neither here nor there. 'I have made over so much, and have saved you so much in death duties, that what I did reserve ought to be paid back to me.' Strictly speaking Osbert ought also to pay interest on what was owing, 'but I shall not claim it if the capital sums are repaid'.[55]

Those sums had now been augmented by certain surface coal rents, which were due to Sir George but which Hollingworth had apparently failed to pay over. 'There is a battle which I believe may end in a legal wrangle,' Edith told a friend. 'My father says that Osbert owes him £2,000. This is a terrible lie.'[56] Osbert, to all except his intimates, professed to bear the whole thing lightly, to find it rather amusing, a source of entertaining anecdotes with which to divert his friends. To David Horner, though, he admitted: 'Life has been undiluted hell, and my nerves are like rags. Ginger is worse than I have ever seen him.'[57] Edith had been right in predicting a legal battle; by mid-August the correspondence was being conducted largely through solicitors. Osbert's champion was Philip Frere, a partner in the firm of Frere Cholmeley and a skilful if not over-scrupulous lawyer who was to become one of Osbert's most trusted friends. By the end of August deadlock seemed to have been reached. Osbert, in despair, wrote to his cousin and the trustee of his estate, William Worsley, to give notice of his intention of abandoning Renishaw. 'This decision has been forced upon me by my Father's sudden demand for £2,000, which he alleges is due to him, by his refusal of arbitration on the matter, and by his threat to leave his money away from me, if I go to law in the matter, or refuse to pay him at once the whole of this large sum.'[58] Both William Worsley and his father, the joint trustees, threatened to resign from their position if Osbert's father insisted on proceeding to a lawsuit, and Sir George had another unpleasant shock when the ultra-respectable firm of Lewis & Lewis refused to act on his behalf.[59] Still he showed no signs of relenting. Osbert urged his sister-in-law to make common cause against the enemy: 'I think it is of vital importance that you and Sachie should stand out at the same time . . . If we show a united front we may possibly get the best of it. It is, I think, the only chance.' All direct communication between father and son had now been severed: 'You don't know what the relief is of not having to see the old beast.'[60]

While Osbert tried to keep Sachie on his side, Sir George worked quite as busily to divide the brothers. Osbert told Sachie that their father had refused to pay one of Osbert's hotel bills, for which he had previously agreed to accept responsibility. As a justification he had pleaded his own poverty, which was due 'in a mysterious way to the enormous expense in which *you* had involved him'.[61] Meanwhile Sir George wrote to Georgia to say how much he wished he could pay the school fees for his grandson, Reresby. Unfortunately, however, 'Osbert's refusal to pay me the small rental reserved to me in my deeds of gift, makes this difficult in my life time'.[62] He was very sorry that Osbert had recently neglected Georgia and Sachie, he told them in the spring of 1933. 'He is unfortunately subject to flattery, and there may be some feeling on his part that I have made better provision than is usual in the case of a younger son.'[63]

And then the crisis passed. The relationship between father and son remained cool but, on the surface at least, the acrimony dwindled. Sir George reduced his financial claims to £1,000 and then seems to have dropped them altogether.[64] The economy began to pick up after the slump, agricultural rents revived, the Renishaw estate reverted to its normal condition of prosperity. And Osbert's income as a writer, for so many years exiguous, now began to make a major contribution to his still precarious finances.

*

It was neither his poetry nor his novels – work in which he really took a pride – which brought about this change, but the increasing flood of demands for material from the newspapers. In 1930 he reported that his income had dropped by some £200 a year: 'But journalism must rectify that. A series of really idiotic articles should put it right.'[65] The remark suggests that he viewed such work with some disdain, which is true, but also that he took little trouble over it, which was far from the case. Osbert as hack was a conscientious craftsman, who drafted and redrafted with the care, if not the love, that he lavished on his poetry. He could produce an article on almost any subject at the right time and of the right length, but the spontaneity was an artefact: few writers can have laboured more diligently to produce the right note of casual chattiness. Ever since 1918 he had written regularly for the more serious journals like the *Nation and Athenaeum*, the *Weekly Westminster Gazette*, or the *Spectator*; in 1924 he began to write for *Vogue*, and from 1926 onwards he appeared increasingly in the *Daily Express* and *Sunday Express*, the *Daily Mail*, the *Evening News*, the *Week-End Review* and, most regularly from 1934, the *Sunday Referee*. His contributions to the *Express* were relatively sparse and seem to have been made against the wishes of the proprietor. In 1929 Beaverbrook protested furiously when Edith Sitwell was hired to write a story for the leader page. For ten years, he said, he had stood in the breach 'defending the paper against the publicity stunts of the Sitwells. His Lordship is betrayed from time to time, and he would like to know who gave the Sitwells the key to the gate ... This family group is less than a band of mediocrities.'[66]

Osbert's range was splendidly eclectic. His first article for the *Sunday Referee*, on 7 January 1934, was called 'Englishmen Love Fogs' (this was referred to in an article about him as 'Englishmen Love Frogs', a subject which he could have tackled with equal ease, whether the frogs had been literal or metaphorical). In the next six months he appeared almost every Sunday, producing pieces with titles like 'I Would Forbid Street Music', 'The Art of Being Rude', 'Belittling the Great', 'Virtue of Laziness' and 'Save Me from My Friends'. The subjects differed, the style was always the same: scattered with epigrams, mellifluous, perverse without being upsettingly so, paradoxical without being too confusing, perfect material for the middle-brows who wanted to feel that they were being offered something slightly adventurous and sophisticated. Once every couple of months or so he would have lunch with the editor and return with a list of subjects scrawled beside each Sunday in his pocket diary. When he went abroad he would leave a stockpile of pieces behind him for use during his absence. Even when he was operating at a higher intellectual level his range was still extensive. When T. S. Eliot pressed him for a contribution to the *Criterion* he offered an essay on eighteenth-century German architecture, another on volcanic cities in Sicily, or a story about a murder. If these did not suit he would be happy to produce something else to order.[67]

Some years before, Osbert had read a review of a book of essays and had been struck by the ease with which journalistic articles were suddenly transformed into works of literature. 'No one ever complains of seeing the grey, featureless, formless, brainless, boring things in print a second time – possibly because they cannot remember having seen them the first time.'[68] Now he had an accumulation of his own 'grey, featureless, formless, brainless, boring things', and he felt that they were worthy of reproduction in a less ephemeral format. His first collection of essays – *Penny Foolish. A Book of Tirades and Panegyrics* – was published by Macmillan in 1935. Of the forty-five or so pieces, all had appeared previously, though many had been worked over and some given new titles. They offer a parade of his familiar prejudices, from the significant – 'No war is ever a "righteous" war. A righteous war is only one degree less wicked than a wicked war' – to the frivolous – trifle is 'the most ill-favoured and excruciating of national dishes'. Probably the essay he most enjoyed writing was 'Prigs', an attack on the Leavises, Geoffrey Grigson and other like-minded critics. He had used to suppose the Leavises to be elderly spinster sisters, he claimed. They were not stupid but 'their minds undoubtedly betray a curious combination of silliness and intelligence. They are altogether without simplicity, and revel in a peculiar, puritan complication which, while they think it austere, in reality lacks all the qualities of natural reaction to thought.'

It was such passages which the novelist Howard Spring must have had in mind when in a review in the *Evening Standard* he said that Osbert's style, 'which can at times voice a delightfully urbane rudeness, has always seemed to me better used in the essay than the novel . . . most of these essays are very good indeed'. Osbert would have been gratified by the praise but not have been best pleased by the implicit criticism of his novels; probably he would have preferred E. B. Osborn's judgment that 'He and his like (if any) are the drops of vinegar in a salad of life and letters which has hitherto contained too much oil from the pacific olive.' The reviews on the whole were good, and more extensive than might have been expected for a collection of light-weight journalism. The *Daily Telegraph* was almost alone in complaining that such 'quotidian jottings' were only worth republication if they would give future generations 'an exact picture of the contemporary scene'. *Penny Foolish* did no more than offer 'a catalogue of those personal likings and antipathies which Mr Sitwell acquired in 1920 . . . neither very original nor very topical'.[69]

Penny Foolish sold unexpectedly well: 'I'm so glad the book is prospering,' Osbert wrote to Harold Macmillan. 'I must say I'm delighted it's being reprinted.'[70] Macmillan's clamoured for a further volume, but though Osbert produced books of travel-writings, the publishing house had to wait ten years before it got a similar collection. Mainly this was because, after 1935, Osbert felt his financial position allowed him to be more selective in his journalism and to write minor pieces, as for *Lilliput* on 'The Old School Tie', only if the fee was handsome enough to be irresistible.[71] His second volume, *Sing High! Sing Low!*, which did not appear until 1944, was very much the mixture as before, with the same unexpected trivialities – how to cook iguana, or female cigar smokers – and one or two more substantial pieces. The essay on Thomas Rowlandson was typical of the latter. It had first appeared in 1929 as part of a series of pamphlets on famous water-colour painters. It was clearly written by a man of taste with a wide knowledge of contemporary cultures but it displayed no evidence of serious research and was heavily dependent on obvious sources like the *Dictionary of National Biography* or A. P. Oppé's book on Rowlandson's drawings and water-colours. Perhaps because he had more time at his disposal, Osbert gave greater thought to rewriting the pieces than he had done with the earlier volume. 'I hear that *Sing High* is selling rapidly,' wrote David Horner. 'Such an easy way of making money; but of course you did *réchauffé* the whole thing very carefully, and that has obviously made all the difference.'[72] Osbert's publishers probably thought that the *réchauffage* had been carried considerably too far. Rache Lovat Dickson, Macmillan's senior editor, complained that the copy submitted had been so extensively corrected that it would have been simpler to have the entire book retyped. Only then, he added resignedly, 'if I know Osbert, he would have corrected the corrected typescript'.[73]

James Agate, who, though a man of wide reading and considerable intelligence, liked from time to time to beat his philistine drum, complained that *Sing High! Sing Low!* made him feel that he was reading above his class, beyond his intellectual means: 'There is in this superb writer a vein of something which in a less sincere artist I should call precious and even high falutin'. He writes adorably about the pictures of Salvator Rosa. Will he believe that I am far more interested in my early photographs of Jimmy Wilde?'[74] Osbert, who was anyway at that time engaged in a literary battle with Agate, would have had no trouble in believing it, and despising Agate accordingly. The book got fewer reviews than its predecessor, but Osbert must have been pleased by Elizabeth Bowen's summary in the *Tatler*, 'as packed with quality as it is diverse in its subjects'.[75] The reading public was unconcerned by the paucity of reviews. The success of *Penny Foolish* had encouraged Macmillan to print 10,000 copies of *Sing High! Sing Low!*, a remarkably large edition for such a book. Within three weeks the publisher was telling Osbert that over 9,000 had already been sold and a new impression was in the press.[76] In the middle of the war new books were a rarity and almost anything would sell, but even allowing for this the result was something of a triumph.

The need to make money led Osbert into other ventures which he would have eschewed in happier circumstances. He had been hired to give a reading, he announced from Montegufoni, 'at the house of Mrs Myron Taylor, wife of the President of some immense corporation in America'. The fee had not yet been paid but he hoped it would be fat; so did his mother, who was acting as his agent and would be taking 10 per cent. Sir George was most put out: 'such a pity, it lets one down so'. 'It will be a dreadful affair,' Osbert concluded gloomily; but the money was needed and, anyway, it was a pleasure to annoy his father.[77] He had sometimes to draw the line, however. Stuart Perowne asked him to contribute a series of talks on 'Great Lovers' for the Arabic service of the BBC – 'stories of Eastern lovers would naturally awaken a more ready sympathy in some of our listeners'. Osbert's reply is lost but his scrawled instruction to his secretary reads: 'v kind; not doing this sort of thing at present'.[78]

He still found time for labours of love. His booklet on Charles Dickens was one of these, for he idolised Dickens as a prophet, a propagandist who actually managed to ameliorate some of the social injustices which he described, and 'a master of sensational plots and continued excitement'. Dickens's delineation of character, wrote Osbert, 'places him ... in a class by himself with no contemporary rival'. He was an innovator, 'wielding with perfect ease a technique towards which others are even now but struggling; the inventor of "expressionism" in fiction – a writer a hundred years ahead of his time'.[79]

The booklet, based on an article he had contributed to the *Week-End Review* in 1931, almost failed to make the transition to hard covers. The article had been entitled 'A Note on Charles Dickens' and it was as such that it fell to the reader for Chatto & Windus, Oliver Warner. 'Osbert Sitwell is right to be modest in his title,' judged Warner with some hauteur. 'This is indeed a note and no more. It reads quite pleasantly, but I can't say I gathered anything fresh whatever from it.' From a lesser name it would have merited rejection. As it was, 'it is very flimsy. What it has is charm.'[80] Fortunately for Osbert, it fitted in well with a series which Chatto & Windus were publishing and was accepted on that ground. On the whole Warner's doubts seem justified: the study, little more than an extended essay, is pleasant to read and vividly captures the imaginative energy and rich vulgarity of Dickens – qualities so remote from Osbert's work. But the judgments are run-of-the-mill and the treatment superficial. 'Mr Sitwell is saying what we have all known for years,' wrote V. S. Pritchett, 'and adding nothing to the interpretative sympathy which Mr G. K. Chesterton gave to the subject some years ago.' But, Pritchett added, Osbert wrote 'with so becoming a simplicity and fervour that we move up and make room for him gladly'.[81] Some were less muted in their praises. Somerset Maugham told Osbert that, to his mind, he had never written better. 'Formerly, I sometimes felt that you were not the master but the instrument of your great gift for words, but now, though you have preserved your very individual talent for using them . . . I think you have acquired a new mastery.'[82] Rebecca West described *Dickens* as delightful and called for a longer book, while the *Morning Post*, with a fervour which cast some doubt on the reviewer's judgment, concluded that it was worth 'all the other books on Dickens ever written, and I hail it as one of the few classics of criticism'.[83]

The anthologies which he compiled with the help of Margaret Barton, a diligent lady who acted as Osbert's secretary and seemed delighted to do most of the work and leave her employer most of the credit, were more mundane hack work. *Sober Truth. A Collection of Nineteenth-Century Episodes, Fantastic, Grotesque and Mysterious* and *Victoriana. A Symposium of Victorian Wisdom* were both devoted to amiable mockery of the standards and shibboleths of Osbert's immediate ancestors. They contain some splendid things – most notably the *Quarterly Review*'s criticism of *Jane Eyre* as 'pre-eminently an anti-Christian composition . . . We do not hesitate to say that the tone of mind and thought which has now overthrown and violated every code human and divine abroad, and fostered Chartism and rebellion at home, is the same which has also written *Jane Eyre*' – but though Osbert made some suggestions and contributed graceful prefaces, the main credit for excavating such gems rested with Miss Barton.

His role was greater in a third book which he and his secretary wrote together, though even there Miss Barton did almost all the research and Henry D. Roberts, the art director at Brighton to whom the book was dedicated, probably contributed as much as either. Most of Osbert's work was done during a visit to China – 'I've managed to finish writing a very bad book on Brighton,' he told Lady Aberconway.[84] He was unduly disparaging: *Brighton*[85] was a slight work but supplemented a pleasant, gossipy history of the town with some vivid character sketches, notably of the Prince Regent, for whose self-indulgence, extravagance and artistic sensibilities Osbert felt great sympathy. Nobody suggested it was a major contribution to history, whether social or architectural, but it was perceptive and often witty. 'I am so glad to see that Osbert has had such excellent reviews for his *Brighton*,' Somerset Maugham told David Horner. 'He must be very much pleased and if he is not in a good temper he is (as my neighbour Mr Rudyard Kipling puts it) not a pukkah sahib, not even a white man, and should be put with his back to a wall and shot at dawn.'[86]

But the most successful of these diversions, in quality if not in sales, was the result of another collaboration, this time with the pugnacious and somewhat louche artist Nina Hamnett. Miss Hamnett had been a pupil of Sickert and a protégée of Augustus John. Osbert went to an exhibition of her work some time in 1927, was impressed by what he saw, and asked her what she was going to do next. She said that she thought it would be interesting to draw the statues of London. 'That's an idea,' said Osbert. 'Let's do a book together of the statues of London; they are so comic. I will write it and you will do the drawing.' Some months later, having mulled over the idea, she telephoned him to ask whether he had been serious. 'Let's start at once,' said Osbert, who then sold the project to Duckworth and procured the artist an advance.[87] His aim, as he made clear, was to ridicule rather than seriously to assess. 'The queerer the statues, the duller the people, the better,' he told Nina Hamnett, 'that is, apart from Royalties. Your Queen Vic as Boadicea sounds quite perfect . . . Whiskered and forgotten peers in top hats and classical togas should be an aim, if you take me.'[88]

The artist took him and took to the idea. Her drawings are delightful, very much in the style later brought to perfection by Osbert Lancaster, funny, even grotesque, yet precise in detail and conveying an impression of what the statue is all about. Osbert's extended captions are more variable; many are excellent, yet he gives the impression of having lost interest in the enterprise towards the end, when the text becomes cursory and the factual details obviously culled from Mrs Esdaile's more substantial work on the same subject. Statues are chosen more for the absurdity of the subject than the merits or demerits of the sculpture. Lyonell Lockyer, from Southwark Cathedral, was a quack doctor and pioneer beautician who claimed he could encapsulate the sun's rays in a pill. Osbert was enchanted by the inscription:

> His virtues and his pills are so well known,
> That envy can't confine them under stone,
> But they'll survive his dust and not expire
> Till all things else at the Universal Fire.

His caption to the drawing of Shakespeare's statue in Leicester Square reads: 'WS or Shakespeare was an Elizabethan poet and journalist, whose plays are still occasionally performed in the poorer parts of London. Miss Clemence Dane has lately immortalised his name by making it the title of a play of her own.' This piece, one of the longer in the collection, rambled on into a discourse on Sir Ashton Lever's Holophusikon or museum, which was full of tropical and antipodean curiosities brought back from his voyages with Captain Cook; a subject which, while entertaining and intriguing, had nothing whatsoever to do with the subject except that it, too, had been in Leicester Square.[89]

While the *Listener* commented severely that *The People's Album of London Statues* was 'a queer jumble of curious information, humour and affectation', of no use to anyone 'seriously interested in English monumental sculpture', most critics saw the point of this whimsical enterprise. Osbert and Nina Hamnett had taken the statues out of their limbo and restored them to life, said the *Times Literary Supplement*: 'We are enchanted with the result.' Clive Bell, a heavy art-critical gun to be brought to bear on so frivolous an enterprise, concluded that Osbert had had two intentions: 'To lead to the overthrow of some of London's more conspicuously hideous statues (in which he will fail)' and 'to give pleasure to intelligent people; and in this he has succeeded'.[90]

Osbert had, of course, a third intention, to make some money – but in this too he failed. He wrote to Sachie from Capri to say that he was feeling 'rotten and depressed': 'before the end of next month I must finish my preface to the new anthology Miss Barton and I have done (I haven't written a word of it yet) and between now and April do my Rowlandson essay . . . And, in spite of reviews in all papers, my statue book has sold only 800!'[91] Things did not improve. A few years later, in 1937, Osbert tried to persuade the publisher to reprint *London Statues*, on the grounds of Nina Hamnett's destitution. A subscription had been got up for her and he had contributed £5, 'but I wondered if it would be possible to obtain more money out of the book, which I like very much'. There was ample stock already, replied Gerald Duckworth. Then couldn't at least some effort be made to sell it, pleaded Osbert. Perhaps there might be special displays 'as a sort of *guide* for colonial and American visitors' who had come to London for the coronation. 'It is very, very difficult to get booksellers to feature old books,' wrote Duckworth, gloomily. Hatchards and Bumpus had taken a few copies on sale or return and little more could be expected.[92] The exchange will be dismally familiar to anyone who has either had books published or has published books. It confirmed Osbert in his belief, only much later to be dispelled, that if he were to make serious money out of writing, then journalism offered the only hope.

11

Wings to Head and Pen

To all writers, whether chiefly concerned with the exterior or the
interior of the world, books of travel are the most stimulating,
lending wings to head and pen.

(Sing High! Sing Low!)

THERE was one form of writing which gave Osbert great gratification and also the chance of a decent financial return. He had
discovered in 1925, when his *Discursions on Travel, Art and Life*
had been a notable success, that travel articles collected in a book appear
more respectable, more considerable in the eyes of the critics, than most
compendiums of journalistic bric-à-brac. He would have found the
money to pay for voyages abroad even though there had been no possibility of reward, it was a pleasure, almost a necessity, which ranked only
after reading in his scale of values. The fact that newspaper editors and
publishers were ready to pay him handsomely for doing what he would
anyway have done gave additional savour to his delight.

Travel, for Osbert, could mean different things. There were protracted
winter sessions in quiet places where serious work could be undertaken;
progresses around Europe or North Africa, usually accompanied by a
little court of like-minded enthusiasts; and long journeys to remoter
parts with no companion except David Horner. So far as the first of these
were concerned, until 1930, except for one season in Rapallo, Amalfi
had always been the chosen spot, but Horner, less dedicated to writing
than Osbert, found the hotel bleak and rather dull. In the winter of
1929/30 William Walton was also in attendance, working as hard as
Osbert. 'So far so good,' Horner reported. 'Only one little row between
Willie and Osbert which I started by accident and hurriedly stopped.' He
may have stopped it, but the accidental nature of its start is more
implausible; starting rows was one of Horner's main diversions, and

with time on his hands he could have been expected to stir things up. Also reappearing in the hotel was Godfrey Winn; 'famous in literary and theatrical circles,' wrote Horner superciliously, 'but until now unknown to me. He is a nuisance and suffers from loquamania – and talks such tosh.' Winn was in love with Walton – or at least Walton claimed he was – a fresh offence in Horner's eyes. Horner poisoned Winn with a triple dose of his new purge, which laid low this unfortunate androgyne for twenty-four hours: 'Willie said I was a cad for doing such a thing, but I finally managed to point out that it was rather funny. Winnie the Pooh is with us for another month, unless I manage to enrage him so much that he leaves. (Also he capers and scampers, wh is unforgivable).'[1]

Winn did not leave; he clung ingratiatingly to the other Englishmen and began to address Osbert as 'Headmaster' – 'He is full of these little, winning, schoolboy affectations,' wrote Horner disgustedly. The party was almost teetotal, which Horner found upsetting, and rose at 7.30 a.m., which was even worse. By way of diversion when they were not working Osbert and Walton would go down to the sea to bathe. The Tyrrhenian Sea in January did not appeal to Horner, so 'I stood on the beach and listened to those little gasps and grunts which bathers always make to show that they are having a "lovely time". They looked very blue when they emerged.'[2]

All in all, it was unsurprising that for the winter of 1930/1 they moved on to Syracuse, in Sicily, and in subsequent years to the Canaries, Cyprus, Corfu and Madeira. For Osbert, at least, a chief object was to find something close to solitude. In Amalfi there had been a constant threat of tourists: 'An old American woman, for example, was very impertinent,' Osbert told Lady Aberconway. He had been enraged, 'and you know how I suffer from suppressed temper'.[3] At least if the impertinence were gross enough there was no need to suppress the temper; worse were the literary bores, who had no wish to cause offence and might even be admirers – 'the sort whom you avoid for years but persist in bouncing out at you, when you least expect them, from behind Gothic screen or Attic pillars – "Do you really think Mr T S Eliot means it?" And "Do tell me, is James Joyce nice?" '[4]

In Corfu he at first thought he had escaped: 'I like this place very much. It's empty of visitors.' He spoke too soon. A few weeks later he still liked Corfu but couldn't 'make out how it is I have come to know so many and so boring people here. They badger one almost as badly as in London.'[5] The visitors, however, were redeemed by the spectacular beauty of the island: 'The town is tiny, and a mixture of Venetian 18th century,

English Regency and Oriental. The landscape is just what that of a large Greek island should be; little sickle bays lying flat on flat blue sea and gentle hills with olive trees and cypresses, and meadows with the smallest lambs, black and white, scampering around and big merino sheep, like poor old Ottoline.'[6] The food was 'very romantic. We live on wild boar and deer and hens and snipe in an almost mediaeval way.' And best of all was the cheapness: 'We live at £5 a week, including all bills and cigarettes and everything.'[7]

Left to himself Osbert would probably have returned to Corfu, or perhaps reverted to Amalfi, when a wintering spot was next needed, but the ever-restless Horner craved for new sensations. 'I wish that bad Osbert wasn't going to Cyprus,' Edith wrote plaintively. 'I am sure we shall have him in Central Africa yet.'[8] In Cyprus Osbert found, as he so often did, that while every prospect pleased, man was singularly vile. 'I don't like the Cypriots,' he complained to Lady Aberconway, 'and would like to give this island back to Turkey. The servants are dirty and stupid.'[9] But at least there were few if any earnest literary ladies to tease and fawn upon him. The little town of Paphos, where he and Horner ensconced themselves, was almost too quiet, there was hardly a mule in the street and because Ramadan was in progress there was not even a wailing from the minarets to call the faithful to prayer. But the work did not go well. Osbert was trying to start a new novel – a project which seems eventually to have been aborted – and finding the effort a misery. 'How I, or anyone else, has *ever* managed to do it, I can't imagine,' he wrote to his old friend, Lady Desborough. 'I see the most horrible risks of headaches, bad temper, and laziness ahead of me, crowned finally by complete exhaustion and no sales.'[10]

This gloomy experience, coupled with Horner's craving for something rather more sociable, sent them the following year to Funchal in Madeira. Here the scene was considerably more animated; the Duke of Sutherland had arrived, Osbert reported, 'but I don't think he knows it. So perhaps one ought *not* to say it, or it might get back to him and give him a shock.'[11] The Duke of Sutherland was felt by Osbert to be vague but nice; Noël Coward's mother, who arrived the following month, did not even have the redeeming feature of niceness. She was 'very deaf and gaga', Osbert told Georgia, 'so deaf and gaga, indeed, that I think she must have helped [her son] with his plays. It's no use trying to explain to her that I don't like her or her son, because she can't hear.'[12] Osbert's rancour against Noël Coward was unabated and he missed no opportunity of expressing it. In *Penny Foolish*, published in 1935, he described Coward as a 'competent but incomparably boring writer of musical comedies and revues' who 'became a playwright, poet and musician'. He had less musical talent than 'the late Mr Adrian Ross, and less talent as a playwright than the late Henry Arthur Jones – both of whom were equally deservedly forgotten. We must not allow ourselves to be blinded by the fact that he does three things rather badly.'[13]

As a variant on such excursions, David Horner and Osbert would from time to time patronise the continental health resorts. There they would take the waters, diet under medical supervision, and generally cosset their fragile constitutions. Such a regime should have left plenty of time for writing. Unfortunately the fashionable spas, which David Horner favoured, were filled with the very kind of people whom Osbert was most anxious to avoid. He was prepared to put up with – just – the 'monsters so obese that they seem to have fallen like H. G. [Wells]'s Martians from another planet', whom he met at Brides-les-Bains in the French Alps. They were cross from starvation and so bored that they had nothing to do except encourage their children to jump and skip directly above Osbert's room, but at least 'they make me feel thin; for which I like them'.[14] But he found it harder to forgive the Swiss lady novelist who, discovering that Osbert was also an author and was called Sitwell, asked him under what name he wrote. 'Clemence Dane,' Osbert replied at random – Miss Dane being a competent novelist and dramatist whose work the Sitwells chose to disparage with particular ferocity. This caused an instant sensation: 'What, you are the Great Dane! Then you are *great* as Galsworthy!' The Swiss lady, a Miss Kramer, later confided in Edith, who was staying in the same hotel, that she had always supposed Clemence Dane to be a woman. 'Oh, no,' said Edith firmly, 'a man, my brother!' In fact, she added, most of the great women novelists in England were in fact men, but preferred this to be unknown. Osbert benevolently granted Miss Kramer permission to translate certain of his books and urged her to write to Clemence Dane's agents, explaining that Osbert Sitwell had authorised her to undertake this task. 'What *will* happen?' he speculated.[15]

This was sedentary travelling, undertaken to provide an opportunity for writing what was already planned, not to gather material for fresh books or articles. Far more enjoyable were the trips which he made around Europe or the fringes of the Mediterranean. Certain places and themes constantly recurred. Venice was the goal of innumerable journeys; 'never did I feel in Florence that same contentment tinged with wonder that always came to me in Venice,' he wrote in his autobiography.[16] Santa Sophia and San Vitale at Ravenna were places of pilgrimage, the most beautiful of Byzantine churches, 'which is to say the most beautiful of all churches'.[17] Baroque remained the school of architecture and painting for which he retained the greatest, almost a proprietary affection; the Sitwells used baroque 'to express something of their own, slightly frivolous, un-English attitude to life', said Kenneth Clark.[18] Osbert's tastes were adventurous and eclectic; though the threat of discomfort or disease increasingly deterred him as he grew older, he was always ready to go anywhere and try anything if he believed the reward would be great enough. Usually, though, he preferred a better beaten track. After Venice, Athens was the most common destination. He was there in April 1929 on the last of the grand tours which he made with Sachie. Georgia came too and described it as 'one of the happiest times of my life. Sach and O have been angels too and equally happy I think.'[19]

Four years later he was there again, this time with Lord Berners, the rich novelist, composer and relentless joker. Gerald Berners, Osbert told Georgia, 'still exists in that peculiar artificial paradise, which he has built for himself . . . paradise in which, since it is always the first of April, neither autumn nor winter can ever enter'. Though he was sometimes supercilious about Berners, Osbert was happy enough to descend from time to time into his gilded play-pen, where good taste and high spirits reigned and only the most lavish standard of comfort was acceptable. On this occasion Berners was, for some reason, pursuing a vendetta against Cyril Connolly, who was in Athens just before the party was due to arrive, lecturing, writing articles and being fêted in a quiet but satisfying way. To his dismay, Connolly now received a letter, apparently emanating from the Director of the Greek Tourist Board, which told him: 'A party of distinguished visitors, to whom your appearance and mentality are equally repulsive, is shortly arriving in Athens. As it is important that they should obtain a pleasant first impression of our city, it is requested that you will leave Greece by 22nd inst.' It seems inconceivable that Connolly was taken in by so transparent a hoax, but according to Osbert he had fled the scene before Berners and his troupe arrived.[20]

In 1932 it was the turn of Spain and Portugal. On earlier visits Osbert had far preferred Spain to Portugal, but the previous year a republic had been proclaimed in Spain and the king driven into exile. The left-wing regime which was now in power was not at all to Osbert's taste: 'The atmosphere is terrible,' he told Lady Desborough, 'and dreadfully sad to anyone who knows the country.'[21] With some relief he and David Horner moved on to Lisbon, where proper order still prevailed. The German minister gave a party for them, with the promise that they would hear some real *fado* singing. They looked forward to it immensely, Osbert reported. It proved to be an enormous party, 'full of black 2ft high Portuguese aristocrats in very flashing clothes, lots of jewels and white waistcoats'. When it came to the *fado* singing, however, all they got was 'a certain Count de Lancastre, only a metre tall, who would not stop singing, in a cockney accent, a song called "I'm for ever blowing bubbles" – a pantomime hit of ten years ago'.[22] It was all very disappointing, but at least somebody had tried to do something in their honour, which was more than had happened in Madrid.

It was journeys of this kind which provided the new material for *Winters of Content*, subtitled *More Discursions on Travel, Art and Life*. It was, as the name suggests, the mixture as before, rambling and relaxed, the reflections of a talented and well-read amateur with a sharp eye and a capacious memory. Osbert deplored travel by train, which induced, he maintained, 'that curious, slow inflexibility of mind' which distinguished the nineteenth-century author from those of any other age. The passenger by train could not spend 'the merest instant on his way for the examination of a wild flower or a bird'.[23] Now flexibility and swiftness had been restored, 'the natural properties of minds that think in terms of motor-car and airplane'. Osbert can be forgiven for not foreseeing the horrors of the autostrada but it is hard to imagine how he supposed the traveller by aeroplane – a conveyance which he was not to use himself for another thirty years – could pause to examine a wild flower or a bird. He was himself, however, a most fruitful dawdler who would form his own opinion as to the merits of any work of art and, if it pleased him, linger over it while neglecting other, better-accredited masterpieces. His prolonged eulogy of the paintings of Tintoretto, Correggio and El Greco – the second at that time unfashionable, the third ignored by almost all the established pundits – is a remarkable demonstration of how an independent-minded man, capable of forming and holding his own heretical opinions, may make himself widely heard even though the voices of received wisdom demand that he be ignored. But it was in the description of buildings – the Castel del Monte in Apulia, the Villa Malcontenta on the Brenta – that Osbert's mastery of the aesthetic and the anecdotal met to best advantage. He and Sachie were two of the few living Englishmen who could describe architecture, judged Evelyn Waugh: 'It is a very gracious gift, requiring a keen visual memory, discernment and enterprise in taste, a sense of social standards, delicate accuracy of expression and, unobtrusive at the back, a full technical scholarship of date and name and material.'[24] In Sachie the 'full technical scholarship' was more soundly based, but Osbert had the ability in his writings to people a building and make it come alive.

Winters of Content deals almost entirely with Italian subjects. Its prime object was to entertain rather than to educate: he was trying, Osbert wrote, 'to convey to the reader a sense of holiday'. Proselytisation was secondary: he would be grateful if his readers in future looked at El Greco with new eyes, but he would not feel that he had failed provided they had passed an enjoyable half-hour with his essay. His efforts to be lively sometimes became a little hectic – the lift in the hotel at Bari and the thinness of the walls receive more attention than they deserve – but the book as a whole is never less than readable and has the great merit of making readers see things for themselves. The essays, wrote Harold Acton, 'seem like twentieth-century sequels to William Beckford's travel books, suavely discursive, imaginatively poetical, but richer than rich Beckford in red corpuscles and humanity'.[25]

The first volume of *Discursions* had been published by Grant Richards; *Winters of Content* was brought out by Duckworth; by the time of Osbert's next and best travel book he had moved on again. As late as 1937 Edith was referring fondly to Duckworth as 'the kindest and friendliest of publishers in the world';[26] but Osbert had been disillusioned by their failure to promote and sell *London Statues* and when his admirer and protector Thomas Balston was driven from the firm, he lost heart and decided to look elsewhere. He considered several possibilities. Faber & Faber had a distinguished list but they were, he concluded wryly, 'a luxury for the rich';[27] besides which, he probably did not relish the thought of playing second fiddle to T. S. Eliot. Rupert Hart-Davis, that paragon among publishers who had given Osbert much helpful advice in the past, tried hard to secure him for his then employer, Jonathan Cape. Osbert told his agent, David Higham, or at least told Hart-Davis that he had told his agent, that 'other things being equal' he would prefer to move to Cape – 'This is due to you. I wonder how it will work out?'[28] Other things were not equal, they never are. Macmillan made a bid far more substantial than Osbert's sales to date could justify – a technique which had recently secured them Storm Jameson and C. P. Snow – and the match was made. He never regretted the decision. Osbert liked both Daniel and Harold Macmillan, who controlled the firm on behalf of the family, and had total confidence in his desk editor, Thomas

Mark, who in his time had looked after Hardy, Kipling and Yeats and whose clear-headed conscientiousness was one of the marvels of the publishing profession.[29] He moved to Macmillan with his volume of essays, *Penny Foolish*, and remained with them for more than twenty years.

It was for Macmillan that Osbert wrote *Escape With Me!*, an account of his visit to Indo-China and China in 1934.[30] The idea of such a journey had come to him when visiting Sachie at Weston in November 1933. He remarked that he felt in the mood for a long journey but did not know where to go or how to pay for it. 'Why not go to Peking?' asked Sachie casually. He had hardly spoken before Osbert had decided that this was the one thing he most longed to do. As for the cost – it would have to look after itself: 'and you, Gentle Reader, would have to look after it in the end,' as he remarked cheerfully in the preface to *Escape With Me!* He set sail with David Horner at the end of 1933 on the French liner, the *D'Artagnan*. Unsurprisingly, he was bored by his fellow travellers – 'all the passengers have names like those in Walter Guilbert's songs of *bourgeoise* life in Paris ... Madame Bonhomme, Madame Bonnard etc.,' he complained to Christabel Aberconway. Equally unsurprisingly, he was entranced by the stops along the way, Ceylon in particular, with 'flowers like an orchid house, and palm trees and elephants and English governesses and all that sort of thing'.[31]

Angkor, in Cambodia, was his first serious stopping place. He went there before it had become widely known, before the exquisite temple of Bantis Sthrea, most perfect building of the whole miraculous complex, had even been discovered, yet the effect on him was overwhelming: Angkor, he wrote, 'ranks as chief wonder of the world today, one of the summits to which human genius has aspired in stone'.[32] Only the inhabitants disappointed; 'very odd', Osbert found them. 'I thought they would be like Indians or Chinese, but, no, they're native tattooed savages.'[33] He and Horner spent more than a week among the ruins; not long enough but lavish compared with the time most contemporary travellers can afford. There was always a leisurely tempo to Osbert's travelling which provokes jealousy in a world ruled by publishers' deadlines and the demands of airline schedules.

Then it was on to Peking – Peiping, Osbert tended to call it in his letters, though he was always casual about nomenclature and wrote both Pekin and Peking on occasion. Harold Acton was living there, teaching and studying; the fact that he would be available to act as cicerone was one of the reasons which had led Osbert to undertake the voyage. Acton did all and more than could have been expected of him: 'Harold is "grand",' Osbert told Sachie enthusiastically. 'Very much nicer and more intelligent than formerly.'[34] With Acton's help they quickly found a house and settled in for more than three months; a lovely house 'with two stone courtyards, full of flowering trees and charming rooms, furnished, for £2.10.0 a week. And very good servants.'[35] The best of those servants, and major-domo of the household, was Chang, 'tall, with an almost episcopal dignity of mien', sweeping around the house in pursuance of his duties and giggling discreetly from time to time as his employer displayed some fresh example of his boundless ignorance.[36] In *Escape With Me!* Osbert built up Chang into a character of almost Henry Moat-ian proportions and made him the source of much recondite information about the habits and characteristics of the Chinese. This got him into some trouble with the *Times Literary Supplement*, whose reviewer commented: 'If Chang actually existed in the flesh, if he is not the product of an artistic imagination, he must have been one of the most inveterate leg-pullers ever produced by a race that loves its joke at the expense of the barbarian. But the fearful and wonderful quasi-pidgin English in which his talk is recorded would seem to suggest what Mr Gladstone called a constructive memory.'[37] Chang did exist, but so did Osbert's constructive memory.

One of the most successful set-pieces in *Escape With Me!*, in which one suspects that the constructive memory plays a large part, is the visit to the Ancestral Hall of the Exalted Brave, the retirement home for distressed eunuchs who had survived from the imperial palace. Osbert brilliantly describes the twittering and gossiping of these pathetic relics, the 'vivacious cackle and prattle and toothless laughter', the consuming curiosity about their unexpected visitors, the gigantic painted effigy of the Eunuch General, 'one of the most superb pieces of sculpture of the Ming Epoch'. All this one can accept. But it is harder to believe in the anonymous Englishman who, Osbert claims, the eunuchs told him had visited them two years before. When they had said sadly to their visitor that they believed people like them were not now to be found anywhere in the world, he replied that there was one place in London where they still survived: in, 'a difficult word for them', Bloomsbury. 'It was, he had said, a Refuge for Eunuchs, like their own. How they longed to visit it, and see for themselves English ways of life.'[38]

Osbert greatly enjoyed Peking. He would spend the morning working on his book on Brighton, then in the afternoon roam around the city, visiting shops or temples, venturing down alleys or into courtyards, sometimes embarking on longer expeditions to the Forbidden City. He enjoyed the social life, though he found fatiguing the way that the Chinese would gather for dinner at 6.45 p.m. but not utter a word until 9.00 or later. Meanwhile they would drink a great deal – 'hot white wine which is made of rice and tastes like a cross between sherry and Chablis with a tintack melted in it', and a vodka-like spirit which 'so far took one's breath away as partially to explain the lack of conversation'. He was pleased, too, by the food, particularly once he had discovered that they liked eating dogs – though more, it seems, because he disliked live dogs than that he enjoyed the taste of dead ones. While still alive the dog had to be plunged into a tank of hot white wine and held there until fully marinated; something which even Osbert felt was going a little far.[39] Otherwise the only thing he found to complain about in Peking was the dust-storm which from time to time would envelop the city in a germ-laden cloud and ensure that he suffered from an unbroken series of colds. Horner was more seriously ill, but, Osbert complained, was not content with his own affliction but took to developing other people's symptoms into the bargain. When Harold Acton was nearly suffocated by his stove one night, Horner at once said that the same thing had happened to him; when Christabel Aberconway complained in a letter about her sinus trouble, he retreated to bed with sinusitis. 'Where, I ask myself, is it leading to?' wrote Osbert darkly.[40] It was while Horner was in bed that Osbert paid a visit to a Chinese face-diviner. After studying his visitor the diviner prophesied that within a few years he would grow a moustache – a sign of his having adopted some position of great responsibility. He would have several sons, who would be headstrong and wayward. And he would be involved in and win a celebrated lawsuit. About the first two predictions Osbert was sceptical; the third seemed much more hopeful and he stored it away for future reference.[41]

Osbert wrote up his Asian experiences for *Harper's Bazaar*, the *Fortnightly* and other journals, but for one reason or another it was not until early 1938 that he settled down to a study of the chewing of betel, the cultivation of rice and other such subjects preparatory to turning his journalism into a book. The delay helped him produce a more considered and carefully constructed piece of travel-writing than anything he had achieved before. He claimed to be finding the work tedious but the result was delectably spontaneous and communicated a sense of almost intoxicating joy. Osbert always delighted in the incantatory quality of words and he never found richer material: the dishes in a restaurant – Boiled Bears' Paws and the Pudding of the Seven Heavenly Flavours;

buildings in the Forbidden City – the Pavilion of Equable Autumn and the Peaceful Cottage among Coiled Mists, a name which, Osbert observed, 'suggests a picture by Salvador Dali – except, perhaps, that then it would be called in the catalogue "Peaceful Mists among Coiled Cottages" '.[42]

His object, as he had insisted in earlier works, was to entertain and not to educate; a disclaimer accepted by all except the censorious reviewer of the *Times Literary Supplement* who took him to task for superficiality and slipshod scholarship. Hugh Walpole called it 'one of the half-dozen best books of travel in English of the last half-century', while in the *Saturday Review* Upton Close described it as a book 'whose body is part of the actual delight of human living', and 'a permanent classic like Marco Polo and Doughty'.[43] It appeared in November 1939, at a time when the English were beginning to realise that for years to come they would have to do their travelling vicariously. Macmillan knew that they had a success on their hands from the moment they received the typescript – 'everyone here thinks that it is your best book, and so do I,' enthused Harold Macmillan.[44] The publisher sent a copy to Stella Gibbons, and the author of *Cold Comfort Farm* replied delightedly that she had not enjoyed a book more for months: 'I particularly like the beautiful kindness that shines in Sitwell's writing. So many people who love beauty better than anything are cruel; he isn't.'[45] The first printing had sold out before Christmas and a new impression was selling briskly by the New Year. The advance had been £250, not over-generous but reasonable by the standards of the age; this had been earned within a few weeks of publication. Given that Osbert was being paid twice over for work that had already appeared in magazines, it was commercially the most successful of his books to date.

He was well satisfied with his publisher's efforts, though there was a moment when he doubted their taste in advertising. Rache Lovat Dickson had proposed some copy which referred to the activities of the Sitwells as an entity. Osbert was not offended but found the approach unpleasing:

> I have been thinking very carefully over the publicity question. I think it is a mistake, really, to stress the *trio* aspect more than necessary. By this time, we have each of us carved out for ourselves a recognisable personality (no easy matter in England where people love 'The Brontës' and all sorts of groups, The Crazy Gang). And if we again label Trio about the place, it may muddle the stampeding herds. Better to exploit the personality of each shepherd separately. What do you think?[46]

It was a far cry from the days when 'the Sitwells' seemed invariably to hunt as a pack, but even then Edith in particular had resented this vision of a trichotomous literary figure. Now it was far too late for such foolery. Edith, Osbert and Sacheverell were still often together, read poetry on the same platforms, attended the same occasions, but they were three independent artists and wished to be recognised as such.

The greater part of *Escape With Me!* was written in Guatemala early in 1939. Osbert had been in apocalyptic mood in the autumn of 1938. One weekend at Renishaw he complained so frequently that everything was happening 'for the last time' that one of the guests complained that it was as bad as being locked up with Edgar Allan Poe's raven, who perpetually quoth 'Nevermore'.[47] The conviction that civilisation was about to end, or at least to put up the shutters for several years, led him to plan one last journey before serious travel was made impossible. That same weekend he decided that he should go west. Angkor had whetted his appetite for crumbling ruins in jungle settings; Central America seemed to promise a cornucopia of such delights. A German liner presented the most convenient way of getting there, and though Osbert professed some doubts about travelling by such means, he overcame them without too much difficulty. In December he and David Horner, with Beverley Nichols by chance also aboard, sailed from Hamburg on the SS *Cordillera*.

According to Nichols, in the course of the voyage he and Osbert conducted many introspective discussions about their literary careers. Osbert is quoted as telling Nichols that he envied him 'his creative ability as an imaginative writer, a quality he believed he lacked'; he in fact had good reason to doubt his ability to create save from a solid base of his own experience, but it does not seem likely that he found much to admire in Nichols's prolific but wholly undistinguished products. Nichols suggested that his companion should write a biography of Edgar Allan Poe, whose macabre Gothic extravagance did indeed appeal to Osbert; the idea was well received but never followed up.[48] Osbert was less receptive to the overtures of a German-Jewish professor who was anxious to engage him in debate about the future of English literature. The professor pursued him around the deck at night, forcing him to take refuge in a wholly spurious interest in astronomy: 'You must study the stars, Professor, you must study the stars!' Eventually the professor became discouraged and renounced the quest.[49]

The first-class section of the boat was crowded with rich Jews fleeing Nazi Germany. 'Poor things,' Osbert remarked with rather perfunctory sympathy. 'However, they seemed as gay as gay, and screamed all the decks down, so that it was impossible to write a letter, and ate all the food and drank all the drinks, took up all the space, and spent enormous sums in the ship's shops, buying things like cameras for fifty pounds which they c'd then sell on landing.'[50] When Osbert turned up at the swimming pool at the hour reserved for first-class passengers he found it crowded with Jews. 'When do you think it is Aryan hour?' he asked Nichols. In a short story which he wrote on this theme, Nichols makes a pretty Jewish girl retort: 'It would be better if you were to ask if there was an hour for gentlemen.'[51] Probably this was a fruit of the 'creative ability' of which Nichols was so proud, indeed he may well have invented the original comment as well, but Osbert was certainly not over-distressed by the plight of the Jews. Nichols exclaimed in indignation at their unjust treatment and said that he was ashamed to be an Aryan; if there were a surgeon on board he would apply to be circumcised. 'Haven't you been circumcised yet?' asked Osbert. 'No. Have you?' 'I have no idea. One day I must take down my trousers and have a look.'[52] Once again according to Nichols, however, Osbert put aside his flippancy when he realised that many of the Jews might not be allowed ashore but instead returned to Germany and persecution. He invited all the adults to champagne receptions and gave parties for their children – hardly adequate consolation but at least a gesture of goodwill.[53]

Once in Guatemala, Osbert and Horner went up-country to Antigua, a remote and ancient Spanish city, 5,000 feet up and in the shadow of two volcanoes. Periodically these erupted: 'I like them,' Osbert told Lady Aberconway, 'as they remind me of life at home with my parents.'[54] Antigua boasted a legion of decaying baroque churches and palaces, orchids and parrots galore, a military band which played Spanish waltzes and *paso dobles* outside the hotel windows at 6.00 a.m. – all that Osbert had hoped for. The hotel allocated him a disused pink kitchen with an octagonal glass dome and lantern, where he could write in peace. The only fault he could find with the establishment was that iguana featured too frequently on the menu. 'The people, except the "upper" classes, are half-Indian and such pets: v much like Spaniards, only darker and not so obstinate and stupid. They spend all their time playing marimbas or flopping down on their knees in church.' Exactly what they were worshipping, Osbert never established. Their religious observances were unconventional by European standards – 'They do the most fantastic things: strew the pavements with rose leaves and throw incense into fires and a thousand pagan ceremonies.'[55]

Unlike his other travels, which had been instantly transformed into newspaper articles and then books, Osbert's Guatemalan experiences were overtaken by the war. Nothing appeared for more than fifteen years, and by then his recollections were transmuted into something more impressionistic, visionary even, than Osbert had essayed before. There was no place for such a mood in the Europe to which he and David Horner returned at the end of April 1939.

He Likes to Write

He likes to write, and write egad he will,
So write he does, writing, as Lesbians flirt,
To amuse himself and – best amusement! – hurt.

(From *Fisbo* by Robert Nichols)

IT is one of the more vexatious features of an author's life that the books which he or she esteems most highly are rarely those most successful with the critics, let alone book-buying readers. By 1939 Osbert had achieved both fame and a modest degree of fortune as a journalist and writer of travel books, yet he still considered himself primarily a poet and after that a novelist. In the ten years before the Second World War he wrote three novels: each one earning him a reasonable amount of critical attention, yet each one leaving him disappointed at the coolness of its reception and the paucity of its sales.

The Man Who Lost Himself, published in 1929, was the novel which Osbert saw as technically his most accomplished. The idea for it – the only idea for it, since it is a book remarkably economical in its plotting – came to Osbert when he wanted to see the interior of a hotel in Granada. Hesitating to enter as an avowed sight-seer, he decided to pretend that he was looking for a friend, and since he knew of one person who would definitely *not* be staying there, he asked the hall-porter whether a Mr Osbert Sitwell was in the hotel. As he did so, it struck him how disconcerting it would be if he were told that Mr Sitwell was indeed there and expecting him.[1] He seized on the concept and at once wrote to Sachie to ask him to track down a description he remembered once reading of Shelley seeing himself – 'I want it for a story.'[2]

There was not much more than that to the final narrative. Tristram Orlander, a brilliant young poet, is crossed in love and goes with the narrator to recover in Granada. All seems to go well, but after the narrator has left him, Orlander grows lonely and calls at the grandest of the town's hotels to see if any friends happen to be staying there. Losing his head, he asks for himself and to his consternation is ushered into a room where he finds his thirty-years-older self awaiting him. After this contretemps he undergoes a personality change and makes a fortune writing the sort of middle-brow novel which, as a radical poet, he had most despised. Rich, famous, yet secretly despising his success, he returns as an old man to Granada, finds himself in reality the vision he had seen thirty years before, and duly dies. The plot would furnish an excellent short story; here it is inflated with much descriptive writing about Granada, a seven-page disquisition on the deaths of authors, and a strikingly stilted and unconvincing philosophical discussion between a group of English visitors to Granada which is spun out over fifteen pages. Often when faced by Osbert's fiction the reader itches to tell him to get a move on, but never more than when battling through *The Man Who Lost Himself*.

The various drafts of this novel in the Berg Collection in New York show how intensely Osbert worked and reworked his creations. His manuscript, already radically rewritten, was typed and pasted into a folio book with marbled boards, each page with a blank page opposite. It was then once more rewritten and, presumably, retyped. Between this third version and the published text, however, another rewrite took place. The order of the first few pages was reversed and almost no sentence survived without amendment. Some of these changes were trifling: 'Whether my conjecture, however fantastic it may seem' became 'Whether my conjecture, fantastic as it may seem' and then 'Whether my conjecture, however fantastic it may appear' – the sort of compulsive fiddling calculated to madden a typist in pre-computer days while making precious little difference to the reader's pleasure. Others were more significant and were not invariably for the better – Mrs Hope Doodle Cope, for instance, an American tourist who was given scant attention in the earlier drafts, was quite unnecessarily embellished and expanded in a way irrelevant to the plot. Names were freely changed for reasons that were no doubt felt compelling by the author: Tristram Orlander was once Hubert; Lord St Asaph became Lord St Donat.

In his preface Osbert claimed to have carried further the method which 'for all his humility, he claims to have originated in *Before the Bombardment*'. An action or series of actions was not enough, 'the adventures of the mind and soul are more interesting', a balance must be struck between the two. He had attempted to write, he announced portentously, 'a Novel of Reasoned Action'. It is hard to see in what way his objective differed from that of a dozen other contemporary writers; some may be economical with the action, others care little about the reason, but reasoned action is surely the material of every novelist of distinction. 'Mr Sitwell cannot write novels, even novels of what he is pleased to call Reasoned Action,' sneered the *Manchester Guardian*, adding forgivingly: 'but he can write.' This was the consensus of the reviews; Osbert's descriptive powers were great, his intelligence unquestioned, but he couldn't write novels. 'Mr Osbert Sitwell has written a very brilliant book, of which the bare story is the least absorbing part,' judged *The Times*. 'The active thing in this book is Mr Sitwell's own intellectual passion for beauty and the powerful use he makes of it.' On the whole the reception was friendly, even flattering – 'There is nothing in contemporary English literature like Osbert Sitwell's prose,' wrote Hugh Walpole – but sometimes a harsher note crept in: 'He makes a very heavy demand on the reader,' observed Vita Sackville-West. 'I do not think the reward justifies the demand.'[3] 'His book is dull,' Stephen Tennant told Cecil Beaton more brutally.[4]

Bryher, the rich and generous illegitimate daughter of the shipping magnate Sir John Ellerman, and herself a historical novelist of distinction, believed that Osbert had written himself into the role of Tristram Orlander and, still more, that he had once had a girlfriend who appeared in the novel as Ursula Rypton, the woman whom Orlander loved and lost.[5] The second point is hard to justify; that Osbert consciously endowed Orlander with some of the characteristics which he saw with greatest satisfaction in himself – his conversational skills, his vitality, the 'slow, animal warmth of his smile' – is easier to accept. Richard Aldington, for his part, complained that the narrator in *The Man Who Lost Himself* was tired, old and disappointed, while Osbert was 'certainly not old, I hope not tired, and has no reason whatever to be disappointed, since many of us look on him as one of the most brilliant writers of our time . . . His place is among the leaders of a new generation of writers, young in spirit, intensely alive, and cheerfully disillusioned beyond any chance of disappointment.'[6]

Osbert was disappointed, all the same, at what he saw as a failure to appreciate the real nature of his achievement as well as at miserable sales. It was two years before he embarked on another novel. Early in 1933 he wrote from Corfu to tell his fanatical admirer Frank Megroz that he was at work, 'but it is the dickens. I've done three quarters of it. The title isn't certain. It is concerned with religion.'[7] The title he then favoured was

'New Commandments', but this had only recently been used, so he settled for *Miracle on Sinai*. A group of disparate characters, mainly invented to serve as butts for Osbert's angrier prejudices, are wintering in a hotel at the foot of the Jebel Mŭsă (Mount Sinai). They picnic near the summit, over which always hangs a mysterious cloud. In this Jehovah manifests himself, producing a set of stone tablets on which the commandments are engraved. But these are new commandments, which appear differently to each of the characters and which are designed to suit their individual predilections: 'Thou shalt commit adultery', 'Thou shalt play golf', 'Thou shalt not buy foreign goods'. Unfortunately the only Arab in the party receives instructions to reinstate the supremacy of Allah. He summons his tribesmen and massacres the guests when they appear reluctant to convert.

The characters were cardboard stereotypes: Major-General Sir Rudyard Ramshakkle, President of the Society for the Prevention of Foreign Artists from Entering Britain; Sir Levy Lollygo, a base and repulsive Jewish financier; Lord Pridian, a newspaper proprietor suffering from Napoleonic illusions; T. L. Enfalon, a writer patently modelled on D. H. Lawrence. At its best, *Miracle on Sinai* was Thomas Love Peacock as remodelled by Aldous Huxley, but the satire was so broad, the characters so predictable, that the excellence of the descriptive writing and the occasional flashes of genuinely amusing wit cannot redeem its crippling weaknesses. Eddy Sackville-West complained about the 'haystack-hitting jokes' and found the book dull and long-winded: 'He really should give up writing if he can't do better than that.'[8] Somerset Maugham told Osbert: 'The *Miracle* is a wonderful piece of writing. I do not think you have ever done anything better. And the end is extremely clever.'[9] His enthusiasm may have owed something to the fact that he was writing for the author's eyes; there is a note of greater sincerity in Evelyn Waugh's comment to Mary Lygon: 'I bought myself Sitwell's new book and found it as heavy as my heart.'[10] Fifteen years later a Mr Bull in the BBC suggested *Miracle on Sinai* to Christopher Sykes for adaptation for radio: 'You may find it cheap and overwritten after all these years, but let me say that this is necessary for *acting* egregious comedy.' The idea appealed to Sykes, and Osbert gave his blessing, provided he did not have to do the work himself.[11] Then the project withered. It was a pity; disembodied voices and a skilful shredding of Osbert's over-explanatory and emphatic prose might have produced an entertaining hour or two of broadcasting. It is doubtful, though, whether it would have revived the fortunes of the novel.

It took another five years and much travail for Osbert to publish his last novel. He began it in Cyprus in early 1935: 'Starting on my new novel – hard! What work, over and over again,' he told Christabel Aberconway.[12] Things did not go smoothly. 'My new novel is incredibly bad,' he told Georgia two months later. 'I couldn't have believed it. But it needn't come out for a long time.'[13] It did not. Family rows, illness and the demands of journalism distracted him; he tore it up and made a fresh start; he dismissed the enterprise as beyond redemption, then took it up once again. In January 1937 from Vevey he told Ettie Desborough that he was still wrestling with it, 'it makes me feel quite ill to think how long it has taken me'.[14] Then at last it fell into shape. 'It comes out on March 1,' he reported in February 1938. 'Perhaps it's a wow! I can't make up my mind.'[15] Privately he had no doubt that it was a wow. He had taken more trouble over it than any other book and was convinced that his efforts had been worthwhile. He wrote a draft blurb for Macmillan: 'Mr Osbert Sitwell's new novel, which has occupied him for three years, is the most ambitious work he has yet attempted ...'[16] 'I am desperately anxious for it to have a real success,' he told his publishers as the first reviews began to appear.[17]

Those Were the Days was not only his most ambitious but by far his longest novel – 544 pages. 'It is an attempt to show the extraordinary rapidity of the convolutions through which people pass today; so that most people change themselves much more thoroughly than bodies, every seven years,' he had written when work was still at an early stage.[18] It is set in Scarborough, London and Florence and takes place over a period of twenty years. Joanna, the heroine, has some of the attributes of his sister, Edith; she is a girl who loves poetry and is lamentably bad at hockey. She marries her cousin Jocelyn and they set up house as a thoroughly progressive couple, thus leaving scope for many Sitwellian jokes about the artists and poets of their acquaintance. Having invented his characters, however, Osbert has no real idea what to do with them – eventually Jocelyn loses his much younger girlfriend to his son, but since neither Jocelyn nor girlfriend nor son has in any way come alive, this contretemps leaves the reader unmoved and largely unamused. There are some familiar scenes – Scarborough/Newborough is bombarded and Joanna's aunt, like Sir George, takes refuge in the undercroft – and some familiar characters are resurrected – Mattie Dean, the caricature version of Edward Marsh, is busy during the war selecting 'a special little anthology of modern poets for the lads to read during their leisure hours; playful, skittish poems about tea and toast and cats and lilac and birds –

ever so many birds'.[19] Excellent turns of phrase abound: Lady Kemble-Freemartin covered her walls with a kind of sacking and her floors with rush mats, 'both of which materials seemed to have been woven from the tresses of dead parlour-maids'; Mrs Kinfoot not only never listened to the person to whom she was talking, but 'she never listened either to what she was saying herself, and that, in conversation, is the one unforgivable sin'. But as always in Osbert's novels, the parts are superior to the whole. Almost the only character who really engages the reader's attention is Vera Marmaduke, a fading actress who is given a new lease of life in the First World War when she declaims popular verse at recruiting rallies. Miss Marmaduke is Miss Cantrell-Cooksey or any one of the scores of dim, sad and underprivileged spinsters who haunt Osbert's pages. He mocked them but he observed them with real compassion and for all their insipidity they are flesh and blood in a way that few of Osbert's characters achieve.

Once again the reviews were appreciative, except for some strictures from James Agate in the *Daily Express* and a curious outburst from the *Jewish Chronicle*: 'wonderful', Osbert described them, with slight but not unpardonable exaggeration.[20] Once again the sales, a little over 3,600 after two months, were not calamitous but still disappointing. Osbert claimed that the growing tension in Europe was responsible – 'of course Hitler is to blame, blast him,' he told Harold Macmillan[21] – but he knew that other writers were still managing to sell merrily. 'I am only so sorry that my first novel with Macmillans should not have had a whopping success,' he wrote despondently. 'I am so tired of "moral success".'[22] Perhaps he would have tried yet once more if the war had not broken the thread of his activities; as it was, he turned away from novels and thus freed himself for the enterprise for which it seemed all his previous writing had been a hard apprenticeship.

In the meantime he could at least console himself by working up into a book the Northcliffe Lectures which he, Edith and Sachie had jointly delivered in the autumn of 1937. Osbert's two subjects had been 'Dickens and the Modern Novel' and 'The Modern Novel: Its Cause and Cure'. The first drew largely on the booklet he had written five years before, the second was more controversial and can have made him few friends. His main theme was the inadequacy of modern novelists compared with Charles Dickens: H. G. Wells was a propagandist, James Joyce wilfully obscure, E. M. Forster and Virginia Woolf were 'the posthumous offspring of a hitherto unsuspected union between George Eliot and Ruskin'.[23] (Not a bad lineage, at that.) It was lively stuff, but not likely to endear him to those whom he disparaged.

He endured some ferocious disparagement himself over these years. The most formidable had been in 1930, when Wyndham Lewis published *The Apes of God*. Lewis had until then been considered a friend and ally by the Sitwells. Probably money was at the root of his disaffection. Perpetually impecunious and sponging ruthlessly off anyone who offered him the least encouragement, Lewis was constantly disgruntled because he felt his rich friends had let him down. In the spring of 1925 he complained to Ezra Pound about his ill treatment. Pound took it for granted that the Sitwells were the culprits. No, wrote Lewis, 'with the constipated Shitwells I have had no economic contretemps'.[24] Since then, however, Osbert had been in financial difficulties himself. Perhaps he had refused a loan, or had been too patronising or insufficiently solicitous. Edith suggested other causes. The genesis of Lewis's disenchantment, she claimed, lay in an incident at Renishaw, when Lewis lost his one, extremely dirty collar and felt unable to come down to dinner. He brooded over this humiliation, concluded that the Sitwells were 'evil symbols of the decay of civilisation' and struck back ferociously.[25] Feuds have begun for sillier reasons, but Edith hinted at another, slightly more substantial cause in a letter to Sidney Schiff. Lewis, she wrote, had 'a mean personal grudge against me, a mean personal reason for hating me – but I shall never tell anyone what that reason is'.[26] Presumably she was suggesting that Lewis made a pass at her and had been rebuffed – perhaps while he was painting the portrait of her which he left unfinished. Something must have happened to poison the relationship. Geoffrey Grigson put the feud on a higher plane when he saw it as being one of 'art as life against art as a game; art as the lonely fight with the intractability and hardness of material and art as the game of taste'.[27] Lewis certainly would have recognised and accepted the dichotomy, but it can hardly account for the savage personal animosity displayed in *The Apes of God*.

This was an enormous, rambling extravaganza, mainly dedicated to an attack on the Bloomsbury Group, but devoting nearly 250 pages to the Sitwells, appearing as the Finnian Shaw family, 'prosperous mountebanks who alternately imitate and mock at and traduce those figures they at once admire and hate'. Osbert was Lord Osmund: 'The senior, more or less male, offspring of the Marquis of Balbriggen, is a master-Ape. It is with him well-nigh a *craft* – he makes of Apehood a true business – not of course that he earns money by it (for no Ape can be an Ape unless he is quite rich, and no one has ever yet been found who is fool enough to pay an Ape a penny-piece for any piece of Apery). But he takes Apery very seriously indeed: whereas his expertness and his method entitle him, in the great freemasonry of Apehood, to the title grand-master craftsman.'[28] Every aspect of Osbert's life and character was mocked: his appearance – 'Lord Osmund is above six foot and is columbiform ... The pouter-inflation seems also to give him a certain lightness – which suspends him like a balloon, while he sweeps majestically forward'; his house – 'Upon the walls the pictures revealed the strange embrace of Past and Present – of so casual a nature as to produce nothing but an effect of bastardy'; his attitude towards his father – 'The family's long-standing joke is that of the male parent, called "Cockeye", a typical nursery persiflage'; his attacks on society hostesses, actuated by no sentiment more noble than his indignation that they treated him not as a proper lion but as an Ape in lion's clothing.

It was grossly unfair – to challenge only one point, Osbert was to earn a great deal more by his pen than Wyndham Lewis – but it was also uncommonly well done and embodied an uncomfortable amount of truth. Cyril Connolly claimed that *The Apes of God* contained 'some of the most vigorous satire, original description and profound criticism produced by the twentieth century',[29] while Richard Aldington described it as one of the cruellest but 'also one of the most tremendous farces ever conceived in the mind of man'. The portraits of Osbert and Sachie were 'really immortal', Aldington told Lawrence Durrell.[30] Osbert professed to be unmoved. He thought the book 'wonderful but dangerous', he told T. S. Eliot. He was 'puzzled and very amused', he wrote. 'But then I am always delighted when people behave as you would expect them to.'[31] He had been more put out than he admitted, Lewis's parody was extremely hurtful. Whether it was also damaging is more doubtful. Literary London read the book and sniggered, but it did not give them any facts that they did not know already and not many people can have changed their views of the Sitwells as a result. The obvious malice weakened the impact of the book; in her review in *Time and Tide* Naomi Mitchison advised people to read *The Apes of God*, but made it plain that she felt Lewis had behaved badly and that 'artistically it has spoilt an important section of his book'.[32]

However dulcet his response, Osbert did not forgive. 'This is a nursery,' a character in *The Apes of God* had protested about life in the Finnian Shaw household. 'This is God's own Peterpaniest family!' Appropriately, Osbert's revenge was childish. An old photograph he had come across at Renishaw showed two men dressed identically, looking exactly alike and bearing a striking resemblance to Wyndham Lewis. Osbert had five hundred postcards made, sent one to Lewis with the perplexing anonymous message 'So there *are* two of you' and despatched copies to all Lewis's friends, so that wherever he went he would find the postcard on the mantelpiece or table. This Osbert followed by the gift of his secretary's recently extracted tooth, enclosed in a box from the jeweller Cartier and sent to Lewis anonymously with a card reading 'With Sir Gerald du Maurier's Compliments'.[33] Osbert was convinced that these jokes would cause Lewis endless mystification and annoyance. Perhaps they did; Geoffrey Gorer thought that Osbert was playing with fire since Lewis was in a dangerously paranoid condition, carried a gun, and might well have fired it at anyone whom he believed to be his persecutor.[34] Fortunately no confrontation took place, and little seemed to have changed when the battle was publicly renewed in the correspondence columns of the *New Statesman*: Osbert described Lewis as 'the venerable artist' and picked up a historical howler in his latest book; Lewis hit back energetically against 'incorrigibly "naughty", delicately shell-shocked, wistfully age-complexed, wartime Peter Pans'; a good time was had by all.[35]

Another diatribe against Osbert, this time from Robert Nichols, was altogether less considerable.[36] Nichols was jealous of Osbert's prosperity and affronted by the Sitwells' habit of dismissing him as a minor member of the Squirearchy. In September 1934 the critic Raymond Mortimer warned Christabel Aberconway that Nichols was about to launch an attack on Osbert. 'I don't know what to think about R. Nichols,' Lady Aberconway told Osbert. 'He is negligible as a writer, but I am a little disturbed as to what he is going to do. (If it was too stupid, Raymond wouldn't mind.)'[37] It was not too stupid, but *Fisbo*, a satirical poem of some 5,000 lines, was intolerably long and often ineffective, like an ill-zeroed shot-gun which mainly missed its target though inflicting a few lacerations in the outer rings. Fisbo/Osbert was an inadequate versifier and tedious satirist –

> The usual literary arriviste
> More fat than some, more fatuous than most.

Having failed in poetry he tried politics, the Church, 'espoused Dame Fashion', became a British institution and ended up praying for salvation to the God of lies. There are a few good hits along the way:

> Who, vowed to register beyond dubiety
> Your attitude to an effete Society,
> Have, in the fury of your will to grieve it,
> Performed all possible outrage save to leave it.

Or

> Fisbo intent on an orchestral score
> His eyebrows beetling, a Beethoven frown
> And little wonder, the score's upside down.

Or

> He likes to write, and write egad he will,
> So write he does, writing, as Lesbians flirt,
> To amuse himself and – best amusement! – hurt.

But most of it is tedious stuff and it never rises above the level of witty doggerel. Eddie Marsh, who had good reason to relish seeing Osbert on the receiving end of abuse, told Francis Brett Young that it was 'a really magnificent piece of satiric writing, full of poetry and wit, tho' I can't be sure that poor Osbert has really deserved all that vitriol'.[38] Nobody else seemed particularly impressed, however. Osbert contemplated suing when John Hayward in the *New York Sun* wrote a review which was extremely derogatory of the poem's victim but his solicitor Philip Frere dissuaded him: Hayward had no money, the paper had only minimal assets in Britain and 'anyway, nobody who mattered took *Fisbo* seriously'.[39]

To add to such irritation, Osbert was in increasingly bad health. By 1934 he was seriously overweight, his teeth plagued him, he suffered from frequent headaches, slept badly, had doubts about the state of his heart and complained of sharp pains in his legs. Some of this was hypochondria; much was not. In 1935 gout was diagnosed; Osbert comforted himself that it was a most distinguished disease which he shared with Ben Jonson, Pitt, Gibbon, Kubla Khan and other such dignitaries and that it was found most frequently in men of pre-eminent intellectual ability.[40] He needed all the consolation he could get when early in 1938 he found himself confined to bed, in acute pain caused by either gout or rheumatism: 'the Dr (who is a bloody imbecile) doesn't know which. In the watches of the night, stricken with frightful agony, I still maintain that champagne is worth it, but what a price to pay!' He was to live on bread and lentils for the rest of his life, with a taste of milk every now and then.[41] A few weeks later he found a less imbecilic Dr Boyet in Monte Carlo who struck an even gloomier note: it *was* hereditary gout; it was incurable though with care the worst effects might be ameliorated; Osbert would never be able to eat meat or drink wine again; if he failed to follow the prescribed regimen he would probably succumb to Bright's Disease and find himself afflicted with diseased kidneys, dropsy and who knew what other hideous complications.[42] Osbert meekly accepted every restriction on his liberty but struck when yet another doctor not merely endorsed everything Dr Boyet had said but insisted he give up *petits suisses* and all smoking into the bargain. 'But I'm *not* going to,' wrote Osbert defiantly.[43] Happily, the doctors soon decided that he was, if anything, rather the worse for the dieting; 'so it's back to living as I like and hoping for the best,' he told Harold Macmillan.[44]

Hopes were soon disappointed. Within a few weeks the trouble flared up again. He was in bed for a fortnight, unable to walk a yard; then, when he did hobble from his room, found himself 'merely a perambulating mass of rheumatic pains'. Taking the waters at Vichy followed, with a promise that there might be a permanent cure if he would religiously follow his doctors' orders. Osbert stayed there for a month, escaped to London and Renishaw for the high summer, then was back at the spa for September. 'I feel deplorably low and ill as one always does half way through a cure,' he told Lady Aberconway. To add to his grounds for discontent, there was 'a world concentration of Jews here, all the ones who used to go to German spas and now can't'.[45] Worst of all, the doctors insisted that any kind of work would do him harm; he was forced to remain in a resentful torpor while itching to write up his Asian travels into something that Macmillan could be asked to publish.

David Horner kept Osbert's father posted on the latest developments. Sir George was suitably disturbed and hastened to point out instructive examples from the past: Sir Sitwell Sitwell took 'Eau Médicinale' in 1811, warranted to drive gout away, and was dead within three days; his mother's grandfather had taken colchicum and had to be removed to an asylum. Good sleep was essential, and the avoidance of all intellectual work, even letter-writing. 'If the overwrought nervous reflexes are quieted down, the kidneys will recover.'[46] Henry Moat, too, wrote to condole on what must be proving an intolerably protracted conval-escence: 'You have Sir George's kind reminder that it killed his grand-father at 41, but you are safely past that age, thank goodness.'[47]

Lady Ida was meanwhile slipping quietly away. Sir George was looking after her, Moat had reported a few years before, 'he being afraid Her Ladyship will get fat has docked her soups meat and sweets from her dinner and of course pays half price, [while] he has to eat double portions to get built up again'.[48] She survived her husband's solicitude, but without enthusiasm. 'How much I should hate to live to be old,' she had told Osbert many years before.[49] Now she was old and tired and bored. One of the few incentives to keep going had been that of outliving her husband. When Henry Moat told her how ill Sir George was looking, 'she would say "poor thing, I have noticed it" and would wipe one eye (but there was no tear there)'. When eventually he told her that her husband was on the mend she indignantly accused him of hoping that she would die first.[50] But now she did not even have the heart to continue the contest. She was brought back to London, already ill, and soon developed pneumonia. Osbert visited her and thought that she was sinking fast – 'She recognised me, but no one else,' he told David Horner.[51] A week later she was dead. 'Well, at least Sir George will know now where Her Ladyship spends her afternoons,' remarked Moat philosophically.[52] Sir George announced that he was too tired to attend the funeral; Osbert was decorously in attendance but if he felt any sense of piercing loss he concealed it well. He had been fond but slightly contemptuous of his mother, since he was a child they had shared no interests and though he had suffered for her at the time of the trial they had never subsequently been close.

His chief concern was lest his father should find that Lady Ida's death left him with time on his hands to take more interest in his children. In the hope of keeping him quiet he and Sachie found him a secretary-cum-companion, Francis Bamford, a serious young man who shared Sir George's passion for genealogy and was quite ready to spend a few years in Italy ministering to the needs of his increasingly eccentric employer. This worked well enough, until late in 1937 Sir George decided that he was being neglected and summoned his eldest son to what he announced would certainly prove to be his deathbed. With some reluctance Osbert yielded and made the journey to Montegufoni. 'I've seldom seen "Ginger" looking so well, and in such high spirits,' he reported indignantly. 'He's good for several years yet, though he looks old and frail.' The food was delicious, which came as a pleasant surprise, 'but I am very depressed by napkin rings (shades of Mother!)'.[53] Apart from his unforgivable remissness in not dying, Sir George was affable and the visit passed off without a row. But from Osbert's point of view it was not a success. 'It was such a disagreeable experience in every way,' he told

Bryher. 'I can't see why disinherited sons, except from a perverted sense of duty, should have to see their fathers.'[54]

Henry Moat kept Osbert posted on developments. Sir George was proving 'a hero for his bed', he reported early in 1938. 'I have known him often being tired of laying in bed and got up to have a *rest* and when he had rested got back into bed again like a martyr.'[55] By all the rules he was unlikely to live for long; equally there seemed no reason why he should not survive indefinitely if the mood took him. At least, after Osbert's visit, he decided that he was not in favour of deathbed scenes. In August 1938 he told his sons that he would prefer them not to rush out when he fell seriously ill, especially if such a visit would involve travel by air. 'The Chinese philosopher's teaching that when one has to go one should make as little fuss about it as possible, should not inflict one's troubles on others, is the only sound doctrine.'[56] It was a doctrine that appealed greatly to Osbert, but he had little doubt that when the time came, he would find himself in the train, if not the plane, for Italy.

The most immediate question was whether Europe would be at war before Sir George felt it time to die. Whatever faint flicker of radicalism Osbert had once felt had long been extinguished. He viewed the new authoritarian regimes which were establishing themselves on the continent with cautious approbation. At home he had seen the advent of the National Government in August 1931 without great enthusiasm – 'three fools aren't better than one' – but considered that it was at least a great deal better than the Labour Government which it replaced.[57] When he got back to England a month later he found that everyone was depressed and expecting imminent revolution. The Labour Party was said to have deliberately insisted on large cuts in the Army and Navy so as to foment discontent in the ranks. 'Whatever you do, don't on any account move your money,' he wrote to David Horner, who had kept his inheritance from d'Hendecourt in Swiss banks. 'Leave it where it is.'[58]

Osbert was wholly unmoved by the swing to the left which was such a marked feature of intellectual life in Britain in the early 1930s. He knew Auden, Isherwood, Spender, and was prepared to take his sister's word for it that they were doing work of importance, but he viewed their poetry with slight enthusiasm and their politics with distaste. In the *Sunday Referee* in March 1934 he wrote an article called 'A Peer's Wartime Prophecies', which reappeared in *Penny Foolish* as 'Is Fascism British?'[59] The piece was supposed to be a commentary on a book written in 1917 by a ferociously right-wing peer, Lord Harberton, who argued that democracy had been a failure and that mass-education had proved at the best a waste of money, at the worst actively damaging. Osbert did not explicitly espouse these views, but made it obvious that he felt they contained a great deal of sense. Fascism, he maintained, judiciously tailored to national needs, could give the people what they really wanted. He had admired Italian fascism from the start; now, he felt, it had proved itself. There might have been some small sacrifice in individual liberties but this was a negligible price to pay for stability, prosperity, trains that ran on time, and a progressive social policy. The only losers were left-wing malcontents and even they were only modestly maltreated.

Italy, it seemed to him, was Britain's natural ally. He was dismayed when Mussolini's sabre-rattling over Abyssinia embittered relations between the two countries. 'The Foreign Office seems bent on war with Italy,' he wrote gloomily to Horner in July 1935. 'There must be some cause (Malta?) of which we are unaware. I am really frightened.'[60] He was still more frightened a month later when he stayed with Philip Sassoon at Lympne. Anthony Eden came over to dinner and persuaded him that Italy was behaving badly. 'A very nice man,' Osbert found him, 'like Sir E Grey but less fond of nature, which may pull us through.'[61] But not even Eden could convince him that Abyssinia – or anything else for that matter – could be worth a war; and it seemed to be Eden's view that war was likely, if not inevitable, in September.

Osbert felt immense relief when resistance in Abyssinia collapsed and British threats of war dwindled into demands for economic sanctions against Italy, but he believed that it was folly to annoy the Italians further now that the fighting was over. The League of Nations should accept the *fait accompli*, he held; to continue to press for sanctions would poison the atmosphere and achieve nothing. J. L. Garvin, editor of the *Observer*, took the same line and at the end of 1935 Osbert wrote to congratulate him on his 'mingled prescience and courage'. Mussolini, said Osbert, whatever his faults, was

incapable of bluffing: and now that the truth has really come out, and the nation finds itself so deeply and publicly humiliated, it will be interesting to see what the bellicose bishops and professors have to say for themselves. I have always been a pacifist and a worker for the League, but hope now never to hear that body spoken of again! It has been a truly sickening three or four months. Pray God the Prime Minister now sticks to his latest policy, and doesn't allow all the old League ladies to drag him back again. I hope the word Sanctions may now drop, to be replaced . . . by the phrase 'Pious Reprimands'.[62]

The Spanish civil war, which more than any other issue divided the radicals and progressives from the reactionaries, illustrated clearly where Osbert's heart really lay. He was too sophisticated to see the question wholly in black and white – martyred Catholic priests against communist murderers – but he had no doubt that Franco offered the best chance for a united and resurgent country. 'Much cheered by Franco's successes in Spain,' Sir George wrote in January 1939,[63] and though Osbert might have been a little more equivocal in his satisfaction, his underlying sentiment would have been the same. Garvin again seemed to him the quintessence of good sense; Osbert wrote to applaud his far-sightedness: 'what a sickening morass of lies and misunderstanding one finds oneself in, with Spain represented as a sort of Gladstonian Liberal democracy fighting against brutal rebels! And how dangerous it is.'[64] Stephen Spender remembered vividly the look of disconcerted dismay on Osbert's face at the suggestion that he should go to Madrid to lend support to the republican government. Partly this stemmed from his disinclination to endure discomfort and danger in such a cause, still more it was because he felt that, if he intervened at all, it should be on the other side.[65]

About the Nazis he was more equivocal. The rampant anti-Semitism of the regime appalled him; he never condoned the brutalities of *Kristallnacht* or the persecution of the German Jews. Yet he knew that, though he had close Jewish friends, there were many more whom he disliked and that, still more, the whole concept of 'Jewishness' displeased him. He believed that, in Germany, they had in part contributed to their own ill-treatment. He tried to quiet his conscience by belittling the scale of the atrocities; they were unpleasant, unforgivable even, but they were much exaggerated by propagandists and were, anyway, no more than a disagreeable phase. 'I think that Germany, for me, now plays the game,' he wrote in a revealing passage. 'That is to say that Hitlerism (I do not mean Fascism, which I admire) is a true development of the English public school spirit. Certainly the descriptions of the concentration camps, called into being by the present regime, read, in our newspapers, very much like a word-picture of life at Eton.'[66] Nobody who knew Osbert's memories of Eton could suppose that this was meant to be flattering to the Nazi Government; equally it showed how grossly he underestimated the threat to the rest of the world posed by Hitler and his acolytes.

It was his admiration for fascism, his respect for Mussolini, which led him to look kindly on Oswald Mosley and his New Party. In *Fisbo*

Nichols had derided Osbert's political ambitions:

> Literature's all very well for the *literati*
> But what this country needs is a New Party.

But when Osbert/Fisbo made overtures to the Mosleyites

> Fisbo reviews the cut of a black shirt,
> But that confounded Captain is so curt.

And Fisbo moves on to try the Communist Party instead. In fact Mosley was not in the least curt. Quite apart from the fact that he had had a love affair with Osbert's sister-in-law Georgia, something which certainly did not prejudice him against the Sitwells, he knew the value of a rich, well-connected and celebrated devotee. He courted Osbert and Osbert was happy to respond. In 1931 he joined the New Party. He had often been asked why, he wrote. 'My chief reason is that I have, for the past thirty-one years, been acutely aware of which century I was living in and ... until I met Sir Oswald Mosley, I had never encountered an English politician who was not living, in his own mind, before the year 1888.' Generously, he excepted Winston Churchill from this generalisation; he belonged to 1899.[67]

In August 1931 he opened the grounds at Renishaw for a New Party rally. According to one report, 40,000 attended.[68] The figure seems improbably high, unless the neighbourhood of Sheffield and Chesterfield was exceptionally well disposed to fascism, but the meeting was certainly a success. Osbert did not play any part but by the autumn he was writing from time to time for *Action*, the weekly journal edited by Harold Nicolson and overtly supporting New Party policies. Other contributors included Alan Pryce-Jones, Raymond Mortimer, Christopher Hobhouse, Peter Quennell, Vita Sackville-West – hardly a roll-call of hard-line totalitarian fanatics.[69] As the New Party blackshirts became more noticeably thuggish, the camp-followers began to fall away, Osbert among them. He did not formally renounce his membership but his role in the party, always small, dwindled still further. In 1935 Lady Mosley discussed with her husband the possibility of turning Sousa's 'Stars and Stripes' into a fascist anthem, with Osbert providing the new words and Walton doing whatever was necessary to the music.[70] It was a beguiling concept, but it does not seem ever to have been put to Osbert. It would have been too late, in any case. By this time he had, to all intents and purposes, left the party.

But though no fascist he was still an ardent appeaser, and convinced that war might be avoided if only the warmonger could be reined in and sensible, right-minded men allowed to direct affairs. For a time Samuel Hoare was his standard-bearer. It was Hoare who concocted with Pierre Laval a plan that would, in effect, have sold out Abyssinia and given the Italians most of what they demanded. The House of Commons and the press turned on him and he was forced into resignation. Osbert was downcast. He wrote to congratulate Hoare on his courage and common sense. 'Nobody really wants a war, especially of my generation, but obviously unless some action such as yours is taken, we shall get one.'[71] But Hoare was gone, and though the confrontation with Italy was avoided the threat of war with Germany seemed ever more imminent. Osbert transferred his allegiance to Neville Chamberlain as the best hope of peace. In March 1938 Hitler took over Austria. 'It isn't a very nice world,' Osbert wrote disconsolately. 'It's so frightful about Austria, and yet I pray to God we don't guarantee Czechoslovakia.' Chamberlain, he felt, was being sensible, but common sense held little popular appeal and he might not be able to control the warmongers. The Germans were set to introduce conscription and were obviously contemplating a major war. 'But we can't afford the best air force, navy and *army*. It's madness. It isn't our job.'[72] Given such views, it was inevitable that he should welcome with enthusiasm the 'peace with honour' that Chamberlain brought back with him from Munich. For once Osbert and his father were in accord. 'I agree with you that it would have been idiotic to have a war,' wrote Sir George, 'and I think Chamberlain by far the most sensible Prime Minister since I can remember – since, that is to say, Lord Salisbury.'[73]

Sensible or not, Osbert did not delude himself that Chamberlain had done more than buy a little time. There was bound to be another war before long, he told Hollingworth gloomily, 'and a much worse one. What *can* one do with the Germans? You see, they *like* being killed: and other races, except the Japs, don't.'[74] There was no single issue which it seemed to him could justify a declaration of war on Germany, certainly not the territorial integrity of Czechoslovakia or Poland, but he accepted that politicians wise enough to share his point of view and persuasive enough to convince the people that they were right were not to be found in London or Paris. At least he would have no part to play himself. The 'concussion' which was a relic of his First World War service should rule him out of any active role, he explained to Horner; 'I may have to give you a good smack when I see you, to do the same for you!'[75] He tried to close his eyes and his mind to the inevitable. But reality kept intruding. 'What about all this gas-mask business?' he asked peevishly. 'Who do you know who's doing it? I absolutely refuse: in any case it isn't the slightest good.'[76] But absolute refusal was not a line that could easily be held to when the authorities were involved. Hollingworth wrote to tell him that Renishaw had been selected by the Chesterfield Council as a suitable place for a hospital and dressing station in case of air raids. Osbert was outraged. Hollingworth must protest vigorously, he instructed. The Hall contained works of art of national importance – the Copley portrait group, Henry Walton's 'The Fruit Barrow' and various pieces of furniture – and was in a most exposed position on the fringes of a prime target like Sheffield. Other houses were far more suitable. 'If necessary, I shall make a holy row.'[77] But he confessed to Lady Aberconway that he had little defence against the council – 'a very Socialist body'. Their intentions had put him in 'a frightful rage. And I don't know the best way to fight it (not my temper, but the proposal).'[78]

At the end of 1938 Osbert wrote to his father to say that he was contemplating emigration:

> I am seriously thinking of settling in America . . . Of course, I don't feel that I want to make an exile of myself, but actually, from the point of view of the whole family, and also from that of my work and pleasure, I think the best thing for us would be to try and secure a small house in Washington . . . I could do all the necessary business for getting my stories and articles accepted better there than in New York, and the place itself is much more agreeable and cosmopolitan . . . If I want to settle in America, it would, of course, involve living there at first for some time, but I have unfortunately no money to invest. However, I wondered whether, from the point of view of the entire family, a good small house would not be a wise investment. If you approved, I would go out to the States and arrange it next summer. I think the armament programme is calculated to get anybody out of any house they are in, and I think the future of Renishaw is most frightfully insecure.[79]

Osbert's relationship with his father was so embroiled that one cannot rule out the possibility that this letter was merely a complex ploy to extract money or cause vexation. It seems more likely, however, that he was in such despair at the state of Europe that he was contemplating a flight across the Atlantic. He would not have been the only literary figure to reach such a conclusion. In the end the idea petered out, but nothing could indicate more strongly the blackness of his mood than his readiness to abandon everything which he loved most in favour of life in a country for which, at that stage at least, he had no particular affection.

In spite of the troubles with his health Osbert, by the last years before the war, had indeed established a pattern of life which suited him admirably. Winters were spent at work in some congenial spot; springs and early summers mainly in London; high summer and early autumn at Renishaw; Montegufoni for the wine-making, or perhaps some other continental trip; then it was time to prepare for the winter migration once again. He told his father that the future of Renishaw was insecure, but it was in fact at the heart of his existence. Though Sir George still had the last word in the gardens, Osbert had remodelled the house to his satisfaction. There was not yet any electric light but the comfort was voluptuous. Beverley Nichols, arriving on a bleak November evening in the late 1930s, felt as if he were stepping into an immense conservatory: 'the heat was almost excessive, and it was the exquisite warmth that comes from log fires smouldering in ancient grates. The bitter-sweet tang of the logs mingled with the perfume of white Parma violets.' Soon the champagne arrived, Louis Roederer 1928 served in Venetian goblets.[80] So radically had Osbert reformed the interior that Sir George, prowling around in his son's absence, announced in dismay that a thief had been at work and that some Sheffield art-dealer must be growing fat on the proceeds. Eventually he was convinced that everything in the inventory could be accounted for, only moved to some other place.[81]

Renishaw, for Osbert, was above all a place for parties; usually for weekends, though in summer guests might linger on for weeks. With his father safely out of the way in Italy, there was an atmosphere of irresponsibility, celebration, even sometimes schoolboy jollity. Rex Whistler wrote in mock indignation: 'What a beast you were, in coming and pulling the clothes off and wrecking my bed every morning. BUT I DON'T FORGET, and that, and the cold water in my bath on the previous visit shall be avenged one day, I promise you.'[82] Charades and other excuses for dressing-up were a regular feature. Once Somerset Maugham was coming to dinner and the house party proposed to put on fancy dress in his honour. Osbert decide at the last minute that it was really too much trouble and countermanded the order. Unfortunately, he omitted to tell one of the guests, the dancer and choreographer Robert Helpmann. Helpmann swept down the stairs splendidly dressed as Queen Alexandra, to find everyone else in conventional evening clothes. Somerset Maugham shook his hand without comment.[83]

But Renishaw was also the family seat, involving responsibilities which Osbert took seriously. Shortly before the outbreak of war the Duke of Devonshire put Osbert's name forward to the Lord Chancellor as a magistrate. Anything less than 40 per cent attendance would be considered slack, he warned Osbert severely. 'I hope you will agree as I think you would make a most admirable magistrate and that your attendance on the Bench would be greatly appreciated by the criminal classes in Eckington.'[84] Osbert did agree and proved most conscientious, rarely missing a meeting of the Bench when he was in England. He became a governor of the school at Staveley, patronised the local church, took a keen interest in the management of the estate. Whenever he was at Renishaw without a house party, two days of the week at least would be given up to local business of one kind or another; even when guests were there they would often notice him slipping away to confer with his agent or some other employee. Sir George found it hard to believe that his son was really performing his duties properly. 'If you could only give a few months, or even weeks, to the study of the estate and to an attempt to make friends with the local powers that be, that might do wonders,' he wrote. Osbert should cultivate the parish council at Eckington and the authorities at Chesterfield. He was already on excellent terms with the Eckington Parish Council, Osbert replied crossly. 'I will try now to captivate the Chesterfield R[ural] D[istrict] C[ouncil], but I feel this will be a more difficult job.'[85]

This was a side of Osbert which his writer friends in London suspected was there yet rarely saw. In spite of his father's objurgations, life in Carlyle Square continued as extravagantly as ever. Osbert and David Horner entertained frequently and expensively. Osbert knew everybody, wrote Alan Pryce-Jones. 'His hospitality was memorable, often washed down by an "old" champagne, not too old, but delightfully darker and flatter than ordinary "fizz".'[86] Mrs Belloc Lowndes lunched there early in August 1934. She was, wrote Osbert:

Dressed as a guinea-fowl, in a long silk robe of black speckled with white. I went first into the dining room, guided by a sort of awful premonition, and walking backwards, as though helping Queen Victoria. I said, in explanation of this apparently curious conduct, 'Mrs Lowndes, I'll go first as I'm always so nervous of people falling.' Mrs Lowndes, almost at the bottom of the steps, replied, 'Well, I never fall,' and at the same time, as though possessed by the spirit of some dead devil-dancer, trod heavily on the classic hem of her guinea-fowl silk crinoline, rolled herself like a hedgehog into a little round ball, and propelled herself irresistibly down the last stair into the corner . . . Picking herself up, she then said, 'Luckily, I fall soft,' and proceeded, with considerable pluck, to eat quite a good luncheon.[87]

Osbert not merely knew everyone, he went everywhere, as likely to be seen in a Bloomsbury *soirée* as a Mayfair ballroom, at an avant-garde ballet in darkest Chelsea as a string quartet in St James's Palace. His presence conferred a seal of respectability on the first and lent a flavour of the agreeably raffish to the second. He was not entirely undis-criminating. Gerald Berners wrote a ballet based on a work by Gertrude Stein. Osbert was invited to the first night but refused. 'You see,' he explained to Christabel Aberconway, his would-be hostess, 'among other things, Edith and I introduced the old lady to England nearly fifteen years ago and got nothing but abuse for it and no help from the Geralds of this world, and now they are behaving as if they had discovered her. So I'd rather not be present.'[88] Sometimes it was he who was rejected. In 1933 Duff Cooper proposed him for membership of the Society of Dilettanti, a small dining club of some antiquity. His election seemed a formality, but the architect to the society was Sir Reginald Blomfield, whose scheme for the redevelopment of Carlton House Terrace Osbert had successfully impeded. Sir Reginald bore a grudge and blackballed Osbert. 'How odd and funny,' Osbert commented. He had always disliked the description of dilettante when applied to him, but was displeased at being excluded from a group which he knew he would find congenial. There was no recourse, however; Osbert had to wait until after Blomfield's death in 1942 before he was elected to a society to which, whatever his reservations about the name, he seemed so naturally to belong.[89]

He was involved as champion in unexpected causes. In September 1939 he was summoned urgently to 44 Bedford Square by Margot Oxford, tempestuous widow of an earlier Prime Minister, Asquith. On arrival he was handed by the butler a letter from Lady Oxford, telling him of a book by Mrs Woodrow Wilson, 'a book which you will never *read*', which was filled with lies about her and her husband. Would Osbert please write to *The Times* or *Daily Telegraph* saying that his attention had been drawn to this work. He was to continue: 'that you have been a friend of mine all your life and resent what [Mrs Wilson] has written, and even doubt whether it is accurate. You can add, "Lady Oxford has never spoken evil of anyone, and though she has known many members of the royal family, she is not a snob." '[90] If Osbert did as he was bid, the letter does not seem to have been published. More probably he prevaricated politely. He disliked looking a fool, and though he had some affection for Lady Oxford he knew that to ride into the lists on her behalf would have been to invite derision.

Running Renishaw and Carlyle Square on the scale he felt appropriate was a costly business. In 1937–8 his income from mineral rents and royalties alone was just under £5,000 – say, £125,000 today – but he still found it hard to make ends meet. 'I feel rather poor, owing to the continued American slump,' he told Horner. 'Overdraft is mounting.'[91] It continued to mount, despite the protests of the long-suffering Coutts Bank. Things got even worse when a coal mine suddenly ceased production and he lost about a third of his income from minerals. 'I do not know what I shall do (but certainly not economise),' he wrote.[92] He continued to indulge himself insouciantly, to the dismay of his agent. He was sorry to hear there were a lot of bills to pay, Hollingworth wrote to Osbert's secretary. 'I do not myself see where the money is to come from. Agricultural Depression is more acute than any time within living memory but Captain Sitwell continues to spend regardless of income.'[93] Osbert remained convinced that something would turn up. It did; but hardly in the form he had hoped for. The war, which he so bitterly deplored, saved him financially by brutally truncating his expenditure. But for this enforced economy there would have been a crisis in 1940 or 1941 and the bank might well have insisted that he sell, or at least lease out, Renishaw.

One of his problems was that many of his friends were much richer than he was, and keeping up with their pattern of life was an expensive business. In 1939 he still owed Siegfried Sassoon £7,500, secured on various life insurance policies and costing him 5 per cent in interest per annum.[94] Meanwhile Siegfried's cousin Philip entertained him lavishly; he expected nothing in return, but Osbert would have felt himself humiliated if he had not been able to return the hospitality. It took some living up to. At Port Lympne, Sassoon's country home near Hythe, Osbert found himself involved with others of Sassoon's guests in the Hythe Venetian Fête, floating up and down in a highly decorated gondola between two rows of spectators. There was a nasty moment at the beginning when somebody laughed offensively (at what must have been a pretty grotesque spectacle), but better feelings prevailed and the rest of the way there were only cheers. Osbert enjoyed it all immensely. Anthony Eden was also in the house party, though not in the gondola since he was suffering from chicken-pox. 'What a complaint for a foreign secretary!' wrote Osbert caustically. 'Can you imagine Palmerston having it? He'll be having teething troubles next!'[95]

It was on a gala occasion at Philip Sassoon's other stately home, Trent Park, that Osbert first had more than a casual meeting with the Duke and Duchess of York. At dawn a cavalcade of carts from Covent Garden delivered a mass of lilies and potted plants, that night there were fireworks over the lake and the celebrated – and inordinately expensive – tenor Richard Tauber sang on the terrace,[96] but for Osbert the presence of the royal couple was the most memorable feature. Osbert attached immense importance to his royal connections, a predilection which confirmed the suspicions of those who saw him as a snob and a socialite rather than an artist. He was not above mild mockery – after a Sunday at Mrs Ronnie Greville's house, Polesden Lacey, he remarked that the Duke of York was 'out of temper and on his dignity, but cocktails and champagne restored him by the fall of night'[97] – but he never missed a chance to hobnob with royalty and rarely failed to refer to such intimacies when an opportunity arose or could be contrived.

The year 1936 was a poor one for a monarchist. Osbert was at first cautiously optimistic about the new reign. 'I must say the photographs of [Edward VIII] are extraordinary and very pathetic,' he wrote to Lady Aberconway. 'Poor man! Is it nice perhaps, all the same, to have a young King, contemporary?'[98] Very soon he concluded that it was not nice at all. He felt nothing but loathing for the empty-headed, philistine crew who made up Edward VIII's entourage at Fort Belvedere. Mrs Simpson he met only once; at Lady Cunard's. He arrived early, to find her alone in the room, dabbing at her face with a small powder-puff. As he approached she looked up and said: 'Emerald isn't down yet so we must introduce ourselves. My name is Wallis Simpson.' To his horror Osbert heard himself respond, 'Yes, I've often heard it lately.'[99] Mrs Simpson seemed unsurprised but Osbert liked her none the more for her sang-froid. To him she exemplified the sort of brazen, wise-cracking vulgarity which he found least congenial. The Duke of York might not be an intellectual but at least he was a gentleman; the duchess had actually read and enjoyed his books; when the crisis came there was no doubt where his sympathies would lie.

The abdication was for Osbert one of 'the two really horrible events' of 1936 (the other being 'the proved fatuity of the League of Nations').[100] Osbert detested the smart set who had encouraged the affair with Mrs Simpson and basked in the favour of the King, then hurriedly claimed to have deplored the relationship all along when Edward VIII went into exile. In this mood he wrote a furious piece of doggerel, in which he denounced Lady Mendl, Lady Colefax, the fashion editor Johnny McMullen, and other such sycophantic and, in due course, treacherous hangers-on. *Rat Week* was not great poetry but it had the merits of being short, sharp and intensely felt:

> Where are the friends of yesterday
> That fawned on Him,
> That flattered Her;
> Where are the friends of yesterday,
> Submitting to His every whim,
> Offering praise of her as myrrh
> To him?

There followed a brisk denunciation of the 'gay, courageous pirate crew' who had danced the night through at Fort Belvedere and wassailed aboard the Nahlin, only to betray their benefactor when the going got too hot:

> What do they say, that jolly crew,
> So new, and brave, and free and easy,
> What do they say, that jolly crew,
> Who must make even Judas queasy?[101]

Osbert realised that this diatribe, if published, might land him in a flurry of libel actions, but he could not resist having a few copies made and distributed to his closer cronies; Mrs Greville, Lady Aberconway, Lady Cholmondeley and Philip Frere among them. They showed it to *their* closer friends, copies were made, word of it passed around, soon it was known to everyone who was anyone in London. Osbert claimed that it was known also to many who were not anyone; it spread 'with the force and urgency of an eighteenth-century ballad ... declaimed in drawing rooms and saloon-bars and the public rooms of hotels ... read aloud in crowded omnibuses or over the subterranean roar of the tube trains'.[102] The boast is not entirely convincing – one would like to know exactly how many buses or underground trains were entertained by recitations of *Rat Week* – but the verses struck a popular chord and enjoyed a readership far beyond their intrinsic merits.

The editor of the popular weekly *Cavalcade* got his hands on a copy and cabled Osbert – then in Vevey suffering one of his blackest bouts of depression – to ask him whether he had written it. This put Osbert in a quandary: if he replied that he had, the newspaper would proclaim his authorship abroad; if he denied parentage, the paper would feel free to publish the poem unattributed. He compromised with the cryptic reply, 'Sez you. Sitwell.' The editor thereupon excised the lines in *Rat Week* which referred specifically to individuals, so as to eliminate the risk of a libel action, and published the truncated poem, with the exchange of telegrams appended as a footnote. Osbert, for once encouraged into action by his usually cautious solicitor, at once demanded damages for breach of copyright, costs, an apology and the withdrawal of all unsold copies of *Cavalcade*. Protracted litigation followed. The matter was complicated by the fact that Osbert's lawyers refused to allow the full text of *Rat Week* to be produced in court, citing precedents such as Oscar Wilde, Lord Byron and Frank Harris. Eventually they won their point, whereupon *Cavalcade* lost heart and settled out of court for £500.[103] In retrospect the whole affair seemed vastly amusing to Osbert but at the time it appeared likely to land him in seriously hot water and he would have been happy if he could have withdrawn the poem and forgotten the matter altogether.

This was not the only difficulty in which *Rat Week* involved him. Sibyl Colefax, hearing that the unexpurgated version mentioned her by name and that Christabel Aberconway had a copy, demanded to be allowed to see it. Osbert advised Lady Aberconway to refuse, or perhaps to proffer a copy with the particularly offensive passages omitted: 'She's a regular old nuisance, poor old thing, and has brought great misfortune to the Crown by being associated with it.'[104] He could endure Lady Colefax's displeasure with equanimity. Diana Cooper was another matter. It was well known that she and her husband Duff had been friends of Edward VIII, had at least condoned the liaison with Mrs Simpson, and had even been on the notorious *Nahlin* cruise. 'I'm afraid I'm a Rat, Sir,' she was supposed to have confessed to George VI, in a moment of slightly disingenuous contrition.[105] What if she too took offence? 'I am not going to worry about Diana, as she *must* know that I would never say anything unpleasant about either her or Duff,' Osbert announced stoutly, but he did worry all the same, about Lady Diana and about others who might feel that he was getting at them and with whom he did not wish to quarrel.

But the reaction about which Osbert was most anxious was that of the new regime in the palace. He had no need to feel concern. When the Queen was staying at Houghton, the Cholmondeley house in Norfolk, her hostess lent her a copy of *Rat Week*. She showed it to the King, and they so enjoyed it that they passed it on to Queen Mary, who also thought it marvellous. 'I'm sure Sibyl wouldn't do anything silly, so it must be all right,'[106] Osbert wrote hopefully, and sure enough, it was all right. Osbert was already in high favour at court; *Rat Week* clinched it. When he wrote to the Queen to condole and congratulate on the accession, she replied warmly with thanks for his encouragement and support. Ten days later she wrote again:

> One can hardly believe that we could have survived such drama and tragedy and yet, here we are, back at the old business – buckling to, doing our best, keeping the old Flag flying hoorah, and of course it is the only thing that is worth doing now. I believe now, more than ever before, that this country is worth sacrificing a good deal for. In fact, if I was exiled, I should die, anyway in the spirit.[107]

Osbert now found himself in demand on royal occasions. In April 1937 he was summoned to Windsor: 'It will be lovely seeing it, and in grand state – Windsor liveries, gold plate, bands etc. – but I'm rather terrified,' he told Georgia. 'I've got no clothes, and I'm sure I've lost my knee-breeches ... And what, I imagine, the tips will cost!!'[108] Whatever they had cost, he would have felt it money well spent. He was equally delighted to visit Balmoral, taking Rex Whistler with him. The King treated him as a licensed jester, teasing him about his lack of interest in sport: he had walked twenty-five miles on the hill that day, he said, and never seen a stag. It would have done Osbert good to do the same. That night Rex Whistler rushed into Osbert's room and said that his own bedroom was next door to the King's and through the wall he could hear George VI talking to himself. 'Well, what did he say?' asked Osbert. 'I've never been so *tired* in my life – it's all these bloody guests!'[109] The King had more than the bloody guests to make him tired. After his marathon on the hill had come the annual ghillies' ball. 'Such fun,' Osbert told Christabel Aberconway. 'The most complicated reels, valetas and odd dances, like Elizabethan times; quite devoid, the whole thing, of class feeling.'[110] Rex Whistler almost disgraced himself on the same visit. As they went into the drawing-room the Queen had said to Osbert: 'I must tell you, *that* is Queen Victoria's chair. It is never sat in.' A few minutes later, after she had left the room, Osbert was dismayed to see Whistler sitting in the chair. 'Rex, that's Queen Victoria's chair, get out of it, quick!' But Whistler was used to Osbert's little jokes and refused to budge. He was persuaded that the matter was serious only seconds before the Queen returned.[111] Georgia lunched with Osbert a few days after the visit to Balmoral. He was full of royal stories, she noted in her diary: 'King peppery but amiable. Queen was an angel. Children utterly charming. O is mad about the Queen.'[112]

One of the pleasures of intimacy with the royal family was the jealousy it aroused among less favoured acquaintances. At a ball at Londonderry House the Queen sent for Osbert and was 'too charming for words . . . I saw one or two people I don't like looking very cross'.[113] At the Duchess of Sutherland's he was less fortunate but he was solaced by a short chat with Queen Mary. Her secretary later told Osbert that he had made 'a great hit' with her. Next day Osbert dictated a letter to David Horner reporting this event. His secretary omitted the word 'great'; Osbert proudly wrote it in. The reason he dictated the letter rather than wrote it was that, as he left the ball, his car had been rammed by a drunken lady driver and he had been severely knocked about. His assailant made matters worse by climbing into Osbert's car, where she rocked to and fro and wailed repeatedly: 'Uncle's much worse. His nose is bleeding!' In the end she had to be forcibly removed by the police.[114] This experience in no way tarnished Osbert's pleasure in the evening nor deterred him from future excursions into the royal circle. Princess Alice, Countess of Athlone, invited him to Brantridge to meet Queen Mary again. The visit was in some ways a strain, since Osbert hated convivial breakfasts and always ate alone; while at Brantridge Queen Mary came down at 8.55 a.m. precisely and expected everyone to be waiting at the foot of the stairs to make their bow.[115] It was worth it, though.

The apotheosis of this relationship should have been achieved in the autumn of 1939, when Queen Mary was to stay with her son-in-law at Harewood and expressed a wish to come over to Renishaw for the day. Anxious to keep her busy so that she did not notice the holes in the carpet and the frayed curtains, Osbert told his agent to gather ivy and hang it over the stables so that she could occupy herself with pulling it off. 'Very good idea,' said the King, when told of this. 'You know Queen Mary once gave me and Lillybet ivy poisoning by making us pick it off walls at Sandringham?'[116] But the ploy was never put to the test. War came before the visit could take place. Next time Osbert saw Queen Mary she would be in retreat at Badminton and the world would be a very different place.

13

We Want – PEACE!

We should be thrown into prison,
Or cast into an asylum,
For we want – PEACE!

(From 'Rhapsode')

OSBERT, as he had done in 1914, began the Second World War with the conviction that it would soon be over. He did not think that it would last more than a month or two, he told Christabel Aberconway. Within a few weeks, though, his natural pessimism was reasserting itself; he prayed for a quick end, he told her, but 'it seems too good to be true'. A few weeks more, again, and he had accepted that it *was* too good to be true. 'I think the war will go on for ever now,' he wrote despairingly in January 1940.[1] At no time during the war did he doubt that it could end and should be ended if only those responsible would show a little good will and common sense. Whether such qualities were to be found on the German side, he could not say, but it was the duty of the British Government to give a lead and at least provide an opportunity for the more conciliatory among the enemy to make their voices heard. Progressively, however, he despaired of anyone of courage and vision being found in Britain to plead the cause of peace. He refused to believe that military victory was a possibility; even when the fighting was almost over he insisted that the end would be indefinitely postponed.

He did not doubt that Germany was more to blame for the Second World War than Britain or France and he would have rejoiced in a rapid Allied victory. He disapproved of the decision of Isherwood and Auden to see the war out in the United States and sneered when told by Alan Searle that Somerset Maugham would also not be returning – 'Really, these patriots!'[2] But his heart was not in it. The Germans might be more to blame but it was only a matter of degree. 'What are we fighting for?'

he asked angrily. 'The Germans say, quite rightly in my opinion, that we are fighting to maintain intact an Empire which we are, at the same time, selling to the United States.'[3] He never weakened in his insistence that a righteous war was only marginally less wicked than an unrighteous one. When Clive Bell towards the end of 1940 wrote a letter to the newspapers questioning the need to continue fighting, Osbert congratulated him; 'I'm appalled to find everyone in London . . . taking their old-war attitudes. Already they are almost beyond the reach of reason . . . and I think public opinion is heading towards intricating us in an intolerable and measureless disaster, beyond repair.'[4]

He did not see what anyone could do to help, or rather hinder, Osbert concluded sadly. He felt impotent, swept away by a torrent which he could not hope to check and from which there seemed no possibility of escape. 'Oh dear, what a hell our lives have become,' he wrote to Cynthia Asquith. 'I used not to believe in hell between the ages of 25–35, but do now. This appalling repetition, sort of recurring decimal, just has the quality of horror combined with eternity. What are we to do? "Set my teeth?", "Clench my fists?", "Show a stiff upper lip?" '[5] None of those postures would have suited Osbert well. His preferred solution was to pretend that nothing was going on, or, better still, that he was not even present. He spent the day in a coma, he told Lady Aberconway; 'my usual tendency towards escapism is emphasised so that I, who normally sleep so little and never in the daytime, can sleep the whole day and night away. It is – and always has been – a symptom of intense misery with me.'[6] It seems unlikely that there were many days on which so satisfactory a stupor was attained; Osbert had a vast range of intellectual interests, a career as a writer to pursue and a plethora of estate or civic duties. He did consciously seek to detach himself, however, from any day-to-day involvement with the war. He was accustomed to say that he felt great sympathy for Nero, who notoriously fiddled while Rome burned. What else was Nero supposed to do? Osbert asked David Horner. 'He was, no doubt, good at the violin, and due to give a concert in a few days time, and didn't want to be bothered about a fire he couldn't put out.' If everyone had had the good sense to do the same, the fire would no doubt have burned itself out more quickly.[7] The only other feasible escape from war seemed to be death, and Osbert admitted to the poet HD (Hilda Doolittle, former wife of Richard Aldington and lover of Bryher) that there were moments when he hankered after the 'eternal peace as advertised by the tombstones in the neighbourhood'. Perhaps it would not be as peaceful as pretended, though; 'One w'd have that *frightful* "new-boy" feeling all over again. But war does fail to interest, though never to horrify me.'[8]

In October 1940 Osbert wrote to Bernard Shaw:

What I don't see is how it's possible to keep one's temper if the war continues. The general incompetence and muddled thinking, the self-complacent braying and boasting, the platitudinous mouthings of poor old Winston, with his 'Woe Betide Them! They Shall Have Short Shrift!' type of oratory ... The roarings about Democracy and Autocracy and Aggression and Sacrifice when everybody knows it's all Poppycock – combined with Days of National Prayer and the consequent and successive 'flops' all wear me down.[9]

The reference to Churchill illuminated one of the reasons why Osbert felt alienated from the war-effort. Since the days of *The Winstonburg Line* and even earlier, Churchill had represented to Osbert all that was most bombastic and warmongering. To see him elevated to the rank of national hero was to confirm every suspicion about the futility and needlessness of the war. Churchill was not the only object of dislike: Bevin was a pet hate, especially when his industrial recruitment campaign seemed to threaten Osbert's liberty; Lord Woolton, the Minister of Food, was guilty of 'brow-beating' insolence; Stafford Cripps was 'a nut-eating *arriviste* ... I hope his raw vegetables will go down the wrong way and choke him'.[10] But these were only bit-part actors, supporting the monstrous Behemoth. Churchill could do no right. The promise of nothing but blood and tears and sweat was 'in a way noble', Osbert grudgingly conceded, but it 'could hardly be surpassed in menace by the threats of foreign autocrats, bellowing across the water what they will do to us'.[11] The Prime Minister's unabashed playing to the gallery, though it won the hearts of the British people, struck Osbert as infinitely vulgar: 'A dreadful spectacle he must be, riding on the hood of a motor, balancing his hat on a stick, and with a "thumb-up". Grock and Nero and Heliogabulus and the Fratellini and a bad hospital case rolled into an inexplicable whole.'[12]

Churchill was not merely a vainglorious buffoon, Osbert maintained; he had almost lost the war through his ineptness and was now prolonging it through his obstinate blood-lust. 'It's time we stopped making tragic fools of ourselves against the German General Staff,' he proclaimed in May 1941. The Army ought to be disbanded and the soldiers employed in making ships and aeroplanes, the two fields in which the British could hold their own. 'I want a Naval Dictatorship, which would know the relative values of land and sea. I fear Winston is bent on *further* adventures of a disastrous kind.'[13] A week or two after writing this letter, presumably prompted by the campaign in Crete, Osbert concluded that the war was now certainly lost. All would be over within a few weeks, at any rate by the autumn. Churchill had 'completely lost touch and grasp'.[14] He had always believed that there was a strong element in the German army which was anxious to oust Hitler and make a reasonable peace; the run of German victories would make it harder for them to get their way but it still seemed inevitable that a peace offer would soon be made. Of course it would be insanity to reject it but, 'I'm sure we shall turn it down,' Osbert concluded gloomily.[15] The only chance seemed to be that the Dominion leaders might gang up and force 'a choice of common sense or competence on the government'.[16]

When Edward Marsh, Churchill's former secretary and butt of so much of Osbert's satire, came over to lunch at Renishaw shortly before Christmas 1940, Osbert restrained himself until just before his guest was about to leave and then launched into a savage diatribe against Churchill and all his works. The 'poor old boy' was nearly reduced to tears, reported Edith – whether Marsh's tears were of grief or rage, she did not relate. The occasion was unusual, since Osbert normally vented his views on Churchill and the war only to people whom he knew or thought were sympathetic to his opinions: Lady Aberconway, David Horner, Violet Woodhouse. Even Edith was not a wholly suitable audience. Her patriotism was more robust than Osbert's; she rejoiced when the German air force suffered heavy losses in the Battle of Britain; 'My God, I hope we continue to give them the thrashing they deserve,' she trumpeted.[17] Osbert would have rejoiced too, but his satisfaction would have been tempered by the fact that such victories could only delay the ending of the war. In public, though, he kept quiet. He encouraged Clive Bell to write subversive letters to the papers but had no intention of doing so himself. 'I now try never to speak my mind,' he told HD, 'and hope that this will become easier if the war continues and my mind disintegrates.'[18] Osbert had no wish to become a martyr, or even to risk the disapproval of his neighbours. In the St James' Club, in the local officers' mess, with any member of the royal family, he would listen blandly to the patriotic rodomontades and keep his real opinion to himself. It was hardly noble, but he knew there was no hope of converting others to his view and to court unpopularity for the sake of a principle would have seemed to him a foolish gesture.

The entry of Russia into the war was cause for qualified celebration.

'I'm delighted with the Bolsheviks,' wrote Osbert, when news of the German invasion was first heard, 'but I suppose we shall have a revolution here now within 2 years.'[19] For a dedicated pessimist the outlook seemed most promising: if the Russians were defeated Britain would lose the war; if they won there would be a revolution. He never veered from his conviction that some sort of violent uprising was imminent. Eighteen months later he was observing the trampled parks and squares of London with shocked dismay: 'I think revolution is very clearly to be felt in the air now.'[20] Eighteen years later he would have said much the same. He would have been appalled if the Germans had established a Nazi government in Britain but saw no reason to revise his opinion that a form of fascism modified to suit the British character would have been an acceptable, even desirable alternative to democratic rule. He felt that Oswald Mosley had been misjudged and, by his imprisonment, was woefully misused. 'To have been deprived, as you have been, of a period of time, is beyond bearing,' he wrote sympathetically to Mosley early in 1945. 'The only comfort for you must be, that it is impossible to blame *you* for anything that happened in those years.'[21]

When stories of Nazi atrocities began to leak out of occupied Europe, Osbert dismissed them as fantasies, dreamt up by propagandists employed by Churchill to foment hatred of the Germans. Cyril Connolly quoted the first-hand accounts of refugees, but Osbert dismissed such evidence. 'Of course, you *may* be right,' he wrote, but experience led him to doubt it. 'If I believe in *Atrocities* – by which I mean 100% atrocities – not 20% which I might believe – then I must believe, too, in the Truth of Revealed Religion. But I belong to a sceptical generation and genus. I will bet you £5 – and you will be the first to be pleased to lose it – that if we are alive 10 years after the war has ended, you will truthfully and willingly admit that you have [been] hoodwinked and nose-led.' Besides, what was an atrocity? Was it not an atrocity to order the incineration of thousands of civilians in raids on German cities?[22]

What interested him, Connolly replied, was *why* Osbert insisted in dismissing what seemed to most people to be overwhelming evidence. Was it because, as a sensitive person, he would suffer so terribly if he did believe it, or because the last war had taught him how easy it was to mislead the people on such a subject?[23] The second explanation was nearer the truth. In the First World War Osbert had been fed on atrocity stories: the Corpse-Rendering Works, where the bodies of soldiers were boiled down into fats for use as an industrial lubricant or even boot polish; the Crucified Canadian, displayed on a cross near Ypres.[24] Osbert had been doubtful then, and proved correct. He was not to be had for a mug this time. 'Do you believe the atrocity stories?' he asked Lorna Andrade. 'The lies in the last war make me sceptical.'[25] He was no more credulous when the excesses of the Japanese were in question. He believed very little of such propaganda, he told Bryher: 'It is merely to try and work up and palm off Puritan measures.'[26]

Given his attitude towards the war, it is hardly surprising that Osbert viewed with dismay any suggestion that he might play a serious part in it. He was forty-six years old in September 1939 so that, even if his health had permitted, there was no question of his being called up for military service. Nor, at the beginning of the war, was there any nation-wide system for directing labour into the war-effort. There was still moral pressure, however, to do *something* to help one's country, and though Osbert had no intention of taking any energetic steps in that direction he did not wish to be seen as standing totally aloof. Many intellectuals in his position, including some who feared that otherwise they might be called upon to fight, turned to the Ministry of Information as being a place where they might find work which would both establish their patriotic credentials and be reasonably congenial. Osbert gingerly made overtures and was ordered to hold himself in readiness for a call; in the meantime, he told Christabel Aberconway, he would remain at Renishaw and 'arrange about breeding pigs and planting the gardens with cabbages'.[27] Eventually he received his summons and was courteously received, but noticed that the official who interviewed him was constantly called to the telephone. Finally his interlocutor slammed down the receiver with an angry: 'No, Madam, I can't tell you. I told you before not to ring me up again. It's not our business.' Osbert asked what the problem was and was told that a woman persisted in confusing the Ministry of Information with Selfridge's Information Bureau and asking when William Rufus planted the New Forest.[28] To his relief no offer of a job followed the interview, only a request that he should write satirical articles on subjects such as the black-out, rumours or other issues of the day: 'In this rather trying period between war and peace, we need to counteract a mood of scared boredom. No propaganda from here can do this as effectively as writers like yourself who can remind the public that normal sanity and normal scepticism are not unpatriotic.'[29]

This was almost the last Osbert heard from the Ministry of Information, whose relaxed approach to the demands of wartime propaganda must have seemed to him unexpectedly civilised. In 1942 he had a letter from the then Minister, Brendan Bracken, politely rejecting a proposal that a panel of authors should be set up to advise the ministry as to which books should be published. Such a mechanism would smack of censorship and enrage publishers, said Bracken.[30] The idea seems to have originated with Cecil Day Lewis, then an editor in the ministry's publications division. It is hard to believe that Osbert viewed its rejection with any real regret.

After this somewhat token gesture to the demands of wartime, Osbert devoted himself to the uphill struggle of guarding his time and energies for his own pursuits. 'Is it frightful to wish to do one's own work, and not somebody else's?' he asked, and answered himself dispiritedly, 'I suppose so.'[31] Frightful or not, he organised no less a doctor than Lord Dawson of Penn, formerly physician to King George V, to attest that his health was such that he would not be able to take on any government job involving long or erratic hours – 'as I gather you would like,' added Dawson somewhat disingenuously.[32] Armed with such an alibi, he was surely immune; yet he never felt he could sleep securely: in March 1941 Edith reported that he was making alarmed telephone calls to his lawyer about a new threat of recruitment for industry; nine months later he was in 'a bit of a call-up stew. *J'y suis, j'y reste* is my motto.'[33]

The most serious threat came in 1942, when shortage of labour in the mines led Ernest Bevin to launch a new campaign for the recruitment of workers from non-essential tasks. The idea of trying to turn Osbert into a coal-miner was so grotesque that it is hard to believe he took it seriously but, though he joked about it, all the evidence suggests that he was genuinely alarmed. He was ordered to register in London on 19 September and wrote apprehensively to Cyril Connolly to explain why he did not know whether he would be able to provide a promised article: 'It looks as though you will shortly have to be singing "Don't go down the mine, daddy" to me.'[34] Even if he were spared the mines, he thought it possible that he would be ordered into a factory. His publishers were instructed to apply for his exemption, on the grounds that he was in the middle of a book which would help bolster the morale of the British public,[35] while the Society of Authors was also invoked. Denys Kilham-Roberts, general secretary of the society, made discreet enquiries and was encouraging: 'I gather there is little prospect of writers of your eminence being called upon, but we must obviously take precautions in case Bevin is tempted to spring a fast one.'[36] Osbert's agent Ann Pearn was equally encouraging; the best policy would be to lie low and do nothing to attract the attention of the authorities; almost certainly he would be left in peace.[37] He remained apprehensive, and set off to register in the conviction that a few days would see him down a mine or at a factory bench. 'My darling, I am terribly distressed for you,' wrote Edith. She was regretful above all that he had to report in London where she would not be present to support and, if necessary, comfort him. But perhaps it was for the best, she reflected. In London no one would know that he was one of the 'hated gentry. Nobody cares so much if one is gentry or not, because they are more used to them.'[38]

And then the danger passed. The Society of Authors was told in confidence that active writers of repute would be left in peace. Osbert was given similarly encouraging advice from a well-placed source. He was not formally exempted, but he was assured that he could count on his call-up being indefinitely postponed. It is easy to feel some irritation at his reluctance to be made use of when so many millions of his fellow countrymen were already doing as much or far more. For someone of his age, health and temperament, however, assignment to a mine or a factory in Sheffield would have been catastrophic; not far from a sentence of death. He spent a sheltered war; rarely in serious danger, enjoying comforts far greater than those available to all but a handful of Britons; but it was still for him an intensely painful experience. If he had been called up, the painful would have become intolerable; it would be hard to begrudge him his exemption.

He did volunteer for one kind of war service which he hoped to combine with his filial duty. Sir George was proposing to see out the war in an Italy that was still neutral but seemed more and more likely to join on the German side if an opportunity occurred to make some pickings without too much risk. He was eighty, his health was failing; there were things to be decided about the estate and his investments overseas. Osbert assumed that, nevertheless, a visit to Italy would be impossible; then the British Council suggested a tour that would enable him to see his father and simultaneously help the Allied effort. To volunteer, he was assured, was his patriotic duty. An old friend, Ian Greenlees, wrote from Rome to say that 'what the Italians want to hear is a lecture by a poet or a novelist they have heard of, and who is representative of the best cultural tradition of England'. Whether the sort of Italian who might want to hear such a lecture was likely to be of much significance when it came to deciding on peace or war was an issue to which neither Mr Greenlees nor the British Council seem to have addressed themselves.

The former at least proved to have been slightly out of touch with the feeling in Rome. His letter was dated 15 April 1940. In it he reported that opinion was very anti-German; 'I should think there is little chance of Italy coming in on the side of Germany.'[39]

Osbert needed little encouragement. An itinerary was devised which would take him to several of Italy's greater cities and give him a free day at Florence which he could devote to a visit to Montegufoni. Sir George was touchingly delighted. 'It will be a joy to me to see you,' he wrote. 'I think you will be very comfortable and you will have whatever dishes you prefer.' He much needed Osbert's advice on certain improvements which he was making to the house and gardens.[40] He was never to get it. The visit was delayed because Edith contracted chicken-pox and Osbert had to wait till the period of incubation was over (one wonders whether he remembered the contempt he had expressed for Eden when the then Foreign Secretary had been afflicted in the same way some years before*). By the time the danger was over the German onslaught in the West was under way. The British Council dithered: 'I would of course let you know if the Council thought it inadvisable for you to go to Italy,' wrote Allen Rose, 'but I am afraid we are no better informed than you are.'[41] Osbert appealed to Harold Macmillan for advice. 'I am most anxious not to get to Italy and then find myself interned.'[42] Macmillan, now a junior minister, presumably had other things on his mind. The Foreign Office on his behalf cautiously recommended that Osbert should set off but keep in touch and be ready to change his plans if the course of the war made it necessary. Apprehensively, Osbert left for the continent on 9 May 1940.

'It was heroic of you to come in spite of the crisis,' wrote his father enthusiastically. 'I do earnestly hope they won't order you home.'[43] If he continued his journey and France fell, he would be perfectly safe in Florence or in Switzerland. By the time this letter was written, Osbert had reached Milan. Even if he had received it he would not have found it reassuring. His earnest hope was that the Foreign Office would order him to do *something*, no matter what. He had cabled them from Paris to ask whether he should continue further and received the reply: 'Advise you to go, but it must be on your own responsibility.' 'Am proceeding,' Osbert retorted, 'but if Tennyson had described the Light Brigade as being told to charge but on their own responsibility, it would have been less impressive!'[44] Unlike the Light Brigade, he checked his charge before

*See p. 234 above.

the guns became too menacing and retreated to Monte Carlo, where he lurked for a few days before heading back to London. Within a fortnight Italy was at war. Osbert had missed his last chance of a farewell visit to his father.

One of the worst features of the war for Osbert was that it entailed separation from David Horner. Horner was thirty-nine when war broke out, not a candidate for early call-up but likely to become involved if there was no early end to the fighting. At one point he volunteered to go and fight for Finland against the Russians but the Finns surrendered before any force could be despatched – the mere news that Horner was threatening to take part made an armistice inevitable, said Osbert's close friend the Tory MP Malcolm Bullock, since neither party 'could stand up to it and its far reaching consequences upon the Army on both sides'.[45] Osbert hoped that Horner would find a billet in the Ministry of Information but nothing was offered, and as the age for call-up moved inexorably upwards it became more and more likely that eventually he would end up in the services. In August 1940 the blow fell – a blow felt more by Osbert than by Horner, who in many ways was quite pleased to escape into a new and perhaps more exciting world. He joined the Royal Air Force and almost at once found himself posted to a camp not far from Renishaw, able to make frequent visits for baths and meals and to spend there whatever weekend leaves he could contrive. To Osbert it seemed a satisfactory solution, but he managed to stifle his dismay when Horner was posted to the Air Ministry in London.

'You have been more than angelic in yr attitude towards the change,' wrote Horner gratefully, 'and psychologically I shall feel so much nearer to you at home in London than in a comparatively nearby hut.'[46] 'Home' was Carlyle Square, which had been lightly scarred by war but was never seriously damaged. Most of the pictures and some of the furniture had been moved to Renishaw, but Miss Noble, who had succeeded Mrs Powell as housekeeper, was still ensconced and Horner was able to squat there in only mild discomfort. For Osbert this at least meant that he could hope to see his friend whenever he came to London. Though familiarity had taken off the edge of passion, Osbert was still emotionally committed to the relationship and counted a day wasted if it was not passed in Horner's company. Unfortunately for Osbert, Horner's work involved a lot of travel. Quite what it entailed remained mysterious – perhaps because it was secret, perhaps because Horner thought it would seem more significant if wrapped in obscurity. Liaison with the Americans, once they had entered the war, was in some way involved. Horner professed contempt for his new allies: 'No words of mine can express the ineptitude of the Yankees. I am not amused, and very worried. I hope that quite a lot of them will get bumped off. They are far worse than we have ever been and quite under-estimated the Japs.'[47] This unattractive rancour was soon modified and, anyway, did not survive the war. It showed, however, that his always formidable capacity for taking – and giving – offence had been exaggerated by the stresses of war. The Americans were not the only victims. He quarrelled increasingly with Edith on his visits to Renishaw and was affronted when 'his' room was given in his absence to another guest.[48]

'I fret dreadfully about poor David in London and ring up continually, which must bore him and Miss Noble,' Osbert confessed to L. P. Hartley.[49] The thought that Horner was growing away from him in London was a constant nagging worry, which was reinforced in 1943 when his friend decided to join the Roman Catholic Church. 'Are you really becoming a Catholic?' Osbert enquired. 'In a way I feel happy about it, for it will be a good source of consolation to you; but unhappy too, as I would not have you changed in any respect.'[50] Horner did not feel that Osbert's attitude reflected the importance of the event – the word 'consolation' in particular piqued him by its inadequacy. Osbert was contrite. 'I suppose, for me, Parish Church religion has been always so depressing that I never imagined one could adopt a faith from joy, strength, only discord and from weakness. Now I do really understand and it makes a *very* great difference to me ... What an idiot I am in those matters.'[51] He was no doubt altogether sincere when he wrote these words, but the mood did not last. He resented Horner's new allegiance and never ceased to poke fun at what seemed to him the excesses of religiosity involved in this adoption of the Roman Catholic faith.

Georgia and Sachie visited Renishaw in September 1939. They found the inhabitants 'comfortable but edgy'. Horner was amiable enough but Edith told Georgia that she was 'not at all happy' and that Osbert was unkind to her.[52] It is probably true to say that, if Osbert had *not* been unkind to her, Horner would have been less amiable. At the outbreak of war Edith had installed herself at Renishaw. Horner made it clear he found her presence at the best irksome, at the worst actively offensive. They coexisted cautiously; Edith being the more cautious because of the weakness of her position – she was dependent on Osbert and so, much though she resented his presence, knew that she could not afford to quarrel with Horner. She was as relieved as Osbert was distressed when Pilot Officer Horner departed for the wars. Alone together in the great house the brother and sister might at times get on each other's nerves, but the most dangerous single cause of friction was safely out of the way. During the day, anyway, they saw little of each other. Edith kept to her room and wrote; Osbert did the same for much of the time but often had to be about his duties. His decision to see out the war at Renishaw made more pressing the responsibilities which he had already begun to take on before the war. His prime preoccupation was still his writing and he begrudged the other pressures on his time; but he played his part in the neighbourhood conscientiously and with good grace.

Robert Herring, the editor of the literary journal *Life and Letters*, spent several months at Renishaw when driven from London by the blitz and was therefore deeply in Osbert's debt; but though his tone was gushing there is no reason to doubt his sincerity when he told Edith: 'I have never known anything like Osbert's nature, and I want to do it honour . . . and then, since I have been up here, I have seen Osbert at work and running Renishaw and learnt to admire that.'[53] He would have seen Osbert presiding at the tenants' dinners: 'Rather fun in a way,' the squire of Renishaw wrote benignly. 'In lots of places they've fallen into disuse, but they've been on here twice a year since the 17th century.'[54] Or hob-nobbing with the Eckington carnival queen, 'whatever she may be'.[55] Or coming back after a session on the magistrates' bench – 'Such a nice lot of drunks. I loved them! They . . . could not have been more jolly and full of fun. It was a shame, I thought, to have to fine them. I'd much rather have asked them to dinner.'[56] He was equally tolerant when the accused were a bunch of hooligans aged between six and ten who had done an impressively good job of wrecking the boat-house on the lake at Renishaw. If only they had been a little older, he wrote, he would have recommended that they be formed into a committee to suggest ideas for the destruction of German cities: 'Our statesmen are too old. Have not the resource of these inimitable youngsters.'[57] Or acting as a governor of Staveley Netherthorpe School: he would expect, he told Horner, in future to be addressed as 'Governor'.[58]

He rarely attended the local church but, as patron of the living, took a proprietary interest in its affairs. He was therefore outraged when he was told that his presence would not be welcome at a presentation that was to be made to a retiring rector. He sent £5 to swell the fund but blasted the unfortunate Mr Kirkham, who was in charge of the affair:

I had never imagined the possibility of receiving such a message – in Eckington, of all places. You will realise that I am an excessively busy man, and that very few authors of eminence allow their time to be taken up with parish matters, but I have always had this place so near my heart that I have been eager to help in any way I can. When I think of the interest which my family have taken for several centuries in the church here, I cannot but feel extremely perturbed, distressed and disgusted. But the matter is more than a personal one. It is most unsatisfactory that any churchgoer, whoever he is, should be subjected to an insult of this sort. It is not likely to encourage churchgoing. I must request an apology from those concerned.[59]

Whether he got the apology is unknown; his church attendance did not improve under the new incumbent.

Renishaw in wartime displayed in an exaggerated form that eccentric compound of luxury and discomfort which had been the tradition of English country houses for many years. Osbert described it to Bernard Shaw as a 'Museum of Inconvenience ... The library is full of 17th century sermons, there is no electric light or heating, the pictures, furniture and gardens are pretty. And it is so uncomfortable in a comfortable old-fashioned way.'[60] Much of the house was shut up, including the gloomier and most ghost-ridden wing, but quite enough was left open to ensure that, when people came to stay, hosts and guests need not meet unless they wanted to. Indeed, visitors were encouraged to spend much of the day in their bedrooms, in which fires burned from October to April. Edith pleaded with T. S. Eliot to come and stay; it would not be at all like paying a conventional visit, she explained: 'You can do whatever you want to do with no interference. Nobody ever comes down to breakfast – people disappear for hours on end if they want to, or stop in by themselves ... Nobody is ever hurried or badgered.'[61] Eliot resisted the temptation, but Harold Acton came and found that the Sitwells were as good as their word: 'They work all day, breakfast in bed, and except for occasional walks we only meet at meals.'[62] After dinner they would listen to the news on an ancient wireless which seemed intent on thwarting its owners; Edith sadly told Stephen Spender that it had broken down when his wife, the pianist Natasha Litvin, had been broadcasting and regularly did so whenever one of Osbert's plays was on the air, but never 'when male choirs are singing the March of the Men of Harlech, or Mr Sandy Macpherson [the celebrated theatre organist] is oozing out warm treacle'.[63]

To some this rarefied and remote existence seemed entirely proper. Evelyn Waugh rejoiced at the spectacle of two people 'still living a private life and doing proper work and being serious about serious things and funny about funny things'.[64] Others, and not just the hearties and the jingoes, were more censorious. William Plomer, the young South African writer who had much admired the Sitwells, saw something selfish and self-indulgent in their behaviour. They lived in luxury and relative safety yet did nothing but complain about the old gardener who talked under their windows, the dog that barked, the clergyman who came to tea, the admirers who sent them poems from all over England.[65] The luxury was relative, and more apparent when guests were present than when they were alone, but they certainly ate a great deal better than most of their fellow countrymen. 'It's difficult to get things to eat here now. There really is little,' Osbert told David Horner, yet only a month earlier Marie Belloc Lowndes, for Christmas lunch, had enjoyed two helpings of turkey, plum pudding, grapes, with a half-bottle of champagne and a prunelle, while for dinner she had had two cocktails, soup, sole, cold turkey, dessert and again a half-bottle of champagne, prunelle and, this time, brandy.[66] 'Here we live on a few strings of desiccated spaghetti,' reported Osbert, yet a month later when Bryher came to lunch: 'We had *quails* (Sucks! Cripps!)'[67] Visitors were expected to bring allowances of the more sternly rationed items – sugar, butter, tea – but the contribution from local sources was lavish: Mrs Belloc Lowndes was entranced by the 'wonderful, unusual vegetables',[68] while Osbert used four wine merchants to supply his needs. In 1941 and 1942 he managed to procure more than 360 bottles of wine and 36 of sherry.

Heating so large a house was a problem in winter since, even though Renishaw was built on coal, the supply to the house was rigidly rationed. There was wood in abundance, though. Life entailed a series of hurried scuttles down draughty corridors from heated bedrooms to heated sitting-rooms. 'There were log fires in the bedrooms,' remembered the painter John Piper, 'and a battery of tall white candlesticks on the chamber-pot cupboards. Aladdin paraffin lamps in the sitting rooms, storm lanterns out of doors.'[69] By the winter of 1943 the little dining-room was the only downstairs room kept warm: 'We sit in it too, now,' complained Osbert. 'It's squalid and middle-class and I hate it, but it's better than being cold.'[70]

One of the reasons Osbert had settled at Renishaw was to protect it from those anxious to take it over and use it as a school, barracks or internment camp. Nothing could keep evacuees at bay, though the first wave did not arrive till August 1940. 'You can't imagine the dirt and helplessness,' Osbert told Sachie. 'They are fried-fish-shop types, and can hardly cook for themselves, and have no windows open. If they are given bread they throw it away. Three loaves were found in the park.'[71] By November there were two mothers and eleven children in the house – they 'might have been designed by Cruickshank', Osbert wrote despairingly[72] – and more followed, 'an Italian woman and a Jewess'. 'I asked if I couldn't have an English person, but they said, No,' he told David Horner.[73] Luckily the evacuees disliked the conditions at Renishaw quite as much as Osbert resented their presence; gradually they moved out to cottages on the estate.

But the evacuees were not the only, or even the most serious, threat. The first onslaught came shortly after the outbreak of war, when a colonel in charge of billeting arrived to inspect the premises. To Osbert's immense relief he decided that the '12th century tapestries' would be too serious a responsibility for the Army to take on. 'The Colonel decided that they were of that epoch and no one contradicted him,' David Horner told Lady Aberconway. 'Aren't the Army a darling lot of aesthetes these days?'[74] Then, while Osbert was in Monte Carlo, Hollingworth was served with a notice to provide beds and food for a party of officers, presumably in anticipation of a retreat from France. Twenty-four of them arrived; just in time to make impossible a long-meditated visit from Max Beerbohm. Everyone had got his own radio, Osbert gloomily reported; the cacophony was fearful.[75] They soon moved on, but the menace of requisition never lifted. In October 1941 the Office of Works took up the attack, looking for somewhere suitable to accommodate a ministry evacuated from Whitehall. *They* were deterred by the lack of heating and electric light.[76] A lull followed, during which Osbert began to feel secure; but then in the summer of 1942 a Captain Ingham arrived from Nottingham planning to take over the whole house to house some of the million Englishmen displaced by the advent of the Americans. All the traditional counter-arguments were brushed aside: 'I tried to throw the golf club at them,' reported Osbert, but even this ploy proved unavailing. 'I'm starting to see what else I can do.'[77] What else he did do remains mysterious but it proved efficacious. The danger of eviction once more receded. He could not keep the house altogether inviolate, there were usually up to half a dozen officers somewhere on the premises, but the heart of Renishaw remained free for the family and their friends. Osbert could never feel wholly safe, though, and his nerves ached under the strain. 'They're starting to try and snatch this house from me again,' he wailed to Robert Herring in 1943. 'I feel quite sick with boredom.'[78]

Earlier in the war boredom, at least, had been alleviated by the bombing. Renishaw was close enough to Sheffield to ensure that, whenever that city was attacked, Osbert would pass a disturbed and possibly dangerous night. 'The bombs have fallen like the rain of an English June,' he told Cyril Connolly in December 1940. 'The noise of Sheffield being destroyed was appalling on Thursday and Sunday. Shops on Thursday, factories on Sunday. This morning we had some machine-gunning for a change.' Sheffield was in ruins, he reported four days later: 'Much worse than London.'[79] The drive was blocked by an unexploded bomb just inside the gates and eleven panes of glass were blown out in these or subsequent raids. Sometimes Osbert took refuge in a dug-out near the front door – 'I should think *very* dangerous,' commented Mrs Belloc Lowndes[80] – sometimes he went up on to the roof to join the fire watchers. 'It is in a way so beautiful,' he told Madame Guéritte, 'the garden below in the full moon, and the lake, glint of water everywhere. And a comforting sense persists that there have been watchers on the roof before, because the house was garrisoned for King Charles I, and it is said you can still see the marks of cannon balls on the wall, though I never have been able to identify them.'[81]

The regular fire watchers – a group to which Osbert evidently felt it unnecessary to belong – consisted of gardeners and estate workers. The footmen who might once have supplemented the squad had vanished with the outbreak of war and the only manservant living in the house was Osbert's old batman, the indefatigable Robins. As well as being indefatigable, Robins was intelligent and ferociously loyal; he was also cantankerous and quick to take offence. Robins's dog was howling, Edith told John Lehmann. 'Robins is our Old Retainer, and at moments he is exactly like Heathcliff's servant in *Wuthering Heights*. Robins likes his dog to howl. He says it is "what dogs are for".'[82] Almost worse than his dog was his daughter, who played the piano and sang with a vigour which far outmatched her competence. If we win the war, Osbert reflected, 'she ought to be made to give a series of concerts in Germany, attendance compulsory'.[83] And yet, with the help of his wife as cook and such casual labour as could be recruited in the neighbourhood, Robins managed to keep Renishaw running: preparing hot baths, laying out warm towels, lighting fires in bedrooms, serving breakfasts there, presiding over meals, valeting for Osbert and the not infrequent visitors. 'I have never in my life seen such devoted, such fierce, such ardent labour,' wrote Lovat Dickson. 'It possessed him as though it were a religious fervour.' Dickson was dismayed by Osbert's apparent failure to appreciate what was being done for him; he would ring bells and shout orders down the stairs as if there were a full complement of servants, 'feeling slightly martyred when he sometimes had to wait to get what he wanted'.[84] Probably Osbert was more appreciative than Dickson imagined: Robins knew he was indispensable, rejoiced in his voluntary servitude and would have been disconcerted if his employer had adopted a more conciliatory approach.

Robins's rebarbative nature and the lure of armaments factories in Sheffield together explained why it was so difficult to find other servants at Renishaw. 'Kitty (housemaid) has her son down with mumps, so we all make our own beds,' Osbert reported in 1942;[85] an imposition which sounds endurable to the post-war generation but to him must have seemed only a short step from revolution and the rumbling of the tumbrils. If Edith and Osbert are to be believed, Renishaw was staffed, when staff existed, by grotesques and lunatics. The gardener's wife played the piano even worse and even louder than Robins's daughter, until Osbert persuaded her that the instrument was permeated with death-watch beetle and must be returned immediately to the manu-facturers.[86] But pride of place for horror was taken by the fourteen-year-old housemaid who was plainly possessed by a poltergeist: 'a piece of broken glass was found near my gouty foot, and my sister found part of a broken china candlestick inside a fried whiting. She then developed a place on one cheek . . . it looked as if she had been transfixed by the Devil with a fiery pitchfork. By this time we had had too much of it and sent her home.'[87] Osbert grumbled endlessly. 'This house is hell now,' he told Lady Aberconway. 'No one to do anything. I wish I could be taken back to 1910, don't you? Or not? I want an enormous house, no trouble, an assured income, lots of servants.'[88] At this time, the enormous house *was* the trouble. 'Edith and I can find nowhere to go while the servants are on their selfish holidays,' he complained to Bryher.[89] Probably he was joking in his use of the word 'selfish', but it is an alarming commentary on his character that one cannot be entirely sure.

Edith was as capable of grumbling as Osbert and took the vicissitudes of life more tragically. In theory she rented the room at Renishaw in which she worked, but this was probably no more than an accounting device, enabling Osbert to set the cost of coal, candles and cleaning against tax.[90] Though Georgia had said that Edith complained Osbert was unkind to her, her usual refrain was one of passionate gratitude. 'It would be stupid even to begin to say what I feel about how wonderfully good you are to me,' she told him in August 1940.

'You have never, in all my life, let me down.'[91] She realised that, if they were too much together, they might begin to regret each other's company. The possibility alarmed her. In the spring of 1941 she refused an invitation to accompany him to stay with the Aberconways. 'Owing to my being here with him so much,' she told Christabel, 'he never gets a real chance to see his greatest friends alone, and I do feel that it is rather a shame – and *cramping*.'[92] She was right in suspecting that her company could be exhausting. Evelyn Waugh reported that Osbert was bland and genial, 'Edith alternating between extremes of venom[?] and compassion'.[93] The plight of Evelyn Wiel – sister of her oldest friend and ally, Helen Rootham – who was battling against hunger and ill-health in occupied Paris, so overcame her that she retreated to her room if visitors came to the house. She 'anyhow cries all through lunch and dinner, which is hardly fair on a stranger', Osbert remarked resignedly. 'If she doesn't cry, she feels, poor darling, that she isn't "doing her bit" for Evelyn.'[94]

Hospitable by nature, and feeling woefully cut off from most of what he loved in life, Osbert eagerly welcomed congenial visitors. He had rather too much of Robert Herring, however. Since Edith wrote regularly for Herring's journal and Osbert's old friend Bryher put up much of the money for it, it seemed reasonable that he should seek refuge in Renishaw after his flat and offices had been made uninhabitable by bombs. However, his fecklessness and susceptibility to drink made him at times an inconvenient guest. Osbert was not sorry when Herring settled in a house in Eckington, but he was good company and, once he had moved out, his presence on the doorstep of Renishaw was a decided asset. Osbert, too, relished flattery, and Herring provided it in lavish dollops. 'One of the many lasting benefits I have drawn from my protracted stay with you', he wrote, 'is that I have been in the same house as so finely tempered and disciplined a quick mind. I think it has done me more good than anything I have ever had, to have seen your mind in daily action . . . These are standards now I can never lose, because they have been seen and touched in Renishaw.'[95]

Herring's presence ensured that his benefactor, Bryher, soon too became a frequent visitor at Renishaw. She had never visited Osbert in the country before and, seeing him and Edith on their native heath, found them comical but still more appealing. She went to Renishaw for the first time in January 1941, walking through the snow to get there. 'Osbert was looking magnificent in corduroys, there was Edith superb in a black quilted gown, David in civilian top and flying fleece-lined boots to his knees and two other guests, one a Lady Aberconway who is apparently O's best girl-friend, and with whom I fell quite in love.'[96] Soon she was quite in love with all of them. Osbert would take her for long walks, scrambling over fences and through hedges, asking her the name of any flower, trotting down the railway line, 'with the big Elephant saying "I wonder if we shall meet a train"'.[97] Bryher, whose generosity seemed as inexhaustible as her fortune, bought Edith a house in Bath and heaped other kindnesses on Osbert. However tiresome Herring might sometimes have been, his presence was a small price to pay for Bryher's friendship.

Leslie Hartley, who was just beginning his career as a successful novelist, was another frequent visitor. Edith criticised his sensibilities and David Horner sneered at him as middle class, but to Osbert he was 'the most charming and sensitive of friends, and I'm devoted to him'.[98] The fact that they were both homosexual certainly drew them together, but though the tone of their conversation, and indeed letters, was camp in style, the friendship seems to have been entirely decorous. Hartley, though notably untidy, was otherwise the perfect guest: entertaining, appreciative, delighted to sight-see or hob-nob with the neighbours but equally happy to get on with his own writing and leave his host to his. He wrote wonderful, gossipy, rambling bread-and-butter letters which alone would have made his visits memorable. Osbert paid him the supreme compliment of urging him, when he was on the look-out for a new house, to 'remember you are always welcome here, and that, though I believe such arrangements are often a flop, I would welcome you here for the rest of the war (or the rest of our liberty)'.[99]

Arthur Waley came to Renishaw several times during the war: 'He is always unexpected,' reported Osbert, 'and this time has produced the most remarkably loud check suits, deliciously inappropriate.'[100] Tom Driberg, journalist, sexual adventurer and future Labour politician, erupted at an hour's notice, 'very louche and furious . . . He has a servant of Italian descent, the illegitimate son of a conjuror.'[101] Anthony and Violet Powell stayed there one winter. They went shopping with Edith in Sheffield and Osbert urged them to look in on the fishmonger, who could sometimes provide a salmon. Edith cross-examined Lady Violet on how to cook a salmon and was given several tips, ending 'Then you make the tail into kedgeree'. On arriving at the fish-shop Edith swept past the queue, probably not noticing it was there, and demanded a salmon 'for making kedgeree'. The queue shuddered in outrage but Edith secured her salmon and swept out again. She then abandoned her prey on the counter of the next shop she visited, so that eventually the salmon had to complete the journey by train.[102]

John Piper, a young, talented but at that date little-known painter, was at Renishaw more than any of them. In April 1940 Osbert wrote to suggest that Piper visit Renishaw and paint a series of pictures of it. Piper was delighted. 'Its beauties look very great from the postcards you send,' he wrote enthusiastically; as to the price, he suggested £10 for a water-colour and £20, £30 or £40 for an oil, according to size and difficulty, 'but I should be very surprised if we could not arrange about fee easily'.[103] He was right; Osbert accepted the terms with alacrity and wrote to Madame Guéritte to report his new venture: 'I suppose you know his work? Old houses, splintered in ancient glory and coruscating in their own decay; they are lovely, I think. And the lightning sketches that he makes, to serve as notes for his pictures, have a wonderful rapidity of movement about them.' The weather had played up most obligingly during Piper's first visit, with dramatic storms and lightning alternating with splashes of brilliant sunlight; almost like *The Ancient Mariner*, Osbert noted approvingly.[104]

Piper was enchanted by the grandeur and romance of Renishaw and Osbert enjoyed showing off, trying out his favourite anecdotes and introducing his protégé to various aspects of gracious living. At midnight he would look at his watch and say: 'It's about time the ghost walked.' Once Piper thought he heard a distant clanking. Osbert 'did his funny hum-hum and giggled, "Some say that it's a ghost but others say it's the noise of the trolleys in the mine below the house." '[105] John Piper's wife Myfanwy occasionally came too but more often stayed at home; she was made welcome but had the impression that Osbert preferred to have her husband to himself. Sometimes she speculated whether there was anything sexual in this possessiveness. She knew her husband well enough to be sure any such feeling on Osbert's part was not reciprocated but once asked Piper whether he had ever been accosted by his host. Piper denied the implication with genuine surprise. He was overwhelmed by the kindness that both Osbert and Edith showed him. 'I loved them for it and basked in their affection. In a sense they answered a fairly desperate need of mine at the time for sophistication, for lively conversation, for some constructive and slightly abrasive experience of literature and painting and music and indeed life . . . And they were frightfully funny. I never laughed so much as in those early days at Renishaw.'[106] Geoffrey Grigson for one believed that Osbert had had a bad effect on Piper's painting, making him socially conscious and encouraging him to practise the trivial and the decorative at the expense of more 'serious' undertakings.[107] The charge is hard to justify. Piper had finished with his foray into abstraction and was dedicated to the painting of buildings long before Osbert took him up; his stay at Renishaw may have improved his technique but certainly did not affect his style.

Not every guest was so welcome. Victor Cazalet, the Tory MP and partisan supporter of Churchill, was a man whom Osbert much disliked. Nevertheless, he felt he could hardly refuse when Cazalet invited himself to tea. He made his feelings clear, however, when Cazalet, who had much admired the chocolate cake, wrote to ask for the recipe. He was, he added, enclosing a stamped and addressed envelope, so as to make it difficult for Osbert to refuse. Osbert replied gleefully: ' Dear Victor, you say you have made it difficult for me to refuse. You haven't!'[108] Alec Guinness, who had become a friend of Edith's before the war, stayed there with his wife Merula. He was a great success, but they were given strict instructions by Edith to keep their three-months-old son secreted since Osbert could not stand babies. The child was smuggled in and only put out in parts of the garden which Osbert never visited. All went well until Robins, at dinner, murmured confidentially but not confidentially enough that 'young Master Guinness' was screaming. Osbert took the news with commendable calm. 'I assure you I do not mind in the least,' he said, 'so long as you will excuse me from looking at him.'[109] Dogs were even worse than babies. A young man brought one and, to add to Osbert's dismay, insisted on talking to it the whole time with cries of 'Who's a Foozie-Woozie?' or 'Woogie-Boozie'. Looking at a picture of St Jerome and the lion the night after his guest had left, Osbert speculated whether the saint had spoken to the animal like that or whether, when he was writing 'one of his bad-tempered, acute books, someone would barge into his cave, shouting "Who's a Foozie Woozie?" I hope the lion ate the intruder if it was so.'[110]

John Lehmann and his sister Rosamond were more of a problem. John Lehmann was always welcome; Osbert enjoyed his company, admired his writing and eventually encouraged him to write a book about the three Sitwells. About Rosamond he was ambivalent. 'She is *really* beautiful, like the rose of Sharon in some way entangled with one of the Fates, her hair has been struck to sculpture.' But he found her humourless and, still worse, possessed at times by 'a terrible spite'.[111] He was therefore put out when Denys Kilham-Roberts told him not only that Rosamond Lehmann was to serve with him on a small committee to administer a scheme for travel grants for authors – hardly an onerous task in 1942 – but that she was 'thrilled at the idea of paying a visit to Renishaw in the Spring'. Osbert crossly annotated the letter, probably for the eyes of Bryher: 'I don't know why Kilham-Roberts should take it upon himself to ask her. I haven't, and don't want her here. She's a bad writer, I think.'[112] Either his views on this last point changed with time or he was no more honest than most of the people who wrote to him about *his* books. In 1945 Osbert wrote to congratulate her in ardent terms on her new book *The Ballad and the Source*, 'and I know what I'm talking about, for novels are what I most like'.[113]

Cecil Beaton would have been still less acceptable at that period. He had caused offence some years before when, without first asking permission, he had changed the preface Osbert had contributed to the catalogue of his 1929 exhibition by substituting American names for English. He then compounded his sin by referring to Sir George as 'Ginger' in his *Scrapbook* of 1935. Finally, in 1941, he included photographs of the Sitwells in his latest book, *Time Exposure*, without first asking them whether they approved, allowed Peter Quennell to make what Osbert considered to be offensive comments about them in the text and, to cap it all, put photographs of Siegfried Sassoon and Anita Loos, the author of *Gentlemen Prefer Blondes*, on the same page.[114] Quennell's comments would, in fact, have appeared offensive only to the hyper-sensitive and it is hard to see why Sassoon's juxtaposition with Miss Loos should have so upset him. Sassoon himself did not mind in the least. 'Osbert's fuss is nonsense,' he told Beaton. 'He really ought to know better at his age and so ought Edith. I suppose they haven't enough to think about as they sit there at Renishaw! Poor dears; how typical it is of their hyper-sensitive egotism. Same as ever!' Lord Berners, too, found the whole affair most comical. He wrote Beaton a letter of mock rebuke for having photographed him standing half in and half out of a doorway, thus suggesting that he was merely poised on the threshold of the Hall of Fame. 'To say nothing', he concluded, 'of your having placed dear Anita's picture on the same page as that *dreadful* Siegfried Sassoon – and why include the Sitwells?'[115]

Osbert, however, was in a mood to take umbrage at almost anything. Beaton was suitably chastened, protesting his 'great affection and admiration' for the Sitwells, and insisting that neither he nor Quennell had meant to give offence. Osbert was reading into the text things that were not there. His apology was handsome but his last sentence unfortunate – 'I had thought that by giving the Sitwells such a "showing" I had shown my respect.'[116] Osbert's dignity was affronted by the suggestion that he should be gratified at receiving a 'showing' from Cecil Beaton but he might still have let the matter drop if Edith had not seen the letter. Always one to pour depth-charges into troubled waters, Edith urged counter-attack. Osbert should reply, beginning his letter: 'You are a nasty little man, as well as a third rate little man. You are impertinent to your superiors . . .'[117] Osbert stopped short of this, but his reply was cool: 'I appreciate your professions of esteem and affection at their full worth,' he began, with deliberate ambiguity.[118] He did not forgive Beaton and his letters to friends like Christabel Aberconway abound in offensive references. 'Imagine him having the mixture of folly and spite', he wrote in early 1943, 'to send me . . . a notice of a charity "do" for the new Coward film . . . But he's a trivial little person and one can't worry about him.'[119] The quarrel lasted till 1947 and the two men were never close friends again.

However many visitors, wanted or unwanted, might come to Renishaw, Osbert was still going to feel himself cut off from London life. Carlyle Square was never closed and, from the time that David Horner was posted to the Air Ministry, was regularly occupied. It became shabby and somewhat frayed at the edges but was not seriously damaged. Ian Greenlees, dining there with Horner in May 1942, rejoiced to see that there were still a few pictures on the walls and bottles of wine in the cellar.[120] Osbert happened to be there for the first days of the blitz and found the experience disagreeable. He came away 'feeling rather like a shuttlecock', he told Bernard Shaw. 'An incendiary bomb fired the gas main just outside on the 3rd day at 3 am and at 6 pm the same evening a land-mine, I suppose, blew up 7 houses within 30 yards of mine. I was in my bath and expected to be drowned.'[121] Fourteen people were buried in the rubble of the square and only two were dug out alive. Osbert returned to Renishaw; he had duties there and nothing to keep him in London: to stay on would have been pointless bravado and he does not seem to have contemplated doing so. He came up again for a week in October, when the blitz was at its height, but endured no misses so near as those he had already experienced. He planned to return in November but Lorna Andrade urged him not to come 'unless it is absolutely necessary. The damage all round your house may not be on the vast scale of, say, John Lewis or Chancery Lane, but it is considerable and *always* increasing.'[122] On reflection, Osbert heeded her advice. 'I feel quite sick from the thought of London being destroyed,' he told Lady Aberconway. 'And the heroism of the civilian population, while wonderful, is rather like the heroism of pheasants on October 1. No way of *directly* hitting back.'[123] There seemed little point in adding to the company of pheasants; Osbert did not return to London, except for two nights at the Savoy en route to and from Badminton, until after the blitz was over.

For the rest of the war he settled into a routine whereby he would spend four or five days in London every two or three months, often combining the visit with a weekend at one of the reduced range of houses still open near the capital. In June 1944 he abruptly cut short a stay in Carlyle Square when the first V1s began to fall on central London: 'I skedaddled from the new kind of bomb,' he admitted to William Plomer, 'which shows ingratitude, I suppose, to the makers of modern blessings.'[124] When he was there he would fit in as many appointments and see as many friends as could be contrived: in one typical period of four days in May/June 1942, he lunched with Malcolm Bullock, Sachie and at Buckingham Palace, dined with Harold Macmillan's elder brother Daniel, Cyril Connolly and Lady Desborough, went to a performance of *Façade* at the Aeolian Hall, and called on his bank, his solicitors, his literary agent and the Society of Authors. He then went on to spend a weekend with the Woodhouses at Nether Lypiatt. It was stimulating stuff, and made the sequestered calm of Renishaw seem tolerable for the next few weeks.

One of Osbert's principal regrets at being forced to live in the country arose from his conviction – commonly held among Londoners – that no competent doctors or dentists were to be found outside the capital. Like it or not, however, he had to resort frequently to their provincial counterparts. He had a severe attack of gout towards the end of 1939 – 'It must add to the pain that Chamberlain also has it,' Malcolm Muggeridge pointed out[125] – and was even worse afflicted in July 1942, when he was unable to leave his room for ten days or more. 'I'm afraid I'm as bad as I was at Hyères,' he told Horner; 'can't move without groaning, can't work, and what worries me is that I don't see how I am to get treatment afterwards and I may be lame for some time.'[126] In fact he was hobbling around within a few days but there was worse to come. Six months later he went to the doctor, complaining of sleeplessness, shortness of breath, mysterious pains. The doctor thought he detected a heart murmur and brought him back for an electro-cardiogram. The results were bad enough for him to be passed on to a specialist, who confirmed the murmur but said that it was a nervous one 'caused by worry, loathing of the war, nostalgia'. He prescribed a day a week in bed, no worry, no writing 'and a general *couleur de rose* existence'.[127] To tell Osbert not to worry, or to look on the rosy side of life, in the middle of the Second World War was not calculated to produce any satisfactory result. Osbert conscientiously spent his day a week in bed but tranquillity was beyond him. 'I haven't been at all well again, feeling very trembling and stupid,' he complained in March 1943.[128] Medically it seems impossible that there could have been any connection between this trembling and the Parkinson's Disease that was to strike him down some seven years later, but it could be that the encephalitis – as it almost certainly had been – from which he had suffered in 1919, was at the root of his troubles. Osbert certainly was convinced that his heart trouble had been with him for many years, longer indeed than the disastrous flu epidemic. 'Why did the medical boards consistently turn me down for service abroad after the summer of 1916?' he asked. Whatever the genesis of his complaint, things had taken a turn for the worse: 'I don't feel well, my worst time is about 5 am.'[129]

His health did not deteriorate significantly in 1943, but nor did he get wholly better. 'I had a sad, even rather disturbing postcard from Osbert,' Leslie Hartley told Horner in December. 'He sounded really bad.'[130] He *was* really bad. The apparent endlessness of the war, isolation at Renishaw, worry about his father, the cold and damp of the loathed English weather, all combined with real physical frailty to reduce him to a state of acute debility. He found relief only in his work. The doctor who recommended that Osbert rest and renounce his writing may have been right in his diagnosis but was grievously wrong in the recommended treatment. In 1943 it was his writing that kept Osbert alive.

14

Beavering Away

How is it possible to do solid work in this epoch, and who wants to read it? Fortunately, such questions occur, but do not prevent the writer from trying. I suppose as well try to prevent a beaver from dam-building.

(Osbert Sitwell, 20 December 1939)

WHEN Osbert told Rosamond Lehmann that 'novels are what I most like', the comment was the more striking as coming from a man who, whether he recognised the fact or not, had put the writing of novels behind him. In his *Who's Who* entry for 1941 he described himself as 'poet, essayist, writer of novels, satires, short stories and art criticism'. He made no mention of the form of writing which was already beginning to absorb his thoughts and energies. Some time in the course of 1940 he had conceived the idea of a monster autobiography sprawling over several volumes and taking him as many or more years to write. By November he was diligently compiling notes – 'but I must live such a long time before I can write it,' he wrote despairingly to Madame Guéritte, 'and living long is not easy, and never more difficult than at the moment'. Nor was the task always a pleasant one. He had been spending the last week looking through old letters, he wrote a month or so later, and 'the miseries of the past have pursued me like the Furies'. How curious it was, he reflected, that members of a family seemed so rarely to write to each other about pleasant things instead of 'mumps and measles, bad school reports, unfortunate events of one sort or another'.[1]

By April 1941 he had so far advanced in his task as to be able to send the first 20,000 words to Lorna Andrade for her to type. He was anxious that she alone should do it, even if it meant delay, 'for it contains remarks about "the living" and it may also have a disagreeable flavour that will need removing. I can't tell till I see it in type.'[2] His agent urged him to sign a contract with Macmillan as soon as possible so as to have more evidence to satisfy the Ministry of Labour that he was hard at work and thus should be excused call-up. Osbert had no objection, especially since Macmillan were prepared to offer him most generous terms, including a top royalty of 20 per cent, but he was not ready to commit himself to any fixed date of delivery. Nor would he take any advance until he had satisfied himself that the book could be published.[3] There was one factor above all which inhibited him from making any firm decision. 'I sincerely hope your father will die soon so that the world can have the pleasure I had by candlelight from your autobiography,' wrote John Piper in mid-1942,[4] stating with some brutality the problem that haunted Osbert. If his book turned out at all as he planned it there could be no question of publication while Sir George was alive. Even if he himself was not particularly worried by the distress that the book would cause his father, he knew that most readers, including some of those whose opinions he greatly respected, would think him heartless and guilty of deplorably bad taste. The fact lent a certain unreality to Osbert's labours, and meant that the work was constantly put to one side when other, more urgent commitments supervened. This they did, with irritating regularity.

At the outset of the war he almost became involved in an enterprise which would both have forced him to spend more time in London and have taken up a great part of his energies. Evelyn Waugh wrote to tell him how much he had enjoyed his new volume of travel-writing, *Escape With Me!* Could they not start a magazine together? he asked. It might be called *Duration*, because it would last only as long as the war and 'its point would be the duration of the things we value – not universal suffrage or disarmament or federalism and all that but good jokes and luxurious writing'. David Cecil and John Betjeman were possible contributors. 'There would be no profit in it. It would be our war work ... It would have no competition and might find numbers of sympathisers hidden in the dark.'[5]

It was an idea that might have appealed to Osbert but, perhaps fortunately, there *were* competitors. Almost at the same time as he received this letter, Osbert heard from Cyril Connolly, to say that he too planned shortly to launch a literary magazine, to be called *Horizon*, to which he hoped Osbert would contribute. Clearly there would not be room for two such magazines. With mingled disappointment and relief, Waugh abandoned the field. Osbert was delighted by Connolly's new venture. 'How nice to hear of something opening, instead of shutting,' he wrote. 'And I feel in my bones that you will make a good editor.'[6] He regularly submitted pieces for publication. Though the two occasionally bickered and each was capable of saying disagreeable things about the other to third parties, Osbert genuinely liked and admired Cyril Connolly, and on the whole the feeling seems to have been reciprocated. 'I do feel intensely for you,' Osbert wrote sympathetically in 1943. '35–40 should be a lovely age, bringing a ripening of the senses and a focusing of the powers. How can it be so now? The only thing we can do is to look at history and at fate, without a loss of nerve, or any weakening that we can help of moral fibre. But it is not easy. Nostalgia lies at the back of every cell in the mind.'[7] He was delighted when Connolly replaced Desmond MacCarthy as lead reviewer on the *Sunday Times*; not only because he believed it would mean better reviews for his own books but because he felt MacCarthy had too narrow a range, particularly in modern poetry, where 'he really likes nothing except Hilaire Belloc's rather smuttier poems'. Anyhow, concluded Osbert, 'you are left with the responsibility for CULTURE, or whatever its new manifestation may be'.[8]

Journalistic work of one kind or another was never hard to find. In 1940 his agent tried to commit him to writing regular pieces for the *Spectator* – short poems, occasional 'light middle articles', book reviews. Graham Greene was the literary editor: 'I know how much you admire Graham's own work, and knowing how in turn he is a keen admirer of yours, I was not surprised to find him enthusiastic.'[9] Greene moved on, and this proposal came to little, but the wartime years saw Osbert contributing also to *Lilliput, Strand Magazine*, the *Times Literary Supplement, Harper's Bazaar* and, most frequently, *Life and Letters*. The BBC he kept at arm's length. George Orwell suggested he do a ten-minute talk on Oscar Wilde for the Indian Service. Osbert replied he was too busy. Orwell then suggested the war poets as a subject. 'My heart has gone wrong, and I am inundated with work, and forbidden to do any for several months,' Osbert pleaded. Roy Campbell took on the charge and asked him to select and read poems from Pope. He was 'snowed under with proofs and books and odds and ends', said Osbert.[10] In time he was rather to fancy himself as a broadcaster but during the war he had no wish to accept the extra strain, especially in view of the exiguous financial reward which was involved. On the same grounds he rejected a proposal that he should write a short book on the ballet for the *Britain in Pictures* series; even in 1942, £50 for all rights did not seem a very satisfactory return for a book of 14,000 words.

He could afford to pick and choose. At the end of 1940 Daniel Macmillan, somewhat cautiously, told him that the current sales figures 'tended to show that you are a successful author'. To date, *Those Were the Days* had sold 4,721 copies, *Escape With Me!* 4,771, and still selling briskly; even the poetry was moving well.[11] Encouraged by this, Osbert tried to extricate from Duckworth the titles that the firm still had in print so that they could be transferred to Macmillan. Duckworth expressed dismay at the thought of Osbert's name disappearing from their list and went on to ask: 'Will you be good enough to tell us what it is in your mind to offer for the acquiring of the copyright?'[12] Eventually they decided that they would charge £1,300 for the assignment of all rights and whatever stock and plant was available; a demand that Macmillan evidently felt was too grasping to be accepted. Osbert was more successful when it came to the royalties from his libretto for *Belshazzar's Feast*. At first the Oxford University Press were sceptical whether he was entitled to a royalty at all – was the text wholly biblical, they asked, or did it contain original material? If the former, no amount of editing and rearranging could justify a claim for copyright. When Osbert managed to convince them on this point, they questioned whether William Walton would agree to a split royalty. Here too their doubts were overcome; Walton was perfectly happy for his collaborator to have a share.[13] From the end of 1942 Osbert was in receipt of a small but long-lasting addition to his income as an author.

One of the books which Daniel Macmillan reported was selling well was *Two Generations*, the diaries of two Sitwell ladies, edited by Osbert, who also contributed a lengthy preface. Together the diaries spanned most of the nineteenth century and presented a vivid and evocative picture of life in that period at a certain level of society. To judge from Osbert's preface they were works of rare genius; phrases like 'unconscious magic', 'a joy to read aloud', 'beauty derived from surprise', 'full of interest and charm', abound in greater quantities than the intrinsic value of the diaries justifies. But they were and are a pleasure to read. Even the usually censorious Virginia Woolf admitted grudgingly: 'I don't care for Osbert's prose; the rhododendrons grow to such a height in it. But it was an amusing book.'[14]

A long short story which Macmillan published as a 2s 6d booklet at the end of 1941 proved more profitable than most of Osbert's full-length books. *A Place of One's Own* was a predictable but still effective ghost story set in the inevitable Newborough/Scarborough. The story tells of a prosperous retired couple from Leeds, a Mr and Mrs Smedhurst, who buy a large Newborough house that has been vacant for several years. Though nobody thinks fit to warn them, the house some years before had been the scene of a grisly tragedy, in which the old lady who lived there apparently hanged herself but was in fact murdered by her two servants. The servants later killed themselves, and this unfortunate trio haunt the house – the old lady manifesting herself by blowing shrilly through the speaking tubes which connect the drawing-room to the servants' quarters. Eventually the Smedhursts' servant, Ellen, who sleeps in the old lady's room, is bullied by the ghosts of the servants into hanging herself from the hook which had been used for the same purpose some years before. The Smedhursts, not unreasonably feeling that enough is enough, retreat post-haste to Leeds.

The prolixity which marred so many of Osbert's novels is strikingly absent here and the result is genuinely chilling, a *Turn of the Screw* though without the added horror of the children. It caught the eye of the film magnate Henry Ostrer, who offered £250 for the cinema rights. Osbert's agent, Ann Pearn's partner Laurence Pollinger, stood out for double, got his way, and the deal was done. 'I feel rich, if worried,' Osbert told Lady Desborough.[15] His worry was partly due to his doubts about whether Ostrer would do justice to his story and partly to his own involvement. Pollinger had told Ostrer that the author had got his own ideas about how the film should be made and would like a chance to write the script.[16] Ostrer agreed readily, and Osbert found himself confronted by a task which, too late, he realised he might find both tedious and difficult. His fears proved justified. The work dragged on, and in 1944 he reported that he was 'nearly cracked from the boredom of wrestling with film-writers' English'.[17] Graham Greene told him not to worry: 'I have suffered so much from films myself that I never expect a picture to bear any relationship to its source.'[18] Osbert found this rather less than comforting but he drew some relief from the fact that Rex Whistler was to do the decor and costumes – a task the painter had barely completed before his death in 1944 – and that the cast included many of the stalwarts of the British cinema of the time: James Mason, Margaret Lockwood, Dennis Price and Dulcie Gray among them.[19] The result was perfectly competent – certainly not something of which Osbert needed to feel ashamed – and the reviews, while not ecstatic about the production as a whole, paid tribute to the imaginative power of the original story.

These years were particularly fruitful for Osbert as a short-story writer. On the first page of *Open the Door!*, which Macmillan published at the end of 1941, Osbert remarked that writing in wartime was like 'the action of the band which played a hymn as the great ship *Titanic* was sinking'. The imminence of a watery death must concentrate the mind and it is tempting to suppose that the hectic pace of events in the world about him inspired Osbert to adopt a brisker tempo in his own writing. The thesis might be more convincing if he had not simultaneously been involved in the early stages of his autobiography, a work in which the protracted digressions, though rarely tedious, take on a luxuriant splendour which even he had not till then attained. If he had embarked on another novel he would no doubt soon have slipped back into his old ways. In the early years of the war, however, he was in no mood to expose himself to the painful and protracted travail which novel-writing for him involved.

He was well served by this circumstance. He was struggling with a want of ideas for short stories, Osbert told David Horner,[20] but *Open the Door!* in fact contained some work of real originality. 'One of the best collections of short stories since the early H. G. Wells,' wrote George Bishop in the *Daily Telegraph*,[21] and though this verged on hyperbole it was not ridiculously extravagant. The collection contained what, in their different ways, were probably the two best short stories Osbert ever wrote. The first, 'Defeat', tells of a captain in the French Army who returns to his home in occupied France after the defeat of 1940 and is humiliated when a German officer, drinking at the same café, protects him from the insolent contempt of a group of his former soldiers. '*Defeat*. Defeat. This was Defeat. And the world lay broken round him.' In twelve extraordinarily poignant pages, Osbert catches the atmosphere of a crushed and humiliated nation, and the burden which it imposes on the soldier who carries the stigma of subjugation. It is a most accomplished performance, remarkable in its simplicity and the sympathy it shows for the unfortunate protagonists. '"Defeat",' Elizabeth Bowen wrote in the *Tatler*, 'I say in all sobriety, is one of the finest, if not the finest, stories that I have read in the English language.' If this is what she writes in all sobriety, one hardly dares surmise what she might not have written if the worse for drink. But Miss Bowen was a fine critic as well as writer and one, incidentally, who scarcely knew Osbert personally and so was not writing for his pleasure. The same cannot be said of L. P. Hartley, who wrote in the *Sketch* that 'Defeat' was a 'masterpiece, one of the best short stories I have ever read'. In letters to third parties, however, he said much the same thing, so there is no reason to doubt that his praise was sincere.[22]

The second story, 'Death of a God', is a touching vignette of an old man who winds the clocks in the stately homes of Derbyshire and Nottinghamshire and who dies when his pony runs away with him and he falls heavily on his head. The 1914 war was declared on the same day; it was not just in Derbyshire that the clocks ran down. Because Osbert invoked the names of Chatsworth and Welbeck, not to mention Renishaw, people tended to assume that the story was drawn from life. 'Of course it was invented and not just observed,' wrote Osbert crossly. 'The clock-winder did not exist, but some of the clocks did.'[23] No doubt the disclaimer was strictly true, but the story nevertheless reads as if it could just as easily have been a chapter from his autobiography.

The same accusation, if accusation it is, was levelled at 'Pompey and some Peaches', a crudely overdrawn picture of a great painter in old age, misunderstood by his wife and neighbours and even more so by his unconvincingly obtuse doctor. Osbert complained to Cecil Day Lewis that his critical review suggested that the story's author was incapable of writing satire. This would be going too far, Day Lewis protested, but he still felt that the doctor was unreal: 'I felt he was just a projection of your own honourable hatred of artist baiting.'[24] Cyril Connolly made the same point when he rejected the story for *Horizon*. 'It seems to me that you are using autobiography to write short stories,' he wrote, 'when it is really autobiography that is the living form and the short story which is the dying one.' If Osbert had not already been so committed to the concept of his autobiography, he might have been more resentful of this rebuff. As it was, he accepted it with meekness as exemplary as it was out of character. Connolly wrote to thank him for his forbearance. 'I am glad you appreciate my perpetual unwillingness to take affront,' Osbert replied blandly. 'Nothing makes a writer such a bore as perpetual high-horsing.'[25]

The producer of *A Place of One's Own*, who also helped Osbert with the script, was R. J. Minney, a former editor of the *Sunday Referee*, which had published many of Osbert's articles in the 1930s. Early in 1942 the two men agreed to co-operate on a play about the last years of the ill-fated Nicholas and Alexandra, murdered tsar and tsarina of Russia. Osbert's delight in the project grew more intense as work progressed: 'The situation is extraordinarily dramatic and moving, I think,' gave way to 'It is a Wow, I think,' and a final, triumphant, 'It really is a wonderful piece of work, though I shouldn't say so.'[26]

Nobody else was likely to if he did not. The first considered reaction to *Gentle Caesar* came from John Gielgud. Osbert had presumably sent him a copy in the hope that he might be tempted to play the part of the tsar – he could hardly have visualised Gielgud as Rasputin. The overture was rebuffed; Gielgud said bluntly that he did not like the play, 'though I have always been attracted by the character of Nicholas and had great hopes of the subject'. The script was historically correct but there was not much else to be said for it. 'Of course it is beautifully written and the detail and much of the quality of the play are charming, but I don't really feel, except for the one curtain with Rasputin, that it is enormously dramatic.' Osbert was displeased. 'What a very tiresome letter,' he told Minney. 'What can we do now? He is quite *wrong* in what he says.'[27]

Gielgud was not quite wrong; indeed he could have been less generous. The script is pitted with long speeches recounting facts which must already have been well known to everybody on the stage – a lady-in-waiting gives the tsarina a detailed account of Rasputin's murder, the tsarina explains to the tsar the medical facts of their son's haemophilia; superfluous recitations made no more convincing by the inclusion of an occasional 'as you know'. Worse still, the play is dominated throughout by the off-stage presence of Rasputin and he runs rampant when he finally makes his appearance. It is a role demanding a major actor of commanding stature. Yet he actually only has some ten minutes on the stage. When he *is* there the play comes alive, otherwise it creaks dustily. Gielgud could have said not merely that it was not 'enormously dramatic' but that it lacked any dramatic quality at all.

C. B. Cochran, whom Osbert hoped would produce the play, professed to like it enormously but refused to handle it as being 'the wrong play for this moment . . . the theme would be unsympathetic and even unpopular'.[28] Any doubts Osbert might have had about Cochran's meaning were dispelled when Tom Driberg sent him a report on *Gentle Caesar* prepared by Andrew Rothenstein, the chief correspondent in London of the Soviet news agency, Tass. The play, Rothenstein concluded, 'whether deliberately or not, is a white-washing of the Tsar, in accordance with the mythology created after his death by the White emigrants. As such, its *objective* effect is to create hostility to the Soviet power.' To put it on or to publish it as a book would certainly be regarded in the Soviet Union as a hostile and offensive act. 'This is authoritative,' Driberg added. 'It seems very hard that you have put so much work into it, but perhaps you will feel that it is wisest to abandon the play, or to revise it drastically.'[29]

Osbert felt nothing of the sort. Rothenstein's strictures were utter nonsense, he told Daniel Macmillan. The play was unbiased and accurate. 'The interpretation of the late Tsar's character is a matter of *opinion*: and in this matter my opinion is worth more than his.'[30] If Macmillan had any doubts about the political correctness of the enterprise, they seem to have suppressed them. *Gentle Caesar* appeared in book form in April 1943. Reviews were sparse but not unfriendly: *John O'London's Weekly* pointed out the obvious weakness of having Rasputin off-stage for nine-tenths of the play but concluded that it was 'an eminently actable stage-piece, authenticated and well-documented in its events'.[31] Theatrical producers were not convinced. *Gentle Caesar* was staged in Birmingham in September 1943: 'We hope a London venture will follow,'[32] Osbert told Christabel Aberconway, but it never did. It was revived, again in the provinces, in 1945 but even Osbert could not convince himself that success was probable: 'The Tsar is being played by Ernest Milton, who is a Jew and a very good actor in the parts of crook murderers, but not so good as Emperor of All the Russias; Rasputin is stone-deaf and wears a head-piece in which he entangles all the other actors; the Tsarina is a wispish Noel Coward figure and all the Ministers have the strongest possible cockney accents.'[33]

Osbert never lost faith in the play or the merits of his collaborator. There was a brief unpleasantness when Minney insisted that his name should come first on the title page of the book version but Macmillan seem to have been more put out than Osbert, who was happy with Minney's proposal that the order be reversed on their next joint play.[34] There never was a next play, however. In mid-1943 Minney suggested that they should collaborate on a play about 'George Elliot [*sic*]. It's a grand idea, I think, if you can possibly bear to embark upon another before the fate of the first is known.'[35] Evidently Osbert could not; the idea came to nothing. *Gentle Caesar* was Osbert's last attempt at a play; drama joined the novel as a line of literature where he had no further contribution to make.

For much of 1940 and early 1941 his energies had been diverted into a libel action against the newspaper *Reynold's News*. A review of an anthology of Edith's verse widened into an attack on the Sitwells as a group, whose 'energy and self-assurance' had pushed them into a prominence beyond their merits. 'One brother wrote amusing political verse. The sister produced a life of Alexander Pope. Now oblivion has claimed them and they are remembered with a kindly if slightly cynical smile.' The reviewer, Hamilton Fyfe, was a little-known young writer out to write an amusing article; most authors would have dismissed it as offensive but unimportant; Osbert and Edith saw it as a challenge to their literary existence. To say they were forgotten, Osbert argued, was like 'saying an actor is too old to act, a very grave professional libel'.[36] Frere was instructed to take counsel's opinion and advised that the review was libellous. Sachie was reluctant to become involved but Edith whipped him into line. If they did not fight back, she urged, every paper in England, indeed the Empire, would be announcing that they were finished. They must go for *Reynold's News* 'in the way in which the Elizabethans went for the King of Spain'.[37] Their counsel, G. O. Slade, favoured a less swashbuckling approach. He advised them that, though they would probably be awarded damages, these were likely to be small. When it seemed that *Reynold's News* might be ready to settle out of court, he urged his clients to accept the offer.[38] Osbert and Edith, whose blood was now up, would have needed some persuading that this was the best course; the matter was never put to the test, however, since *Reynold's News* decided that they did not feel conciliatory after all. By November 1940 Frere was reporting that they were not ready to settle on any terms. The action must go on, if the Sitwells were not to lose face altogether.

For months the case was the chief pleasure of literary London. 'Dear me, can you account for the Sitwells?' Virginia Woolf asked Mary Hutchinson. 'Maliciously, I'm amused; but professionally – I must not say what, for fear I shall be hauled into the Law Courts.'[39] In court Sachie proved a slightly lack-lustre witness but Edith – or so she told Lady Aberconway – gave 'a really beautiful performance of a sweet sunny-natured old lady, smelling of lavender and looped with old lace', while 'Osbert was marvellous and kept his head to a degree we couldn't believe'.[40] They assembled a strong supporting cast, including Mr Wilson, the manager of the bookshop Bumpus, Arthur Waley, Daniel Macmillan and the novelist and critic Charles Morgan. Daniel Macmillan was probably the most valuable witness, arguing with irrefutable logic that, if the Sitwells were really has-beens, they would not be so prominent and successful on the Macmillan list. Charles Morgan made an excellent impression. He had volunteered to testify to the Sitwells' standing as serious authors of high reputation and he was, wrote Osbert, '*magnificent* in the box: so plainly a man of distinction, whose testimony *must* be believed, and so evidently too, a diffident man, uneager to appear except for the sake of truth and good writing'.[41]

Not all their fellow writers were so co-operative. Stephen Spender considered that the action was silly and ill-conceived and, worse still, that it challenged the right of the critic to state his views without fear of censorship or prosecution.[42] '*Of course* I am not reproaching you for not appearing as a witness,' wrote Edith, who was in fact doing that very thing, but could he not at least have abstained from writing a letter to the *New Statesman* which might have encouraged the defendants to appeal against the verdict? Desmond MacCarthy caused even greater offence. Frere had said it would be useful to have a journalist as witness and Osbert thought MacCarthy had the necessary *gravitas*. He would be delighted to testify to the Sitwells' indisputable status, MacCarthy replied cautiously by telegram, but he considered 'even fools have right to say good authors' day over. If quoted phrase peak of offence, anxiously recommend ignoring attack.'[43] Osbert interpreted this as a refusal to appear; 'owing to some cringing fear of his,' he told Alan Pryce-Jones some years later. 'I have never felt myself to like him since.'[44]

The judge, Mr Justice Cassels, was a man of sophistication, who mildly teased Edith over some of her more far-fetched analogies but was conspicuously fair and ready to see the point of view of the affronted artists. The Sitwells were awarded £350 each and costs, a satisfactory if unsensational result which enabled them to claim that they had won a famous victory. Osbert must have spent a large part of his damages entertaining the various witnesses at Renishaw. Bryher was there the weekend that it was the turn of Charles Morgan. She had never in her life witnessed so much '*cher maître* stuff', she told Hilda Aldington. 'He discoursed in a tired voice of "sentence form" and Walter Pater. Edith did her best until, getting desperate, she remarked what she really enjoyed was the *News of the World*. It was the kind of lunch that could only have been described by Proust ... Osbert became quite gay when the others had left.'[45]

Osbert and Edith's other major contribution to the entertainment of their fellow authors was the royal poetry reading of April 1943. 'Morale is low at the moment,' Osbert told Bryher, and 'the time has come to do something to keep the arts alive: I have decided to organise a Poet's Reading.'[46] Once he had persuaded the Queen to attend, the poets fell readily into line. Precedence could pose problems, so it was decided that they should read in alphabetical order. Laurence Binyon should have taken the lead but he died a few weeks before the reading, so a poem was read in his memory. Edmund Blunden followed, and so through the alphabet of English poesy. The standard of performance varied. Harold Nicolson loyally thought his wife, Vita Sackville-West, was by far the best and that most of the others were inaudible; particularly Walter de la Mare, who was so small that he was entirely hidden behind the monstrous Victorian lectern that Osbert had procured in the Caledonian Market for the occasion.[47] Osbert was generally judged to be competent; Edith spectacular, a little too much so for the taste of some of her audience. The Queen sat in the front row, flanked by the two Princesses. The Princesses kept their eyes on the performers with decorous and disconcerting fervour, except when T. S. Eliot incanted from 'The Waste Land', at which point they had to try hard not to giggle. They enjoyed it even more when W. J. Turner exceeded by far his allotted span of six minutes and was loudly heckled by his fellow poets.

The liveliest entertainment of the evening was provided by Lady Gerald ('Dottie') Wellesley. Though she later hotly denied it, the opinion of everyone else in a position to judge was that she had drunk far too much so as to soothe her nerves and was as a consequence unfit to read aloud. She first refused to mount the platform, then repented and had to be physically restrained. Outraged, she mistook Harold Nicolson for Osbert and began to belabour him with her stick. The poets clucked ineffectively, but Beatrice Lillie, who had been selling programmes, took control and led the unfortunate Lady Gerald to the back of the hall. Raymond Mortimer then got her into the street, seated her on the pavement which she beat at fretfully with her stick, and went back to seek the aid of Vita Sackville-West. By the time he had found her, Lady Gerald was back in the hall again, threatening to renew the assault on Harold Nicolson. Subsequently she wrote a furious letter to Osbert, complaining about the suggestion that she had drunk anything stronger than water. 'Who started this rumour? Perhaps you can tell me that? You, as the promoter of this Reading, are the proper person to make this enquiry ... If you will not undertake to do this, I shall be compelled to put the matter into the hands of my solicitors.'[48] Christabel Aberconway offered to come to Osbert's help should need arise; if Lady Gerald sued for slander she would give witness about her condition and the glass under the chair. 'Only it will be a cruel nuisance for you, and we must not let her bring the action. Indeed – I think when her lawyers heard my story, they wouldn't let her bring it.'[49]

Either Lady Gerald's lawyers or her common sense prevailed. No more was heard of her action and Osbert, forgiven, was invited to a reading she had organised in Tunbridge Wells. 'I shall read "Yo-ho-ho and a bottle of rum",' he told Horner.[50] Osbert at least was convinced the royal poetry reading had been a vast success. Some thought differently. Edith's protégé, Denton Welch, was struck by the 'utter incompetent dreariness of the whole thing'.[51] But most people seem to have enjoyed it, particularly Hilda Aldington. 'We have had parties every day since,' she wrote; 'it has quite broken us up, as the IDEA of happiness and such sheer delight comes like a real resurrection.'[52] The occasion may not have done much for national morale, or even helped significantly to keep the arts alive, but it was a defiant gesture to show that civilisation could still thrive in the most unpromising circumstances. In times of peace Osbert had prided himself on keeping the flag of culture flying in the face of onslaught from the barbarians and philistines. Now he could boast that he would do the same even though the barbarians came bearing bombs.

15

A Devoted Family

Was there ever a family who had more in common, was there ever a family more truly devoted?

(Edith to Sachie Sitwell, 18 May 1945)

THOUGH the battle against his father had been fought and largely won, there was still much residual bitterness between Osbert and Sir George. The years before Osbert's abortive dash to Montegufoni in 1940 had been marked by intermittent outbursts of hostility. Usually Osbert was the aggressor; he rarely missed a chance to frustrate his father or to pillory him for some fresh extravagance or display of vanity. Such opportunities arose with some regularity. In 1938 Christopher Hussey wrote an article on Renishaw for *Country Life* which relied heavily on Sir George for its information. The resultant draft, which Hussey sent to Osbert for approval, contained references to Osbert's great-grandfather, 'known as the Scottish Sir George, because . . .' and to his father 'known as the Italian Sir George, because . . .'. Osbert recognised his father's hand and furiously cut out the appellations. 'No one had ever called them anything of the sort,' he told Hussey; the present text made them all look fools. He had thought of substituting 'known as the tax dodging Sir George,' he told Sachie. 'If he is ever known as anything, it will be as father of his children, so that's that.'[1]

'Do you suppose "Ginger" will be furious?' Osbert continued. If he was, he made no reference to it in his letters. Perhaps his fury was subsumed into the greater outrage caused by his conviction that he was being cheated out of those parts of the English estate he had reserved for himself. The running of the golf club at Renishaw was one source of constant contention; the exploitation of the park collieries another. The interests of the two men were incompatible and it would have taken goodwill on both sides to bring about a mutually satisfactory solution.

Such goodwill was singularly lacking. The lawyers did their best to smooth things over. 'I have no intention of suggesting any step which might cause ill feeling between Captain Sitwell and yourself,' one solicitor protested to Sir George, 'and I feel confident, that if I did it would not receive the approval of Captain Sitwell, whom I have invariably found . . . anxious to consider your interests.'[2] The indignant baronet received this assurance with the scepticism it deserved; Osbert felt that his father was more than competent to consider his own interests and that any assistance would be superfluous.

In December 1939 Sir George delivered another of his solemn rebukes to his peccant son, rehearsing all the reasons he had to feel aggrieved: the huge investments he had made in the Renishaw estates, the work he had done on the house, the debts he had had to pay off on Osbert's account, Osbert's unscrupulousness in selling the house in Scarborough when it had been understood between them that it should be put into a settlement. 'I do value most highly what you have done for the family by your literary career,' he went on, 'but I have already done far more for you than any other father in England has been able to do for his eldest son.'[3] It seemed that the first barrage had been fired in a fresh campaign but before things could get even worse the real war made such family skirmishings an impossibility. France fell, Italy entered the war, Osbert's plans to meet his father were suspended for the duration. Henceforth all correspondence between father and son would be erratic and conducted through neutral countries.

The Italian authorities left Sir George in peace and for a time did not even take any steps to sequestrate Montegufoni. No doubt they would eventually have found some reason to evict the old man and take over the castle, but Sir George made such a move unnecessary. At the end of 1940 he fell seriously ill and had a series of blood transfusions. Bulletins were gloomy; the doctors reported that haemorrhages were continuing and that they had no great hopes of a recovery. 'I think poor "Ginger" is dying,' Osbert told Christabel Aberconway. If he had known of his son's remark Sir George might well have echoed that other self-pitying parent: 'Thy wish was father, Harry, to that thought.' In this case too the expectation proved premature. 'That monster – poor, poor monster – is recovering!' the dutiful son was reporting a few days later. 'After all those operations and with no hope!' Such lack of consideration seemed hardly credible. For what must have been almost the only time in his life, Osbert spared a thought for the forces which had made his father what he was. 'I think he was always cold-blooded,' he went on, 'though an entry I found in an old notebook here explained much: "George has been naughty a second time." 1864. His mother made him write it.'[4] This flash of sympathy had no sequel. Osbert was openly put out when, early in 1941, a report said that Sir George was better, both in mind and body. He could not expect to leave hospital in the immediate future, though, since he still needed a lot of attention, 'for instance, having every day a full-blown lunch at 4 oc in the morning'.[5]

The bulletin came from Bernard Woog, who had appointed himself Sir George's friend and guardian. Woog was a former bank manager from Zurich – the bank in which Sir George had deposited the capital which supplemented his income from the estates at Montegufoni, the '*Stiftung*'. Woog happened to be resident in Florence at the beginning of the war. Still more fortunate, he was married to a Chandos-Pole, a Derbyshire family which was distantly related to the Sitwells. For Osbert, who in spite of his apparent callousness had twinges of conscience about his father's welfare, it was a relief to know that someone reliable was on the spot, to give whatever help was needed. Woog seemed a god-sent ally, a 'charming, practical, quiet Swiss', Edith described him.[6] His attentions continued when the invalid left hospital and returned, not to Montegufoni but to the Blue Nuns nursing home. The reason for this, Sir George assured Woog, was not that he needed the attention of the nuns, but because they would be so hurt if he did not come.

Gradually things got more difficult. The Bank of England was loath to transfer funds to an enemy country in time of war and it became increasingly hard to secure the income from Sir George's Swiss investments. The deserted Montegufoni was requisitioned, for some as yet unknown purpose. The bare necessities of life – as envisaged by Sir George at least – became more scarce; his appetite had fully returned, and he insisted on starting every day with a tin of sardines. He was convinced that the Blue Nuns were cheating him rapaciously and quarrelled with the Mother Superior. Finally the Italian authorities began to question whether he was really ill or could not be interned with the other British prisoners. And yet he showed no signs of solving all these problems by a rapid death – indeed he told Woog that he planned to live to a hundred: 'I do not want to die for a very long time.'[7]

The best way out seemed to be to get him over the frontier into Switzerland, where his money was and he could see out the war undisturbed. The Italians made it clear they would have no objection. Sir George, however, at first felt otherwise. 'I dislike running away from difficulties even if threatened with starvation if I stay,' he told Osbert defiantly in a letter forwarded from Geneva.[8] Finally he succumbed and, escorted by Woog, moved to Locarno. There he made fresh difficulties. Coutts got permission from the Bank of England to send him £75 a month, but only on condition that he signed a declaration that he would not return to enemy territory.[9] This at first he refused to do, saying that it would be the equivalent of signing his death warrant. Woog pointed out that this was a ridiculous line to take, 'as the dagos will not let Sir George go back at all'.[10] Eventually he yielded on this point as well. According to Marie Belloc Lowndes, Osbert was not best pleased by the Bank of England's generosity;[11] presumably feeling that his father should have been able to manage on the income from his *Stiftung*, which at the outbreak of war had been worth £75,000 and, even in early 1943, was believed to contain £27,500 in British or American securities and some £40,000 in Italian lira. At last the matter was safely regulated. With his supply of sardines thus apparently secure, Sir George seemed rejuvenated: 'I have never known anything like his zest for life,' wrote Osbert. 'I keep on getting telegrams demanding books and saying how happy he is. He is especially anxious to get Dr Hay's *Way to Health*.'[12]

In the autumn an old man's fancy lightly turned to thoughts of love. Sir George conceived a senile passion for his German nurse, a persuasive lady who had a reputation for extracting money from her more vulnerable patients. Woog suspected that she had kept for herself large sums of money which Sir George claimed to have given to the Red Cross.[13] She was promised an annuity of £500 a year and, worse still, liked the idea of becoming Lady Sitwell. 'I am getting very cross now about the prospect of a German step-mother,' Osbert told David Horner, viewing with dismay the possibility that this harpy would batten on the family for many years to come.[14] Woog acted swiftly, and persuaded the Swiss authorities that the nurse's residence papers should not be renewed. She departed, grumbling; he did not believe the annuity document could possibly be valid, Frere reassured Osbert.[15] Sir George was at first disconsolate but soon adjusted himself to the new situation. By the end of 1942 Woog was reporting that he was now beginning to fall in love with his new nurse.[16]

And then, in July 1943, with an unobtrusiveness that was wholly out of character, Sir George died. 'I am not unmindful of the news I read in the *Times* the other day,' wrote Queen Mary, with measured solicitude, 'but I gather that it was a happy release.'[17] It was, for Sir George presumably, for his children without doubt. Yet it was also a shock. For nearly fifty years Osbert's life had largely been shaped in reaction to his father, an inordinate amount of time had been devoted to opposing his will, frustrating his ploys, ridiculing his pretensions. The Sir George that Osbert had created was largely mythical, but mythical or not he had become an obsession which dominated Osbert's life and would continue to do so, after death, until partly exorcised in the autobiography. Even then he would not disappear altogether: for if Osbert disliked, perhaps even hated, his father, he also felt alarmingly close to him. Among the hundreds of letters he received after Sir George's death, one of the most telling came from Lord Crawford, whose father had also recently died, leaving a fearsome financial mess behind. 'Do people tell you how like your father you have become and how wonderful and good and wise he was? They tell me so constantly and I try to look modest and at the same time pleased and flattered. And behind it all, there is the lurking terror that perhaps they are quite right.'[18]

Most of the letters, even from those who knew him well, deferred to the rule of *de mortuis nil nisi bonum* and assumed that Osbert was wrapped in decorous grief. 'I know the charming and tolerant humour with which you regarded your Father, had affection and understanding in it,' wrote Violet Woodhouse,[19] basing her certitude on little more than an instinct for propriety. Understanding perhaps, but little if any affection; Osbert put a good face on it, but the deftly cryptic nature of his standard reply showed his real feelings: 'Those who knew my father best will not find it easy to forget him.' Lady Cholmondeley was one of the few who wrote to him with brutal honesty: 'My first impression was "Now Osbert can publish his autobiography" – and I cannot feign any sympathy at the news.'[20] Osbert's principal reaction to his father's death was one of overwhelming satisfaction. 'Oh, the freedom in the air, the rollicking carefree feeling, and the general sense of relief,' he wrote to Christabel Aberconway. 'But I dare not say so except to you . . . for to the world I wreathe my top hat with crêpe.'[21] He had gained freedom; freedom not just from financial bickering and endless recriminations but to publish the book which he knew would be his masterpiece. He had told would-be sympathisers that those who had known Sir George would find it hard to forget him. He meant to make sure that they would have no chance. He would raise a monument to his father's memory which would give him all the more pleasure because of the outrage it would have caused its subject.

The euphoria was short-lived. Sir George's death in exile and in wartime involved endless legal complications. Under his will Osbert inherited nothing, though the Renishaw and Montegufoni estates were already in large part his and he could not be deprived of certain additional properties which came to the eldest son under the marriage settlement and which Sir George had hitherto retained – two railways worth about £600 a year and a farm. Osbert took his exclusion from the will as a token of hostility, but accepted its justice: 'I can frankly say I do not mind and expected it,' he wrote. 'Years ago, I made up my mind that one quarter existed from which I could not be hurt, nor can I pretend to think myself badly treated, for my father handed over these estates to me many years ago.'[22] His only personal regret was that Sir George had appointed Francis Bamford as his literary executor: 'I do hope he won't be difficult about the letters of Father's I'm publishing in my autobiography.'[23] The principal beneficiary under the will was Sachie's son Reresby; Sachie himself was left £10,000; Edith a mere £1,000. 'To my mother,' Osbert told Lady Aberconway, 'he had left £100 "in token of his life-long devotion". Cheap, I call it, at £2 per annum.'[24]

But the will was only the beginning of the problems. In theory Sir George should have left a large estate in Switzerland. Even before he died his children were in some doubt about how much of this survived. 'I am absolutely in the power of the people around me,' Sir George told Sachie in 1941, 'and Osbert, who understands men, motives and business best, should fly over to Switzerland to see Bernard Woog. Otherwise I fear that we may find that the *Stiftung* is an empty shell, all its value having disappeared.'[25] Osbert, of course, could never have flown out to Switzerland in wartime on such a quest, and even if he had he would probably have been too late. Woog, with the active or passive co-operation of the Swiss bank involved, had pillaged the *Stiftung*; no doubt he acted partly in the interests of Sir George, but it would be surprising if he had not reaped a substantial advantage for himself along the way. A few weeks after Sir George's death, Woog began to break it to Osbert how many of the securities had been sold and how little remained, not nearly enough to meet all the payments which had been allowed for in the latest will.[26] Soon it became clear that the principal beneficiary was Woog himself. 'It is now possible to sum up the damage,' Osbert concluded bleakly. 'In 1939 the *Stiftung* held shares worth between £71,000 and £75,000: it now holds shares worth between £10,000 and £12,000, the income of which goes to Woog or Mrs Woog for life. Result for us – nil – and after all those economy preachings.'[27]

At first Osbert had believed Woog to be a shrewd and reliable ally, then he began to doubt his competence, then to suspect dishonesty. Finally came the blackest suspicion of all. In the spring of 1944, by which time it had become obvious that the *Stiftung* was almost empty and that the only hope of redress lay in proving negligence on the part of the Swiss bank, Osbert became more and more uncertain whether they knew the real facts about Sir George's death. 'Do you know, I'm not convinced that he wasn't *murdered*,' he told Lady Aberconway. 'The thing against it is that people don't murder old men of 83. The thing for it, that the moment there was nothing more to be got out of him, he died.'[28] From this it was only a step to convincing himself that his father was indeed the victim of a cruel crime. The British consul was persuaded to investigate and reported that Woog had no private means, had retired early from his bank as the result of a motor accident, had lost and then recovered his memory, had obtained a power of attorney over Sir George's affairs in 1941 – 'In fact, a perfect sketch of a murderer,' Osbert concluded knowingly. 'It has a horrible aroma.'[29]

Whether or not these suspicions were the wildest phantasmagoria or possessed some substance, the vision of a sick, frightened old man, surrounded by enemies, trusting nobody, without anybody to whom he could turn for help, despoiled and finally done to death, haunted the imaginations of Osbert and Edith. Bryher, lunching at Renishaw in March 1944, noticed that Osbert seemed always to be on the telephone and had the feeling that there was 'some crisis or some particular loneliness and that they are both rather desolate'. Two days later she was there again and Osbert told her the whole story. He seemed jumpy and anxious, she wrote. Things soon got worse. A month later again Bryher reported: 'I am beginning to be awfully worried about Osbert, as he looked ill and so worried . . . the whole atmosphere was awfully subdued and depressed.'[30] In a bid to obtain some sort of certainty Osbert, whose desperation drove him from his usual attitude of robust scepticism, adopted Edith's idea that they should consult the celebrated medium Mrs Nell St John. Lorna Andrade was despatched with letters from Sir George and Woog – 'I don't know if you may have a prejudice,' Osbert wrote to her apologetically. 'I have none, only, combined in equal proportions, superstition and disbelief.'[31] Mrs St John was asked to use her skills as graphologist as well as crystal-gazer. On both counts the prognosis was bad; though her report does not survive, it seems that she detected emanations of evil from Woog's letter and a premonition of violent death in Sir George's. One does not know how far she had been told about the background to the enquiry, but Miss Andrade possessed more than a fair share of caution and common sense and it seems unlikely that she gave away too much. Osbert's more rational instincts reasserted themselves when Mrs St John's house was hit by a bomb a few weeks later and she was killed.[32] It was a case, he felt, of the physician signally failing to heal herself: a clairvoyant who was unable even to foresee her own imminent end could not really be trusted on the fates of other people.

Though Philip Frere contended that there was not the slightest reason to suspect foul play, Osbert was unconvinced. Any remaining doubts were extinguished when Dr Witstein, the Swiss doctor who might have provided evidence of the Woogs' manipulations, also died suddenly. 'My immediate reaction, as apparently was yours, was to charge Woog with the deed,' wrote David Horner. ' I wonder if it can be so?'[33] Even if it could be so, there was no way of proving it. Reluctantly, Osbert had to accept that his father's death must go unavenged. But the circumstances of Sir George's end haunted his son for years. 'He had a tremendous will power and an intellect,' Osbert told Madame Guéritte, 'and it is peculiarly horrible that someone like that should have been quite friendless and surrounded by people who were plotting against him ... The whole thing is tinged with nightmare.'[34] It is much more likely that Frere was right and Sir George died a natural death, but even if Osbert had brought himself to accept this intellectually, his doubts would have remained. Meanwhile his father continued to plague him from beyond the grave. Even in April 1945 Osbert was still having to find an extra £500 to send to the lawyer in Switzerland: 'What an old booby-trap layer Dad was!' he complained.[35] And the legacy was not only financial; five years on again at Montegufoni, looking through some notes which Sir George had written shortly before he left, Osbert came across the chill and curiously disturbing words: 'There is no such person as Captain Francis Osbert Sacheverell Sitwell.' What Sir George meant by this gnomic pronouncement it is hard to tell, but as Osbert remarked, there was a Lear-like quality about it. Whether or not he was sped on his way, his final years were bleak and unhappy; a fitting end, perhaps, for a lifetime of almost unwavering selfishness, but one which could hardly fail to inspire pity, even in the most censorious.

Another legacy of Sir George was dissension between his sons. The trouble really started when the will was read after the memorial service on 18 July. Till then the full realisation of how little Sachie was to get had not sunk in, but that night at Renishaw disappointment and pique spilled over into a scene of concentrated bitterness such as only a close-knit family could produce. In fact, Sachie himself behaved well, accepting that it made good sense that his son should be preferred to him and making no claims for any special treatment. Georgia, however, as Osbert told Horner, 'proceeded for 3 hours to dance heavily on any corn that Edith and I had ever possessed. Corns, as it were, literary, parental, friendly, every sort. She went out of her way to say how frightful all our relations were.'[36] The immediate cause for her pique was, presumably, that no specific mention had been made of her in Sir George's will; but this was no more than a trigger to release the bile that had been building up for years. She was a proud woman, and on her husband's as well as her own behalf she resented fiercely that Sachie was only a younger son, with a younger son's portion, dependent first on his father and now on his brother for the livelihood which he had failed to make himself.

What hurt most was the knowledge that this dependence would never end. Sachie and Georgia would have to rely on Osbert's generosity not only for holidays and the luxuries of life, but for the education of their children. She accepted that Osbert must be propitiated, and from time to time she tried. 'Your interest and help mean everything to Sach,' she told Osbert after one particularly generous present. 'He has this hero-worship for you, and nothing that anyone else says or does means anything by comparison.'[37] But then her sharp tongue and jealous nature would reassert themselves. She could never resist reminding her brother-in-law that it was *their* son who would eventually inherit Renishaw and the title. Her relationship with Osbert had always been precarious; now it became dangerously strained. They could still coexist in apparent amity but even a minor disagreement would quickly blow up into a storm and blast apart the fragile façade of family togetherness.

Left to himself Sachie would probably have resented his dependence on his elder brother but learned to live with it. Georgia did not leave him to himself, however, and convinced him that he was not merely unfortunate but monstrously ill-used. 'I think Sachie seems so *sad* now,' Osbert told Horner, 'and therefore leaves one feeling sad oneself. He certainly has a great capacity for depression, poor darling.'[38] His readiness to take offence was formidable even without his wife's encouragement. Once he decided that Osbert's remarks about one of his books constituted an attack on his style and choice of subject. Edith rushed to heal the breach. 'Osbert *frequently* urges me to write a long poem upon a given theme,' she assured Georgia. 'He suggested, for instance ... that I should write a long poem about the discovery of America. He frequently urges me to try completely a *new style*. This is not because he does not admire my present style, for he admires it greatly, but because he thinks it is good for one's work, because it keeps it more than ever living.'[39] It was so obvious that this was Osbert's own practice, and that therefore he could be forgiven for preaching it to his siblings, that on this occasion the explanation seems to have been accepted. The good effects soon wore off, however. By the middle of 1945 Sachie was feeling hopelessly estranged from his elder brother. Once again it was Edith who tried to put matters right. The distance between them was imaginary, she insisted. 'Osbert is absolutely and completed devoted to you, there isn't *any* change in him ... That old devil of a father of ours has, naturally, caused the most ghastly worry and unhappiness.' Whenever the two brothers met, that unhappiness bubbled to the surface and only their problems were discussed, with the result that they parted in deep despair. 'You are worried to death with anxiety,' she went on. Osbert for his part was 'nearly off his head with worry and over-work, trying to recover the money. In that, you are in his mind, you, and you, and you again.' What the brothers must do now was to meet and talk without any mention of their gloomier concerns, talk only of the things in which they were deeply, permanently interested: 'After all, was there ever a family who had more in common, was there ever a family more truly devoted?'[40] With the end of the war and the gradual resolution of the worst of the financial problems, the relationship between Osbert and Sachie slowly returned to something nearer normality, but it was never glad confident morning again. The love which had withered after Sachie's marriage was now a sorry-looking growth indeed.

Sir George's death did not bring only misery. Osbert exulted in his new distinction. 'I *love* being a baronet,' he told Christabel Aberconway. 'It's the most heavenly new toy.' The only problem was that 'the Baronets' College, or whatever it's called' were insisting that they must have proof his parents had been properly married, and the marriage certificate had gone astray.[41] It seems that it soon came to hand; anyway, Osbert renewed life as Sir Osbert without any demur from his fellow baronets. The title distanced him yet further from the young poet who had outraged the bourgeoisie in the 1920s. He revelled in his role as local magnate and proudly told David Horner that he was becoming a well-known and popular figure. 'What a change,' he added. 'You have a genius for misinterpreting a situation,' Horner retorted:

It is not that you were *unpopular* before; merely that you were *unknown* ... The people who knew you at Renishaw – such as Hollingworth, the Game-keeper, etc – all liked you, but they were just a few. The others in the village and the county knew of you and probably hated Ginger. They may have disliked the *idea* of you; but they could not have had personal animosity. I think that your daily prowl, dressed in tatters, through the village, is enjoyed as much by 'them' as you admit enjoying it. You have a good many useful cards up your sleeve. You have put the locality on the map in *many* ways – and that fact is certain to be appreciated locally. Gossip is (though inaccurate) very wide-spreading; and probably many people are aware that Renishaw is plastered with photographs of the two Queens. And all those sorts of things give the locals a second-hand thrill. Apart from parliament (wh is tedious) you might do well to increase your activities on councils etc. You can do so much more in that way, and it is important.[42]

The photographs of the Queens were one indication of how sedulously Osbert fostered the royal connection. 'Great excitement here when a box of grouse arrived with a huge red printed "From the King" on it!' he told Horner proudly. 'I think it sent my shares up.'[43] Heywood Hill, the bookseller, was set to work each autumn to find suitable presents for the Queen – the sketch book of the Duke of Saxe-Weimar; a coloured print of Queen Victoria; 'would £12 be too much for the Queen's present? I have just bought a very pretty exquisite little album containing 24 coloured views of St Petersburg.'[44] When Osbert visited London he would warn the Queen in advance in the hope that an invitation to the palace would be forthcoming – 'Do you think it's sauce?' he asked Horner anxiously.[45] When the Duke of Kent was killed in 1942 he wrote letters of condolence to the King, the Queen, Queen Mary and the Duchess of Beaufort as well as to the duke's widow; a few weeks later he reported with satisfaction that he had had 'a charming letter from the Queen. What a sensitive and perspicacious woman she is.'[46]

But it was Queen Mary of whom he saw most during the wartime years. In October 1939 she had migrated, with seventy pieces of personal luggage and a retinue of attendants, to Badminton, the home of the Duke of Beaufort. She needed constant entertainment, and Osbert was summoned for the first time in January 1941. He proved a great success and the invitation was soon repeated. 'Osbert is off to stay with Queen Mary *again* next week,' Edith reported a few months later. 'It is becoming a habit.'[47] There were hazards about such hob-nobbing with the mighty. He was to bring a suit of 'very old clothes', the lady-in-waiting, Cynthia Colville, told him ominously before his second visit.[48] Sure enough, he was soon put to work cutting trees. Queen Mary kept her team at it with total indifference to comfort or even safety; by the end of the day, according to Osbert anyway, a chauffeur and a woodsman had retired with concussion, several others wore slings and black patches over their eyes, and a tree had fallen on the Princess Royal.[49] No doubt the reality was somewhat less colourful. Osbert was as ready as ever to elaborate for the sake of a good story. On the same visit there was an expedition to Bath, in the course of which Queen Mary gave a lift to a young airman, who was overcome by embarrassment on discovering the identity of his benefactor. Describing the incident in a letter that night Osbert remarked how amusing it would have been if the young man had in fact wanted to go in a quite different direction but had been too shy to point this out. Within a few days fancy had become fact; the victim had been taken fifteen miles out of his way. The airman told Queen Mary that before the war he had worked in a maternity ward. 'How very odd,' said Queen Mary after he had got out. 'What *could* he have been doing?' asked the Princess Royal.[50] 'I dread Badminton,' Osbert told Leslie Hartley just before his third visit, 'and think Queen M has a down on me and means to persecute me.'[51] He thought nothing of the sort, and was most gratified when the Duchess of Beaufort urged him to make sure that Queen Mary was sent an advance copy of the *Burlington Magazine* which contained an article by Osbert on some pictures at Badminton: 'She thinks (and probably is quite right) that she should come first in your life.'[52]

Osbert's last visit to wartime Badminton was at Christmas 1944. There was a ritual by which all members of the house party assembled their presents in heaps around the drawing-room and opened them at a given moment, Queen Mary taking a keen interest in what everyone had received. The finding of enough suitable presents in wartime promised to be a nightmare. 'If you will kindly bring me something of your own for me to give you I will supply two things for you to give us!' suggested the duchess. 'Isn't that the best, don't you think?'[53] Osbert brought 200 cigarettes and a book on Sickert for the Beauforts to give him and presented them with a book on hunting from the Badminton Library and a green shagreen *étui* which the duchess had dug up in a lumber room. The exchange duly took place, to much surprised gratification, though Queen Mary caused a problem by cross-examining Osbert about the source of the *étui*. No such economy was possible in the case of Queen Mary herself; Osbert gave her a 'fine baroque book', profusely illustrated, describing Lord Castlemain's embassy to the Pope on behalf of James II.[54] But the present-giving was only one hurdle in what must have proved a traumatic day. 'Then there's that haunting Communion trouble,' Osbert told Lady Aberconway. 'You know, darling, I was never confirmed (refused to be as part of non-conformity at Eton). But now, I'm so old to be confirmed. And I dread being told to attend Holy Communion. But I suppose it's not likely. It's a free country. But such a phobia!'[55]

Keeping up with the Beauforts was an expensive business, and Osbert at the outbreak of war was convinced that he was close to bankruptcy. He was in fact in some difficulty. Though his outgoings, perforce, fell away sharply, his income from minerals slumped, rentals were precarious and his overdraft at Coutts became mountainous. When the bank protested he sent them an unhelpful telegram reading: 'Never before has so much been owed by so many to so few.'[56] He over-reacted, however. He tried to extricate himself from his hire-purchase arrangement for his motor-car, and when this proved impossible, at least gave up membership of the Automobile Association. He resigned from the Marlborough Club, cut off his subscriptions to several charities, and kept his grocers, wine-merchants, shirt-makers and other such purveyors of the necessities of life waiting for their money even longer than was his wont. But all was not black. Bryher came to lunch in December 1941 and out of the blue produced a cheque for £1,000 – half for Osbert and half for David Horner. 'She really is an extraordinary woman,' wrote Osbert gratefully.[57]

He did even better a year or so later, when Mrs Ronnie Greville died. First reports were that she had left everything to the National Trust. Mrs Keppel was the source of the rumour: 'A notorious liar,' remarked Osbert, 'but I expect nothing.'[58] A few days later he heard that he had been left £10,000. His immediate reaction was to send a telegram to the antique dealers Partridge, ordering a coveted piece of furniture at a cost of 190 guineas.[59] Almost as good as the money was the chagrin that it caused his enemies. Cecil Beaton went around proclaiming that Osbert had been left 'an enormous fortune', probably round £250,000. On no account disabuse him, Osbert instructed: 'It will annoy him by just that amount of multiplication the more.'[60] James Agate too admitted to jealousy. 'You will not, I imagine, buy an honour, but what will you do?' he speculated. 'Add a wing to Renishaw? Start an intellectual theatre at Sheffield? Keep a boxer? Finance an orchestra? Head a fund on behalf of ballet dancers suffering from rheumatoid arthritis?'[61] Osbert did none of those things, but thanked God that rescue had come in the nick of time. Not merely had Sir George's death brought him little extra income and cost him a fortune in lawyers' bills, but the business in which it involved him absorbed his time and energies. Trying to retrieve bits and pieces of Sir George's fortune, wrote Osbert, 'takes up as much time as I should need to write half a book'.[62] For a man who was accustomed to make a large part of his income by his pen, this was a serious deprivation.

In his *Who's Who* entry for 1941 Osbert included: 'for the past 22 years has conducted, in conjunction with his brother and sister, a series of skirmishes and hand-to-hand battles against the Philistine. Though outnumbered, has occasionally succeeded in denting the line; though not without damage to himself.' In March 1943, in *Horizon*, he flung himself into one of the most hectic of these engagements. *Letter to My Son* was a long essay – 10,000 words or so – about the status of the artist in time of war.[63] This polemic was no more temperate though rather wittier than the preface to *All At Sea* which he had written sixteen years before. Osbert argued that it was the artists and writers in a country who comprised its true greatness, not the generals and statesmen; that 'Shakespeare outdistances Waterloo as an English triumph'. In time of war they should be left in peace to get on with their own pursuits: what a hideous waste it would have been if Mozart had been made to spend four years of his life under arms, Shelley conscripted as a fireman, Byron forced to work at the BBC. This thesis, provocative enough in time of war, was made still more offensive by a fusillade of insults directed at all Osbert's most cherished *bêtes noires*: 'the vapid and unimaginative public'; 'the fat middle classes'; 'the chic giggling modistes who write on art and literature'; public schools, 'vile concentration camps'; 'the beaked and bloated tribes of the great capitalists'; 'civil servants, dons, masters-of-hounds, school-masters, professional football players and all friends to national sclerosis everywhere'.

'How much homage do I owe to the dreary-dearies who try to set the world right? and how much to art?' E. M. Forster had asked in a letter to Osbert at the end of 1941. 'I work for the dreary-dearies a bit, because I think the effort good, though seldom in the direction, and never to the extent, that they expect. Lately, however, I have got so horrified with the world and so bored with its practitioners, that I have reverted to the other line for a bit, and am at the moment reading, reading, reading, Molière.[64] Osbert would have used a harsher term than 'dreary-dearie' and have been less sanguine about their intentions, but the priority Forster gave to art was wholly to his liking. He dedicated his diatribe to 'my friend Duff Cooper', a curious choice, since Cooper had recently been Minister of Information – surely the dreary-deariest of all occupations? He was 'in almost complete agreement with you', Cooper responded with a trace of caution. Kenneth Clark was less equivocal: 'I agree with every word,' he wrote.[65] George Orwell shared the hesitation of Duff Cooper, though on different grounds. He had read it, he said, 'with, I think, more agreement than disagreement'. He promised to try to mention it in the weekly column he wrote for *Tribune*, and duly did so. Osbert, he wrote, had managed to say some penetrating things about the position of the artist in a modern centralised society. 'These are not my views. They are the views of an intelligent Conservative. But all the same there is much in what Sir Osbert Sitwell says.'[66]

Orwell's comments were provoked not by the *Horizon* article but by the somewhat revised version which Osbert published as a pamphlet in August 1944. He had hoped that Macmillan would take it on but was quickly disabused; he hated pamphlets, his editor Rache Lovat Dickson said, 'horrid, trivial things' which were neither books nor journalism. Forgivingly, Osbert inscribed a copy for him: 'This letter, which he despised and rejected, from a devoted author.'[67] It had been published instead by the small firm of Home & van Thal. 'I'm excited about my letter as though it were my first book,' Osbert told van Thal. 'I attach importance to it. I wonder what reaction there will be, if any, in the press.'[68] He soon found out. James Agate reviewed the pamphlet with some hostility in the *Daily Express* and followed this up with a counter-pamphlet, *Noblesse Oblige*, which was also published by Home & van Thal. Agate quoted Baudelaire's remark: 'The immoderate taste for beauty and art leads men into monstrous excesses,' and took exception to Osbert's contention that the artist was a man apart who must concentrate exclusively on his speciality if he were to fulfil his destiny. What about Rubens the diplomat, Fielding the magistrate, Burns the ploughman? 'Art is not "arty" and the people who must retire to an ivory tower before they can produce it come perilously near to being dilettante.'

It was presumably this last phrase which so infuriated Osbert. He was unreasonably enraged by an essay which, though certainly challenging his thesis, was couched in affectionate, even admiring terms. 'Agate's conduct has made me very angry,' he stormed, when he first heard that the pamphlet was on the way. 'He is a publicity hound of the worst kind!' and then two months later, 'James Agate's stupid *Noblesse Oblige* is out. So stupid and boring.'[69] An added irritant was that Osbert had previously regarded Agate as one of his most ardent fans. Agate had given consistently excellent reviews to Osbert's fiction and only two years before had included him with Proust, Virginia Woolf and Dylan Thomas as being the contemporary authors whom he most admired.[70] Osbert in 1942 had contributed a preface to an anthology of Agate's work which stressed the differences between the two writers but was extremely friendly in tone and called him 'a very clever writer, he is also full of character'.[71] But this proved to have been the high-water mark of their relationship. Agate offended him in 1943 when he told Osbert: 'I write too much, you too little.' 'Me!' Osbert exploded to Madame Guéritte. '(I refuse to use the first person) *Moi, qui parle*. You know that it is a rage, that I am in the coils and toils of my writing continually, and never have a holiday.'[72] From then on things had got worse. Agate's review and subsequent pamphlet merely confirmed Osbert's view that he was a crass philistine who might occasionally make a sensible judgment but was unfit to rule on any of the finer things of life.

The *Manchester Guardian* considered the rival pamphlets. *A Letter to My Son*, it concluded, 'contained many true and percipient things about art. Its chief message, however, that the artist should be exempt from the obligations of citizenship, was surely wrong.' *Noblesse Oblige*, on the other hand, abounded in 'rash statements about life and art, but the main argument is surely right'.[73] It is difficult to argue with this judgment. As so often, Osbert ruined a reasonable case by ranting and exaggeration. One of the most telling criticisms of his pamphlet came from the pen of the popular novelist Angela Thirkell. 'Sir Osbert', she wrote, 'has done us the disservice of presenting to us a large number of our own prejudices with such venom that we are almost tempted to reconsider them.'[74] To overstate a case so dramatically that even its defenders doubt its reliability is indeed a grave failing; it was far from being the only time that Osbert was guilty of it.

A Letter to My Son appeared the following year in the magazine *Fontaine*. Osbert had authorised this but was annoyed because he was not invited to approve the French translation. What really offended him, however, was that the issue of *Fontaine*, which purported to be a guide for the French on contemporary British literature and was sponsored by the British Council, seemed to him to have treated the Sitwells with scant respect. 'The clue to the whole performance is given in the Index,' Osbert told Malcolm Robertson of the British Council. Auden, for instance, 'who went to America before the War and only returned after it had finished, like Noah's dove released from the Ark, and dressed in an American uniform, is mentioned nine times; Aldous Huxley, also in America, fifteen times; myself twice and my brother once. This is not strictly in accordance with our comparative stature.' It was not just the Sitwells who were mistreated; Forster was insulted, Arthur Waley ignored, 'but whenever one of the Leftie boys is mentioned, there is general prostration and kow-towing'.[75] It might have been hoped that the mellowing effects of age would have made Osbert less sensitive to slights and criticism. On the contrary, his skin seemed to grow thinner with the years. At almost the same time as he was doing battle with the British Council, he remonstrated with Stephen Spender for giving a good review to a book on modern poetry which had spoken slightingly of the Sitwells. Spender replied that he too had thought those comments rather silly but went on: 'It seems to me that though remarks may offend one occasionally, offensiveness is not so damaging to one as having a reputation that one does not permit oneself to be offended. I am quite sure that the most damaging thing that can possibly be said about one is that one is "touchy".'[76]

Spender can hardly have supposed that Osbert was likely to pay much attention to this admirable advice. He could rarely resist an excuse to be affronted. When F. L. Lucas made some disparaging comments about the Sitwells and T. S. Eliot in a pamphlet published by the PEN Club, Osbert wrote in fury to the general secretary of PEN, Hermon Ould, threatening resignation. 'I know nothing of Mr Lucas, and though I have asked several people, no one seems to be able to enlighten me as to his identity. Is it a pen name? Someone said it was a man called Dr Leavis.' Ould replied with some levity, saying that PEN was not responsible for the views of its contributors, that it stood for freedom of expression, and that Lucas – as Osbert must have known perfectly well – was an eminent scholar, poet and critic. Osbert was outraged. Ould's letter contained no expression of regret, did not even seem to admit that offence had been given. This would not do. 'The position at present', he protested, 'is that I subscribe to a Society which publishes personal attacks on my sister and myself.' Ould on the whole stuck to his guns but ended on a conciliatory note: 'Believe me when I add that I should be really upset if you thought me lacking in consideration.' Osbert at this point either re-read Lucas's pamphlet and decided that it was not so dreadful after all or, more probably, got bored by the whole affair. Ould's latest letter, he said, had greatly pleased him, 'So I say no more.'[77]

His literary judgments, too, seemed to grow more cantankerous with the years. Many other writers thought badly of Evelyn Waugh's *Brideshead Revisited*, but Osbert was particularly spiteful in his comments. He started off with excellent intentions. When Nancy Mitford told him how wonderful it was, Osbert replied benignly that he was 'jealous of all writers except Evelyn, whom I regard as being on our side'.[78] Waugh then sent him an advance copy and he began to read it. 'It is full of Catholic points of view, which you will like,' he told David Horner, 'but with all my gt admiration and warm friendship for Evelyn, I think it is a bad book. It reveals unpleasant snobbishness etc in the author.' One of the few good points, he felt, was the caricature of Harold Acton as the aesthete Anthony Blanche. 'Very good rendering of his talk,' said Osbert, but, 'I can't think Harold will like it.'[79] To William Plomer he was even more severe: he found the book 'overwhelmingly, *amazingly* bad'.[80] Nancy Mitford reported his attitude to Waugh as being, 'Jealous, doesn't like talking about it.'[81] Jealousy was never to be ruled out, but it seems more likely in this case that he could not think of anything polite to say to someone whom he knew would pass on his words. (It is only fair to add that, at about the same time, Waugh was being quite as offensive about Osbert's work. Cellini, he told Miss Mitford, was a bad painter: 'Well, he was as bad at painting as Osbert is at writing; for Christ's sake don't repeat that comparison to *anyone*.')[82]

Osbert deplored the snobbishness of *Brideshead*, but he was still more likely to be offended by the excesses of democracy – a term which he increasingly used to denounce anything he saw as philistine or vulgar. The people who would have forced Mozart or Shakespeare to join the Army were democrats; so were the local councillors who tried to requisition Renishaw. In February 1945 he went to see the new musical film *Fantasia* and, unsurprisingly, found it '*appalling* and think Walt Disney should be tortured and then killed ... It is the Greek world of mythology seen through a bungalow window, between the stone mushrooms and the gnomes. And the meanness, real democratic meanness, of poking fun at Stravinsky, and then making use of his tremendous music.'[83]

The BBC, it seemed to him, was an organisation fatally tainted by democracy, relentlessly reducing culture to its lowest common denominator. Its control, he believed, was firmly in the hands of 'Lefties', determined to do down the honest artist. He agonised over the labour of rewriting his short story 'The Man Who Lost Himself' for radio – a process which seemed to him to remove all the sparkle and subtlety of the original. 'I am beginning to wish the brute had never lost himself,' he wrote peevishly.[84] It seemed to him, too, that the BBC were trying to underpay him and demand too many rights over his work. He appealed to Bernard Shaw for help but got little satisfaction. 'I don't see what I can do,' replied Shaw, 'for I have nothing to complain of . . . When they want to broadcast a play of mine I say "37 guineas, please". They pay without a word . . . If you ask why 37, I can only guess that it seems cheap because it is less than 50.'[85]

As the war neared its end there were new reasons for anxiety. Osbert found himself unexpectedly preoccupied by the invasion. 'I've been off work lately from fussing,' he told David Horner. 'It's as bad as Dunkirk for worry, I think.'[86] But the fighting in Italy caused him more immediate concern. Early in July the news came that Allied troops had taken Poggibonsi and were advancing on Empoli. 'Montegufoni must be today in the firing line,' Osbert wrote. 'I have not *much* hope for it. It is such a target, and looks more important than it is.' His agony continued for several weeks. 'I dread seeing "Ancient Tuscan Castle Liberated" and then a photograph of a mound of rubble,' he told Horner.[87] It was a near thing. A young New Zealand officer in an armoured car shelled the farm buildings on either side of the castle, prepared to open fire on the castle itself, then decided that it was definitely unoccupied and could be spared.[88]

It was Field Marshal Alexander who put Osbert out of his misery. The two men had been colleagues as subalterns and had kept in touch. Osbert had always admired his soldier friend and realised that the jovial, even hearty façade concealed acute sensibilities and a good brain. Once he had looked at him suspiciously and asked: 'Alex, between ourselves, you are really a very clever man, aren't you?' A few months before the liberation of Montegufoni they had met in the street in London and Osbert, overwhelmed by his friend's new grandeur, had blushed and babbled foolishly. To try to remedy his ineptitude he had sent Alexander a magnum of champagne.[89] Now the gesture was returned with interest. A telegram from Alex was quickly followed by a letter. He had visited Montegufoni and found it unharmed, though dirty and neglected. It had been used by the Italians to shelter pictures evacuated from Florence; a curator was now in charge of these and no troops would be billeted there. 'I still have that magnum of champagne – we will celebrate the final victory, which won't be long now.'[90] Further news soon arrived: the pictures had been the cream of the collection from the Uffizi; Montegufoni had played host to paintings by Giotto and Piero della Francesca, to Botticelli's *Primavera* and Uccello's *Battle of San Romano*. 'It is so lovely to think of the guests I have been entertaining,' wrote Osbert exultantly. 'Surely they will leave, in gratitude, something of themselves in the house. For if they hadn't been there, they'd probably have been destroyed. What a house party!'[91]

The final victory which Alexander had predicted was delayed longer than the Field Marshal had believed possible. Osbert had been convinced that negotiations could have avoided the Second World War, he was equally certain that negotiations ought to end it. 'No peace that is not negotiated is likely to endure more than five years,' he told Cyril Connolly; the mistakes which, in 1918, had set the scene for 1939 must not be repeated.[92] He despaired when Stalin, Churchill and Roosevelt jointly declared that only Unconditional Surrender would be acceptable. Now, unless the Germans were already in a state of total collapse, the war would go on for another ten years. From Churchill such folly was to be expected, but 'I'd like to strangle old Roosevelt. He ought to know better.'[93] Meanwhile he was preoccupied by the need to extract David Horner from the Royal Air Force. Horner was very clear what was needed. Osbert was to write him a formal letter, offering him a post as secretary at a salary of 'what do you think? £850? Perhaps £840. The letter should express a certain urgency. I think that this, together with my two contracts with Macmillans, should help in my eventual demobilisation . . . Can you somehow make clear in your letter that you are a Baronet?'[94]

In spite of Osbert's dire prophecies, Germany surrendered. He spent VE evening with Bryher in her flat in Lowndes Square. 'We were all solemn at first,' she remembered, 'but it turned afterwards into one of the most hilarious parties of my life.'[95] Hilarity did not survive for long. In August 1945 the first atom bomb fell on Japan – a 'final present from Churchill', Osbert called it bitterly. The horror of the event dispelled what was left of Osbert's euphoria. It was, he told Madame Guéritte, 'infinitely laden with echoes of wickedness; it resembles the moment in Faust when the earth spirit is summoned up – but at least Dr Faustus dismissed the djinn. The only relief to be found is that the pass to which science has brought us is so evident.'[96] He never wavered in his conviction that the end did not justify the means; whatever the military arguments the atom bomb should never have been used. He played no part in politics after the war, least of all in any political activity which seemed tainted by the support of communism, but the Campaign for Nuclear Disarmament was the one movement of generally left-wing tendencies which he would whole-heartedly have supported.

Though not prepared to put himself out to work for any political party, Osbert was by disposition a socially conscious Conservative. In

Thatcherite terms he would unequivocally have been classed as wet. R. A. Butler, who was to become the architect of the new Conservatives, was the politician whom he most admired. Butler had stayed at Renishaw during the war and had impressed Osbert and Edith by his intelligence, open-mindedness, and readiness to sympathise with the plight of the young poets.[97] The future of the party, Osbert felt, would be safe in such hands; the only pity was that Churchill seemed to have no intention of retiring to make way for progressives. He watched with dismay as a series of by-elections towards the end of the war showed how hostile the electorate had become towards the Tories. He was especially outraged by the West Derbyshire election of early 1944 when the Duke of Devonshire's son was defeated by a radical cobbler. 'I hate democracy more every day and don't in the least believe in it,' he stormed to Lady Desborough. 'As I once heard Duff say about it, "It's splendid – as long as it doesn't work".'[98] His prediction for the state of Britain after the war was 'poverty for all and unlimited Bolshevism'.[99] The election campaign – even though, like most people, he believed that the Tories were bound to win – had done little to relieve his mood. He was affronted when the local Labour candidate pointed derisively at Renishaw Hall and announced that its owner wallowed every night in a bath plated with gold. Since the boiler was going through one of its periodic bouts of digestive difficulties at the time and Osbert was consequently unable to wallow in anything, the slur seemed particularly unjust.[100] The landslide to Labour disconcerted him. At 5.30 on the morning after the election results were announced, he had to get out of bed to chase the cows off the lawn: 'It is their way of claiming equal opportunities, I suppose. They've no doubt been encouraged by the Labour success.'[101] But the Conservative Party was the party of Winston Churchill and anything that frustrated Churchill must have its redeeming side. Osbert took the results philosophically. 'I don't think it will be so bad,' he told Bryher. 'The new government will probably make an appalling mess of things in the space of two years; and, much as I *loathe* Bevin, he may be quite good with Stalin.'[102] To Georgia, perhaps because he hoped it would annoy her, he went even further. 'Personally, I think it's a good thing that Labour is in,' he declared. 'If it is a good government, then it deserves to be in – if bad, it can't put the blame on the Tories.'[103] This benevolence did not last long; it was only a matter of months before he was at a loss to decide whether the viciousness of the Labour Government was more reprehensible than its incompetence, or vice versa. For the moment, though, he was ready to give it the benefit of the doubt.

In the autumn of 1945, he would, anyhow, have been ready to give the benefit of the doubt to a government of baboons and chimpanzees. The war was over, life could begin again. Most satisfactory of all, the continent was reopening. 'I doubt if there's much chance of getting abroad,' Osbert had written in the summer of 1945, '– and yet – it's possible.'[104] Then the war with Japan had still seemed a formidable obstacle to foreign travel. Now that war too was over. There were still difficulties to overcome, but before too long it must happen. Labour Government or no Labour Government, the way ahead looked bright.

16

Anatomy of an Age

In England we have . . . almost no great writers about Society – its historical and monumental aspects, its rich and authoritative consciousness, its shifting values. In this aspect alone the almost unique importance of Sir Osbert Sitwell cannot be over-rated: he anatomises not a single life but an age.

(Elizabeth Bowen, *Tatler*)

THE five volumes of Osbert Sitwell's autobiography were the focus of his literary life from the spring of 1941 until the end of 1950. The fact that he could not even consider publication until his father was safely dead, however, meant that he diversified during the war years into a wide range of minor enterprises: many poems and short stories, the play *Gentle Caesar*, the polemic *A Letter to My Son* and a flurry of articles some of which, particularly those for *Horizon* or the *Burlington Magazine*, were quite substantial. It was in *Horizon*, in March 1945, that appeared *The True Story of Dick Whittington*, a first example of the genre that he was later to make particularly his own – the updated fairy story with a sardonic twist to its tail. He made no pretence that the stories were written for children; his technique was to take a well-known narrative and look at it from a different point of view, so that it seemed simultaneously familiar and disconcerting. The approach was one which Tom Stoppard was to use to great effect twenty years later in *Rosencrantz and Guildenstern are Dead*; Osbert's efforts seem somewhat clumsy in comparison, though they are filled with ingenious ideas and some witty phrases.

In Osbert's version of Dick Whittington, the cat, Roxy, has the starring role. A consummate ratter, it clears the palace of Tongador of plague-bearing vermin and wins its master a fortune in diamonds as a reward. Whittington uses this to found an armaments firm, grows immensely rich and in due course rises to be Lord Mayor of London. Roxy, however, becomes an embarrassment to its master and falls foul of the snobbish and ambitious Lady Mayoress. In an effort to dispose of his feline benefactor, Whittington sets up cats' homes in various parts of the country; to the fury of his wife, however, Roxy always escapes and returns to London. Lady Whittington manages to make Roxy's life a misery, but when the Lord Mayor dies it is found that he has left all his money to found more cats' homes. Roxy has the last laugh. Osbert used this flimsy vehicle as a means of belabouring armaments manufacturers, belligerent bishops, capitalists and his other traditional bugbears; if he had delayed it by another six months the cats' homes would probably have been nationalised and a new set of pet hates introduced to be mocked and vilified.

'I have written an exquisite story (though it may not make me popular),' Osbert wrote to Lady Aberconway.[1] It cannot be said to have made him either popular or unpopular. Cyril Connolly reported that the article had been well received – 'The best-written thing he has done,' Raymond Mortimer was quoted as having said – but not much attention was paid to it. When the story appeared as a booklet nearly a year later, Osbert sent copies to most of his friends and got the usual amiable comments, but there was no pretence of rapturous enthusiasm. E. M. Forster apologised for the long delay in acknowledging, explaining that his copy had been hidden by his cat, but found no more to say than a rather cool: 'Thank you very much. I enjoyed the book.'[2] Edward Marsh had to pay for his copy and thus felt himself entitled to be more acerbic in his comments. He was disappointed, he wrote. The story had been heavily revised since it appeared in *Horizon*, but it still struck Marsh as being 'very slapdash, both in substance and style. He has some *disgracefully* bad sentences, but all the critics butter him up for his elegance.'[3]

Even if Osbert had read Marsh's comments he would have been relatively undisturbed. Long before *Dick Whittington* appeared his thoughts and hopes were almost entirely centred on another enterprise. From the moment of its conception Osbert had no doubt that his autobiography was going to be the most important book he would write and should also prove the most popular. The first volume, *Left Hand, Right Hand!* – the name, also, of the autobiography as a whole – was first published in June 1944 in the United States; more than three years after he had begun to jot down rough notes at Renishaw. The fifth and final volume did not appear until September 1950. The entire work, excluding the extensive appendices, ran to more than 1,500 pages or 600,000 words. It was, at the least, a considerable feat of stamina and determination.

'I shall look forward to the Autobiography. Keep it clean!' wrote William Walton in May 1941;[4] one of the first references to the work to be found in Osbert's correspondence. Walton must have known that his enjoinment was uncalled for. Osbert was not the sort of man to expose the sexual peccadilloes of others to the world, still less to dwell upon his own. He gave away virtually nothing about his emotional life; said not a word to indicate that he was homosexual; mentioned David Horner only three times and fleetingly, though referring to him once as 'a very dear friend of mine'[5] (in fact the leisurely tempo of the sequence, which effectively dwindled away in the 1930s, meant that chronologically Horner would anyway not have deserved a place until well on into the fourth volume). Nor was this to be a chronicle of great deeds done, of moving accidents or hair-breadth 'scapes. Osbert planned a history of his times and his society, of a social order which when he was born seemed immutable and all-powerful yet which, by the time he wrote, appeared to be, if not dead, then at least in terminal decline. Elizabeth Bowen, in her review of *The Scarlet Tree*, the second volume of the series, which is quoted in the epigraph to this chapter, got to the heart of what Osbert was seeking to achieve. 'It seems to me notable that in England we have, as compared to France, almost no great writers about Society – its historical and monumental aspects, its rich and authoritative consciousness, its shifting values. In this aspect alone the almost unique importance of Sir Osbert Sitwell cannot be over-rated: he anatomises not a single life but an age.'[6]

The reference to France is particularly apt. The writer whom Osbert believed had most influenced him and with whom he would most have liked to be compared was Marcel Proust. The parallels are obvious. Both were obsessed by the social minutiae of their age; both fascinated by the shadowy, evanescent relationship between the façade and the reality; both masters of the long, discursive sentence which apparently rambles on but is in fact subject to the most meticulous control. In his review of the fourth volume, *Laughter in the Next Room*, V. S. Pritchett agreed that the inspiration was clearly Proustian but argued that there was a fundamental difference in the two approaches: 'in Proust the drama is in the act of memory, in Sir Osbert it lies in what he will impose next'. Osbert's formal method was 'made to control a rich memory, a rioting fancy and fast wit, and to light only where he conducts ... To the

English comic tradition, Sir Osbert has added the tremendous.' Osbert, in his discursiveness, his apparent self-indulgence, owed as much to Sterne as he did to Proust. Yet there is another way in which Osbert differed from, perhaps fell below the level of, Proust. *Albertine Disparue – The Sweet Cheat Gone –* agonisingly conveys the horrors of jealousy and frustrated love. Osbert does not deal with passion; the pains of loneliness, of misunderstanding, of rejection, are often evoked with brilliant sympathy, but love is kept at arm's length. The autobiography is a cool and rational work, strongly felt, certainly, but never portraying ungovernable emotion. 'He is indeed a Social Historian, and one of a rare kind,' wrote Desmond MacCarthy, 'aesthete, aristocrat, wit, poet, psychological observer, master of the art of prose.' Saint-Simon would have enjoyed *Left Hand, Right Hand!*, so would Robert de Montesquiou, the original of Baron Charlus. MacCarthy suggests that Montesquiou was the nearest equivalent to Osbert in either French or British literature, though the Frenchman's 'lack of common-sense kept him (unlike Sir Osbert) from co-ordinating remarkable but quarrelsome gifts'.[7]

'I *want* my memories to be old-fashioned and extravagant – as they are,' wrote Osbert. 'I *want* this work to be full of detail, massed or individual ... I *want* this to be gothic, complicated in surface and crowned with turrets and with pinnacles, for that is its nature.'[8] His method, as Pritchett pointed out, was visual: 'The superficial is never to be neglected and his is a kind of superficiality in depth.'[9] Osbert's achievement was to vest the trivial with significance, or, perhaps more correctly, to demonstrate that the trivial *was* significant. Now at last the style which Osbert had painstakingly evolved over more than twenty years had finally fused with his innate creativity, so that the prose was not merely the servant of the writer but almost *was* the writer. Osbert was accustomed to say that he conceived every book as a poem. Peter Fleming, in his review of the third volume, *Great Morning*, pointed out that the value of the book lay in its execution, not its conception:

> He is before everything else a stylist. This book, and its predecessors, may have been conceived as poems, and the least sensible reader must apprehend that they were written by a poet, but their importance – as literature, not as social history – lies in the author's ability to write the very best prose. Ornate yet pellucid, obliquely evocative yet unfailingly precise, full of colours and images and *tours de force*, yet subordinating always *panache* to *tenue*, so that its effects, though seen to be deliberate, are not felt as spectacular or ostentatious, this poet's prose moves forward with the

rhythm, the assurance, the occult discipline and the brave state of a fleet under full sail.[10]

Osbert's prose style seems to have provoked the florid in his reviewers. In a still more excited review of *Great Morning* Maurice Collis compared it to a long tapestry, a river, a glittering and jingling cavalry procession, and invoked artists such as Rubens, Goya, Rowlandson who shared Osbert's temperament: 'Such artists are vital rather than geometric; their energies flow out towards the living complexities of the world, their gift is the accumulation of detail.'[11] Such praise explains why others did not find the writing to their taste. Virginia Woolf was not the only writer to complain that in Osbert's prose 'the rhododendrons grow to such a height'.[12] 'It isn't bad in a podgy way, his rigmarole,' Lawrence Durrell wrote grudgingly to Richard Aldington, 'but God, it is depressing, the airs and manners. Compare it to 18th century memoirs. No tang. No punch. Just feeble mannered anecdotes. The Beau Nash of Rickshaw Hall.'[13] Osbert never read Durrell's abuse but he had no such freedom from Desmond Shawe-Taylor in the *New Statesman*, who questioned not the style but the author's competence to handle it. 'The truth seems to be that Sir Osbert is a gifted and copious writer, who can write well . . . when he happens to be in the vein. Like some actors, he doesn't know when he's giving a good performance, and when a bad.'[14] The victim of these strictures wrote a furious rejoinder to the editor, Kingsley Martin. With considerable altruism – for the letter would have provided excellent copy – Martin said that he would print it if Osbert insisted but that it would be much better left unpublished. 'I expect your advice is good,' Osbert wrote regretfully. 'You are – or so it has struck me when I met you – a wise man.' But Martin, he claimed, had misunderstood his motives in hitting back. He did not resent the criticism as such; what offended him was 'a youngish man, of no great powers (which are, as a rule, I think confined to an analysis of gramophone records . . .) popping into the wrong column to air his fancy views on a work which has taken many years of labour and experience'.[15]

The pace of the autobiography was leisurely and deliberate. To Evelyn Waugh this was a large part of its charm; Osbert refused to be hurried, he wrote. 'He knew he had a valuable message to deliver – one of urbane enjoyment . . . He knew he had an uniquely rich experience to develop – a lifetime lived in and for the arts. These five volumes have given him a secure place in English literature.'[16] The narrative wound its serpentine, digressive way, stopping here to admire the view, stepping aside there to visit some neglected monument or forgotten ancestor, moving with such apparent inconsequence as to seem to be going nowhere yet always arriving miraculously at the intended spot. In his intelligent, entertaining yet inevitably – since it was written when all three of them were very much alive – reticent study of the Sitwells, *A Nest of Tigers*, John Lehmann analyses the two parts of *Great Morning*.[17] The first, 'The House of Mars Victoryall' (a phrase applied to the Tower of London by William Dunbar in his poem 'To the City of London'), begins with Osbert as a young Grenadier officer mounting guard at the Tower; he moves on to his father's eccentricities, then provides portraits of Sir Edwin Lutyens, Lady Colvin – Oscar Wilde's 'parrot with a tongue of zinc' – and the gamekeeper at Renishaw, Mark Kirkby. A description of the Derbyshire countryside and its traditional life gives way to Sir George's purchase of Montegufoni. Then it is back to the author's own life, when he is wondering what to do and finds himself shanghaied into the Yeomanry. The horror-comic episode of life in barracks at Aldershot is relieved by vivid descriptions of the Russian Ballet on its first performances in London. And so it goes on, occasionally making readers wish that Osbert would get a move on, but far more often beguiling them into delighted acquiescence in his stately but labyrinthine progress.

Osbert had two particular concerns about the reception of his work. 'Do you think the first, ancestral part *sounds* snobbish,' he wrote anxiously to Lorna Andrade in 1942. 'It is not, but might it seem so? In any case I shall leave it as it is, though I think in a month or two to have even a father may be a capital offence.'[18] Snobbishness was not a charge which the reviewers often levelled at him, though the *Cleveland Plain Dealer* praised *Left Hand, Right Hand!* as 'A really beautiful book, witty and frank and rich' but went on to live up to its name by regretting that so much space had been given to 'a lot of stuffy aristocrats for whom most of us do not care one single damn'. If ever 'this sheltered son of fortune' had been deprived of his castles and servants and had had to work for a living, concluded the *Plain Dealer*, 'his autobiography might have had more punch and suspense' – a judgment which was perfectly tenable but seemed at variance with the almost rhapsodic praise with which the review began.[19] Most people felt that the aristocratic grotesques who featured among Osbert's ancestors were one of the most enjoyable features of the book. It is, perhaps, *prima facie* snobbish to claim the Duchess of Beaufort as a forebear, but the charge of ancestor worship is surely mitigated when that ancestor is presented as a comical old lady who has slipped over the borders of eccentricity on to the uplands of the higher craziness. Every afternoon the duchess would be taken for a drive around the New Forest. In theory a different route was followed each day; in practice, since she was too blind to see where she was going, the coachman never left the grounds of her house. For company she took her parrot. The bird had died and been stuffed some years before, but she firmly believed it to be alive and enjoying the outing as much as she did.[20]

His other fear was that people would be offended by what he said about his parents. 'Its frankness may displease you,' he told Madame Guéritte when promising her a copy of the first volume, 'for the French are so discreet about their relations.'[21] One of his prime objects in writing his autobiography was to exorcise his father's memory by presenting him as a grotesque figure of fun, not without ability and even a certain grandeur, but of monumental selfishness and a range of eccentricities so flamboyant that in a man less rich and well connected they would probably have led to his confinement in a mental home. The portrait was not entirely unfair but it was encrusted with so much rococo detail, much of it embellished, some of it invented, that the reality beneath sometimes disappeared from view. Osbert's siblings differed sharply in their reaction to this caricature. Edith believed *Left Hand, Right Hand!* to be a masterpiece, 'and the portrait of my father is quite terrific'. She told Stephen Spender that 'in this wonderful book, I feel something has been made of my parents' useless lives'.[22] Sachie on the other hand was distressed: 'It is most painful to realise your hatred for your father. It is, I know, useless to try and persuade you that, in his heart, he was in his queer way devoted to you.'[23] To someone like Leslie Hartley, who was close to the family, and to Osbert in particular, but not a member of it, it was the conflict between the author and his father which gave the work 'its most dramatic and consecutive interest'.[24] Whether Edith or Sachie was more nearly right was a secondary issue. Sir George was a work of art, and the autobiography would have been immeasurably weakened by his absence.

Quixote Sir George, with his Sancho Panza, Henry Moat, for a time at least entered the national consciousness like Falstaff, Mrs Malaprop or Sam Weller – equally larger than life, equally convincing. They gave immense pleasure to innumerable readers. Few stopped to consider what bitterness must lie behind this pillorying of a parent, or whether it was proper for a son to decry his father with such gusto. One person who did was a Mr R. Dymond, who wrote to the *Spectator* to point out that Osbert and Edith's reputations would never have been gained but for the

David Horner. Osbert praised his 'lovely "nigger" face', but it is hard to see
much negroid in the surviving photographs of the period.

Edith, Osbert and Sacheverell outside the New Chenil Galleries before the
performance of *Façade* in April 1926

Osbert with
Christabel McLaren,
later Lady
Aberconway, at a
reception at the
Egyptian Legation
in 1930

Osbert and David Horner with the staff of their house in Peking in 1933.
Chang, the major-domo 'with an almost episcopal dignity of mien', is second
from the left in the front row.

Osbert, Georgia, Edith and Sacheverell outside the High Court in
February 1941 during their libel action against *Reynolds News*.

Osbert and Edith at Renishaw in the winter of 1943, wearing their overcoats to protect themselves against the cold.

The royal poetry reading at the Aeolian Hall in April 1943. Arthur Waley and Walter de la Mare flank the Queen, Osbert and the two Princesses.

Osbert at Renishaw,
photographed by
Hamish Magee in 1949.
The manuscript in front
of him is probably that
of *Noble Essences*.

Osbert photographed on a
visit to New York, *c*.1950

Osbert in New York drawn by his
friend Dan Maloney. The ruffled hair
was most untypical of the subject.

Osbert on the set at Gainsborough Studios, with James Mason, star of the film based on Osbert's story *A Place of One's Own*.

(*Opposite page, lower*) Osbert and Edith on the set of *This Is Your Life* in November 1962. Those standing, from left to right, are Cecil Beaton, Baroness de Bosmelet, Antony Bernard, Tom Driberg, Sachie, Marjorie Proops, Georgia, Veronica Gilliat, Francis Sitwell, Velma LeRoy, John Robins, Geoffrey Gorer and Reresby Sitwell.

Edith and Osbert at the Gotham Book Mart in New York in 1948. In the left foreground is William Rose Benét, behind him are Stephen Spender and, against the bookcase, Horace Gregory and his wife Marya Zaturenska. The four men behind the Sitwells are Tennessee Williams, Richard Eberhart, Gore Vidal and José Garcia Villa. Up the ladder is W. H. Auden, with Elizabeth Bishop in front of him and Marianne Moore seated further forward. Randall Jarrell, with the moustache, and Delmore Schwartz are on the right in front, and Charles Henri Ford is seated in the centre.

Frank Magro reading aloud in the last years of Osbert's life

austere upbringing which their father had given them and about which they now complained: 'The success they have attained would hardly have followed from the usual indulgent upbringing given to spoiled children.' Osbert's response was characteristically aggressive. Affecting to believe that R. Dymond was an elderly spinster, he wrote that he could make no sense of her letter. He and Edith had, however, at least learned good manners from their upbringing, 'and never to be rude to an inferior – a fact for which Miss Dymond should be thoroughly thankful'. Robert Dymond, as he now signed himself, wrote to the *Spectator* a second time. He admitted that he could never compete with Osbert for rudeness but persisted: 'I still think an artist ought not to make capital out of the idiosyncrasies of his relatives or friends, and, if they are dead, there is the proverb *de mortuis* etc.' Osbert struck back to claim that he had 'conferred on my father immortality, the greatest gift which I, or any other artist, can bestow'. The last person who should claim immortality was the author himself, thought Mr Dymond, 'and if immortality has been conferred on the late Sir George Sitwell, it must seem a bitter gift'. Osbert was allowed the last word before the editor closed the correspondence. Sir George, who with all his faults was a man of intellect, would have been dismayed to have had Mr Dymond as his champion. 'Nothing remains to be said, excepting that I may have conferred a measure of immortality upon Mr Dymond also and for this I should be sorry.'[25]

On the whole Mr Dymond comes rather better out of the exchange, but it is doubtful whether Osbert was in the least moved by his strictures. He had feared that others might condemn his behaviour, but he had no doubt that it was fully justified. It would have taken far more than Mr Dymond, or even the protests of Sachie, to make him question his decision.

That the autobiography might be caviare to the general was another source of worry. Osbert craved not just the praise of his peers but popular success. Reviewing *Left Hand, Right Hand!* in New York, Richard Aldington concluded that 'to those who have the requisite knowledge and predisposition, it will be irresistible'.[26] The suggestion that it might be an arcane masterpiece, accessible only to a sensitive and well-educated minority, must have dismayed Osbert. He had no cause for concern. Macmillan's immediate reaction when they received the typescript of the first volume was that they had got a best-seller on their hands. They printed 20,000 – an enormous number for the memoirs of somebody who was neither royal nor a prominent politician nor a film star; were reprinting even before publication, and by 1948 had sold 141,500. By the same date *The Scarlet Tree*, published fifteen months after *Left Hand, Right Hand!*, had sold a still more remarkable 171,600. For the Reprint Society the series was to be one of the most successful of all its ventures. The autobiography was to be found in virtually every English house which bought books with any regularity; matching in popularity the Bible and Shakespeare, the histories of Arthur Bryant and the novels of Evelyn Waugh. It had till then been a matter of doubt whether or not the public would have considered that Osbert played second fiddle to his sister. Between 1945 and 1950, when *Noble Essences* completed the quintet, there was no doubt that Edith had been eclipsed.

Because of the self-imposed embargo on publication while his father was still alive, Osbert was well ahead with the second volume before the first had even been submitted to his publishers. He found this to be curiously debilitating; his new book, he told Madame Guéritte, seemed like an ancient cathedral which needed underpinning and the bringing-out of the colours on the surface. It was beginning to look better but 'how odd to write a book which I have no idea *when* it can be published'.[27] By the beginning of 1944 it too was nearly finished. To start on a third volume while the first was still unpublished seemed almost inconceivable; then inexplicably he had 'one of those days, so rare, perhaps one or two every few years, when you see the perspective of your work, and are able to plan the further volumes'.[28] Suddenly the way ahead seemed clear. *The Scarlet Tree* was finished six months later, 'so it's a red letter day for me,' Osbert told the novelist Cecil Roberts triumphantly.[29] Almost before the last pages had reached the typist, Osbert was at work on the third volume. By the time *Left Hand, Right Hand!* was published in the United States in June 1944, the first chapters of what was to be *Great Morning* were well advanced.

Sterne's Tristram Shandy, though he referred to himself from time to time, was in effect unborn until Book Three of his eponymous romance. Osbert did rather better, appearing at the beginning of Book Two of *Left Hand, Right Hand!* Book One had been given up to his ancestry: 'the lines of the left hand are incised inalterably at birth,' Osbert wrote in his Introduction, and it was not until Book Two, devoted to his childhood at Scarborough and Renishaw, that the right hand, whose lines 'are modified by our actions and environment', began to play its part. It was this second book which contained one of Osbert's greatest set pieces, the painting of the family group by J. S. Sargent. At first glance this seems to be no more than an entertaining account of a fashionable painter at work on what proves to be an onerous commission. Osbert, however, cunningly uses the episode to illustrate the internal dynamics of the Sitwells, contrasting Sir George's vision of a sedate and contented family with the tensions and miseries which underlie the surface and which Sargent contrives to hint at on his canvas. The interplay of image and reality was a Proustian theme and Osbert's handling of it disclosed his vision of the autobiography as a whole.

Osbert attached great importance to the American publication of this book. Though his reputation had grown modestly in the more anglophile cities of the East Coast he had never achieved any sort of popular success and would have been virtually unheard of in San Francisco or Los Angeles, let alone St Louis or Kansas City. He had turned down out of hand an offer by Macmillan to publish it there: 'The book, I hope, will be a classic,' he wrote; 'it is a book of a lifetime, and the Americans, who appreciate success, will only despise me if I do not obtain the best possible offer.'[30] His confidence had been bolstered when Ted Weeks, the editor of the *Atlantic Monthly*, was shown a typescript by Logan Pearsall Smith and eagerly bought the serial rights: 'He likes it quite as much as I do, he is in love with it,' reported Pearsall Smith.[31] But though the eventual publishers, Little Brown, professed great enthusiasm, they printed only a cautious 2,000 copies. Within two months, they had reprinted twice and had already sold 8,000 copies. 'How wonderful your American reviews are,' wrote Horner, '. . . it's so reassuring to have the great heart of Uncle Sam beating for you or at you. And all before you were 9 years old, wh is so sweet.'[32] The British reviewers a few months later were still more enthusiastic, even the *New Statesman* was conspicuously polite, while Elizabeth Bowen announced that it would 'occupy a unique place in the literature of this generation; and, I think, a permanent one in the literature of this country'.[33] Only Godfrey Winn struck a cautious note, warning the readers of *Woman's Illustrated* that it was 'not an easy book but my mother was enthralled by it and urged me to recommend it to you'.[34]

The second volume, *The Scarlet Tree* – the tree being, one is told, that of 'the singing blood in the young veins'[35] – was originally conceived by Osbert as 'The Running Shadow'. Shadows don't run, complained Horner, they glide or fade. He countered with 'The Shadow of Time', taken from a line of Swinburne's. 'I think that the Shadow of Time is a really wonderful title now I come to think of it!! But I may be wrong.'[36] Osbert evidently felt he was; what is more, 'The Running Shadow' survived as the title of the first chapter. Once again the volume was divided into two; the first book taking Osbert through childhood, the second, ironically entitled 'The Happiest Time of One's Life', dealing with his years at boarding school. The treatment is boldly impressionistic; Rose Macaulay in her review compared it with Pater's 'Child in the House'; it was 'a book where memory has flowered into poetry and irony while keeping the authentic flavour of truth. Its dominating quality, among many, is beauty.'[37] What Pater lacked, could indeed hardly have handled, was the splendidly grotesque figure of Sir George who in *The Scarlet Tree* emerged in full refulgence. The book was a masterpiece, wrote John Betjeman. 'And I think I have only used that word once before in describing a modern book.'[38] Reviews ranged between the appreciative and the ecstatic. 'I *suppose*,' wrote Osbert to Lady Aberconway with ill-concealed delight, 'but how difficult to judge oneself, an immense success with *The Scarlet Tree* ... I've had a tremendous fan-mail (to which, as a rule, I send a typewritten reply, always the same).'[39]

For those who had loved the nostalgic glow of the first two volumes, his third, *Great Morning*, was treading on more dangerous and controversial ground. It dealt for the most part with his time in the Army in the years before the First World War, and abounded in references to bone-headed cavalry officers and blinkered generals. Brigadier T. Rose Price wrote furiously from the Guards Club to remonstrate. The incidence of incompetence was no higher among generals than among writers, he protested. But he professed to be comforted by Osbert's references to Oscar Wilde and Frank Harris: 'I feel that we bone-headed survivors need not worry over much about the opinion of an author who can still write of Wilde and Harris as celebrities. I suggest that "notorieties" would fit them better.'[40] It was in this book also that Osbert dealt with his mother's imprisonment for fraud. On the whole he handled skilfully his self-appointed task of convincing the reader that his father had behaved outrageously while not actually saying anything in condemnation of his conduct. But it would have been impossible for the uninitiated to work out from this sketchy narrative what had actually happened. 'He treads gingerly about Lady Ida's criminal record,' Evelyn Waugh told Nancy Mitford, continuing, 'Whenever he writes about Ginger he is splendid but there are some awful drab panegyrics of Edwardian hostesses.'[41] Once more the critics were vastly appreciative, though Desmond Shawe-Taylor's harsh comments on Osbert's prose made a conspicuous exception. James Lees-Milne read his *New Statesman* with interest and was struck by these 'animadversions upon the man's style. He is right. It is not so pure as I thought. Perhaps this book falls short of its predecessors. They were surely magnificent. The style flowed like a clear river in spate.'[42] Viewed from fifty years on, it is hard to detect any marked difference in style. The material was perhaps more intractable, less easily moulded by Osbert's urbane mellifluousness, but for this very reason it is easy to agree with A. L. Rowse, who wrote: 'The book is wonderful . . . it has moved me and gripped me far more powerfully than the previous volumes. Beautiful and touching and nostalgic as they were, this has generated far more energy and emotion.'[43]

Great Morning appeared in America in 1947 and London in 1948; by now Macmillan's first printing had risen to 40,000. *Laughter in the Next Room*, the fourth and final volume of the chronological sequence, followed a year later. Its title was inspired by the small inner chamber behind the main dining-room at Montegufoni. Here Sir George would lurk when his children were entertaining their friends, haunted, he is supposed once to have said, by the sound of laughter in the next room. *Great Morning* had broken off at the start of the First World War; its successor effectively began when Osbert returned from the Western Front to London. References to the fighting in France are so cursory as scarcely to be noticeable. Partly, no doubt, this was because of Osbert's deep loathing for this period of his life and a reluctance to review it; even more, he may have felt that the horrors of trench warfare did not fit in with his grand design. To deal with his experiences at the Front would have been to throw the book off balance, slipping uneasily from *À la recherche du temps perdu* to *Götterdämmerung*. As it was, the book concentrates on his early years as a writer, with other cultural adventures such as *Façade* and the Modern French Art exhibition, and a bombastic piece, ill-suited to the rest of the volume, dealing with the General Strike and Osbert's role in settling it.

Nancy Mitford found the book pretentious, arrogant even: 'I can't make up my mind about it. The *Tatler* bits seem to me rather terrible and the bits about Henry Moat perfunctory.' Among the '*Tatler* bits' she found least palatable a fulsome tribute to Lady Aberconway. Probably it was the bit Osbert most liked himself, she reflected – 'Perhaps one should always cut out what one likes best oneself.' Evelyn Waugh agreed that the book was queer: 'It is extraordinary that a man of his humour can write like that of Lord Wimborne and the general strike.'[44] As his memoirs came closer to the present day, Osbert found himself dealing more and more with people still prominent on the London scene. He treated almost all of them with gingerly politeness; insults there were, but they were usually directed towards a type rather than at an individual. T. S. Eliot wrote to say that he was 'highly gratified by the portrait of myself, for which you exercised a merciful talent for selection ... I am impressed by the magnanimity of your attitude, and the gracefulness of your allusions to several men who, with great merits, have also traits which lend themselves almost irresistibly to caricature and humour.'[45] As an Envoy, Osbert indulged himself in a somewhat over-excited appeal to the future, recalling in its rhetorical exuberance the 'Sound out, proud trumpets, And you, bugles, blow' of the 'Grand Finale' to *England Reclaimed*. 'I, a Citizen of the Sunset Age, an Englishman, who saw the world's great darkness gathering, salute you, Stranger, across the Chasm': rich stuff, indeed, but it would not have occurred to Osbert that many among his readers – not just the brutish philistines – might not in the spring of 1949 have found the future so alarmingly dark or the Sunset Age so invincibly attractive. Nostalgia is a respectable emotion but it is best when not exploited in so magniloquent a style.

As a coda to his great work Osbert in 1950 added a fifth volume, *Noble Essences*, consisting of essays on writers or artists whom he had known. Most of the pieces had been published before, though in some cases the original had been amended or expanded. In a way, though, the interest of the book lay in the extent to which the original had been retained: 'It is the rare portraitist', judged the *Times Literary Supplement*, 'who, able to recall one of these mighty hunters of lions or shadows at the top of golden hours, blandly ignores the wisdom that comes after the event and dares to treat his subject as the fiery unexpended force that he appeared to his contemporaries.'[46] V. S. Pritchett was struck by the way Osbert had sought out as subjects such 'great fellow egotists' as Gosse, Sickert and Arnold Bennett. Osbert may not have been gratified by his classification as a great egotist, but he must have been relieved by Pritchett's conclusion that this was 'living portraiture at its best'.[47]

And so the great enterprise was behind him. Osbert could legitimately look with pride on his extraordinary creation. A. L. Rowse wrote to tell him that he had produced 'a superb work of art, a monument indeed which you have reared in a decaying time, like a vast Vanbrugh house towering above the pre-fabs and filling stations of our age'.[48] What is perhaps most remarkable is that, though it may have lost a slate or two and suffered the occasional cracked window, this Blenheim among autobiographies has survived remarkably well. It is still a delight to read, evocative, sensitive, often enormously amusing, sometimes genuinely moving. The social assumptions occasionally jar, the mannerisms grate, but for the most part they would have jarred and grated fifty years ago. The autobiography has not dated, because it was conceived dated, or perhaps dateless. It will be as vividly redolent of an age and a society in a hundred years' time as it was when it was written.

A final postscript was still to be appended. In the winter of 1956, at Montegufoni, Osbert began to dictate an amiable, anecdotal book, to be called *Tales My Father Taught Me*, which was implausibly presented as stories about Sir George that it had proved impossible to fit into the autobiography proper. The fragments of a precious stone left after the gem is cut, Osbert described it; 'scrapings from a barrel' might be more accurate, Philip Toynbee observed, though he went on to say that this would be unfair to a book filled with splendid material and comic anecdotes.[49] Any pretence at verisimilitude has vanished: the Sir George of *Left Hand, Right Hand!* was already a grotesque; in this last book he takes off into Cloud-cuckoo-land. For example, the reader is told that Osbert was urged by his father not to have anything to do with selfish and disreputable people like Friar Tuck and Robin Hood, who set out to rob the rich, the only people who knew what to do with money, so as to give it to the poor, who would have no use for it. It was all right to plunder the monks, perhaps, but Robin Hood should then have passed on the money to the rich. As for Maid Marian, Sir George happened to know that she was a bad lot who was blackmailing Robin Hood.[50] This is another of Osbert's inverted nursery tales, like *Dick Whittington*; to attribute it to Sir George and suggest that it was put forward in all seriousness destroys the authenticity of what, in the autobiography proper, had been a far-fetched yet still not totally implausible creation.

Toynbee in his review went on to complain that, though Osbert was a writer of great natural talent, he seemed to have adopted a style which was ill-suited for his purposes. 'In his more recent prose he has decided to adopt a tone which is so pompously mandarin that the earlier delicacies are almost drowned in sonorous vocables . . . this is not Lord Emsworth speaking: it is the voice of Jeeves.' He meant, presumably, the voice of Beach – no less an authority on social minutiae than Kenneth Rose has also accused Osbert of writing like a butler. In fact the charge seems to apply as much if not more to the earlier books. As Rupert Hart-Davis remarked to George Lyttelton, the stories in *Tales My Father Taught Me* were 'short enough to prevent O's getting involved in those endless sentences that made some of his autobiography such heavy going'.[51] Hart-Davis said he had enormously enjoyed them and the public agreed; the book rose to the top of the best-seller charts, above such formidably popular novelists as Howard Spring and Nigel Balchin.[52] It was almost as much a work of fiction as either of these produced; Nigel Dennis in his review remarked that many fathers could claim to have created their sons, but there were few sons who could claim to have invented their parents.[53]

The startling success of the autobiography, combined with Edith's reviving reputation as a poet and the acclaim awarded to her dramatic and highly subjective account of Queen Elizabeth I, *Fanfare for Elizabeth*, combined to cause a renaissance for the Sitwells as an entity. The edition of *Horizon* for July 1947 was dedicated to the three Sitwells and included an extract from the autobiography and an essay on Edith's poetry by Kenneth Clark. When Cyril Connolly wrote a foreword to a new edition of *Enemies of Promise* in 1949 he said that his literary judgments remained substantially unchanged, except that 'the Sitwells have since 1938 grown enormously in stature'.[54] Max Beerbohm swelled the hymn of praise. 'If I were still by way of being a caricaturist,' he told Osbert, 'I should do a drawing of you and Sachy on either side of Dr Edith, and from the clouds above, three sisters gazing down rather sadly and sourly. For you three have quite definitely now surpassed the Brontës.'[55] Osbert would still have preferred not to be subsumed into a triad, but his own literary identity and standing were sufficiently secure for him to accept Beerbohm's tribute with equanimity. False modesty was never one of his failings. Duckworth tried to persuade him to write a preface for a new edition of Firbank's work. The terms were not very attractive, wrote Osbert reprovingly. 'I am a very, very highly paid author.'[56]

His self-esteem was reinforced when in 1947 he was awarded the *Sunday Times* Book Prize of £1,000 and a gold medal. One of Osbert's more attractive features was the unaffected delight with which he greeted every fresh honour or recognition of his work. 'I am enchanted,' he wrote to Christabel Aberconway, 'and feel rather ill as a consequence of excitement. Unlike really nice people, anything like that pleases me ecstatically, quite apart from the thousand pounds – which is needed, goodness knows!'[57] Better still, after some toing and froing, the inspector of taxes ruled that such awards were not subject to income tax, a decision which, in 1947, saved Osbert from being mulcted of at least three-quarters of the money.[58] It was the *Sunday Times* who should be congratulated, rather than Osbert, wrote Anthony Powell, but 'you can now be sure of at least one square meal on the Black Market'.[59] There were differing ideas about how the money should be spent. In the recent past Osbert had refused to contribute to the Development Fund for Sheffield University, on whose governing body he had sat for some years. A Mr G. W. Keeling now wrote to ask whether, in view of the prize, he might not feel disposed to change his mind. 'I really cannot give both money and time,' Osbert replied coldly. 'I could earn many hundreds of pounds in the hours I spend in the building. I appreciate your initiative in writing me a letter directly you see I have made a little money, but it is the kind of enterprise I do not like.'[60] Keeling might have been tempted to reply that if the university had to choose between Osbert's time and his money they would settle for the latter, but discretion saved him from such brutal honesty.

Fame brought other importunities. A female admirer began to bombard him with letters and announced her intention of moving into Renishaw; it must be 'Fulfilment or Destruction', she declared. Frere eventually saw her in London and told her that it would have to be the latter; he dissuaded her from drowning herself in the Round Pond in Kensington Gardens on the ground that she would obstruct the sailing of model yachts but recommended Westminster Bridge as a picturesque alternative – though preferably when the weather had grown a little warmer. Such callousness deterred her: 'I have this morning a letter from her stating that she will hold off, though reiterating her undying affection for you and asking me to assure you of this, which, of course, I have much pleasure in doing.'[61] A more acceptable gesture was that of the Scarborough Council, who proposed to turn part of the old family home, Wood End, into a museum of Sitwelliana. The rest of the house, Osbert wrote, was to accommodate a collection of dodos, dinosaurs' teeth and other such curiosities.* 'I suppose we had better lend books and manuscripts. Even with the extinct animals, it is well-meant and go-ahead, and an unusual compliment.'[62] Osbert and Edith went on a state visit to the opening and were conducted around by the Mayor and Town Clerk. Sir George, Osbert was convinced, was there as well. As the party entered the house a brick shot out of the ceiling, bounced on Osbert's head, ricocheted by way of the Mayor to the Town Clerk and finally felled the Clerk of the Works. 'They were so astonished – but I know that kind of trick.'[63]

---

*Now a lively and well-run museum of natural history or, as Sir Reresby Sitwell puts it: 'A collection of fossils with one room devoted to the Sitwells.'

He was much sought after as a participant in cultural congresses but usually found reason to refuse. In the summer of 1948 he and T. S. Eliot were both approached on behalf of a Conference of Intellectuals and Artists to be held at Wratislav in Poland. After one glance, Osbert told Eliot, the organisers decided that he was greedy and tried to lure him by descriptions of the excellent cuisine. 'Tom, with one of his grave smiles and his usual precision of diction, observed: "And they told *me* I should find a number of earnest Christians." '[64] But though Osbert did not put himself far out for the sake of institutions, whether Polish conferences or Sheffield University, he could still be generous to individual writers whom he admired and who were in need. There are many letters in the archive at Renishaw acknowledging such generosity, including several from Dylan Thomas. One, in August 1946, thanked him for a gift of money, which paid for a holiday in Ireland, and for Osbert's praise for his poetry. 'Poetry, perhaps, is the love it makes, but, like you, I am scared of the old toad that croaks and pomps in the middle of such generalisations. Here, in my father's house in a drizzled and windless valley by a woeful estuary there is such bloody blanketing quietness that my heart, to me, thumps like a gong in a bog summoning to dinner wet and woollen trolls.'[65]

One institution to which he did devote himself with good effect was the Society of Authors. Osbert had been on the Committee of Management since 1938 and in 1944 was appointed deputy chairman with the intention that he should succeed the chairman, John Strachey, three years later. 'Osbert has become a Trades Union boss,' Nancy Mitford told Evelyn Waugh,[66] and the description, provided it was implicitly hedged about by inverted commas, was not one Osbert would have rejected. '*Do* join the Society of Authors,' he urged Cyril Connolly. 'We must pretend to be a Trades Union or perish.'[67] As usual when he played an executive role, he was energetic and efficient. He worked hard at recruiting members from the literary establishment – Nigel Balchin, Maurice Bowra, C. S. Lewis, A. L. Rowse, Philip Toynbee and Evelyn Waugh among them[68] – and was almost as ferocious in defence of the society as of his own family. Henry Reed, a poet and dramatist chiefly celebrated for his much anthologised poem 'Naming of Parts', wrote cantankerously to complain that his income from the BBC had been halved since the society had intervened on his behalf. Osbert took offence and wrote him a savage rebuke. 'I don't, myself, see how friendship survives an official encounter as rude and cold as that,' Reed replied mournfully. 'Perhaps, however, you did not intend that it should.' Osbert's cool reply said that the matter was now closed and their friendship unimpaired; it had never been close, however, and now it perished.[69]

Osbert retired as chairman in 1949 but was back on the committee the following year and chairman once more in 1951. When he finally gave up in 1953 Rex Warner wrote to express admiration for the 'wisdom and charm with which you have always conducted our affairs. If you were yourself willing to remain in office, I should support any revolution or *coup d'état* by which the constitution of the Society could be amended so that you could become Permanent Consul.'[70] The job was time-consuming, but at least it enabled him to refuse other chores, like joining the Committee of the National Book League; not merely was he running the Society of Authors, he explained, but 'my name is associated with a great many other public authorities'.[71] Fellowship of the Royal Society of Literature was another matter, since it seemed to involve no duties. 'If only it was the Garter!' Osbert wrote wistfully. 'Still, I love distinctions – and I suppose it is one.'[72] He accepted with alacrity, was asked what 'degrees and other description' he would like listed and replied, with vainglorious modesty: 'I possess no degrees, no honours; nothing except brains and a baronetcy. Will you enter me as Author?'[73] 'I have nothing to declare except my genius,' as a still greater egoist announced to the New York customs.

He did not even contemplate refusing an invitation, issued on behalf of the King, to join the committee which recommended recipients for the Royal Medal for Poetry. Other new members were Vita Sackville-West, Maurice Bowra, Charles Morgan and Nevill Coghill. In his letter,[74] John Masefield said that it was the King's wish that Osbert should take over from him as chairman, but two years later the Poet Laureate was still in charge. Osbert possibly made some enemies by his habit of insisting that no poet was worthy of the honour. In 1950, for example, Bowra favoured Laurie Lee; Coghill, de la Mare; Masefield, Patric Dickinson; Charles Morgan, David Wright; Vita Sackville-West, John Waller; while Osbert and Gilbert Murray were for no award. In 1955 Coghill voted for Betjeman; Masefield and Murray for Ruth Pitter; de la Mare (now a judge) and Morgan for Edmund Blunden; Sackville-West for James Kirkup; Osbert again considered no one deserved the prize.[75]

Osbert himself, who had written little poetry over the last ten years, was reactivated in 1948 and 1949. 'I've been the victim of an acute attack of poetry,' he told William Plomer. 'Not for years have I been so much on the telephone wire to the Muse, and I feel very exhausted.'[76]

Four Songs of the Italian Earth were published first in the *Cornhill* in the spring of 1948 and then in a tiny edition by the Banyan Press. The four seasons in Italy are evoked in pleasant, unambitious terms; the poems mark no progress – indeed, if anything, some regression – from the sort of pastoral verse that he was writing in the 1930s.

Demos the Emperor, described as 'A Secular Oratorio' and published in April 1949, is altogether more interesting, from the point of view of Osbert's personal philosophy, at least. It was an angry rant against post-war society. 'A novel democratic folly possessed the educated, making them prize virtues that did not exist,' Osbert had written in the Envoy to his autobiography.[77] *Demos the Emperor* picked up and dwelt loathingly upon the theme. The world is the battleground on which Demos and Autork wage a titanic struggle for mastery. Autork, Osbert told Siegfried Sassoon, 'serves equally for Hitler or Stalin';[78] on the whole Osbert gives the impression that Demos was the more distasteful of the two:

> The Emperor Demos!
> Sired by Caliban,
> Demos the Emperor
> Uprises from his couch of bluebells,
> Mosaicked with cigarette ends
> And bits of oily papers, newspaper and cartons.
> Thus does he love to lie,
> With cigarette stub clamped to loose lips of blubber
>
> For hours together . . .

Osbert's contempt for the ordinary man, above all the urban proletariat, was never so nakedly displayed:

> I am the bloated, flat group-ghost
> Of all the Little Men in all the world,
> I am your Lord, your Hope.

'Your quarry is of course Cultural Democracy (not to be confused with Political or Economic Democracy),' wrote J. B. Priestley, basing this benevolent interpretation on who knows what evidence, 'and I have attacked this over and over again. The common mistake, made by people of various opinions, is to assume that one kind of Democracy necessarily involves another.'[79] It seems unlikely that the distinction was very clear to Osbert. The *Times Literary Supplement* accused him of setting up a false target and then tilting at it. The Emperor Demos would not just rise from a couch of cigarette ends and oily paper, he would also, 'with blunt pencil but earnest eyes, listen to a WEA lecture on modern poetry'. The evils that Osbert attacked had no intrinsic connection 'with either the theory or the practice of political democracy; nor even in a wider sense with the popular mould'.[80]

The poem contained one of Osbert's livelier satires, the 'Journalist's Song':

> Who will buy my pretty wares,
> Weeds and tares
> Prospering on blood alone
> And the marrow of the bone.
>
> All tricked out with pretty favours,
> Heigh-ho, Heigh-ho!
> Words, according to their flavours,
> Heigh-ho, Heigh-ho!
>
> Seductive words for which men die
> Every day more willingly,
> 'Liberty', 'Democracy',
> And – foul fiend I – 'Autocracy'.

But though this shot-gun peppering of the target slightly relieved the intensity of the poem's attack, it was a black and bilious production. Its author was unlikely to find life to his taste in the brave new world of post-war Socialist Britain.

17

England's Most Celebrated Living Literary Family

'IT'S icy here, and I'm getting elderly,' wrote Osbert in gloom from Renishaw at the end of 1945. 'What we all need is what we want – and how to get it? I want, this house, electric light and heating unstinted, works of art, champagne, caviare (I'll let *foie gras* go), mangoes, peaches, Southern climate, and *masses* of money as well as fame. Not much to ask. And, of course, no gout.'[1]

The wry resignation with which Osbert had greeted the Labour victory in 1945 quickly faded. Logically he accepted that Renishaw would have been no warmer, the caviare as expensive, the Southern climate almost if not quite as unattainable, had the government been Conservative, but logic played no part in his splenetic indignation. 'Oh, how I hate the Government,' he told Lady Aberconway. 'It's becoming an obsession with me. That dreary kill-joy crankiness which I've always so much hated.'[2] Some of his resentment was aimed at specific targets; he was dismayed by the attitude of Ernest Bevin – the 'sole whale or buffalo in ... the Government of all the Nitwits' – toward the Jewish would-be emigrants to Palestine: 'No man of feeling or who knew how to behave, would do such a thing.'[3] He was still more outraged by Attlee's decision to develop an all-British hydrogen bomb. 'Over the whole extent of the Government's complete, enormous, and apparently almost irremediable failure in foreign policy,' he wrote indignantly to *The Times*, 'no single incident stands out as more entire and gigantic than its listless inability to bring about any accord between the two halves of the world.'[4] More often, however, he seethed with a generalised fury against an administration which seemed determined to frustrate his every wish and confine him to abject poverty and discomfort. In September 1947 a Mr H. G. Hoskins of the Halfway and District Federation of Labour Parties wrote to ask if his group could hold a rally the following June in the park at Renishaw. Osbert's reply was spirited and, in the circumstances, not ungenerous:

> I must inform you that I consider that your Government has done more evil to the country than any collection of previous Governments in English history. As, however, I believe in Free Speech, which the Government you support is doing so much to suppress and destroy, I will allow you to hold your meeting in my park. I hope, however, that it may prove an unmitigated disaster to your party, and that already, by the time it is held, the Government will have met at the polls the crushing defeat it so obviously deserves.
>
> I should be glad of an undertaking from you that your speakers will tell no lies about me personally, or by reference or inference. I am sorry to say that one of the local Labour paladins told the most outrageous 'whoppers' about me at the last elections; among them, that I had a gold bath (I wish I had; I'd sell it and give the proceeds to your opponents).[5]

Long before the meeting was held, Osbert had decided, by calculations based more on hope than political analysis, that the Labour Government was tottering towards an early rout. In August 1947 he gave it a maximum of six months before it fell – 'But, I suppose I'm wrong,' he added gloomily.[6] Two years later he was still convinced the end was near; the Socialists were 'terrified of having their dull and pernicious state-paradise snatched from them. The best thing is to snub them well and pay no more attention.'[7] He told Christabel Aberconway that he was so depressed by the government's activities that he would even prefer to see Churchill back in power.[8] Violet Bonham Carter wrote to ask him whether he would become president of the Chesterfield Liberal Association. 'I expect you will reply that you have ceased to take any interest in politics – that Liberalism is a lost cause – that we are all anyway hurtling to perdition . . . Still, I go through the ritual of writing.'[9] Osbert's reply has not yet been traced. If Lady Violet had not put the words in his mouth he might well have replied as she predicted. But he would not have been telling the truth if he said that he took no interest in politics; on the contrary, he felt about them so intensely as sometimes to leave room for little else.

He seems genuinely to have believed that socialism was only a step towards a police state. His *Who's Who* biography for 1947 for the first time included the entry: 'Advocates compulsory Freedom everywhere, the suppression of Public Opinion in the interests of Free Speech, and the rationing of brains, without which there can be no true democracy.' His heavy irony illustrated his uncertainty as to whether socialism was more dangerous as a threat to true liberty in itself, or as the creator of the chaos on which the extreme right wing might build. 'I suppose we shall have a fascist government within ten years,' he wrote in 1947. 'Not a Mosley fascist, but some other brand.'[10] He was convinced that another and yet more frightful war was imminent in which the communists would almost inevitably triumph. 'Oh for the German army to be in existence to help us!' he wrote to his publisher. 'A labour camp in Omsk will be cold, but not much colder than here – and there will be reindeer to look at and even eat.'[11] As the general election of 1950 approached he became less confident of Conservative victory. He was absorbed by the campaign, and yet simultaneously resented his absorption – 'What a pestilence it is. Nobody will be sane – I least of all – for weeks.'[12] The result when it came – a Labour majority, but vastly reduced – was not what he had hoped for but better than he had feared.

Mrs Greville's bequest and the money paid in compensation for the nationalised coal mines meant that Osbert, however much of his income might be taken away from him by the government, possessed substantially more capital in the years after the war than he had before or during it. The complications of Sir George's *Stiftung* too had finally been resolved and though not much was left, the Swiss bank which had sadly mismanaged the affair was bullied into paying substantial compensation. Osbert felt prosperous enough in 1946 to buy himself a painting by Tiepolo. He had doubted whether he should diminish his capital, he told David Horner, 'because of leaving it to you. But the picture can be left instead.'[13]

His continued and lavish generosity towards David Horner cannot be questioned. Whether he was mean where his brother and sister were concerned is harder to decide. Edith not merely never complained but constantly praised Osbert's kindness to her. She was frugal by instinct, wanted money only so as to give it away or to entertain her friends, and would have been perpetually impoverished however munificent an allowance Osbert had given her. She had lived at Renishaw, almost entirely at her brother's expense, throughout the war and still largely made her home there or at Montegufoni. Osbert could perhaps have done more for her in the 1930s but during the war and afterwards it is hard to reproach him.

Sachie, on the other hand, complained constantly, not merely about the hard lot of a younger son in a society where primogeniture ruled supreme, but also about Osbert's insensitivity and failure to consider a younger brother's problems. Viewed from Weston it is easy to see how such feelings could have arisen, but from Renishaw things looked very different. Osbert felt that he had done as much as, perhaps even more than, could reasonably have been expected. He had preached the virtues of Sachie's writing to all and sundry and had done his best to further his brother's career by preparing the ground for him to move to Macmillan. They were, he told Georgia – to whom, presumably so that she would not take umbrage at being excluded, he wrote far more often than he did to Sachie – 'much the best and richest publishers'. They were mean, like everybody else in the profession; but they were honest, 'and they do sell books'.[14] It was not his fault if Sachie proved unable or unwilling to write the kind of book that would enable them to display their talents to advantage.

He had also taken a more than casual interest in his nephews, helping pay for Reresby's schooling and giving generous presents. He was not the sort of uncle who would take the boys to visit museums or churches, still less to a cricket match, but he was genuinely concerned about their future. Reresby, who would one day inherit the baronetcy, was a subject of particular interest. Though Osbert did not try to bring any undue pressure, he made clear his doubts when his nephew elected to join the Guards. 'I do feel,' he told Georgia, 'much as I honour the Brigade, that going voluntarily into it as an officer is like joining of one's own accord a company of Dodos.' Reresby had much better learn something about business, 'for unless the Socialists nab everything, he should, at my and Sachie's deaths, still come into a substantial inheritance'.[15]

But casual benevolence of this kind was not going to be enough. Sachie habitually lived far beyond his income and seemed unable to economise and put his house in order. When Osbert helped out with gifts or interest-free loans, his brother was genuinely grateful but found it almost impossible to express his feelings. Georgia, for her part, resented being patronised and, though she tried to curb her tongue, could not always conceal the fact that she found Osbert's charity both inadequate and offensive. This in turn left Osbert feeling ill-used. Some time early in 1945 he gave Sachie £500. Since then, he told Georgia indignantly, he had not 'had a word of acknowledgement or thanks from either him or you. What's it all about? It is *not* encouraging . . . I had the feeling at the time that I had been clever and useful to you, but now feel an utter flop. I feel, moreover, very sad and extremely distressed and rather angry.'[16]

There was sadness, distress and anger all round. Sachie, who had originally expected to get almost £100,000 from his father's *Stiftung*, in the end saw what little was recovered devoted to the upkeep of Montegufoni. His disappointment was heavily tinged with resentment. By the end of 1949 he was financially in disastrous straits. Philip Frere was asked by Osbert to organise a rescue operation, and enraged Sachie by his assumption – or so Sachie saw it – that the only sensible thing to do was leave Weston and live 'in a bungalow on the Great West Road ... I think that is entirely dictated by personal spite against me ... He is so very unfair to me, and so prejudiced, that I do think I *had* to have another lawyer.'[17] It was back to the bad old days when Sir George and Osbert communicated only through solicitors.

In the end a deal was done by which Sachie sold his reversionary interest in Renishaw and Osbert bought the Weston estate for the Renishaw trust, with Sachie as tenant for life. It was a generous settlement, valuing Weston at well above market estimates and leaving Sachie some £20,000 better off. All problems had been resolved, Osbert told a rich American admirer, Alice Hunt, but 'Georgia and I are not on speaking terms, and she is abusing me like a pickpocket'.[18] Left to herself, indeed, Georgia would probably have rejected the terms and faced the consequences of a final split between the brothers. 'I don't think we can accept Osbert's very grudging charity,' she told her husband. 'I really think he would even like to contaminate our love ... Poor Osbert, he is warped and tortured ... and cannot bear to see others happy – though poor! ... He writes like a caricature of his own version of your father's fulminations. Spite, condescension, recriminations, *threats*.'[19] Fortunately Sachie was a better judge of his brother's true intentions and was also more disposed to settle for a quiet life.

Osbert and Georgia, who at the best of times had never advanced far beyond armed neutrality, now lived in a state of constant and embittered acrimony. In 1948 Georgia took offence because Osbert would not let her use the family jewels at some great London occasion: 'It is such balm to one's inferiority complex ... to feel that people think *you* like to see me in them.'[20] In his reply, Osbert reminded her that she had already lost several pieces of family jewellery. 'When I saw how wounded you were, I felt extremely sorry,' he went on unconvincingly, 'but it is impossible always to give way on every point.' And while they were about it, he went on, 'why, *why* did you tell John Lehmann about the incident with Coward at Buckingham Palace when I specially asked you not to mention it to anyone?'[21]

The background to this piece of Georgia's mischief-making was that Osbert had met Coward on the staircase at Buckingham Palace. According to Osbert, whose version of events became noticeably more ornate with repetition, he had already refused to shake hands with him once that evening, but when Coward came cringing up to him a second time, he failed to recognise him and shook hands before he realised what he was doing. 'If he writes to me,' he told John Lehmann, 'I shall just write back "That I spoke to you proves I was drunk."' The important thing was that Edith should not know. She had never forgiven Coward for the insults supposedly levelled at her in his revue *London Calling* and if she heard that Osbert had been reconciled with the arch-enemy it would 'stop her working for a year'.[22] Whether it was Osbert himself, Georgia or John Lehmann who told her, within a few days Edith did know about the meeting. She swallowed without question the story about Osbert failing to recognise Coward – 'he sees very badly, it was in a dark passage' – and appeared unconcerned. She was never going to have anything to do with Noël Coward herself but 'I think it's a good thing, *for my family*, that this has happened'.[23]

Another reconciliation, though after far less turbulent a separation, was with William Walton. When Walton married in 1948, his Argentine wife Susana noticed that Osbert and David Horner were the first of her new husband's friends who seemed to be genuinely pleased to welcome her. Only later did Walton tell her that he had not spoken to any of the Sitwells for several years.[24] If he did tell his wife this he exaggerated, but the relationship had certainly been tenuous and for professional reasons if no other it was desirable that the two men should become friends again. It was Walton who seems to have started the rumour that Osbert was being seriously considered as a candidate to replace Kenneth Clark as Director of the National Gallery. He told Horner of this, who at once passed it on to Osbert. 'I find this very interesting,' wrote Horner.[25] Osbert found it interesting too. 'The more I think of the National Gallery idea the more I LIKE it!' he replied enthusiastically. 'It would mean chauffeur, car, £1,800 a year, duty and dignity. Red carpets. It's them I feel the want of.'[26] The suggestion came to nothing. Perhaps Walton was romanticising. When John Pearson, many years later, asked Lord Clark about the possibility it was dismissed with derision. Osbert would never even have been considered for the directorship, said Clark; anyway, red carpets and chauffeur-driven cars were unknown at the National Gallery.

National Gallery or not, life slowly returned to something near peacetime normality. Carlyle Square needed only a little patching-up to make it fully habitable and Osbert and David Horner were soon entertaining again. Brinsley Ford dined there with his wife early in 1948. It was, he wrote in his diary, an evening 'of concentrated enchantment'. Sherry was taken in the downstairs sitting-room; above the chimneypiece was Osbert's recently acquired Tiepolo of *Rinaldo and Armida* in 'a beautiful carved frame which our host was convinced was Austrian', to its right hung a copy of Brueghel's *Triumph of Death* in the Prado, 'a picture crammed full of all that fantastic and inexplicable detail most calculated to appeal to the bizarre imagination of a Sitwell'. 'The excitement of so many different pictures and objects, the witty remarks made about them, seemed to fill the air with an infectious intellectual electricity.'

They moved on to the dining-room, a room 'of dazzling originality, the innermost hall of Prosperine can hardly have been more striking, for contrasted against walls of ebony blackness were chairs which resembled vast glittering oysters' shells, and the light of the candles fell on pictures chosen for their gaudy sparkle'. The conversation was as glittering as the chairs, but the two things the Fords remembered most clearly were 'the way both our host and David Horner gave themselves up entirely to making themselves agreeable with all the art at their command, and the way we felt that Osbert Sitwell observed everything in the nuance of one's thoughts ... Both he and Horner are strange contradictions, their sensibility is extremely developed, and their intuition very perceptive, and yet with an understanding which could make them very sympathetic to human character, they are too critical, and the judgments they pass on people, who can never have harmed them, too harsh. And yet Osbert Sitwell is capable of great kindness.'[27]

Things had not quite got back to what they had been before the war. A friend recorded meeting Osbert on the upper deck of a No. 19 bus, not a conveyance in which he would commonly have been sighted in 1939.[28] But the bus was probably taking him to old haunts: to have his hair cut at Trumper's; or to Heywood Hill, the bookshop next door; or to some Bond Street gallery; or to lunch with Lady Aberconway at the Ritz; or to the St James' Club. Brinsley Ford, again, met him at lunch at the club and noted in his diary: 'I adore his company, though it alarms me sometimes as I feel I must bore him.' Osbert, for his part, told Ford that he was dismayed to find how many of his father's most irritating characteristics he was adopting – extreme fussiness over trains, for instance. But he was able to announce proudly that he had just acquired a new servant by asking the agency to find someone used to dealing with mental cases. 'The servant arrived,' Ford concluded his diary entry, 'and he had never had anyone in his service with such a sympathetic understanding of human nature and of himself.'[29]

Sympathetic servants were particularly in demand at Renishaw, where conditions were still primitive and Robins, though as industrious as ever, was growing increasingly malign. There was clearly little chance of obtaining the foreign currency to winter in Italy in the years after the war, so Osbert resigned himself to carrying on in Derbyshire. It was not ideal. He returned from a brief stay abroad in 1947 to find the house a ruin: '*all* the pipes had burst, all roofs had collapsed, the usual stories. One feels quite like the old Italians one used to see, living in ruined houses, with nothing to eat except their pride and their words.'[30] When an American admirer wanted to visit him at Renishaw in December, he turned her down decisively. There was nothing personal, he subsequently explained, he had done the same to the Duchess of Kent. 'An enormous house like this, with all the statues veiled against frost, and all the rooms closed, no electric light, no heating, is not suitable to be shown in the winter. Besides, what is more important, I was *trying* to settle down to my winter's work, though letters and ill-health have made this difficult. And I can, as a matter of principle, allow no one to break this rule.'[31]

There were compensations for even the bleakest winters. When the lake froze, people came from miles around to skate there. Three years running the sister of the local Master of Foxhounds skated backwards into the hole kept open for the swans. 'This year I fairly *roared*!' Osbert told William Plomer. 'I didn't even pretend to be sorry. I ought to give her a challenge cup, I suppose.'[32] But it was better in the summer, when the house thawed out and the gardens, freed from the shackles of vegetables, slowly regained their former glory. The large house parties of before the war were still impracticable but old friends and casual visitors abounded and there were few summer weekends when Osbert and David Horner found themselves alone. The annual flower and agricultural show in the park was always a great occasion. In 1949 a frizzy white poodle shot out and bit the prize bull on the ankle just as it was being paraded in front of Edith. The bull decided Edith was responsible and tried to charge her. He was restrained but fixed her 'with a fearful look of disapproval, until she succeeded in staring him out of countenance'.[33]

Osbert continued to enjoy playing the part of local dignitary. In 1949 he was re-elected chairman of the magistrates; by a complete vote, he noted proudly, 'including the local Bolsheviks'.[34] He was invited to serve as high sheriff but refused because of the expense involved and fears about his health.[35] But local affairs did not always run smoothly and Osbert had not lost his capacity for writing offensive letters which hurt and annoyed people far more than he had expected. At the end of 1945 the Eckington Parish Council passed a resolution deploring 'a scathing letter', which Osbert had published in a local paper, 'concerning their remissness in not complaining about the distasteful water'. It would have been more courteous, they felt, if he had approached the council himself rather than burst into print without any warning. 'The Parish Council expresses grave concern at the flippant language concerning cows in the reservoir, which was only hearsay.'[36] It was perhaps flippant language or something similar that provoked the displeasure of Staveley Grammar School. Osbert took considerable pride in his role as a governor of the school: 'One of my parents [*sic*] was one of the three founders in about 1560 or 1570. So it is gratifying to me to be connected with it.'[37] He served as chairman for several years. But in 1952 the clerk to the governors wrote to say that the question of his reappointment had been considered at the last meeting: 'I regret to inform you that you were not re-elected.' No explanation was offered. Osbert presumably knew what lay behind the snub; it must have been one of the first in a series of minor tribulations which were in the end to induce him to abandon Renishaw and make his home in Italy.[38]

In 1946, however, he had barely contemplated such a possibility. It was at the end of that year that he conceived the idea of buying the ruins of the eighteenth-century mansion Sutton Scarsdale, not far from Renishaw, which was threatened by demolition. James Lees-Milne inspected the site for the National Trust and found it wanting. 'Classic ruins in England not as satisfactory architecturally as Gothic ruins,' he ruled firmly. 'They lack the picturesque gloom.'[39] Osbert's local solicitor, William Elmhirst, was even more disapproving. The owner wanted £900 for the ruins and six acres surrounding it; no way was it worth so much, Elmhirst considered. It had no easy access, no development potential and did not even rank as an ancient building: 'I am sorry to appear to disagree with you so entirely on this matter but I . . . feel that I must point this all out to you.'[40] Osbert was unrepentant. He bought the ruins and put in hand the minimum needed to prevent further deterioration. He cheerfully admitted to Maynard Hollingworth that it was a white elephant, but then so was Montegufoni and 'I'm not at all sure that another white elephant won't soon be in our stable'.[41] What he had in mind when he made this threat is unknown; it seems, anyway, to have come to nothing. This was just as well; Sachie's economic plight was dire enough without the added chagrin of seeing his brother squandering fortunes on the purchase of picturesque but unusable heaps of brick and stone.

Meanwhile Osbert had at last got back to that Italian white elephant which had so miraculously survived the war. He was fond of Montegufoni but it was too closely associated with his father to be at first altogether comfortable. He told Lady Desborough that he knew he would never be able to live there – indeed, did not really want to do so – but would have to visit it so as to take it over from the Italian authorities.[42] 'I love it dearly,' he told Eric Linklater, who had been one of the first to visit it after the Liberation, 'but my father so hashed up his affairs, that I may have to sell it . . . But then, who wd buy an enormous house, on an island site, in a country tottering on the edge of a revolution?'[43] He got there on a fleeting visit in June 1946, having devoted the greater part of his time on the continent to trying to sort out his father's affairs in Switzerland. Montegufoni was just the same, he told Christabel Aberconway. At one time not merely had the Uffizi pictures been on the ground floor but nearly a thousand locals had sheltered in the cellars below. Now all was peaceful again, with remarkably little damage done. 'Only the peasants to look after us, and Guido always drunk by dinner so that one held one's breath when a dish appeared. But, all the same, he saved the castle by his courage and devotion and hid 2 English soldiers while the Germans were there.'[44] He planned to go on to the Lido at Venice. 'But is my figure suitable for bathing?' he asked David Horner in anxiety. 'I wish I were an athlete and not a black-collar worker (which is what I am, *not* white).'[45] In the event the visit to Venice fell through and his figure was not put to the test.

He had hopes for more ambitious travel the following year, but one of the current sterling crises led the government to allow only the most meagre funds for would-be voyagers. He did manage to get permission to go back to Montegufoni, though, so as to put the estate in order, and brought with him John Piper, whom he had commissioned to paint a set of pictures to match those already done at Renishaw. They arrived in a balmy Tuscan October, to find the garden 'a bower of plumbago and zinnias – a forest of zinnias tall as trees – and only the ghost of my father, walking about a little at night, disturbs tranquillity and makes the dog howl'.[46] 'Osbert works all day and so do I,' Piper told his wife. 'I like the life as there is no society whatever and no going out except for an evening walk.'[47] It was 1949 before Osbert got back to Amalfi, his first visit for twenty years. 'I have always adored the place, the landscape and sea, more than anywhere,' he told Alice Hunt,[48] and it had its customary effect. He was hardly installed in his old rooms at the Cappuccini before he was writing poetry and the spate endured for the fortnight that he was there.

'I have just discovered', wrote Ethel Sands to Logan Pearsall Smith in October 1944, ' "The Importance of Being Osbert". The fame of Osbert has been carried across that waste of water and now all America is a-jump behind me and the Gospel is being spread all over Russia and the Middle East and translations are being made into Arabic, Persian, Demotic Greek and Russian. There has been nothing like it since Catherine the Great had *The Rambler* translated into Russian and Dr Johnson could boast that he was being read on the banks of the Volga.'[49] This flight of fancy had a base of fact; *Left Hand, Right Hand!* had achieved a remarkable success in the United States, not in the mass market or deep into those vast regions where European culture hardly penetrated, but among the intellectuals, the literati, all those who claimed acquaintance with the latest fashions from across the Atlantic. At the end of the war and in the years that immediately followed, the Sitwells were in vogue and their reputation grew with striking speed.

Plans for a state visit to the United States and Canada were soon being discussed. Osbert and Edith decided to make the tour in partnership. By October 1948 the Bank of England had agreed to make available nearly £1,500 in dollars to finance the trip and plans were being laid for several months of lectures and readings around the country. The agent who was arranging the tour, Colston Leigh, was sternly told that the Sitwells did not wish to accept private hospitality but would prefer hotels.[50] 'I shall come back liking my own country more,' Osbert told Lorna Andrade. 'There's nothing like a visit to the States for that.'[51] Osbert and Edith, with David Horner in attendance, sailed for New York in the *Queen Elizabeth* on 15 October 1948. They were confident that they would give a good account of themselves but had some doubts whether the Americans were worthy of them and whether they would be properly appreciated.

From the moment they arrived all fears were quieted. They were met by the agent, Leigh, a reassuring giant of a man according to Edith,[52] who told them that over the whole of their itinerary the demand for tickets was overwhelming. New York, Buffalo, Baltimore, Washington, Boston, Toronto, Hamilton, Sarasota, Lynchburg, Kansas City: the story was everywhere the same. America was ready for them; were they ready for America? They could hardly have been better designed for the job. Edith was the more extravagant in appearance and melodramatic in manner, but Osbert played the urbane English aristocrat to perfection; formidably self-assured, capable of being offensive in the politest possible way, witty in a style for which the readers of America were unprepared. 'How can you tell good poetry from bad?' he was asked. 'In the same way as you can tell fish,' he replied. 'If it's fresh, it's good; if it's stale, it's bad; and if you're not certain, try it on the cat.' At the same lecture a woman at the back called out, 'We can't hear!' 'Pay attention, madam, and you will,' Osbert replied dismissively.[53] Not everyone took such treatment meekly. The *Toronto Globe* complained that he mumbled into his shirt-front. Now and again somebody would shout, 'Louder!' 'Then like a tired horse at the flick of a whip, he would raise his voice momentarily only to let it subside to an almost inaudible soporific monotone.'[54] Such criticism was rare, however. The audience, as in Gladstone's Midlothian campaign, had come not so much because it expected to hear as to see and to participate. It was an occasion, something not to be missed, to be discussed for months thereafter; and the Sitwells played their part with enthusiasm.

It was exhilarating and exciting, but it was hard work. 'We are having a terrific success,' Osbert reported from Kansas. 'All lectures sold out 3 times over. I was told we were having more success than any English lecturer for 50 years. But I grow tired (more of the functions than the lectures).'[55] The audiences who met him at receptions after the lectures were amazed to find that he smiled, shook hands, behaved quite as though he were a human being. 'I have put my best foot forward here,' he told Lady Aberconway proudly. 'I have had to behave rather as if I were a diplomat instead of a writer – one has to be so careful what one says.'[56]

A measure of their popular success was the huge illustrated feature which the magazine *Life* devoted to them in December. 'We are the only two people to whom *Life* has ever been polite,' Edith told John Lehmann;[57] and though she overstated her case a little, the tone of the piece was still unusual in its adulation. They were referred to as 'the senior members of England's most celebrated living literary family who gave the New York literary set its biggest thrill in years'.[58] The Sitwells were being lionised and in response they behaved like lambs. They seemed unable to do wrong. A performance of *Façade* was put on in New York. Beverley Nichols, who happened also to be in the city, begged them not to persist in this wild endeavour, but they were obdurate. 'It was even worse than I feared,' he wrote. 'Something went wrong with the microphone, Edith had to recite her little jingles from the background, and when Osbert tried to walk on he got mixed up with the curtain behind the stage and plunged around like a captive elephant.'[59] But nobody minded. Every seat was sold and could have been sold several times over. A more elitist occasion was staged at New York's most celebrated book-store, the Gotham Book Mart, where the cream of the literary world assembled to honour the visitors. Auden and Spender were there; among the Americans were Tennessee Williams, Gore Vidal, Richard Eberhart, William Carlos Williams, Marianne Moore. William Saroyan was said to have been so offended at being excluded from the group picture that he vowed never to enter the store again.

Osbert and Edith are having 'one hell of a time', Evelyn Waugh, who was on a brief visit to New York, reported to Nancy Mitford. Osbert had grown his hair, so that he looked like Einstein. 'Every magazine has six pages of pictures headed "The Fabulous Sitwells". They have hired the Philharmonic Orchestra, which in this town is something very big indeed, to play while they recite poetry. Goodness, how they are enjoying it.' 'Are you a little bit gel-gel of the Sitwells?' Nancy Mitford asked. 'Gel-gel be buggered,' Waugh replied robustly. 'No sane man could envy Sir Osbert his ostentatious progress through USA. Nor do the Americans respect him for it. Perhaps I told you that I asked his publisher whether there had been any increase in his sales as a result of all the ballyhoo. "Yes, 18 copies." The point is that at last Sir Osbert has found the life that he has groped after all his life.' Waugh had reason to be a little bit gel-gel; as he well knew, Osbert *was* respected by the Americans and his sales had gone up by a great deal more than eighteen copies. But he was right when he said that Osbert was having the time of his life. He adored adulation, and here he was getting it in a heady dose.[60]

Glenway Westcott, the novelist, told John Pearson that four powerful New York figures had been above all important in creating the success of the Sitwells' visit: Lincoln Kirstein, of the New York City Ballet; Monroe Wheeler of the Museum of Modern Art; Mrs Vincent Astor, supreme among New York hostesses; and Mrs Crane, the rich, ancient bluestocking widow of a Senator.[61] To these could be added Alice Hunt, less distinguished than the others but immensely rich and far more devoted. Mrs Hunt was one of that little band of worshipping women –

Madame Guéritte was another – whom Osbert bullied, made fun of, complained about, and yet on whom he was curiously dependent. Over 200 letters from him to her survive;[62] a total which suggests she had some importance in his life, and yet he unkindly christened her '*La Chasseresse*' and tended to go into hiding when she arrived in Europe. She bombarded him with presents badly needed in impoverished England – coffee, tea, rice, sugar, caviare, Chesterfield cigarettes. All were accepted and more solicited. Only the medicines were treated cautiously; he kept the cortisone in reserve until after he had consulted his specialist, as 'I'm rather frightened of it'. At one time she wanted to commission Graham Sutherland to paint a portrait of Osbert for presentation to the Tate. 'I said I would let her know – but it does no harm to keep her waiting for her refusal,' he told David Horner. Horner suggested that Osbert plead sickness – that he would not be able to sit still for long enough – an excuse which his deteriorating health would by then have justified. 'Why can't she take up good works, or something?' he asked crossly. He missed the point. Osbert *was* Alice Hunt's good work and she loved it with the devotion which all great philanthropists bring to the causes they have espoused.[63]

One unfortunate by-product of Osbert and Edith's triumph was that David Horner found himself far from the limelight, a position to which he was not accustomed and which displeased him greatly. Osbert reported hopefully from New York that Horner had been fêted and had a 'frightful swollen head' in consequence,[64] but though he was not ignored he was in no way the star. Freya Stark met them and wrote subsequently to Horner to apologise: 'It was a very short glimpse in N York and I was so enraptured at meeting Osbert Sitwell (I do think he is the best living writer of English prose) that I rather neglected you.'[65] If Freya Stark, an old friend, neglected Horner, how much worse must it have been with the army of Sitwell-worshippers who were meeting him for the first time? Horner was left with a sense of vague displeasure, which was to cost Osbert much in future visits.

In 1949, however, this lay ahead. When Osbert and Edith returned to Southampton in mid-March they knew that they had been established as major stars on the American literary and social scene. Any time that they wanted to return to resume their triumphal progress, they would be more than welcome. Osbert was euphoric. 'I have now lost my sense of values,' he told Lincoln Kirstein, 'and like *every* American; though I don't like every Englishman, Wop or Frog.'[66] One thing only marred the pleasure of their return. Sachie, egged on by Georgia, felt that he had been deliberately left behind and excluded by his siblings. Evelyn Waugh, in New York, had asked Osbert why Sachie was not in the party. Because, Osbert answered, 'he is High Sheriff of his county and therefore cannot leave England'.[67] One can imagine Osbert making this reply, but not his believing it. Sachie was left behind because he would not greatly have enjoyed the expedition and, more important, because he would not have been nearly as good at showing off to Americans as either his brother or his sister. Most of all, he would not have made the journey without Georgia. Edith suggested that perhaps they might come on the next visit. Osbert flatly refused. 'You see,' Edith explained to Geoffrey Gorer, 'G has really been very difficult.'[68] Osbert took it for granted that Georgia's rancour was as much on her own behalf as on Sachie's and roundly remonstrated with her. They had not greedily been skimming the cream off the milk as she alleged, he protested. 'We have worked very hard for many years to establish ourselves there, and one of our objects is to get Sachie his rightful position. But at first it especially requires no socialite or Mae West business – only boring literary politics. And you have been there and had a good time already.'[69] The reference to 'socialite or Mae West business' was hardly calculated to appease an already fuming Georgia; and if Georgia remained unappeased it was unlikely that Sachie would be allowed to rest at ease. The grievance about the United States was added to the grievances about money and festered viciously over the following decade. Sachie's unhappiness caused Osbert real regret, but he did not see that there was anything he could do about it. He did not allow it to destroy his delight in his transatlantic triumph.

18

Parkinson's

FROM 1950 the state of Osbert's health began so to dominate his life as progressively to limit and finally to render impossible nearly all those activities which made his life worth living. 'I do hope that the gout is not troubling you too much,' Evelyn Waugh wrote sympathetically in 1949. 'I suffer mainly from nervous nausea, insomnia, irrational rages, noises in the head, melancholy and deafness.'[1] Presumably this catalogue of woes was intended to cheer up Osbert by reminding him how much worse things might have been, but without too much difficulty he could muster an equally formidable list. By then most of Osbert's teeth had gone, but the gums still gave constant trouble. His eyes were deteriorating rapidly; reading, even with spectacles, became more and more of a problem. His winters were still made horrible by periodic bouts of bronchitis; the condition of his heart was a constant if usually unobtrusive threat. John Lehmann asked Edith why Osbert had seemed so strange when he met him in July 1947. It was just that he was ill, said Edith; in constant pain and finding it difficult to sleep.[2] The 'hinges of one leg' had gone wrong, he reported, owing to the fact that he was nearly double-jointed. The doctors noted 'Great lateral movement in the legs'. In other words, commented Osbert dryly, 'I can kick sideways like a cow (But can a cow?).'[3]

Compared with all this, the intermittent tremors, particularly noticeable in his hands, seemed a trifling matter. Osbert had complained several years before of waking in the small hours of the morning and feeling 'very trembly'.[4] This may have been some passing ailment; it was not until August 1949 that he told Alice Hunt of 'a tiresome tremor' in his left arm: 'A real old fashioned palsy; but I hope it will pass. Probably partly nerves.'[5] It did not pass. He endured a miserable winter and in the spring told Sachie that he could do nothing except sit and tremble and wish that he could work.[6] His Derbyshire doctor told him that his condition was connected to his gout and that he should not take it too seriously. Osbert accepted the diagnosis, but attached more importance to the fact that he was sent on to see a specialist. The expert was kind and cautious, but Osbert was thoroughly alarmed by 'his lengthy and esoteric examination' and his refusal to make any suggestion as to what the trouble might be. Osbert got home to find a letter from Philip Gosse, son of his old friend Sir Edmund. Gosse was sending him a copy of a medical magazine, *Bart's Quarterly*, which contained a reference to the Sitwells. While you are about it, suggested Gosse, you might like to look at the testimonial of a very brave man on page 81. 'Turning to p. 81 I found a full description of all my own symptoms, only aggravated, written by a doctor, of what I either have or haven't got, in the last stages of his disease.'[7]

Osbert moved on to another specialist, who refused to confirm his patient's self-diagnosis though feeding his blackest fears. He 'said things to me that should be said to no patient', wrote Osbert indignantly. 'And how should he know how anyone's case will develop?'[8] Osbert was told, with what appears to have been some brutality, that his condition was certainly incurable and would probably deteriorate. A third specialist was recommended. For a few weeks Osbert revolted, refused to see any more doctors and claimed to feel much better as a result. Edith wrote despairingly to tell Sachie that the news was bad. 'Osbert can't bear it being discussed,' she told her brother; 'naturally it is all right when we are together; I only mean I know he would hate me to *write* about it.'[9] But Osbert's defiance soon petered out. Early in August 1950 he went to Liverpool to consult Sir Henry Cohen. The diagnosis was unequivocal. His condition probably had its origins in the encephalitis which Osbert had suffered when at Montegufoni shortly after the First World War – an aftermath of the Spanish influenza which had so nearly killed him. He was now in the early stages of Parkinson's Disease.

The news was almost a relief, so unbearable had been the uncertainty. Besides, Cohen was cautiously cheerful. There was no reason why Osbert should get rapidly worse; indeed it was reasonable to hope that he might stay more or less the same for ten or fifteen years. He was to carry on with his normal life so far as possible.[10] In the long term the prospect looked grim; the tremors waxing till they made almost any normal activity impossible, muscular deterioration, partial blindness, speech becoming progressively more inaudible, long periods of depression and alienation from other people. But this event might be almost indefinitely postponed and meanwhile some new technique for coping with Parkinson's might be devised. The disease need not destroy his life. Indeed, it could even be of some service as providing an alibi for not taking on unwelcome chores. Four days after his fate was confirmed he refused to succeed Desmond MacCarthy as president of the English Centre of PEN. His doctor, he explained, had told him 'to give up all work and activities not immediately connected with my own books'.[11] Cohen had issued no such embargo but it is hard to blame Osbert for extracting a little advantage from the catastrophe that had so cruelly overwhelmed him.

In August 1950 Osbert was fifty-seven years old. He had never appeared particularly young for his age but now, Aldous Huxley told Isherwood, he looked 'suddenly rather old and tired'.[12] He could realistically look forward to nothing except charting the relentless crumbling of his faculties. 'I have always liked your handwriting,' Bryher had told him, 'it is so clear and easy to read, and yet so full of character.'[13] His handwriting was one of the first victims of the disease. In 1950 it was becoming markedly cramped and ungainly, within a few years he was having to dictate even the most personal of letters or else risk being entirely incomprehensible. For a man who took great pride in his appearance it was particularly hard to see himself become bent and shrivelled, to slop food over his clothes, to feel the victim of pitying eyes as he shuffled across a room or clattered his knife and fork uncontrollably against his plate. Most of these tribulations were still a long way off, there would be periods of remission, even of modest improvement, but every day Osbert was taking stock in case some new evidence of decay was becoming manifest.

Endlessly, he cast around in search of rescue. Usually he looked for it in drugs. In May 1951 he refused to stay with Duff and Diana Cooper at Chantilly because he was taking a course of pills from the United States and had to lead a quiet life while doing so. 'I have to take one a day for a week, then two, and so on – and sometimes the effects are what they call "distressing".'[14] But he did not exclude the possibility of finding some more arcane remedy. 'Between you and me,' he later the same year told Zozia Kochanski, a close friend of both Osbert and Edith and wife of a Polish violinist, 'I am going next week to see a "healer", a priest from Arezzo, who is said to be marvellous.'[15] The marvel did not follow; once more he looked elsewhere. No two experts seemed to agree on the best course of action. On a visit to Sicily, from where he told David Horner that he felt 170 years old and slept a lot, 'like very old people do', he went to see a doctor at Messina, who was supposed to be an authority on Parkinson's, and was told to do everything that his English doctor had forbidden.[16] The possibility of surgery always existed, but Osbert thrust it to the back of his mind as being a remedy of last resort. When Alice Hunt in 1953 wrote to tell him about a marvellous new brain operation which offered instant relief, Osbert replied coolly that he had already been sent two newspaper cuttings about it but had not been convinced. 'It necessitates two three-inch holes being made in the skull, which does not seem to me an attractive proposition, and the results are very meagre – a hand which does not move instead of one which shakes.' 'But it was most kind of you to send it,' he added as an afterthought.[17] In time he would change his mind but for the first few years he favoured a less drastically physical approach. At the end of 1955 Osbert got in touch with Harry Edwards of the Spiritual Healing Sanctuary at Shere in Surrey. Initially he convinced himself that the treatment was doing good: 'We are so pleased', wrote Edwards, 'to see that through the power of Spiritual Healing the ill-conditions are easier and new strength is coming to you.'[18] Whether or not the improvement was illusory, it anyway soon passed. Osbert abandoned spiritualism as he had already abandoned so many other hopeful approaches. For somebody who prided himself on his robust scepticism and distrust of mumbo-jumbo it must anyway have been painful to have recourse to such methods. Richard Aldington heard in Florence that Osbert had cancer, then was told that it was Parkinson's. 'Most humiliating,' he commented.[19] For Osbert the humiliation must have lain not merely in his physical condition but in the way it drove him to have recourse to those whom at other times he would have shunned as charlatans or quacks.

Meanwhile the decay went on. He would not become helpless until he was ninety, the American neurologist Desmond Laurence assured him.[20] But where did clumsiness end and helplessness begin? Harold Nicolson told Gladwyn Jebb that he had sat next to Osbert at a literary dinner. 'He was sitting on his hand to keep it from wobbling. He is very depressed about himself and told me that he had no hopes in life at all except to await a slow and gradual death. I mind about this since, although I have had trouble with Osbert in the past, I really do admire and like him very much.'[21] By the middle of 1953 Osbert was apologising to Zozia Kochanski for being so long in writing, the physical effort of using his right hand was too great to bear. And yet he hated to dictate letters to close friends. Sachie, a fellow writer, realised only too well how great the privation must be. 'I can't bear to think of it,' he wrote. 'You used to dash off such marvellously amusing letters in a few seconds. It must be agony to have your mind work so much quicker than your hand.'[22] To Rache Lovat Dickson, in 1954, Osbert complained that he was now suffering from housemaid's knee on top of all his other afflictions. 'It seems to make writing letters more difficult than ever and I shall soon have to start signing letters with my right foot.' 'Poor OS!' Thomas Mark commented in a scribbled note at the top of the letter. 'It seems heartless to suggest another volume – *Left Foot, Right Foot!*'[23]

Second only to Osbert, indeed in some ways even more acutely, Edith suffered for her brother's misfortune. Capable of dealing the most ferocious blows at others, she was invariably dismayed if forced to witness their suffering. When those she loved were involved she was inconsolable. She never stopped worrying about Osbert's health and happiness. In 1951 she refused to write her autobiography. 'I think it might upset Osbert,' she told John Lehmann. 'His Autobiography is in one way his greatest life work. And I couldn't bear for him to feel I was in any way trying to rival him over it. I couldn't, anyhow, because it is a masterpiece.'[24] In 1955 she was accepted into the Roman Catholic Church, a conversion that to some extent reconciled her to Osbert's travail. 'I am greatly cheered by what you say of Osbert,' Evelyn Waugh wrote to her. 'Suffering is by nature bad, but it is the work of the redemption that it can be turned to good. I am very hopeful that with your help he too will find the truth.'[25] Waugh claimed to have found signs in Osbert's writing that suggested he was 'near the truth'. Father Caraman, Edith's instructor in her conversion, had similar hopes. They were not well justified. Osbert accepted his sister's conversion as he had accepted David's; indeed, he may even have approved it. He told Frank Magro, the companion of his final years and himself a Roman Catholic, that if he believed he would follow her example.[26] But he could not believe at all. He might make overtures to a spiritualist or a priest-healer, but he could never commit himself to such an undertaking. Like Henri IV he would have felt that Paris was worth a mass. If he had believed that conversion to Roman Catholicism would rid him of Parkinson's Disease, then he would have made the move without hesitation. But he could not see that the two were in any way connected, and was not prepared to feign faith to gratify even those whom he loved most. He envied his friend and his sister their new-found happiness, but knew he could not share it.

Sachie too felt great sympathy for Osbert, but this was not enough to assuage the bitterness between them. David Horner worked

industriously to ensure there was no rapprochement. In October 1951
Sachie lost the job of writing the up-market gossip column, 'Atticus', in
the *Sunday Times* – a task which he had performed with idiosyncratic
zest for some nine months. With it he lost £2,000 a year. 'This means a
new financial crisis just after Osbert has forked out £25,000 for them,'
Horner told Christabel Aberconway. 'They are a very tiresome couple.'[27]
Sachie had long considered Horner an enemy and Lady Aberconway as,
at the best, a dangerous friend. It seems that she wrote him a letter
suggesting that Osbert's illness was in some way related to his worry
over his brother's affairs. Sachie recoiled in rage. 'I do not think you can
realise what a wicked and monstrous load you are fastening on me. I
cannot possibly see or speak to you again. It is, of course, as always, that
fatal and horrible David Horner (who has been such a disastrous
influence in Osbert's life) whom I have to thank for this. He was a
wicked evil creature long before he came into poor Osbert's life.'[28] Lady
Aberconway, of course, felt it her duty to show this letter to Osbert.
Then came a scene in the St James' Club, when Horner deliberately
settled at a table opposite where Sachie was sitting. Sachie ignored him.
'Very soon,' Horner told Lady Aberconway, 'as I made it quite clear that
I was enjoying the situation, he left the Irish stew and went out. He was
certainly looking rather odd.' This too was faithfully reported. 'I do not
mind being cut,' Horner told Osbert, 'but only regret that guilty
conscience is masked by excessive bad manners.'[29] Against two such
accomplished mischief-makers Edith could do little to reconcile the
brothers. Osbert and Sachie never quarrelled openly and met from time
to time, but their intimacy was over. Many years later Sachie told Philip
Frere's successor, Hugo Southern, that he and Georgia did not go to
Montegufoni for twenty-five years for the simple reason that they were
never asked. 'For the same reason we never went to Renishaw for sixteen
years. It does seem a strange waste of time.'[30]

James Lees-Milne had met Horner at dinner with the Princess de
Polignac towards the end of the war, 'invited because apparently the
Princess thought he was E. M. Forster. He is a slightly epicene, elderly
young man who lives with Osbert Sitwell. He has a soothing low voice,
but his manner is embarrassingly affected.'[31] Horner's prime social assets
had always been his charm and his good looks, both reinforced by the
appearance of extreme youthfulness which he retained long after the
demands of nature should have wreaked their usual havoc. Like the
Duke of Windsor, however, that other would-be Peter Pan, his youthful
freshness suddenly began to seem artificial. By the mid-1950s Lees-

Milne's 'elderly young man' had become unequivocally middle-aged. Osbert loved him no less, however, and could see no change. A damp, dark, gloomy July at Renishaw, Edith told Bryher, was relieved only by 'the presence of David, whose pretty golden curls light the landscape'.[32] She wrote satirically, but she knew that to Osbert the golden curls glowed as radiantly as ever.

Horner was still the beneficiary of Osbert's largess. In July 1948 Osbert had sent him £110 as a final instalment of 'this year's covenant'. 'Goodness knows when you'll get the next,' he warned, but financially speaking his affairs were on the mend and it is unlikely that the covenant was allowed to lapse.[33] It seems that at one point Horner was also in line to inherit much of Edith's estate in the event of Osbert predeceasing her. This is a mysterious episode. Edith loathed Horner and loved Sachie; one would have expected that, even if Osbert were named as heir, her younger brother would have been next in line to inherit. Yet a draft will in Osbert's hand, written in the early 1950s, left £3,000 or a house to Osbert, with remainder to Horner after Osbert's death.[34] Whether Edith briefly acceded to this project, and what pressure if any was brought on her to do so, is uncertain; the fact that Osbert contemplated it, however, shows not only how devoted he still was to Horner but also how bitterly he felt towards his brother or, perhaps more accurately, his brother's wife. This was borne out still more forcibly when for a time Osbert planned to leave to Horner not merely the castle of Montegufoni but also certain outlying farms which had been bought from the residue of Sir George's *Stiftung*.[35] Legally Edith and Sachie had a strong case for claiming that a share of these farms was theirs; morally the argument was overwhelming. Even after Horner had disappeared from the scene, the way that Osbert chose to dispose of Montegufoni caused much distress to his brother. If Sachie had known what was intended at this period he would have been beside himself with grief and fury.

Osbert's bounty was as much a payment for loyalty in the future as an acknowledgment of affection in the past. He was acutely conscious that, while he had aged beyond his years and must expect to become more and more of a cripple as time went on, Horner was younger, better preserved and socially and sexually more ambitious. He feared that his friend might grow discontented with his lot and reassert his independence. He knew that Horner was genuinely fond of him and would be reluctant to hurt him; but he suspected also that, if he allowed himself to be too easily hurt, Horner would grow impatient. If he tried too hard to keep his friend he risked losing him altogether; a tacit compromise by which

Horner roamed at will but returned eventually to base was the best that he could hope for. 'David comes in late, looking strangely tired but happy,' he told an American friend.[36] Where he had been, and why he looked tired but happy, was not something into which Osbert thought it judicious to enquire.

That escapade, whatever it may have been, took place in London; it was in the United States that Horner first put the relationship under serious strain. Osbert, Edith and David Horner left for New York in September 1950. The visit, though not a failure, did not repeat the triumph of its predecessor. Osbert was preoccupied with his health, called on several specialists, and was disappointed by their prognoses. Edith too was far from well for much of the time, among other things contracting amoebic dysentery while in Mexico. Determined to provide a flamboyant follow-up to the *Façade* of January 1949, she elected to put on a reading of *Macbeth* at the Museum of Modern Art, with herself as Lady Macbeth, various friends playing the other roles and David Horner in a tartan dinner-jacket as MacDuff. 'Cheapest seats £5. I wish I could be there,' wrote Evelyn Waugh; adding that Osbert looked like a tottering corpse.[37] The result was memorably grotesque and received enough harsh criticism in the press to shake the confidence of the hyper-sensitive Edith. True to form, she reacted with indignation, denouncing all those who complained of her performance as philistine dullards unfit to appreciate a work of art.

They moved on to Mexico, and thence to Hollywood, where Edith was supposed to be negotiating with the director George Cukor, over a film of her *Fanfare for Elizabeth*. 'Do you like Los Angeles or hate it?' Osbert asked a friend. 'For a few days I found it most amusing. But I suppose after a week it would fade on one.'[38] The chief event, from his point of view, was a poetry reading to an audience of 2,000 who included Aldous Huxley, Dorothy Parker and Harpo Marx. The presence of the last of these so pleased him that he boasted of it in letters to at least half a dozen of his usual correspondents. But when they moved on to Florida for the next stage of their pilgrimage David Horner, bored by perpetually playing second fiddle and tending to the needs of an invalid, defected and went off to stay with friends in Kansas. Osbert was left to the care of a new acquaintance, Daniel Maloney, a young Irish painter whose relaxed charm, unconventionality and affectionate nature made him irresistibly attractive to the older man. Maloney was never a substitute for Horner; he could not and would not have wanted to fit in with life at Renishaw, Carlyle Square or Montegufoni, but for the United

States he was all that Osbert could have hoped for. To Maloney, Osbert was sage, benefactor, father figure. He wrote to Osbert after his hand had been badly hurt in an accident: 'Physical wounds have nothing on wounds of the heart, as you know. I'm in the process of pulling myself together. How I wish we were sitting on a park bench by the zoo this moment – I wouldn't demand a "pep talk", just sitting beside you would be enough . . . I know you're there, Osbert, and you'll not betray my heart – that's a treasure to me.'[39]

It was not till the tour of the United States in 1954/5 that Horner's increasingly semi-detached attitude to the relationship provoked something close to an explosion – and then it was Edith who both created most of the blast and was the principal victim of the fall-out. Far from Edith's growing more dulcet with old age, her propensity to react with disproportionate fury to real or imagined slights had grown more marked year by year. Early in 1954, for instance, she wrote in outrage to Stephen Spender to report that 'Mr Peter Ustinov has *criminally* libelled Osbert and me in a play in which we were shown as sex-maniacs and given the name of D'Urt!!!! There is no possible doubt that it was meant for us – and most of the papers said so, in so many words. And Osbert is desperately ill – as this creature knows.' To make matters worse, the Sitwells' traditional enemy, the *New Statesman*, went into raptures over the wit and ingenuity of the play.[40] Osbert, so far as one can tell, was relatively unmoved – with good reason, since Edith was relying solely on the exaggerated reports of others and there was nothing in Ustinov's play, *No Sign of the Dove*, to cause more than mild irritation. No doubt Philip Frere, to whom Edith appealed, consulted with Osbert before he persuaded the would-be litigant that to sue Ustinov would lead to endless anxiety and annoyance to little end. Edith grumblingly let the matter drop, and Ustinov was not even aware of Edith's wrath until several years later.[41]

At the beginning of 1955 it was on behalf of Osbert that her fury was vented. On 17 January she wrote to Sachie a letter headed 'Private and Confidential':

Dear Little Lord Fauntleroy has *not* been in New York during the whole of our stay, but has been staying with a friend in the country. Nor has he gone with O to Florida. O has gone with a very nice young man, a friend of Lincoln's, who was a naval nurse during the war. I am afraid I really let myself go to O on the subject of the Little Lord's behaviour, and this has not made me popular. To have chosen this moment to let O be looked after by strangers!!! I did not tell you until I could control myself, because it is dangerous for us if we fall into rages over it; because he will come back when there is something to be got out of it. After all, any social position he has comes through us.

Sachie was not to tell anyone about the episode.

You see, the creature is coming back to England with us, and will infest the house again. O says we have to behave the same, otherwise our domestic life will be hell – because we will have him there, just the same, but hating us. O says one must show nothing.[42]

Osbert's sad but apathetic resignation was for Edith almost the worst part of the imbroglio. Every instinct urged her to rise in his protection, to rend what she saw as the cruel and treacherous Horner. But if she did, she knew that she would end up the most severely wounded. Though he might resent Horner's conduct, Osbert was not ready to lose him. If Edith could not bear to live with them together, then she would have to live apart. She was not the only one to see and deplore what was going on. People gossiped, and surmised that Osbert and David Horner were on the point of breaking up. Though the letter does not survive, it seems that Horner must have written to Osbert to ask that such rumours should be quashed. 'About what you tell me, what can I say, what can I do?' asked Osbert plaintively. 'There was bound to be talk.'[43] When the time came to return to London and Horner appeared to claim his berth on the *United States*, Edith's fury was renewed. She claimed Horner had told her brother that he did not care whether Osbert lived or died. Again she made a scene, again Osbert repressed her. 'Don't mention it to Osbert, unless he does to you,' she told Sachie. 'I have put my foot in it again by saying what I think of the creature.'[44] Back in England she confessed to Father Caraman that she felt daily temptation to great anger 'because of something terribly cruel that has been done to my dear Osbert'. Caraman tried to persuade her that Horner had given a great deal to Osbert in the past and no doubt would again in the future; grudgingly she conceded: 'He hasn't, I think, any idea of the terrible thing he has done. Osbert always tried to find excuses for him.'[45]

Unless he was more adept than usual at concealing his emotions, Osbert did not find it so very terrible himself. Of course he would have preferred to have Horner always with him but Maloney was more than acceptable as a stopgap and he was realistic enough to understand that Horner would have felt stifled if he had not been able to make occasional breaks for freedom. Life in his absence was not inevitably sad and dull.

In April 1955 Osbert and Edith were fêted in Boston. They went to a party given by an undergraduate club. On the way downstairs one of the hosts proudly pointed out the head of an enormous rhinoceros which had been presented by Theodore Roosevelt in 1901; then exclaimed in dismay: 'Oh! Its horn is missing. What can have happened to it?' When they returned to their hotel they found three young men waiting for them, dressed in Elizabethan costume. Their spokesman announced: 'Sitwells, we were not invited to the party for you, but we love beautiful words and nice people, so we have brought you presents. Here, Sitwell, [to Edith] is a swan!' Whereupon he produced a large stuffed duck with a bandage round its foot. 'And here, Sitwell,' to Osbert, 'is a rhinoceros horn.' Evidently the young men, put out at being excluded from the party, had broken in and stolen the horn as a trophy. Osbert and Edith accepted the tributes gracefully, and when Osbert reported the incident to Bryher the duck and the horn had just arrived at Renishaw.[46]

By then the pattern of life there had changed considerably. Ever since Osbert had taken over the house it had been dominated by Robins as butler and his wife as housekeeper. Robins, however, had been growing increasingly hard to live with. He was organising a new hate campaign, Osbert told Horner, 'against all foreigners, all "gentry", all estate workers, all workers of any sort, all other servants, and anyone who lives in this district. "Really," he said to me, "you'd think there was something wrong with Mother and me, the way folk go on. Always picking quarrels and shunning us." '[47] Horner for many years had disliked Robins and been resented by him; left to himself he would have pensioned him off, but Osbert was loyal to his old soldier servant, who had worked for him so conscientiously for so long. Then, early in 1952, Mrs Robins was diagnosed as having inoperable duodenal cancer. 'It is awful to be able to do nothing for poor Susan,' Osbert wrote, 'except to try to see that she is given enough drugs.'[48] A fortnight later she was dead. Her husband had been with Osbert more than forty years, she twenty-eight. Osbert had doubts whether he would be able to find anyone to replace her.

One thing was obvious: no housekeeper could be prevailed on to stay at Renishaw while Robins was in residence. He was already long past retirement age and Osbert at last accepted that he must go. Hollingworth was instructed to give him notice in the most delicate way and Osbert wrote to tell him what was planned. He was set up in a cottage in the park and retired with a semblance of good grace. Briefly, Renishaw was dependent on a handful of cleaners from the village – 'But oh, the divine peace without poor Robins,' Osbert wrote gratefully.[49] The employment agencies were circularised. Many possible applicants must have found the job description unappealing. Renishaw, they were told, was a large old house much of which was shut up. There was some Calor gas and an Aga cooker in the servants' quarters, but the rest of the house had neither gas nor electric light. Two housemaids, one kitchenmaid and an odd-job man to look after lamps, wood and coal came each day from Eckington. 'There are two in the family, Sir Osbert and his sister Dr Edith Sitwell (his sister takes no part in the running of the house), and a friend, Mr David Horner, is frequently there. Sir Osbert requires some valeting and he appreciates very good cooking.' The hall was large, Lorna Andrade warned potential employees, and the work was hard while Osbert was in residence; but he was rarely there for more than three or four months in the year. A couple would be paid £7 a week and would be welcome to bring a child.[50] Miss Noble, the veteran housekeeper at Carlyle Square, threatened to apply for the job herself and was told benignly by Hollingworth that this would be most welcome, 'but you will have to provide the other half of the married couple advertised for. So get busy.'[51] The quest went on until the middle of 1953 but in the meantime there was no shortage of stopgap staff. 'Having had no servants here for months,' Osbert told Leslie Hartley in July, 'I now have nine, and two more coming this weekend.'[52]

Though he was producing more poetry than he had done for many years, the end of the 1940s had been a barren period for Osbert so far as prose was concerned. He told Alice Hunt in September 1949 that he had no sooner arrived at Montegufoni than he fell ill, 'but it's only nerves, heat, overwork, exhaustion . . . I shall be better when I have a big new idea for a *book* and when, when will that come? It nearly arrived last year, but on the crucial day a party of people arrived, demanded to see me, and broke it up for ever.'[53] What train of creative thought those people from Porlock so disturbed is uncertain, though it was probably the book of travel-writing on which he eventually embarked. In the meantime he rejected Harold Macmillan's somewhat eccentric suggestion that he should write the biography of Lord Mildmay of Flete, a man of great character and courage but remembered primarily for having almost won the Grand National on a 100–1 outsider. He found the idea most attractive, Osbert told Macmillan, but he feared he would find Mildmay's sporting activities 'too much outside my range of knowledge and appreciation'.[54] It was not till the spring of 1951 that he reported with relief: 'Thank heavens, I've actually started a new book. It means months of work, but I'm so greatly relieved.'[55]

This was *The Four Continents*, which can best be described as a travel book though the discursive and visionary rambles which it describes make so mundane a description misleading. The reader at Macmillan commented that it was 'a kind of meditation distilled from Sir Osbert's travels, on the Four Elements and the part they played in the life of men, on the different continents, on Magicians, Towers, Bells, Flowers and a hundred other things'.[56] It was, the reader pertinently remarked, more the sort of book one would have expected Sachie to have produced. Osbert had written much of it in Amalfi – 'My eye, my mind, my memory and my imagination, seem to work better here than elsewhere' – but it was marked most clearly by his new love affair with the Americans. There is praise for their warm-heartedness, their hatred of oppression, their generosity, their sense of responsibility: 'For these reasons, among others, I love America and Americans.'[57]

There is much excellent and perceptive writing in *The Four Continents*, and some good jokes too, but perhaps because his deteriorating health forced him to dictate almost all the text, the passages of clotted-cream lyricism seem to have become more highly seasoned, sometimes almost rancid. In a passage on night-time New York, describing the sleeping visions of the various ethnic groups, Osbert writes:

> And all these acronychal dreams and countless others, all this amorphous weight of nostalgia, all these longings so evident in the syncopated popular music of the epoch, made concrete in Tin Pan Alley, are in the silent night most plainly to be felt. There the air is loaded with sorrow and ambition, with regrets forlorn and white as the bones of dead men and with hopes bright as their youth: and all these are as apparent to the nocturnal antennae of the senses as in the daytime are the names written over the doors of the shops, and indicate race in the same way that goods sold in the stores, or the food in the restaurant, the *spaghetti*, the *smörgåsbord*, the German sausage, similarly declare the various nationalities of the tradesmen and their customers and indicate their aims.[58]

It must have been writing of this kind that led Michael Holroyd, describing another of Osbert's books, to say that 'at its most elaborate and elongated his prose reads like that of Sir Thomas Browne, after being translated into French by Proust and subsequently rendered back into English by Henry James'.[59] The critics of *The Four Continents* were almost invariably enthusiastic: 'the book of a poet, a book of wonders', wrote Elizabeth Bowen, while Evelyn Waugh described it as 'Ruskinian, but with a larger heart than Ruskin's'.[60] But even in Raymond Mortimer's prolonged panegyric of Osbert as 'the supreme example in our time of a man whose life has been in itself a work of art and who has transmuted that life into literature',[61] there seems to be a suspicion that art is as much the root of the word 'artificial' as of 'artistic', and that Osbert's florid *longueurs* were beginning to incline too often to the former. A generation of angry young writers, who prided themselves on being sternly honest and down-to-earth, rejected these urbane circumlocutions. 'Many years ago,' wrote Philip Larkin in 1984, 'Kingsley [Amis] and I devised a literary award for the book of the year combining the greatest pretension and the least talent: it was called the Osbert.'[62]

Such views were still very much those of a minority. Macmillan printed 5,000 copies, realised they had miscalculated badly when they read the early reviews, reprinted immediately, and had sold as many again within two months. 'Personally, I have never seen a 25/- book sell at such an astonishing daily rate,'[63] Lovat Dickson told the Reprint Society, who had already done enormously well with the autobiography and were now to do the same with *The Four Continents*. It was welcome news to Osbert, but he felt more concern for what were to be his final two volumes of poetry. It was a quarter of a century since Osbert's collection of rural portraits, *England Reclaimed*, had first appeared and he had always planned to complement it with a second volume which would do for the characters of Scarborough what his first book had done for Renishaw and Blankney. He called *Wrack at Tidesend* 'A Book of Balnearics', because the people moving through its pages 'are essentially those belonging to a health resort, and who might, in the later period of the Roman Empire, have spent their time in attending the Baths'.[64]

The poems were disagreeable, he told the jacket-designer, 'concerned with snobs, failures, murderers, etc., as opposed to the innocence of the earlier volume'.[65] He seems to have been curiously preoccupied with the nastiness of the characters whom he depicted: the poems were 'not very agreeable', he told Lady Aberconway, while 'few are pleasant' was his comment to an American friend.[66] Perhaps he was preparing himself for the indignation shown many years before by the inhabitants of Scarborough when he mocked them in *Before the Bombardment*. His fears were exaggerated. *Wrack at Tidesend* was in nature very similar to

England Reclaimed: nostalgia, mild ridicule of retired colonels and pompous clergymen, the same ingenious word-play:

> Clumsy Mrs Humbleby,
>> Rumbled like a bumble-bee
>> Round the town.
>> When the morn was crumbling
>> She stumbled into sick rooms, mumbling . . .

'Lousy Peter', a portrait of a mentally retarded beggar whose terror was the Workhouse, shows real compassion and understanding for those who find it impossible to come to terms with society. But the most disagreeable, or certainly the most chilling, poem is 'The Ballad of Sister Anne'. Sister Anne is the companion of the bed-ridden Miss Wetherby, sent repeatedly to the window to report on what is going on outside. Her accounts become ever more gnomic and sinister until finally she turns on her patient with what is presumably a hypodermic syringe in her hand:

> Miss Wetherby, Miss Wetherby, my love,
>> It's time to wake you from your dream.
> Now I'll tell you what you heard.
>> The thin stranger in the cards
> Was Death, drawing near and nearer:
>> It is Death you feared –
>> Try not to scream!

'I have read enough to be sure that I shall read it all,' wrote T. S. Eliot, in what Osbert might have felt to be somewhat economical praise. 'It is in any case a relief to open a book of poems which is something different from a mere assemblage of odds and ends, which has consistency and design as a whole; and in which the pieces support each other and build up something.'[67] He might have said as much, and certainly would have said no more, about Osbert's final volume of poems, *On the Continent*. *Wrack at Tidesend* had come out in 1952, *On the Continent* followed six years later. Osbert described it as 'A Book of Inquilinics', derived from 'inquiline', a word described as rare by the *Oxford English Dictionary* and meaning a person living in a place not his own. The people in this case were, Osbert said in his preface, the English in Italy just before or just after the First World War – though in fact more than half the portraits were of Americans, Italians or others. He had been writing poems again, he had told Christabel

Aberconway some years before, 'if they are poems'.[68] His doubts were justified. Except for the 'Grand Finale', where a rather hysterical rhythm takes control –

> Howl, crowds, howl
>   For your own heads!
> Scream, sirens, scream,
>   Your sound shall come to be
> The signature tune of the century.
>   Scream, sirens, scream!
>   Scream!
>   Scream!

these portraits are deft, entertaining, sometimes perceptive, but bear little relationship to poetry. The book contains several recognisable real characters: Donald McDougal – 'he was, I suppose, an Ogre, or, alternatively and more pleasantly, a survival from pagan Rome' – is clearly Norman Douglas; Algernon Braithwaite, who 'wherever he went, he carried with him, the atmosphere of London in the 1890s', owed much to Reggie Turner. More often, however, Osbert tilts at the stereotypes who had haunted his pages for so many years, like Mrs Battoni: 'a voluminous and enveloping Englishwoman':

> 'I'm afraid I don't care for Modern Art –
>   In fact, I *loathe* it!'
> Mrs Battoni would confide at a certain stage.
> 'Perhaps I don't understand it; but I *like* things to be *like*
>   If you see what I mean.'
> Did she never entertain a suspicion that, as the years went by,
>   She came exactly to resemble
>   A portrait by Matisse . . . ?

The poems, wrote Cyril Connolly in the *Sunday Times*, were 'full of wisdom, compassion and an unforced nostalgia for the palmy days of expatriation'.[9] They deserved such praise; but it did not make them considerable as poetry. By the time that they appeared, Osbert's illness was far advanced. It was impressive that he found the physical and mental resources to complete them; it would have been unreasonable to expect much more.

On the Continent was Osbert's last original work of any significance; there would be more to come but it would consist of trivia or scrapings from the bottom of the barrel. He himself claimed that the poems had, in many cases, been written to be read aloud and benefited greatly from such performance. To judge by the success he still enjoyed on his less and less frequent appearances on a platform, he could command an audience and give pleasure merely by his presence. Beverley Nichols wrote that intellectuals nearly always made bad speakers and that Osbert was among the worst; the two men had once had a row in New York when Nichols tried to persuade his friend not to perform in public.[70] The enthusiasm of many audiences suggests that Nichols was wrong, yet recordings of Osbert reading his own poetry leave the listener wondering where the charm lay; his enunciation was precise but a little affected, the vocal range limited, the pace monotonous. It seems that he had to be there to convince. Though he broadcast with some frequency, the BBC did not esteem him highly as a performer; when the Canadian Broadcasting Corporation asked for a confidential report on his abilities the reply stated tersely: 'Most indifferent broadcasting ... somewhat plummy, aristocratic Oxford voice. Pitched baritone to bass. Somewhat slow and formal. Osbert requires quantities red carpet, insists on title, feeds on literary admiration but only if admirers detailedly acquainted Sitwell's writings.'[71]

His powers were waning, and he knew it, but Osbert was by no means yet disposed to go gentle into that good night. He still hurled himself into battles and only asked himself afterwards whether the provocation had really justified the pains. In July 1951 Constant Lambert's ballet *Tiresias* was attacked by the critics, most ferociously by Richard Buckle in the *Observer*. A few weeks later Lambert died of pneumonia and diabetes aggravated by heavy drinking. Osbert believed, and stated in an obituary of Lambert, that he had been sped on his way by the cruelty of the critics, pointing an accusatory finger at the *Observer* in particular. Buckle, whom Osbert had seen only a day or two before the obituary appeared but who had been given no indication of what was in the wind, indignantly responded that his review was fair and had anyway not contributed to Lambert's death. 'Critics must write what they think, in any way they think best, and it is monstrous that Sir Osbert – renowned as a doughty champion of literary integrity – should suggest their doing otherwise.' There is no reason to suppose that Osbert repented of his onslaught but at least he did not seek to renew it. The matter dropped, though Osbert and Buckle never spoke to each other again.[72]

A few years later he was reassured that he was not yet forgotten when he was offered the CBE in the New Year's Honours of 1956. He at once accepted; 'I would rather have the OM, though, but I didn't say so,' he told Lorna Andrade.[73] David Horner was outraged that L. P. Hartley was awarded the same honour. Agatha Christie, another recipient in the same list, was perhaps acceptable, he grudgingly admitted; she, after all, was 'an international figure'. But it was ridiculous for Hartley to be given anything, 'really, the suburbs of Peterborough and Bath are not international'. Hartley, though no doubt with rather less sincerity, professed to feel the same. 'Quite frankly, I don't rate my achievement as a writer with yours,' he wrote, when congratulating Osbert on his new distinction and apologising for his own.[74] Evelyn Waugh went further, and thought Osbert should have rejected so trivial an honour. When Anthony Powell was similarly rewarded in the following list, Waugh was still more put out. 'No sour grapes,' he told Nancy Mitford, 'but I think it very WRONG that politicians should treat writers as second grade civil servants. Osbert Sitwell opened the breach by accepting this degrading decoration.'[75] Though Osbert may have felt some disappointment that he was not better rewarded, on the whole pleasure prevailed – after all, he could hope for promotion in the future. His main concern was that his inability to control his movements might cause havoc at the investiture. 'I'm terrified of running amok at Buckingham Palace,' he told Lincoln Kirstein. 'It should cause a sensation if I enter at a run and can't stop.'[76] In the event all went well, but the worry, though flippantly expressed, was real enough. By the mid-1950s, Osbert was already unable to do many of the things that he most enjoyed and every year infringed more cruelly upon his remaining liberties. No honour, however glorious, could compensate for that.

19

A Good Deal of Time in Bed

He spends a good deal of time in bed . . . It is restful and prevents
him from being bored.

(Lorna Andrade from Montegufoni to Christabel Aberconway,
20 April 1962)

'ABOUT giving up my domicile in England,' Osbert wrote to his
solicitor some time in the late 1950s, 'I must point out this
Castello is enormously large and there is a great shortage of
servants in Italy now. In any case, I have no intention of giving up my
domicile in England. I had too many money difficulties as a young man,
and now that I've got the Renishaw Estate into order I do not wish to
give it away.'[1] The decade between 1955 and 1965 marks the gradual
erosion of this resolution. Little by little arguments of money, health and
personal affections made him not merely ready but eager to put England
behind him and make his home in Italy.

The scene in London seemed to him unappealing. The Conservatives
were still in power and to that extent life was noticeably easier but he
had little confidence that they would survive. At first the growing crisis
of Egypt's nationalisation of the Suez Canal seemed to him unfortunate
but not particularly threatening; 'if it is not one thing it is another,' he
wrote resignedly to Hollingworth.[2] Soon, however, he was as vociferous
as anyone in denouncing the follies of the government. It was the
ineptitude of the attack on Egypt which offended him, not the
immorality; in particular he deplored the fact that the British should have
undertaken such an operation without first ensuring that the Americans
were approving, or at least acquiescent. 'We are obviously going to have
a new departure from the gold standard and the Labour Party in power,
and one won't be able to blame anyone for voting for the Labour Party,

horrible though it is,' he wrote gloomily to Sachie. He had no doubt where the responsibility should be put. 'Do you remember I always used to say that, if Anthony Eden became Prime Minister, I shall emigrate?'[3] If he had indeed said this, he signally failed to act on it in April 1955, but now, if a long period of Labour rule lay ahead, it was perhaps time to give some thought to doing so.

The Russian invasion of Hungary only deepened his gloom. Stephen Spender passed on to him and Edith a request from Budapest that they, with a group of other writers, should hasten there to lend support to the revolution. The telegram found them at Montegufoni. Osbert and she were both 'horribly distressed', Edith told Spender. But they could do nothing. Her sciatica would make it impossible for her to get down quickly enough to avoid Russian bullets, while Osbert 'has this terrible illness and it would, of course, be utterly impossible for him to go'.[4] Osbert himself professed distaste for the tortured souls who sat around wringing their hands over what was going on while doing nothing to help the Hungarians except send bandages and food, but he admitted that he had no idea what such people, or indeed the governments of the West, were actually to do. Another war must at all costs be avoided: 'In my more cynical moments I know that there won't be another war until the Germans are ready for one, and they aren't yet, though much has been done to arm them. A war in Europe without the Germans fighting in it is unthinkable.'[5]

The lease of Carlyle Square, which had seemed so long when it had last been renewed twenty years before, was due to run out early in 1963. The owner, Lord Cadogan, had decided to sell his houses in the square as freeholds and asked £20,000 – too much, in Osbert's view, for a house that was tumbling down. Horner and he endlessly debated the possibilities: freehold or leasehold, house or flat, SW1, 3, 5 or 7? Two sitting-rooms, one large; four bedrooms; two bathrooms: these were the minimum; and nowhere north of the Park, Horner insisted. Lady Aberconway was enlisted to join the hunt, but everywhere seemed too small, too distant, too inconvenient.[6] Osbert had lived in Carlyle Square for more than forty years, to leave it would not only be a breach with the past but sever another of the ties that kept him bound to England.

The new house or flat would need to be secure. After a burglary in the area Osbert decided to insure individually some of the pictures which he had acquired since moving in. He was disconcerted when he was told how much these pictures were now worth. Colin Agnew, from the dealers Agnews, did the valuation and the Atlas Insurance Company accepted his figures without demur. The Tiepolo *Rinaldo and Armida* was valued at £7,000; the Brueghel at £3,500; the 'Picture of St John the Baptist by Sebastiano Pimbo Jumbo' at £1,500. 'The picture of St John', Osbert obligingly pointed out, 'has been attributed to Raphael and also to Sebastiano del Piombo (not Pimbo Jumbo as you humorously state), but Mr Agnew thinks it is probably by Giulio Romano.'[7] Osbert took a childish delight in malapropisms: Pimbo Jumbo gave him almost as much pleasure as the discovery of 'strawberry mouse' on the menu at the St James' Club.

The Renishaw estate, which Osbert so proudly told his lawyer had been successfully put in order, now consisted of some fifty tenanted farms, 120 cottages and 600 acres of woodland. It had become an extremely valuable and prosperous concern. Mainly this was the doing of Maynard Hollingworth and the local solicitor William Elmhirst, but Osbert underpinned an artistic temperament with a sound financial brain and he had taken a keen and informed interest in the purchases of farmland from the compensation paid after the nationalisation of coal and the paying-off of mortgages by the sale of building sites. The Renishaw estate, at the end of the war, had been a crippled giant, now it was fully healed and thriving. The house, too, had been fitted up with electricity in 1957 at a cost of £1,591 and was now more spruce than at any time since the golden days of Sir Sitwell Sitwell. There were far fewer house parties than before the war but August was still a month for entertaining. 'May I, without impertinence, say how enormously I admire the high spirit in which you accept your illness?' wrote Evelyn Waugh, after the annual weekend party for the agricultural show. 'How kind you are to your guests and how solicitous of their comfort. I am becoming a grudging, crotchety host. You taught me many lessons in civility, which I will try to profit from.'[8] Standards were kept up; Osbert put on a dinner jacket even when only the family were at home, though as the effort of changing from one set of clothing to another became more arduous and the humiliating irritation of spilling food and drink oppressed him more and more, his dress became less formal and stained, sloppy jerseys began to appear and reappear.

At Montegufoni, too, Osbert continued to welcome carefully selected friends. He was 'always a munificent host', wrote his neighbour, Harold Acton, 'lavish with wine, good cheer and conversation'.[9] The wine of Montegufoni, both red and white, had for centuries enjoyed a high reputation; in the years after the war it was recognised as being among the better of Italian wines. But such pleasures did not come cheaply.

Until the late 1950s and even sometimes thereafter, Osbert was constantly wondering whether he could afford to keep the great house going. When the travel allowance was only a meagre £40 a year and all the revenue from the estate was swallowed up by essential maintenance, the equation seemed almost impossible to balance; he could not even afford to pay the postage on letters to England, he told Lorna Andrade in despair.[10]

There were other annoyances, too. A local industrialist bought one of the few bits of land within view of the castle which did not belong to Osbert and built on it a small but extremely conspicuous red-brick factory. 'It annoys me so much that I don't usually refer to it at all,' he wrote to Georgia; a sensible resolution to which in practice he paid little attention.[11] Feline influenza ravaged the countryside near Montegufoni and, among many other victims, slew Savonarola, Osbert's favourite cat, who in spite of its name had turned out to be a female and had recently given birth to a charming kitten. She was 'very beautiful, highly intelligent and very funny. We shall all miss her frightfully,' Osbert wrote sadly. Her kitten followed her to the grave.[12] Savonarola's decease perhaps led to an upsurge in the numbers of the castle's mice, or the resident poltergeist, often remarked on in the past, may have indulged in one of its periodic outbursts of activity; in any case Osbert noticed that his bedroom became more turbulent. 'A purple light got into his room at 2.30 am and gave him gyp for ten minutes one night,' Edith reported, 'and next he heard a dead person being wheeled in a trolley along the passage outside his room.'[13] He was more irritated than alarmed by these manifestations; he already found it hard to sleep and a purple light or books flying around the room created an intolerable extra hazard. Eventually he summoned a holy woman, who arrived with a blind medium in attendance and did a thorough job of exorcism on his bedroom and the adjoining rooms. 'I understand . . . they are now free from devils,' reported Lorna Andrade, continuing cautiously, 'I hope so.'[14] This was not the first time that Montegufoni had been plagued by supernatural visitors. John Piper reported the apparition of a ghost hound, which howled in the passages, passed through apparently closed doors and was seen in silhouette against the moonlight through the windows. This caused Osbert a sleepless night, though the discovery next morning of an extremely large dog mess outside his bedroom door to some extent relieved the tension.[15]

Osbert's Italian, never fluent, got worse as his disease strengthened its hold. Edith described a drive to Florence when a hornet got into their chauffeur-driven car and drove her to distraction. Osbert tried to tell the driver to stop but forgot the word for hornet – *calabrone* – and produced a substitute which meant either an inhabitant of Calabria or a species of cabbage. The driver could see no Calabrian and was unconcerned about the cabbage. It took some time before he could be induced to stop and the hornet successfully evicted. But though he made little effort to accommodate himself to the customs or habits of the region, Osbert loved the place no less. He delighted in playing the squire, peering benevolently at the vineyards, inspecting the wine-presses, patronising the tenants. They, for their part, seemed genuinely fond of him; he was an interloper, but one whom they had known all their lives and his extravagantly eccentric father before him. When he had guests the local brass band would assemble in the Great Court to entertain them. Most of its members were communists but this did not discourage them from playing 'God Save the King' very slowly and with many, possibly intentional, variations. The guests were less numerous as Osbert found the business of entertaining become more onerous, but certain habitués came again and again. Leslie Hartley was the most regular, both at Renishaw and at Montegufoni. David Horner treated him with outward friendliness, but in private became more and more splenetic. Hartley had arrived, he told Christabel Aberconway in October 1951, 'bringing the most disreputable luggage I have ever seen outside a third class carriage in a French train'. He went to bed with a cold, but soon was up again, snorting and puffing and wheezing. 'I cannot say that he has been a welcome guest, as he spends his time creeping into bedrooms and writing rooms to read all one's letters, inspect one's clothes. It is such a bore having to lock everything up.'[16]

The household could not have run without the energy and organising genius of Luigi Pestelli, who not only carried out all the functions of a butler but supervised the making of the wine and olive oil, gave Osbert his injections and sat on the council of the nearby town of Montespertoli. 'An angel', Lorna Andrade called him, as opposed to the other Luigi, the Sardinian Luigi Palitta, the devil, Osbert's manservant, whom everyone else viewed with mingled fear and loathing. David Horner disliked him so much that he would neither look at nor speak to him, and insisted that he had the Evil Eye. In the end Horner and all the others prevailed and Palitta was driven from the castle, but Osbert was obstinately attached to him and took a lot of convincing before he let him go. Even the angelic Luigi had his drawbacks, however. His father-in-law Guido was a notorious drunk and bully who would roam the countryside with a shot-gun, causing palpitations among the more nervous peasants. Several times Osbert was warned to lock all his doors since Guido was on the rampage and threatening to shoot the inhabitants of the castle. Osbert would shrug his shoulders and retreat resignedly to bed; as he said, all the locks were either broken or far too rusty to move, so what was there to be done?[17]

As travel became more difficult, Osbert began to spend more of the winter at Montegufoni; from the late 1950s he was almost always there for Christmas and the early months of the following year. It was not ideal. The truth of the matter was, Osbert told a friend, 'that this is not a winter place. Gradually the cold weather gets colder, until we are all forced to live only in the hottest room in the house. It just happens to suit me. A lot of people wouldn't care to live here.'[18] One of those people was Lorna Andrade, who was growing increasingly disaffected. 'Both in colour and expression,' David Horner told Georgia, Miss Andrade 'looks daily more and more like a maggot emerging from an exceptionally sour apple.'[19] Her sourness owed more to Horner than any tribulations her employer inflicted on her; she found his demands on her time unreasonable and his discourtesy intolerable. Osbert may have sympathised but was not prepared to risk a row by taking her side. She made her displeasure evident. Miss Andrade would not be able to type out a letter, Osbert told an American friend in 1963, 'as she has withdrawn, an epitome of huffiness, into private life'.[20] The phrase suggests a breach more final than had in fact occurred. Lorna Andrade continued to hold the fort in London and do much work for Osbert. But the main need for her services, the typing of Osbert's manuscripts or the taking of dictation, was rapidly diminishing. Osbert, as an author, was drying up.

An author's output, still less the quality of his writing, cannot necessarily be gauged by the size of the royalty cheques, but these are still a useful indication of his standing. For several years after the end of the war, Osbert's annual literary earnings had run at between £8,000 and £12,000 – say, something near £200,000 a year at present values.[21] Given the sort of book he wrote, that was a remarkable, even astonishing figure. By 1955 that had dropped to about £1,000, a level at which it stayed until his death. It was still a respectable total, but showed how little new work of any substance he was producing. Apart from *Tales My Father Taught Me* (a postscript to his autobiography)* and *Pound Wise*,

*See pp. 313–14 above.

which consisted almost entirely of previously published articles, Osbert effectively published only one book after *On the Continent*. This was *Fee Fi Fo Fum!*, a book which picked up on his idea of rewriting the Dick Whittington legend and treated a handful of other fairy stories in the same way. He had been playing around with the subject for more than a decade. 'I've been through all the fairy story books from the London Library, and *can't, can't* find what I want,' he wrote despairingly to Lorna Andrade. Could she track down and do a précis of 'Beauty and the Beast', 'The Three Bears', 'Red Riding Hood'? 'I want the barest outline . . . leaving it to me to elaborate on the facts, the characters and the rest of it.'[22]

Miss Andrade did her bit, but it took a long time for Osbert to complete his part of the operation. The final product was witty, ingenious but somewhat predictable. Jack of the Beanstalk became greedy as well as rich. He sponsored the 'Golden Egg' Radio and Television Programmes and founded the 'Golden Egg Bonus Company'. He became Lord Beanstalk but could never get out of the habit of climbing trees and eventually broke his neck falling from a tree in Kensington Gardens. After Bluebeard was killed and Lucille inherited the castle, the Inland Revenue dunned her for death duties on the estate of her murdered predecessors, with compound interest. She was forced to open the castle to the public, eventually sold it to the National Trust, and lived happily ever after on the proceeds.

'A most brilliant idea,' Maurice Bowra told Osbert, 'carried out with incomparable skill – a task that you alone could do . . . you give these remarkable stories a new, brilliant and fascinating life.'[23] Brilliant or not, the book fell between two stools. The editor of *Good Housekeeping*, representing one stool, refused to take an extract. Personally, she had enjoyed the stories, she wrote, 'but I felt that the satire and somewhat sardonic humour might go unappreciated by readers with less than average literary taste. To certain of our readers, alas, life is chaste and moral – a bed of roses not to be disturbed. Sometimes we do disturb them, but I don't think we should do it in the Sitwell manner.'[24] Most reviewers, however, took the opposite view and felt that the satire was not sharp enough and that the social observations which permeated the stories were over-tendentious and decidedly outdated: 'The comment has been somewhat overdone,' said the *Daily Telegraph*, while *The Times* relegated the book to a 'Shorter Notice' and concluded that Osbert's 'constant complaints, obliquely but heavily made in almost every story in the book, about the dreariness of the Welfare State, are more than a little stale after all these years'.[25] By 1959, after nearly eight years of Conservative government, he might indeed have found a new windmill at which to tilt.

Fee Fi Fo Fum! was the last book Osbert published with Macmillan. Most authors attribute falling sales and inadequate reviews to the shortcoming of their publishers rather than their own waning powers. Osbert felt that Macmillan had grown sleepy and complacent and was flattered when Hutchinson tempted him with promises of a large advance and furious activity on his backlist. The official reason given for the move was that Macmillan had shown no interest in republishing his earlier titles while Robert Lusty of Hutchinson had professed himself eager to do so.[26] Macmillan were affronted at what they saw as an act of gross disloyalty but the damage was more to their pride than to their balance sheet. They would have done well with *Tales My Father Taught Me* but otherwise no new books were to come from the illustrious defector. The rest of his writing life contained nothing but a series of aborted enterprises: the libretto for another oratorio by William Walton – 'I suppose we shall go to the Bible again for it,' Osbert told Alice Hunt vaguely; a synopsis for a play about the Dreyfus case which he contemplated writing in partnership with Lincoln Kirstein.[27] The one project that might have made a lot of money – a single-volume edition of his autobiography – he sternly vetoed: 'The only abridgement to which I could consent would be to cut out the notes and appendices.'[28] Though he never admitted the fact, and from time to time even professed to be hard at work, by the early 1960s his writing career was over.

His career as a lecturer was over too. The visit to America in 1956 was the last on which he ventured on any serious public performance. By the time he sailed home in the *United States* – 'I met Mr Truman and found him delightful and with a certain presence, which I hadn't expected'[29] – he had concluded that the mental and physical strain involved in appearances on a platform was more than he could endure. Noël Coward met him at a cocktail party in New York and was dismayed by his convulsive shaking. 'I felt suddenly dreadfully sorry for him and also admiring because he is not allowing it to get him down. We had a long talk and he couldn't have been nicer. It seems at long last that the age-old feud will be resolved.'[30] Certainly the feud was not renewed, and Osbert would have had little appetite for it if it had been, but his retreat from social life was to gather pace over the next few years; there is no evidence that he and Coward ever met again.

*

From the mid-1950s Osbert's life was dominated by his battle against the inexorable march of Parkinson's Disease. There were occasional false dawns, when he seemed to be improving and could even dream of recovery, but year by year the decline was dreadfully apparent. Each new treatment seemed to offer grounds for hope, each time the hope was dashed. More and more his visits to the United States were concerned not with lectures or the promotion of his books but an ever more despairing pursuit of the latest miracle cure. In 1959 he spent six weeks in New York at the Institute of the Crippled and Disabled and convinced himself that he was vastly the better for the experience; then, on the morning of the day he was to leave for England, he fell heavily, 'a misfortune which has put me back'.[31] He continued to fall from time to time; each time telling himself that the accident had checked a steady improvement in his condition rather than that it was merely a symptom of his progressive deterioration. 'He falls almost as well as an actor on the stage,' Lorna Andrade told Georgia, 'but he has two grazed legs and a cut over one eye. Cuts and grazes don't matter much, but falls however slight must give him an unpleasant shock, both conscious and unconscious.'[32] He went more rarely into public places or other people's houses but could not resist the occasional invitation. In July 1960 it was to Chatsworth. 'Antrim and Devonshire carried Osbert Sitwell into lunch,' Anne Fleming told Evelyn Waugh; 'their first effort failed and poor O fell back upon the sofa all of a tremble; during the meal his fork started knocking against his plate, the din was awful, and it was difficult to maintain unembarrassed conversation.'[33]

For some years he had been considering the possibilities of an operation on the brain. As early as 1958 he had been to see the American surgeon Dr Irving Cooper, who was supposed to be the supreme practitioner of this sort of operation. According to Osbert, Dr Cooper had urged the case for the operation but had failed to convince him that it was likely to yield good results; a letter from Dr Desmond Laurence, however, suggests that Cooper had thought the case was unsuitable and had refused to operate.[34] Dr Laurence's letter was written closer to the event and it seems likely that his version was the correct one; whatever the cause, however, two years later Osbert was still dithering. The operation might achieve nothing; still worse it might kill him or reduce him to a vegetable; could the risk be worth taking? 'Your old pal, Osbert, sinks deeper into the horrors of Parkinson's and refuses all treatment,' Richard Aldington told Lawrence Durrell.[35] Osbert was, on the contrary, eagerly on the look-out for any new treatment that looked remotely hopeful; it was only at surgery that he balked, and by August 1961 when Aldington wrote his letter, he had convinced himself that things were so bad that even a botched operation could hardly make them worse.

By September, when he lunched with Sachie at Weston – 'Oh! What poor Osbert was like'[36] – he had succumbed to what was now the almost unanimous advice of his friends. He was booked into the National Hospital, Queen Square, for four or five days' observation; 'which makes me feel awfully like an animal in the zoo,' he told Christabel Aberconway ruefully.[37] The understanding was that, if there was no last-minute change of heart on either his part or the surgeon's, the operation would take place on 4 October. It duly did so. Sachie visited him two days later: 'his right hand was lying on the sheet, *quite still*. He was very dopey, of course, and a little tearful (can you wonder!)' A day later he was out of danger and sitting up in bed, reading; a week later again the doctors were still hedging about the long-term success of the treatment but Sachie was detecting a marked improvement.[38] Edith, typically, having been more worried than either of her brothers while Osbert was preparing for the operation, was the first to hail a miracle. 'Osbert can now use his right hand,' she told Stephen Spender exultantly. 'It seems unbelievable. The last few years have been nightmares for everyone concerned.'[39] The word spread that an astonishing cure had been achieved. Osbert 'has had pins stuck into his noddle by the quacks and is on the road to recovery,' wrote Aldington, with some brutality. 'It could have been done years ago, if he hadn't been such a mule.'[40]

There had been no miracle, but the improvement was substantial enough to give grounds for real hope. From Montegufoni, where he retreated to convalesce, Osbert wrote to Christabel Aberconway to describe his time in hospital. It had been a curious experience since, apart from a Chinese boy from Hong Kong, only he among the patients could speak English. The rest – Turks, Syrians, Lebanese, Egyptians, Abyssinians – could communicate only by groans: 'It was a terrible sound, the universal language of the sick.' In the margin of the letter Lady Aberconway noted that it was the first letter she had received from Osbert in his own hand 'for many years' – in fact since 1956. The incomprehensible jottings of a few months before had indeed given way to a handwriting which, though still uncertain and ill-formed, was perfectly legible.[41] Osbert was 'extraordinarily well', Lorna Andrade reported in the spring of 1962. Friends who had been to lunch the day before had thought that he looked fifty and the picture of health. He had

charm was fading, the twisted and curmudgeonly figure who survived in 1964 bore little relationship to the brilliant creature whom Osbert had so loved forty years before. And yet they were the same. Osbert had shared his existence with David Horner for half a lifetime: he owed him much happiness; parting would have been an agonising wrench even if both parties had thought it best.

Both parties did not think it best. Though the bickering and mutual recriminations became ever more painful, it never occurred to Horner that they would be wise to break up the household. He felt sure that he would eventually be able to drive Magro from the field; even if he did not, he saw no reason why he should abandon his comfortable bases in London and Renishaw. Besides, he was genuinely fond of Osbert and had probably never stopped to think whether his conduct might make Osbert less fond of him. But a dangerous alliance was forming against him. Sachie and Christabel Aberconway had sunk their suspicions of each other in their shared concern for Osbert and their fears that Horner's presence in his life was making intolerable an old age which disease had already rendered disagreeable enough. 'What an absolute curse and nuisance he is!' Sachie wrote splenetically to his new ally in September. 'And such a dangerous one, too! . . . I am not sure whether it would not be a good idea for me to ask Osbert outright if he would not like David Horner to be asked to leave – this could be done when O is alone at Montegufoni this winter.'[26] Lady Aberconway thought it would definitely be a good idea and the two plotted busily. Towards the end of October, Osbert was summoned to lunch at Lady Aberconway's house to be told of their deliberations. Sachie warned him that he would arrive to find a conference already in progress. 'He is not in the least alarmed,' Sachie told Lady Aberconway, 'as indeed how could he be, because he knows perfectly well we are the two most devoted to him. But I think he will take it better from you . . . I do hope we can do some good – and am only afraid he will say it's too late, and not worth it.'[27]

He said nothing of the sort; indeed he seemed to be unsurprised by and even to welcome the initiative. It was agreed that Philip Frere should write Horner a friendly but firm lawyer's letter, enclosing a report which Dr Gottfried had prepared saying that, for the sake of his health, Osbert must live apart.[28] Horner's response was uncompromising: if they must live apart, so be it, but there could be no question of his leaving York House. *His* doctor had assured *him* that a move at the moment would be most unwise. Besides, the flat was half his; it was purely by chance that Osbert had signed the lease. He went to lunch with Christabel

Aberconway and told her that Osbert had been getting on his nerves for five years or more and he was not surprised to hear that the reverse was true. But he was 'terribly hurt' that Osbert had not spoken to him or even written a letter rather than choosing to communicate through a solicitor. How could Osbert, who was now at Montegufoni, dictate a letter of this kind to Frank Magro? asked Lady Aberconway. He could perfectly well have taken some action before he left England, retorted Horner – 'had he done so I should feel quite different'. As it was, whatever the outcome of the negotiations, 'I shall never speak to him again.'[29]

Fresh complications soon arose. Osbert was reluctantly prepared to accept that he would have to pay half the rent and rates for the remainder of the lease of York House but proposed to remove to Renishaw all the pictures, ornaments and furniture that did not belong to Horner. He told Peter Hollingworth, who had taken over as agent at Renishaw from his father, that in future Horner would be responsible for all expenses at the flat and that he should prepare to receive a consignment of goods from York House, including such items as a new refrigerator and gas cooker. But Horner insisted that all the contents of the flat were his, that they had been handed over to him by deed of gift many years before. 'I am quite clear in my mind that if anything was drawn up it was done during the war,' Osbert commented cautiously to Hugo Southern, who had taken over the case when Philip Frere found his friendship with both parties made it too embarrassing for him to act.[30] The truth is probably that Osbert had intended Horner to have the contents of Carlyle Square, may even have promised to transfer them legally by deed of gift, but did not ever get round to taking the necessary steps. Certainly Horner was unable to produce any document to prove his case. The last thing that Osbert wanted, however, was that the matter should come to court. Even if he won, it would be painful and degrading; if he did not, and he had an uneasy suspicion that his legal position was not entirely secure, then he would be publicly humiliated as well. 'Poor Osbert has of course behaved far from well over this,' Sachie told Bryher. 'A lawsuit would be disastrous – and the lawyers tell me Osbert would probably lose it.'[31]

Horner was certainly holding out for his full deserts or more but he had reason to feel himself misused. He had paid, if not half, then at least a substantial part of the rent of York House in the past and it seemed rather hard that he should now unexpectedly be required to find the whole of it in the future as well as to refurnish it almost from scratch. Osbert's failure to confront him openly, though his health offered some excuse, was still ignoble. It would not have been surprising if Horner had changed the locks on the doors at York House and held on to the contents, defying Osbert to have recourse to the law. Instead he meekly allowed the movers to take everything they wanted, including several items which he was subsequently to reclaim. The explanation may lie in a letter Osbert wrote to Philip Frere about this time. 'I think it important that David should know that I intend to pay him £8,000 when the money comes in from the sale of my manuscripts. If you agree that this is a good thing, please tell Southern to do so. Though David is so grasping that it might go against the grain to pay him this large sum.'[32] If Horner knew that this handsome *douceur* was coming his way he would have felt far more ready to sacrifice the furnishings of York House, valuable though some of these must have been.

He made his protest, though, in his own way. Many years before, in Amalfi, he had tried to commit suicide, but the attempt had been so half-hearted that Osbert was satisfied his object had only been to attract attention and sympathy. From the end of 1964 he began to revert to this technique, writing letters to all and sundry hinting that if he were pushed any further he would take his own life. Bryher was one of the targets of this campaign. Georgia Sitwell urged her not to take the threat too seriously. Horner had talked of suicide in the past, she said, and always it came to nothing, 'and an anonymous letter, sent to Frank, of a very unpleasant nature was almost certainly written by him . . . Whether or not he deserved the *manner* in which he was thrown out may be questionable – so is capital punishment.'[33] Then, at the beginning of February 1965, he took an overdose of sleeping pills and had to be removed to hospital. 'Of course he has threatened it continually, but I never thought he would do it again,' wrote Osbert wearily. 'It is a sad business, but I am determined not to be intimidated by it.'[34] Horner did not win much sympathy by his action; indeed Lady Aberconway dismissed it as 'sheer blackmail' and took Osbert's side still more robustly. 'I can't but be sorry for the wretch. But, truly, he had been so horrid to "underlings" that I can't pay too much attention to him now. How Robins, who loved you, loathed David (the things your Mr Hollingshead [*sic,* presumably she had Hollingworth in mind] complained about to me re David is a whole document).'[35]

Horner did find one champion, however. To the great embarrassment of Philip Frere, his wife Vera exploded in a vengeful letter: 'You unspeakable swine, Osbert. Only the most unutterable cad will hit a man who is broken in mind and body – and that is what you have done to David whom you called your dearest friend. May God's curse be on you for the rest of your days, and don't you ever dare set foot in this house again.'[36] Osbert was more surprised than upset by this richly cliché-ridden epistle. He showed it to Frere, to explain why he was suggesting meeting in a restaurant rather than their usual venue of the Frere home. Frere was aghast, and explained that his wife was schizophrenic and that he should have left her years before – 'What about her leaving me and going to look after David? I should be the last to impose any barrier.'[37] Christabel Aberconway had a simple explanation: Vera Frere had been in love with Horner for years and had already offered him all the furniture he needed to replace what Osbert had removed from York House.

Several of their mutual friends regretted the separation and made tentative overtures towards a reconciliation. Harold Acton kept Horner posted on events at Montegufoni. He had lunched the day before with Ian Greenlees, director of the British Institute in Florence, he told Horner in November 1965, and they had both spoken with regret of the old days. At least Osbert seemed to be well looked after, he wrote; an observation which can hardly have given Horner unmixed satisfaction.[38] Father Caraman, on the other hand, saw only the bright side of events. 'Perhaps it is Edith's first work in heaven,' he surmised hopefully.[39] Lady Aberconway, as usual, contrived to have it both ways, congratulating Osbert on his liberation, condoling with Horner on his harsh treatment. But on balance she made it clear to everyone that she thought things had turned out for the best. She outraged Horner by telling him that Osbert was 'marvellously well' and that Frank Magro was proving 'a tower of strength'. He had heard from other friends that Osbert was very far from 'marvellously well', Horner replied, and as for Magro, 'how you can describe a dwarf Maltese as being a tower of strength, even meta-phorically, is difficult to understand'.[40]

Horner's detestation of Frank Magro showed no signs of waning as a result of their forced separation. Osbert's dependence on the 'odious Maltese' reminded him of Sir George's relationship with Mr Woog, he told Peter Hollingworth. 'Nobody trusts Frank at all, and I warn you to be very careful of him . . . There was always a mystery about Sir George's demise and I say again that in my humble opinion Frank is not in any way to be trusted.'[41] Hollingworth was far from being a partisan of Magro's, but he could see the absurdity of such insinuations. Through Lady Aberconway word got back to Magro of the attacks to which he was being subjected. 'So long as he confines his remarks to you, Mr Sachie, Mr Harold Acton and two other gentlemen in Florence who all know that he is "bonkers", it is not so bad,' Magro told her, 'but if anything decidedly unpleasant comes out into the open, then I shall make sure that he is dragged into court.'[42] Luckily for everyone concerned, it never came to that. But there was no hint of a reconciliation between Osbert and Horner. As late as 1967 the campaign still stuttered on; Horner demanding the return of various pictures at Renishaw which he claimed were his. They had never belonged to Horner, Osbert complained, and anyway were now the property of Reresby. Eventually Horner lapsed into quiescence; by the time Osbert died, there was little left to mark their many years of intimate friendship.

Reresby had come into the picture because he was now the owner of Renishaw. Osbert had not found this process easy. He recognised that, to avoid death duties, it would make good sense to hand on the estate to the next generation, but when it came to the point he found that he disliked the idea intensely. He was feeling a little like King Lear, he told Lady Aberconway, as 'after David tried to get off with my furniture, Reresby sent me an unsolicited letter from young Dashwood [Francis Dashwood of West Wycombe], telling me how to divest myself of my interest in the Renishaw estates in favour of Reresby'.[43] To his surprise his friend, while sympathetic, made it clear that she thought the proposal was eminently sensible. Osbert should follow his father's example and retire to Montegufoni. But he had already sold most of the possible building sites and handed over much of the purchase price to Reresby, he protested. He did not feel inclined to do the same by the house and agricultural land.[44] Lady Aberconway persisted and gradually he weakened. Renishaw had been a gloomy place over the last few years. Nancy Mitford had gone over there from Chatsworth in 1963 with her sister Deborah, Duchess of Devonshire. 'Oh *dear*,' she wrote to Evelyn Waugh afterwards, 'two shades in a ghastly house. It was tragic. Debs said cheerfully as we drove away: "Last time we see the dear old place under that management I bet!" If Reresby takes it on I salute him – I never saw such ingrained gloom.'[45] Since then, one of the two shades had disappeared, but the gloom had not appreciably lifted.

The turning point came when Osbert stayed at Renishaw in the summer of 1965. Magro had now been promoted to private secretary and Osbert was anxious that his new status should be recognised. The pair were shortly to go to stay with the Aberconways at their Welsh home, Maenan. Christabel has been more than ready to treat Frank Magro as Osbert thought appropriate and had thoughtfully tried to ease his passage by saying that dinner jackets would not be worn. 'I am sure you must have been thinking of Frank,' Osbert wrote, '. . . but, just for the record, he has got one, of which he is intensely proud, and is only too willing to wear it if given half a chance.'[46] Renishaw, he recognised, would pose trickier problems. In an effort to forestall them he had written to Peter Hollingworth to set out the position. Magro was now his private secretary, he explained – a task for which, at his own request, he was to receive no extra pay. He would eat with Osbert at all times but would continue to wait on him at table as well as to look after his clothes and minister to all his other needs. 'While he is prepared to do all this, he draws the line at doing any washing up or laying the table. I hope there will not be any jealousy about this. The trouble is that I need somebody with me the whole time: the house is a big one and I can't even reach for bells.'[47]

In the eyes of the traditionally minded staff at Renishaw – cook-housekeeper and two maids – there was a fearful ambiguity about Magro's position. Was he a servant like them but with additional duties and privileges, or had he been elevated above their heads? The former they could have borne; the latter would be intolerable. It seems to have been the dinner jacket which provoked revolution. There were complaints to Hollingworth, a furious letter of protest to Sachie, then the staff left the house. One of the maids, Kitty, loyally stayed on for a few days to cook lunch, but then peer pressure became too great and she too abandoned ship. Obstinately Osbert clung on for a while longer, with Magro catering for his needs as best he might, but it could not last. On 7 August 1965 he left Renishaw for the last time, en route to Maenan and thence to the Metropole Hotel at Brighton.

Once there he set in train the procedures for transferring the estate to his nephew. Hugo Southern was summoned and told to draw up the necessary documents; the whole thing had become a most dreadful bore, Southern was told.[48] Osbert told Bryher that he had finally been convinced such a step was necessary by the enormous increase in the value of the property which would have taken it into a new and punitive band when it came to paying death duties.[49] Such considerations were certainly in the background, but it was the unpleasant memory of his final visit which decided him. It was a relief when he had made up his mind but none the less he hated doing it. 'I find the relinquishing of Renishaw so painful that I can hardly mention it,' he told Hollingworth. 'But as facts must be faced I have to do it.'[50] He sent his agent a farewell message to the tenants which was to be read at the next suitable occasion:

The time has come for me, if death duties are not to swallow everything, to say goodbye to you. I do so now with a sore heart at leaving many friends, but with the feeling that my successor, my elder nephew, Reresby Sitwell, whom I recommend to you warmly, is a person you will like. Goodbye and God bless you![51]

He was not just leaving Renishaw, he was leaving England. Visits would of course be possible in the future but only subject to the rules laid down by the Inland Revenue. If he was to establish domicile in Italy, he was told, it would be desirable for him even to give up his clubs. The sacrifice was more symbolic than real; by the end of 1965 he paid only infrequent visits to the St James' Club. Actually to resign from it, though, was to resign from London life. Once the decision was made, he cleared away the detritus of the past with some ruthlessness. Some years before he had refused a request from Lord Scarbrough that the Renishaw archive should be deposited at the County Record Office on the grounds that he had promised his father, 'a man of unusual ideas, never to let the Archives that I possess out of my possession. As he made them over to me I do not like to break my promise.'[52] So far as the family papers were concerned, he kept his word, but he sold many of his personal and literary papers to the University of Texas at Austin. He was equally decisive with his books, leaving at Renishaw all that he had found there, taking a limited number to Montegufoni, but selling most of the more valuable items at Sotheby's. Lot 680 had been bought by Agnews for £19,000, he reported delightedly. 'I paid £40 for it fifteen years ago.'[53] Osbert was already a rich man; by the time that he left England he knew that there was no whim he could not indulge if it would make what remained to him of life less painful.

The Faces that I Love

If I must leave the faces that I love,
Let it be when every dove
  Is crooning, swinging in the soft June trees,
And roses rise on every breeze.

(From 'Grand Finale' to England Reclaimed)

THE eviction of David Horner did not bring Osbert and Sachie noticeably closer. The differences between them ran too deep for that, and those between Osbert and his sister-in-law deeper still. 'I am sure Georgia fills Sachie with the idea that I wallow in luxury while she and he have no enjoyment,' Osbert told Bryher.[1] The truth was that he *did* wallow in luxury, denying himself little that he thought might ease his troubles. Sachie lived well too – decidedly better than his means permitted – but he was haunted always by the spectre of destitution. He continued to resent his elder brother's wealth and to resent still more being so largely dependent on Osbert's charity. The archives at Renishaw abound in letters thanking Osbert for his generosity: from Sachie at Weston, 'I want to thank you, darling, for helping me in this way, which I think should make all the difference to our life here'; from Georgia at Baden-Baden thanking him for a holiday 'which you have so angelically made possible'.[2] Each time the thanks were sincere, each time the burden of gratitude became more onerous. Osbert was not prepared to make any substantial settlement which might have solved Sachie's problems; arguing, not unreasonably, that it would soon turn out not to have achieved its end. 'Giving money to Sachie is like pouring money down a well,' he told Bryher. Not merely was Sachie improvident and Georgia extravagant, but there was no hope of any serious improvement in their finances. His brother, he went on, 'bless his heart, won't settle to work as I do'.[3] The note of affectionate contempt which he struck in this

Georgia sent Osbert an alarmist telegram. After reading it, Magro wrote, Osbert 'became visibly disturbed and refused to get out of bed for the rest of the day. Do you think that in future telegrams of that nature could be addressed to me . . . so that I, in conjunction with the doctor, could decide whether Sir Osbert ought to be told or not? After all, I know you will agree with me, there is no earthly use in making someone who is already very ill, worse, when that someone can do nothing to help the newly indisposed person.'[15] Magro had a perfectly valid point, but he was not likely to win much affection by his manner of expressing it.

Sachie was determined that, as Osbert's brother, it was his right to receive the first news of any crisis and regular bulletins on the state of his health. Magro was often slow in doing this; if only because 'I always seem to get the kind of reply from Weston that seems to put me in my place, not so much from Mr Sachie as from Mrs Sachie'.[16] Towards the end of 1967 Georgia insisted that Magro should telephone once a week. With some satisfaction Magro told Lady Aberconway that Osbert had forbidden him to do anything of the sort: 'He is terrified that in case of real emergency she and not Mr Sachie will decide on a matter of life-and-death.'[17] Sachie now entered the battle. He had been piqued to discover that Magro had been writing direct to Reresby about Osbert's health, sometimes giving news that had not yet been divulged to Sachie. He must be the first to hear. '*I* am his brother and next of kin. Mr Reresby is *my* son and *his* nephew. He must be let know, of course; but *I* should come first.'[18] Incensed, Magro retorted that he found this letter 'cold, thankless and ungrateful'. He told Lady Aberconway that there was no member of Osbert's family who could or would do as much for him. Osbert slept lightly and woke frequently, he would ask Magro the time or simply enquire how he was, 'this at two, three or four o'clock in the morning. He also feels the need for companionship and I often have to put on my dressing-gown and sit beside him for about three-quarters of an hour.' Since his days were taken up with unremitting duties, Magro was seriously short of sleep: 'But the realisation that I am looking after such a great and delightful gentleman makes it all so worthwhile.'[19]

Magro had feared that Sachie, and still more Georgia, would find his reproachful reply 'impertinent'. He was all too right. The scene was set for a turbulent confrontation when the couple came to Montegufoni in 1968. As it turned out, it was not so much Georgia's off-hand treatment of Magro which incensed Osbert as her bossiness and lack of tact. 'They hadn't been near Osbert for years,' Harold Acton told John Pearson. 'Then, when they heard he was dying, they descended, and Georgia was lifts would not take Osbert's wheelchair, the deck steward was surly and unhelpful. But worst of all was the lack of stabilisers, which caused fearful problems when the ship hit rough weather on the return journey. Osbert fell four times, once from his bed, and injured his arm, but he suffered little compared with a gentleman of eighty-two – gallantly embarked on his honeymoon – who was scalped by a steel hook, or a younger man who had an artery in his leg severed by a flying tumbler. 'Your letter expressed most graphically experiences unequalled since the wreck of the *Hesperus*,' wrote Sybil Cholmondeley sympathetically. 'It was a real *scandal* that an expensive cruise should have been in a ship so unstabilised as to result in these dreadful and frightening accidents.'[26] They had planned to disembark in Lisbon but Osbert was in no mood to face the Bay of Biscay and instead they jumped ship at Vigo. The only respectable hotel was being restored and conditions were dire. To remain there seemed inconceivable, to take the local train still worse. Osbert, who had once been advised by a Dutch seer that he should never fly, viewed the prospect of stepping into an aeroplane with some apprehension, but Magro convinced him that it was the least painful of the various possibilities. They flew to Santiago de Compostela, where Osbert made up for the deficiencies of Vigo by sleeping in a vast suite normally reserved for General Franco, and thence, by way of Madrid, to Rome. 'I flew from Madrid to Rome in two hours and five minutes,' Osbert told Peter Hollingworth with some pride. 'I still find myself wondering where I am.'[27] The experience was not as daunting as he had feared it might be, but he saw no reason to repeat it in the future.

Indeed, this was his last long journey. He was not cured of his taste for travel, however, though most of it was now connected with his quest for new doctors and new treatments. In April 1966 it was Zurich, then four months later Monte Carlo, where a Dr Jacques Grasset, who had looked after Winston Churchill, seemed to be dramatically successful. Osbert could now walk unaided for short distances, Magro reported excitedly. As so often before, however, the improvement proved fleeting and illusory.[28] Soon all was as it had been. But his stay in Monte Carlo reminded him of the delights of other cities. In May 1967, with some apprehension, he set out for Asolo and Venice. He had not been to Venice for years, he told a friend, 'and very much looked forward to it, though getting in and out of gondolas will prove a difficult proposition. More amusing for bystanders than for me.'[29] Prudently, when it came to the point, he stuck to motorboats, and Magro wheeled him to and fro, facing problems with the steeper bridges but thanking God they were not in San Francisco. The trip was an immense success. 'I enjoyed it particularly at night with all the illuminations, which made everything look so gay(!),' he wrote to Lincoln Kirstein.[30] The '(!)' is of interest as being – presumably – the only overt reference to his homosexuality to appear in any of his letters. He was, of course, writing to an American; Leslie Hartley, Malcolm Bullock and other such English friends had no illusions about his proclivities but would have been disconcerted if he had put in writing anything which reflected on them.

So much had he enjoyed this outing that the following year he decided to repeat it. This time it led to disaster. In Venice Osbert got pneumonia and was rushed to hospital, where he stayed for more than two weeks. For several days he was delirious and his life was in danger. The nurses seemed to have decided that, since they could not communicate with him, there was not much point in going into his room, and Magro had to appeal to them if anything was wanted. Luckily the doctors were more able to cope and there was no lasting damage except a slightly distended heart. More seriously, Sachie told Bryher, 'I am afraid that his memory will be permanently affected.'[31] The experience left him weakened in spirit and disinclined to venture forth. He returned to Montegufoni by ambulance on 21 September 1968. He never left there again.

Since the sinister Sardinian with the Evil Eye had finally been coaxed from the castle, life at Montegufoni had settled down to an agreeably undemanding routine. Osbert inhabited only a corner of the vast house but he lived there in considerable comfort, especially after Magro persuaded him to move downstairs, so that he slept in what had once been his father's bedroom with a bathroom newly installed alongside. Servants were, as so often, a serious problem. Osbert had the gift of attracting to him people who would serve him for many years with total dedication – Luigi at Montegufoni, Robins at Renishaw, Mrs Powell and Miss Noble in London – but perhaps because they were so loyal they grew possessive and resented the incursions of underlings who might threaten their exclusive relationship with their employer. This was the case at Montegufoni until Luigi fell ill and died of cancer. After that the staff came and went; some barely perceptible, some all too conspicuous. A manservant seemed promising, then one morning announced that he must leave that evening because one of his feet was growing larger than the other. As an excuse for so precipitate a departure this seemed inadequate but worse was to follow. A few hours later he decided after all to stay on, but as an invalid. So stout was his resistance that in the end the Carabinieri were summoned; they saw him off the premises, investigated, and reported a few days later that he had escaped from the lunatic asylum at Volterra. 'It is so difficult to get any servants around here, apart from mad ones,' Osbert noted sadly.[32]

Because the burden on Frank Magro was already great, and his condition made him anyway unwilling to expose himself to new acquaintances, Osbert's last years became more and more reclusive. He told John Lehmann that he was most welcome to come to stay but not with the friend whom he had asked to bring. 'I find it very difficult to entertain people who are not my intimate friends. Also, as you know, there is nothing at Montegufoni for a young man.'[33] There were few who ranked as intimates. Malcolm Bullock was one, whose arrival seemed to rekindle in Osbert the spirit of rollicking 1930s house parties. 'We are still working on your bedroom,' Osbert wrote in the spring of 1966. 'I can't get the arrangements of the hidden alarm clocks, set for every hour of the night, quite as I should wish to. But the priest will be doing his bit with the church bells.'[34] In the event, however, the priest was not troubled. Bullock was killed in a motor accident while on his way to Italy. Arthur Waley died within a few days of him. 'It is terrifying the way the birds are falling off their perches,' Osbert told William Plomer.[35] 'I shall miss him very much,' Osbert wrote of Bullock, but there were few of whom he would have said as much. Even an old friend like Anthony Powell was discouraged from coming to stay. Harold Acton was the most regular visitor, doubly welcome because he would come over for lunch and thus not put too severe a strain on the depleted household. 'His inability to control his movements was humiliating for him and harrowing to witness,' Acton remembered, 'but he was quite without bitterness or self-pity, and his patience under strain was exemplary.'[36]

Anything which involved dressing up or even a modest degree of formality had become an intolerable burden by the spring of 1968. An exception was made for the visit of Princess Margaret, who was staying with Harold Acton at his Tuscan villa and suggested that she might come over on what she suspected would be a farewell visit. Osbert had not been enthusiastic when she had married Antony Armstrong-Jones eight years before. 'I did not know what you told me about polio, or something of that sort,' he told Christabel Aberconway. 'It certainly doesn't make it better . . . I wonder how Lady Rosse likes her son to be referred to as "working class".'[37] He had long been reconciled to the match, however, and was delighted when he was rung up at 3.00 p.m. to be told that the princess would like to come to tea. She arrived at half past five, by which time every hand had been enlisted to make the castle spruce. Osbert did his best to entertain his guest, but he was more than usually incomprehensible and Princess Margaret found the visit something of a strain; the first sign of spontaneous enjoyment coming when a turkey cackled at her in the lemon house and she cackled back.[38] But she too did her bit gallantly, and though the visit was in some ways painful to all concerned, it achieved its object of making Osbert feel that he was still remembered.

Not that such reminders should have been necessary. As is sometimes the way with living writers, Osbert's reputation had continued to grow even though he was producing little or nothing new. In the New Year's Honours of 1963 he had become a Companion of Honour, a far more elegant distinction than the CBE, confined as it was to sixty-five members of varied but individual merit. Then four years later he became a Companion of Literature, an honour of somewhat uncertain status which nevertheless gave its holder the right to describe himself as 'C Litt'. 'Sir Osbert is immensely proud of being a Companion of Literature,' Magro told the secretary of the administering body, the Royal Society of Literature, 'and naturally he is keen on using the initials C Litt whenever the opportunity presents itself.'[39] But where should they appear in relation to his other honours? After the CH and the CBE but before the honorary degrees, was the answer; and there it duly appeared whenever Osbert felt – as he often did – that his distinctions could do with an airing.

Frank Magro continued to read him the English newspapers; he grew more detached but no more liberal in his views. *The Times* was his regular source of information; he stuck to it *faute de mieux* even though he felt that William Haley was a very bad editor; he had made it, he complained, into 'a duller, dingier annexe of the *Manchester Guardian*, a paper which I have always disliked'.[40] Any radical gesture, even if it was disguised in the wider context of a protest against war, was now eschewed. Graham Greene in 1967 urged him to resign his honorary membership of the American Academy in protest against US intervention in Vietnam. Magro replied on his behalf: 'Much as he values your friendship and much as he admires you as a splendid writer, he doesn't think that he can do what you ask of him, particularly as he sees things from a different point of view.'[41] The following year Enoch Powell made his notorious 'rivers of blood' speech which outraged every liberal in the British Isles. Osbert could not see what all the fuss was about. 'I too am all for Enoch Powell,' he assured Leslie Hartley. 'All he said was that it was high time we stopped allowing more coloured people into the country as if our resources were limitless. I can't see how anybody could disagree with that.'[42]

Even in the last few months of his life he was still capable of coming to life in sympathetic company. He was not gloomy or melancholy, said his old friend, the British Consul in Florence, Christopher Pirie Gordon; 'He liked a good laugh and was full of stories.'[43] But when alone, he relapsed into an apathetic torpor. 'I have given up any idea of writing,' he told Christabel Aberconway as early as April 1967, 'as my complex of maladies makes it too difficult. I shake so much that I cannot do much in the line of dictation and what I do is unsatisfactory. *Between ourselves*, my eyesight is going due to inoperable cataract, and so on, and so forth. In fact I seem to be an involuntary candidate for Job's crown.'[44] By the time Sachie reached Montegufoni in 1968 his eyes had grown still worse: 'he has double vision, and even sees the lovely landscape like that'.[45] His speech was now so severely impaired that Magro had to act as interpreter in almost every conversation and even he was occasionally at a loss to know what was being said. Shortly before his first visit to Venice, Osbert suffered prostate trouble; no operation was possible and he knew that he would have to live the rest of his life with a rubber tube inside him. He had physically shrunk, said his literary agent, David Higham. Frank Magro had to wheel him to the lavatory every hour and hold him there like a baby. 'But his dignity survived, his courtesy still shone through.' Worse than any of this for Osbert was his failing memory. It was 'appalling and chaotic', reported Hugo Southern at the end of 1968. 'He forgets half way through a sentence what he has been saying.'[46] The suspicion that his mind too might be collapsing was for Osbert the most fearful threat of all.

His dependence on Frank Magro was now complete. The burden, for Magro, was a crushing one, but he knew it could not last for long and did not begrudge a moment. Indeed, he resisted any suggestion that he might seek temporary relief. Leslie Hartley offered to send his servant to take over for a week or two. 'My relationship with Sir Osbert is on a higher level than that which exists between father and son,' Magro replied. 'So I just cannot make him suffer by getting a new person.'[47] Georgia persisted in her belief that Magro had ambitions to be the master of Montegufoni and might yet turn up in that capacity when Osbert's will was finally read. The suspicion was ridiculous, but Osbert's appreciation of his friend and servant was generously shown. As well as the life-interest in the flat, he left Magro $30,000 in a Swiss bank, the Dobson bust and the Piper paintings of Montegufoni. He also, which to

Magro was the most important thing of all, appointed him his literary executor. David Higham hoped that Sachie's younger son, Francis, would be given the task, so that Osbert and Edith's papers could be under joint control. Osbert paid no heed. Sachie was particularly indignant. 'Frank has been very good with Osbert,' he rather grudgingly admitted; 'he must, of course, be given a good present. But now it means his permission has to be obtained for anything of Osbert's to be published. It ... just shows how weak Osbert is, and how much in Frank's power!'[48]

Almost the only person to whom Magro would willingly delegate his role was Osbert's nephew, Reresby. In July 1958 he went on a two-week cure, while Reresby held the fort at Montegufoni. 'I know Sir Osbert likes Mr Reresby very much, and I also know that Mr Reresby cares very much about his uncle,' Magro told Lady Aberconway.[49] Osbert liked to feel that he was still in touch with Renishaw. Peter Hollingworth sent him periodic bulletins, and Reresby, on his visits, would outline plans for the future and put up at least a decent semblance of being keen to have his uncle's comments and advice.

Father Caraman continued to hope that Osbert would find consolation in religion. He was invited to Montegufoni a few months before Osbert died and concluded that his host was well on the way to conversion. 'I have no doubt at all that had he lived on longer he too would have become a Catholic. The point is that he didn't expect to die so soon.'[50] The question can hardly be settled one way or the other, but it seems more probable that Osbert was merely displaying his customary courtesy. Frank Magro reported to Lady Aberconway that Father Caraman was about to arrive: 'I shall see to it that Sir Osbert is not converted,' he reassured her. 'I like Sir Osbert as he is and any change in him could only be for the worse.' Osbert was much more preoccupied by the television which had at last been installed in the castle. 'Last night we saw Billy Smart's Circus from London – we both felt nostalgic.'[51] Though Osbert in his final years was even more inscrutable and disinclined to reveal his deeper thoughts, there is no reason to suppose that he gave much time to God, still less to conversion. When the Bishop of Gibraltar turned on him after twenty minutes of desultory conversation and asked, 'May I give you my blessing?' Osbert, so far as his disease permitted, recoiled in dismay. The bishop presumably did not notice, or perhaps thought that his blessing was even more necessary than had at first appeared. 'However, The Master doesn't seem to be suffering any adverse effects,' Magro reported.[52]

Until the very end, Osbert never lost hope that medical science might make some miraculous breakthrough which would check the disease or, best of all, reverse its course. Early in 1967 there were reports that a new cure for Parkinson's was being developed in Boston, while the *Corriere della Sera* reported that advances were also being made in Europe. 'I ought to bear in mind that I am now 74, and these things might not be suitable for me,'[53] Osbert wrote, but when it came to the point, such cautious thoughts were at the back of his mind. Early in 1967 he approached Professor Anna Aslan to ask whether her celebrated Gerotival H3 might help his condition. She assured him that it would and a supply of pills was sent for from Switzerland. Sachie urged restraint. 'Be sensible and don't expect too much,' he wrote. 'Miracles seldom happen. But I do think it could just make all the difference, and restore your mobility.'[54] Harold Acton was soon reporting that he could see a definite improvement,[55] and fleetingly Osbert did seem able to move more easily, but the improvement was probably more psychological than physical and did not last. Even that did not extinguish all his hopes, however. In March 1969 he told Tom Driberg that Dr Yahr of the Neurological Institute in New York had said that he would be willing to take Osbert on if he cared to make the journey. 'That, of course, depends on many things,' Osbert wrote tentatively, 'but I am willing and eager to have a go if the doctors thought it would greatly benefit me.'[56] A few weeks later he had decided on the venture, and plans were being made on the assumption that the treatment would succeed. 'After Sir Osbert has been cured of the symptoms of Parkinson's Disease in New York,' Magro told Lady Aberconway, 'we might visit London, and you some time afterwards.'[57]

Frank Magro wrote these exuberant prognostications on 19 April 1969. Only a week or so before, Christabel Aberconway and Reresby and Penelope Sitwell had been staying at Montegufoni. Reresby was struck by how well his uncle appeared to be, 'his voice seemed much stronger, his memory more reliable, his look in the eye brighter, his wit as sharp as ever and even his awful "wobble" less distressing'.[58] All went well till the end of the month and then an infection of the bladder brought on a recurrence of the prostate trouble. On Friday, 2 May, Magro went to the sick man's bedroom with the day's correspondence to be told by the Italian nurse that Osbert had suffered a heart attack. By the time the doctor arrived he had sunk into a coma, and it seemed unlikely that he would regain consciousness.

When speaking of the death of the Greek poet Demetrios Capetanakis,

Osbert had remarked that he had seen a great many people die and he believed that all they wanted, when the moment came, was 'not to be surrounded. No human contact can appear to them real, and it is only an added cruelty.'[59] No such dispensation was to be granted to him. Hugo Southern, his lawyer, happened to be already there; Reresby arrived late at night on the Friday; Sachie, Georgia and Francis appeared the next day. Frank Magro suggested to Reresby that the Anglican vicar should be summoned from Florence. Reresby asked his father what he felt; 'Well, if it's going to make anyone happy, I don't mind,' said Sachie unenthusiastically. The vicar had once been a chaplain to the Queen, which entitled him to wear a purple cassock, making him look very like a Roman Catholic cardinal. Encouraged by this, Magro, himself a Roman Catholic though at that time hardly practising, joined him in reciting the Lord's Prayer and the Creed. During the prayers he noticed two large tears rolling down Osbert's cheeks. 'Sir Osbert was not totally devoid of religious feeling,' Magro recorded, 'and therefore those two tears could have been due to repentance, or to a full appreciation of his extreme condition.' Other possibilities occur to one. Osbert was never to have the chance to explain; at 7.15 that evening he died without recovering consciousness.

Frank Magro dressed the body in a dinner jacket and carefully tied the bow tie. Throughout Monday and Tuesday morning Osbert lay in the hall of the castle, attended by workers from the estate. Magro had been reading *Before the Bombardment* to him in the days before his last illness; he placed it in the coffin, from which it was removed before cremation and deposited later in the marble urn with his ashes. His final home was the Allori Protestant cemetery on the outskirts of Florence. Harold Acton was among the mourners at the funeral. No one could have wished Osbert a longer life, he reflected, but he would still miss him. The last few years had been painful 'but I believe he still had moments of enjoyment'.[60]

In 'Grand Finale', the climax to *England Reclaimed*, Osbert wrote:

> If I must leave the faces that I love,
> Let it be when every dove
>   Is crooning, swinging in the soft June trees,
> And roses rise on every breeze:
>   Thus would I love the faces that I leave
>   And need not so much grieve.

He had died a month too early, and it was wisteria that rose on every breeze; but more than that, where were the faces that he loved? Osbert had only fully loved three people in his life: Edith was dead; Sachie was resentful and grown apart; from David Horner, for whom he had felt the most intensely, he had long been bitterly estranged. He had grown very fond of his nephew, Reresby, but nobody could replace his former intimates. Frank Magro mourned him whole-heartedly, but in the lives of all his other friends and relations it cannot be said that he left a serious gap. He had always been semi-detached, a man apart; in death he had merely become by one step more remote.

'By their fruits shall ye know them.' Osbert would have said that he did not expect to live on as an object of love or even affection; it was his books that would survive. So what is left? Some competent verse, yet with hardly a single line striking enough to linger obstinately in the mind. A handful of good short stories. Some fine and colourful travel-writing. One unequivocal masterpiece, his autobiography, a triumphant evocation of an age and a gallery of grotesques on a heroic scale. This, surely, should still be read in a hundred years, if books, in one form or another, are still to be found by then. And yet will there be many sufficiently interested in this remote and esoteric corner of society to ensure that *Left Hand, Right Hand!* is still taken from the shelves or reproduced in whatever modish style the literary-minded of the year 2098 may find convenient?

Is Osbert Sitwell therefore worth a book? It is a question all biographers must sometimes ask themselves, and often over the past few years I have wondered if I were writing only for my own entertainment and for a handful of kindred spirits who are happy to grub around among such disregarded fossils. The question did not worry me much – the entertainment was so great, the *dramatis personae* so bizarre, the background so rich, that I would happily have carried on even if I had known that only the smallest possible chorus of indolent reviewers would cursorily scan my work. Yet at the end, I am satisfied that Osbert *is* worth a book; not so much for what he did as for what he was. Osbert was an odd man out in many worlds: an aesthete among philistines, an aristocrat among bohemians, an Englishman among Italians. In all he played an active and conspicuous role: it was possible to dislike Osbert Sitwell, to mock him, even to despise him, but it was very difficult to ignore him.

In the 1920s the Sitwells were an inspiration for the younger generation: brilliant, provocative, inventive. Today it is easy to see that they were not Pounds, Eliots or Joyces, innovators of seminal importance, but to Evelyn Waugh or Cyril Connolly they seemed the acme of modernity, a challenge to the established values and an inspiration to all who wished to blaze a new artistic trail. In the years after the Second World War, Osbert and Edith in particular achieved a renaissance; acclaimed as the Grand Old Man and Woman of contemporary letters, still rebarbative, still claiming the cultural high ground as their rightful territory, but now bathed in the twilight refulgence reserved for relics of an earlier age. Even between these two golden periods they were never forgotten and could not safely be dismissed as inconsiderable. For forty years, mutually and individually, they were an important presence on the literary scene. Whether Osbert Sitwell can be called a major writer is a matter of definition; it can hardly be denied, though, that twentieth-century English letters would have looked very different if he had not existed.

Source Notes

Abbreviations used in notes

CA	Christabel Aberconway
DH	David Horner
ES	Edith Sitwell
FM	Frank Magro
GM	*Great Morning*
GS	George Sitwell
Georgia S	Georgia Sitwell
HD	Hilda Doolittle (Aldington)
HRCA	Harry Ransom Humanities Research Center, Austin, Texas
HRO	Hertfordshire Record Office
IS	Ida Sitwell
JPN	John Pearson Notes
LA	Lorna Andrade
LHRH	*Left Hand, Right Hand!*
LITNR	*Laughter in the Next Room*
NE	*Noble Essences*
OS	Osbert Sitwell
QMAO	*Queen Mary and Others*
RW	*Rat Week*
SHSL	*Sing High! Sing Low!*
SS	Sacheverell Sitwell
TFC	*The Four Continents*
TMFTM	*Tales My Father Taught Me*
TST	*The Scarlet Tree*

For the location of manuscript sources cited in these notes, see the Bibliographical Notes on pp. 438–40.

1: The Eye of Childhood

1 *The Diaries of Evelyn Waugh*. ed. Michael Davie. London, 1976. p. 784.
2 *The Letters of Evelyn Waugh*. ed. Mark Amory. London, 1980. p. 274.
3 John Pearson. *Façades*. London, 1978. p. 19. (All references are to Fontana paperback edition of 1980.)

4 Anthony Powell. *Messengers of Day*. London, 1978. pp. 160–1; Interview with Anthony Powell.
5 John Pearson Notes (henceforth JPN). Sitwell Collection VI, Box 3. Tulsa, Oklahoma.
6 JPN.
7 Alan Pryce-Jones. *The Bonus of Laughter*. London, 1987. p. 64.
8 JPN.
9 Sir George Sitwell. *On the Making of Gardens*. London, 1951. pp. 6–7.
10 Preface to Osbert Sitwell's *Queen Mary and Others* (henceforth QMAO). London, 1974. p. 10; Peter Quennell. *Daily Mail*. 31 March 1945.
11 Osbert Sitwell. *Left Hand, Right Hand!* (henceforth *LHRH*). London, 1945. p. 184.
12 *LHRH*. pp. 100–1.
13 Beverley Nichols. *The Sweet and Twenties*. London, 1958. p. 49.
14 Powell. *Messengers of Day*. p. 165.
15 *LHRH*. p. 26.
16 JPN.
17 George Sitwell (henceforth GS) to Osbert Sitwell (henceforth OS). 29/10/39. Renishaw papers. Box 502.
18 Edith Sitwell (henceforth ES). *Taken Care Of*. London, 1965. p. 20.
19 Constance Sitwell. *Bright Morning*. London, 1942. pp. 56–7.
20 Interview with Anthony Powell.
21 *LHRH*. p. 4.
22 Osbert Sitwell. *England Reclaimed*. London, 1927. p. 7.
23 ES to Spender. 6/1/44. Berg Collection.
24 Victoria Glendinning. *Edith Sitwell*. London, 1981. p. 9.
25 *LHRH*. p. 90.
26 Glendinning. *Edith Sitwell*. p. 5.
27 *LHRH*. p. 164.
28 ES to Spender. 6/1/44. Berg Collection.
29 Sacheverell Sitwell (henceforth SS). *All Summer in a Day*. London, 1926. pp. 19–20.
30 Osbert Sitwell. *The Scarlet Tree* (henceforth TST). London, 1946. p. 22.
31 *LHRH*. p. 114.
32 Osbert Sitwell. *Great Morning* (henceforth GM). London, 1948. p. 9.
33 Sunderland Rollinson. Renishaw papers. Box 567/1.
34 GS to Georgia Sitwell (henceforth Georgia S). 4/4/36. Harry Ransom Humanities Research Center, Austin, Texas (henceforth HRCA). SS papers. Box 25.
35 *TST*. p. 19.
36 18/7/42. Renishaw papers. Box 502.
37 30/10/19. HRCA. Sitwell papers. Misc.
38 Peter Quennell. *The Marble Foot*. London, 1976. p. 131.
39 *Edith Sitwell. Selected Letters*. ed. John Lehmann and Derek Parker. London, 1970. p. 221.
40 11/1/38. HRCA. OS papers. Recip; cf. *LHRH*. p. 93.
41 Renishaw papers. Box 577/9.
42 Margaret Barton and Osbert Sitwell. *Sober Truth*. London, 1930. p. 14.
43 *LHRH*. p. 104.
44 30/9/40. Sitwell Collection. University of Boston. 1/5.
45 JPN.
46 Nichols. *The Sweet and Twenties*. p. 49.
47 *Wrack at Tidesend*. London, 1952. p. 88.
48 *TST*. p. 85.
49 Constance Sitwell. *Frolic Youth*. London, 1964. pp. 55–6.

50 OS to Lady Desborough. 6/5/43. Lady Desborough papers. Hertfordshire Record Office (henceforth HRO) ref. D/ERVC 2407/19.
51 *LHRH*. p. 167.
52 *LHRH*. p. 159.
53 GS to Georgia S. 21/5/39. HRCA. SS papers. Box 25.
54 *LHRH*. p. 219.
55 *LHRH*. p. 161.

2: Educated in the Holidays from Eton

1 OS to Lady Desborough. 10/1/38. Desborough papers. HRO ref. D/ERVC 2407/6.
2 Elizabeth Salter. *The Last Years of a Rebel*. London, 1967. p. 15.
3 *GM*. p. 115.
4 *GM*. p. 37.
5 *TST*. p. 119.
6 *LHRH*. p. 241.
7 *TST*. p. 121.
8 Preface to *QMAO*. p. 14.
9 Osbert Sitwell. *Penny Foolish*. London, 1935. p. 187.
10 GS to OS. 3/2/03. Renishaw papers. Box 501.
11 GS to OS. 3/2/03. Renishaw papers. Box 501.
12 *TST*. p. 69.
13 *TST*. p. 162.
14 Sarah Bradford. *Sacheverell Sitwell*. London, 1993. p. 41.
15 'Mulberry or Morus'. From SS's *An Indian Summer*. London, 1982.
16 SS to OS. 23/1/08 and 16/9/08. Renishaw papers. Box 501.
17 OS to GS. Undated. Renishaw papers. Box 508/5.
18 OS to GS and Ida Sitwell (henceforth IS). 23/1/03, 25/1/03, 9/7/05. Renishaw papers. Box 508; and HRCA. OS papers. Letters to IS.
19 OS to IS. 23/1/03. HRCA. OS papers.
20 OS to IS. 25/1/03. HRCA. OS papers.
21 30/3/04. Renishaw papers. Box 501.
22 22/2/03, 1/3/03, 8/11/03. HRCA. OS papers.
23 John Hoare to OS. 14/8/50. Renishaw papers. Box 571/2.
24 *TST*. p. 226.
25 W. D. Joyce to GS. June 1905. Renishaw papers. Box 501.
26 Report of December 1905. Renishaw papers. Box 508/5.
27 Osbert Sitwell. *Dumb Animal*. London, 1930. p. 234.
28 *TST*. p. 257.
29 *Penny Foolish*. p. 12.
30 Osbert Sitwell. *Sing High! Sing Low!* (henceforth *SHSL*). London, 1944. p. 26.
31 *Dumb Animal*. p. 129.
32 John Langdon–Davies to OS. 3/3/64. Renishaw papers. Box 572/2.
33 *The Lyttelton–Hart-Davis Letters*. ed. Rupert Hart-Davis. Vol. 1. London, 1978. p. 170.
34 27/3/07. Renishaw papers. Box 508/4.
35 *TST*. p. 267.
36 Renishaw papers. Box 501.
37 David Horner papers. Eton College Library.
38 Answers to questionnaire. Frank Megroz mss. University of Reading.
39 *TST*. p. 269.
40 Answers to questionnaire. Frank Megroz mss.

41 Undated. Renishaw papers. Box 508/5.
42 Constance Sitwell. *Frolic Youth*. pp. 19–23.
43 Constance Sitwell. *Frolic Youth*. p. 56.
44 26/8/39. Macmillan papers. Sitwell, uncatalogued. British Library.
45 OS to William Plomer. 13/3/44. Plomer mss. Durham University Library. 306/9.
46 Constance Sitwell. *Bounteous Days*. London, 1976. p. 33.
47 *TST*. p. 86.
48 30/3/41. Aberconway papers. Add mss 70834. f. 164.
49 *TST*. p. 295.
50 27/3/07. Renishaw papers. Box 508/4.
51 *TST*. p. 228.
52 SS to OS. 24/4/65. Renishaw papers. Box 504.
53 GS to Lady Sitwell. 30/4/08. Renishaw papers. Box 508/6.
54 GS to OS. 1/5/01. Renishaw papers. Box 501.
55 IS to OS. 14/4/09 and 23/1/08. Renishaw papers. Box 501.
56 IS to OS. 13/5/08. Renishaw papers. Box 501.
57 IS to OS. 29/5/08. Renishaw papers. Box 501.
58 IS to OS. 10/6/09. Renishaw papers. Box 501.
59 IS to OS. 28/10/08. Renishaw papers. Box 501.

3: The Great Free World

1 OS to Bryher. 1/11/40. Bryher papers. Beinecke Library, Yale.
2 *GM*. p. 55.
3 *Dumb Animal*. pp. 227–349.
4 OS to GS. 29/9/09. Renishaw papers. Box 508/5.
5 OS to GS. 29/9/09. Renishaw papers. Box 508/5.
6 *Dumb Animal*. pp. 270–1.
7 *GM*. p. 41.
8 JPN.
9 *LHRH*. p. x.
10 *Two Generations*. With a Preface and edited by Osbert Sitwell. London, 1940. p. vii; though cf. Roger Fulford. *Osbert Sitwell*. Supplement to *British Book News*. London, 1951. p. 8.
11 GS to OS. 6/10/09. Renishaw papers. Box 501.
12 *Dumb Animal*. p. 289.
13 Nevill Meakin to Lady Sitwell. 10/11/09[?]. Renishaw papers. Box 501.
14 *GM*. p. 115.
15 OS to GS. 14/9/09. Renishaw papers. Box 508/5.
16 OS to GS. Undated. Renishaw papers. Box 508/4.
17 OS to GS. Undated. Renishaw papers. Box 508/4.
18 *Dumb Animal*. p. 254.
19 David Horner papers; *GM*. p. 34.
20 Miss E. Lloyd to OS. 9/3/11. Renishaw papers. Box 501.
21 Blanche Sitwell to OS. 31/10/11. Renishaw papers. Box 501.
22 Interview with Mrs Myfanwy Piper.
23 Miss E. Lloyd to OS. 29/10/10. Renishaw papers. Box 501.
24 *GM*. p. 92.
25 *GM*. pp. 121–2.
26 *Dumb Animal*. p. 334.
27 Paul Fussell. *The Great War and Modern Memory*. London, 1975. p. 157.
28 Louis Spears to OS. 7/5/48; OS to Spears. Undated. Renishaw papers. Box 501.

29 *GM.* pp. 11–13; cf. Nigel Nicolson. *Alex.* London, 1973. pp. 24–5.
30 OS to IS. 21/9/13. Renishaw papers. Box 508/7.
31 Interview with Anthony Powell.
32 JPN.
33 ES to Georgia S. Undated. HRCA. SS papers. Box 24.
34 *The Denton Welch Journals.* ed. Jocelyn Brooke. London, 1952. p. 64.
35 Beverley Nichols. *The Unforgiving Minute.* London, 1978. pp. 50–1; *The Diary of Virginia Woolf.* ed. Anne Olivier Bell. Vol. 4. London, 1982. p. 225.
36 Osbert Sitwell. *The People's Album of London Statues.* London, 1928. p. 116.
37 Duncan Fallowell. *To Noto.* London, 1989. p. 110.
38 Diana Cooper. *The Rainbow Comes and Goes.* London, 1959. p. 140.
39 JPN.
40 Frank Megroz mss.
41 *LHRH.* p. xii; *TST.* p. 14.
42 *GM.* p. 141.
43 Foreword to James Agate's *Here's Richness.* London, 1942. p. 8.
44 *LHRH.* p. 185.
45 Frank Megroz mss.
46 SS to OS. 5/3/11. Renishaw papers. Box 501.
47 Pearson. *Façades.* p. 77.
48 Interview with Frank Magro (henceforth FM).
49 Gordon Bottomley to OS. 1945. Renishaw papers. Box 503.
50 GS to OS. 26/11/09. Renishaw papers. Box 532/1.
51 *GM.* p. 76.
52 Constance Sitwell. *Bounteous Days.* p. 40; JPN.
53 OS to GS. 17/11/38. Renishaw papers. Box 567/1.
54 OS to Christabel Aberconway (henceforth CA). 20/2/52. Aberconway papers. Add mss 70836.
55 ES to SS. November 1910. cit. Bradford. *Sacheverell Sitwell.* p. 42.
56 ES to OS. 8/10[?]/10. Renishaw papers. Box 501.
57 Bradford. *Sacheverell Sitwell.* p. 50.
58 GS to OS. 25/7/19. Renishaw papers. Box 501.
59 GS to OS. 6/10/09. Renishaw papers. Box 501.
60 GS to OS. 6/3/13. HRCA. OS papers. Recip.
61 GS to OS. 6/3/13. HRCA. OS papers. Recip.
62 GS to OS. 6/3/13. HRCA. OS papers. Recip.
63 GS to OS. 15/3/13. HRCA. OS papers. Recip.
64 *GM.* p. 278.
65 IS to OS. 13/2/11. Renishaw papers. Box 501.
66 SS to OS. Jan. 1911[?]. Renishaw papers. Box 501.
67 OS to IS. Undated. Renishaw papers. Box 501.
68 Pearson. *Façades.* p. 65. Pearson provides the most lucid and convincing exposition of the Lady Ida scandal.
69 JPN.
70 Lord Grimthorpe to GS. 15/11/13. Renishaw papers. Box 508/7.
71 GS to OS. 9/11/12. Renishaw papers. Box 501.
72 Lady Londesborough to GS. Undated. Renishaw papers. Box 508/7.
73 IS to OS. 1/11/13. Renishaw papers. Box 508/7.
74 SS to OS. 28/12/13. HRCA. OS papers. Recip.
75 Report by Dr James. 14/11/13. Renishaw papers. Box 508/7.
76 IS to GS. 10/12/13. Renishaw papers. Box 508/7.
77 GS to OS. 17/12/13. Renishaw papers. Box 501.

4: Splendid Soldier Strife

1 Renishaw papers. Box 508/7.
2 From 'Peace'. *Collected Poems of Rupert Brooke*. London, 1931. p. 144.
3 OS to GS. 5/8/14. Renishaw papers. Box 508/7.
4 Osbert Sitwell. *Tales My Father Taught Me* (henceforth *TMFTM*). London, 1962. pp. 54–5.
5 *GM*. p. 187.
6 Osbert Sitwell. *Laughter in the Next Room* (henceforth *LITNR*). London, 1949. pp. 76–8.
7 Renishaw papers. Box 508/4.
8 Alistair Horne. *Macmillan 1894–1956*. London, 1988. p. 31.
9 Bradford. *Sacheverell Sitwell*. p. 59; IS to OS. Undated. HRCA. OS papers. Recip.
10 *LITNR*. p. 87; *TMFTM*. p. 101.
11 GS to OS. 5/8/14, 26/8/14, 8/1/15. Renishaw papers. Box 501.
12 Rt Hon. Sir Frederick Ponsonby. *The Grenadier Guards in the Great War of 1914–1918*. Vols. 1–3. London, 1920.
13 *Atlantic Monthly*. February 1948.
14 OS to GS. Undated. Renishaw papers. Box 508/7.
15 OS to GS. 28/12/14. Renishaw papers. Box 508/6.
16 OS to Mme Guéritte. 1/1/42. Renishaw papers. Box 550.
17 *LITNR*. p. 84.
18 'Hymn to Moloch'. From Osbert Sitwell's *Collected Satires and Poems*. London, 1931. p. 26.
19 *LITNR*. p. 85.
20 GS to OS. Undated. Renishaw papers. Box 501.
21 JPN.
22 Interview with Frank Magro.
23 Renishaw papers. Box 548/1.
24 JPN. Interview with David Horner (henceforth DH).

5: We Are Poets and Shall Tell the Truth

1 cit. Richard Davenport-Hines. *Auden*. London, 1995. p. 3.
2 Osbert Sitwell. *Triple Fugue*. London, 1924. p. 184.
3 Thomas Hardy. *The Dynasts*. Part Third, Act V, Scene v.
4 *Sunday Referee*. 25/3/34.
5 Osbert Sitwell. *Those Were the Days*. London, 1938. p. 398.
6 *Penny Foolish*. p. 88.
7 cit. Fussell. *Great War and Modern Memory*. p. 99.
8 *GM*. p. 298.
9 *LHRH*. p. 179.
10 *LITNR*. p. 118.
11 *GM*. p. 135.
12 JPN.
13 JPN.
14 Nichols. *The Unforgiving Minute*. p. 52.
15 *Collected Satires and Poems*. p. 23. First published in the *Nation*. 2/2/18.
16 *LITNR*. p. 116.
17 *Collected Satires and Poems*. pp. 9–10. First published in *The Times*. 11/5/16.
18 Draft letter to the *Bookseller*, covering contribution to 'My First Poem' series. Renishaw papers.

19 Frank Megroz mss.
20 *Collected Satires and Poems.* pp. 14–17. First published in the *Nation*. 27/7/17.
21 Among the many studies of poetry of this period I would particularly commend Robert H. Ross's *The Georgian Revolt*. London, 1967; cf. Alan Pryce-Jones. *Georgian Poets*. London, 1959; and the invaluable *Georgian Poetry 1911–1922*. ed. Timothy Rogers, in the Critical Heritage Series. London, 1977.
22 ed. Edward Marsh. London, 1912.
23 *England Reclaimed*. p. 34.
24 Alfred Noyes. *Collected Poems*. London, 1950. p. 367.
25 Osbert Sitwell. *Miracle on Sinai*. London, 1933. p. 91.
26 T. S. Eliot. 'Verse, Pleasant and Unpleasant'. *The Egoist*. March 1918. pp. 43–4.
27 Frank Megroz mss.
28 HD [Hilda Doolittle (Aldington)] papers. Beinecke Library, Yale.
29 *Times Literary Supplement*. 4/1/17; *The Egoist*. March 1918. p. 44.
30 21/6/17. *Ottoline at Garsington*. ed. Robert Gathorne-Hardy. London, 1974. p. 207.
31 3/8/17. *Letters of Aldous Huxley*. ed. Grover Smith. London, 1969. p. 132.
32 Evan Charteris. *The Life and Letters of Sir Edmund Gosse*. London, 1951. p. 434.
33 Osbert Sitwell and Edith Sitwell. *Twentieth Century Harlequinade*. Oxford, 1916; Osbert Sitwell. *The Winstonburg Line*. London, 1919.
34 *Daily Herald*. 22/7/19, 28/7/19 and the *Nation*. 5/7/19.
35 *Daily News*. 19/11/19.
36 Chatto & Windus mss. University of Reading.
37 'Cornucopia'. From *Argonaut and Juggernaut*. Book 1. London, 1919.
38 Aldington to OS. 24/11/19. Sitwell Collection. University of Boston. 1/5; *Globe*. 30/10/19.
39 *Athenaeum*. 28/11/19; *Daily News*. 19/11/19; Blunden to OS. Sitwell Collection. University of Boston. 1/5.
40 *The Times*. 27/11/19.
41 *London Mercury*. Vol. 1, No. 2. December 1919.
42 *The Letters of Virginia Woolf*. Vol. 4. ed. Nigel Nicolson. London, 1978. p. 307.
43 Harold Monro. *Some Contemporary Poets*. London, 1920. p. 137; cf. Joy Grant. *Harold Monro and the Poetry Bookshop*. London, 1967.
44 JPN.
45 Lady Cynthia Asquith. *Diaries*. London, 1968. p. 421.
46 Ann Thwaite. *Edmund Gosse*. London, 1984. pp. 471–2.
47 *The Letters of T. S. Eliot*. ed. Valerie Eliot. Vol. 1. London, 1988. p. 221.
48 *Letters of T. S. Eliot*. Vol. 1. p. 240.
49 Sassoon to OS. 3/7/17. HRCA. OS papers. Recip.
50 Sassoon to OS. 3/7/17. HRCA. OS papers. Recip.
51 Osbert Sitwell. *Noble Essences* (henceforth *NE*). London, 1950. p. 104.
52 Siegfried Sassoon. *Siegfried's Journey*. London, 1946. p. 71.
53 *Wilfred Owen. Collected Letters*. ed. Harold Owen and John Bell. London, 1967. p. 562.
54 OS to Mrs Owen. Undated. English Faculty, Oxford. OEF 532.
55 OS to Mrs Owen. Undated. English Faculty, Oxford. OEF 534.
56 *NE*. p. 109.
57 Interview with Anthony Powell.
58 *Letters of Aldous Huxley*. p. 141.
59 Thwaite. *Gosse*. p. 472.
60 *Letters of T. S. Eliot*. p. 206.
61 *Letters of Aldous Huxley*. p. 141.
62 Cynthia Asquith. *Diaries*. p. 379.

63 OS to Maynard Hollingworth. 25/3/17. Renishaw papers. Box 335/1.
64 Nina Hamnett. *Laughing Torso*. London, 1932. p. 104.
65 Colonel Repington. *The First World War*. Vol. 1. London, 1920. p. 314.
66 Bradford. *Sacheverell Sitwell*. pp. 57 and 73.
67 IS to Maynard Hollingworth. 5/4/17. Renishaw papers. Box 335/1.
68 Maynard Hollingworth to IS. 11/4/17. Renishaw papers. Box 335/1.
69 OS to Maynard Hollingworth. Undated. Renishaw papers. Box 335/1.
70 Maynard Hollingworth to OS. 21/12/17. Renishaw papers. Box 335/1.
71 *The Journals of Arnold Bennett*. Vol. 2. 1911–1921. ed. Newman Flower. London, 1932. p. 251.
72 Sassoon. *Siegfried's Journey*. p. 163.
73 *A Free House or The Artist as Craftsman. Being the Writings of Walter Richard Sickert*. ed. Osbert Sitwell. London, 1947. p. xxi.
74 Nichols. *The Unforgiving Minute*. pp. 50–1.
75 Cynthia Asquith. *Diaries*. p. 267.
76 *A Durable Fire. The Letters of Duff and Diana Cooper*. ed. Artemis Cooper. London, 1983. p. 99; Diana Cooper. *The Rainbow Comes and Goes*. p. 195.
77 *A Durable Fire*. p. 92.
78 Cynthia Asquith. *Diaries*. p. 278; David Garnett. *The Flowers of the Forest*. London, 1955. p. 185.
79 *Ottoline at Garsington*. p. 209.
80 C. R. W. Nevinson. *Paint and Prejudice*. London, 1937. p. 88.
81 Ellen Moers. *The Dandy*. London, 1962. p. 13; cf. Martin Green. *Children of the Sun*. London, 1977. pp. 23–31.
82 *LITNR*. p. 17.
83 *Carrington. Letters and Extracts from her Diaries*. ed. David Garnett. London, 1970. p. 113.
84 *The Diary of Virginia Woolf*. ed. Anne Olivier Bell. Vol. 3. London, 1980. pp. 24–5.
85 Garnett. *Flowers of the Forest*. p. 141.

6: The Delightful but Deleterious Trio

1 ES to Rache Lovat Dickson. 14/7/49. *Edith Sitwell. Selected Letters*. p. 168.
2 *NE*. p. 41.
3 *LITNR*. p. 61; ES to Robert Nichols. March 1919. *Edith Sitwell. Selected Letters*. p. 15.
4 *Sunday Times*. 7/12/52.
5 Powell. *Messengers of Day*. p. 35.
6 Sylvia Gosse to OS. 17/10/50. David Horner mss.
7 Wyndham Lewis to OS. 10/3/22. Sitwell Collection. University of Boston. 1/5.
8 *The Adelphi*. August 1923.
9 OS to Lincoln Kirstein. Lincoln Kirstein Collection. Library for the Performing Arts. Lincoln Center, New York.
10 *Letters of T. S. Eliot*. p. 358.
11 John Gross. *The Rise and Fall of the Man of Letters*. London, 1969. pp. 240–1; Patrick Howarth. *Squire. 'Most Generous of Men'*. London, 1963.
12 *Who Killed Cock-Robin? Remarks on poetry, on its criticism, and, as a sad warning, the story of Eunuch Arden*. London, 1921.
13 Geoffrey Grigson. *The Crest on the Silver*. London, 1950. p. 115.
14 Chatto & Windus mss. 5/9/21.
15 OS to Edward Thompson. 23/2/29. Bodleian Library, Oxford. MS Eng c 5315. f. 17.
16 *Letters of Leonard Woolf*. ed. Frederic Spotts. London, 1990. p. 561.

17 David Higham. *Literary Gent*. London, 1978. p. 218.
18 W. J. Turner. *Smaragda's Lover – a Dramatic Phantasmagoria*. London, 1924.
19 OS to Grant Richards. 26/12/24 and 14/1/25. HRCA. OS papers. Letters to Grant Richards.
20 Sassoon. *Siegfried's Journey*. p. 160.
21 *Siegfried Sassoon Diaries 1920–1922*. ed. Rupert Hart-Davis. London, 1981. pp. 254–5.
22 *Sassoon Diaries 1920–1922*. pp. 90–103.
23 *Sassoon Diaries 1920–1922*. p. 155.
24 *Sassoon Diaries 1920–1922*. p. 110.
25 *The Journals of Arnold Bennett*. Vol. 3. *1921–1928*. ed. Newman Flower. London, 1933. p. 59.
26 *Siegfried Sassoon Diaries 1923–1925*. ed. Rupert Hart-Davis. London, 1985. p. 253.
27 *Sunday Times*. 7/12/52.
28 JPN.
29 *Vita and Harold. The Letters of Vita Sackville-West and Harold Nicolson*. ed. Nigel Nicolson. London, 1992. p. 151.
30 *LITNR*. p. 182.
31 Noël Coward. *Present Indicative*. London, 1937. p. 197.
32 OS to SS. 26/11/26. Renishaw papers. Box 21.
33 Cole Leslie. *Noël Coward*. London, 1976. p. 104.
34 Michael Kennedy. *Portrait of Walton*. Oxford, 1989. p. 30.
35 Susana Walton. *William Walton. Behind the Façade*. Oxford, 1988. p. 61.
36 *Sacheverell Sitwell. A Symposium*. ed. Derek Parker. London, 1975. pp. 1–3.
37 *Sacheverell Sitwell. A Symposium*. p. 66.
38 Renishaw papers. Undated. Box 335/6.
39 OS to Georgia S. Undated. HRCA. SS papers. Box 25.
40 OS to SS. 1/10/25. Renishaw papers. Box 21.
41 4/9/25. Aberconway papers. Add mss 70837. A.1.
42 17/8/25. HRCA. OS papers.
43 OS to Georgia S. 2/8/25. HRCA. SS papers. Box 26.
44 OS to SS. 1/10/25. Renishaw papers. Box 21.
45 *LHRH*. p. 95.
46 JPN.
47 Letters from Lady Mosley of 11/2/97 and 13/3/97.
48 Green. *Children of the Sun*. pp. 65 and 71.
49 *Sassoon Diaries 1920–1922*. p. 75.
50 GS to OS. 22/6/19. Renishaw papers. Box 501.
51 *GM*. p. 36.
52 Mrs Powell to Maynard Hollingworth. April 1921. Renishaw papers. Box 335/1.
53 GS to OS. 14/7/20. Renishaw papers. Box 501.
54 Aberconway papers. Add mss 70831.
55 OS to Ronald Firbank. 20/3/19. Sitwell Collection. University of Iowa.
56 Maynard Hollingworth to OS. 5/1/22. Renishaw papers. Box 335/3.
57 OS to Arnold Bennett. Undated. Arnold Bennett papers. Beinecke Library, Yale.
58 Wyndham Lewis to Violet Schiff. 30/8/22. Schiff papers. Add mss 52922. f. 30.
59 OS to CA. Aberconway papers. Add mss 70831. f. 7.
60 *Sassoon Diaries 1920–1922*. pp. 75–8.
61 OS to Mme Guéritte. 20/11/46. Renishaw papers. Box 550.
62 Pearson. *Façades*. p. 154.
63 Susana Walton. *Walton*. p. 47.
64 *LITNR*. p. 57.

65 *Letters of Arnold Bennett.* Vol. 3. ed. James Hepburn. London, 1970. p. 121.
66 Powell. *Messengers of Day.* p. 41.
67 Philip Hoare. *Serious Pleasures. The Life of Stephen Tennant.* London, 1990. p. 96.
68 *Letters of Virginia Woolf.* Vol. 4. p. 108.
69 Michael Holroyd. *Lytton Strachey.* Vol. 2. London, 1968. p. 440.
70 Holroyd. *Strachey.* Vol. 2. p. 559.
71 OS to Lytton Strachey. Undated. Strachey papers. Add mss 60699. f. 15.
72 David Garnett. *The Familiar Faces.* London, 1962. pp. 22–4.
73 Peter Quennell. *The Sign of the Fish.* London, 1960. p. 31.
74 Christabel Aberconway. *A Wise Woman?* London, 1966. p. 81.
75 Interview with Lady Violet Powell.
76 OS to Lady Desborough. 24/4/38. HRO ref. D/ERVC 2407/11.
77 OS to CA. 8/5/35. Add mss 70833. f. 128.
78 Osbert Sitwell. *Rat Week* (Henceforth *RW*). London, 1986. p. 61.
79 JPN.
80 Violet Wyndham. *The Sphinx and Her Circle.* London, 1963. p. 84; Julie Speedie. *Wonderful Sphinx.* London, 1993. pp. 240–4.
81 Quennell. *Marble Foot.* p. 132.
82 Speedie. *Wonderful Sphinx.* pp. 249 and 259.
83 *LITNR.* p. 52.
84 *RW.* p. 33.
85 Renishaw papers. Box 335/1 and 3; Robert Graves. *Goodbye to All That.* Revised edition. London, 1959. p. 274.
86 *Observer.* 11/2/62.
87 Kennedy. *Walton.* p. 44.
88 JPN.
89 Hoare. *Stephen Tennant.* p. 61.
90 Andrew Motion. *The Lamberts.* London, 1986. p. 138.
91 JPN.
92 Susana Walton. *Walton.* p. 67.
93 OS to T. S. Eliot. 10/12/23. T. S. Eliot papers.
94 Quennell. *Marble Foot.* p. 142.
95 ES to Richard Aldington. 26/11/22. Berg Collection.
96 *LITNR.* pp. 137–8.
97 *Sassoon Diaries 1920–1922.* p. 275.
98 OS to CA. 10/1/25. Add mss 70831. f. 81.
99 OS to Alida Monro. 14/12/24 and 10/1/25. Alida Monro papers. Add mss 57752. ff. 10 and 11.
100 OS to Maynard Hollingworth. 12/1/25. Renishaw papers. Box 335/6.
101 ES to Sydney Schiff. Schiff papers. Add mss 52922. f. 20.
102 Holroyd. *Strachey.* Vol. 2. p. 397; *Letters of Aldous Huxley.* pp. 168 and 202.
103 Gino Severini. *The Life of a Painter.* trans. Jennifer Franchina. Princeton, 1996. p. 254.
104 *TST.* p. 50.
105 OS to SS. Undated. HRCA. SS papers. Box 20.
106 David Pryce-Jones. *Cyril Connolly.* London, 1983. p. 74.
107 JPN.
108 Wyndham. *The Sphinx and Her Circle.* p. 92.
109 *LITNR.* p. 5.
110 Osbert Sitwell. *Discursions on Travel, Art and Life.* London, 1925. pp. 217–41. First published in the *Nation.* 1/1/21.
111 Osbert Sitwell. *Before the Bombardment.* London, 1926. p. 153.

112 *Miracle on Sinai.* p. 67.
113 OS to David Horner. 29/8/34. HRCA. OS papers; OS to Mme Guéritte. 24/10/42. Renishaw papers. Box 550.
114 JPN. Interview with Geoffrey Grigson.
115 OS to CA. March 1933. Add mss 70831. f. 17.
116 OS to DH. 19/11/28. HRCA. OS papers.
117 Hollingworth to OS. 20/11/18. Renishaw papers. Box 335/1.
118 Glendinning. *Edith Sitwell.* p. 54.
119 GS to OS. 17/7/19. Renishaw papers. Box 501.
120 OS to Sydney Schiff. 12/10/21. Schiff papers. Add mss 52922. f. 50.
121 GS to OS. 5/9/19. Renishaw papers. Box 501.
122 *Aldous Huxley. A Memorial Volume.* ed. Julian Huxley. London, 1965. p. 33.
123 Constance Sitwell. *Bounteous Days.* p. 20.
124 *LITNR.* p. 68.
125 Hollingworth to OS and OS to Hollingworth. 11 and 23/3/25. Renishaw papers. Box 335/6.

7: Not a Story but a Sketch

1 *LITNR.* p. 148.
2 *Nation.* 16/8/19.
3 *Nation.* 8/9/19; *Everyman.* 30/8/19. p. 489; *LITNR.* p. 158.
4 Bradford. *Sacheverell Sitwell.* p. 135.
5 Osbert Sitwell. 'The Magnasco Society'. *Apollo.* 1963. pp. 378–90.
6 OS to Frank Megroz. 21/7/25. Frank Megroz mss.
7 Borenius to OS. 14/5/29. HRCA. OS papers. Recip.
8 JPN.
9 Cyril Connolly. *Enemies of Promise.* London, 1938. p. 55.
10 Herbert Read. *The Contrary Experience.* London, 1963. pp. 139–41.
11 Bennett to OS. 23/10/18. Arnold Bennett papers.
12 Read. *Contrary Experience.* p. 146.
13 Bennett to OS. 20/1/19. Arnold Bennett papers.
14 Graves to OS. 27/1/19. Sitwell Collection. University of Boston.
15 *Richard Aldington and HD. The Early Years in Letters.* ed. Caroline Zilbourg. Indiana, 1992. p. 185.
16 OS to Firbank. 20/3/19. Sitwell Collection. University of Iowa.
17 Victoria Glendinning. *Vita.* London, 1983. p. 102.
18 Michael De-la-Noy. *Denton Welch.* London, 1984. p. 147.
19 OS to Sydney Schiff. 17/10/19. Schiff papers. Add mss 52922. f. 44.
20 *Letters of T. S. Eliot.* Vol. 1. p. 340.
21 OS to T. S. Eliot. 19/10/19. T. S. Eliot mss.
22 OS to Sydney Schiff. 19/10/19. Schiff papers. Add mss 52922. f. 44.
23 Osbert Sitwell. Unpublished essay on T. S .Eliot. Renishaw papers. Box 533.
24 Eliot to OS. 11/8/30. Renishaw papers. Box 501.
25 *The Tyro.*
26 *Letters of T. S. Eliot.* pp. 358 and 378.
27 OS to Horace Liveright. Undated. HRCA. OS papers. Misc.
28 OS to Sydney Schiff. Late Sept. 1922. Schiff papers. Add mss 52922. f. 51.
29 Lewis to Schiff. Undated. Add mss 52922. f. 35.
30 OS to Grant Richards. 29/8/24. HRCA. OS papers.
31 Osbert Sitwell. *Three-Quarter-length Portrait of Michael Arlen.* London, 1931.
32 Aldous Huxley. *Crome Yellow.* London, 1921.

33 Aldous Huxley. *Mortal Coils*. London, 1922.
34 OS to Mme Guéritte. 24/1/42. Renishaw papers. Box 550.
35 Osbert Sitwell. *Collected Stories*. London, 1953. pp. viii–ix.
36 Osbert Sitwell. *Triple Fugue*. London, 1924, First published in *English Review*. Dec. 1922.
37 *NE*. p. 152; Speedie. *Wonderful Sphinx*. p. 152.
38 *Collected Stories*. p. x.
39 OS to Arnold Bennett. Undated. Arnold Bennett papers.
40 *Collected Stories*. p. ix.
41 JPN.
42 Duchess of York to OS. 14/11/30. Weston papers.
43 OS to Grant Richards. Undated. HRCA. OS papers.
44 OS to Lytton Strachey. 9/7/24. Strachey mss. Add mss 60699. f. 16.
45 OS to CA. 28/2/30. Add mss 70832. f. 12.
46 Miranda Seymour. *Ottoline Morrell*. London, 1992. p. 323.
47 *Sassoon Diaries 1923–1925*. p. 142.
48 *Times Literary Supplement*. 19/6/24.
49 *Collected Stories*. p. ix.
50 *Dumb Animal*. London, 1930.
51 JPN. Interview with Francis Bamford.
52 OS to CA. 22/12/30. Add mss 70832. f. 52.
53 OS to CA. 27/1/31. Add mss 70832. f. 64.
54 OS to DH. 16/2/31. David Horner mss.
55 OS to CA. 17/2/31. Add mss 70832. f. 71.
56 Thomas Balston to OS. 16/2/31. Sitwell Collection. University of Boston.
57 OS to CA. 18/11/25. Add mss 70331. f. 18.
58 OS to Grant Richards. June 1926. HRCA. OS papers.
59 OS to Bryher. 13/4/33. Bryher papers.
60 *The Letters of D. H. Lawrence*. Vol. 6. ed. J. T. and M. Boulton. Cambridge, 1991. p. 68.
61 Interview with Lord Horder.
62 Powell. *Messengers of Day*. p. 37; Interview with Anthony Powell.
63 *SHSL*. p. 98.
64 *Discursions*. p. 28. First published in the *Nation*. 27/5/22 and 3/6/22.
65 Green. *Children of the Sun*. p. 212.
66 OS to Alice Hunt. Undated. Renishaw papers. Box 550.
67 OS to CA. 16/5/27. Add mss 70831. f. 47.
68 John to CA. 13/12/26. Add mss 52526 (Vol. 2). f. 42.
69 OS to Maynard Hollingworth. 7/8/24. Renishaw papers. Box 335/6.
70 Cecil Beaton. *The Wandering Years*. London, 1961. p. 150.
71 Siegfried Sassoon to Henry Festing-Jones. 18/6/27. Add 8484. Cambridge University Library.
72 OS to Grant Richards. 13/4/25. HRCA. OS papers.
73 4/4/27. Frank Megroz mss.
74 Sassoon. *Siegfried's Journey*. p. 171.
75 *Journals of Arnold Bennett*. Vol. 3. 1921–1928. p. 168.
76 *QMAO*. p. 99; JPN; Interview with Glenway Prescott.
77 OS to CA. 16/5/27. Add mss 70831. f. 49.
78 *Daily Express*. 24/2/27.
79 OS to SS. 12/12/26. HRCA. SS papers. Box 21.
80 *Letters of D. H. Lawrence*. Vol. 6. p. 73.
81 25/8/45. Renishaw papers. Box 550.

8: No Love and No Buried Treasure

1 Frank Megroz mss.
2 OS to Rebecca West. 19/1/42. Rebecca West Collection. Series 1. Box 46. Folder 11. Tulsa, Oklahoma.
3 Osbert Sitwell. 'The Modern Novel: Its Cause and Cure'. In Osbert Sitwell, Edith Sitwell and Sacheverell Sitwell. *Trio. Some Aspects of National Genius*. London, 1938. p. 56.
4 *Trio*. p. 54.
5 OS to Howard Moss. 19/11/63. Berg Collection.
6 *Trio*. pp. 92–3.
7 *Daily Sketch*. 12/10/26.
8 Powell. *Messengers of Day*. p. 164.
9 *QMAO*. p. 78.
10 *Diary of Virginia Woolf*. Vol. 3. p. 114; *Journals of Arnold Bennett*. Vol. 3. p. 162.
11 Renishaw papers. Box 501.
12 *Daily Express*. 27/5/44; *Bookman*. Christmas 1926.
13 A collection of reviews figured in an appendix to *Dumb Animal*.
14 Berg Collection.
15 D. H. Lawrence. *Lady Chatterley's Lover*. Italian edition of 1928. p. 15.
16 OS to Alice Hunt. 20/4/49. Renishaw papers. Box 567/5.
17 *The Letters of D. H. Lawrence*. Vol. 5. ed. J. T. Boulton and L. Vasey. Cambridge, 1989. pp. 468–74.
18 ES. *Taken Care Of*. p. 107.
19 *Letters of D. H. Lawrence*. Vol. 6. pp. 65–7.
20 Pearson. *Façades*. pp. 227–32.
21 Geoffrey Elborn. *Edith Sitwell. A Biography*. London, 1981. p. 254.
22 ES. *Taken Care Of*. p. 109.
23 *Letters of D. H. Lawrence*. Vol. 6. p. 579.
24 OS to SS. Undated. Sitwell Collection. University of Boston.
25 OS to Hollingworth. 26/9/33. Renishaw papers. Box 302; Edward Nehls to OS. 23/5/57. Renishaw papers. Box 561/6.
26 OS to Edward Nehls. 6/6/57. Copy in Renishaw papers. Box 561/6.
27 *Miracle on Sinai*. pp. 29–31.
28 Glendinning. *Edith Sitwell*. p. 126.
29 OS to John Lehmann. 17/1/46. HRCA. John Lehmann papers.
30 P. G. Lear and L.O. Cayme Press Pamphlets. No. 2. London, 1926.
31 'A Few Days in an Author's Life'. Published as Preface to *All At Sea*. London, 1927.
32 OS to John Lehmann. 17/1/46. HRCA. John Lehmann papers.
33 OS to CA. 30/1/30. Add mss 70832. f. 3.
34 Gertrude Stein. *The Autobiography of Alice B. Toklas*. London, 1933. pp. 313–15.
35 *A Romantic Friendship. The Letters of Cyril Connolly to Noel Blakiston*. London, 1975. p. 191.
36 David Pryce-Jones. *Cyril Connolly*. London, 1983. p. 266.
37 Gladwyn Jebb to Connolly. 26/5/27. Gladwyn papers.
38 Festing-Jones papers. Add 8484.
39 Beaton. *The Wandering Years*. p. 166.
40 Christopher Hassall. *Edward Marsh*. London, 1959. p. 563.
41 OS to CA. Undated. Add mss 70831. f. 69.
42 OS to SS. 5/2/27. HRCA. SS papers. Box 21.
43 OS to CA. Sept. 1939. Add mss 70834. f. 115.
44 OS to SS. 24 and 27/12/27. HRCA. SS papers. Box 21.

45 Bradford. *Sacheverell Sitwell*. pp. 180–7.
46 Bradford. *Sacheverell Sitwell*. p. 190.
47 Godfrey Winn. *The Bend of the River*. London, 1949. pp. 30–1.
48 Bradford. *Sacheverell Sitwell*. p. 154.
49 OS to CA. 23/11/28. Add mss 70831. f. 137.
50 OS to SS. Undated. HRCA. SS papers. Box 20.
51 OS to DH. 26/2/29. HRCA. OS papers.
52 OS to CA. Undated. Add mss 70831. f. 75.
53 OS to CA. 2/5/30. Add mss 70832. f. 18.
54 OS to SS. 27/4/27. HRCA. SS papers. Box 20.
55 Festing-Jones papers. Add 8484.
56 OS to Grant Richards. 4/2/25. HRCA. OS papers.
57 OS to David Higham. 15/2/62. Renishaw papers. Box 521; OS to Samuel Chotzinoff. 20/3/63. Samuel Chotzinoff Collection. University of Boston.
58 *Arnold Bennett's Letters to his Nephew*. ed. Richard Bennett. London, 1936. p. 205.
59 *Dumb Animal*. Appendix.
60 Report by Mrs Helena Wood. 15/6/43. BBC Written Archives. Caversham.
61 Siegfried Sassoon to OS. Undated. HRCA. OS papers. Recip.
62 Sassoon to CA. 5/12/27. Add mss 70837 B. f. 106.
63 OS to SS. 11/4/27. HRCA. SS papers. Box 21; OS to S. J. G. Ervine. Undated. HRCA. S. J. G. Ervine Collection.
64 *The Autobiography of William Plomer*. ed. Rupert Hart-Davis. London, 1975. p. 267; Peter F. Alexander. *William Plomer. A Biography*. Oxford, 1989. p. 158.
65 *The Letters of Edwin Lutyens to his Wife Lady Emily*. ed. Clayre Percy and Jane Ridley. London, 1985. p. 411.
66 Maynard Hollingworth to OS. 14/2/28. Renishaw papers. Box 335/6.
67 OS to CA. 12/9/30. Add mss 70822. f. 38.
68 Laurence Whistler. *The Laughter and the Urn. The Life of Rex Whistler*. London, 1985. p. 123.
69 OS to SS. 30/3/27. HRCA. SS papers. Box 21.
70 OS to Virginia Woolf. Undated. Leonard Woolf papers. Sx Ms 13 II DSA. University of Sussex.
71 GS to OS. 8/7/28. Renishaw papers. Box 501.
72 OS to DH. 19/12/29. HRCA. OS papers.
73 Osbert Sitwell. *The Man Who Lost Himself*. London, 1929. p. 244.
74 *LITNR*. p. 206.
75 Lady Wimborne to OS. 7 and 8/5/26. Renishaw papers. Box 568/4.
76 Lady Wimborne to OS. 9/5/26. Renishaw papers. Box 568/4.
77 *Journals of Arnold Bennett*. Vol. 3. p. 133.
78 Lady Wimborne to OS. 12/5/26. Renishaw papers. Box 568/4.
79 *LITNR*. p. 242.

9: Enter a Golden Squirrel

1 *LITNR*. p. 62.
2 *Letters of Conrad Russell*. ed. Georgina Blakiston. London, 1987. pp. 246–7.
3 *The Diary of Virginia Woolf*. Vol. 4. p. 225
4 Wyndham Lewis. *Blasting and Bombardiering*. London, 1937. p. 96.
5 Richard Church to OS. 11/10/50. David Horner mss; W. S. Maugham to DH. 24/3/47. HRCA. OS papers. Misc.
6 JPN.
7 JPN.

8 *LITNR.* p. 37.
9 Lovat Dickson. *The House of Words.* London, 1963. p. 273.
10 JPN.
11 Susana Walton. *William Walton.* p. 52.
12 OS to Alice Hunt. 31/3/49. Renishaw papers. Box 567/5.
13 Ethel Mannin. *Confessions and Impressions.* London, 1930. pp. 242–3.
14 Ethel Mannin to OS. 20/5/36. David Horner mss.
15 *Sunday Times.* 7/12/52.
16 *SHSL.* p. 189.
17 *Sacheverell Sitwell. A Symposium.* p. 66.
18 JPN; Interview with Philip Frere.
19 Adrian Wright. *Foreign Country. The Life of L. P. Hartley.* London, 1996. p. 103.
20 Bradford. *Sacheverell Sitwell.* p. 182.
21 Osbert Sitwell. *Winters of Content.* London, 1932. p. 218.
22 Osbert Sitwell. *Selected Poems Old and New.* London, 1943.
23 Bradford. *Sacheverell Sitwell.* p. 195.
24 *All At Sea.* p. 15.
25 OS to Bryher. 1932[?]. Bryher papers.
26 Renishaw papers. Box 575/8b.
27 John Lehmann. *I Am My Brother.* London, 1960. p. 178.
28 *A Free House.* p. xvi.
29 Gordon Woodhouse to Dorothy. August 1949. Violet Woodhouse papers.
30 *Trio.* p. 11.
31 OS to Val Gielgud. 1/1/42. BBC Written Archives.
32 OS to J. H. Hutchinson. 22/6/43. HRCA. OS papers. Misc.
33 JPN.
34 Powell, *Messengers of Day.* p. 38.
35 Nevinson, *Paint and Prejudice.* p. 179.
36 Brinsley Ford diary. 2/6/47.
37 Higham. *Literary Gent.* p. 204.
38 Renishaw papers. Box 511.
39 Lovat Dickson. *The House of Words.* p. 274.
40 *Diaries of Evelyn Waugh.* p. 327.
41 Interview with Sir Brinsley Ford.
42 23/11/46. Renishaw papers. Box 532/6.
43 HRCA. OS papers. Misc.
44 *Sunday Times.* 22/3/64.
45 9/6/47. Renishaw papers. Box 340/2.
46 JPN.
47 *Diaries of Evelyn Waugh.* p. 327.
48 Preface to *QMAO.* p. 14.
49 JPN.
50 *TST.* p. 209.
51 *GM.* pp. 227–8.
52 Somerset Maugham to DH. 15/6/35. HRCA. OS papers. Misc.
53 Glendinning. *Vita.* p. 83.
54 Pearson. *Façades.* p. 203.
55 JPN; Letter from Anne Chisholm of 6/9/96.
56 De-la-Noy. *Denton Welch.* p. 5.
57 Susana Walton. *Walton.* p. 51.
58 Interview with Anthony Powell.

59 Quennell. *The Marble Foot.* p. 142.
60 Mannin. *Confessions and Impressions.* p. 241.
61 OS to SS. 12/12/26. HRCA. SS papers. Box 21.
62 JPN.
63 DH to OS. 7/6/44. Renishaw papers. Box 570/7.
64 James Agate. *Ego 6.* London, 1944. p. 3.
65 *LITNR.* p. 208.
66 OS to DH. Undated. HRCA. OS papers.
67 OS to DH. Undated. HRCA. OS papers.
68 OS to DH. April 1929. HRCA. OS papers.
69 OS to DH. 12/5/29. HRCA. OS papers.
70 OS to DH. 19/12/29. HRCA. OS papers.
71 JPN.
72 David Horner mss.
73 DH to CA. 18/9/29. Add mss 70837. Vol. 7/5.
74 Interview with Nicolas Barker.
75 Interview with Frank Magro.
76 OS to DH. 7/8/30 and 9/5/32. HRCA. OS papers.
77 OS to DH. 26/4/43. HRCA. OS papers.
78 OS to DH. 22/7/43. HRCA. OS papers.
79 DH to OS. 17/11/44. Renishaw papers. Box 570/8.
80 OS to DH. 3/6/45 and 10/6/45. HRCA. OS papers.
81 JPN.
82 OS to CA. April 1938. Add mss 70834. f. 71.
83 David Horner. *Through French Windows.* London, 1938; and *Was it Yesterday?* London, 1939.
84 DH to CA. Undated. Add mss 70834. f. 72.
85 OS to DH. Undated. HRCA. OS papers.
86 Bradford. *Sacheverell Sitwell.* p. 237.
87 Pryce-Jones. *The Bonus of Laughter.* p. 85.
88 OS to Alan Pryce-Jones. 28/1/34. Beinecke Library, Yale. Alan Pryce-Jones papers.
89 OS to CA. 14/2/32. Add mss 70832. f. 137.

10: Phantoms

1 OS to Grant Richards. 26/11/22. HRCA. OS papers.
2 Speedie. *Wonderful Sphinx.* p. 251.
3 *Collected Satires and Poems.* p. 4.
4 *Collected Satires and Poems.* p. 64.
5 *Collected Satires and Poems.* pp. 69–74.
6 A selection of reviews, hostile as well as favourable, is printed as an appendix to *Triple Fugue.*
7 *Collected Satires and Poems.* p. 141.
8 *Collected Satires and Poems.* p. 130.
9 *Collected Satires and Poems.* p. 132.
10 *Collected Satires and Poems.* p. 116.
11 Preface to *Selected Poems Old and New.* p. 8.
12 *Letters of Virginia Woolf.* Vol. 4. p. 307.
13 *Wrack at Tidesend.* p. 1.
14 OS to Dr Connie Guion. Undated. HRCA. OS papers. Misc.
15 OS to Dr Guion. Undated. HRCA. OS papers. Misc.

16 Jon Stallworthy. *Louis MacNeice*. London, 1995. p. 163.
17 Reprinted in Osbert Sitwell. *Poems about People or England Reclaimed*. London, 1965. pp. 41–2.
18 20/10/27, 27/10/27 and 4/11/27.
19 Preface to *Three-Quarter-length Portrait of Michael Arlen*.
20 Max Wykes-Jones. *Triad of Genius*. London, 1953. p. 103.
21 Osbert Sitwell. *Three-Quarter-length Portrait of Viscountess Wimborne*. Privately printed. 1931.
22 OS to Joe Ackerley. 24/9/32. BBC Written Archives, Caversham.
23 Kennedy. *Walton*. p. 78.
24 Walton to OS. 25/8/29. Aberconway papers. Add mss 70831. f. 200.
25 OS to CA. Undated. Add mss 70831. f. 199.
26 Kennedy. *Walton*. p. 82.
27 JPN.
28 Lord Aberconway to OS. 25/10/37. David Horner mss.
29 Susana Walton. *Walton*. p. 82.
30 Kennedy. *Walton*. pp. 54–5; Susana Walton. *Walton*. pp. 71–2.
31 DH to CA. 8/1/30. Add mss 70837A. f. 67.
32 *Yorkshire Post*. 7/10/31.
33 *The Times*. 10/10/31.
34 Edward Ricco. 'The Sitwells at the Ballet'. *Ballet Review*. Vol. 6. No. 1 (1977–8). p. 75; Kennedy. *Walton*. p. 81.
35 Graham Greene to OS. Undated. Renishaw papers. Box 512/6.
36 Francis Bamford to OS. 1/6/48. Renishaw papers. Box 548/6.
37 SS to OS. Undated. Renishaw papers. Box 567/1.
38 GS to OS. 14/4/33. Renishaw papers. Box 567/1.
39 OS to Georgia S. 12/4/33. HRCA. SS papers. Box 26.
40 OS to Maynard Hollingworth. 5/1/34. Renishaw papers. Box 312.
41 Preface to *QMAO*. p. 10.
42 GS to OS. 12/7/31. Renishaw papers. Box 567/1.
43 OS to Georgia S. Undated. HRCA. SS papers. Box 26.
44 DH to CA. 24/9/29. Add mss 70837A. f. 57.
45 GS to OS. 3/5/29. Renishaw papers. Box 501.
46 OS to CA. 9/4/29. Add mss 70831. f. 194.
47 GS to OS. 21/4/29. Renishaw papers. Box 501.
48 OS to Maynard Hollingworth. 16/2/30. Hollingworth to OS. 21/2/30. Renishaw papers. Box 333/10.
49 OS to Georgia S. 24/12/31. Renishaw papers. Box 233/10.
50 OS to CA. 14/4/32. Add mss 70832. f. 150.
51 OS to CA. March 1933. Add mss 70833. f. 15.
52 OS to CA. June 1933. Add mss 70833. f. 33.
53 OS to SS. 25/1/33. Sitwell Collection. University of Boston. Box 1/F/1.
54 GS to OS. 3/4/33. Renishaw papers. Box 567/1.
55 GS to OS. 14/4/33. Renishaw papers. Box 567/1.
56 ES to Choura Tchelitchew. 15/8/33; Elborn. *Edith Sitwell*. p. 107.
57 OS to DH. 13/8/33. HRCA. OS papers.
58 OS to William Worsley. 31/8/33. Renishaw papers. Box 333/10.
59 OS to DH. 9/9/33 and 14/9/33. HRCA. OS papers.
60 OS to Georgia S. 21/9/33. HRCA. SS papers. Box 26.
61 OS to SS. 25/1/33. Sitwell Collection. University of Boston. Box 1/F/1.
62 GS to Georgia S. 13/6/34. HRCA. SS papers. Box 25.
63 GS to Georgia S. 8/3/33. HRCA. SS papers. Box 25.

64 OS to DH. 19/8/36. HRCA. OS papers.
65 OS to CA. 13/4/30. Add mss 70832. f. 16.
66 A. J. P. Taylor. *Beaverbrook*. London, 1972. p. 264.
67 OS to T. S. Eliot. 10/12/23. T. S. Eliot papers.
68 OS to Grant Richards. 11/12/22. HRCA. OS papers.
69 *Evening Standard*. 19/9/35; *Morning Post*. 17/9/35; *Daily Telegraph*. 20/9/35.
70 OS to H. Macmillan. 10/10/35. Macmillan papers. Uncatalogued. British Library.
71 *Lilliput*. Vol. 5. No. 1. pp. 79–82. July 1939.
72 DH to OS. 26/6/44. Renishaw papers. Box 503.
73 Rache Lovat Dickson to OS. 28/10/43. Renishaw papers. Box 561/4.
74 *Daily Express*. 27/5/44; James Agate. *Ego 7*. London, 1945. p. 99.
75 *Tatler*. 31/5/44.
76 Rache Lovat Dickson to OS. 9/6/44. Renishaw papers. Box 503.
77 OS to CA. May 1931. Add mss 70832. f. 99.
78 Renishaw papers. Box 502.
79 Osbert Sitwell. *Dickens*. London, 1932.
80 Report of 16/10/31. Chatto & Windus mss.
81 *Christian Science Monitor*. 8/4/32.
82 Somerset Maugham to OS. 6/6/32. Sitwell Collection. University of Boston. Box 1/F/1.
83 *Daily Telegraph*. 26/3/32; *Morning Post*. 18/2/32.
84 OS to CA. May 1934. Add mss 70833. f. 52.
85 Osbert Sitwell and Margaret Barton. *Brighton*. London, 1935.
86 Somerset Maugham to DH. 22/3/35. HRCA. OS papers. Misc.
87 Nina Hamnett. *Is She a Lady?* London, 1955. pp. 37–9.
88 OS to Nina Hamnett. Undated. HRCA. OS papers. Misc.
89 *The People's Album of London Statues*. pp. 64–6 and 73–9.
90 *Listener*. 16/1/29; *Times Literary Supplement*. 14/12/28; *Nation and Athenaeum*. 8/12/28.
91 OS to SS. 22/1/29. HRCA. SS papers. Box 21.
92 OS to Duckworth. 20/2/37 and 19/4/37; Duckworth to OS. 26/2/37 and 21/4/37. Duckworth archive. General Correspondence.

11: Wings to Head and Pen

1 DH to CA. 8/1/30. Add mss 70537A. f. 66.
2 DH to CA. 27/1/30. Add mss 70537A. f. 72.
3 OS to CA. 6/12/28. Add mss 70831. f. 142.
4 OS to Marie Belloc Lowndes. *Diaries and Letters of Marie Belloc Lowndes*. ed. Susan Lowndes. London, 1971. p. 126.
5 OS to CA. 10/2/33. Add mss 70833. f. 10.
6 OS to CA. 24/12/32. Add mss 70832. f. 204.
7 OS to CA. 2/1/33. Add mss 70833. f. 3
8 ES to CA. Undated. Add mss 52556 (Vol. 2). f. 191.
9 OS to CA. 9/2/35. Add mss 70833. f. 104.
10 1/1/35. Lady Desborough papers. HRO ref. D/ERVC 2407/7.
11 12/2/36. Lady Desborough papers. HRO ref. D/ERVC 2407/8.
12 OS to Georgia S. 18/3/36. HRCA. SS papers. Box 26.
13 *Penny Foolish*. p. 214.
14 OS to Marie Belloc Lowndes. *Diaries and Letters*. p. 126.
15 OS to CA. August 1934. Add mss 70833. f. 72.
16 *TST*. p. 241.
17 *Discursions*. p. 194.

18 JPN.
19 Bradford. *Sacheverell Sitwell*. p. 200.
20 OS to Georgia S. 8/5/33. HRCA. SS papers. Box 26.
21 20/2/32. Lady Desborough papers. HRO ref. D/ERVC 2407/5.
22 OS to CA. Undated. Add mss 70832. f. 15.
23 *Winters of Content*. p. 12.
24 *The Spectator*. 7/12/34.
25 Preface to *QMAO*. p. 9.
26 ES to Mr Lewis. 16/6/37. Duckworth archive. General Correspondence.
27 Edith Olivier to OS. 11/7/39. Renishaw papers. Box 502.
28 OS to Rupert Hart-Davis. Undated. Rupert Hart-Davis papers.
29 Higham. *Literary Gent*. p. 163; Interview with Mr T. M. Farmiloe.
30 Osbert Sitwell. *Escape With Me! An Oriental Sketch Book*. London, 1939. First published as articles in *Harper's Bazaar, Fortnightly, Queen, John O'London's* and *Life and Letters Today*.
31 OS to CA. 5/1/34. Add mss 70833. f. 40.
32 *Escape With Me!* Pan edition of 1948. pp. 65–6.
33 OS to CA. 22/1/34. Add mss 70833. f. 42.
34 OS to SS. 27/3/34. HRCA. SS papers. Box 21.
35 OS to Maynard Hollingworth. 7/3/34. Renishaw papers. Box 312.
36 *Escape With Me!* pp. 163–4.
37 *Times Literary Supplement*. 11/11/39.
38 *Escape With Me!* pp. 280–8.
39 OS to CA. Undated. Add mss 70833. f. 52.
40 OS to CA. 22/1/34. Add mss 70833. f. 58.
41 Osbert Sitwell. *The Four Continents* (henceforth *TFC*). London, 1954. p. 94.
42 *Escape with Me*. p. 238.
43 *Saturday Review*. 20/7/40.
44 Harold Macmillan to OS. 17/10/39. Renishaw papers. Box 502.
45 Harold Macmillan to OS. 11/1/40. Renishaw papers. Box 502.
46 OS to Rache Lovat Dickson. 26/9/39. Macmillan papers.
47 Nichols. *The Unforgiving Minute*. p. 270.
48 Brian Connon. *Beverley Nichols*. London, 1991. p. 206.
49 Beverley Nichols. *All I Could Never Be*. London, 1949. pp. 330–1.
50 OS to Lady Desborough. 22/2/39. Lady Desborough papers. HRO ref. D/ERVC 2407/12.
51 Connon. *Nichols*. p. 206.
52 Nichols. *The Unforgiving Minute*. p. 273.
53 Connon. *Nichols*. p. 206.
54 OS to CA. 1/2/39. Add mss 70834. f. 103.
55 OS to CA. 22/1/39. Add mss 70834. f. 101.

12: He Likes to Write

1 OS to Mme Ronchaud. 17/1/58. Renishaw papers. Box 561/6.
2 OS to SS. 22/11/28. HRCA. SS papers. Box 21.
3 *Manchester Guardian*. 6/12/29; *The Times*. 6/12/29; *Book Society News*. 22/12/29; *The Listener*. 14/12/29.
4 Hoare. *Stephen Tennant*. p. 146.
5 Bryher to HD. 31/1/41. HD papers.
6 *The Referee*. 1/12/29.
7 OS to Megroz. 21/2/33. Frank Megroz mss.

8 Michael De-la-Noy. *Eddy. The Life of Edward Sackville-West*. London, 1988. p. 174.
9 Maugham to OS. Undated. Sitwell Collection. University of Boston.
10 28/10/33. Selina Hastings. *Evelyn Waugh*. London, 1994. p. 270.
11 Memo by E. J. King Bull; Christopher Sykes to OS. 12/8/48. BBC Written Archives, Caversham.
12 OS to CA. 12/1/35. Add mss 70833. f. 96.
13 OS to Georgia S. 2/3/35. HRCA. SS papers. Box 26.
14 OS to Lady Desborough. 6/1/37. Lady Desborough papers. HRO ref. D/ERVC 2407/9.
15 OS to CA. Feb. 1938. Add mss 70834. f. 58.
16 OS to F. J. Ratcliffe. 24/1/38. Macmillan papers.
17 OS to Harold Macmillan. 10/3/38. Macmillan papers.
18 OS to CA. 11/2/35. Add mss 70833. f. 108.
19 *Those Were the Days*. p. 257.
20 OS to CA. 30/4/38. Add mss 70834. f. 76.
21 OS to Harold Macmillan. 26/4/38. Macmillan papers.
22 OS to Harold Macmillan. 3/5/38. Macmillan papers.
23 *Trio*. pp. 54–6.
24 *The Correspondence of Ezra Pound and Wyndham Lewis*. ed. Timothy Maturin. London, 1988. p. 143.
25 ES to Tom Driberg. 3/9/62. Driberg mss.
26 ES to Sydney Schiff. 26/9/30. Schiff papers. Add mss 52922. f. 35.
27 Grigson. *The Crest on the Silver*. p. 166.
28 Wyndham Lewis. *The Apes of God*. London, 1931. p. 322.
29 Connolly. *Enemies of Promise*. p. 60.
30 *Literary Lifelines. The Richard Aldington–Lawrence Durrell Correspondence*. ed. Ian S. MacNiven and Harry T Moore. London, 1987. p. 8.
31 OS to T. S. Eliot. 22/5/34. T. S. Eliot papers.
32 Elborn. *Edith Sitwell*. p. 89.
33 *TMFTM*. pp. 91–3.
34 JPN.
35 *The Letters of Wyndham Lewis*. ed. W. K. Rose. London, 1963. pp. 229–30.
36 Robert Nichols. *Fisbo*. London, 1934.
37 CA to OS. 9/9/34. Add mss 70833. f. 78.
38 Hassall. *Marsh*. p. 239.
39 Frere to OS. 21/5/35. Renishaw papers. Box 568/12.
40 *LHRH*. pp. 77–8.
41 OS to CA. Undated. Add mss 70834. f. 59.
42 OS to Lady Desborough. 22/4/38. Lady Desborough papers. HRO ref. D/ERVC 2407/11; OS to CA. Undated. Add mss 70834. ff. 60 and 64.
43 OS to DH. 10/4/38. HRCA. OS papers.
44 OS to Macmillan. 3/5/38. Macmillan papers.
45 OS to CA. 21/5/38 and 5/9/38. Add mss 70834. ff. 60 and 64.
46 GS to DH. 8/3/38 and 20/4/38. Renishaw papers. Box 501.
47 Moat to OS. 21/4/38. HRCA. OS papers. Recip.
48 Moat to OS. 23/9/29. HRCA. OS papers. Recip.
49 *LITNR*. p. 303.
50 Moat to OS. 26/2/37. Sitwell Collection. Tulsa, Oklahoma.
51 OS to DH. Undated. HRCA. OS papers.
52 ES. *Taken Care Of*. p. 23.
53 OS to DH. 20/11/37 and 21/11/37. HRCA. OS papers.

54 OS to Bryher. 18/2/38. Bryher papers.
55 Moat to OS. 11/1/38. HRCA. OS papers. Recip.
56 GS to OS. 19/8/38. Renishaw papers. Box 501.
57 OS to CA. 30/8/31. Add mss 70832. f. 108.
58 OS to DH. 24/9/31. HRCA. OS papers.
59 *Sunday Referee*. 4/3/34. Reprinted in *Penny Foolish*. pp. 308–12.
60 OS to DH. 19/7/35. HRCA. OS papers.
61 OS to CA. 14/8/35. Add mss 70833. f. 143.
62 OS to J. L. Garvin. 15/12/35. HRCA. J. L. Garvin Collection.
63 GS to OS. 11/1/39. Renishaw papers. Box 312.
64 OS to J. L. Garvin. 26/1/37. HRCA. J. L. Garvin Collection.
65 Interview with Sir Stephen Spender.
66 *Penny Foolish*. p. 24.
67 *Week-end Review*. 27/6/31.
68 Nicholas Mosley. *Rules of the Game*. London, 1982. p. 191.
69 *Harold Nicolson. Diaries and Letters 1930–39.* ed. Nigel Nicolson. London, 1966. p. 86; Mosley. *Rules of the Game*. p. 201.
70 Mosley. *Rules of the Game*. p. 232.
71 OS to Samuel Hoare. 22/2/36. Templewood papers. 8, 5a.
72 OS to CA. Undated. Add mss 70834. ff. 62 and 67.
73 GS to OS. 7/10/38. Renishaw papers. Box 567/1.
74 OS to Maynard Hollingworth. Undated. Renishaw papers. Box 312.
75 OS to DH. 9/6/37. HRCA. OS papers.
76 OS to SS. Undated. Sitwell Collection. University of Boston.
77 Maynard Hollingworth to OS. 16/3/37; OS to Hollingworth. 18/5/37. Renishaw papers. Box 213.
78 OS to CA. 20/3/37. Add mss 70834. f. 21.
79 OS to GS. 8/11/38. Renishaw papers. Box 567/1.
80 Nichols. *The Unforgiving Minute*. p. 296.
81 Maynard Hollingworth to OS. 21/7/39. Renishaw papers. Box 312.
82 Whistler to OS. Undated. HRCA. OS papers. Recip.
83 Salter. *The Last Years of a Rebel*. p. 186.
84 Undated. Renishaw papers. Box 502.
85 GS to OS. 29/4/37; OS to GS. 3/5/37. Renishaw papers. Box 567/1.
86 Pryce-Jones. *The Bonus of Laughter*. p. 64.
87 OS to CA. 8/8/34. Add mss 70833. f. 63.
88 OS to CA. 11/4/37. Add mss 70834. f. 31.
89 OS to CA. 13/1/33. Add mss 70834. f. 4; Interview with Sir Brinsley Ford.
90 Lady Oxford to OS. 22/9/39. HRCA. OS papers. Recip.
91 OS to DH. 4/6/37. HRCA. OS papers.
92 OS to CA. 26/7/39. Add mss 70834. f. 109.
93 Maynard Hollingworth to Hester Leggatt. 18/1/39. Renishaw papers. Box 213.
94 Frere to OS. 28/9/39. Renishaw papers. Box 502.
95 OS to Lady Desborough. 4/9/36. Lady Desborough papers. HRO ref. D/ERVC 2407/4.
96 James Knox. Introduction to Houghton sale at Christie's. 1994.
97 OS to DH. 30/7/30. HRCA. OS papers.
98 OS to CA. 5/2/36. Add mss 70833. f. 164.
99 *RW*. p. 35.
100 OS to CA. 5/1/37. Add mss 70834. f. 1.
101 *RW*. pp. 59–60.
102 *RW*. p. 66.

103 Memorandum by Philip Frere. 4/8/50. Renishaw papers. Box 503.

104 OS to CA. 5/1/37. Add mss 70834. f. 1.

105 *RW.* p. 70.

106 OS to CA. 6/2/37. Add mss 70834. f. 10.

107 Queen Elizabeth to OS. 7/12/36 and 17/12/36. Weston papers.

108 OS to Georgia S. 14/4/37. HRCA. SS papers. Box 26.

109 *RW.* p. 45.

110 OS to CA. 21/9/37. Add mss 70834. f. 45.

111 OS to Mme Guéritte. 6/8/44. Renishaw papers. Box 550.

112 Bradford. *Sacheverell Sitwell.* p. 272.

113 OS to DH. 3/6/37. HRCA. OS papers.

114 OS to DH. 18/5/37. HRCA. OS papers.

115 *QMAO.* p. 24.

116 *QMAO.* p. 37.

13: We Want – PEACE!

1 OS to CA. September 1939 and 12/1/40. Add mss 70834. ff. 113 and 115.

2 OS to DH. 6/9/41. HRCA. OS papers.

3 OS to Violet Woodhouse. 27/11/40. Violet Woodhouse papers.

4 OS to Clive Bell. 1/10/40. Sitwell Collection. Tulsa, Oklahoma. Box 1.

5 OS to Cynthia Asquith. 2/1/40. Sitwell Collection. Tulsa, Oklahoma. Box 1.

6 OS to CA. Undated. Add mss 70834. f. 115.

7 OS to DH. 30/10/41. HRCA. OS papers.

8 OS to HD. 20/11/39. HD papers.

9 OS to Shaw. 3/10/40. Shaw papers. Add mss 63186.

10 OS to SS. 8/3/42. HRCA. SS papers. Box 22.

11 Osbert Sitwell. *A Letter to My Son.* First published *Horizon.* March 1943.
    Republished in pamphlet form, August 1944 and in *Pound Wise.* London, 1963.
    pp. 293–318.

12 OS to CA. Undated. Add mss 70834. f. 180.

13 OS to CA. May 1941. Add mss 70834. f. 179.

14 OS to CA. Undated. Add mss 70834. f. 180.

15 OS to CA. 5/6/41. Add mss 70834. f. 173.

16 OS to Bryher. 16/4/41. Bryher papers.

17 *Edith Sitwell. Selected Letters* (1970). p. 72.

18 OS to HD. 20/11/39. HD papers.

19 OS to CA. June/July 1941. Add mss 70834. f. 177.

20 OS to CA. Early 1943. Add mss 70835. f. 8.

21 Jonathan Guinness. *House of Mitford.* London, 1984. p. 538.

22 OS to Connolly. 25/12/43. Cyril Connolly Collection. Tulsa, Oklahoma. 1.17.6.

23 Connolly to OS. January 1944. Renishaw papers. Box 504.

24 Fussell. *Great War and Modern Memory.* pp. 116–17.

25 OS to Lorna Andrade (henceforth LA). 12/3/42. HRCA. OS papers.

26 OS to Bryher. 12/3/42. Bryher papers.

27 OS to CA. Undated. Add mss 70834. f. 115.

28 OS to Lady Desborough. 7/10/39. Lady Desborough's papers. HRO ref. D/ERVC
    2407/13.

29 H. V. Rhodes to OS. 22/9/39. Renishaw papers. Box 502.

30 Bracken to OS. 9/6/42. Renishaw papers. Box 502.

31 OS to LA. 6/12/41. HRCA. OS papers.

32 Lord Dawson to OS. 22/7/40. Renishaw papers. Box 502.

33 ES to SS. March 1941. HRCA. SS papers. Box 19; OS to DH. 4/12/41. HRCA. OS papers.
34 OS to Connolly. 11/7/42. Cyril Connolly Collection. Tulsa, Oklahoma. 1.17.6.
35 OS to DH. 25/6/42. HRCA. OS papers; OS to Lovat Dickson. 8/7/42. Macmillan papers.
36 Kilham-Roberts to OS. 11/8/42. Renishaw papers. Box 502.
37 Pearn to OS. 18/8/42. Renishaw papers. Box 502.
38 ES to OS. Undated. Renishaw papers. Box 511.
39 Greenlees to OS. 15/4/40. Renishaw papers. Box 502.
40 GS to OS. 14/4/40. Renishaw papers. Box 502.
41 Rose to OS. 18/4/40. Renishaw papers. Box 502.
42 OS to Macmillan. 20/4/40. Macmillan papers.
43 GS to OS. 16/4/40. Renishaw papers. Box 502.
44 Interview with Lady Violet Powell.
45 Bullock to OS. 13/3/40. Renishaw papers. Box 502.
46 DH to OS. 10/7/41. Renishaw papers. Box 511.
47 DH to OS. 8/12/41. Renishaw papers. Box 511.
48 Glendinning. *Edith Sitwell*. p. 218.
49 OS to L. P. Hartley. 6/7/44. L. P. Hartley papers. John Rylands University Library.
50 OS to DH. 3/2/43. HRCA. OS papers.
51 OS to DH. 3/4/43. HRCA. OS papers.
52 Bradford. *Sacheverell Sitwell*. p. 284.
53 Herring to ES. December 1940. Renishaw papers. Box 502.
54 OS to CA. December 1939. Add mss 70834. f. 121.
55 OS to CA. 18/2/40. Add mss 70834. f. 133.
56 OS to CA. Undated. Add mss 70834. f. 156.
57 OS to Mme Guéritte. 11/5/41. Renishaw papers. Box 550.
58 OS to DH. 27/10/41. HRCA. OS papers.
59 OS to Kirkham. 22/10/42. Copy in Renishaw papers. Box 502.
60 OS to Shaw. 3/10/40. Shaw papers. Add mss 63186.
61 ES to T. S. Eliot. 1/7/45. *Edith Sitwell. Selected Letters* (1970). p. 131.
62 Harold Acton to Mrs Acton. October 1939. Edward Chaney papers.
63 ES to S. Spender. 6/1/44. Berg Collection.
64 E. Waugh to OS. Undated. Renishaw papers. Box 511.
65 Alexander. *William Plomer*. p. 241.
66 OS to DH. 29/1/42 and 26/12/41. HRCA. OS papers.
67 OS to DH. 8/3/42 and 18/2/42. HRCA. OS papers.
68 Belloc Lowndes. *Diaries and Letters*. p. 213.
69 'Notes on Life at Renishaw'. John Piper papers.
70 OS to DH. 11/12/43. HRCA. OS papers.
71 Elborn. *Edith Sitwell*. p. 146.
72 OS to SS. 19/11/40. HRCA. SS papers. Box 22.
73 OS to DH. Undated. HRCA. OS papers.
74 DH to CA. 21/11/39. Add mss 70837A. f. 102.
75 OS to Max Beerbohm. 17/2/41. Beerbohm papers.
76 Hollingworth to OS. 7/10/41. Renishaw papers. Box 312.
77 OS to DH. 24/6/42. HRCA. OS papers.
78 OS to Herring. 10/8/43. HRCA. OS papers. Misc.
79 OS to Connolly. 22/12/40 and 26/12/40. Cyril Connolly Collection. 1.17.6.
80 Belloc Lowndes. *Diaries and Letters*. p. 222.
81 OS to Mme Guéritte. 19/3/41. Renishaw papers. Box 550.
82 *Edith Sitwell. Selected Letters* (1970). p. 124.

83 OS to LA. 2/11/41. HRCA. OS papers.
84 Lovat Dickson. *House of Words.* pp. 275–9.
85 OS to DH. March 1942. HRCA. OS papers.
86 ES to Ree Gorer. 21/6/43. *Edith Sitwell. Selected Letters* (1970). p. 101.
87 OS to Mme Guéritte. 17/8/42. Renishaw papers. Box 550.
88 OS to CA. June 1944. Add mss 70835. f. 65.
89 OS to Bryher. 1944. Bryher papers.
90 Burke, Covington, Nash to ES. 19/8/42. Renishaw papers. Box 502.
91 ES to OS. August 1940. Renishaw papers. Box 502.
92 ES to CA. 2/4/41. Add mss 52556 (Vol. 2). f. 209.
93 *Letters of Evelyn Waugh.* p. 163.
94 OS to Georgia S. 27/8/41. HRCA. SS papers. Box 26.
95 Herring to OS. Jan. 1941. Renishaw papers. Box 511.
96 Bryher to HD. 26/1/41. HD papers.
97 Bryher to HD. 7/7/42 and 29/9/43. HD papers.
98 OS to Mme Guéritte. 2/12/44. Renishaw papers. Box 550.
99 OS to L. P. Hartley. 9/8/41. L. P. Hartley papers.
100 OS to DH. 8/5/43. HRCA. OS papers.
101 OS to DH. 9/3/41. HRCA. OS papers.
102 Powell. *Messengers of Day.* pp. 166–7.
103 Piper to OS. 17/4/40. Renishaw papers. Box 502.
104 OS to Mme Guéritte. 22/6/42. Renishaw papers. Box 550.
105 JPN.
106 Interview with Mrs Myfanwy Piper; 'Notes on Life at Renishaw'. John Piper papers.
107 JPN.
108 OS to Lady Desborough. Undated. Lady Desborough papers. HRO ref. D/ERVC 2407/41.
109 Alec Guinness. *Blessings in Disguise.* London, 1985. p. 148.
110 OS to Lady Desborough. 10/4/42. Lady Desborough papers. HRO ref. D/ERVC 2407/16.
111 OS to Mme Guéritte. 2/12/44. Renishaw papers. Box 550.
112 Kilham-Roberts to OS. 22/12/44. Renishaw papers. Box 570/1.
113 11/2/45. Rosamond Lehmann papers. King's College, Cambridge.
114 OS to Beaton. 7/9/41. Cecil Beaton papers; Hugo Vickers. *Cecil Beaton.* London, 1985. pp. 251–2.
115 Sassoon to Beaton. 20/9/44; Berners to Beaton. Undated. Cecil Beaton papers (Hugo Vickers).
116 Beaton to OS. Undated. Renishaw papers. Box 511; draft in Cecil Beaton papers.
117 ES to OS. Undated. Renishaw papers. Box 511.
118 OS to Beaton. Undated. Cecil Beaton papers.
119 OS to CA. Undated. Add mss 70835. f. 23.
120 Greenlees to OS. 26/5/42. Renishaw papers. Box 502.
121 3/10/40. Shaw papers. Add mss 63186.
122 LA to OS. 14/10/40. Renishaw papers. Box 502.
123 OS to CA. 20/9/40. Add mss 70834. f. 147.
124 Undated. William Plomer mss. 306/8.
125 14/11/39. Renishaw papers. Box 502.
126 OS to DH. 17/7/42. HRCA. OS papers.
127 OS to Rache Lovat Dickson. 24/1/43. Macmillan papers.
128 OS to Mme Guéritte. 7/3/43. Renishaw papers. Box 550.
129 OS to DH. 18/1/43. HRCA. OS papers.
130 Hartley to DH. 11/12/43. HRCA. OS papers. Misc.

14: Beavering Away

1 OS to Mme Guéritte. 1/11/40 and 22/12/40. Renishaw papers. Box 550.
2 OS to LA. 8/4/41. HRCA. OS papers.
3 Anne Pearn to OS. 13/8/41 and 16/12/41. Renishaw papers. Box 550.
4 Piper to OS. 20/6/42. Renishaw papers. Box 501.
5 Waugh to OS. Undated. Renishaw papers. Box 503; Martin Stannard. *Evelyn Waugh. The Early Years*. London, 1986. p. 502.
6 OS to Connolly. 1/11/39. Cyril Connolly Collection. Tulsa, Oklahoma. 1.17.6.
7 OS to Connolly. 25/3/43. Connolly Collection. 1.17.6.
8 OS to Connolly. 23/4/42. Connolly Collection. 1.17.6.
9 Ann Pearn to OS. 8/11/40. Renishaw papers. Box 550.
10 BBC Written Archives. 1/4/43, 13/4/43, 18/4/43.
11 D. Macmillan to OS. 30/12/40. Renishaw papers. Box 501.
12 George Milsted to OS. 15/7/42.
13 OUP Music Dept to OS. 20/7/42 and 9/11/42. Renishaw papers. Box 550.
14 *The Letters of Virginia Woolf*. Vol. 6. ed. Nigel Nicolson. London, 1980. p. 466.
15 OS to Lady Desborough. 10/4/42. Lady Desborough papers. HRO ref. D/ERVC 2407/16.
16 Pollinger to Ostrer. 27/3/42; Pollinger to OS. 26/3/42. Renishaw papers. Box 501.
17 OS to CA. 14/3/44. Add mss 70835. f. 52.
18 Greene to OS. 23/3/45. Renishaw papers. Box 503.
19 John Lehmann. *A Nest of Tigers*. London, 1969. p. 112.
20 OS to DH. 22/9/40. HRCA. OS papers.
21 *Daily Telegraph*. 21/11/41.
22 *Tatler and Bystander*. 13/12/41; *Sketch*. 17/12/41.
23 OS to Max Wykes-Jones. 23/8/53. Berg Collection.
24 Day-Lewis to OS. 20/11/41. Renishaw papers. Box 550.
25 Connolly to OS. 8/11/40. Renishaw papers. Box 550; OS to Connolly. 12/11/40. Connolly Collection. 1.17.6.
26 OS to DH. 19/4/42, 22/4/42, early May 1942. HRCA. OS papers.
27 Gielgud to OS. 2/7/42. Renishaw papers. Box 511.
28 Cochran to OS. 22/6/42. Renishaw papers. Box 511.
29 Driberg to OS. 11/11/42. Renishaw papers. Box 570/1.
30 OS to Macmillan. 20/11/42. Macmillan papers.
31 *John O'London's Weekly*. 9/4/43.
32 OS to CA. 1/8/43. Add mss 70835. f. 30.
33 OS to L. P. Hartley. 23/10/45. L. P. Hartley papers.
34 Rache Lovat Dickson to OS. 12/8/42. Renishaw papers. Box 570/1.
35 Minney to OS. 30/6/43. Renishaw papers. Box 532/6.
36 OS to CA. 24/12/40. Add mss 70834. f. 153.
37 ES to SS. 15/1/41. HRCA. SS papers. Box 19.
38 'Advice' of 19/3/40. Renishaw papers. Box 502.
39 *Letters of Virginia Woolf*. Vol. 6. p. 472.
40 ES to CA. 2/4/41. Add mss 52556 (Vol. 2). f. 210.
41 OS to Rache Lovat Dickson. 17/2/41. Macmillan papers.
42 Interview with Sir Stephen Spender.
43 MacCarthy to OS. 24/1/41. Renishaw papers. Box 502.
44 OS to Pryce-Jones. 28/12/47. Alan Pryce-Jones papers.
45 Bryher to HD. 3/3/41. HD papers.
46 Bryher. *The Days of Mars*. London, 1972. pp. 79–80.

47 *Harold Nicolson. Diaries and Letters 1939–1945*. ed. Nigel Nicolson. London, 1967. p. 290.
48 Lady Gerald Wellesley to OS. 21/4/43. Weston papers.
49 CA to OS. 23/4/43. Renishaw papers. Box 570/3.
50 Pearson. *Façades*. p. 359.
51 De-la-Noy. *Denton Welch*. p. 160.
52 HD to Mary Sarton. 21/4/43. Berg Collection.

15: A Devoted Family

 1 OS to SS. 26/4/38. Sitwell Collection. University of Boston. F/1.
 2 R. B. Blaker to GS. 20/12/39. Renishaw papers. Box 504.
 3 GS to OS. 1/12/39. Renishaw papers. Box 501.
 4 OS to CA. Undated. Add mss 70834. ff. 154 and 155.
 5 Bernard Woog to OS. 4/3/41. Renishaw papers. Box 503.
 6 *Selected Letters of Edith Sitwell*. ed. Richard Greene. London, 1997. p. 226.
 7 Georgia S to OS. 27/1/42. Renishaw papers. Box 511.
 8 GS to OS. 20/1/41. Renishaw papers. Box 511.
 9 Coutts to OS. 23/6/42. Renishaw papers. Box 511.
10 Woog to OS. 18/7/42. Renishaw papers. Box 503.
11 Belloc Lowndes. *Diaries and Letters*. p. 228.
12 OS to CA. 11/7/42. Add mss 70834. f. 208.
13 Woog to OS. 4/9/42. David Horner papers.
14 OS to DH. 1/10/42. HRCA. OS papers.
15 Frere to OS. 5/10/42. Renishaw papers. Box 503.
16 OS to DH. 20/11/42. HRCA. OS papers.
17 Queen Mary to OS. 22/7/43. Weston papers.
18 Crawford to OS. 7/7/43. Renishaw papers. Box 503.
19 Woodhouse to OS. 10/7/43. Renishaw papers. Box 501.
20 Lady Cholmondeley to OS. 13/7/43. Renishaw papers. Box 570/4.
21 OS to CA. 3/7/43. Add mss 70835. f. 27.
22 OS to Stephen Spender. 14/8/43. Berg Collection.
23 OS to DH. 15/7/43. HRCA. OS papers.
24 OS to CA. 3/7/43. Add mss 70835. f. 27.
25 GS to SS. 21/1/41. Renishaw papers. Box 511.
26 Woog to OS. 16/8/43. Renishaw papers. Box 503.
27 OS to DH. 24/4/44. HRCA. OS papers.
28 OS to CA. 14/3/44. Add mss 70835. f. 52.
29 OS to DH. 6/4/44. HRCA. OS papers.
30 Bryher to HD. 17/3/44, 19/3/44, 25/4/44. HD papers.
31 OS to LA. 13/3/44. HRCA. OS papers.
32 JPN.
33 DH to OS. 1/2/45. Renishaw papers. Box 548.
34 OS to Mme Guéritte. 8/4/44. Renishaw papers. Box 550.
35 OS to DH. 5/4/45. HRCA. OS papers.
36 OS to DH. 19/7/43. HRCA. OS papers.
37 Georgia S to OS. 11/9/44. Renishaw papers. Box 570/8.
38 OS to DH. Early 1944. HRCA. OS papers.
39 ES to Georgia S. Undated. HRCA. SS papers. Box 24.
40 ES to SS. 18/5/45. HRCA. SS papers. Box 24.
41 OS to CA. 19/7/43. Add mss 70835. f. 25.
42 DH to OS. 30/3/45. Renishaw papers. Box 550.

43 OS to DH. 10/5/41. HRCA. OS papers.
44 Heywood Hill to OS. 15/10/40, 22/10/42. Renishaw papers. Box 1.
45 OS to DH. 24/9/41. HRCA. OS papers.
46 OS to DH. 1/10/42. HRCA. OS papers.
47 *Selected Letters of Edith Sitwell* (1970). p. 82.
48 Cynthia Colville to OS. 24/4/41. Renishaw papers. Box 503.
49 OS to DH. 10/5/41. HRCA. OS papers.
50 *QMAO*. pp. 47–8.
51 OS to Hartley. 9/8/41. L. P. Hartley papers.
52 *Burlington Magazine*. Vol. 80. Nos. 469 and 470; Duchess of Beaufort to OS. 7/4/42. Renishaw papers. Box 1/3.
53 Duchess of Beaufort to OS. 29/11/44. Weston papers.
54 *QMAO*. pp. 57–8.
55 OS to CA. Undated. Add mss 70834. f. 75.
56 JPN.
57 OS to DH. 11/12/41. HRCA. OS papers.
58 OS to DH. 2/10/42. HRCA. OS papers.
59 OS to CA. Undated. Add mss 70835. f. 22.
60 OS to DH. 1/11/42. HRCA. OS papers.
61 Agate to OS. 11/1/43. Renishaw papers. Box 570/2.
62 OS to D. S. MacColl. 26/6/45. University of Glasgow. MacColl S199.
63 Osbert Sitwell. *Letter to My Son. Horizon*. Vol. 7. No. 39. pp. 159–77. March 1943; revised as pamphlet August 1944; included in *Pound Wise*. London, 1963. pp. 293–320.
64 Forster to OS. 27/12/41. Renishaw papers. Box 511.
65 Cooper to OS. 27/3/43; Clark to OS. 27/3/43. Renishaw papers. Box 570/2.
66 Orwell to OS. 29/8/44. Renishaw papers. Box 503; *Tribune*. 8/9/44.
67 Neil Ritchie archive.
68 Neil Ritchie archive.
69 OS to DH. 11/9/44 and 28/11/44. HRCA. OS papers.
70 James Agate to Cyril Connolly. 8/12/40. Cyril Connolly Collection.
71 Foreword to Agate. *Here's Richness*. p. 8.
72 OS to Mme Guéritte. 31/10/43. Renishaw papers. Box 550.
73 *Manchester Guardian*. 28/11/44.
74 *Foy Libra*. September 1944.
75 OS to Malcolm Robertson. 17/6/45. Copy in Renishaw papers. Box 550/8.
76 Spender to OS. 5/5/45. Renishaw papers. Box 550.
77 OS to Ould. 21/1/43, 28/1/43 and 7/2/43; Ould to OS. 23/1/43 and 1/2/43. PEN Collection. Osbert Sitwell. Tulsa, Oklahoma.
78 *The Letters of Nancy Mitford and Evelyn Waugh*. ed. Charlotte Mosley. London, 1996. p. 12.
79 OS to DH. 29/1/45. HRCA. OS papers.
80 OS to Plomer. 27/1/45. Plomer mss 306/14.
81 *Letters of Nancy Mitford and Evelyn Waugh*. p. 16.
82 *Letters of Nancy Mitford and Evelyn Waugh*. p. 13.
83 OS to LA. Feb. 1945. HRCA. OS papers.
84 OS to Miss Burnham. 29/4/43. BBC Written Archives.
85 Shaw to OS. 10/5/43. Sitwell Collection. University of Boston. 1/5.
86 OS to DH. 10/6/44. HRCA. OS papers.
87 OS to CA. 7/7/44. Add mss 70835. f. 61; OS to DH. 14/7/44. HRCA. OS papers.
88 Alwyn Warren to OS. 19/10/48. Renishaw papers. Box 503.
89 Harold Nicolson. *Diaries and Letters 1939–1945*. p. 300.

90 Alexander to OS. 5/8/44. Sitwell Collection. University of Boston. 1/5.
91 OS to CA. 20/8/44. Add mss 70835. f. 61.
92 OS to Connolly. Undated. Cyril Connolly Collection. 1.17.6.
93 OS to DH. 13/2/45. HRCA. OS papers.
94 DH to OS. 11/9/44. Renishaw papers. Box 570/8.
95 Bryher. *Days of Mars*. pp. 156–7.
96 OS to Mme Guéritte. 12/8/45. Renishaw papers. Box 550.
97 ES to Stephen Spender. 19/5/43. Berg Collection.
98 OS to Lady Desborough. 1/3/44. Lady Desborough papers. HRO ref. D/ERVC 2407/42.
99 Lord Grey de Ruthyn to OS. 8/3/42. Renishaw papers. Box 511.
100 OS to Bryher. 7/7/45. Bryher papers.
101 OS to LA. 28/7/45. HRCA. OS papers.
102 OS to Bryher. Undated. Bryher papers.
103 OS to Georgia S. 20/8/45. HRCA. SS papers. Box 25.
104 OS to DH. May 1945. HRCA. OS papers.

16: Anatomy of an Age

1 OS to CA. 3/12/44. Add mss 70835. f. 76.
2 Forster to OS. 25/3/46. Renishaw papers. Box 548/2.
3 *Ambrosia and Small Beer. Edward Marsh's Letters.* ed. Christopher Hassall. London, 1964. p. 300.
4 Walton to OS. 18/5/41. Renishaw papers. Box 511.
5 LITNR. p. 208.
6 *Tatler.* 11/9/46.
7 *New Statesman.* 2/7/49; *Sunday Times.* 2/5/48.
8 LHRH. p. x.
9 *New Statesman.* 30/9/50.
10 *Spectator.* 30/4/48.
11 *Time and Tide.* 1/5/48.
12 *Letters of Virginia Woolf.* Vol. 6. p. 466.
13 *Literary Lifelines.* p. 240.
14 *New Statesman.* 15/4/48.
15 OS to Kingsley Martin. 20/5/48. Kingsley Martin papers.
16 *Sunday Times.* 7/12/52.
17 Lehmann. *A Nest of Tigers.* pp. 225–7.
18 OS to LA. Feb. 1942. HRCA. OS papers.
19 *Cleveland Plain Dealer.* 28/5/44.
20 LHRH. p. 74.
21 OS to Mme Guéritte. 2/9/44. Renishaw papers. Box 550.
22 ES to Spender. 6/4/45. Berg Collection.
23 SS to OS. Undated. Renishaw papers. Box 567/1.
24 *Times Literary Supplement.* 6/8/54.
25 *Spectator.* 14/5/48, 21/5/48, 28/5/48, 4/6/48, 18/6/48 and 25/6/48.
26 *Saturday Review of Literature.* 2/9/44.
27 OS to Mme Guéritte. 8/10/42. Renishaw papers. Box 550.
28 OS to Mme Guéritte. 16/1/44. Renishaw papers. Box 550.
29 OS to Roberts. 2/6/44. Cecil Roberts papers. RBTS 2/32.
30 OS to Mrs Rice. 19/8/43. Macmillan papers.
31 Pearsall Smith to OS. 7/8/43. Renishaw papers. Box 570/5.
32 DH to OS. 28/7/44. Renishaw papers. Box 503.

33 *New Statesman.* 14/4/45; *Tatler.* 11/4/45.
34 *Woman's Illustrated.* 28/4/45.
35 Wykes-Jones. *Triad of Genius.* p. 219.
36 DH to OS. 17/2/45. Renishaw papers. Box 503.
37 *Observer.* 4/8/46.
38 *Daily Herald.* 14/8/46.
39 OS to CA. Undated. Add mss 70835. f. 117.
40 Rose Price to OS. 23/5/48. Renishaw papers. Box 571/5.
41 *Letters of Nancy Mitford and Evelyn Waugh.* p. 93.
42 James Lees-Milne. *Midway on the Waves.* London, 1987. p. 58.
43 Rowse to OS. 1/5/48. Renishaw papers. Box 571/5.
44 *Letters of Nancy Mitford and Evelyn Waugh.* pp. 136–8.
45 Eliot to OS. 11/6/49. Sitwell Collection. University of Boston. 1/5.
46 *Times Literary Supplement.* 29/9/50.
47 *New Statesman.* 30/9/50.
48 Rowse to OS. 2/11/50. David Horner mss.
49 *Observer.* 11/2/62.
50 TMFTM. pp. 40–1.
51 *The Lyttelton–Hart-Davis Letters.* ed. Rupert Hart-Davis. Vol. 6. London, 1984. p. 174.
52 *Sunday Times.* 4/3/62.
53 *Sunday Telegraph.* 11/2/62.
54 Green. *Children of the Sun.* p. 420.
55 Beerbohm to OS. June 1949. HRCA. OS papers. Recip.
56 OS to Mervyn Horder. Undated. Renishaw papers. Box 501.
57 OS to CA. 7/12/47. Add mss 70835. f. 143.
58 Lord Kemsley to OS. 11/4/49. Renishaw papers. Box 501.
59 Powell to OS. 9/12/47. Renishaw papers. Box 501.
60 OS to G. W. Keeling. 10/12/47. Renishaw papers. Box 501.
61 ES to Zozia Kochanski. 12/5/49. Sitwell Collection. Tulsa. Box 11, folder 9; Frere to OS. 13/5/49. Renishaw papers. Box 571.
62 OS to Bryher. 22/8/49. Bryher papers.
63 OS to Diana Cooper. 12/10/50. Duff and Diana Cooper mss. Eton College Library.
64 Essay on T. S. Eliot. Renishaw papers. Box 533.
65 Thomas to OS. 27/8/46. Renishaw papers. Box 548/3.
66 *Letters of Nancy Mitford and Evelyn Waugh.* p. 85.
67 Undated. Cyril Connolly Collection. Tulsa. 1.17.6.
68 Society of Authors papers. HRCA.
69 Henry Reed to OS. 13/6/48; Rosamond Lehmann to OS. 24/6/48. Renishaw papers. Box 548/6.
70 Warner to OS. 15/7/53. Renishaw papers. Box 572.
71 OS to John Hadfield. 14/11/47. Renishaw papers. Box 501.
72 OS to CA. Undated. Add mss 70835. f. 62.
73 23/8/44. Royal Society of Literature archives.
74 Masefield to OS. 25/6/48. Renishaw papers. Box 501.
75 Masefield to OS. 2/5/51 and 28/5/55. Renishaw papers. Box 571/1 and Box 571/7.
76 OS to Plomer. 30/10/49. William Plomer mss. 26.
77 LITNR. p. 326.
78 OS to Sassoon. 28/5/49. Neil Ritchie archive.
79 Priestley to OS. 14/5/49. Renishaw papers. Box 501.
80 *Times Literary Supplement.* 13/5/49.

17: England's Most Celebrated Living Literary Family

1 OS to CA. 26/11/45. Add mss 70835. f. 99.
2 OS to CA. 9/12/46. Add mss 70834. f. 127.
3 OS to John Lehmann. 6/9/47. Sitwell Collection. University of Boston. Box 1 F/4.
4 *The Times.* 2/2/50.
5 OS to Hoskins. 15/9/47. Renishaw papers. Box 340/2.
6 OS to DH. 7/8/47. HRCA. OS papers.
7 OS to Alice Hunt. 22/8/49. Renishaw papers. Box 550.
8 OS to CA. mid-1947. Add mss 70835. f. 144.
9 Violet Bonham Carter to OS. 25/7/47. Renishaw papers. Box 561/2.
10 OS to CA. 2/3/47. Add mss 70835. f. 135.
11 OS to Thomas Mark. 2/3/46. Pearson. *Façades.* p. 382.
12 OS to William Plomer. 14/1/50. William Plomer mss. 306/27.
13 OS to DH. 10/1/46. HRCA. OS papers.
14 OS to Georgia S. 30/2/46. HRCA. SS papers. Box 25.
15 OS to Georgia S. 15/11/45. HRCA. SS papers. Box 25.
16 OS to Georgia S. Undated. HRCA. SS papers. Box 25.
17 SS to OS. 19/1/50. Renishaw papers. Box 571/2.
18 OS to Alice Hunt. 12/6/50. Renishaw papers. Box 550.
19 Bradford. *Sacheverell Sitwell.* pp. 344–5.
20 Georgia S to OS. 29/4/48. Renishaw papers. Box 571.
21 OS to Georgia S. Undated. HRCA. SS papers. Box 25.
22 OS to John Lehmann. 11/12/47. HRCA. John Lehmann papers.
23 OS to John Lehmann. 14/12/47. HRCA. John Lehmann papers.
24 Susana Walton. *William Walton.* pp. 46–7.
25 DH to OS. 4/8/45. Renishaw papers. Box 548/1.
26 OS to DH. 7/8/45. HRCA. OS papers.
27 Brinsley Ford diary. 21/3/48.
28 Guy Lovell to OS. 6/5/48. Renishaw papers. Box 571/5.
29 Brinsley Ford diary. 28/5/47.
30 OS to Lady Desborough. 2/5/47. Lady Desborough papers. HRO ref. D/ERVC 2407/39.
31 OS to Alice Hunt. 1/12/49. Renishaw papers. Box 550.
32 OS to Plomer. 13/3/46. Plomer mss. 306/19.
33 OS to Alice Hunt. 7/8/49. Renishaw papers. Box 550.
34 OS to Alice Hunt. 3/12/49. Renishaw papers. Box 550.
35 OS to SS. 15/8/50. HRCA. SS papers. Box 22.
36 13/12/45. Renishaw papers. Box 548/1.
37 OS to Mme Guéritte. 26/11/45. Renishaw papers. Box 550.
38 3/10/52. Renishaw papers. Box 532/10.
39 Lees-Milne. *Midway on the Waves.* p. 81.
40 Elmhirst to OS. 21/11/46. Renishaw papers. Box 503.
41 OS to Hollingworth. 23/10/50. Renishaw papers. Box 532.
42 OS to Lady Desborough. 12/9/47. Lady Desborough papers. HRO ref. D/ERVC 2407/40.
43 OS to Linklater. 18/8/47. National Library of Scotland. Acc. 10282 no. 2.
44 OS to CA. 16/6/46. Add mss 70835. f. 114.
45 OS to DH. Undated. HRCA. OS papers.
46 OS to LA. Early Oct. 1947. HRCA. OS papers.
47 John to Myfanwy Piper. 9/10/47. John Piper papers.
48 OS to Alice Hunt. 19/10/49. Renishaw papers. Box 550.

49 17/10/45. Copy in Renishaw papers. Box 572/4.
50 David Higham to OS. 5/4/48. Renishaw papers. Box 550/9.
51 OS to LA. 8/2/48. HRCA. OS papers.
52 ES. *Taken Care Of*. pp. 174–5.
53 Lehmann. *Nest of Tigers*. p. 244.
54 *Toronto Globe*. 8/1/49.
55 OS to Hollingworth. 9/2/49. Renishaw papers. Box 550.
56 OS to CA. 25/12/48. Add mss 70835. f. 145.
57 Lehmann. *Nest of Tigers*. p. 241.
58 *Life*. 13/12/48.
59 Nichols. *The Unforgiving Minute*. p. 103.
60 *Letters of Nancy Mitford and Evelyn Waugh*. pp. 113–17.
61 JPN.
62 All in Renishaw papers. Box 550.
63 OS to DH. 16/9/53. HRCA. OS papers; DH to OS. 11/9/53. Renishaw papers. Box 571/5.
64 OS to CA. 25/12/48. Add mss 70835. f. 145.
65 Stark to DH. 18/8/49. HRCA. OS papers. Misc.
66 OS to Kirstein. 5/5/49. Lincoln Kirstein Collection.
67 *The Letters of Evelyn Waugh and Diana Cooper*. ed. Artemis Cooper. London, 1992. p. 104.
68 *Selected Letters of Edith Sitwell* (1997). p. 313.
69 OS to Georgia S. Undated. HRCA. SS papers. Box 25.

18: Parkinson's

1 Waugh to OS. 26/5/49. Renishaw papers. Box 503.
2 Pearson. *Façades*. p. 391.
3 OS to CA. 7/8/47. Add mss 70835. f. 138.
4 OS to DH. 18/1/43. HRCA. OS papers.
5 OS to Alice Hunt. 11/8/49. Renishaw papers. Box 550.
6 OS to SS. 16/3/50. Bradford. *Sacheverell Sitwell*. p. 345.
7 OS to William Plomer. 17/8/50. William Plomer mss. 306/29.
8 OS to Alice Hunt. 22/7/50. Renishaw papers. Box 550.
9 ES to SS. 5/6/50. HRCA. SS papers. Box 20.
10 ES to SS. 2/8/50. HRCA. SS papers. Box 20.
11 OS to Hermon Ould. 4/8/50. Tulsa. PEN Collection. OS papers.
12 *Letters of Aldous Huxley*. p. 627.
13 Bryher to OS. 25/6/41. Renishaw papers. Box 511.
14 OS to Diana Cooper. 26/5/51. Duff and Diana Cooper mss.
15 OS to Zozia Kochanski. 23/9/51. Tulsa. Sitwell Collection. Box 2.
16 OS to DH. 4/2/52 and 7/3/52. HRCA. OS papers.
17 OS to Hunt. 27/6/53. Renishaw papers. Box 550.
18 Edwards to OS. 9/11/55. Renishaw papers. Box 515.
19 *A Passionate Prodigality. Letters to Alan Bird from Richard Aldington*. ed. Miriam Benkovitz. New York, 1975. pp. 148 and 152.
20 Laurence to OS. 25/10/55. Houghton Library, Harvard. Brus. Eng. 1293(19).
21 22/6/52. Gladwyn papers.
22 SS to OS. 25/9/53. Renishaw papers. Box 571/5.
23 OS to Lovat Dickson. 26/8/54. Macmillan papers.
24 ES to John Lehmann. 21/5/51. *Selected Letters* (1970). p. 174.
25 *Letters of Evelyn Waugh*. pp. 445 and 441.

26 Interview with Frank Magro.
27 DH to CA. 30/10/51. Add mss 70837A. f. 106.
28 SS to CA. 16/12/51. Add mss 70837B. f. 7.
29 DH to CA. 6/4/52. Add mss 70837B. f. 10; DH to OS. 5/4/52. Renishaw papers. Box 571/4.
30 JPN.
31 James Lees-Milne. *Ancestral Voices*. London, 1975. p. 211.
32 ES to Bryher. Late July 1956. Bryher papers.
33 OS to DH. 8/7/48. HRCA. OS papers.
34 Renishaw papers. Box 80.
35 Hans Berger to OS. 11/11/52. Renishaw papers. Box 80.
36 OS to Ed Hewitt. 31/5/53. Berg Collection.
37 *Letters of Nancy Mitford and Evelyn Waugh.* p. 204.
38 OS to Zozia Kochanski. 3/2/51. Tulsa. Sitwell Collection. Box 2.
39 Maloney to OS. Undated. Renishaw papers. Box 571/2.
40 ES to Spender. 26/2/54. Berg Collection; ES to Tom Driberg. 4/2/54. Driberg mss.
41 Letter from Sir Peter Ustinov to the author. May 1995.
42 ES to SS. 17/1/55. HRCA. SS papers. Box 20.
43 OS to DH. 5/2/55. HRCA. OS papers.
44 Elborn. *Edith Sitwell*. p. 223.
45 Elborn. *Edith Sitwell*. p. 226.
46 OS to Bryher. 27/4/55. Bryher papers.
47 OS to DH. 25/7/47. HRCA. OS papers.
48 OS to Alice Hunt. 10/3/52. Renishaw papers. Box 550.
49 OS to L. P. Hartley. 25/7/52. L. P. Hartley papers.
50 LA to Captain J. J. Anderson. 26/5/52. Renishaw papers. Box 532.
51 Renishaw papers. Box 550.
52 OS to Hartley. 25/7/52. L. P. Hartley papers.
53 OS to Hunt. 14/9/49. Renishaw papers. Box 550.
54 OS to Macmillan. 11/7/50. Macmillan papers.
55 OS to Alice Hunt. 26/4/51. Renishaw papers. Box 550.
56 Unsigned and undated report. Macmillan papers.
57 *TFC.* p. 62.
58 *TFC.* p. 131.
59 *The Spectator.* 2/3/62. Review of *Tales My Father Told Me.*
60 *The Tatler.* 18/8/54; Waugh to OS. 15/7/54. Renishaw papers. Box 571/6.
61 *Sunday Times.* 18/7/54.
62 *Selected Letters of Philip Larkin.* ed. Anthony Thwaite. London, 1992. p. 711.
63 Lovat Dickson to J. L. Barrett. 20/7/54. Macmillan papers.
64 Osbert Sitwell. *Wrack at Tidesend.* p. vii.
65 OS to Ted Dorn. 19/1/51. Sitwell Collection. University of Boston. Box 1 F/3.
66 OS to CA. December 1949. Add mss 70835. f. 150; OS to Zozia Kochanski. 22/5/50. Sitwell Collection. Tulsa. Box 2.
67 Eliot to OS. 12/6/52. Renishaw papers. Box 571/4.
68 OS to CA. Undated. Add mss 70835. f. 153.
69 *Sunday Times.* 11/2/62.
70 Nichols. *The Unforgiving Minute.* p. 103.
71 Report by V. Marley. 29/10/48. BBC Written Archives.
72 *New Statesman.* 1/9/51; *Ballet.* Vol. 11. No. 10. Nov. 1951; Ricco. 'The Sitwells at the Ballet'. *Ballet Review.* Vol. 6. No. 1 (1977–8).
73 OS to LA. Undated. HRCA. OS papers.
74 DH to OS. 8/1/56; Hartley to OS. 13/1/56. Renishaw papers. Box 571/8.

75 *Letters of Nancy Mitford and Evelyn Waugh.* p. 394.
76 OS to Kirstein. 20/1/56. Lincoln Kirstein Collection.

19: A Good Deal of Time in Bed

1 OS to Hugo Southern. Undated. HRCA. OS papers. 70B.
2 OS to Maynard Hollingworth. 8/11/56. Renishaw papers. Box 335.
3 OS to SS. 6/12/56. Renishaw papers. Box 530/1.
4 ES to Spender. 16/11/56. Berg Collection.
5 OS to Alice Hunt. 20/11/56. Renishaw papers. Box 550.
6 DH to CA. 11/2/62 and 25/2/62. Add mss 70837A. ff. 110 and 113.
7 Atlas Insurance Co. to OS. 1/7/63; OS to AIC. 2/7/63. Renishaw papers. Box 335.
8 Waugh to OS. 15/8/57. Renishaw papers. Box 571/9.
9 Harold Acton. *More Memoirs of an Aesthete.* London, 1970. p. 304.
10 OS to LA. HRCA. OS papers.
11 OS to Georgia S. 25/12/60. HRCA. SS papers. Box 23.
12 OS to Lincoln Kirstein. 20/2/61. Lincoln Kirstein Collection.
13 *Selected Letters of Edith Sitwell* (1997). p. 323.
14 LA to Peter Hollingworth. 22/5/62. Renishaw papers. Box 335/4.
15 John to Myfanwy Piper. 12/10/54. John Piper papers.
16 DH to CA. 30/10/51. Add mss 70837A. f. 104.
17 LA to Peter Hollingworth. 30/5/62. Renishaw papers. Box 335/4.
18 OS to Denys Kilham-Roberts. 20/12/56. Renishaw papers. Box 570.
19 DH to Georgia S. 9/1/61. HRCA. SS papers. Box 23.
20 OS to Chotzinoff. 25/9/63. Samuel Chotzinoff Collection.
21 OS to Robert Elmhirst. 3/3/60. Renishaw papers. Box 530/1.
22 OS to LA. 19/3/50. HRCA. OS papers.
23 Bowra to OS. 6/2/59. Renishaw papers. Box 571/11.
24 Jean Le Roy to OS. 28/7/58. Renishaw papers. Box 571.
25 *Daily Telegraph.* 13/2/59; *The Times.* 3/2/59.
26 David Higham to Lovat Dickson. 10/5/61. Macmillan papers.
27 OS to Alice Hunt. 27/12/57. Renishaw papers. Box 550; Lincoln Kirstein Collection
    (Sitwell, Osbert, misc.).
28 OS to Lovat Dickson. 5/8/55. Macmillan papers.
29 OS to Lincoln Kirstein. 27/5/56. Lincoln Kirstein Collection.
30 *The Noël Coward Diaries.* ed. Graham Payn and Sheridan Morley. London, 1982.
    p. 318.
31 OS to Bryher. 9/7/59. Bryher papers.
32 LA to Georgia S. 31/7/60. HRCA. SS papers. Box 23.
33 *The Letters of Anne Fleming.* ed. Mark Amory. London, 1985. p. 264.
34 OS to Chotzinoff. 11/8/60. Samuel Chotzinoff Collection; Laurence to OS. 31/3/58.
    Sitwell papers. Houghton Library, Harvard.
35 *Richard Aldington–Lawrence Durrell Correspondence.* p. 187.
36 SS to Bryher. 18/9/61. Bryher papers.
37 OS to CA. 31/7/61. Add mss 70836. f. 75.
38 SS to Bryher. 6/10/61, 8/10/61, 25/10/61. Bryher papers.
39 ES to Spender. 9/10/61. Berg Collection.
40 *Aldington–Durrell Correspondence.* p. 192.
41 OS to CA. Probably mid-November 1961. Add mss 70836. f. 81.
42 LA to CA. 20/4/62. Add mss 70836. f. 99.
43 LA to Georgia S. 10/5/63. HRCA. SS papers. Box 23.
44 Salter. *Last Years of a Rebel.* p. 34.

45 ES to Amardo Child. 20/5/56. Elborn. *Edith Sitwell*. p. 227.
46 Wright. *Foreign Country*. p. 186.
47 ES to SS. March 1957. Elborn. *Edith Sitwell*. p. 230.
48 ES to Georgia S. 2/5/57. HRCA. SS papers. Box 25.
49 ES to Georgia S. 21/12/57. HRCA. SS papers. Box 25.
50 OS to SS. 31/12/59. HRCA. SS papers. Box 23.
51 DH to Georgia S. 20/7/60. HRCA. SS papers. Box 23.
52 Elborn. *Edith Sitwell*. pp. 251–2.
53 Hartley to DH. 15/9/60. HRCA. OS papers. Misc.
54 DH to OS. 4/11/58. Renishaw papers. Box 571/10.
55 Bradford. *Sacheverell Sitwell*. p. 392.
56 OS to CA. 9/3/62. Add mss 70836. f. 84.
57 JPN.
58 OS to CA. 9/3/62. Add mss 70836. f. 84.
59 LA to Georgia S. 14/3/62. HRCA. SS papers. Box 23.
60 OS to CA. 15/3/62 and 9/4/62. Add mss 70836. ff. 86 and 97.
61 OS to Bryher. 21/6/62. Bryher papers.
62 OS to CA. 31/5/62. Add mss 70836. f. 105.
63 Georgia S to OS. 9/9/62. Renishaw papers. Box 572/2.
64 ES to CA. 9/7/62. Add mss 52556 (Vol. 2). f. 230.
65 OS to Kirstein. Undated. Lincoln Kirstein papers; OS to CA. 22/9/64. Add mss 70838. f. 2.
66 Interview with Frank Magro.

20: Exit a Rose-Red Cissy

1 Interview with Frank Magro, who provided much of the material for this and the following chapter.
2 OS to LA. 5/12/67. HRCA. OS papers.
3 FM to CA. 6/4/66. Add mss 70838. f. 109.
4 FM to CA. 13/7/65. Add mss 70838. f. 82.
5 FM to CA. 9/6/65. Add mss 70838. f. 71.
6 DH to CA. 13/9/64. Add mss 70838. f. 4.
7 SS to CA. 25/9/64 and 7/10/64. Add mss 70838. ff. 5 and 7.
8 FM to CA. 12/7/65. Add mss 70838. f. 81.
9 LA to Peter Hollingworth. 22/12/64 and 31/12/64. Renishaw papers. Box 335.
10 LA to Peter Hollingworth. 11/2/65. Renishaw papers. Box 335.
11 CA to OS. Undated. Add mss 70836. f. 129.
12 OS to Kirstein. 28/1/63. Lincoln Kirstein Collection.
13 Letter from Sir Rupert Hart-Davis to the author. 8/2/96.
14 ES to OS. 5/12/64. Add mss 70837A. f. 9.
15 LA to Peter Hollingworth. 14/12/64. Renishaw papers. Box 335.
16 OS to SS. Undated. HRCA. SS papers. Works 69.
17 OS to Lehmann. Undated. HRCA. John Lehmann papers.
18 SS to Bryher. 5/2/65. Bryher papers.
19 OS to Henry Newnham. Undated. HRCA. OS papers. 70B.
20 OS to Pryce-Jones. 7/5/65. Alan Pryce-Jones papers.
21 OS to Tom Driberg. 25/10/65. Driberg mss.
22 OS to Bryher. 2/1/66. Bryher papers.
23 OS to Driberg. 24/3/69. Driberg mss.
24 SS to OS. 24/12/64. Renishaw papers. Box 504.
25 Thekla Clark. *Wystan and Chester*. London, 1995. pp. 27–8.

26 SS to CA. 25/9/64. Add mss 70838. f. 5.
27 SS to CA. 13/10/64. Add mss 70838. f. 8.
28 SS to CA. 13/1/65. Add mss 70838. f. 9.
29 CA to OS. 31/1/65. Add mss 70838. f. 35.
30 OS to Southern. Undated. HRCA. OS papers. Misc.
31 SS to Bryher. 15/1/65. Bryher papers.
32 OS to Frere. Undated. HRCA. OS papers. Misc.
33 Georgia S to Bryher. 27/12/64. Bryher papers.
34 OS to CA. 7/2/65. Add mss 70838. f. 40.
35 CA to OS. 12/2/65. Add mss 70838. f. 44.
36 Vera Frere to OS. 16/2/65. Add mss 70838. f. 51.
37 OS to Frere. Undated. HRCA. OS papers. 70B; Frere to OS. Undated. Renishaw papers. Box 572/6.
38 Acton to DH. 22/11/65. David Horner mss.
39 Bradford. *Sacheverell Sitwell.* p. 400.
40 DH to CA. 18/11/66. Add mss 70838. f. 129.
41 DH to Hollingworth. 27/5/65. Renishaw papers. Box 335.
42 FM to CA. 29/11/66. Add mss 70838. f. 133.
43 OS to CA. 3/2/65. Add mss 70838. f. 37.
44 OS to CA. 15/2/65. Add mss 70838. f. 47.
45 *Letters of Nancy Mitford and Evelyn Waugh.* p. 484.
46 OS to CA. 27/7/65. Add mss 70838. f. 116.
47 OS to Hollingworth. 12/6/65. Renishaw papers. Box 335.
48 JPN.
49 OS to Bryher. 25/9/65. Bryher papers.
50 OS to Hollingworth. 24/10/65. Renishaw papers. Box 335.
51 OS to Hollingworth. 10/11/65. Renishaw papers. Box 335.
52 OS to Scarborough. Undated. HRCA. OS papers. Box 70B
53 OS to Anthony Hobson. Undated. HRCA. OS papers. Box 70B

21: The Faces that I Love

1 OS to Bryher. 15/11/49. Bryher papers.
2 SS to OS. 24/5/59; Georgia S to OS. 27/9/68. Renishaw papers. Box 504.
3 OS to Bryher. 15/11/49. Bryher papers.
4 OS to CA. 3/2/65. Add mss 70838. f. 37.
5 SS to Bryher. 10/5/67. Bryher papers.
6 OS to Hartley. 26/11/67. L. P. Hartley papers.
7 OS to Lehmann. 23/1/64. HRCA. John Lehmann papers.
8 OS to Lehmann. 1/3/67. HRCA. John Lehmann papers.
9 Magro to Lehmann. 6/5/68. HRCA. John Lehmann papers.
10 SS to OS. 20/8/68. Renishaw papers. Box 504.
11 Magro to CA. 9/7/68. Add mss 70838. f. 189.
12 SS to Kirstein. 12/10/65. Lincoln Kirstein Collection.
13 Magro to Georgia S. 15/10/66. HRCA. SS papers. Box 23.
14 Magro to CA. 26/9/67. Add mss 70838. f. 158.
15 Magro to Georgia S. 17/11/66. HRCA. SS papers. Box 23.
16 Magro to CA. 17/1/67. Add mss 70838. f. 138.
17 Magro to CA. 1/10/67. Add mss 70838. f. 161.
18 SS to Magro. 17/10/67. Add mss 70838. f. 170.
19 Magro to SS. 17/1/67; to CA. 29/10/67. Add mss 70838. ff. 169 and 171.
20 JPN.

21 OS to CA. 14/2/69. Add mss 70838. f. 211.
22 Magro to CA. 30/11/68. Add mss 70838. f. 204.
23 SS to Bryher. 12/5/69 and 24/6/69. Bryher papers.
24 LA to Hollingworth. 13/8/65. Renishaw papers. Box 335.
25 OS to Lehmann. 14/12/65. HRCA. John Lehmann papers.
26 Lady Cholmondeley to OS. 13/3/66. Renishaw papers. Box 572/4.
27 OS to Hollingworth. 9/3/66. Renishaw papers. Box 335.
28 Magro to CA. Undated. Add mss 70838. f. 119.
29 OS to 'Jack'. Undated. HRCA. OS papers. 70B.
30 OS to Kirstein, Undated. Lincoln Kirstein Collection.
31 SS to Bryher. 7/10/68. Bryher papers.
32 OS to Hartley. 22/5/66. L. P. Hartley papers.
33 OS to Lehmann. 13/12/68. HRCA. John Lehmann papers.
34 OS to Bullock. Undated. HRCA. OS papers. 70B.
35 OS to Plomer. 28/6/68. William Plomer mss. 56.
36 Harold Acton. Preface to *QMAO*. pp. 16–17.
37 OS to CA. 3/3/60. Add mss 70836. f. 70.
38 Magro to CA. 17/8/68. Add mss 70838. f. 193.
39 Magro to Mrs Patterson. 21/7/67. Royal Society of Literature archives.
40 OS to Denys Kilham-Roberts. 20/12/56. Renishaw papers. Box 520.
41 Magro to Greene. 31/8/67. Magro papers.
42 OS to Hartley. 10/5/68. L. P. Hartley papers.
43 JPN.
44 OS to CA. 17/4/67. Add mss 70838. f. 146.
45 SS to Bryher. 11/12/68. Bryher papers.
46 SS to Bryher. 5/11/68. Bryher papers.
47 Wright. *Foreign Country*. p. 232.
48 SS to Kirstein. 23/10/66. Lincoln Kirstein Collection.
49 Magro to CA. 4/4/68. Add mss 70838. f. 179.
50 JPN.
51 Magro to CA. 6/1/69. Add mss 70838. f. 208.
52 Magro to CA. 29/1/68. Add mss 70838. f. 175.
53 OS to CA. 3/3/67. Add mss 70838. f. 144.
54 SS to OS. 14/2/69. Renishaw papers. Box 572/6.
55 Acton to DH. 13/2/69. David Horner mss.
56 OS to Driberg. 24/3/69. Driberg papers.
57 Magro to CA. 19/4/69. Add mss 70838. f. 214.
58 Reresby Sitwell to David Carver. Undated. PEN Collection. OS.
59 ES to John Lehmann. 15/3/44. *Edith Sitwell. Selected Letters* (1970). p. 120.
60 Acton to DH. 5/7/69. David Horner mss.

Books by Osbert Sitwell

Year of publication, title and English publisher

1919 *Argonaut and Juggernaut* (Chatto & Windus)

1919 *The Winstonburg Line* (Hendersons, 66 Charing Cross Road)

1921 *At the House of Mrs Kinfoot* (Favil Press)

1921 *Who Killed Cock-Robin?* (C. W. Daniel)

1923 *Out of the Flame* (Grant Richards)

1924 *Triple Fugue* (Grant Richards)

1925 (with Edith and Sacheverell Sitwell) *Poor Young People* (The Fleuron)

1925 *Discursions on Travel, Art and Life* (Grant Richards)

1926 *Before the Bombardment* (Duckworth)

1927 *Winter the Huntsman* (Poetry Bookshop)

1927 *England Reclaimed. A Book of Eclogues* (Duckworth)

1927 (with Sacheverell Sitwell) *All At Sea* (Duckworth)

1928 *The People's Album of London Statues* (Duckworth)

1929 *The Man Who Lost Himself* (Duckworth)

1929 *Miss Mew* (Mill House Press)

1930 (with Margaret Barton) *Sober Truth. A Collection of Nineteenth-Century Episodes, Fantastic, Grotesque and Mysterious* (Duckworth)

1930 *Dumb Animal* (Duckworth)

1931 (with Margaret Barton) *Victoriana. A Symposium of Victorian Wisdom* (Duckworth)

1931 *Collected Satires and Poems* (Duckworth)

1931 *Three-Quarter-length Portrait of Michael Arlen* (Heinemann)

1931 *Belshazzar's Feast* (libretto) (Oxford University Press)

1932 *Dickens* (Chatto & Windus)

1932 *Winters of Content. More Discursions on Travel, Art and Life* (Duckworth)

1933 *Miracle on Sinai* (Duckworth)

1935 (with Margaret Barton) *Brighton* (Faber & Faber)

1935 *Penny Foolish. A Book of Tirades and Panegyrics* (Macmillan)

1937 *Mrs Kimber* (Macmillan)

1938 *Those Were the Days* (Macmillan)

1938 (with Edith and Sacheverell Sitwell) *Trio. Some Aspects of National Genius.* Northcliffe Lectures (University of London)

1939 *Escape With Me! An Oriental Sketch Book* (Macmillan)

1940 *Two Generations* (Macmillan)

1941 *Open the Door!* (Macmillan)

1941 *A Place of One's Own* (Macmillan)

1943 (with R. J. Minney) *Gentle Caesar* (Macmillan)

1943 *Selected Poems, Old and New* (Duckworth)

1944 *Sing High! Sing Low!* (Macmillan)

1944 *A Letter to My Son* (Home & Van Thal)

1945 *Left Hand, Right Hand!* (Macmillan)

1946 *The True Story of Dick Whittington* (Home & Van Thal)

1946 *The Scarlet Tree* (Macmillan)

1947 *The Novels of George Meredith* (Oxford University Press)

1948 *Great Morning* (Macmillan)

1948 *Four Songs of the Italian Earth* (Banyan Press)

1949 *Laughter in the Next Room* (Macmillan)

1949 *Demos the Emperor* (Macmillan)

1949 *Death of a God* (Macmillan)

1950 *Noble Essences* (Macmillan)

1952 *Wrack at Tidesend* (Macmillan)

1953 *Collected Stories* (Duckworth and Macmillan)

1954 *The Four Continents* (Macmillan)

1958 *On the Continent* (Macmillan)

1959 *Fee Fi Fo Fum!* (Macmillan)

1962 *Tales My Father Taught Me* (Hutchinson)

1963 *Pound Wise* (Hutchinson)

1965 *Poems about People or England Reclaimed* (Hutchinson)

1986 *Rat Week* (Michael Joseph)

(For a complete list of all Osbert Sitwell's published writings, including articles and edited works, see Richard Fifoot's invaluable *Edith, Osbert and Sacheverell Sitwell. A Bibliography*. London, 1965. Revised Edition 1971.)

Books about Osbert Sitwell
or the Sitwell Family

Sarah Bradford. *Sacheverell Sitwell*. London, 1993

Geoffrey Elborn. *Edith Sitwell*. London, 1981

Richard Fifoot. *Edith, Osbert and Sacheverell Sitwell. A Bibliography* London, 1971

Roger Fulford. *Osbert Sitwell*, supplement to *British Book News*. London, 1951

Victoria Glendinning. *Edith Sitwell*. London, 1981

John Lehmann. *A Nest of Tigers*. London, 1969

R. L. Megroz. *The Three Sitwells*. London, 1927

John Pearson. *Façades*. London, 1978

Elizabeth Salter. *The Last Years of a Rebel*. London, 1967

Edith Sitwell. *Taken Care Of*. London, 1965

Edith Sitwell. Selected Letters, ed. John Lehmann and Derek Parker. London, 1970

Selected Letters of Edith Sitwell, ed. Richard Greene. London, 1997

Francis Sitwell. *Weston Hall*. Privately printed

Reresby Sitwell. *Renishaw Hall and the Sitwells*. Privately printed

Reresby Sitwell. *The Garden at Renishaw Hall*. Privately printed

Sacheverell Sitwell. *All Summer in a Day*. London, 1926

Sacheverell Sitwell. A Symposium, ed. Derek Parker. London, 1975

Max Wykes-Jones. *Triad of Genius*. London, 1953

Bibliographical Notes

Manuscript sources

The largest single collection of Sitwell papers is in the Harry Ransom Humanities Research Center at the University of Texas at Austin. This includes over a thousand letters between different members of the family as well as 951 letters from Osbert Sitwell to David Horner and 330 to Lorna Andrade.

An enormously important collection of family and other papers remains at Sir Reresby Sitwell's home, Renishaw Hall, in Derbyshire. This includes several hundred letters from Osbert Sitwell to Mrs Alice Hunt and Madame Guéritte, which were returned after the death of the recipients. The Renishaw papers are assembled in boxes in rough chronological order and usually divided into bundles within those boxes. They are listed in the notes as, e.g., 'Box 501/6'. A smaller but most valuable collection is in the possession of Mr Francis Sitwell of Weston Hall.

There are large 'Sitwell Collections' in the McFarlin Library at the University of Tulsa, Oklahoma; the University of Iowa Library; and the Mulgar Memorial Library at Boston University. The first of these contains the extensive notes made by Mr John Pearson while researching for his study of the Sitwell family, *Façades*. The Berg Collection in the New York Public Library is particularly rich in manuscripts of Osbert Sitwell's published works.

The most important single collection of Osbert Sitwell's letters outside Austin, Texas and Renishaw is that in the Aberconway papers in the British Library. Another very substantial series is to L .P. Hartley in the John Rylands Library at the University of Manchester. As well as many papers of David Horner's, the Eton College Library contains the unpublished poems dedicated to Horner by Osbert Sitwell and the latter's reading list for the period when he was at Eton and immediately thereafter.

Other manuscript collections which contain letters from Osbert Sitwell or papers of particular relevance to his life are: the Harold Acton papers (Eton College Library); BBC Written Archives, Caversham; Cecil Beaton papers (St John's College Library, Cambridge, reproduced by kind permission of the literary executors of the late Sir Cecil Beaton, or in the possession of Mr Hugo Vickers); Max Beerbohm papers (Merton College Library, Oxford); Arnold Bennett papers (Beinecke Library, Yale); Bryher papers (Beinecke Library, Yale); Chatto & Windus papers (Reading University Library); Samuel Chotzinoff Collection (University of Boston Library); Cyril Connolly Collection (University of Tulsa Library); Duff and Diana Cooper papers (Eton College Library); Lady Desborough papers (Hertfordshire Record Office); Tom Driberg papers (Christ Church, Oxford); Duckworth archive (London University Library); T. S. Eliot papers (in the possession of Mrs Valerie Eliot or at King's College, Cambridge); S. J. G. Ervine Collection (Harry Ransom Humanities Research Center, Austin); Henry Festing-Jones papers (Cambridge University Library); Brinsley Ford diary (Sir Brinsley Ford); J. L. Garvin Collection (Harry Ransom Humanities Research Center, Austin); Geoffrey Gorer papers (University of Sussex Library); Gosse family papers (Brotherton Library, University of Leeds); Grenadier Guards archive (Regimental HQ); Hart-Davis papers (Sir Rupert Hart-Davis); HD (Hilda Doolittle [Aldington]) papers (Beinecke Library, Yale); Brian Howard papers (Eton College Library); Gladwyn Jebb papers (Lord Gladwyn); J. M. Keynes papers (King's College, Cambridge); Lincoln Kirstein Collection (Library for the Performing Arts, Lincoln Center); Desmond Laurence papers (Houghton Library, Harvard); John Lehmann papers (Harry Ransom Humanities Research Center, Austin); Rosamond Lehmann papers (King's College, Cambridge); MacColl papers (University of Glasgow); Macmillan Publishers papers (British Library – in the process of cataloguing when consulted); Frank Magro papers (Frank Magro); Kingsley Martin papers (University of Sussex Library); Frank Megroz papers (University of Reading Library); Alida Monro papers (British Library); Wilfred Owen papers (English Faculty Library, Oxford); PEN Collection (University of Tulsa Library); John Piper papers (Mrs Clarissa Lewis); William Plomer papers (Durham University Library); John Cowper Powys papers (University of Wales Library); Alan Pryce-Jones papers (Beinecke Library, Yale); Neil Ritchie archive (Neil Ritchie); Cecil Roberts papers (Churchill College Library, Cambridge); Royal Society of Literature archive; Schiff papers (British Library); G. B. Shaw papers (British

Library); Society of Authors archive (Harry Ransom Humanities Research Center, Austin); Louis Spears papers (Churchill College Library, Cambridge); W. J. H. Sprott papers (King's College, Cambridge); Gertrude Stein papers (Beinecke Library, Yale); Lytton Strachey papers (British Library); Templewood papers (Cambridge University Library); Rebecca West Collection (University of Tulsa Library); Violet Woodhouse papers (Mrs Jessica Douglas-Home); Leonard Woolf papers (University of Sussex Library); Brett Young papers (University of Birmingham Library).

Index